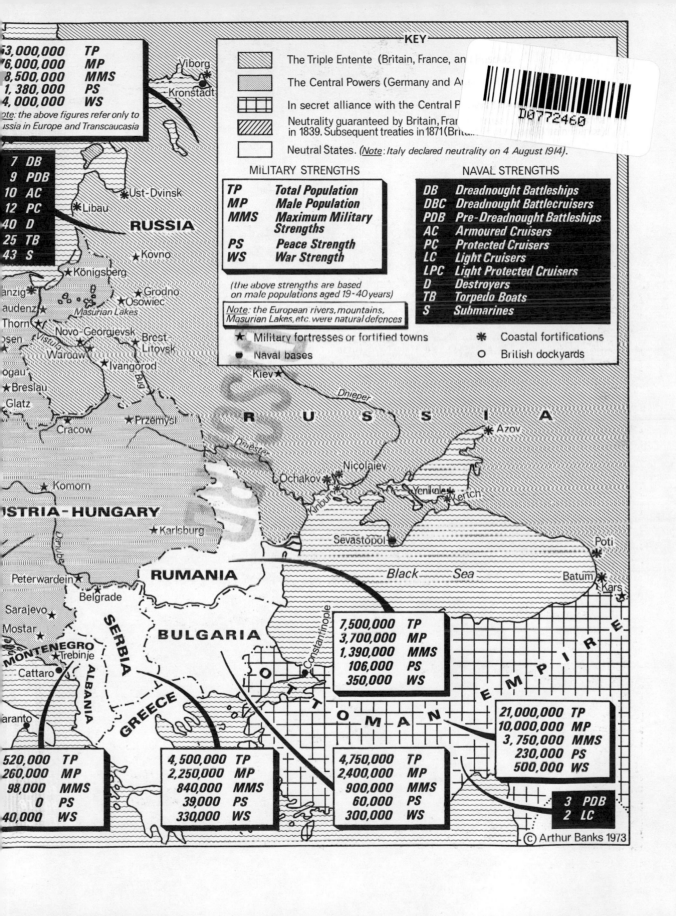

KEY

(diagonal lines)	The Triple Entente (Britain, France, and)
(stipple)	The Central Powers (Germany and A)
(grid)	In secret alliance with the Central P
(hatched)	Neutrality guaranteed by Britain, Fran in 1839. Subsequent treaties in 1871(Britai
(blank)	Neutral States. (*Note*: Italy declared neutrality on 4 August 1914).

MILITARY STRENGTHS

TP	**Total Population**
MP	**Male Population**
MMS	**Maximum Military Strengths**
PS	**Peace Strength**
WS	**War Strength**

(the above strengths are based on male populations aged 19-40 years)

Note: the European rivers, mountains, Masurian Lakes, etc. were natural defences

NAVAL STRENGTHS

DB	**Dreadnought Battleships**
DBC	**Dreadnought Battlecruisers**
PDB	**Pre-Dreadnought Battleships**
AC	**Armoured Cruisers**
PC	**Protected Cruisers**
LC	**Light Cruisers**
LPC	**Light Protected Cruisers**
D	**Destroyers**
TB	**Torpedo Boats**
S	**Submarines**

★ Military fortresses or fortified towns   ✳ Coastal fortifications

● Naval bases   ○ British dockyards

(Top-left Russia box)

53,000,000	TP
76,000,000	MP
8,500,000	MMS
1,380,000	PS
4,000,000	WS

Note: the above figures refer only to Russia in Europe and Transcaucasia

(Russia naval box)

7	DB
9	PDB
10	AC
12	PC
40	D
25	TB
43	S

RUSSIA

Viborg
Kronstadt
Ust-Dvinsk
Libau
Kovno
Königsberg
Danzig
Grodno
raudenz
Osowiec
Masurian Lakes
Thorn
Novo-Georgievsk
osen
Warsaw
Brest-Litovsk
ogau
Ivangorod
Breslau
Bug
Glatz
Cracow
Przemysl
Kiev ★
Dnieper

R U S S I A

Dniester
Azov ✳
Nicolaiev
Ochakov
Yenikale
Kerch
Kinburn
AUSTRIA-HUNGARY
Komorn
Karlsburg
Sevastopol
Poti ✳
RUMANIA
Black   Sea
Batum ✳
Peterwardein
Kars ★
Belgrade
Danube
Sarajevo
BULGARIA
Mostar
MONTENEGRO
Trebinje
SERBIA
Constantinople
Cattaro
ALBANIA
O T T O M A N   E M P I R E
GREECE
aranto

(Ottoman box, centre)

7,500,000	TP
3,700,000	MP
1,390,000	MMS
106,000	PS
350,000	WS

(Ottoman box, right)

21,000,000	TP
10,000,000	MP
3,750,000	MMS
230,000	PS
500,000	WS

(Montenegro box, lower-left)

520,000	TP
260,000	MP
98,000	MMS
0	PS
40,000	WS

(Serbia box)

4,500,000	TP
2,250,000	MP
840,000	MMS
39,000	PS
330,000	WS

(Bulgaria box)

4,750,000	TP
2,400,000	MP
900,000	MMS
60,000	PS
300,000	WS

(Ottoman naval box)

3	PDB
2	LC

© Arthur Banks 1973

A Military Atlas of the First World War

A map history of the War of 1914–18 on land, at sea and in the air

A Military Atlas

commentary by ALAN PALMER

Arthur Banks

of the
First World War

TAPLINGER PUBLISHING COMPANY

NEW YORK

Maps © Arthur Banks 1975
Commentary © Alan Palmer 1975
First published in the United States in 1975 by
Taplinger Publishing Co., Inc.
New York, New York

ISBN 0-8008-5242-7
L.C. No 77-179660

To the memories of my father, Arthur Thomas Banks,
who served his country throughout the Mesopotamian
Campaign and my uncle, Charles Banks, who fell
at Mons

Printed and bound in Great Britain

PREFACE

It is now nearly a quarter of a century since I entered the specialised field of cartography and during that time I have been able to direct much of my effort into the fascinating, but technically complicated, area of military and historical map-production.

I soon discovered that the research material I needed was very widely scattered through many different libraries and military institutions and that much of my time would be spent in sifting through material and consulting veterans of past campaigns. At one time I longed to find some clear, reasonably-priced atlases of battles accompanied by succinct texts, tables, and diagrams. No such volumes seemed to exist, so far as I could discover. The idea of producing such an atlas myself took shape; from my researches and discussions with those who planned and took part in some of the actions I decided to compile my own cartographical record. This was the genesis of this present book.

In these times economy seems to dictate much that we do; therefore, my original plan to give detailed coverage to most of the important military campaigns has had to be modified. As a result, this book is necessarily briefer than the one I originally designed.

However, I hope that the book will be a convenient reference work which deals with those areas where a more detailed examination in cartographical terms has long been demanded.

Arthur Banks

ACKNOWLEDGEMENTS

During the research involved in the preparation of this atlas, I consulted some 1,300 historical reference works, examined and cross-checked 4,000 large- and small-scale maps (many of them of German or French origin), inspected several hundred technical manuals plus individual drawings, and attended numerous discussions with experts and veterans of the First World War.

Consequently, this must of necessity be a blanket appreciation of all those who were interested enough in my project to proffer advice and information in order to advance my work at various stages of the scheme.

In particular, I should like to thank General Sir James Marshall-Cornwall, Mr Michael Willis, and Mr Alan Palmer; all three went to enormous lengths to assist me and I am tremendously indebted to them.

In addition, the following persons deserve special mention and my gratitude: Dr R. Banks, Captain G. Bennett, Rear-Admiral P. Buckley, Captain L. Boswell, Captain E. Bush, Mrs J. Campbell, Miss R. Coombs, Major-General P. Essame, Miss S. Glover, Mr R. Holmes, Dr I. Nish, Mr V. Rigby, and Mr R. Welsh. Mr P. Richardson, Mr A. Hill, and Mr D. Heap of Heinemann Educational Books Limited extended endless encouragement and support to aid me in my task.

The librarians and staffs of the following organisations were generous in the facilities they placed at my disposal:

Imperial War Museum, Ministry of Defence, Royal Science Museum, Royal United Services Institute for Defence Studies, Royal Air Force Museum, H.M.S. *Vernon*, Hydrographic Department of the Admiralty, l'École Royale Militaire (Brussels), Turkish Naval Attaché's Office (London), United States Embassy (London), Belgian Embassy (London), and Surrey County Council Headquarters (Study and Information Department).

Finally, and above all, my wife deserves my deepest thanks: her devotion to my cause succoured me on so many occasions during the years of toil entailed in the research and preparation of this volume.

BIBLIOGRAPHICAL NOTE

Owing to the enormity of the research involved, it has proved impossible to itemise every reference work consulted, and the author feels that it would be unfair to specify particular accounts for recommended reading. However, he states that an essential first step for the serious student is to inspect the various military, naval, and aerial official histories of the belligerent powers. Usually these can be obtained from a central reference library or inspected at museums and institutions which specialise in military history and warfare.

CONTENTS

THE PERIPHERAL CAMPAIGNS

WEAPONS

THE WAR AT SEA

THE WAR IN THE AIR

THE PRE-WAR SITUATION

The coming of the Great War took the European peoples by surprise. In the spring of 1914 the nations of western and central Europe had been at peace with each other for forty-three years, a longer period free from conflict than ever before in their histories. Except in the south-eastern corner of the continent, where the Balkan peoples still sought complete independence from Turkish rule, frontiers had remained inviolate since the Franco-Prussian War. Two traditional battle cockpits, the Polish plains and the low-lying fields of Flanders, had escaped war not merely for forty years, but for a full century. Small wonder if the long European Peace lulled ordinary people into a false sense of security. Economists argued war was commercially so disruptive that no industrialised nation would resort to it; intellectuals maintained that international society was enlightened enough to scorn its folly.

Statesmen and generals remained less sanguine. There had, after all, been colonial campaigns throughout the armed peace. By 1914 the army of every European Great Power, except Germany and Austria-Hungary, had already been engaged in fighting since the turn of the century. If colonial disputes had not led to a general conflict it was because, as yet, they had never affected the vital interests of more than two Great Power rivals at the same time; but potentially they were dangerous, as the Agadir Crisis showed in 1911. Moreover no one could ignore the significance of the arms race. Naval and military expenditure by the Great Powers doubled in the last twenty years of the nineteenth century; it doubled again in the first decade of the twentieth. Where could the arms race finish, if not on the battlefield?

There was, too, uncertainty over the ability of the diplomats to safeguard peace much longer. By 1900 Europe was divided by rival alliances, with the Central Powers (Germany, Austria-Hungary, Italy) on one side and with France and Russia on the other. So long as potential opponents seemed equally strong, these alliances made for continuance of the peace rather than war. But by 1905 Russia, defeated in the Far East by Japan and weakened by the threat of revolution, had ceased to be militarily formidable. There was no genuine balance of strength between the Powers. Too many imponderables accumulated. What would the British do? The Liberal Government gave diplomatic support to its Entente partners, France and Russia, but evaded formal military obligations: in the last resort, only the 1839 pledge to uphold Belgium's neutrality counted in British reckoning. What, too, of Italy? Rivalry with Austria over territorial interests in the Adriatic made the Italians uncomfortable members of the Triple Alliance. Was Italy still a 'Central Power'? There was no doubt that the diplomatic system of 1900 had changed by 1914.

Yet mutual antagonism was growing in intensity rather than diminishing. The French still sought recovery of Alsace-Lorraine; the British were increasingly suspicious of Germany's naval shipbuilding programmes; Russian Pan-Slavism seemed to threaten the integrity of Austria-Hungary; and the Germans resented the web of encirclement which they believed others were weaving around them. Already these issues had provoked diplomatic crises, for which solutions were improvised by statesmen unready for war. But everyone in authority knew that once orders were given for mobilisation, the alliance system would work against any localisation of the conflict. Peace was fragile: the Sarajevo crime was to show it lay ultimately at the mercies of chance. The heir to the Austrian throne and his consort were assassinated in the Bosnian capital by a Serbian student on 28 June 1914. By the middle of August five European Great Powers and two of lesser standing were locked in battle from the Flanders Plain to the eastern foothills of the Carpathians.

© Arthur Banks 1973

MAIN REASONS WHY THE FIVE MAJOR EUROPEAN POWERS WENT TO WAR IN 1914

KEY

- The Triple Entente.
- The Central Powers.

RUSSIA

1. To ensure that Serbia was not crushed by Austria-Hungary.
2. To dominate the Balkans.
3. To strengthen the position of the Tsar at home; the ruling classes feared growing semi-revolutionary murmurs. A foreign victorious war seemed a good insurance against any internal strife.

GERMANY

1. To protect Austria-Hungary from the consequences of her attack on Serbia.
2. To preserve German security; the Kaiser feared an "encircle-ment" by the Triple Entente powers.
3. To demonstrate Germany's emergence from a continental role to world power status.
4. To gain advantage from a surprise attack. Britain appeared pre-occupied in Ireland and India and with the suffragette movement. Furthermore, Germany was sceptical of Britain's full determination to honour her obligations to Belgium.

AUSTRIA - HUNGARY

1. To crush Pan-Serb movement.
2. To dominate the Balkans by crushing Serbia, thus securing Austrian control of the route to Salonika on the Aegean.

BRITAIN

1. To honour treaty obligations to Belgium dating back to 1839.
2. To preserve world naval supremacy.
3. To support France; under a naval agreement, Britain "protected" the English Channel and North Sea zones, thus releasing the French fleet for possible Mediterranean operations.
4. To avoid a continental shift in the balance of power.

? MORAL OBLIGATION. BRITISH CABINET INFLUENCED BY THE MILITARY STAFF TALKS?

FRANCE

1. To combat growing military importance of Germany.
2. To fulfill treaty obligations to Russia.
3. To regain Alsace and Lorraine.

0   300
Miles

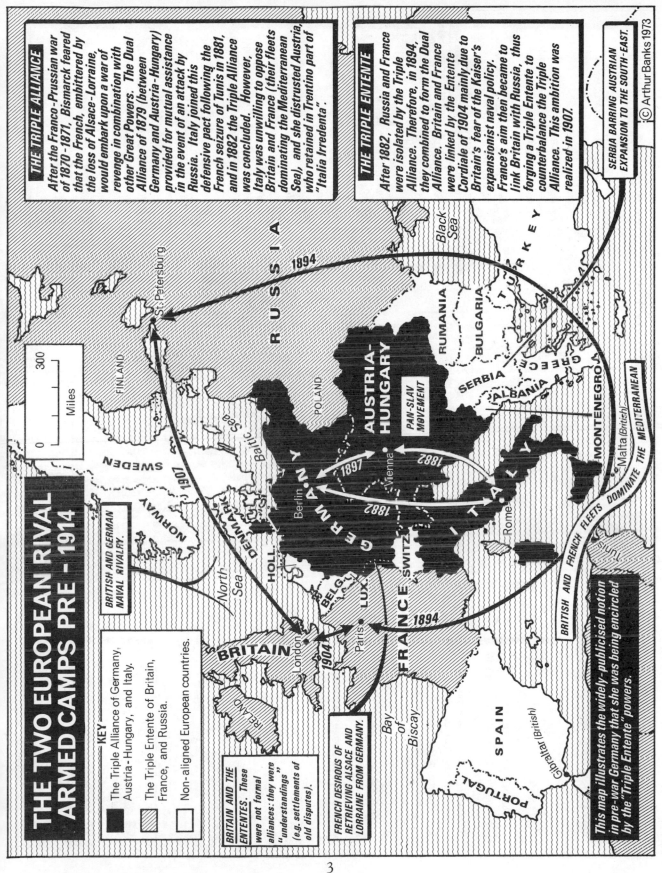

THE TWO EUROPEAN RIVAL ARMED CAMPS PRE – 1914

KEY
- The Triple Alliance of Germany, Austria-Hungary, and Italy.
- The Triple Entente of Britain, France, and Russia.
- Non-aligned European countries.

BRITISH AND GERMAN NAVAL RIVALRY.

BRITAIN AND THE ENTENTES. These were not formal alliances: they were "understandings" (e.g. settlements of old disputes).

FRENCH DESIROUS OF RETRIEVING ALSACE AND LORRAINE FROM GERMANY.

THE TRIPLE ALLIANCE

After the Franco-Prussian war of 1870-1871, Bismarck feared that the French, embittered by the loss of Alsace-Lorraine, would embark upon a war of revenge in combination with other Great Powers. The Dual Alliance of 1879 (between Germany and Austria-Hungary) provided for mutual assistance in the event of an attack by Russia. Italy joined this defensive pact following the French seizure of Tunis in 1881, and in 1882 the Triple Alliance was concluded. However, Italy was unwilling to oppose Britain and France (their fleets dominating the Mediterranean Sea), and she distrusted Austria, who retained in Trentino part of "Italia Irredenta".

THE TRIPLE ENTENTE

After 1882, Russia and France were isolated by the Triple Alliance. Therefore, in 1894, they combined to form the Dual Alliance. Britain and France were linked by the Entente Cordiale of 1904 mainly due to Britain's fear of the Kaiser's expansionist naval policy. France's aim then became to link Britain with Russia, thus forging a Triple Entente to counterbalance the Triple Alliance. This ambition was realized in 1907.

SERBIA BARRING AUSTRIAN EXPANSION TO THE SOUTH-EAST.

© Arthur Banks 1973

This map illustrates the widely-publicised notion in pre-war Germany that she was being encircled by the "Triple Entente" powers.

PAN-SLAV MOVEMENT

BRITISH AND FRENCH FLEETS DOMINATE THE MEDITERRANEAN

3

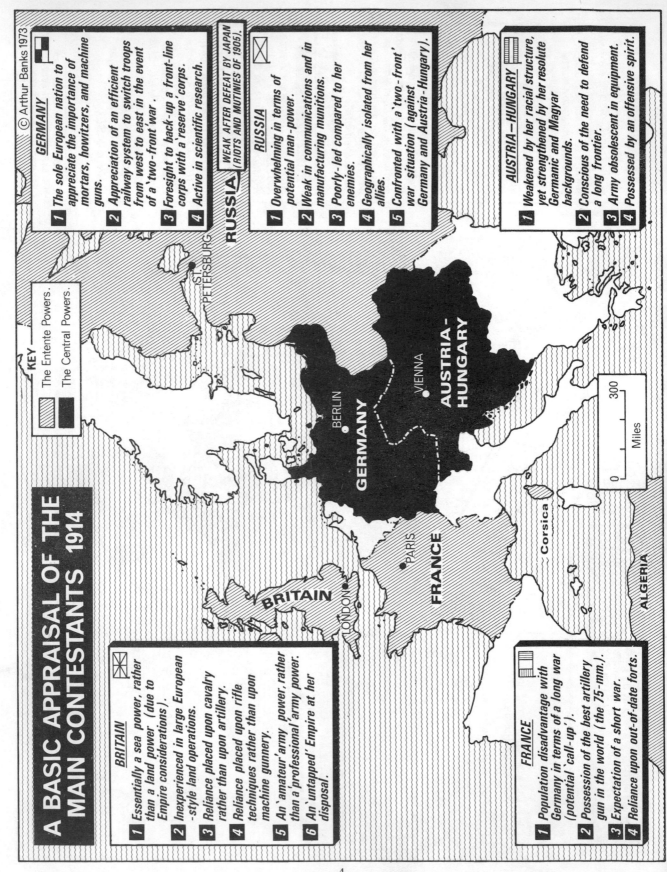

A BASIC APPRAISAL OF THE MAIN CONTESTANTS 1914

© Arthur Banks 1973

GERMANY

1 The sole European nation to appreciate the importance of mortars, howitzers, and machine guns.

2 Appreciation of an efficient railway system to switch troops from west to east in the event of a 'two-front war'.

3 Foresight to back-up a front-line corps with a 'reserve' corps.

4 Active in scientific research.

RUSSIA — WEAK AFTER DEFEAT BY JAPAN (RIOTS AND MUTINIES OF 1905).

1 Overwhelming in terms of potential man-power.

2 Weak in communications and in manufacturing munitions.

3 Poorly-led compared to her enemies.

4 Geographically isolated from her allies.

5 Confronted with a 'two-front' war situation (against Germany and Austria-Hungary).

AUSTRIA – HUNGARY

1 Weakened by her racial structure, yet strengthened by her resolute Germanic and Magyar backgrounds.

2 Conscious of the need to defend a long frontier.

3 Army obsolescent in equipment.

4 Possessed by an offensive spirit.

KEY

The Entente Powers.

The Central Powers.

BRITAIN

1 Essentially a sea power, rather than a land power (due to Empire considerations).

2 Inexperienced in large European-style land operations.

3 Reliance placed upon cavalry rather than upon artillery.

4 Reliance placed upon rifle techniques rather than upon machine gunnery.

5 An 'amateur' army power, rather than a professional army power.

6 An 'untapped' Empire at her disposal.

FRANCE

1 Population disadvantage with Germany in terms of a long war (potential 'call-up').

2 Possession of the best artillery gun in the world (the 75-mm.).

3 Expectation of a short war.

4 Reliance upon out-of-date forts.

ST. PETERSBURG

BERLIN

VIENNA

GERMANY

AUSTRIA–HUNGARY

BRITAIN

LONDON

PARIS

FRANCE

Corsica

ALGERIA

0   300
Miles

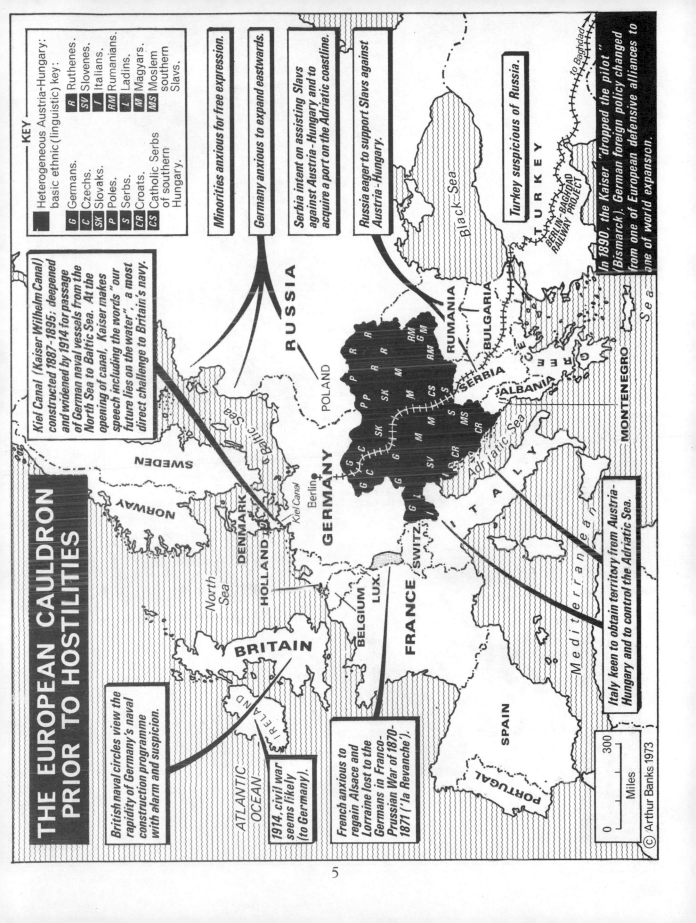

THE EUROPEAN CAULDRON PRIOR TO HOSTILITIES

KEY

■ Heterogeneous Austria-Hungary: basic ethnic (linguistic) key:

G Germans.　*R* Ruthenes.
C Czechs.　*SV* Slovenes.
SK Slovaks.　*I* Italians.
P Poles.　*RM* Rumanians.
S Serbs.　*L* Ladins.
CR Croats.　*M* Magyars.
CS Catholic Serbs of southern Hungary.　*MS* Moslem southern Slavs.

Kiel Canal (Kaiser Wilhelm Canal) constructed 1887-1895: deepened and widened by 1914 for passage of German naval vessels from the North Sea to Baltic Sea. At the opening of canal, Kaiser makes speech including the words "our future lies on the water", a most direct challenge to Britain's navy.

British naval circles view the rapidity of Germany's naval construction programme with alarm and suspicion.

1914, civil war seems likely (to Germany).

French anxious to regain Alsace and Lorraine lost to the Germans in Franco-Prussian War of 1870-1871 ('la Revanche').

Minorities anxious for free expression.

Germany anxious to expand eastwards.

Serbia intent on assisting Slavs against Austria-Hungary and to acquire a port on the Adriatic coastline.

Russia eager to support Slavs against Austria-Hungary.

Turkey suspicious of Russia.

In 1890, the Kaiser "dropped the pilot" (Bismarck). German foreign policy changed from one of European defensive alliances to one of world expansion.

Italy keen to obtain territory from Austria-Hungary and to control the Adriatic Sea.

© Arthur Banks 1973

0 ⎯ 300 Miles

BERLIN-BAGHDAD RAILWAY PROJECT   to Baghdad

5

WORLD EMPIRES OF BRITAIN, FRANCE, AND GERMANY 1914

KEY

■	British Empire in 1914 (total population: 400,000,000).
▨	French Empire in 1914 (total population: 95,638,000).
▢	German Empire in 1914 (total population: 68,745,000).

Note: by the end of 1914, the only German overseas possession remaining uncaptured by the Allies was German East Africa.

Empire troops played a large part in the war, notably those of Britain.

© Arthur Banks 1973

6

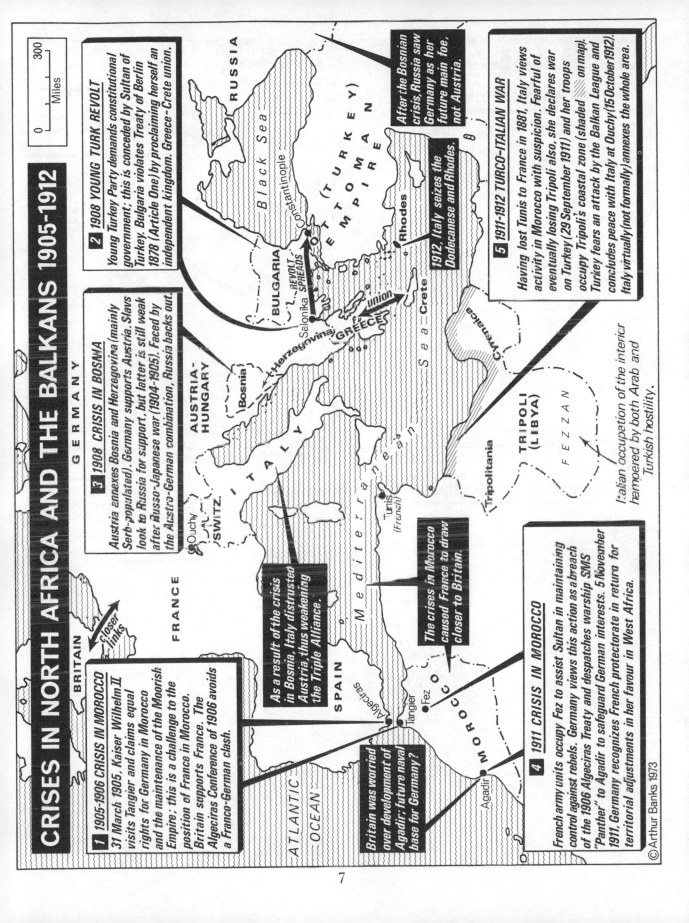

CRISES IN NORTH AFRICA AND THE BALKANS 1905–1912

1 **1905–1906 CRISIS IN MOROCCO**
31 March 1905, Kaiser Wilhelm II visits Tangier and claims equal rights for Germany in Morocco and the maintenance of the Moorish Empire; this is a challenge to the position of France in Morocco. Britain supports France. The Algeciras Conference of 1906 avoids a Franco-German clash.

2 **1908 YOUNG TURK REVOLT**
Young Turkey Party demands constitutional government; this is conceded by Sultan of Turkey. Bulgaria violates Treaty of Berlin 1878 (Article One) by proclaiming herself an independent kingdom. Greece–Crete union.

3 **1908 CRISIS IN BOSNIA**
Austria annexes Bosnia and Herzegovina (mainly Serb-populated). Germany supports Austria. Slavs look to Russia for support, but latter is still weak after Russo-Japanese war (1904–1905). Faced by the Austro-German combination, Russia backs out.

4 **1911 CRISIS IN MOROCCO**
French army units occupy Fez to assist Sultan in maintaining control against rebels. Germany views this action as a breach of the 1906 Algeciras Treaty and despatches warship SMS "Panther" to Agadir to safeguard German interests. 5 November 1911, Germany recognizes French protectorate in return for territorial adjustments in her favour in West Africa.

5 **1911–1912 TURCO-ITALIAN WAR**
Having lost Tunis to France in 1881, Italy views activity in Morocco with suspicion. Fearful of eventually losing Tripoli also, she declares war on Turkey (29 September 1911) and her troops occupy Tripoli's coastal zone (shaded //// on map). Turkey fears an attack by the Balkan League and concludes peace with Italy at Ouchy (15 October 1912). Italy virtually (not formally) annexes the whole area.

After the Bosnian crisis, Russia saw Germany as her future main foe, not Austria.

1912, Italy seizes the Dodecanese and Rhodes.

As a result of the crisis in Bosnia, Italy distrusted Austria thus weakening the Triple Alliance.

The crises in Morocco caused France to draw closer to Britain.

Britain was worried over development of Agadir: future naval base for Germany?

closer links

Italian occupation of the interior hampered by both Arab and Turkish hostility.

© Arthur Banks 1973

0 — 300 Miles

7

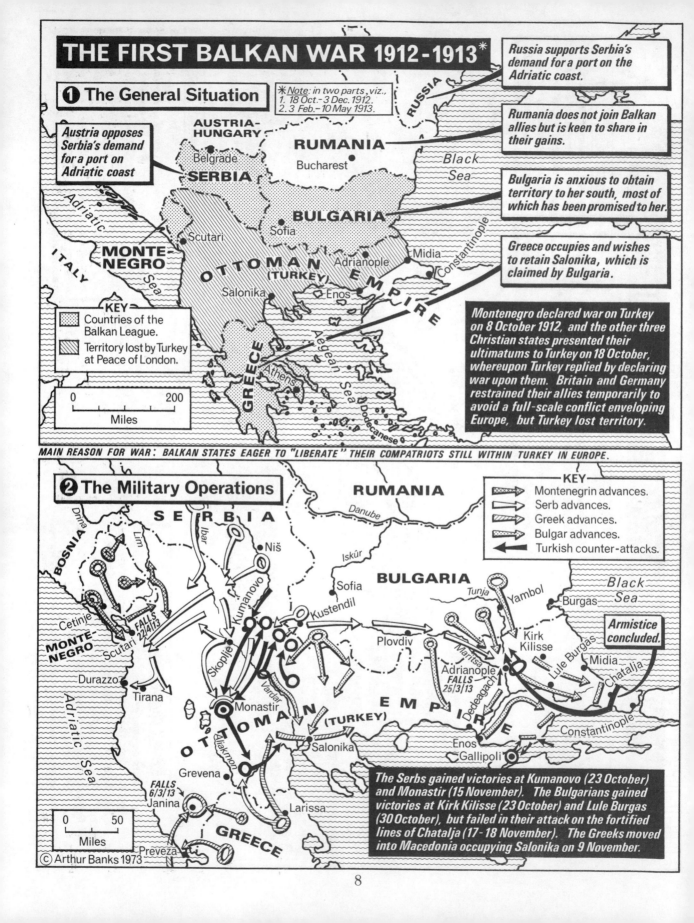

THE FIRST BALKAN WAR 1912-1913*

❶ The General Situation

*Note: in two parts, viz.,
1. 18 Oct.– 3 Dec. 1912.
2. 3 Feb.– 10 May 1913.

Russia supports Serbia's demand for a port on the Adriatic coast.

Austria opposes Serbia's demand for a port on Adriatic coast

Rumania does not join Balkan allies but is keen to share in their gains.

Bulgaria is anxious to obtain territory to her south, most of which has been promised to her.

Greece occupies and wishes to retain Salonika, which is claimed by Bulgaria.

AUSTRIA-HUNGARY
RUSSIA
RUMANIA
Belgrade
Bucharest
Black Sea
SERBIA
BULGARIA
Sofia
Adriatic Sea
Scutari
MONTE-NEGRO
Adrianople
Midia
ITALY
OTTOMAN (TURKEY) EMPIRE
Constantinople
Salonika
Enos
Aegean Sea
GREECE
Athens
Dodecanese

KEY
- Countries of the Balkan League.
- Territory lost by Turkey at Peace of London.

0 — 200
Miles

Montenegro declared war on Turkey on 8 October 1912, and the other three Christian states presented their ultimatums to Turkey on 18 October, whereupon Turkey replied by declaring war upon them. Britain and Germany restrained their allies temporarily to avoid a full-scale conflict enveloping Europe, but Turkey lost territory.

MAIN REASON FOR WAR: BALKAN STATES EAGER TO "LIBERATE" THEIR COMPATRIOTS STILL WITHIN TURKEY IN EUROPE.

❷ The Military Operations

KEY
- ⟫⟫⟫ Montenegrin advances.
- ➯ Serb advances.
- ⟋⟋➯ Greek advances.
- ⟫⟫⟫ Bulgar advances.
- ⬅ Turkish counter-attacks.

RUMANIA
Danube
SERBIA
BOSNIA
Drina
Lim
Ibar
Niš
Iskûr
BULGARIA
Sofia
Black Sea
Tunja
Yambol
Burgas
Cetinje
Kumanovo
Kustendil
MONTE-NEGRO
FALLS 22/4/13
Scutari
Plovdiv
Kirk Kilisse
Durazzo
Skopje
Vardar
Adrianople
FALLS 25/3/13
Maritsa
Lule Burgas
Midia
Chatalja
Tirana
Monastir
OTTOMAN EMPIRE
(TURKEY)
Dedeagach
Armistice concluded.
Adriatic Sea
Aliakmon
Salonika
Enos
Constantinople
Grevena
Gallipoli
FALLS 6/3/13
Janina
Larissa
Preveza
GREECE

The Serbs gained victories at Kumanovo (23 October) and Monastir (15 November). The Bulgarians gained victories at Kirk Kilisse (23 October) and Lule Burgas (30 October), but failed in their attack on the fortified lines of Chatalja (17-18 November). The Greeks moved into Macedonia occupying Salonika on 9 November.

0 — 50
Miles

© Arthur Banks 1973

8

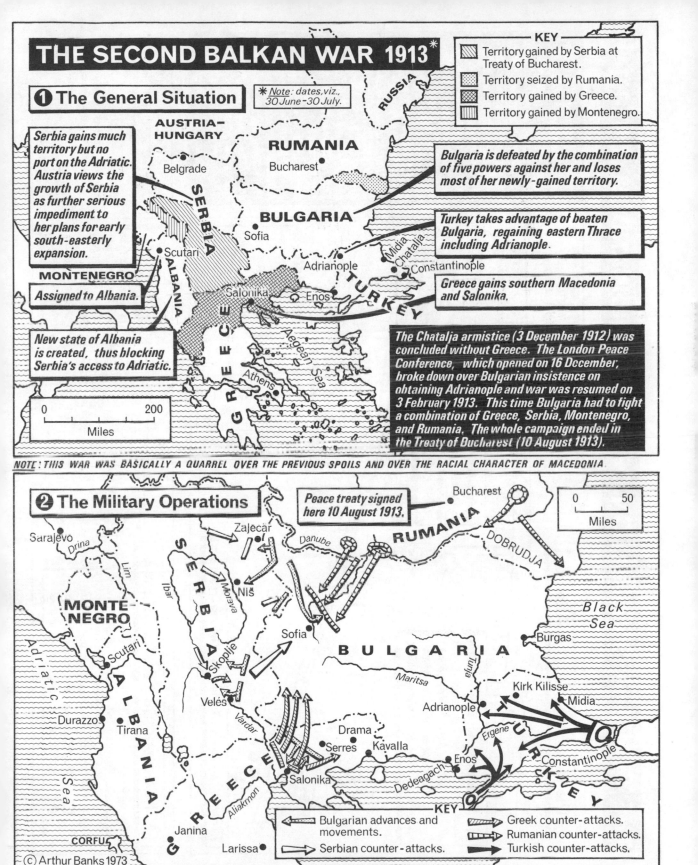

THE SECOND BALKAN WAR 1913*

❶ The General Situation

*Note: dates, viz., 30 June – 30 July.

AUSTRIA–HUNGARY

RUMANIA

Bucharest

Belgrade

SERBIA

Sofia

Scutari

BULGARIA

MONTENEGRO

ALBANIA

Salonika

Midia
Chatalja

Adrianople

Constantinople

TURKEY

Enos

GREECE

Aegean Sea

Athens

0 ____ 200
Miles

Serbia gains much territory but no port on the Adriatic. Austria views the growth of Serbia as further serious impediment to her plans for early south-easterly expansion.

MONTENEGRO
Assigned to Albania.

New state of Albania is created, thus blocking Serbia's access to Adriatic.

Bulgaria is defeated by the combination of five powers against her and loses most of her newly-gained territory.

Turkey takes advantage of beaten Bulgaria, regaining eastern Thrace including Adrianople.

Greece gains southern Macedonia and Salonika.

The Chatalja armistice (3 December 1912) was concluded without Greece. The London Peace Conference, which opened on 16 December, broke down over Bulgarian insistence on obtaining Adrianople and war was resumed on 3 February 1913. This time Bulgaria had to fight a combination of Greece, Serbia, Montenegro, and Rumania. The whole campaign ended in the Treaty of Bucharest (10 August 1913).

KEY
- Territory gained by Serbia at Treaty of Bucharest.
- Territory seized by Rumania.
- Territory gained by Greece.
- Territory gained by Montenegro.

RUSSIA

NOTE: THIS WAR WAS BASICALLY A QUARREL OVER THE PREVIOUS SPOILS AND OVER THE RACIAL CHARACTER OF MACEDONIA.

❷ The Military Operations

Peace treaty signed here 10 August 1913.

Bucharest

0 ____ 50
Miles

Sarajevo

Drina

Zaječar

Danube

RUMANIA

DOBRUDJA

SERBIA

Lim

Ibar

Morava

NIS

MONTE NEGRO

Black Sea

Scutari

Skopje

Sofia

BULGARIA

Burgas

ALBANIA

Veles

Vardar

Maritsa

Tunja

Kirk Kilisse

Midia

Durazzo

Tirana

Drama

Serres

Kavalla

Adrianople

Ergene

TURKEY

Adriatic Sea

GREECE

Salonika

Aliakmon

Enos

Dedeagach

Constantinople

Janina

Larissa

CORFU

© Arthur Banks 1973

KEY
- Bulgarian advances and movements.
- Serbian counter-attacks.
- Greek counter-attacks.
- Rumanian counter-attacks.
- Turkish counter-attacks.

9

THE 'SPARK'—ASSASSINATION OF FRANZ FERDINAND 28 JUNE 1914

The assassination of Archduke Franz Ferdinand (heir to the throne of Austria–Hungary) and his wife at Sarajevo, capital of Bosnia, was the spark igniting a chain reaction sequence that led to the outbreak of war in 1914. A group of conspirators associated with two Balkan Slav societies (the 'Black Hand' and the 'Young Bosnia') were involved in the plot, which was put into operation on St. Vitus' Day (a Serbian festival).

The first attempt failed, but the Archduke, who was on an official visit to Sarajevo, went on to the Town Hall as arranged. The return route was altered but the driver of the Archduke's car misunderstood the change of plan (due to poor briefing) and followed the leading car into Franz Josef Street. Princip, one of the conspirators, saw the car reversing into Appel Quay, ran into the road and shot the Archduke and Duchess.

CLARIFICATION NOTE : 'BLACK HAND' WAS A SECRET SERBIAN SOCIETY, WHEREAS 'YOUNG BOSNIA' WAS A MOVEMENT, PARTLY CULTURAL.

THE TRAGIC FAMILY HISTORY OF FRANZ JOSEF (EMPEROR OF AUSTRIA)

1867. His brother, Emperor of Mexico, was executed.
1889. His son, Crown Prince Rudolf, died mysteriously.
1898. His wife, Empress Elizabeth, was assassinated.

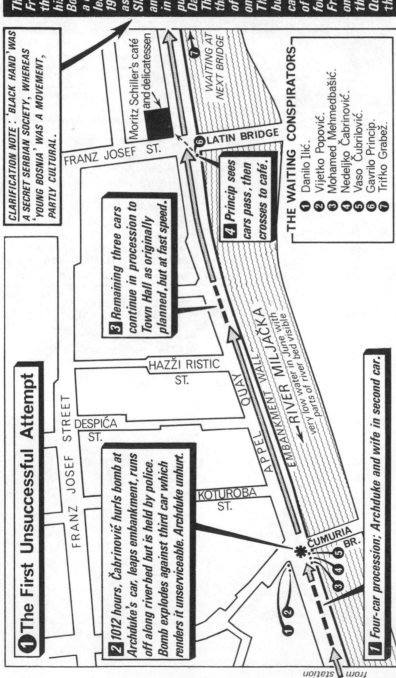

① The First Unsuccessful Attempt

2 1012 hours, Čabrinović hurls bomb at Archduke's car, leaps embankment, runs off along river bed but is held by police. Bomb explodes against third car which renders it unserviceable. Archduke unhurt.

3 Remaining three cars continue in procession to Town Hall as originally planned, but at fast speed.

4 Princip sees cars pass, then crosses to café.

Moritz Schiller's café and delicatessen

FRANZ JOSEF ST.

LATIN BRIDGE

WAITING AT NEXT BRIDGE

RIVER MILJAČKA with very low water in June with parts of river bed visible

EMBANKMENT

QUAY WALL

APPEL QUAY

HAZŽI RISTIC ST.

FRANZ JOSEF STREET

DESPIĆA ST.

KOTUROBA ST.

CUMURIA BR.

from station

THE WAITING CONSPIRATORS

① Danilo Ilić.
② Vijetko Popović.
③ Mohamed Mehmedbašić.
④ Nedeljko Čabrinović.
⑤ Vaso Čubrilović.
⑥ Gavrilo Princip.
⑦ Trifko Grabež.

1 Four-car procession; Archduke and wife in second car.

② The Second Successful Attempt

Princip (positioned at Schiller's store) fires two shots from Browning automatic at five yards range (1045 hours). Archduke and wife mortally wounded.

MILJAČKA

LATIN BR.

STREET

RIVER

FRANZ JOSEF

APPEL QUAY

visit to museum

KEY
- — — Return route from Town Hall as originally planned (before Čabrinović's bomb action).
- ······ Revised return route (after bomb action).
- **S** Moritz Schiller's delicatessen/café shop.
- **c** Position of car during Princip's action.

© Arthur Banks 1973

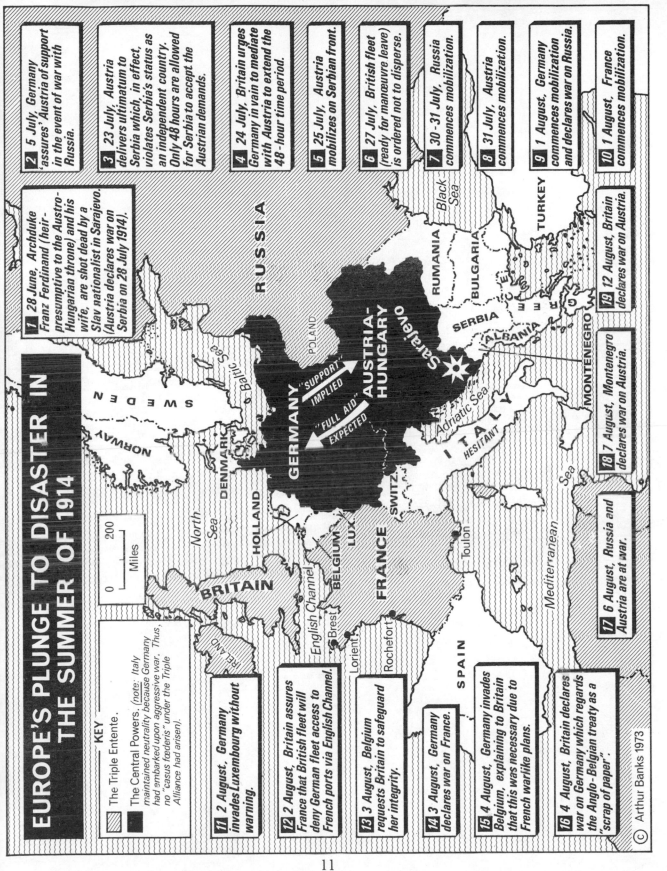

EUROPE'S PLUNGE TO DISASTER IN THE SUMMER OF 1914

KEY

- ⬜ The Triple Entente.
- ⬛ The Central Powers. *(note: Italy maintained neutrality because Germany had embarked upon aggressive war. Thus, no "casus foederis" under the Triple Alliance had arisen).*

0 — 200 Miles

1 28 June, Archduke Franz Ferdinand (heir-presumptive to the Austro-Hungarian throne) and his wife, are shot dead by a Slav nationalist in Sarajevo. (Austria declares war on Serbia on 28 July 1914).

2 5 July, Germany 'assures' Austria of support in the event of war with Russia.

3 23 July, Austria delivers ultimatum to Serbia which, in effect, violates Serbia's status as an independent country. Only 48 hours are allowed for Serbia to accept the Austrian demands.

4 24 July, Britain urges Germany in vain to mediate with Austria to extend the 48-hour time period.

5 25 July, Austria mobilizes on Serbian front.

6 27 July, British fleet (ready for manoeuvre leave) is ordered not to disperse.

7 30-31 July, Russia commences mobilization.

8 31 July, Austria commences mobilization.

9 1 August, Germany commences mobilization and declares war on Russia.

10 1 August, France commences mobilization.

11 2 August, Germany invades Luxembourg without warning.

12 2 August, Britain assures France that British fleet will deny German fleet access via English Channel.

13 3 August, Belgium requests Britain to safeguard her integrity.

14 3 August, Germany declares war on France.

15 4 August, Germany invades Belgium, explaining to Britain that this was necessary due to French warlike plans.

16 4 August, Britain declares war on Germany which regards the Anglo-Belgian treaty as a "scrap of paper".

17 6 August, Russia and Austria are at war.

18 7 August, Montenegro declares war on Austria.

19 12 August, Britain declares war on Austria.

© Arthur Banks 1973

11

WAR ON THE WESTERN FRONT IN 1914

There had never been so great a concentration of military forces as in August 1914. A little over a century before, Napoleon (who, with Voltaire, believed fortune favoured 'the big battalions') staggered his contemporaries by gathering a Grand Army of 500,000 men to invade Russia. Yet, within a fortnight of the outbreak of war in 1914, the Germans had three times that number in France and Belgium alone. At the same time there were over a million Frenchmen on the Western Front, with three million reservists on call; both the Russians and the Austrians had more than a million and a quarter field troops along their frontiers; and by the end of the year a million volunteers in Britain had come forward for Kitchener's 'New Army'. Napoleon's Marshals counted their big battalions in hundreds of thousands; the commanders of 1914 thought in millions.

These huge numbers determined the character of the war. Military theorists in both France and Germany had long believed victory would come to the nation able rapidly to mobilise its mass of manpower and deploy its forces effectively in the field. It was assumed that the key to success lay in an offensive spirit and that the outcome of the war would be decided by a single campaign on each Front. Kitchener warned the British Cabinet the war would last for at least three years, but his colleagues doubted his powers of judgment. In Berlin that August the Kaiser told departing troops, 'You will be home before the leaves have fallen from the trees'; and few public figures in London, Paris or St Petersburg (soon to be renamed Petrograd) believed the fighting would continue for more than six months. The great tragedy for Europe is that when rapid victory eluded the combatants, the armies—still massive in numbers—became deadlocked in trench warfare, the big battalions checked by the unexpected defensive power of machine guns and exposed to the fury of weapons which the authorities had underrated. It was this transformation of the battlefield which wasted so many lives. Casualties were heavy during the 'war of movement': they were heavier still during the long agony of the 'war of attrition'. At a conservative estimate over the world as a whole—with land fighting in three continents and with warships engaged on every

ocean—one sailor, soldier or airman was killed for every ten seconds the war lasted; and it continued in the end for fifty-one months.

Yet, at the outset, it seemed as if the fighting would indeed 'all be over by Christmas'. The Schlieffen Plan, finally adopted by the German General Staff at the end of 1905, proposed a holding operation against the Russians (who, it was assumed, would be slow to mobilise) in the East while the bulk of the German Army struck against France with an enveloping movement through Flanders and Picardy which would invest Paris from the west and south and thus force the French armies eastwards on to their own defences from Nancy to Belfort. British intervention, though regarded as probable once Belgium was invaded, was discounted as negligible. France defeated, the Germans planned to use the network of railways to move their forces eastwards and destroy the Russian menace. This plan, which was modified by Moltke (Chief of the German General Staff since 1906) in the three years immediately preceding the war, came within an ace of success. The French grand design—Plan XVII—to some extent played into German hands, for it committed two armies to an attack on Lorraine, away from the principal threat to the heart of France. Even when amended after the German invasion of Luxembourg, Plan XVII still ignored the strength of the enemy's thrust into western Belgium. So successful were the Germans that on 30 August the readers of *The Times* in England were startled to learn that 'the investment of Paris cannot be banished from the field of possibility'. What the public was not told was that the French, exhausting themselves by courageous counter-attacks in the spirit of Napoleonic battle panoramas, had already suffered nearly a third of a million casualties (dead, missing, wounded). One out of every ten officers in the whole French army (not merely the regiments in the field) was killed or incapacitated before the end of August 1914.

Moltke's variation on the Schlieffen Plan failed for three principal reasons. He lost touch with his army commanders, who showed excessive independence of manoeuvre; he was so worried by reports of the

Russian advance into East Prussia that he weakened his right wing by detaching troops to the East (compare pages 19, 88 and 89); and he failed to see that three weeks of forced marches in intensive heat and blazing sunshine had reduced the efficiency of the invading armies. When General von Kluck began to move his tired troops south-eastwards, exposing the right flank of the German First Army to the Paris garrison (page 54), the fate of the whole war was in the balance. The French commander-in-chief, Joffre, supported by the Military Governor of Paris, General Gallieni, ordered the French Sixth, Fifth and Ninth Armies (Generals Maunoury, Franchet d'Espèrey and Foch) together with the British Expeditionary Force (Field-Marshal Sir John French) to counter-attack across the lower Marne and its tributaries on 5–6 September. There followed the series of inter-related engagements, the legendary 'miracle of the Marne', fought along a front of more than 125 miles. Momentarily the nerve of the German High Command seemed to crack; Paris and France were saved; the German knock-out blow—which had stunned France in 1870 and which was to stun France again in 1940—was thrust aside.

If the Allies had not themselves been so weary and cautious that September, they might well have turned the German retreat from the Marne into a sensational defeat. As it was, the Germans found they could stabilise their line north of Rheims and along the river Aisne. Moltke retired from active service and was replaced as Chief of the German General Staff by General von Falkenhayn, who at once determined to consolidate the German hold on Belgium, through which the invaders had passed like a scythe in the first weeks of war. When Brussels was occupied on 20 August five divisions of the Belgian Army (80,000 men) fell back on Antwerp, the great fortress-port on the Schelde. So long as the Belgians held Antwerp (from which they made a number of sorties to relieve pressure on the French and British on the Marne and the Aisne) there was a possibility of using the city as a point from which to attack the German right flank. This threat the Germans were determined to eradicate. The First Lord of the Admiralty, Churchill, sought to stiffen resistance in Antwerp by a personal visit and by sending from England a naval division, which was hastily trained and inadequately armed. In the event, the Belgians placed excessive reliance on outdated forts and redoubts which could not withstand the pounding of German artillery. Antwerp duly surrendered to General von Beseler on

9 October, but the main Belgian army withdrew by way of Ghent and Bruges to the line of a canalised small river, the Yser. There, inspired by their courageous King Albert, the Belgians resisted a German advance towards Dunkirk, eventually opening the sluices of Nieuport and bringing the North Sea in flood to the aid of the defenders.

While Beseler was besieging Antwerp, both the Germans and the Allies were engaged in a complicated movement from the Aisne to cover the Channel ports. At times during this 'race for the sea' it seemed as if both sides were risking envelopment by the other during their outflanking operations. Briefly there was hope that the British would capture Lille and open up a route towards Brussels, but they failed to penetrate the town in strength. All six divisions of the B.E.F. were moved northwards from the Aisne to Flanders. By the end of the second week in October they had established a salient around Ypres, Armentières and Neuve Chapelle. It was here that they faced Falkenhayn's principal attempt to break through the Allied positions and take Calais and Boulogne.

The first battle of Ypres (October–November 1914) virtually destroyed the old peacetime British regular army and began to take heavy toll of the new territorial infantry battalions as well. 50,000 British soldiers fell at Ypres that autumn, one division losing two-thirds of its infantry in three weeks of combat. Hardest hit were the original 'old contemptibles', the men who had gone forward to Mons in August (page 47) and retreated for a gruelling fortnight before turning back south of the Marne and forcing the Germans northwards to the Belgian frontier. By the end of November over half of the men who had crossed to France three months previously were casualties, one in ten of them dead. The Germans lost twice as many soldiers as the British at Ypres, yet they never broke through. They penetrated the British line at Gheluvelt on the Menin Road (31 October) but were ejected in a surprise counter attack by the 2nd Battalion of the Worcestershire Regiment, subsequently supported by French units. The city of Ypres was never captured by the Germans, even though fighting raged continuously around the ruined mediaeval cloth town for four years. Ypres and its salient acquired a symbolic significance for the British which was out of all proportion to its strategic value. There were two later battles within the Ypres Salient: in the spring of 1915 (pages 138–143) and from June to November 1917 (pages 172–173); and a final penetration of the German positions in September 1918 (page 196).

Winter set in before the First Battle of Ypres was over. There was no longer any danger of an outright German victory, but equally there was little prospect of an Allied breakthrough. First Ypres marked the end of open warfare: henceforth the opposing armies on the Western Front were paralysed by barbed wire, by entrenchments, by minefields, and by machine-gun emplacements. In another sense, too, First Ypres marked a change of character in the war. The first month of fighting had shown divisions and suspicion between the Allied commanders, especially between the British and the French. The close proximity of British, French and Belgian lines around Ypres helped to weld together the Allied command, although it was difficult to forget old prejudices. The mud-filled disease-ridden trenches bred a sense of communal adversity. At the same time First Ypres showed the extent of Allied resources, for in the line were not only the first battalions of Kitchener's 'new army', but Zouave regiments from French Algeria and Indians from Lahore. Before the fighting died away at the salient in 1918, they were to be joined by units from Canada, Senegal and finally the United States. The cemeteries around Ypres, and the great monument to those 'with no known grave', bear silent testimony to the world-wide character of this most wasteful of wars.

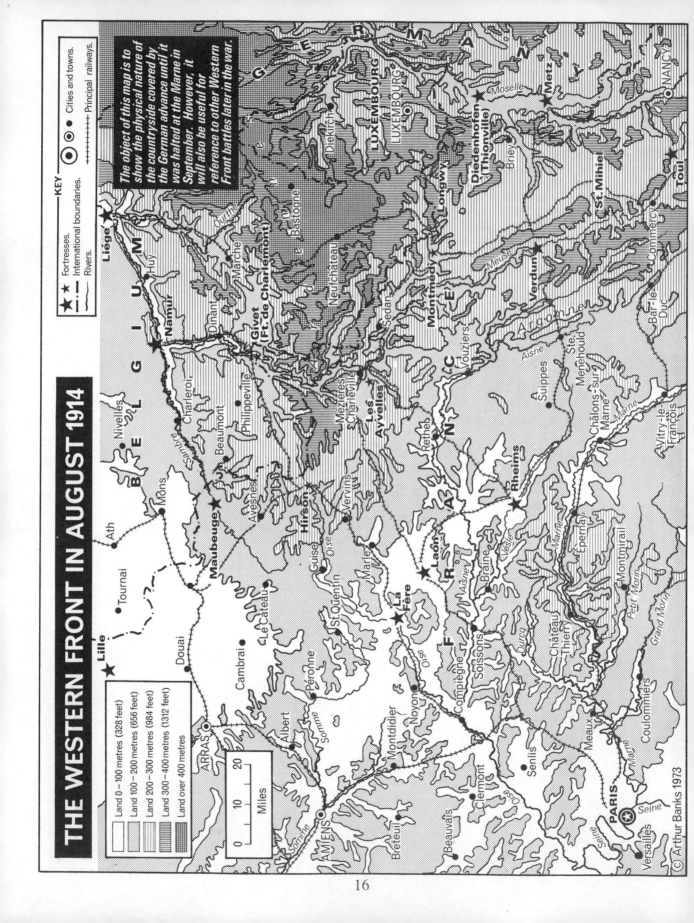

THE WESTERN FRONT IN AUGUST 1914

KEY

★ ★	Fortresses.
·—·—·	International boundaries.
———	Rivers.
⊙ ⊙ ●	Cities and towns.
┼┼┼┼┼	Principal railways.

The object of this map is to show the physical nature of the countryside covered by the German advance until it was halted at the Marne in September. However, it will also be useful for reference to other Western Front battles later in the war.

Land 0 – 100 metres (328 feet)
Land 100 – 200 metres (656 feet)
Land 200 – 300 metres (984 feet)
Land 300 – 400 metres (1312 feet)
Land over 400 metres

Miles
0   10   20

© Arthur Banks 1973

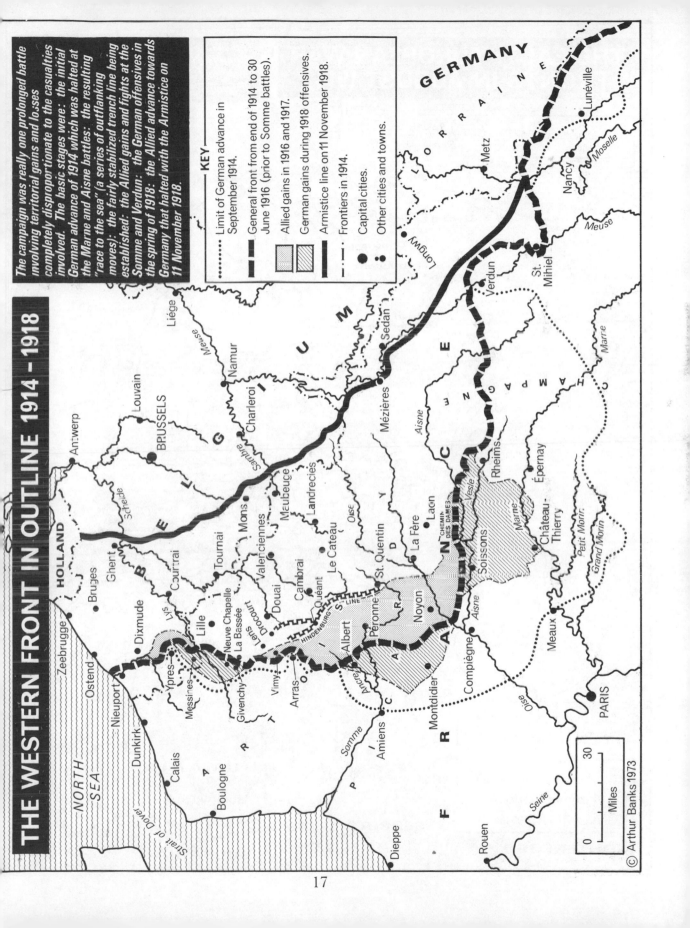

THE WESTERN FRONT IN OUTLINE 1914 – 1918

The campaign was really one prolonged battle involving territorial gains and losses completely disproportionate to the casualties involved. The basic stages were: the initial German advance of 1914 which was halted at the Marne and Aisne battles: the resulting "race to the sea" (a series of outflanking moves): the fairly stabilized trench line being established: the Allied gains and fights at the Somme and Verdun: the German offensives in the spring of 1918: the Allied advance towards Germany that halted with the Armistice on 11 November 1918.

KEY

Limit of German advance in September 1914.	
General front from end of 1914 to 30 June 1916 (prior to Somme battles).	
Allied gains in 1916 and 1917.	
German gains during 1918 offensives.	
Armistice line on 11 November 1918.	
Frontiers in 1914.	
Capital cities.	
Other cities and towns.	

GERMANY

LORRAINE

Lunéville
Metz
Nancy
Moselle
Meuse
Verdun
St. Mihiel
Longwy
Sedan
Mézières
Rheims
Épernay
Château-Thierry
Soissons
Laon
La Fère
St. Quentin
Péronne
Noyon
Montdidier
Compiègne
Meaux
PARIS
Amiens
Albert
Arras
Vimy
Lens
Douai
Cambrai
Le Cateau
Maubeuge
Landrecies
Valenciennes
Mons
Tournai
Courtrai
Lille
La Bassée
Neuve Chapelle
Givenchy
Messines
Ypres
Dixmude
Nieuport
Ostend
Zeebrugge
Dunkirk
Calais
Boulogne
Dieppe
Rouen
Bruges
Ghent
BRUSSELS
Louvain
Antwerp
Namur
Charleroi
Liège

HOLLAND
BELGIUM
FRANCE
CHAMPAGNE
ARTOIS
PICARDY

NORTH SEA
Strait of Dover

Scheldt
Sambre
Meuse
Lys
Somme
Ancre
Oise
Aisne
Vesle
Marne
Petit Morin
Grand Morin
Seine

HINDENBURG LINE
CHEMIN DES DAMES
Quéant
Drocourt

NORTH SEA

0   30
Miles

© Arthur Banks 1973

17

THE EAST-EUROPEAN WAR FRONTS IN AUGUST 1914

This map gives a general impression of the countryside to be fought over. It should be noted that German and Russian railway lines differed in gauges.

Baltic Sea

Libau

Memel

Dvinsk

Königsberg

Niemen

Kovno

Vilna

Danzig

EAST PRUSSIA

Stettin

Minsk

Graudenz

Grodno

Berlin

Thorn

Bialystok

Notec

Posen

Novo-Georgievsk

Bug

Oder

Warsaw

Elbe

Breslau

Lodz

Warta

POLAND

Vistula

Brest-Litovsk

Ivangorod

Kovel

Prague

Lublin

San

Lemberg

Brody

Cracow

Tarnov

Przemysl

GALICIA

VIENNA

AUSTRIA-

Carpathian

Komoron

Danube

BESSARABIA

Budapest

Tisza

Pruth

Dniester

HUNGARY

Danube

Sereth

TRANSYLVANIA

Carpathian Mountains

RUMANIA

DOBRUDJA

Tisza

Black Sea

BELGRADE

BUCHAREST

SERBIA

Danube

BULGARIA

MONTENEGRO

GERMANY

RUSSIA

KEY

- ✪ Forts or fortified towns.
- ★ Smaller forts.
- ┼┼┼┼ Railways.
- ⊔⊓⊔⊓ German "fortified zone".
- Land over 600 feet.
- Land over 3000 feet.

© Arthur Banks 1973

18

THE EASTERN FRONT IN OUTLINE
1914 – 1918

The battle fronts were not continuous and therefore, the lines on map are generalized. The trench system was not so detailed as on the Western Front and the limits of advances or retreats were not contemporaneous. For example, the Russian advance into East Prussia in 1914 was ended at Tannenberg before their large gains in Galicia were achieved.

KEY
— ·— ·— Frontiers in 1914.
● Capital cities.
● Other cities and towns.

0   200
Miles

Baltic Sea
Gulf of Finland
ST. PETERSBURG (Petrograd)
Revel
Narva
Gulf of Riga
Pskov
Riga
Libau
Dvinsk
Moscow
Memel
Kovno
Königsberg
Dvina
Danzig
Vilna
Smolensk
EAST PRUSSIA
Tannenberg
Masuria
Grodno
Minsk
Narew
Niemen
Prasnysz
R U S S I A
Vistula
Warsaw
Brest-Litovsk
Pinsk
Desna
P O L A N D
Pripet
Lodz
Pripet Marshes
Radom
Lublin
Lutsk
GERMANY
Cracow
Lemberg
Rovno
Kiev
Jaroslav
Brody
Vorskla
G A L I C I A
Przemysl
Tarnopol
San
Dnieper
Carpathian Mountains
Stanislau
AUSTRIA-
Dniester
Budapest
Czernovitz
Bug
BUKOVINA
HUNGARY
Kishinev
Nikolaiev
Drava
Danube
Tisza
Prutt
MOLDAVIA
BESS-ARABIA
Odessa
Sava
TRANSYLVANIA
R U M A N I A
KEY
Belgrade
WALLACHIA
BUCHAREST
MONTE-NEGRO
SERBIA
DOBRUDJA
Danube
BULGARIA

KEY
▬ ▬ ▬ Limit of Russian advances 1914 - 1915.
· · · · · Limit of German advances 1915 - 1916.
▨ Territory regained by Brusilov, June-August 1916.
▧ German gains in September 1917.
▬▬▬ Extent of German penetration into Russia by 3 March 1918 (Treaty of Brest-Litovsk).

©Arthur Banks 1973

GERMANY'S PRE-WAR NIGHTMARE OF HAVING TO FIGHT A LAND CAMPAIGN ON TWO FRONTS AT ONCE

© Arthur Banks 1973

❶ The Elder Moltke's Appraisal (1879)

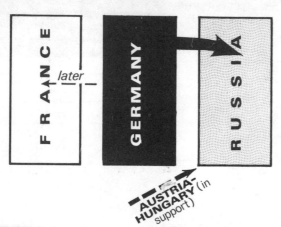

RUSSIA *must be dealt with* **FIRST**. Count von Waldersee (Moltke's successor) agreed with this provided that the offensive against Russia be conducted in summer weather.

❷ Schlieffen's Appraisal (1905)

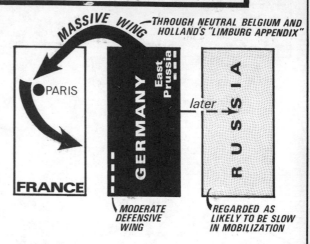

FRANCE *must be dealt with* **FIRST** *in a rapid campaign while Russia is kept at bay by means of a holding or delaying operation in East Prussia. Austria in support.*

❸ Schlieffen's Revised Appraisal (1912)

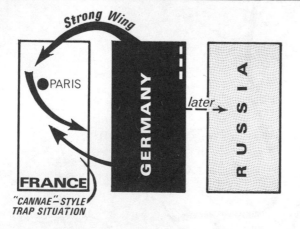

Apparently Schlieffen studied Hannibal's victory at Cannae (216 B.C.) in detail and, as a consequence, revised his own plan. But the German right wing was to be kept strong.

❹ The Younger Moltke's Appraisal (1914)

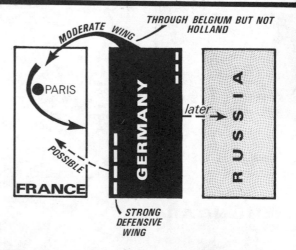

Moltke (nephew of Bismarck's general) strengthened his defensive wing at the expense of his right wing: he omitted ersatz "back up" formations at rear of right wing armies.

In all plans, Germany had to attack first to obviate her fighting an all-out war on two fronts simultaneously: the two potential enemies had to be fought in sequence to avoid splitting Germany's main effort. Everything hinged upon her ability to switch troops from front to front with speed and precision. Even in August 1914, Germany was not powerful enough to launch two major offensives at the same time. Her fear was that SHE might be attacked first!

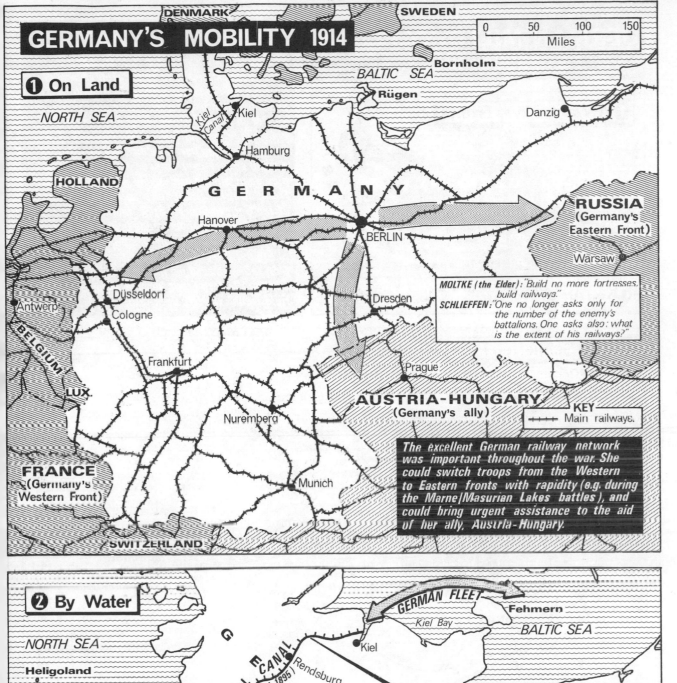

GERMANY'S MOBILITY 1914

① On Land

0   50   100   150
Miles

DENMARK   SWEDEN

BALTIC SEA

Bornholm

Rügen

NORTH SEA

Kiel

Danzig

Hamburg

HOLLAND

G E R M A N Y

BERLIN

Hanover

RUSSIA
(Germany's
Eastern Front)

Warsaw

Düsseldorf

Antwerp

Cologne

Dresden

> **MOLTKE (the Elder):** "Build no more fortresses, build railways."
> **SCHLIEFFEN:** "One no longer asks only for the number of the enemy's battalions. One asks also: what is the extent of his railways?"

BELGIUM

Frankfurt

LUX.

Prague

Nuremberg

AUSTRIA-HUNGARY
(Germany's ally)

KEY
┼┼┼┼ Main railways.

FRANCE
(Germany's
Western Front)

Munich

> The excellent German railway network was important throughout the war. She could switch troops from the Western to Eastern fronts with rapidity (e.g. during the Marne/Masurian Lakes battles), and could bring urgent assistance to the aid of her ally, Austria-Hungary.

SWITZERLAND

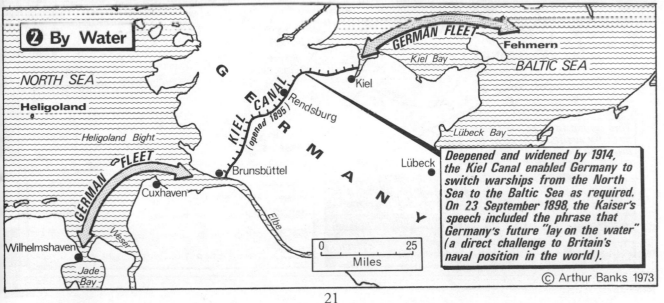

② By Water

GERMAN FLEET

Fehmern

Kiel Bay

BALTIC SEA

NORTH SEA

Heligoland

KIEL CANAL (opened 1895)

Rendsburg

Kiel

G E R M A N Y

Heligoland Bight

Lübeck Bay

GERMAN FLEET

Brunsbüttel

Lübeck

> Deepened and widened by 1914, the Kiel Canal enabled Germany to switch warships from the North Sea to the Baltic Sea as required. On 23 September 1898, the Kaiser's speech included the phrase that Germany's future "lay on the water" (a direct challenge to Britain's naval position in the world).

Cuxhaven

Elbe

Weser

Wilhelmshaven

Jade Bay

0   25
Miles

21

GERMAN MILITARY PLANS 1905-1914

In the years before 1914, German military planners were haunted by fear of an all-out war on two fronts simultaneously (that is, against Russia and France). In 1905, Field-Marshal Graf Alfred Schlieffen prepared a plan based on an assumption that Russia (calculated to be slower in mobilization than France) could be held temporarily at bay, while the bulk of German military power be directed at securing a rapid victory over France. Thus, Schlieffen's plan dealt almost exclusively with the Western Front. Moltke, Schlieffen's successor as Chief of the German General Staff, modified the scheme on several occasions before the war, and an amended version was put into operation in August 1914. Despite initial successes, the plan failed to produce the expected quick victory, and the Western Front became a scene of almost rigid trench warfare until 1918.

❶ A War on Two Fronts

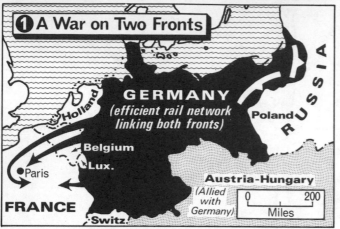

GERMANY (efficient rail network linking both fronts)

Holland · Belgium · Lux. · Paris · FRANCE · Switz. · Poland · RUSSIA · Austria-Hungary (Allied with Germany)

0 — 200 Miles

❷ The Schlieffen Plan

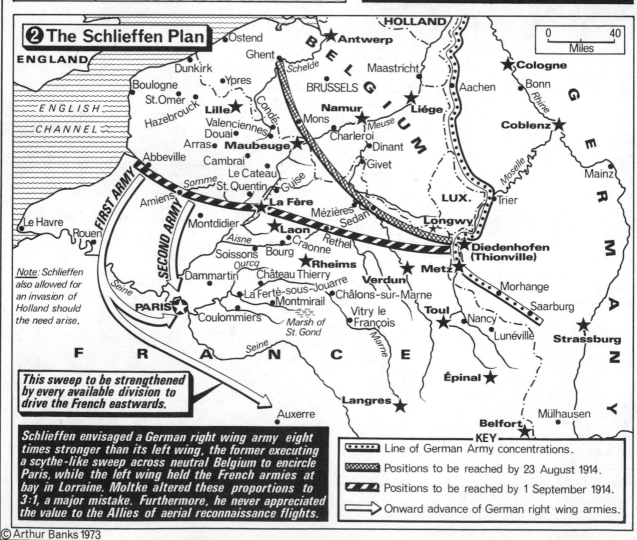

Note: Schlieffen also allowed for an invasion of Holland should the need arise.

This sweep to be strengthened by every available division to drive the French eastwards.

Schlieffen envisaged a German right wing army eight times stronger than its left wing, the former executing a scythe-like sweep across neutral Belgium to encircle Paris, while the left wing held the French armies at bay in Lorraine. Moltke altered these proportions to 3:1, a major mistake. Furthermore, he never appreciated the value to the Allies of aerial reconnaissance flights.

KEY

- ▪▪▪▪ Line of German Army concentrations.
- ▧▧▧ Positions to be reached by 23 August 1914.
- ▨▨▨ Positions to be reached by 1 September 1914.
- ⟹ Onward advance of German right wing armies.

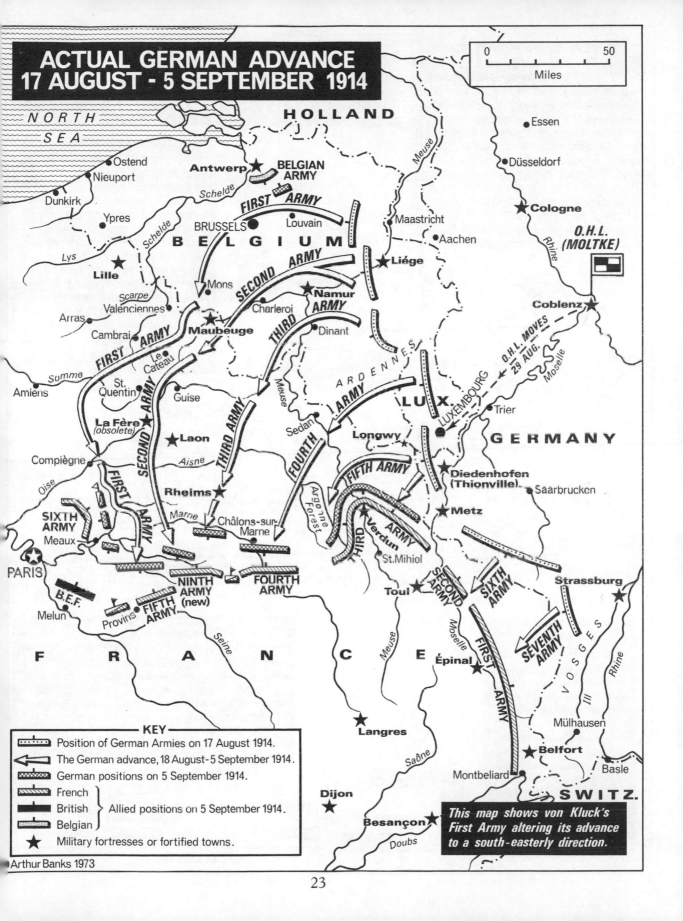

ACTUAL GERMAN ADVANCE 17 AUGUST – 5 SEPTEMBER 1914

0   50

Miles

NORTH SEA

HOLLAND

Essen

Düsseldorf

Ostend
Nieuport
Dunkirk
Ypres

Antwerp ★ BELGIAN ARMY

Schelde

FIRST ARMY

BRUSSELS ● Louvain

Maastricht

Aachen

Cologne ★

O.H.L. (MOLTKE)

Rhine

B E L G I U M

Lille ★

Scarpe
Valenciennes
Arras
Cambrai

SECOND ARMY

Mons ●

Maubeuge ★

Charleroi

Namur ★ ARMY

THIRD

Dinant ●

Liége ★

Coblenz ★

FIRST ARMY

Le Cateau
St. Quentin

Summe

Guise ●

Meuse

Sedan

A R D E N N E S

LUX.

ARMY

LUXEMBOURG

O.H.L. MOVES 29 Aug.

Trier

Moselle

G E R M A N Y

La Fère (obsolete)

SECOND ARMY

Laon ★

Aisne

THIRD ARMY

FOURTH

Longwy ●

Diedenhofen (Thionville)

Saarbrucken

Metz ★

Compiègne

Oise

FIRST ARMY

Rheims ★

Marne

FIFTH ARMY

Argonne Forest

THIRD ARMY

Verdun

St.Mihiol

SIXTH ARMY
Meaux

Châlons-sur-Marne

NINTH ARMY (new)

FOURTH ARMY

Toul ★

SECOND ARMY

SIXTH ARMY

Strassburg ★

PARIS

B.E.F.

Melun

Provins FIFTH ARMY

Seine

Meuse

Épinal ●

FIRST ARMY

Moselle

SEVENTH ARMY

V O S G E S

Rhine

Ill

F   R   A   N   C   E

Langres ★

Mülhausen

Belfort ★

Basle

Saône

Dijon ★

Montbeliard

S W I T Z.

Besançon ★

Doubs

KEY

- ┄┉ Position of German Armies on 17 August 1914.
- ⟵ The German advance, 18 August–5 September 1914.
- ▨ German positions on 5 September 1914.
- ▧ French ⎫
- ▬ British ⎬ Allied positions on 5 September 1914.
- ▤ Belgian ⎭
- ★ Military fortresses or fortified towns.

This map shows von Kluck's First Army altering its advance to a south-easterly direction.

© Arthur Banks 1973

23

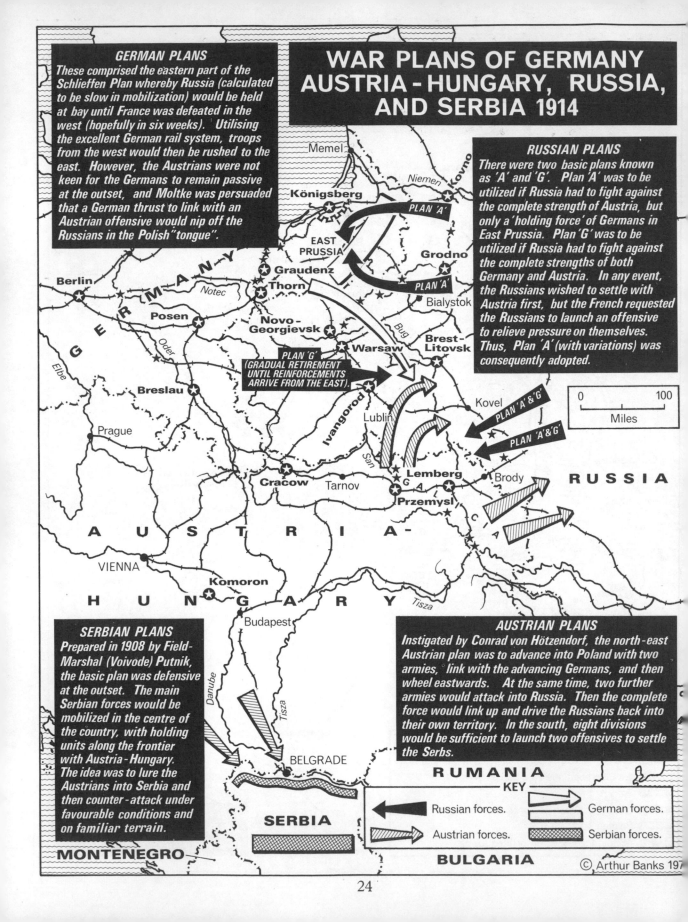

GERMAN PLANS

These comprised the eastern part of the Schlieffen Plan whereby Russia (calculated to be slow in mobilization) would be held at bay until France was defeated in the west (hopefully in six weeks). Utilising the excellent German rail system, troops from the west would then be rushed to the east. However, the Austrians were not keen for the Germans to remain passive at the outset, and Moltke was persuaded that a German thrust to link with an Austrian offensive would nip off the Russians in the Polish "tongue".

WAR PLANS OF GERMANY AUSTRIA - HUNGARY, RUSSIA, AND SERBIA 1914

RUSSIAN PLANS

There were two basic plans known as 'A' and 'G'. Plan 'A' was to be utilized if Russia had to fight against the complete strength of Austria, but only a 'holding force' of Germans in East Prussia. Plan 'G' was to be utilized if Russia had to fight against the complete strengths of both Germany and Austria. In any event, the Russians wished to settle with Austria first, but the French requested the Russians to launch an offensive to relieve pressure on themselves. Thus, Plan 'A' (with variations) was consequently adopted.

Memel
Niemen
Kovno
Königsberg
PLAN 'A'
EAST PRUSSIA
Grodno
Graudenz
PLAN 'A'
Berlin
Thorn
Bialystok
Notec
Posen
Novo-Georgievsk
Bug
Oder
Warsaw
Brest-Litovsk
Elbe
PLAN 'G'
(GRADUAL RETIREMENT UNTIL REINFORCEMENTS ARRIVE FROM THE EAST).
Kovel
PLAN 'A' & 'G'
Breslau
Lublin
PLAN 'A' & 'G'
Prague
San
Ivangorod
Lemberg
Brody
Cracow
Tarnov
Przemysl
RUSSIA

0   100
Miles

VIENNA
A U S T R I A -

H U N G A R Y
Komoron
Tisza
Budapest

SERBIAN PLANS

Prepared in 1908 by Field-Marshal (Voivode) Putnik, the basic plan was defensive at the outset. The main Serbian forces would be mobilized in the centre of the country, with holding units along the frontier with Austria - Hungary. The idea was to lure the Austrians into Serbia and then counter-attack under favourable conditions and on familiar terrain.

AUSTRIAN PLANS

Instigated by Conrad von Hötzendorf, the north-east Austrian plan was to advance into Poland with two armies, link with the advancing Germans, and then wheel eastwards. At the same time, two further armies would attack into Russia. Then the complete force would link up and drive the Russians back into their own territory. In the south, eight divisions would be sufficient to launch two offensives to settle the Serbs.

Danube
Tisza
BELGRADE

RUMANIA

KEY

← Russian forces.		German forces.
Austrian forces.		Serbian forces.

SERBIA

MONTENEGRO
BULGARIA

© Arthur Banks 19

24

FRENCH PRE-WAR MILITARY PLANS 1914

© Arthur Banks 1973

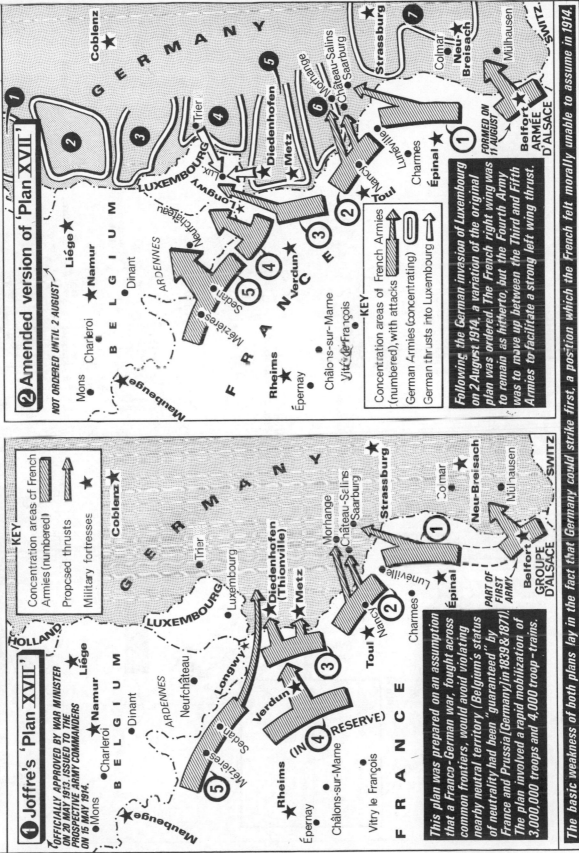

① Joffre's 'Plan XVII'

OFFICIALLY APPROVED BY WAR MINISTER ON 20 MAY 1913. ISSUED TO THE PROSPECTIVE ARMY COMMANDERS ON 15 MAY 1914.

This plan was prepared on an assumption that a Franco-German war, fought across common frontiers, would avoid violating nearby neutral territory (Belgium's status of neutrality had been "guaranteed" by France and Prussia (Germany) in 1839 & 1871). The plan involved a rapid mobilization of 3,000,000 troops and 4,000 troop-trains.

② Amended version of 'Plan XVII'

NOT ORDERED UNTIL 2 AUGUST

Following the German invasion of Luxembourg on 2 August 1914, a variation of the original plan was ordered. The French right wing was to remain as hitherto, but the Fourth Army was to move up between the Third and Fifth Armies to facilitate a strong left wing thrust.

KEY
- Concentration areas of French Armies (numbered), with attacks
- German Armies (concentrating)
- German thrusts into Luxembourg

KEY
- Concentration areas of French Armies (numbered)
- Proposed thrusts
- ★ Military fortresses

The basic weakness of both plans lay in the fact that Germany could strike first, a position which the French felt morally unable to assume in 1914.

25

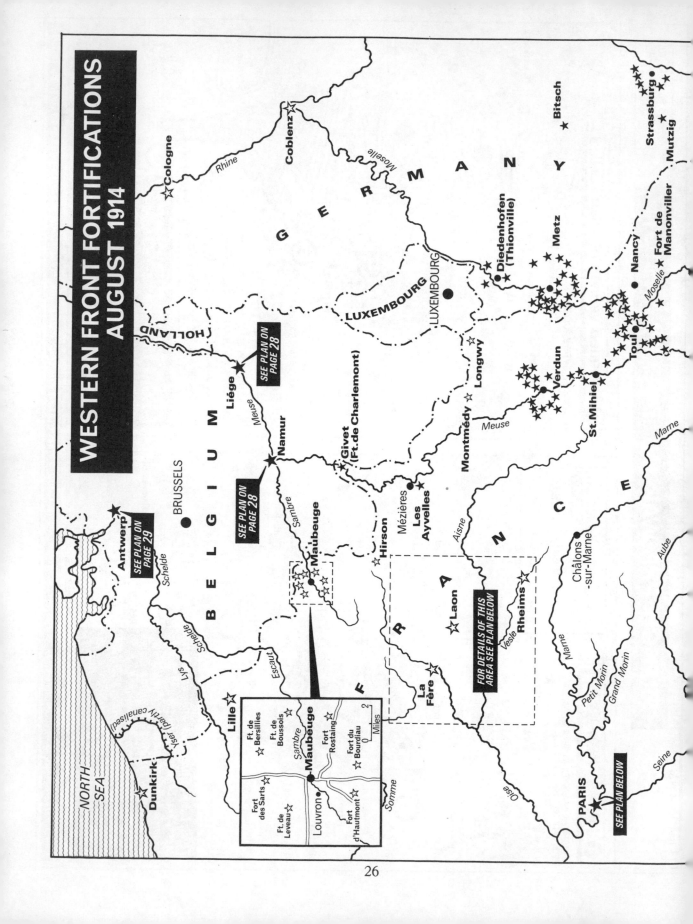

WESTERN FRONT FORTIFICATIONS AUGUST 1914

NORTH SEA

Dunkirk

Lille

Antwerp
SEE PLAN ON PAGE 29

BRUSSELS

B E L G I U M

Cologne

Coblenz

Rhine

Moselle

G E R M A N Y

(HOLLAND)

Liége
SEE PLAN ON PAGE 28

Namur
SEE PLAN ON PAGE 28

Maubeuge

Givet
(Ft. de Charlemont)

Hirson

Mézières
Les Ayvelles

LUXEMBOURG

LUXEMBOURG

Diedenhofen
(Thionville)

Bitsch

Metz

Montmédy

Longwy

Verdun

St.Mihiel

Nancy

Strassburg

Mutzig

Fort de Manonviller

Toul

La Fère

Laon

Rheims

FOR DETAILS OF THIS AREA SEE PLAN BELOW

F R A N C E

Aisne

Vesle

Meuse

Marne

Châlons -sur-Marne

Aube

Marne

Petit Morin

Grand Morin

Oise

Seine

PARIS
SEE PLAN BELOW

Schelde

Lys

Yser (partly canalised)

Escaut

Sambre

Meuse

Sambre

Somme

Maubeuge inset

Ft. de Bersillies

Ft. de Boussois

Fort Rostaing

Fort du Bourdiau

Maubeuge

Fort des Sarts

Ft. de Leveau

Louvron

Fort d'Hautmont

0   2
Miles

26

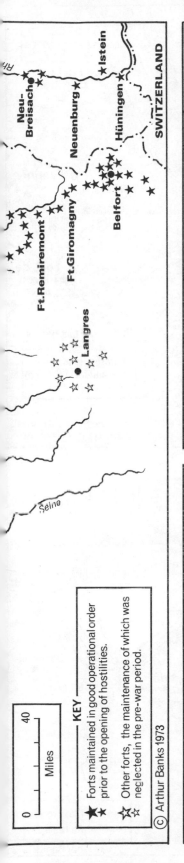

KEY

★★ Forts maintained in good operational order prior to the opening of hostilities.

☆☆ Other forts, the maintenance of which was neglected in the pre-war period.

0 — 40
Miles

Neu-Breisach ●
Istein ★
Neuenburg ★
Hüningen ★
Belfort ●
Ft.Giromagny ★
Ft.Remiremont ★
Langres ●

SWITZERLAND

FORTIFICATIONS TO THE NORTH-EAST OF PARIS

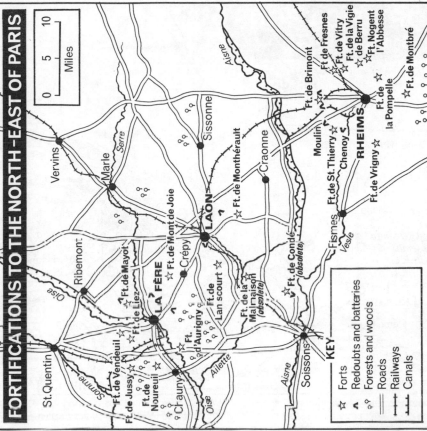

St.Quentin
Vervins
Marle
Serre
Ribemont
Oise
Ft.de Vendeuil
Ft.de Jussy
Ft.de Noureuil
Cl. auny
Ft. d'Aurigny
Ft.de Liez
Ft.de Mayot
Ft.de Mont de Joie
Crépy
LA FÈRE
Ft.de Lan scourt
Ailette
Ft.de la Malmaison (obsolete)
Aisne
Soissons
LAON
Ft.de Monthérault
Craonne
Ft.de Brimont
Ft.de Condé (obsolete)
Sissonne
Moulin
Ft.de St.Thierry
Chenoy
Ft.de Vrigny
Fismes
Vesle
RHEIMS
Ft.de la Pompelle
Ft.de Vitry
Ft.de la Vigie de Berru
Ft.de Fresnes
Ft.Nogent l'Abbesse
Ft.de Montbré
Aisne

KEY
☆ Forts
∧ Redoubts and batteries
ϙϙ Forests and woods
═══ Roads
┼┼┼ Railways
∙∙∙∙ Canals

0 5 10
Miles

DEFENCES OF PARIS

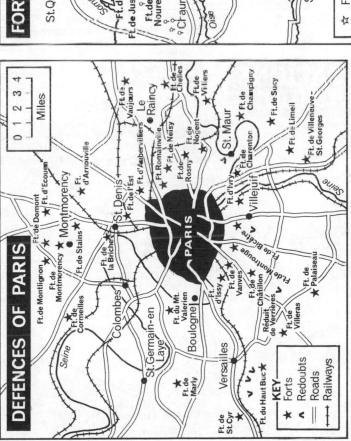

Ft.de Montlignon
Ft.de Domont
Ft. d'Ecouen
Ft.de Montmorency
Montmorency
Ft.de Stains
Ft. d'Arnouville
Ft.de la Briche
St.Denis
Ft.de l'Est
Ft.d'Aubervilliers
Ft.de Vaujours
Le Raincy
Ft.de Chelles
Ft.de Romainville
Ft.de Noisy
Ft.de Villiers
Ft.de Nogent
St. Maur
Ft.de Rosny
Ft. de Champigny
Ft. de Sucy
Ft. de Limeil
Ft.d'Ivry
Ft.de Charenton
Ft.de Villeneuve-St.Georges
Villejuif
Ft.de Bicêtre
Ft.de Montrouge
PARIS
Ft. de Vanves
Ft. d'Issy
Ft. de Châtillon
Réduit de Verrières
Ft.de Palaiseau
Ft.de Villeras
Ft.du Mt. Valerien
Boulogne
St.Germain-en Laye
Colombes
Ft.de Cormeilles
Seine
Ft.de Marly
Ft.du Haut Buc
Versailles
Ft.de St.Cyr
Seine

KEY
★ Forts
∧ Redoubts
═══ Roads
┼┼┼ Railways

0 1 2 3 4
Miles

This map depicts the system of fortifications that adorned the Western Front area prior to the commencement of hostilities. Many of the northern French fortresses were virtually obsolete or in a state of disrepair and the three Belgian fortresses had been designed in the 1880's and 1890's, long before the advent of "Dicke Bertha" and "Schlanke Emma".

27

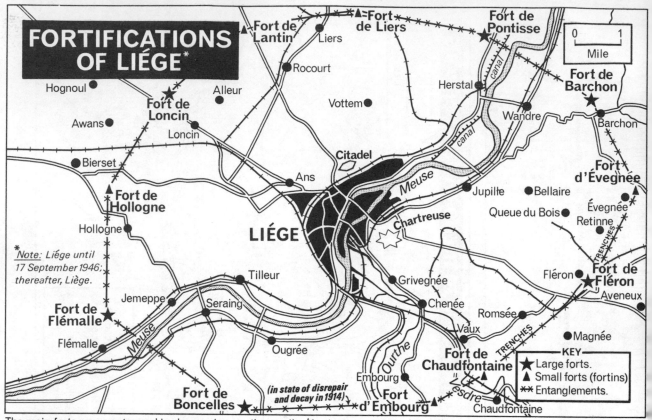

FORTIFICATIONS OF LIÉGE*

0 — 1 Mile

▲ Fort de Lantin
▲ Fort de Liers
★ Fort de Pontisse
★ Fort de Barchon

Hognoul
Liers
Rocourt
Herstal
Vottem
Wandre
Barchon

★ Fort de Loncin
Alleur
Awans
Loncin
Bierset
Ans
Citadel
Meuse
canal
canal
Jupille
Bellaire
Queue du Bois
Évegnée
Retinne
★ Fort d'Évegnée

▲ Fort de Hollogne
Hollogne
LIÉGE
Chartreuse
Fléron
★ Fort de Fléron
Aveneux

*Note: Liége until 17 September 1946; thereafter, Liège.

Tilleur
Grivegnée
Romsée
Vaux
Magnée

★ Fort de Flémalle
Jemeppe
Seraing
Chenée

Flémalle
Ougrée

KEY
★ Large forts.
▲ Small forts (fortins).
✳ Entanglements.

★ Fort de Boncelles
(in state of disrepair and decay in 1914)
Embourg
Fort d'Embourg ▲
Fort de Chaudfontaine
Chaudfontaine

Ourthe
Vesdre

The main forts were pentagonal in shape, whereas the smaller 'fortins' were triangular. All consisted of works beneath ground level, with the guns being housed in steel cupolas which could be raised and lowered again at will. The designer was Henri Brialmont.

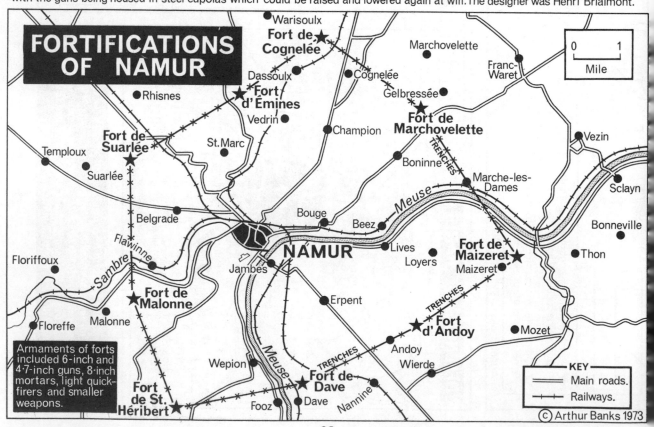

FORTIFICATIONS OF NAMUR

0 — 1 Mile

Warisoulx
★ Fort de Cognelée
Marchovelette
Franc-Waret

Dassoulx
Cognelée
Gelbressée
Rhisnes
★ Fort d'Émines
Vedrin
Champion
★ Fort de Marchovelette
Vezin

Temploux
★ Fort de Suarlée
St. Marc
Boninne
Marche-les-Dames
Sclayn

Suarlée
Meuse
Bonneville

Belgrade
Bouge
Beez
★ Fort de Maizeret
Thon

Floriffoux
Flawinne
NAMUR
Lives
Loyers
Maizeret

Sambre
Jambes

★ Fort de Malonne
Erpent
★ Fort d'Andoy
Mozet

Floreffe
Malonne
Andoy
Wierde

Armaments of forts included 6-inch and 4·7-inch guns, 8-inch mortars, light quick-firers and smaller weapons.

Wepion
★ Fort de Dave
★ Fort de St. Héribert
Fooz
Dave
Nannine

KEY
━━ Main roads.
┼┼ Railways.

© Arthur Banks 1973

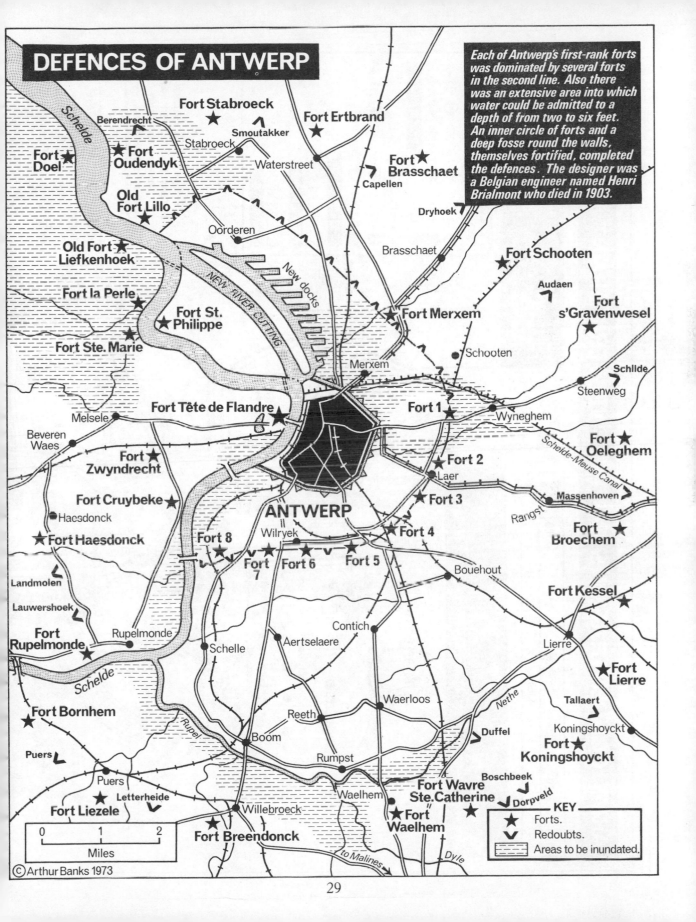

DEFENCES OF ANTWERP

Each of Antwerp's first-rank forts was dominated by several forts in the second line. Also there was an extensive area into which water could be admitted to a depth of from two to six feet. An inner circle of forts and a deep fosse round the walls, themselves fortified, completed the defences. The designer was a Belgian engineer named Henri Brialmont who died in 1903.

Schelde

Fort Stabroeck
Berendrecht
Smoutakker
Stabroeck
Waterstreet

Fort Ertbrand

Fort Brasschaet
Capellen

Dryhoek

Fort Doel
Fort Oudendyk

Old Fort Lillo
Oorderen

Brasschaet

Fort Schooten

Audaen

Fort s'Gravenwesel

Old Fort Liefkenhoek

NEW RIVER CUTTING

New docks

Fort Merxem
Schooten

Schilde
Steenweg

Fort la Perle

Fort St. Philippe

Fort Ste. Marie

Merxem

Fort 1
Wyneghem

Fort Oeleghem

Fort Tête de Flandre
Melsele

Beveren Waes

Fort Zwyndrecht

Fort 2
Laer

Scheide-Meuse Canal

Fort Cruybeke
Haesdonck

ANTWERP

Wilryek

Fort 3

Fort 4

Massenhoven

Rangst

Fort Broechem

Fort Haesdonck

Fort 8

Fort 7

Fort 6

Fort 5

Bouehout

Fort Kessel

Landmolen

Lauwershoek

Fort Rupelmonde
Rupelmonde

Contich
Aertselaere

Lierre

Fort Lierre

Schelle

Nethe

Tallaert

Koningshoyckt

Fort Bornhem

Reeth

Waerloos

Fort Koningshoyckt

Rupel

Boom

Duffel

Puers

Rumpst

Boschbeek

Puers
Letterheide

Waelhem

Fort Wavre Ste. Catherine

Dorpveld

Fort Liezele

Willebroeck

Fort Waelhem

Fort Breendonck

to Malines

Dyle

KEY
★ Forts.
ᐯ Redoubts.
▨ Areas to be inundated.

0   1   2
Miles

© Arthur Banks 1973

29

ARMY CONCENTRATIONS ON THE WESTERN FRONT AUGUST 1914

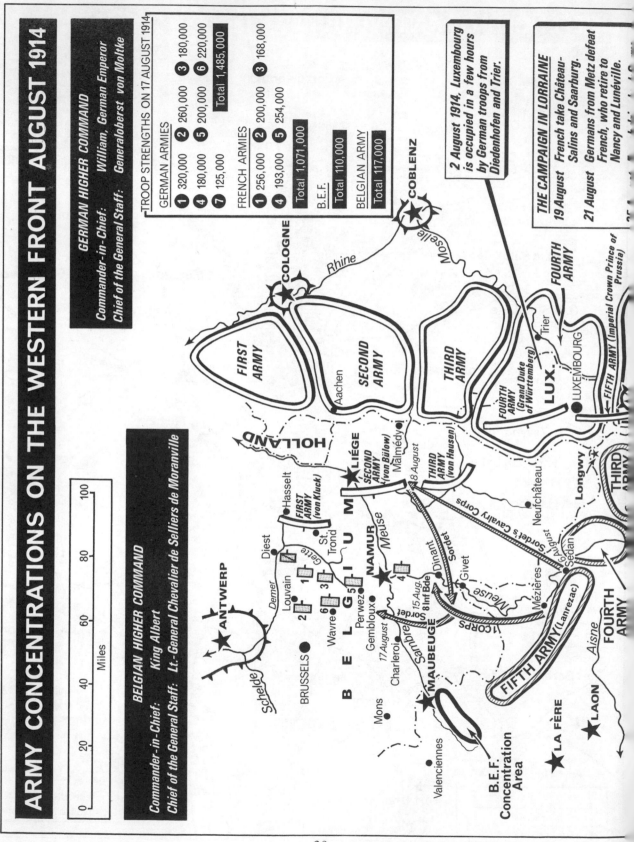

BELGIAN HIGHER COMMAND

Commander-in-Chief: King Albert

Chief of the General Staff: Lt.-General Chevalier de Selliers de Moranville

GERMAN HIGHER COMMAND

Commander-in-Chief: William, German Emperor

Chief of the General Staff: Generaloberst von Moltke

TROOP STRENGTHS ON 17 AUGUST 1914

GERMAN ARMIES

1 320,000	**2** 260,000	**3** 180,000
4 180,000	**5** 200,000	**6** 220,000
7 125,000		Total 1,485,000

FRENCH ARMIES

| **1** 256,000 | **2** 200,000 | **3** 168,000 |
| **4** 193,000 | **5** 254,000 | |

Total 1,071,000

B.E.F.   Total 110,000

BELGIAN ARMY   Total 117,000

2 August 1914. Luxembourg is occupied in a few hours by German troops from Diedenhofen and Trier.

THE CAMPAIGN IN LORRAINE

19 August French take Château-Salins and Saarburg.

21 August Germans from Metz defeat French, who retire to Nancy and Lunéville.

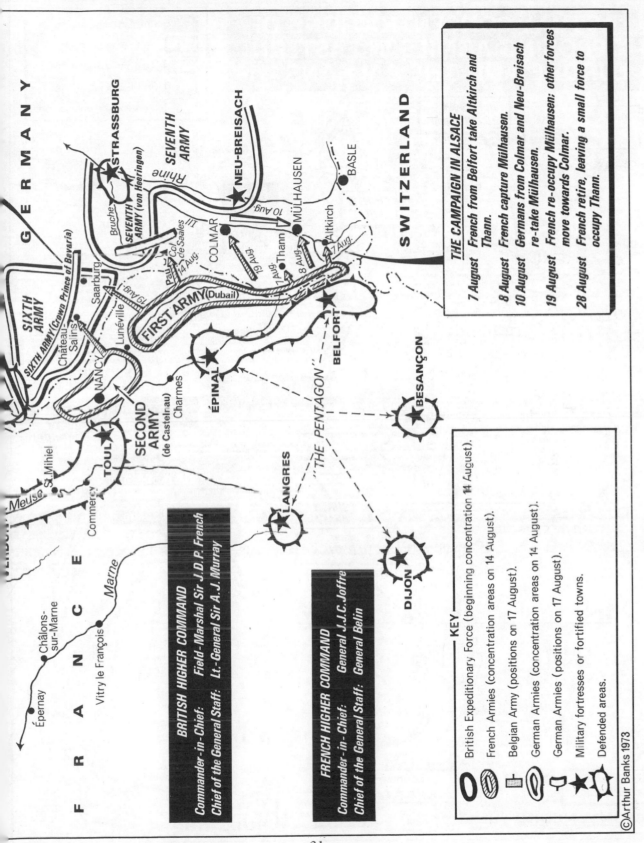

THE CAMPAIGN IN ALSACE

7 August	French from Belfort take Altkirch and Thann.
8 August	French capture Mülhausen.
10 August	Germans from Colmar and Neu-Breisach re-take Mülhausen.
19 August	French re-occupy Mülhausen; other forces move towards Colmar.
28 August	French retire, leaving a small force to occupy Thann.

BRITISH HIGHER COMMAND

Commander-in-Chief: Field-Marshal Sir J.D.P. French
Chief of the General Staff: Lt.-General Sir A.J. Murray

FRENCH HIGHER COMMAND

Commander-in-Chief: General J.J.C. Joffre
Chief of the General Staff: General Belin

KEY

British Expeditionary Force (beginning concentration 14 August).

French Armies (concentration areas on 14 August).

Belgian Army (positions on 17 August).

German Armies (concentration areas on 14 August).

German Armies (positions on 17 August).

Military fortresses or fortified towns.

Defended areas.

© Arthur Banks 1973

GERMANY

STRASSBURG

SEVENTH ARMY

SEVENTH ARMY (von Heeringen)

NEU-BREISACH

Rhine

Bruche

COLMAR

MÜLHAUSEN

BASLE

SWITZERLAND

Altkirch

Thann

Paul Col. de Saales

SIXTH ARMY (Crown Prince of Bavaria)

Saarburg

SIXTH ARMY

Château-Salins

Lunéville

FIRST ARMY (Dubail)

BELFORT

"THE PENTAGON"

BESANÇON

NANCY

SECOND ARMY (de Castelnau)

Charmes

ÉPINAL

LANGRES

TOUL

St. Mihiel

Commercy

Meuse

DIJON

FRANCE

Marne

Châlons-sur-Marne

Vitry le François

Épernay

VERDUN

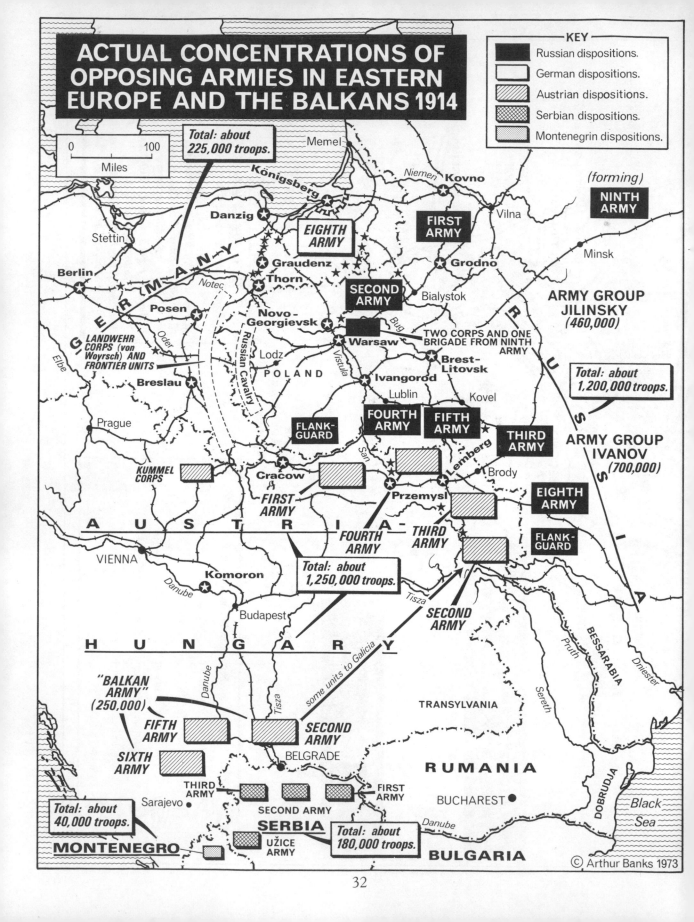

ACTUAL CONCENTRATIONS OF OPPOSING ARMIES IN EASTERN EUROPE AND THE BALKANS 1914

KEY
- Russian dispositions.
- German dispositions.
- Austrian dispositions.
- Serbian dispositions.
- Montenegrin dispositions.

0   100
Miles

Total: about 225,000 troops.

Memel

Königsberg

Niemen   Kovno

(forming)

NINTH ARMY

Danzig

FIRST ARMY

Vilna

Stettin

Minsk

EIGHTH ARMY

Grodno

Berlin

Graudenz

Thorn

SECOND ARMY

Bialystok

ARMY GROUP JILINSKY (460,000)

Posen

LANDWEHR CORPS (von WOYRSCH) AND FRONTIER UNITS

Novo-Georgievsk

Notec

Russian Cavalry

Lodz

P O L A N D

Warsaw

TWO CORPS AND ONE BRIGADE FROM NINTH ARMY

Breslau

Vistula

Ivangorod

Brest-Litovsk

Prague

FLANK-GUARD

FOURTH ARMY

Lublin

Kovel

FIFTH ARMY

THIRD ARMY

Total: about 1,200,000 troops.

ARMY GROUP IVANOV (700,000)

KUMMEL CORPS

Cracow

FIRST ARMY

San

Przemysl

Lemberg   Brody

EIGHTH ARMY

A U S T R I A -

VIENNA

FOURTH ARMY

THIRD ARMY

FLANK-GUARD

Komoron

Danube

Total: about 1,250,000 troops.

Tisza

SECOND ARMY

R U S S I A

Budapest

H U N G A R Y

some units to Galicia

TRANSYLVANIA

Pruth

BESSARABIA

Dniester

"BALKAN ARMY" (250,000)

Danube

Tisza

FIFTH ARMY

SECOND ARMY

Sereth

SIXTH ARMY

BELGRADE

R U M A N I A

Total: about 40,000 troops.

THIRD ARMY

Sarajevo

SECOND ARMY

FIRST ARMY

BUCHAREST

DOBRUDJA

Black Sea

MONTENEGRO

UŽICE ARMY

SERBIA

Total: about 180,000 troops.

Danube

BULGARIA

© Arthur Banks 1973

32

THREE IMPORTANT GUNS IN 1914

French 75-mm. field gun (Model 1897)

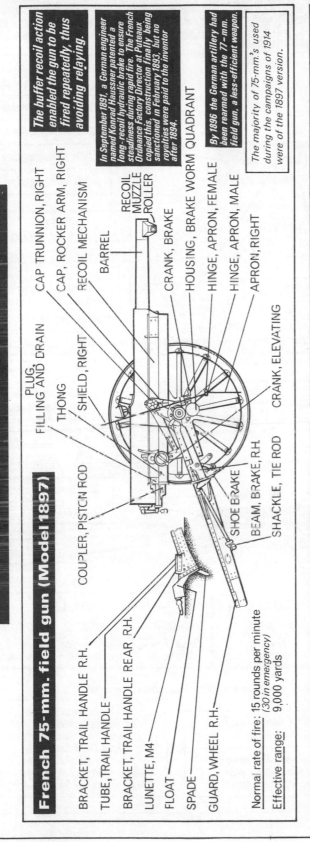

BRACKET, TRAIL HANDLE R.H.

TUBE, TRAIL HANDLE

BRACKET, TRAIL HANDLE REAR R.H.

LUNETTE, M4

FLOAT

SPADE

GUARD, WHEEL R.H.

COUPLER, PISTON ROD

PLUG, FILLING AND DRAIN

THONG

SHIELD, RIGHT

SHOE BRAKE

BEAM, BRAKE, R.H.

SHACKLE, TIE ROD

CAP TRUNNION, RIGHT

CAP, ROCKER ARM, RIGHT

RECOIL MECHANISM

BARREL

RECOIL MUZZLE ROLLER

CRANK, BRAKE

HOUSING, BRAKE WORM QUADRANT

HINGE, APRON, FEMALE

HINGE, APRON, MALE

APRON, RIGHT

CRANK, ELEVATING

Normal rate of fire: 15 rounds per minute
(30 in emergency)

Effective range: <u>9,000 yards</u>

The buffer recoil action enabled the gun to be fired repeatedly, thus avoiding relaying.

In September 1891, a German engineer named Konrad Haussner patented a long-recoil hydraulic brake to ensure steadiness during rapid fire. The French Ordnance Factory Director at Puteaux copied this, construction finally being sanctioned in February 1893, but no royalties were paid to the inventor after 1894.

By 1896 the German artillery had been rearmed with the 77-mm. field gun, a less-efficient weapon.

The majority of 75-mm.'s used during the campaigns of 1914 were of the 1897 version.

Austrian 30·5-cm. howitzer (Model 1911)

Normal rate of fire: 1 round every 6 minutes

Effective range: <u>13,000 yards</u>

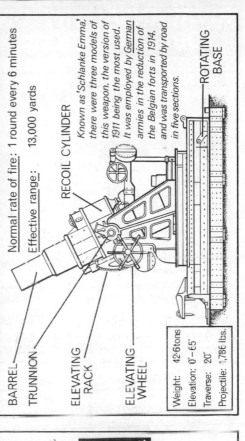

RECOIL CYLINDER

ROTATING BASE

BARREL

TRUNNION

ELEVATING RACK

ELEVATING WHEEL

Known as 'Schlanke Emma,' there were three models of this weapon, the version of 1911 being the most used. It was employed by German armies in the reduction of the Belgian forts in 1914, and was transported by road in five sections.

Weight:	42·6 tons
Elevation:	0°–65°
Traverse:	20°
Projectile:	1,786 lbs.

German 15-cm. field howitzer (Model 1913)

Normal rate of fire: 5 rounds per minute

Effective range: <u>9,300 yards</u>

BARREL

SHIELD

SIGHT BRACKET

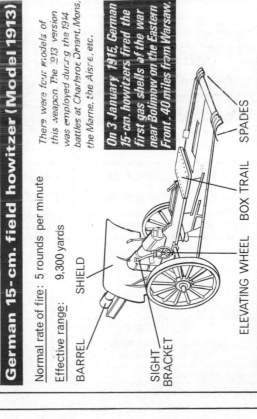

SPADES

ELEVATING WHEEL   BOX TRAIL

There were four models of this weapon. The 1913 version was employed during the 1914 battles at Charleroi, Dinant, Mons, the Marne, the Aisne, etc.

On 3 January 1915, German 15-cm. howitzers fired the first gas shells of the war near Bolinow on the Eastern Front, 40 miles from Warsaw.

RIVAL INFANTRY DIVISIONAL ORGANIZATIONS IN 1914

The infantry division was the standard component of corps and armies. These diagrams give approximate comparisons between the main contending forces.

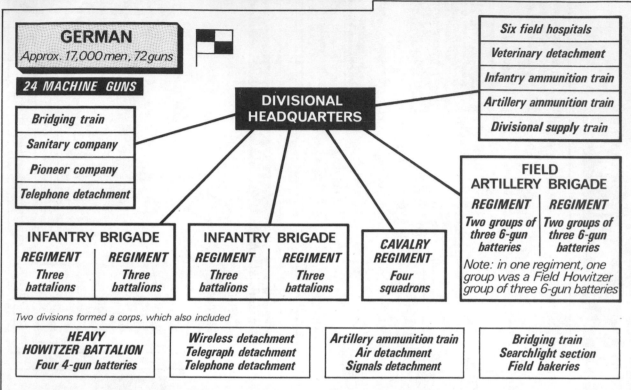

GERMAN
Approx. 17,000 men, 72 guns

24 MACHINE GUNS

DIVISIONAL HEADQUARTERS

- Bridging train
- Sanitary company
- Pioneer company
- Telephone detachment

- Six field hospitals
- Veterinary detachment
- Infantry ammunition train
- Artillery ammunition train
- Divisional supply train

INFANTRY BRIGADE
REGIMENT	REGIMENT
Three battalions	Three battalions

INFANTRY BRIGADE
REGIMENT	REGIMENT
Three battalions	Three battalions

CAVALRY REGIMENT
Four squadrons

FIELD ARTILLERY BRIGADE
REGIMENT	REGIMENT
Two groups of three 6-gun batteries	Two groups of three 6-gun batteries

Note: in one regiment, one group was a Field Howitzer group of three 6-gun batteries

Two divisions formed a corps, which also included

HEAVY HOWITZER BATTALION			
Four 4-gun batteries	Wireless detachment Telegraph detachment Telephone detachment	Artillery ammunition train Air detachment Signals detachment	Bridging train Searchlight section Field bakeries

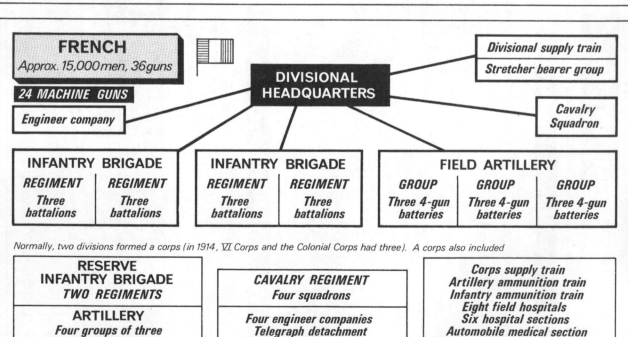

FRENCH
Approx. 15,000 men, 36 guns

24 MACHINE GUNS

DIVISIONAL HEADQUARTERS

- Engineer company

- Divisional supply train
- Stretcher bearer group

- Cavalry Squadron

INFANTRY BRIGADE
REGIMENT	REGIMENT
Three battalions	Three battalions

INFANTRY BRIGADE
REGIMENT	REGIMENT
Three battalions	Three battalions

FIELD ARTILLERY
GROUP	GROUP	GROUP
Three 4-gun batteries	Three 4-gun batteries	Three 4-gun batteries

Normally, two divisions formed a corps (in 1914, VI Corps and the Colonial Corps had three). A corps also included

RESERVE INFANTRY BRIGADE TWO REGIMENTS ARTILLERY Four groups of three 4-gun batteries	CAVALRY REGIMENT Four squadrons Four engineer companies Telegraph detachment Searchlight section	Corps supply train Artillery ammunition train Infantry ammunition train Eight field hospitals Six hospital sections Automobile medical section Corps stretcher bearer section

© Arthur Banks 1973

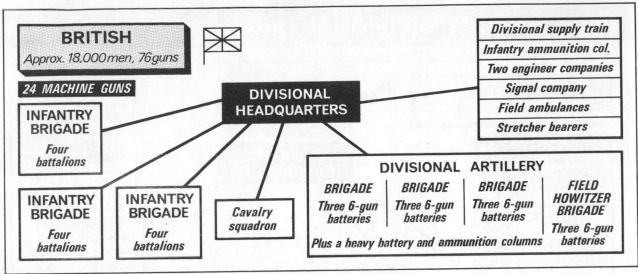

BRITISH
Approx. 18,000 men, 76 guns

24 MACHINE GUNS

DIVISIONAL HEADQUARTERS

Divisional supply train

Infantry ammunition col.

Two engineer companies

Signal company

Field ambulances

Stretcher bearers

INFANTRY BRIGADE
Four battalions

INFANTRY BRIGADE
Four battalions

INFANTRY BRIGADE
Four battalions

Cavalry squadron

DIVISIONAL ARTILLERY

BRIGADE	BRIGADE	BRIGADE	FIELD HOWITZER BRIGADE
Three 6-gun batteries	*Three 6-gun batteries*	*Three 6-gun batteries*	*Three 6-gun batteries*

Plus a heavy battery and ammunition columns

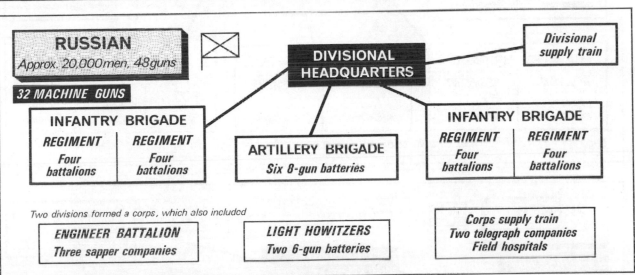

RUSSIAN
Approx. 20,000 men, 48 guns

32 MACHINE GUNS

DIVISIONAL HEADQUARTERS

Divisional supply train

INFANTRY BRIGADE

REGIMENT	REGIMENT
Four battalions	*Four battalions*

ARTILLERY BRIGADE
Six 8-gun batteries

INFANTRY BRIGADE

REGIMENT	REGIMENT
Four battalions	*Four battalions*

Two divisions formed a corps, which also included

ENGINEER BATTALION
Three sapper companies

LIGHT HOWITZERS
Two 6-gun batteries

Corps supply train
Two telegraph companies
Field hospitals

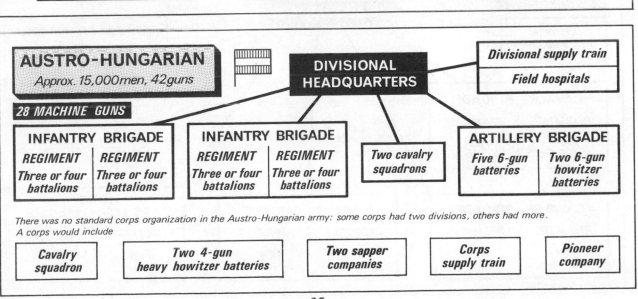

AUSTRO-HUNGARIAN
Approx. 15,000 men, 42 guns

28 MACHINE GUNS

DIVISIONAL HEADQUARTERS

Divisional supply train

Field hospitals

INFANTRY BRIGADE

REGIMENT	REGIMENT
Three or four battalions	*Three or four battalions*

INFANTRY BRIGADE

REGIMENT	REGIMENT
Three or four battalions	*Three or four battalions*

Two cavalry squadrons

ARTILLERY BRIGADE

Five 6-gun batteries	Two 6-gun howitzer batteries

There was no standard corps organization in the Austro-Hungarian army: some corps had two divisions, others had more. A corps would include

Cavalry squadron

Two 4-gun heavy howitzer batteries

Two sapper companies

Corps supply train

Pioneer company

RIVAL CAVALRY DIVISIONAL ORGANIZATIONS IN 1914

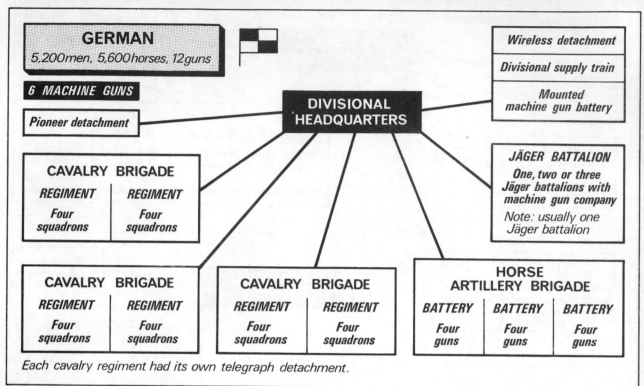

GERMAN
5,200 men, 5,600 horses, 12 guns

6 MACHINE GUNS

Pioneer detachment

DIVISIONAL HEADQUARTERS

Wireless detachment

Divisional supply train

Mounted machine gun battery

JÄGER BATTALION
One, two or three Jäger battalions with machine gun company
Note: usually one Jäger battalion

CAVALRY BRIGADE
REGIMENT — Four squadrons
REGIMENT — Four squadrons

CAVALRY BRIGADE
REGIMENT — Four squadrons
REGIMENT — Four squadrons

CAVALRY BRIGADE
REGIMENT — Four squadrons
REGIMENT — Four squadrons

HORSE ARTILLERY BRIGADE
BATTERY — Four guns
BATTERY — Four guns
BATTERY — Four guns

Each cavalry regiment had its own telegraph detachment.

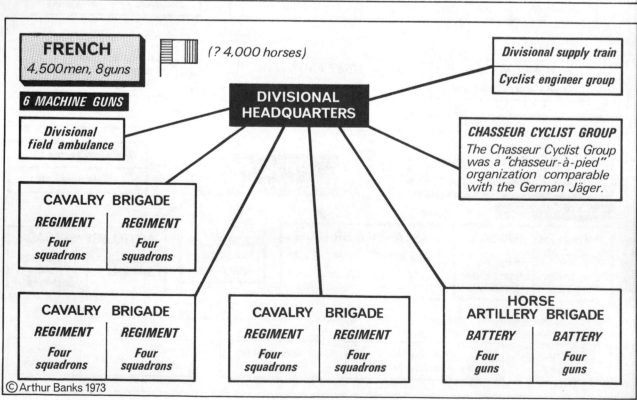

FRENCH
4,500 men, 8 guns

(? 4,000 horses)

6 MACHINE GUNS

Divisional field ambulance

DIVISIONAL HEADQUARTERS

Divisional supply train

Cyclist engineer group

CHASSEUR CYCLIST GROUP
The Chasseur Cyclist Group was a "chasseur-à-pied" organization comparable with the German Jäger.

CAVALRY BRIGADE
REGIMENT — Four squadrons
REGIMENT — Four squadrons

CAVALRY BRIGADE
REGIMENT — Four squadrons
REGIMENT — Four squadrons

CAVALRY BRIGADE
REGIMENT — Four squadrons
REGIMENT — Four squadrons

HORSE ARTILLERY BRIGADE
BATTERY — Four guns
BATTERY — Four guns

© Arthur Banks 1973

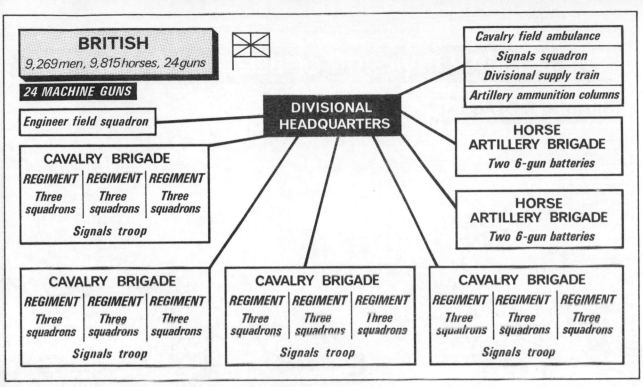

BRITISH
9,269 men, 9,815 horses, 24 guns

24 MACHINE GUNS

Engineer field squadron

Cavalry field ambulance
Signals squadron
Divisional supply train
Artillery ammunition columns

DIVISIONAL HEADQUARTERS

HORSE ARTILLERY BRIGADE
Two 6-gun batteries

HORSE ARTILLERY BRIGADE
Two 6-gun batteries

CAVALRY BRIGADE

REGIMENT	REGIMENT	REGIMENT
Three squadrons	Three squadrons	Three squadrons

Signals troop

CAVALRY BRIGADE

REGIMENT	REGIMENT	REGIMENT
Three squadrons	Three squadrons	Three squadrons

Signals troop

CAVALRY BRIGADE

REGIMENT	REGIMENT	REGIMENT
Three squadrons	Three squadrons	Three squadrons

Signals troop

CAVALRY BRIGADE

REGIMENT	REGIMENT	REGIMENT
Three squadrons	Three squadrons	Three squadrons

Signals troop

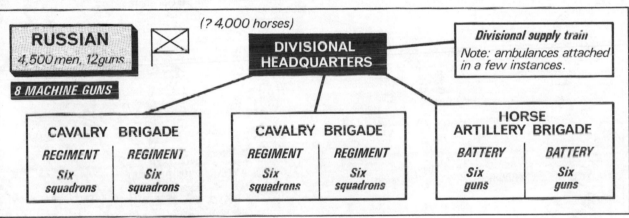

RUSSIAN
4,500 men, 12 guns

8 MACHINE GUNS

(? 4,000 horses)

DIVISIONAL HEADQUARTERS

Divisional supply train
Note: ambulances attached in a few instances.

CAVALRY BRIGADE

REGIMENT	REGIMENT
Six squadrons	Six squadrons

CAVALRY BRIGADE

REGIMENT	REGIMENT
Six squadrons	Six squadrons

HORSE ARTILLERY BRIGADE

BATTERY	BATTERY
Six guns	Six guns

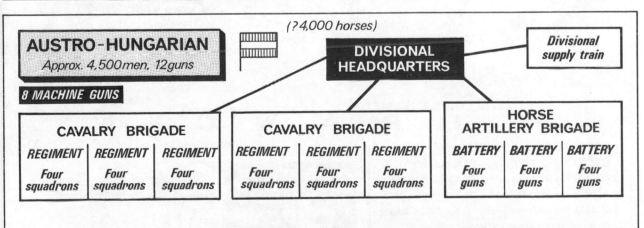

AUSTRO-HUNGARIAN
Approx. 4,500 men, 12 guns

8 MACHINE GUNS

(? 4,000 horses)

DIVISIONAL HEADQUARTERS

Divisional supply train

CAVALRY BRIGADE

REGIMENT	REGIMENT	REGIMENT
Four squadrons	Four squadrons	Four squadrons

CAVALRY BRIGADE

REGIMENT	REGIMENT	REGIMENT
Four squadrons	Four squadrons	Four squadrons

HORSE ARTILLERY BRIGADE

BATTERY	BATTERY	BATTERY
Four guns	Four guns	Four guns

THE GERMAN INVASION OF BELGIUM AUGUST 1914

Situation 17-24 August

NORTH SEA

HOLLAND

OSTEND

BRUGES

Nieuport

DUNKIRK

Dixmude

Bergues

81 Territorial Division

Yser

Roulers

Schelde

GHENT

Schelde

Dendre

B   E   L   G

Ypres

Courtrai

Lys

Oudenarde

Grammont

FIRST ARM.

Cassel

Warneton

Renaix

Enghien

Hazebrouck

Armentières

LILLE

Cysoing

Lys

82 Territorial Division

Béthune

Lens

88 Terr. Div.

23 August

Douai

Scarpe

ARRAS

HQ, GROUP D'AMADE

GROUP D'AMADE (Reserve)

II Cav. Corps

TOURNAI

Antoing

II Cav. Corps (von der Marwitz)

Marchiennes

St. Amand

84 Terr. D.

Leuze

Peruwelz

Condé

Ath

Dendre

24 Aug.

19 Inf. Bde.

Cav. Div.

Valenciennes

MONS

II

B. E. F.

5 Cav. Bde.

Bavai

MAUBEUGE

53 & 69 R.Ds.

53 R.D.

XVIII

Le Quesnoy

Cambrai

Solesmes

Sambre

Helpe

Avesnes

Landrecies

Le Cateau GHQ, B.E.F.

F R A N C E

KEY TO ALLIED DISPOSITIONS

French Fifth Army, 21 August position.
French Fifth Army, 22 August positions.
French Fifth Army, 24 August positions.
British Expeditionary Force, 22/23 August.

Note: Corps are shown by Roman numerals

Royal Flying Corps HQ was at Maubeuge aerodrome. It consisted of 63 aeroplanes and 860 personnel.

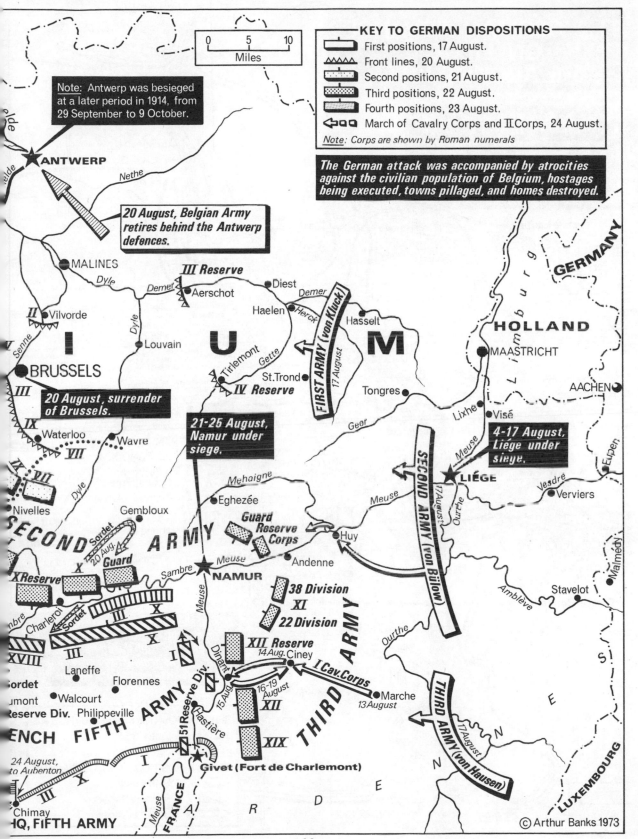

KEY TO GERMAN DISPOSITIONS

First positions, 17 August.
Front lines, 20 August.
Second positions, 21 August.
Third positions, 22 August.
Fourth positions, 23 August.
March of Cavalry Corps and II Corps, 24 August.

Note: Corps are shown by Roman numerals

The German attack was accompanied by atrocities against the civilian population of Belgium, hostages being executed, towns pillaged, and homes destroyed.

Note: Antwerp was besieged at a later period in 1914, from 29 September to 9 October.

ANTWERP

20 August, Belgian Army retires behind the Antwerp defences.

MALINES

GERMANY

III Reserve

Aerschot   Diest

Haelen

Hasselt

HOLLAND

MAASTRICHT

II Vilvorde

Louvain

I   **U**   **M**

BRUSSELS

Tirlemont

St.Trond

FIRST ARMY (von Kluck)

AACHEN

Tongres

17 August

20 August, surrender of Brussels.

IV Reserve

Lixhe Visé

21-25 August, Namur under siege.

Geer

4-17 August, Liége under siege.

Waterloo   Wavre

VII

Mehaigne

Eghezée

SECOND ARMY (von Bülow)

LIÉGE

Verviers

Nivelles

Gembloux

ARMY

Guard Reserve Corps

Huy

17 August

SECOND

Sordet

20 Aug.

Guard

Meuse

Andenne

Stavelot

X Reserve

X   Guard

NAMUR

38 Division

XI

22 Division

Charleroi   Sordet   III   X

XVIII   III   X

XII Reserve

14 Aug. Ciney

I Cav.Corps

THIRD ARMY (von Hausen)

Laneffe

Florennes

Dinant

15 Aug.

16-19 August

XII

Marche

13 August

17 August

Walcourt

Sordet

Reserve Div.   Philippeville

51 Reserve Div.

XIX

Givet (Fort de Charlemont)

24 August, to Aubenton

FIFTH ARMY

Hastière

ENCH FIFTH ARMY

I

X

III

Chimay

HQ, FIFTH ARMY

FRANCE

© Arthur Banks 1973

LUXEMBOURG

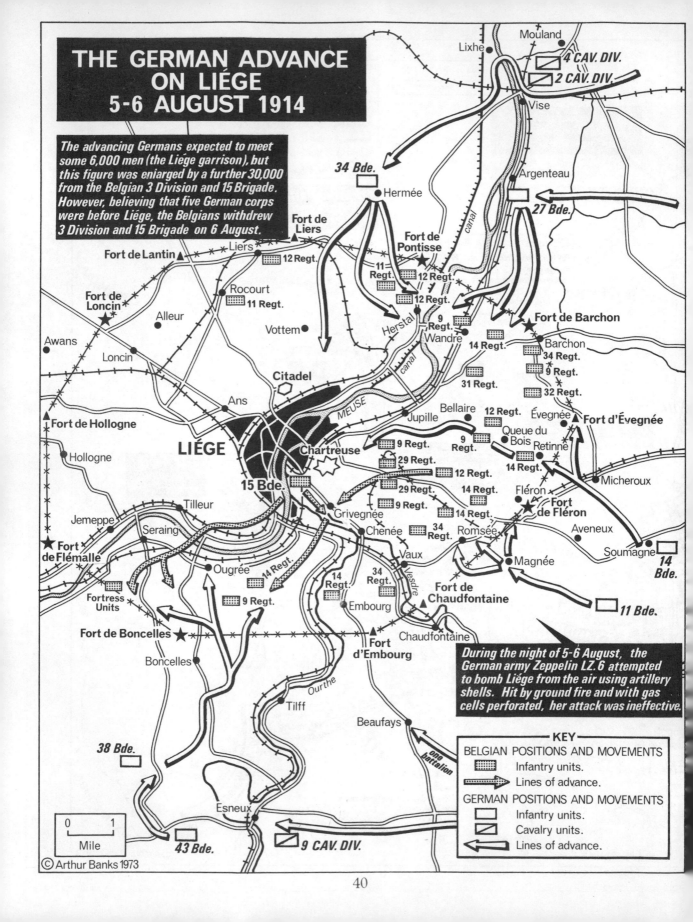

THE GERMAN ADVANCE ON LIÉGE 5-6 AUGUST 1914

The advancing Germans expected to meet some 6,000 men (the Liége garrison), but this figure was enlarged by a further 30,000 from the Belgian 3 Division and 15 Brigade. However, believing that five German corps were before Liége, the Belgians withdrew 3 Division and 15 Brigade on 6 August.

During the night of 5-6 August, the German army Zeppelin LZ.6 attempted to bomb Liége from the air using artillery shells. Hit by ground fire and with gas cells perforated, her attack was ineffective.

Mouland
Lixhe
4 CAV. DIV.
2 CAV. DIV.
Vise
Argenteau
34 Bde.
27 Bde.
Hermée
canal
Fort de Liers
Fort de Pontisse
Liers
12 Regt.
Fort de Lantin
11 Regt.
Fort de Barchon
Rocourt
11 Regt.
12 Regt.
12 Regt.
Fort de Loncin
Alleur
9 Regt.
Barchon
Vottem
Herstal
14 Regt.
34 Regt.
Awans
Wandre
9 Regt.
Loncin
32 Regt.
Citadel
31 Regt.
canal
Fort de Hollogne
MEUSE
Ans
Jupille
Bellaire
12 Regt.
Évegnée
Fort d'Évegnée
Hollogne
Queue du Bois
Retinne
9 Regt.
9 Regt.
LIÉGE
Chartreuse
29 Regt.
12 Regt.
14 Regt.
Micheroux
15 Bde.
29 Regt.
14 Regt.
Fléron
9 Regt.
Fort de Fléron
Tilleur
Grivegnée
14 Regt.
Avenux
Jemeppe
Chenée
34 Regt.
Romsée
Seraing
Vaux
14 Bde.
Fort de Flémalle
Ougrée
14 Regt.
34 Regt.
Magnée
Soumagne
Fortress Units
9 Regt.
14 Regt.
Fort de Chaudfontaine
11 Bde.
Embourg
Fort de Boncelles
Chaudfontaine
Boncelles
Fort d'Embourg
Ourthe
Tilff
Beaufays
38 Bde.
one battalion

0   1
Mile

Esneux
43 Bde.
9 CAV. DIV.

KEY
BELGIAN POSITIONS AND MOVEMENTS
  Infantry units.
  Lines of advance.
GERMAN POSITIONS AND MOVEMENTS
  Infantry units.
  Cavalry units.
  Lines of advance.

40

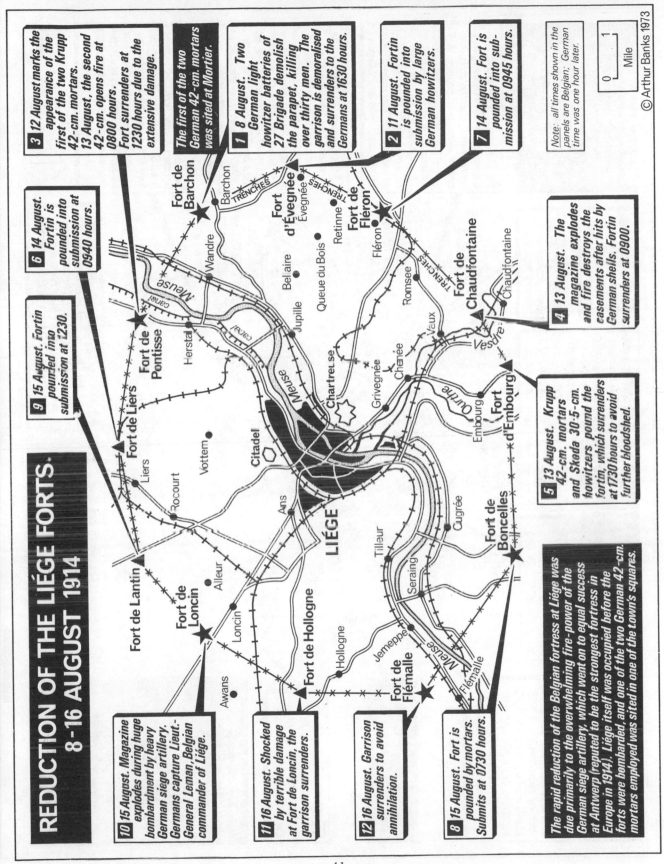

REDUCTION OF THE LIÉGE FORTS. 8-16 AUGUST 1914

3 12 August marks the appearance of the first of the two Krupp 42-cm. mortars. 13 August, the second 42-cm. opens fire at 0800 hours. Fort surrenders at 1230 hours due to the extensive damage.

The first of the two German 42-cm. mortars was sited at Mortier.

1 8 August. Two German light howitzer batteries of 27 Brigade demolish the parapet, killing over thirty men. The garrison is demoralised and surrenders to the Germans at 1630 hours.

2 11 August. Fortin is pounded into submission by large German howitzers.

7 14 August. Fort is pounded into submission at 0945 hours.

6 14 August. Fortin is pounded into submission at 0940 hours.

9 15 August. Fortin pounded into submission at 1230.

4 13 August. The magazine explodes and fire destroys the casemates after hits by German shells. Fortin surrenders at 0900.

5 13 August. Krupp 42-cm. mortars and Skoda 30·5-cm. howitzers pound the fortin, which surrenders at 1730 hours to avoid further bloodshed.

10 15 August. Magazine explodes during huge bombardment by heavy German siege artillery. Germans capture Lieut.-General Leman, Belgian commander of Liége.

11 16 August. Shocked by terrible damage at Fort de Loncin, the garrison surrenders.

12 16 August. Garrison surrenders to avoid annihilation.

8 15 August. Fort is pounded by mortars. Submits at 0730 hours.

Note: all times shown in the panels are Belgian; German time was one hour later.

© Arthur Banks 1973

0 __ 1
Mile

The rapid reduction of the Belgian fortress at Liége was due primarily to the overwhelming fire-power of the German siege artillery, which went on to equal success at Antwerp (reputed to be the strongest fortress in Europe in 1914). Liége itself was occupied before the forts were bombarded, and one of the two German 42-cm. mortars employed was sited in one of the town's squares.

Fort de Barchon · Barchon · TRENCHES · Fort d'Évegnée · Évegnée · TRENCHES · Retinne · Fort de Fléron · Fléron · Bel-aire · Queue du Bois · Jupille · Ronsee · Chaudfontaine · Fort de Chaudfontaine · Vaux · TRENCHES · Wandre · Meuse · Canal · Herstal · Fort de Pontisse · Chartreuse · Grivegnée · Chénée · Vesdre · Ourthe · Embourg · Fort d'Embourg · Fort de Liers · Liers · Rocourt · Vottem · Citadel · Ans · LIÉGE · Cugnée · Tilleur · Fort de Boncelles · Fort de Lantin · Fort de Loncin · Loncin · Alleur · Awans · Seraing · Jemeppe · Fort de Hollogne · Hollogne · Fort de Flémalle · Flémalle · Meuse

THE BOMBARDMENT OF NAMUR 21–25 AUGUST 1914

Namur was defended by the fortress garrison and 4 Belgian (Mobile) Division, plus two companies of the French 45 Infantry Brigade. The German investing forces included the Guard Reserve Corps and XI Corps, plus the heavy siege artillery moved up from Liège.

2 Morning 21 Aug., German field guns fire on trenches in intervals of forts.

1 Night 20 August, three preliminary infantry attacks.

3 1000 hours 21 August, the German "mörser" bombardment commences, rapidly inflicting severe damage to cupolas and magazines. By dusk, telephonic apparatus is unserviceable. Throughout 22 August concrete shells continue falling on sole operational cupola. Fort finally succumbs on 23 August.

4 1000 hours 21 August, the German siege artillery opens fire. By dusk, cupolas remain in working order, but telephonic apparatus is unserviceable. Shelling continues throughout night and on following day. By dusk on 22 August fort is in ruins, and garrison decides to evacuate the position.

5 1000 hours 21 August, the German heavy artillery opens fire. By dusk the structure of fort is honeycombed by large cracks in the concrete structure. By dusk all telephonic apparatus is unserviceable. Fort succumbs on 23 August.

Note: all times shown in the panels are Belgian; German time was one hour later.

6 Shelling opens at 1000 hours on 21 August. Early-morning infantry attack repulsed on 23 August, but fort falls at 1230 due to damage.

7 Morning 22 August, German artillery opens fire, but by dusk is only slightly damaged. On 23 August, German heavy howitzers switch fire from Forts d'Andoy and Maizeret. Destruction follows swiftly.

11 23 August, "mörser" shell attack commences, and heavy damage soon results. 3,600 shells are rained on the fort's position, the majority from 42-cm. weapons. Fort falls at 1700 hours on 25 August.

8 23 August, fire shifted from Fort de Cognelée; fort falls at 1630, 24 Aug.

Namur itself was shelled for four hours on 21 August, and again on 22 August.

10 24 August, howitzer attack commences. Fort succumbs at 1430 hours on the following day.

9 24 August, German 15-cm. field howitzers open bombardment. Fort is shelled continuously for 90 minutes, and then succumbs after main part of garrison is evacuated.

The bombardment of Namur followed the pattern established by the German heavy siege artillery at Liège. As before, the forts facing east were attacked first by the German 42-cm. "mörsers" and Austrian-produced 30.5-cm. howitzers; likewise, they were destroyed systematically. Belgian 4 Division was extricated from the holocaust at night on 23 August, and although the rearguard was trapped at Ermeton-sur-Biert, 12,000 men eventually reached Antwerp via Mariembourg on 30 August.

0 — 1 Mile

GERMAN GUARD RESERVE CORPS

GERMAN XI CORPS

Germans

Franc-Waret
Gelbressée
Marche-les-Dames
Maizeret
Mozet
Fort de Maizeret
22 DIVISION 23 Aug.
Wierde
Marchovelette
Cognelée
Fort de Marchovelette
Boninne
TRENCHES
Meuse
Lives
Loyers
Fort d'Andoy
23 Aug.
TRENCHES
Andoy
Naninne
Champion
Beez
Bouge
2 GUARD DIV. 23 Aug.
3 GUARD DIV. 23 August
Fort de Cognelée
Dassoulx
Vedrin
38 DIVISION 23 August
NAMUR
Jambes
Erpent
Fort de Dave
Dave
Fooz
Warisoulx
1 GUARD RES. DIV. 23 Aug.
Fort d'Émines
St. Marc
Sambre
Belgrade
Meuse
Wepion
Rhisnes
Fort de Suarlée
Flawinne
Fort de Malonne
Malonne
Fort de St. Héribert
TRENCHES

© Arthur Banks 1973

42

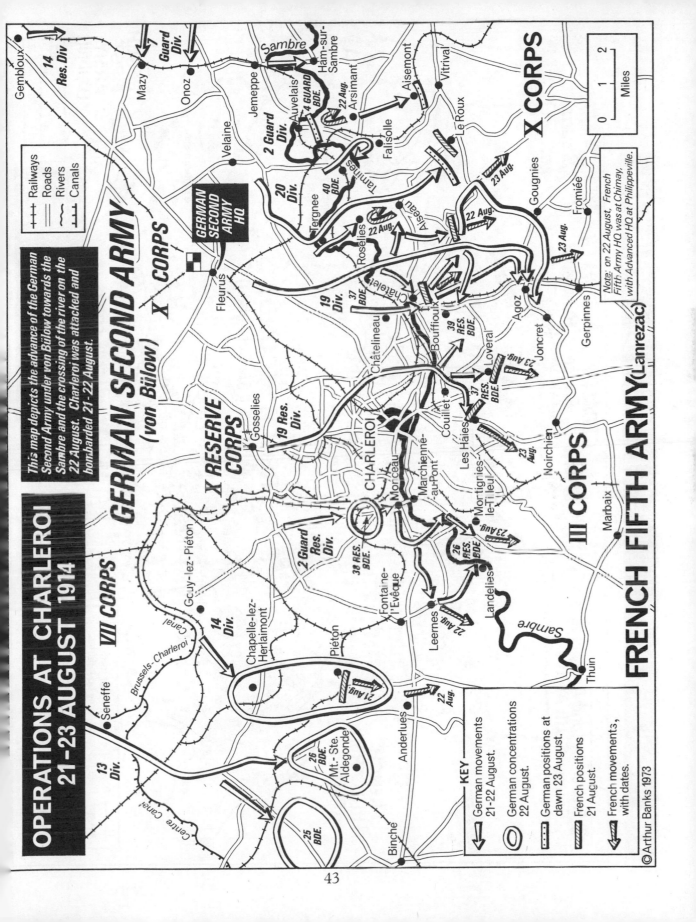

OPERATIONS AT CHARLEROI 21–23 AUGUST 1914

VII CORPS

GERMAN SECOND ARMY (von Bülow)

X CORPS

X RESERVE CORPS

X CORPS

X CORPS

III CORPS

FRENCH FIFTH ARMY (Lanrezac)

This map depicts the advance of the German Second Army under von Bülow towards the Sambre and the crossing of the river on the 22 August. Charleroi was attacked and bombarded 21–22 August.

GERMAN SECOND ARMY HQ

Note: on 22 August, French Fifth Army HQ was at Chimay, with Advanced HQ at Philippeville.

KEY

- German movements 21–22 August.
- German concentrations 22 August.
- German positions at dawn 23 August.
- French positions 21 August.
- French movements, with dates.

Railways
Roads
Rivers
Canals

0 1 2 Miles

© Arthur Banks 1973

Gembloux
14 Res. Div.
Guard Div.
Mazy
Onoz
Sambre
Jemeppe
Auvelais
Ham-sur-Sambre
Arsimant
4 GUARD BDE.
22 Aug.
Aisemont
Vitrival
Velaine
2 Guard Div.
Falisolle
Le Roux
20 Div.
40 BDE.
Tamines
23 Aug.
Gougnies
Fromiée
Tergnee
Aiseau
22 Aug.
Roselies
22 Aug.
Fleurus
19 Div.
37 BDE.
Châtelet
Agoz
23 Aug.
Joncret
Gerpinnes
Châtelineau
Bouffioulx
39 RES. BDE.
22 Aug.
Loveral
23 Aug.
Gosselies
19 Res. Div.
37 RES. BDE.
Couillet
Les Hâies
CHARLEROI
Morceau
Marchienne-au-Pont
Noirchien
2 Guard Res. Div.
38 RES. BDE.
Mortgries-le-Tilleul
26 RES. BDE.
23 Aug.
Marbaix
Gouy-lez-Piéton
Chapelle-lez-Herlaimont
Piéton
Fontaine-l'Evêque
Leernes
22 Aug.
Landelies
Brussels-Charleroi Canal
14 Div.
21 Aug.
22 Aug.
Sambre
Seneffe
13 Div.
Anderlues
Thuin
26 BDE.
Mt.-Ste.-Aldegonde
25 BDE.
Binche
Centre Canal

THE FRONTIER BATTLES IN LORRAINE 10 - 28 AUGUST 1914

① French Second Army versus German Sixth Army

HQ, GERMAN SIXTH ARMY
Hellimer

SIXTH ARMY (Crown Prince Rupprecht of Bavaria)

GERMAN

I BAVARIAN RESERVE CORPS

Grostenquin
Francaltroff
Baronville
Marthille
MORHANGE

XXI CORPS

II BAVARIAN CORPS

III BAV. CORPS

Buchy
Soigne
Morville
DELME

33 Landwehr Division

72 Res. Div.

70 Res. Div.

68 Res. Div.

Laneuveville
Viviers
Fonteny
Burlioncourt
Gerbecourt
CHÂTEAU-SALINS

XX CORPS

39 Div. Brehain
Oron Dalhain
11 Div. Conthil

30 Div. DIEUZE

29 Div.
Bidestroff
Lidrezing

31 Div.
Loudrefing
Rorbach
32
Division

XVI CORPS

Maizières
Moussey
Avricourt
Donnelay

FRENCH FIRST ARMY (Dubail)

Blâmont
Réchicourt le Château
Domèvre
Vezouze

XV CORPS

Juvelize
Moyenvic
Xanrey
Moncourt
Bézange la Petite

Gondrexon
Embermenil

Fort de Manonviller

31 Division

XVI CORPS

LUNÉVILLE

32 Div.

FRENCH SECOND ARMY (de Castlenau)

Nomény

IX CORPS

Mont Toulon

59 Reserve Division

Ste. Geneviève

GRAND COURONNÉ

FORÊT DE HAYE

DE NANCY

Laneuveville-devant-Nancy

Pont St. Vincent

TOUL

FRENCH THIRD ARMY (Ruffey)

DIEULOUARD

PONT-À-MOUSSON

73 Reserve Division

Moselle

KEY

— · — Franco-German frontier in 1914.
▬▬ French Second Army boundaries.
· · · · French corps boundaries.
◁▭ French positions at dawn, 20 August.
⬜ German attacks at dawn, 20 August.
▤ French positions at dusk, 21 August.

The initial progress of Foch's XX Corps was frustrated by withdrawal of its left flanking guard and the slow advance of XV Corps on its right. Following the German attacks on 20 August, XX Corps covered Second Army's retreat.

© Arthur Banks 1973

44

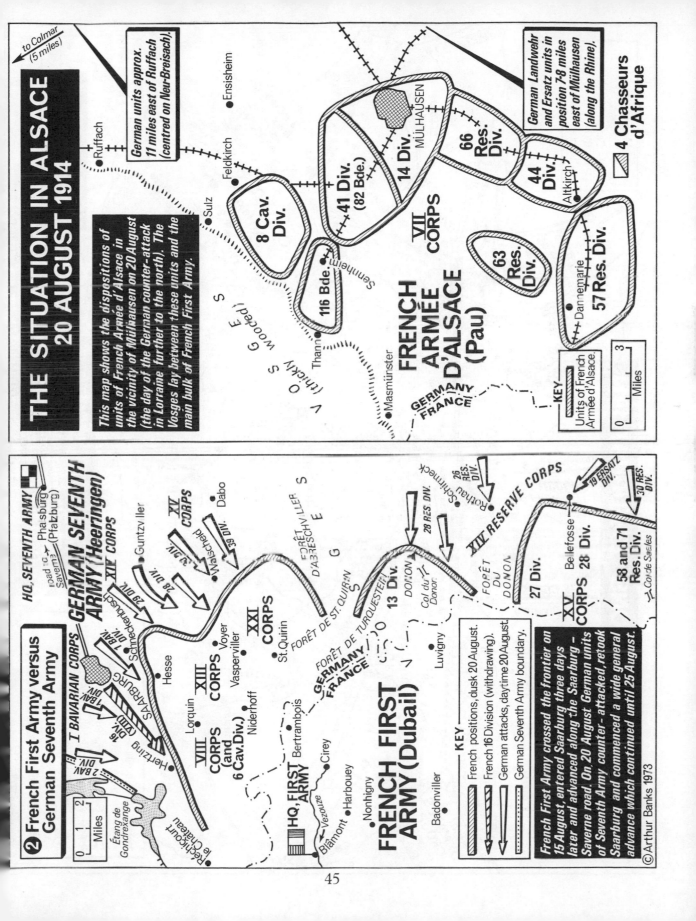

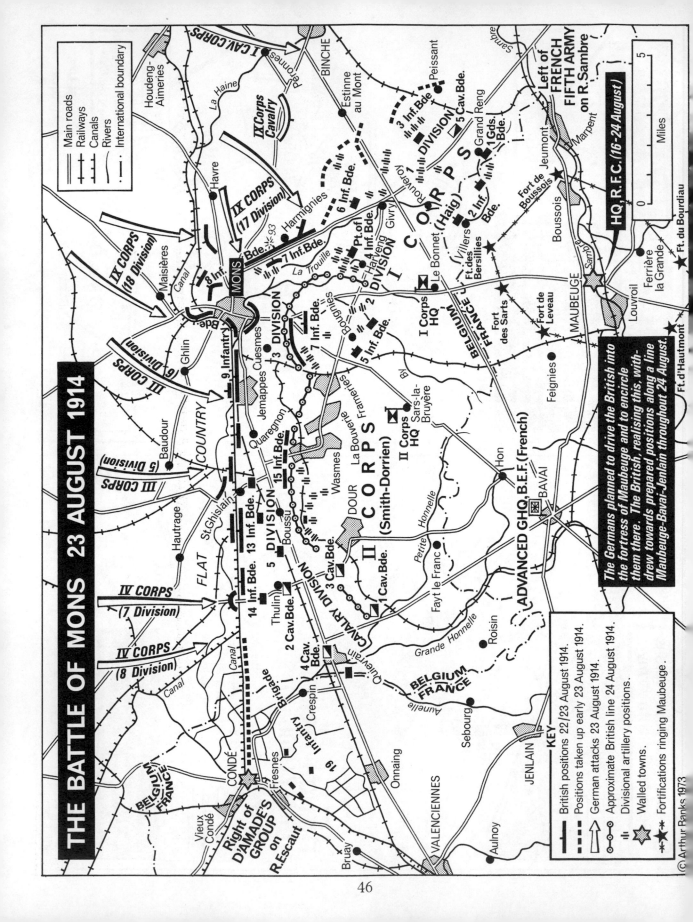

THE BATTLE OF MONS 23 AUGUST 1914

Main roads ⊢⊢⊢
Railways ⊢⊢⊢⊢
Canals ⊢⊢⊢
Rivers
International boundary ·—·—·

I CAV.CORPS

Houdeng-Aimeries

BINCHE

Estinne au Mont

Peissant

3 Inf. Bde.

IX Corps Cavalry

Havre

La Haine

IX CORPS (17 Division)

Harmignies

6 Inf. Bde.

Rouveroy

DIVISION

5 Cav. Bde.

Grand Reng

1 Gds. Bde.

Left of FRENCH FIFTH ARMY on R.Sambre

C O R P S

Marpent

IX CORPS (18 Division)

Maisières

Canal

Bde. 93

7 Inf. Bde.

8 Inf.

MONS

La Trouille

Pt. of 4 Inf.Bde.

Harveng

Givry

2 Inf. Bde.

(Haig)

I

Villers

Ft.des Bersillies

Fort de Boussois

Boussois

HQ, R.F.C. (16-24 August)

Miles

0   5

Bde.

Ghlin

9 Infantry

6 Division

III CORPS

Baudour

5 Division

III CORPS

FLAT

COUNTRY

Hautrage

St.Ghislain

13 Inf. Bde.

14 Inf. Bde.

Thulin

Jemappes

Cuesmes

3 DIVISION

Quaregnon

15 Inf. Bde.

BOUSSU

DOUR

La Bouverie

Wasmes

Frameries

II

7 Inf. Bde.

Bougnies

8 Inf. Bde.

5 Inf. Bde.

Le Bonnet

I Corps HQ

BELGIUM FRANCE

Fort des Sarts

Fort de Leveau

Feignies

MAUBEUGE

Louvroil

Ferrière la Grande

Ft. du Bourdiau

C O R P S

Sars-la-Bruyère

II Corps HQ

(Smith-Dorrien)

Honnelle

Petite Honnelle

Hon

BAVAI

ADVANCED GHQ, B.E.F. (French)

Ft.d'Hautmont

5 Cav. Bde.

3 Cav. Bde.

1 Cav. Bde.

CAVALRY DIVISION

Quiévrain

Fayt le Franc

Grande Honnelle

Roisin

2 Cav. Bde.

4 Cav. Bde.

Infantry Brigade

Crespin

Onnaing

19

Annelle

BELGIUM FRANCE

Sebourg

JENLAIN

CONDÉ

Canal

Canal

Fresnes

BELGIUM FRANCE

Vieux Condé

Right of D'AMADE'S GROUP on R.Escaut

Bruay

Aulnoy

VALENCIENNES

IV CORPS (7 Division)

IV CORPS (8 Division)

The Germans planned to drive the British into the fortress of Maubeuge and to encircle them there. The British, realising this, with-drew towards prepared positions along a line Maubeuge-Bavai-Jenlain throughout 24 August.

KEY

⊢⊢⊢⊢ British positions 22/23 August 1914.
⊢⊢⊢⊢ Positions taken up early 23 August 1914.
⟹ German attacks 23 August 1914.
○=○=○ Approximate British line 24 August 1914.
⊨⊨ Divisional artillery positions.
✦ Walled towns.
✶—✶ Fortifications ringing Maubeuge.

© Arthur Banks 1973

46

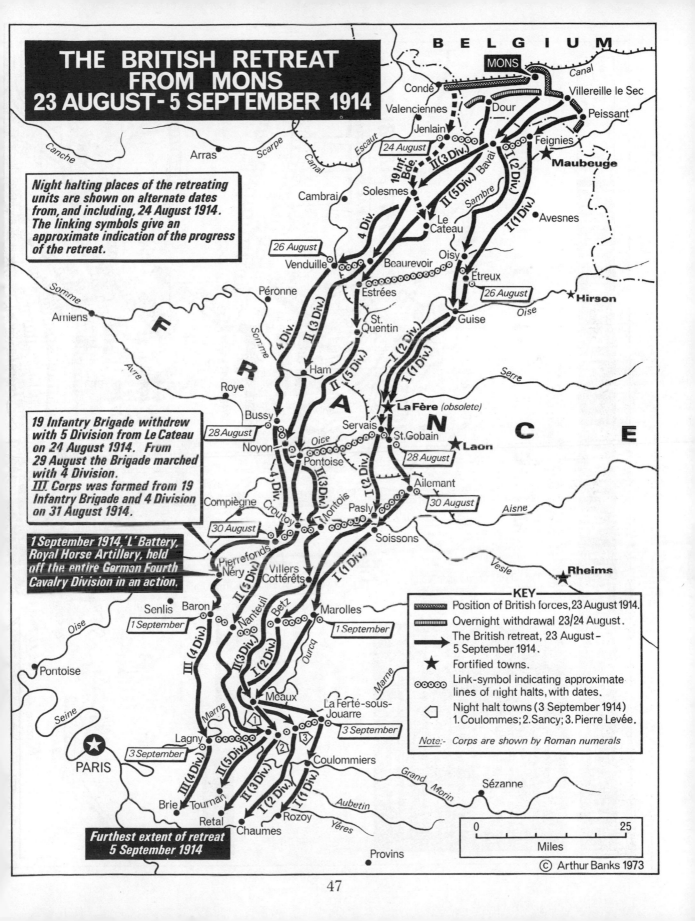

THE BRITISH RETREAT FROM MONS 23 AUGUST – 5 SEPTEMBER 1914

Night halting places of the retreating units are shown on alternate dates from, and including, 24 August 1914. The linking symbols give an approximate indication of the progress of the retreat.

19 Infantry Brigade withdrew with 5 Division from Le Cateau on 24 August 1914. From 29 August the Brigade marched with 4 Division.
III Corps was formed from 19 Infantry Brigade and 4 Division on 31 August 1914.

1 September 1914, 'L' Battery, Royal Horse Artillery, held off the entire German Fourth Cavalry Division in an action.

Furthest extent of retreat 5 September 1914

KEY

- ꙮꙮꙮ Position of British forces, 23 August 1914.
- ꙮꙮꙮ Overnight withdrawal 23/24 August.
- → The British retreat, 23 August – 5 September 1914.
- ★ Fortified towns.
- ⚬⚬⚬⚬ Link-symbol indicating approximate lines of night halts, with dates.
- ⬠ Night halt towns (3 September 1914) 1. Coulommes; 2. Sancy; 3. Pierre Levée.

<u>Note</u>:- Corps are shown by Roman numerals

0 — Miles — 25

© Arthur Banks 1973

47

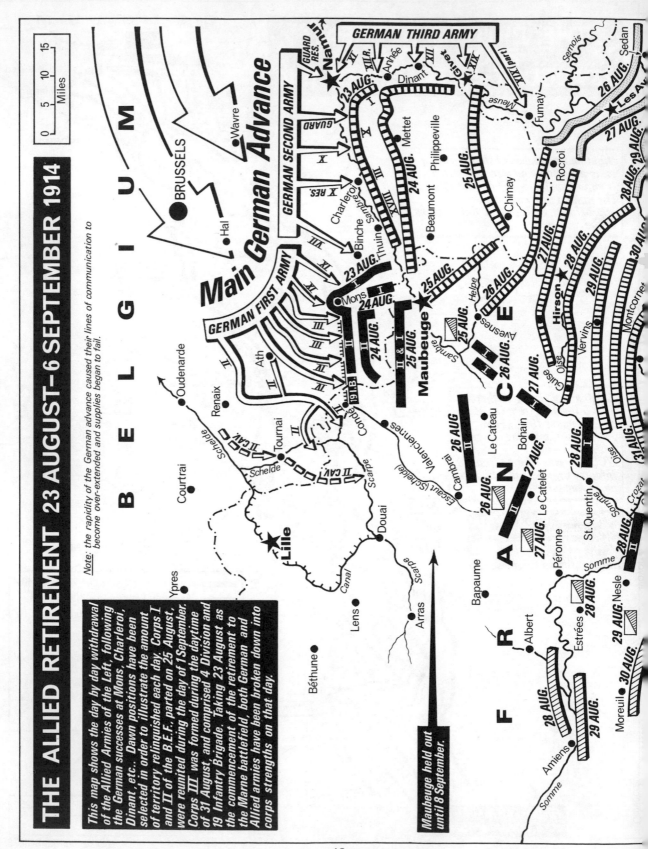

THE ALLIED RETIREMENT 23 AUGUST–6 SEPTEMBER 1914

This map shows the day by day withdrawal of the Allied Armies of the Left, following the German successes at Mons, Charleroi, Dinant, etc.. Dawn positions have been selected in order to illustrate the amount of territory relinquished each day. Corps I and II of the B.E.F., parted on 25 August, were reunited during the daytime of 1 September. Corps III was formed during the daytime of 31 August, and comprised 4 Division and 19 Infantry Brigade. Taking 23 August as the commencement of the retirement to the Marne battlefield, both German and Allied armies have been broken down into corps strengths on that day.

Note: the rapidity of the German advance caused their lines of communication to become over-extended and supplies began to fail.

GERMAN THIRD ARMY

GERMAN SECOND ARMY

GERMAN FIRST ARMY

Main German Advance

Maubeuge held out until 8 September.

BELGIUM

FRANCE

Miles
0 5 10 15

BRUSSELS

Wavre

Hal

Namur

Anhée

Dinant

Givet

Sedan

Les Av.

Fumay

Semois (part)

Meuse

Mettet

Philippeville

Beaumont

Chimay

Rocroi

Charleroi

Binche

Thuin

Sambre

Mons

Maubeuge

Avesnes

Helpe

Hirson

Vervins

Montcornet

Oise

Ath

Oudenaarde

Renaix

Tournai

Schelde

Scarpe

Valenciennes

Escaut (Schelde)

Cambrai

Le Cateau

Bohain

Le Catelet

Guise

St. Quentin

Péronne

Somme

Nesle

Crozat

Courtrai

Ypres

Lille

Douai

Canal

Scarpe

Scarpe

Bapaume

Albert

Estrées

Moreuil

Béthune

Lens

Arras

Amiens

Somme

Somme

48

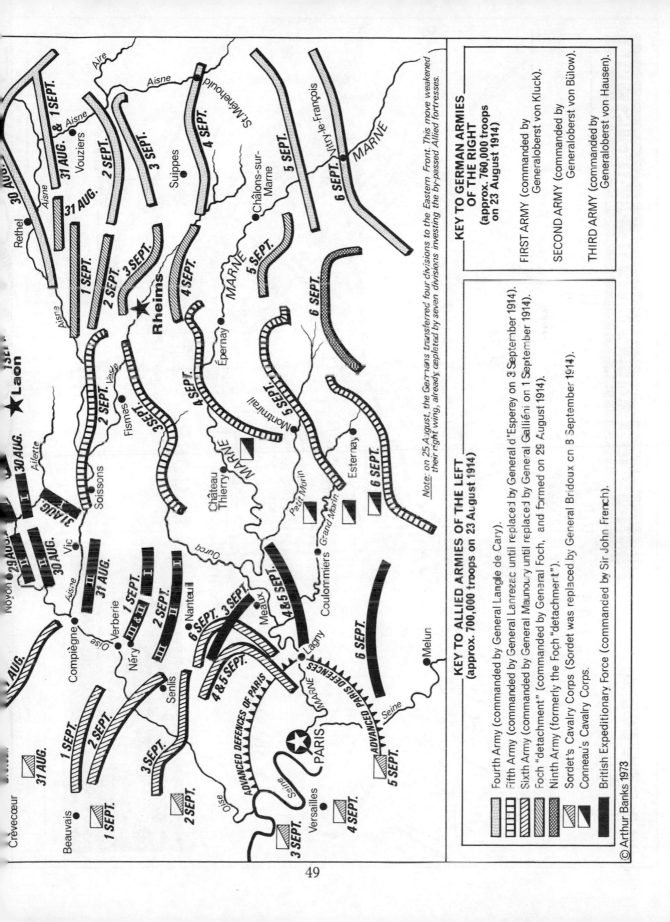

KEY TO GERMAN ARMIES OF THE RIGHT
(approx. 760,000 troops on 23 August 1914)

FIRST ARMY (commanded by Generaloberst von Kluck).

SECOND ARMY (commanded by Generaloberst von Bülow).

THIRD ARMY (commanded by Generaloberst von Hausen).

Note: on 25 August, the Germans transferred four divisions to the Eastern Front. This move weakened their right wing, already depleted by seven divisions investing the by-passed Allied fortresses.

KEY TO ALLIED ARMIES OF THE LEFT
(approx. 700,000 troops on 23 August 1914)

Fourth Army (commanded by General Langle de Cary).

Fifth Army (commanded by General Lanrezac until replaced by General d'Esperey on 3 September 1914).

Sixth Army (commanded by General Maunoury until replaced by General Galliéni on 1 September 1914).

Foch "detachment" (commanded by General Foch, and formed on 29 August 1914).

Ninth Army (formerly the Foch "detachment").

Sordet's Cavalry Corps (Sordet was replaced by General Bridoux on 8 September 1914).

Conneau's Cavalry Corps.

British Expeditionary Force (commanded by Sir John French).

© Arthur Banks 1973

49

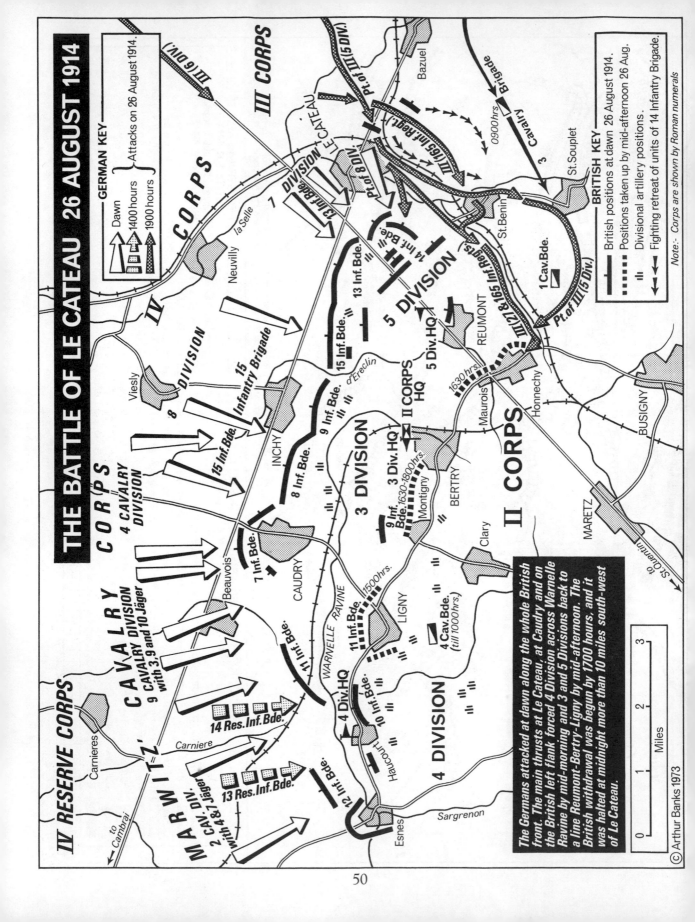

THE BATTLE OF LE CATEAU, 26 AUGUST 1914

GERMAN KEY

Dawn
1400 hours } Attacks on 26 August 1914.
1900 hours

BRITISH KEY

British positions at dawn 26 August 1914.
Positions taken up by mid-afternoon 26 Aug.
Divisional artillery positions.
Fighting retreat of units of 14 Infantry Brigade.

Note:- Corps are shown by Roman numerals

The Germans attacked at dawn along the whole British front. The main thrusts at Le Cateau, at Caudry and on the British left flank forced 4 Division across Warnelle Ravine by mid-morning and 3 and 5 Divisions back to a line Reumont-Bertry-Ligny by mid-afternoon. The British withdrawal was begun by 1700 hours, and it was halted at midnight more than 10 miles south-west of Le Cateau.

Miles
0   1   2   3

© Arthur Banks 1973

50

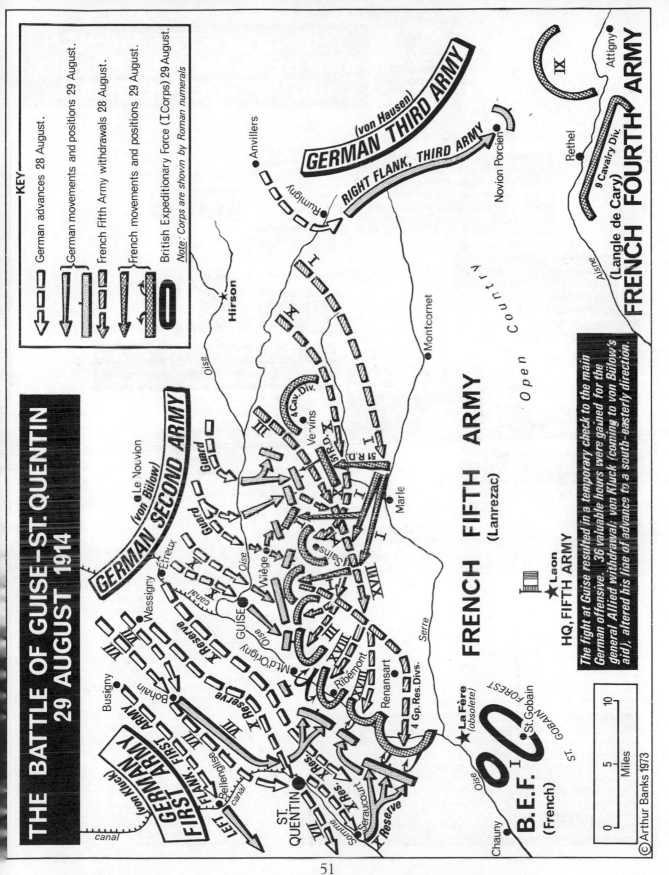

THE BATTLE OF GUISE–ST. QUENTIN 29 AUGUST 1914

KEY

German advances 28 August.

German movements and positions 29 August.

French Fifth Army withdrawals 28 August.

French movements and positions 29 August.

British Expeditionary Force (I Corps) 29 August.

Note: Corps are shown by Roman numerals.

GERMAN THIRD ARMY (von Hausen)

RIGHT FLANK, THIRD ARMY

FRENCH FOURTH ARMY (Langle de Cary)

9 Cavalry Div.

GERMAN SECOND ARMY (von Bülow)

GERMAN FIRST ARMY (von Kluck)

FRENCH FIFTH ARMY (Lanrezac)

Open Country

HQ, FIFTH ARMY — Laon

The fight at Guise resulted in a temporary check to the main German offensive. 36 valuable hours were gained for the general Allied withdrawal: von Kluck (coming to von Bülow's aid), altered his line of advance to a south-easterly direction.

Anvillers

Rumigny

Novion Porcien

Rethel

Attigny

Aisne

Montcornet

Marle

4 Cav. Div.

Ve-vins

51 R.D.

Sains

Le Nouvion

Guard

Guard

Étreux

Wiège

Wassigny

Hirson

Oise

canal

GUISE

Mt. d'Origny

Ribémont

Renansart

Serre

4 Gp. Res. Divs.

La Fère (obsolete)

St. Gobain

ST. GOBAIN FOREST

Busigny

Bohain

Bellenglise

Séraucourt

ST. QUENTIN

Somme

Chauny

Oise

B.E.F. (French)

Reserve

Reserve

Reserve

Reserve

canal

LEFT FLANK

0   5   10
|___|___|
Miles

© Arthur Banks 1973

51

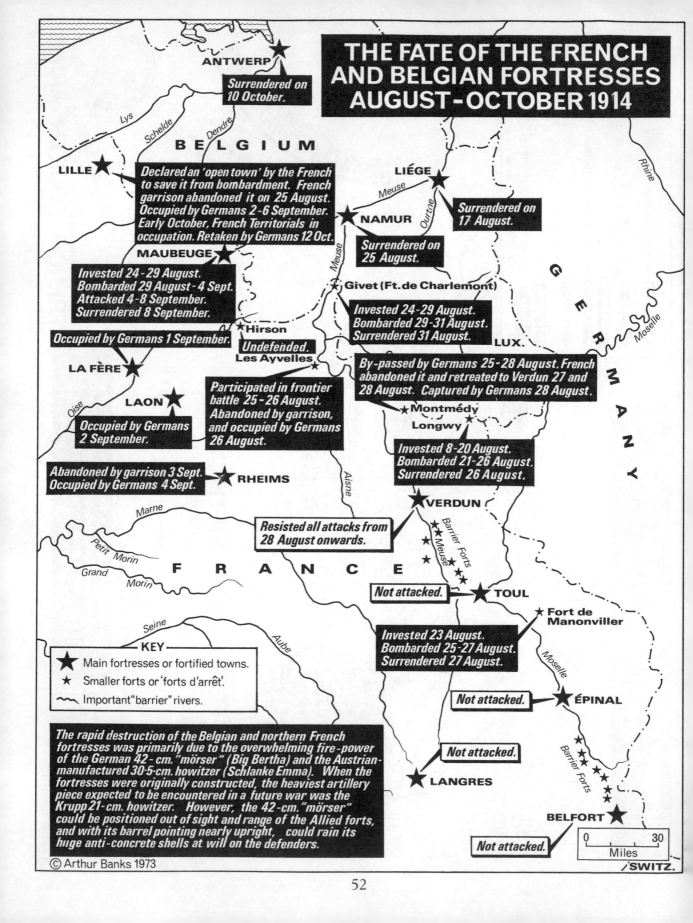

THE FATE OF THE FRENCH AND BELGIAN FORTRESSES AUGUST–OCTOBER 1914

ANTWERP
Surrendered on 10 October.

BELGIUM

LILLE
Declared an 'open town' by the French to save it from bombardment. French garrison abandoned it on 25 August. Occupied by Germans 2–6 September. Early October, French Territorials in occupation. Retaken by Germans 12 Oct.

LIÉGE
Surrendered on 17 August.

NAMUR
Surrendered on 25 August.

MAUBEUGE
Invested 24–29 August. Bombarded 29 August–4 Sept. Attacked 4–8 September. Surrendered 8 September.

Givet (Ft. de Charlemont)
Invested 24–29 August. Bombarded 29–31 August. Surrendered 31 August.

LUX.

Occupied by Germans 1 September.

Hirson
Undefended.
Les Ayvelles

LA FÈRE

LAON
Participated in frontier battle 25–26 August. Abandoned by garrison, and occupied by Germans 26 August.

Occupied by Germans 2 September.

By-passed by Germans 25–28 August. French abandoned it and retreated to Verdun 27 and 28 August. Captured by Germans 28 August.

Montmédy
Longwy
Invested 8–20 August. Bombarded 21–26 August. Surrendered 26 August.

Abandoned by garrison 3 Sept. Occupied by Germans 4 Sept.
RHEIMS

VERDUN
Resisted all attacks from 28 August onwards.

Barrier Forts

Not attacked.
TOUL

Fort de Manonviller
Invested 23 August. Bombarded 25–27 August. Surrendered 27 August.

Not attacked.
ÉPINAL

Not attacked.

LANGRES

Barrier Forts

BELFORT
Not attacked.

KEY
★ Main fortresses or fortified towns.
★ Smaller forts or 'forts d'arrêt'.
〰 Important "barrier" rivers.

The rapid destruction of the Belgian and northern French fortresses was primarily due to the overwhelming fire-power of the German 42-cm. "mörser" (Big Bertha) and the Austrian-manufactured 30·5-cm. howitzer (Schlanke Emma). When the fortresses were originally constructed, the heaviest artillery piece expected to be encountered in a future war was the Krupp 21-cm. howitzer. However, the 42-cm. "mörser" could be positioned out of sight and range of the Allied forts, and with its barrel pointing nearly upright, could rain its huge anti-concrete shells at will on the defenders.

© Arthur Banks 1973

0   30
Miles

SWITZ.

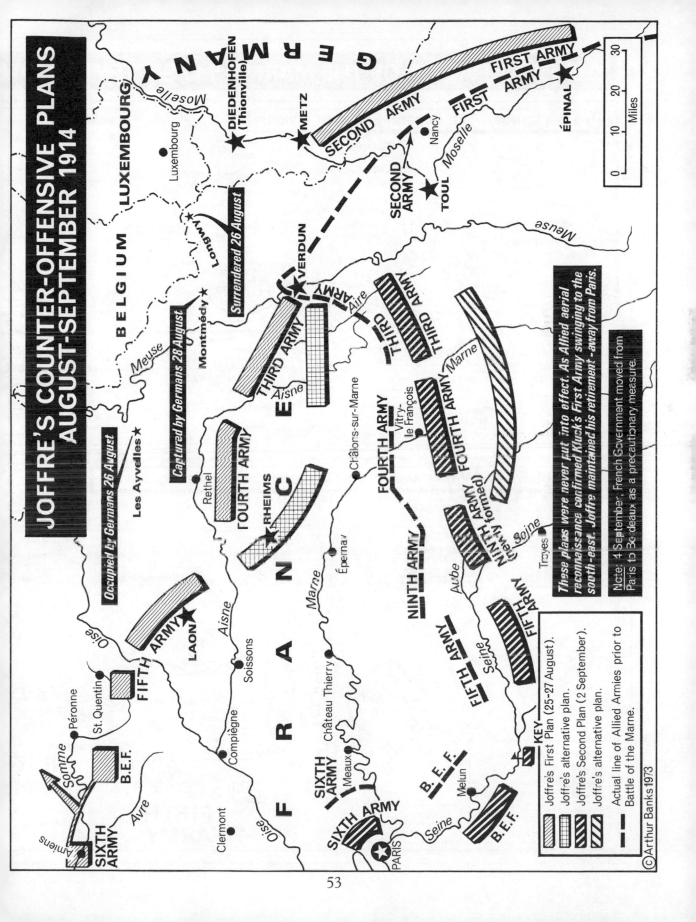

JOFFRE'S COUNTER-OFFENSIVE PLANS AUGUST–SEPTEMBER 1914

GERMANY

LUXEMBOURG

BELGIUM

FRANCE

DIEDENHOFEN (Thionville)

METZ

Moselle

Luxembourg

Longwy — Surrendered 26 August

VERDUN

Montmédy — *Captured by Germans 28 August*

Meuse

Aisne

THIRD ARMY

SECOND ARMY

Nancy

TOUL

ÉPINAL

FIRST ARMY

SECOND ARMY

FIRST ARMY

Moselle

Meuse

Les Ayvelles ★ — *Occupied by Germans 26 August*

Rethel

FOURTH ARMY

RHEIMS ★

THIRD ARMY

THIRD ARMY

Aire

Marne

Châlons-sur-Marne

Vitry-le-François

FOURTH ARMY

FOURTH ARMY

Épernay

Marne

NINTH ARMY

NINTH ARMY (newly formed)

Aube

Seine

Troyes

LAON ★

FIFTH ARMY

Aisne

Soissons

Château Thierry

FIFTH ARMY

FIFTH ARMY

Seine

St. Quentin

Péronne

Somme

B.E.F.

Compiègne

SIXTH ARMY

Meaux

SIXTH ARMY

SIXTH ARMY

Clermont

Oise

Avre

Amiens

SIXTH ARMY

B.E.F.

Melun

B.E.F.

Seine

PARIS ★

These plans were never put into effect. As Allied aerial reconnaissance confirmed Kluck's First Army swinging to the south-east, Joffre maintained his retirement – away from Paris.

Note: 4 September, French Government moved from Paris to Bordeaux as a precautionary measure.

KEY:

▨	Joffre's First Plan (25–27 August).
▤	Joffre's alternative plan.
▨	Joffre's Second Plan (2 September).
▨	Joffre's alternative plan.
▬ ▬	Actual line of Allied Armies prior to Battle of the Marne.

© Arthur Banks 1973

0 10 20 30 Miles

THE FIRST BATTLE OF THE MARNE 5-10 SEPTEMBER 1914

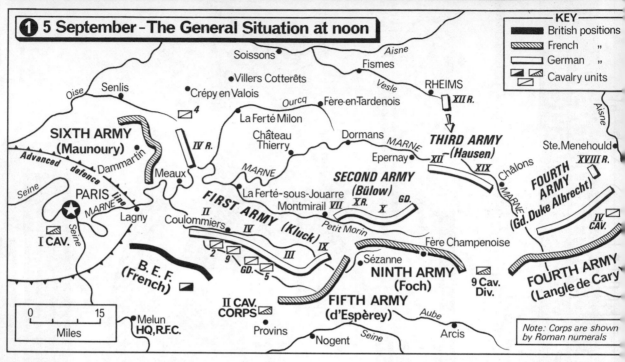

1 5 September – The General Situation at noon

KEY
- British positions
- French   "
- German   "
- Cavalry units

Soissons · Villers Cotterêts · Fismes · Aisne

Senlis · Crépy en Valois · Fère-en-Tardenois · RHEIMS · XII R.

Oise · La Ferté Milon · Ourcq · Vesle

4 · Château Thierry · Dormans · MARNE · THIRD ARMY (Hausen) · XII · Ste. Menehould · XVIII R.

SIXTH ARMY (Maunoury) · IV R. · Epernay · XIX · Châlons · FOURTH ARMY (Gd. Duke Albrecht)

Advanced defence · Dammartin · Meaux · MARNE · SECOND ARMY (Bülow) · MARNE · IV CAV.

Seine · PARIS · MARNE · La Ferté-sous-Jouarre · X R. · GD. · X

I CAV. · Lagny · Coulommiers · FIRST ARMY (Kluck) · Montmirail · VII · Petit Morin · Fère Champenoise · FOURTH ARMY (Langle de Cary)

II · IV · III · IX · Sézanne · NINTH ARMY (Foch) · 9 Cav. Div.

B.E.F. (French) · 2 · 9 · GD. · 5

II CAV. CORPS · FIFTH ARMY (d'Espèrey) · Aube · Arcis

0 — 15 Miles · Melun HQ, R.F.C. · Provins · Nogent · Seine

Note: Corps are shown by Roman numerals

2 6 September – Withdrawal of the German First Army's Right Wing

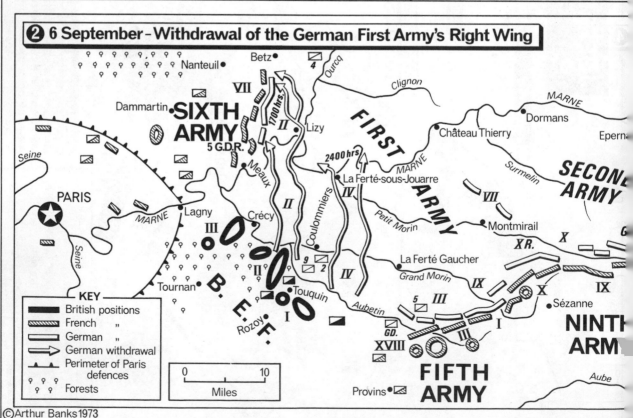

Nanteuil · Betz · 4 · Ourcq · Clignon · MARNE · Dormans · Epern

VII · 1700 hrs. · Lizy · FIRST · Château Thierry

Dammartin · SIXTH ARMY · II · 5 G.D.R. · Meaux · 2400 hrs. · La Ferté-sous-Jouarre · MARNE · Surmelin · SECOND ARMY

Seine · PARIS · MARNE · Lagny · Crécy · II · IV · ARMY · VII · Montmirail · X R. · X

III · II · Coulommiers · Petit Morin · La Ferté Gaucher · IX · X

Tournan · B. E. F. · Touquin · 9 · 2 · IV · Grand Morin · IX

Rozoy · I · Aubetin · 5 · III · X · Sézanne · NINTH ARMY

GD. · III · I

XVIII · FIFTH ARMY · Provins · Aube

KEY
- British positions
- French   "
- German   "
- German withdrawal
- Perimeter of Paris defences
- Forests

0 — 10 Miles

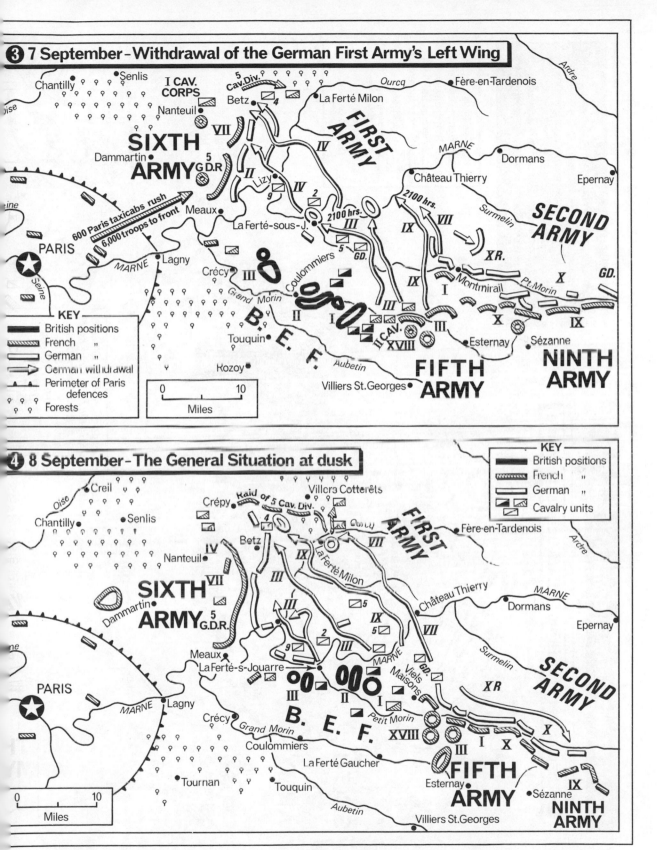

3 7 September – Withdrawal of the German First Army's Left Wing

4 8 September – The General Situation at dusk

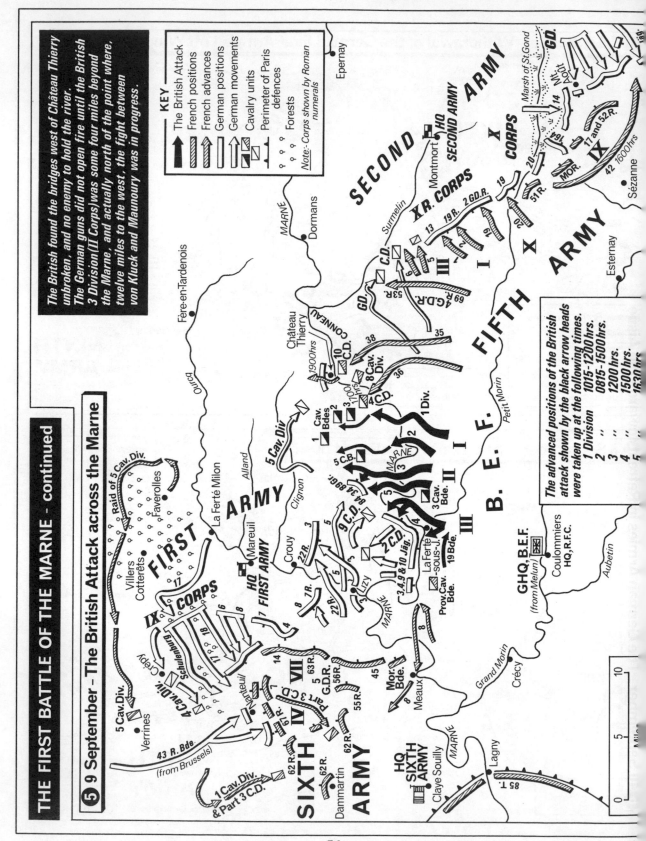

THE FIRST BATTLE OF THE MARNE - continued

The British found the bridges west of Château Thierry unbroken, and no enemy to hold the river. The German guns did not open fire until the British 3 Division (II Corps) was some four miles beyond the Marne, and actually north of the point where, twelve miles to the west, the fight between von Kluck and Maunoury was in progress.

KEY

The British Attack	
French positions	
French advances	
German positions	
German movements	
Cavalry units	
Perimeter of Paris defences	
Forests	
Note:- Corps shown by Roman numerals	

⑤ 9 September – The British Attack across the Marne

The advanced positions of the British attack shown by the black arrow heads were taken up at the following times.

1 Division	..	1015-1200 hrs.
2 "	..	0815-1500 hrs.
3 "	..	1200 hrs.
4 "	..	1500 hrs.
5 "	..	1630 hrs.

SECOND ARMY

FIFTH ARMY

FIRST ARMY

SIXTH ARMY

B. E. F.

GHQ, B.E.F. (from Melun)

HQ SIXTH ARMY

Epernay

Sézanne

Esternay

Dormans

Fère-en-Tardenois

Château Thierry

Coulommiers HQ, R.F.C.

Crécy

Lagny

Claye Souilly

Meaux

Dammartin

Verrines

Crépy

La Ferté Milon

Villers Cotterêts

Faverolles

Mareuil

Crouy

Lizy

La Ferté-sous-J.

56

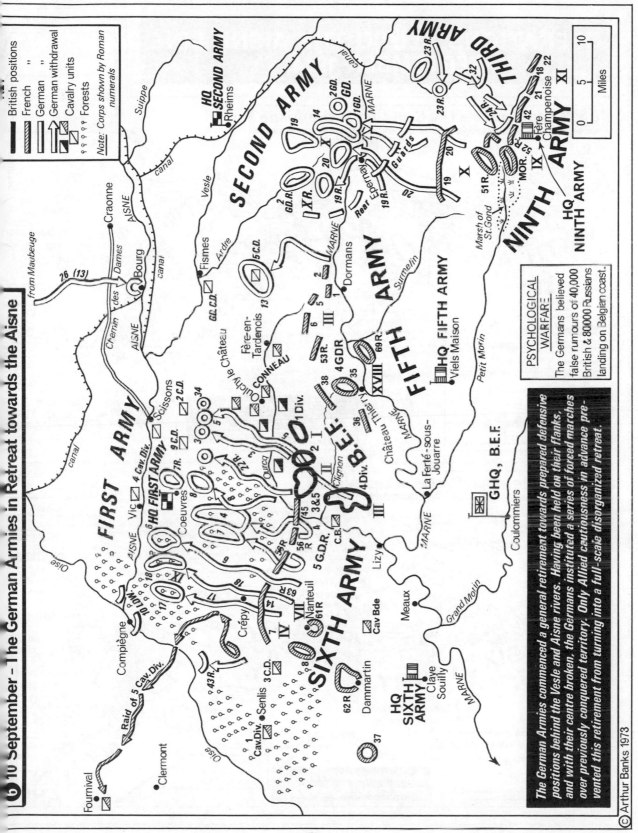

6 1U September – The German Armies in Retreat towards the Aisne

British positions
French "
German "
German withdrawal
Cavalry units
Forests

Note: Corps shown by Roman numerals

PSYCHOLOGICAL WARFARE.

The Germans believed false rumours of 40,000 British & 80000 Russians landing on Belgian coast.

The German Armies commenced a general retirement towards prepared defensive positions behind the Vesle and Aisne rivers. Having been held on their flanks, and with their centre broken, the Germans instituted a series of forced marches over previously conquered territory. Only Allied cautiousness in advance prevented this retirement from turning into a full-scale disorganized retreat.

FIRST ARMY

SECOND ARMY

THIRD ARMY

NINTH ARMY

FIFTH ARMY

SIXTH ARMY

B.E.F.

HQ SECOND ARMY — Rheims

HQ NINTH ARMY

HQ FIFTH ARMY — Viels Maison

HQ FIRST ARMY

HQ SIXTH ARMY — Claye Souilly

GHQ, B.E.F.

Miles
0   5   10

© Arthur Banks 1973

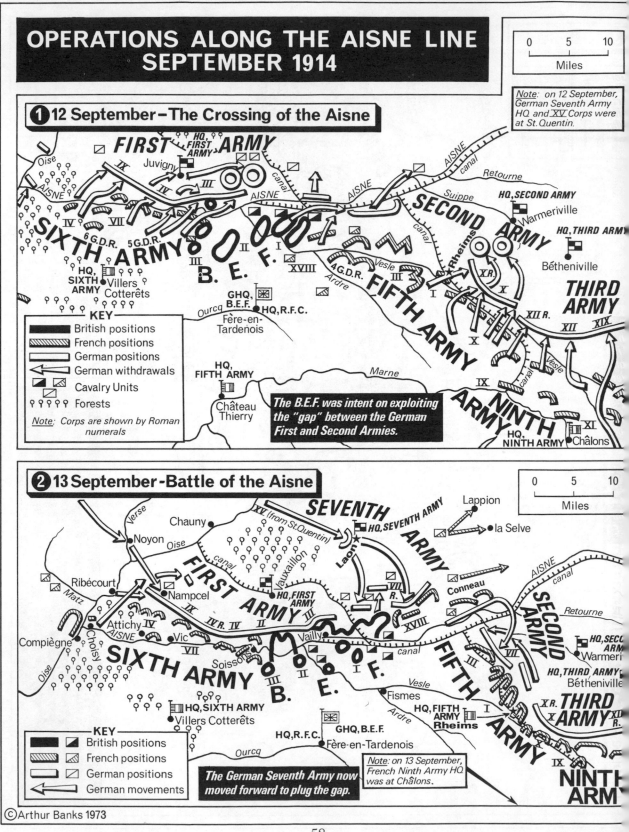

OPERATIONS ALONG THE AISNE LINE SEPTEMBER 1914

0 — 5 — 10 Miles

Note: on 12 September, German Seventh Army HQ. and XV Corps were at St.Quentin.

❶ 12 September – The Crossing of the Aisne

The B.E.F. was intent on exploiting the "gap" between the German First and Second Armies.

FIRST ARMY
HQ, FIRST ARMY
Juvigny
Oise
AISNE
canal
AISNE
Retourne
Suippe
SECOND ARMY
HQ, SECOND ARMY
Warmeriville
HQ, THIRD ARMY
Bétheniville
THIRD ARMY
SIXTH ARMY
6 G.D.R. 5 G.D.R.
B. E. F.
HQ, SIXTH ARMY
Villers Cotterêts
Rheims
Vesle
Ardre
FIFTH ARMY
GHQ, B.E.F.
HQ, R.F.C.
Ourcq
Fère-en-Tardenois
HQ, FIFTH ARMY
Château Thierry
Marne
NINTH ARMY
HQ, NINTH ARMY
Châlons

KEY

- ▬ British positions
- ▨ French positions
- ▭ German positions
- ← German withdrawals
- Cavalry Units
- ♀♀♀♀ Forests

Note: Corps are shown by Roman numerals

❷ 13 September – Battle of the Aisne

0 — 5 — 10 Miles

The German Seventh Army now moved forward to plug the gap.

SEVENTH ARMY
HQ, SEVENTH ARMY
Lappion
la Selve
Verse
Chauny
XV (from St.Quentin)
Laon
Noyon
Oise
canal
Vauxaillon
FIRST ARMY
HQ, FIRST ARMY
Conneau
SECOND ARMY
HQ, SECOND ARMY
Warmeri
Ribécourt
Matz
Nampcel
Attichy
AISNE
Vic
Compiègne
Choisy
Oise
SIXTH ARMY
Soissons
Vailly
canal
B. E. F.
Vesle
Fismes
Ardre
Retourne
HQ, THIRD ARMY
Bétheniville
THIRD ARMY
FIFTH ARMY
HQ, FIFTH ARMY
Rheims
Villers Cotterêts
HQ, SIXTH ARMY
Ourcq
HQ, R.F.C.
GHQ, B.E.F.
Fère-en-Tardenois
NINTH ARMY

KEY

- ▬ ◪ British positions
- ▨ ◪ French positions
- ▭ ◪ German positions
- ← German movements

Note: on 13 September, French Ninth Army HQ. was at Châlons.

© Arthur Banks 1973

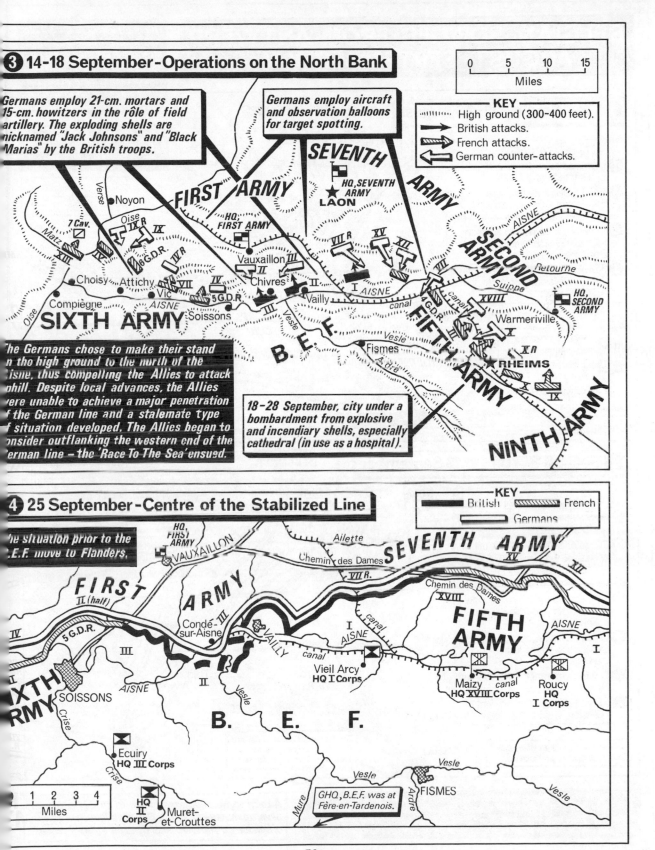

③ 14-18 September - Operations on the North Bank

0   5   10   15
Miles

KEY
.... High ground (300–400 feet).
→ British attacks.
⇒ French attacks.
⇐ German counter-attacks.

Germans employ 21-cm. mortars and 15-cm. howitzers in the rôle of field artillery. The exploding shells are nicknamed "Jack Johnsons" and "Black Marias" by the British troops.

Germans employ aircraft and observation balloons for target spotting.

SEVENTH ARMY

HQ, SEVENTH ARMY
LAON

FIRST ARMY

HQ, FIRST ARMY

7 Cav.
Noyon
Oise
Verse
IX R
IX
Matz
XIII
IV
5 G.D.R.
AISNE
VII R
XV
XII
SECOND ARMY
AISNE
Retourne
Suippe
XVIII
HQ, SECOND ARMY
Warmeriville

Choisy
Attichy
Vic
Compiègne
Soissons
Oise
AISNE
5 G.D.R.
Vauxaillon
Chivres
Vailly
II
III
IV
III
II
I AISNE
4 G.D.R.
canal
canal
III
II
X
X R
IX

SIXTH ARMY

Vesle
B.E.F.
Fismes
Ardre
RHEIMS
FIFTH ARMY

The Germans chose to make their stand on the high ground to the north of the Aisne, thus compelling the Allies to attack uphill. Despite local advances, the Allies were unable to achieve a major penetration of the German line and a stalemate type of situation developed. The Allies began to consider outflanking the western end of the German line – the 'Race To The Sea' ensued.

18–28 September, city under a bombardment from explosive and incendiary shells, especially cathedral (in use as a hospital).

NINTH ARMY

④ 25 September - Centre of the Stabilized Line

KEY
▬▬▬ British   ▨▨▨ French
▭▭▭ Germans

The situation prior to the B.E.F. move to Flanders.

HQ, FIRST ARMY
VAUXAILLON
Ailette
Chemin des Dames
SEVENTH ARMY
XV
XII
VII R.

FIRST ARMY

II (half)
IV
5 G.D.R.
Condé-sur-Aisne
III
VAILLY
I AISNE
canal
II
Chemin des Dames
XVIII
I
FIFTH ARMY
AISNE
I

SIXTH ARMY
SOISSONS
Crise
AISNE
II
Vesle
Vieil Arcy
HQ I Corps
canal
Maizy
HQ XVIII Corps
Roucy
HQ I Corps

B. E. F.

Ecuiry
HQ III Corps
Crise

Vesle
Vesle
Ardre
FISMES
Vesle

1   2   3   4
Miles

HQ II Corps
Muret-et-Crouttes
Mure

GHQ, B.E.F. was at Fère-en-Tardenois.

59

BELGIAN SORTIES FROM ANTWERP AUGUST-SEPTEMBER 1914

The main object of the sorties was to divert part of German strength from their main lines of advance into France. There was also the minor hope that some sort of breakthrough in the German rear might be won.

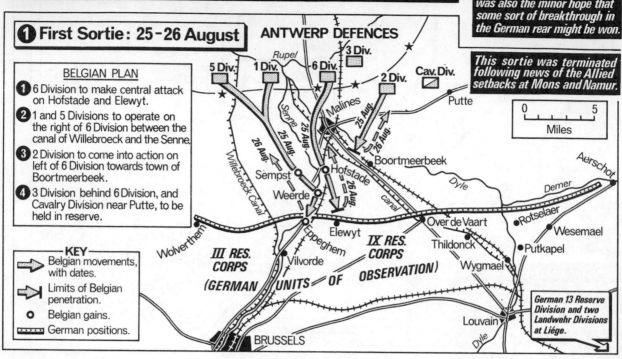

1 First Sortie: 25-26 August

ANTWERP DEFENCES

BELGIAN PLAN

1. 6 Division to make central attack on Hofstade and Elewyt.
2. 1 and 5 Divisions to operate on the right of 6 Division between the canal of Willebroeck and the Senne.
3. 2 Division to come into action on left of 6 Division towards town of Boortmeerbeek.
4. 3 Division behind 6 Division, and Cavalry Division near Putte, to be held in reserve.

KEY
- Belgian movements, with dates.
- Limits of Belgian penetration.
- o Belgian gains.
- German positions.

This sortie was terminated following news of the Allied setbacks at Mons and Namur.

0 ___ 5 Miles

German 13 Reserve Division and two Landwehr Divisions at Liége.

(Map labels: 5 Div., 1 Div., 6 Div., 3 Div., 2 Div., Cav. Div., Rupel, Senne, Malines, Putte, Boortmeerbeek, Dyle, Aerschot, Demer, Hofstade, Sempst, Weerde, Over de Vaart, Rotselaer, Wesemael, Elewyt, Thildonck, Putkapel, Eppeghem, Wolverthem, Vilvorde, Wygmael, III RES. CORPS (GERMAN UNITS OF OBSERVATION), IX RES. CORPS, Louvain, BRUSSELS, 25 Aug., 26 Aug.)

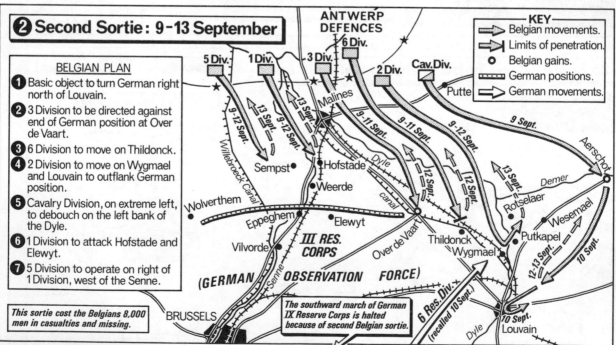

2 Second Sortie: 9-13 September

ANTWERP DEFENCES

BELGIAN PLAN

1. Basic object to turn German right north of Louvain.
2. 3 Division to be directed against end of German position at Over de Vaart.
3. 6 Division to move on Thildonck.
4. 2 Division to move on Wygmael and Louvain to outflank German position.
5. Cavalry Division, on extreme left, to debouch on the left bank of the Dyle.
6. 1 Division to attack Hofstade and Elewyt.
7. 5 Division to operate on right of 1 Division, west of the Senne.

This sortie cost the Belgians 8,000 men in casualties and missing.

KEY
- Belgian movements.
- Limits of penetration.
- o Belgian gains.
- German positions.
- German movements.

The southward march of German IX Reserve Corps is halted because of second Belgian sortie.

(Map labels: 5 Div., 1 Div., 3 Div., 6 Div., 2 Div., Cav. Div., Malines, Putte, Willebroeck Canal, Sempst, Hofstade, Weerde, Dyle, canal, Wolverthem, Eppeghem, Elewyt, Over de Vaart, Thildonck, Wygmael, Vilvorde, III RES. CORPS, (GERMAN OBSERVATION FORCE), Rotselaer, Demer, Aerschot, Wesemael, Putkapel, 6 Res. Div. (recalled 10 Sept.), 10 Sept. Louvain, BRUSSELS, Senne, 9 Sept., 9-11 Sept., 9-12 Sept., 12 Sept., 13 Sept., 12-13 Sept., 10 Sept.)

On 22 September, 700 Belgian cyclist volunteers arranged in seven detachments, left Antwerp to destroy railway lines of communication in enemy-occupied region outside the fortress. Main lines were severed in Limbourg, Brabant and Hainaut provinces, disrupting German transport. Most cyclists returned to Antwerp, but some were captured.

A third sortie, requested by Joffre on 24 September, never materialised as the Germans launched their offensive on Antwerp shortly after Joffre's request.

© Arthur Banks 1973

60

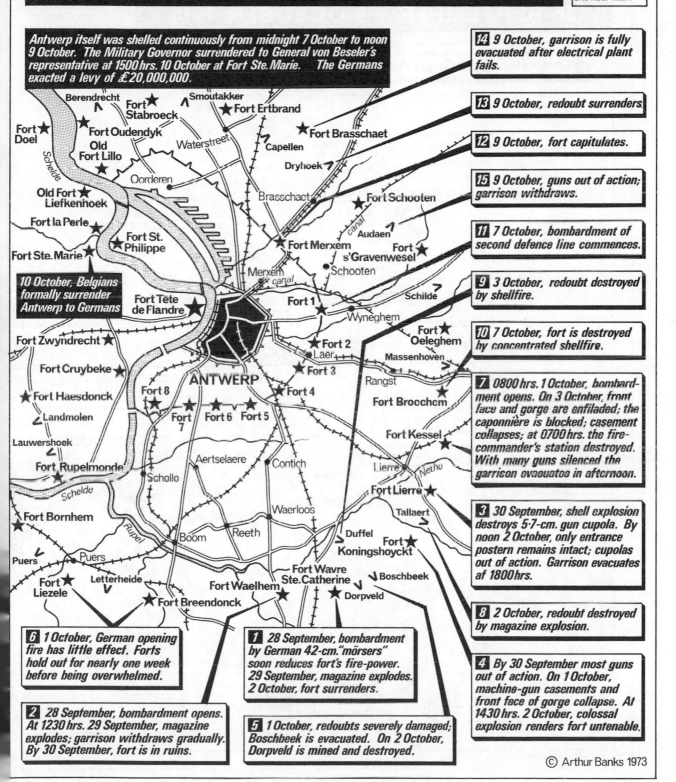

BOMBARDMENT OF THE ANTWERP FORTS
28 SEPTEMBER–9 OCTOBER 1914

Note: all times shown in panels are Belgian; German time was one hour later.

Antwerp itself was shelled continuously from midnight 7 October to noon 9 October. The Military Governor surrendered to General von Beseler's representative at 1500 hrs. 10 October at Fort Ste. Marie. The Germans exacted a levy of £20,000,000.

14 9 October, garrison is fully evacuated after electrical plant fails.

13 9 October, redoubt surrenders.

12 9 October, fort capitulates.

15 9 October, guns out of action; garrison withdraws.

11 7 October, bombardment of second defence line commences.

9 3 October, redoubt destroyed by shellfire.

10 7 October, fort is destroyed by concentrated shellfire.

7 0800 hrs. 1 October, bombardment opens. On 3 October, front face and gorge are enfiladed; the caponnière is blocked; casement collapses; at 0700 hrs. the fire-commander's station destroyed. With many guns silenced the garrison evacuates in afternoon.

3 30 September, shell explosion destroys 5·7-cm. gun cupola. By noon 2 October, only entrance postern remains intact; cupolas out of action. Garrison evacuates at 1800 hrs.

8 2 October, redoubt destroyed by magazine explosion.

10 October, Belgians formally surrender Antwerp to Germans

4 By 30 September most guns out of action. On 1 October, machine-gun casements and front face of gorge collapse. At 1430 hrs. 2 October, colossal explosion renders fort untenable.

6 1 October, German opening fire has little effect. Forts hold out for nearly one week before being overwhelmed.

1 28 September, bombardment by German 42-cm. "mörsers" soon reduces fort's fire-power. 29 September, magazine explodes. 2 October, fort surrenders.

2 28 September, bombardment opens. At 1230 hrs. 29 September, magazine explodes; garrison withdraws gradually. By 30 September, fort is in ruins.

5 1 October, redoubts severely damaged; Boschbeek is evacuated. On 2 October, Dorpveld is mined and destroyed.

© Arthur Banks 1973

THE GERMAN VICTORY AT ANTWERP 26 SEPTEMBER – 9 OCTOBER 1914

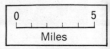

0 — 5 Miles

❶ Operations 26 September–2 October

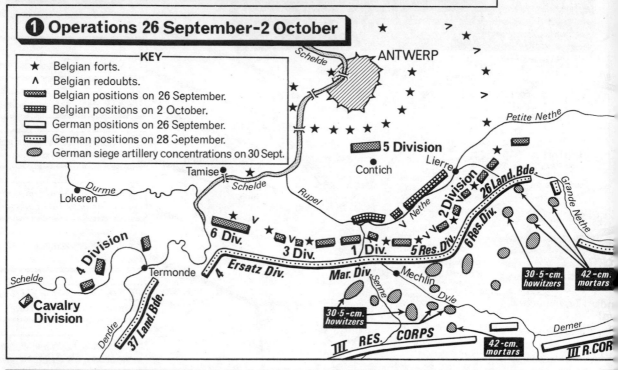

KEY
- ★ Belgian forts.
- ∧ Belgian redoubts.
- Belgian positions on 26 September.
- Belgian positions on 2 October.
- German positions on 26 September.
- German positions on 28 September.
- German siege artillery concentrations on 30 Sept.

ANTWERP — Schelde — Petite Nethe — 5 Division — Contich — Lierre — 2 Division — 26 Land. Bde. — Grande Nethe — Tamise — Schelde — Rupel — Nethe — 5 Res. Div. — 6 Res. Div. — 30·5-cm. howitzers — 42-cm. mortars — Durme — Lokeren — 6 Div. — 3 Div. — 1 Div. — Ersatz Div. — Mar. Div. — Mechlin — Senne — Dyle — 4 Division — Termonde — Schelde — Cavalry Division — Dendre — 37 Land. Bde. — 30·5-cm. howitzers — III. RES. CORPS — 42-cm. mortars — Demer — III R.COR.

❷ Operations 3–8 October

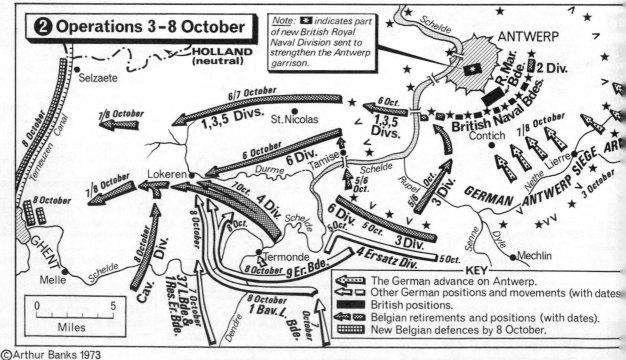

Note: ✱ indicates part of new British Royal Naval Division sent to strengthen the Antwerp garrison.

HOLLAND (neutral) — Selzaete — Terneuzen Canal — 6/7 October — 7/8 October — 1,3,5 Divs. — St.Nicolas — 6 October — 8 October — 7/8 October — Lokeren — Durme — Tamise — 6 Div. — 7 Oct. — 4 Div. — 8 Oct. — Schelde — Cav. Div. — GHENT — Melle — Schelde — Termonde — 8 October — 9 Er. Bde. — 37 L.Bde. & 1 Res.Er. Bde. — Dendre — 1 Bav. L. Bde. — 7 October — ANTWERP — R. Mar. Bde. — 2 Div. — British Naval Bdes. — Contich — 6 Oct. — 1,3,5 Divs. — 7/8 October — 5/6 Oct. — Rupel — 3 Div. — GERMAN ANTWERP SIEGE ART. — Nethe — Lierre — 3 October — 6 Div. — 5 Oct. — 3 Div. — 5 Oct. — 4 Ersatz Div. — 5 Oct. — Senne — Dyle — Mechlin

0 — 5 Miles

KEY
- The German advance on Antwerp.
- Other German positions and movements (with dates)
- British positions.
- Belgian retirements and positions (with dates).
- New Belgian defences by 8 October.

©Arthur Banks 1973

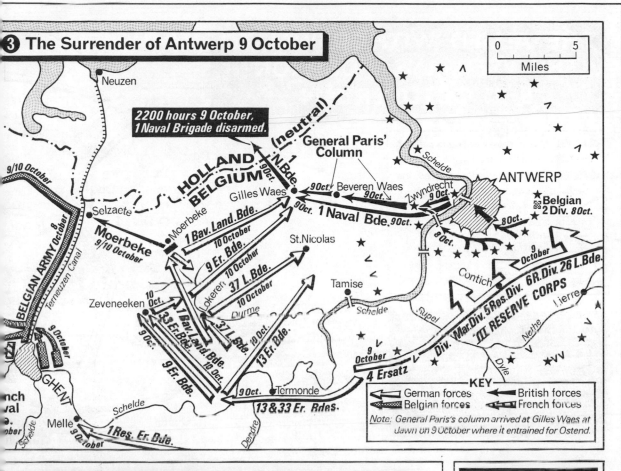

❸ The Surrender of Antwerp 9 October

0 — Miles — 5

2200 hours 9 October, 1 Naval Brigade disarmed.

1 N.Bde.

HOLLAND (neutral)

BELGIUM

Neuzen

9/10 October

Selzaete

Moerbeke 9/10 October

BELGIAN ARMY 8 October

Terneuzen Canal

Moerbeke

Gilles Waes

General Paris' Column

90ct. Beveren Waes 90ct.

1 Bav. Land. Bde.

10 October 9 Er. Bde.

90ct. 1 Naval Bde. 90ct.

Schelde

Zwyndrecht 9 Oct

ANTWERP

⊞ Belgian 2 Div. 80ct.

80ct.

80ct.

St.Nicolas

10 October 37 L. Bde.

10 October

Zeveneeken 10 Oct.

1 Bav. Land Bde.

33 Er.Bde.

90ct.

9 Er. Bde.

Lokeren

37 L.Bde.

10 October

Durme

Tamise

Schelde

Contich

9 October

6 R.Div. 26 L.Bde.

Lierre

Div. Mar.Div. 5 Res.Div.

"III RESERVE CORPS

Rupel

Nethe

GHENT

9 October

Melle

1 Res. Er. Bde.

Schelde

Derdre

13 Er. Bde.

90ct. Termonde

13 & 33 Er. Bdes.

9 October

4 Ersatz

Dyle

KEY

| ⟵ German forces | ⟵ British forces |
| ⟵ Belgian forces | ⟵ French forces |

Note: General Paris's column arrived at Gilles Waes at dawn on 9 October where it entrained for Ostend.

German 42-cm. (16·5-inch) L/16 Mortar "Gamma"

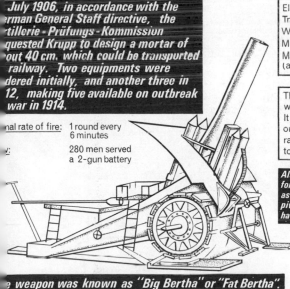

July 1906, in accordance with the German General Staff directive, the Artillerie - Prüfungs - Kommission requested Krupp to design a mortar of about 40 cm. which could be transported by railway. Two equipments were ordered initially, and another three in 12, making five available on outbreak of war in 1914.

...nal rate of fire: 1 round every 6 minutes

280 men served a 2-gun battery

...e weapon was known as "Big Bertha" or "Fat Bertha".

Elevation:	43°–66°
Traverse:	45°
Weight with platform:	75 tons
Muzzle velocity:	1,312 ft·secs
Maximum range: (anti-concrete shell)	15,500 yards

The mortar had a recoiling barrel and was mounted on an iron platform. It was transported in separate loads on ten normal-gauge 25/30-ton railway wagons, and took ten hours to mount.

Although named a 'Mörser' by the German forces, the 42 was technically a howitzer as it was capable of being elevated and pivoted on trunnions, whereas mortars have rear trunnions on fixed beds.

The first naval battery to be armed with the original two mortars was formed and trained in the summer of 1912.

German 42-cm. H.E. Shell

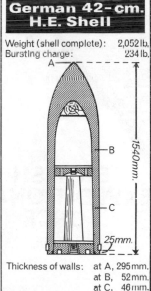

| Weight (shell complete): | 2,052 lb. |
| Bursting charge: | 234 lb. |

A — B — C — 25 mm.

1540mm.

Thickness of walls:	at A,	295mm.
	at B,	52mm.
	at C,	46mm.
Thickness of base:		95mm.
Width of driving band:		50 mm.
Construction material:		Steel

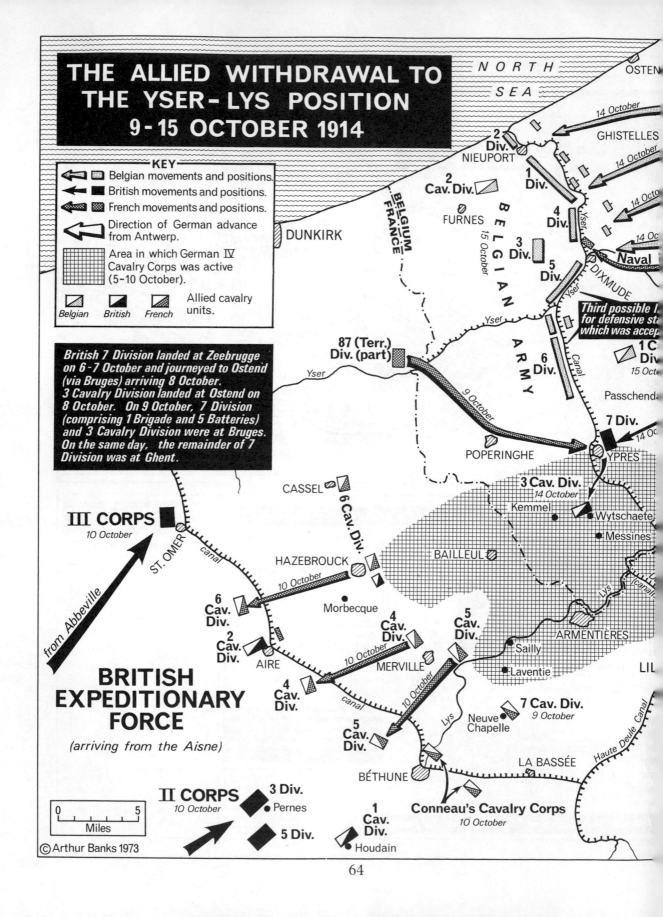

THE ALLIED WITHDRAWAL TO THE YSER-LYS POSITION 9-15 OCTOBER 1914

KEY
- Belgian movements and positions.
- British movements and positions.
- French movements and positions.
- Direction of German advance from Antwerp.
- Area in which German IV Cavalry Corps was active (5-10 October).

Belgian   British   French   Allied cavalry units.

British 7 Division landed at Zeebrugge on 6-7 October and journeyed to Ostend (via Bruges) arriving 8 October. 3 Cavalry Division landed at Ostend on 8 October. On 9 October, 7 Division (comprising 1 Brigade and 5 Batteries) and 3 Cavalry Division were at Bruges. On the same day, the remainder of 7 Division was at Ghent.

NORTH SEA

OSTEN

GHISTELLES

14 October

14 October

14 Oct

14 Oc

2 Div.
NIEUPORT

2 Cav. Div.

1 Div.

4 Div.

Naval

FURNES

3 Div.

5 Div.

DUNKIRK

BELGIUM
FRANCE

15 October

DIXMUDE

Yser

Third possible l. for defensive sta. which was accep

87 (Terr.) Div. (part)

Yser

6 Div.

BELGIAN ARMY

Canal

1 C Div.

15 Oct

Yser

9 October

Passchenda

POPERINGHE

7 Div.

14 Oc

YPRES

CASSEL

6 Cav. Div.

3 Cav. Div.
14 October

Kemmel

Wytschaete

Messines

III CORPS
10 October

ST. OMER

canal

HAZEBROUCK
10 October

BAILLEUL

Lys

canal

from Abbeville

6 Cav. Div.

Morbecque

4 Cav. Div.

5 Cav. Div.

ARMENTIÈRES

Sailly

LIL

2 Cav. Div.

AIRE

10 October

MERVILLE

Laventie

BRITISH EXPEDITIONARY FORCE

(arriving from the Aisne)

4 Cav. Div.

canal

10 October

5 Cav. Div.

Lys

Neuve Chapelle

7 Cav. Div.
9 October

LA BASSÉE

Haute Deule Canal

BÉTHUNE

Conneau's Cavalry Corps
10 October

0   5
Miles

II CORPS
10 October

3 Div.
Pernes

1 Cav. Div.

Houdain

5 Div.

© Arthur Banks 1973

64

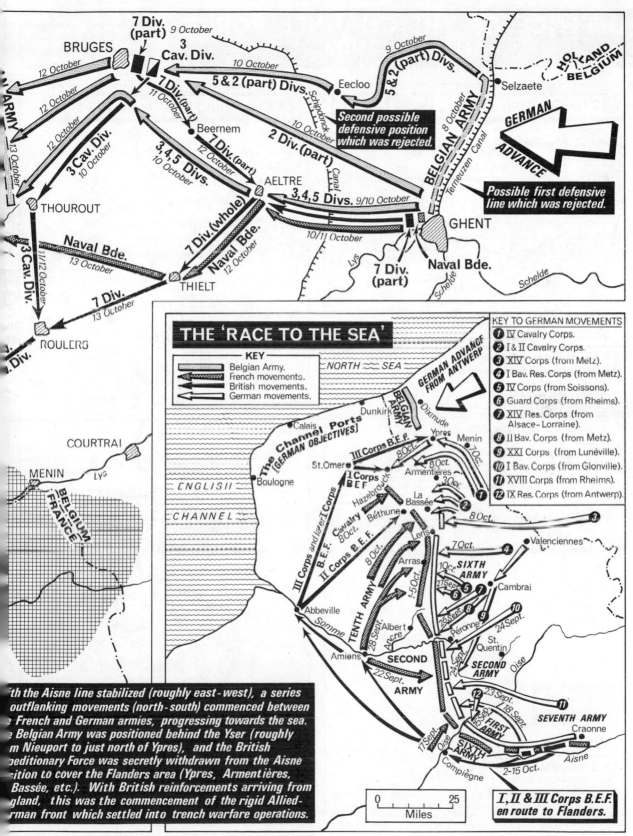

DEFENCE OF THE CHANNEL PORTS AUTUMN 1914

With Antwerp and also Ostend behind them, the German aim was to sever the sea link with England.

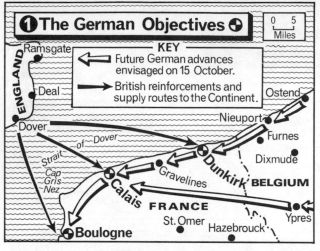

❶ The German Objectives ✚

KEY

⬅ Future German advances envisaged on 15 October.

➡ British reinforcements and supply routes to the Continent.

0 — 5 Miles

ENGLAND — Ramsgate, Deal, Dover, Strait of Dover, Cap Gris Nez, Calais, Boulogne

Ostend, Nieuport, Furnes, Dixmude, Dunkirk, Gravelines, BELGIUM, FRANCE, St. Omer, Hazebrouck, Ypres

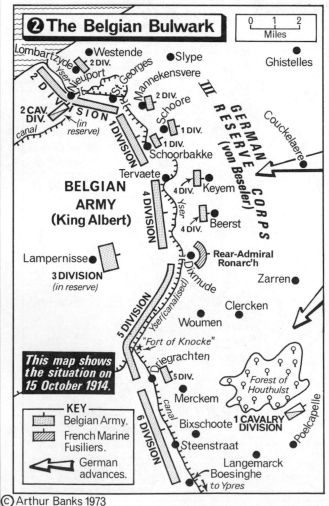

❷ The Belgian Bulwark

0 — 1 — 2 Miles

This map shows the situation on 15 October 1914.

Lombartzyde, Westende, Slype, Ghistelles, 2 DIV., Yser, Nieuport, St. Georges, Mannekensvere, 2 DIV., III, 2 DIVISION, 2 CAV. DIV. (in reserve), canal, 1 DIVISION, Schoore, 1 DIV., 1 DIV., Schoorbakke, GERMAN RESERVE CORPS (von Beseler), Couckelaere, Tervaete, 4 DIVISION, 4 DIV., Keyem, Yser, 4 DIV., Beerst, BELGIAN ARMY (King Albert), Lampernisse, 3 DIVISION (in reserve), Rear-Admiral Ronarc'h, Dixmude, Zarren, 5 DIVISION, Yser (canalised), Clercken, Woumen, "Fort of Knocke", Driegrachten, 5 DIV., canal, Merckem, Forest of Houthulst, 6 DIVISION, Bixschoote, 1 CAVALRY DIVISION, Steenstraat, Poelcapelle, Langemarck, Boesinghe, to Ypres

KEY

▦ Belgian Army.

▨ French Marine Fusiliers.

⬅ German advances.

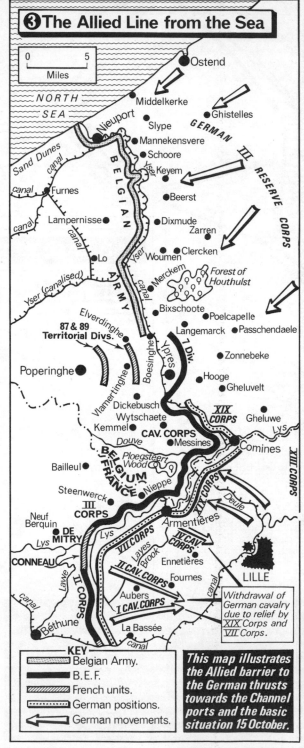

❸ The Allied Line from the Sea

0 — 5 Miles

NORTH SEA

Sand Dunes, Ostend, Middelkerke, Ghistelles, Nieuport, Slype, Mannekensvere, GERMAN III RESERVE CORPS, Schoore, Keyem, canal, Furnes, Beerst, canal, Lampernisse, Dixmude, Zarren, BELGIAN ARMY, canal, Clercken, Lo, Woumen, Yser (canalised), Merckem, Forest of Houthulst, Yser canal, Bixschoote, Poelcapelle, Elverdinghe, Langemarck, Passchendaele, 87 & 89 Territorial Divs., Boesinghe, Ypres, 7 DIV., Zonnebeke, Poperinghe, Vlamertinghe, Hooge, Gheluvelt, Dickebusch, Wytschaete, XIX CORPS, Gheluwe, Kemmel, CAV. CORPS, Messines, Lys, Douve, Comines, Ploegsteert Wood, BELGIUM, FRANCE, Bailleul, Nieppe, XIII CORPS, Steenwerck, Armentières, III CORPS, Deule, Neuf Berquin, DE MITRY, Lys, IV CAV. CORPS, CONNEAU, VII CORPS, Lys, Layes Brook, Ennetières, II CAV. CORPS, Fournes, LILLE, Aubers, I CAV. CORPS, canal, II CORPS, Lawe, canal, Béthune, La Bassée, canal

Withdrawal of German cavalry due to relief by XIX Corps and VII Corps.

KEY

▦ Belgian Army.

▬ B.E.F.

▨ French units.

┄ German positions.

⬅ German movements.

This map illustrates the Allied barrier to the German thrusts towards the Channel ports and the basic situation 15 October.

© Arthur Banks 1973

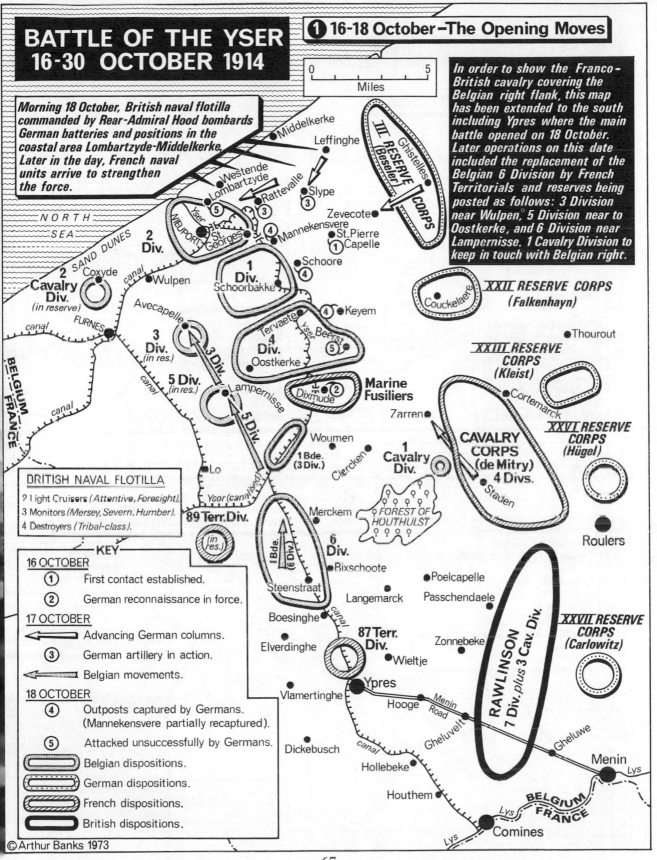

BATTLE OF THE YSER 16-30 OCTOBER 1914

① 16-18 October – The Opening Moves

0 ─── 5
Miles

In order to show the Franco-British cavalry covering the Belgian right flank, this map has been extended to the south including Ypres where the main battle opened on 18 October. Later operations on this date included the replacement of the Belgian 6 Division by French Territorials and reserves being posted as follows: 3 Division near Wulpen, 5 Division near to Oostkerke, and 6 Division near Lampernisse. 1 Cavalry Division to keep in touch with Belgian right.

Morning 18 October, British naval flotilla commanded by Rear-Admiral Hood bombards German batteries and positions in the coastal area Lombartzyde-Middelkerke. Later in the day, French naval units arrive to strengthen the force.

NORTH SEA

Middelkerke
Leffinghe
III RESERVE (Beseler) CORPS
Ghistelles
Westende
Lombartzyde
Rattevalle
Slype
Zevecote
SAND DUNES
NIEUPORT
St. Georges
Mannekensvere
St. Pierre Capelle
2 Div.
Schoore
2 Cavalry Div. *(in reserve)*
Coxyde
Wulpen
Schoorbakke
1 Div.
Couckelaere
XXII RESERVE CORPS *(Falkenhayn)*
canal
Avecapelle
Keyem
FURNES
3 Div. *(in res.)*
Tervaete
4 Div.
Beerst
Oostkerke
Thourout
XXIII RESERVE CORPS *(Kleist)*
canal
5 Div. *(in res.)*
Lampernisse
Dixmude
Marine Fusiliers
Cortemarck
Zarren
XXVI RESERVE CORPS *(Hügel)*
Woumen
CAVALRY CORPS (de Mitry) 4 Divs.
Staden
1 Bde. (3 Div.)
Clercken
1 Cavalry Div.

BRITISH NAVAL FLOTILLA
2 Light Cruisers *(Attentive, Foresight).*
3 Monitors *(Mersey, Severn, Humber).*
4 Destroyers *(Tribal-class).*

Lo
Yser (canalised)
89 Terr. Div. *(in res.)*
Merckem
FOREST OF HOUTHULST
Roulers

6 Div.
Bixschoote
1 Bde. (6 Div.)
Steenstraat
Poelcapelle
Passchendaele
Langemarck
Boesinghe
Elverdinghe
Zonnebeke
87 Terr. Div.
Wieltje
Ypres
Vlamertinghe
Hooge
Menin Road
Gheluvelt
Dickebusch
Hollebeke
Houthem
Gheluwe
Menin
Lys
XXVII RESERVE CORPS *(Carlowitz)*
RAWLINSON 7 Div. plus 3 Cav. Div.
BELGIUM FRANCE
Lys
Comines

KEY

16 OCTOBER
① First contact established.
② German reconnaissance in force.

17 OCTOBER
⬅ Advancing German columns.
③ German artillery in action.
⬅ Belgian movements.

18 OCTOBER
④ Outposts captured by Germans. (Mannekensvere partially recaptured).
⑤ Attacked unsuccessfully by Germans.
▭ Belgian dispositions.
▭ German dispositions.
▭ French dispositions.
▭ British dispositions.

BELGIUM FRANCE

© Arthur Banks 1973

67

BATTLE OF THE YSER – continued

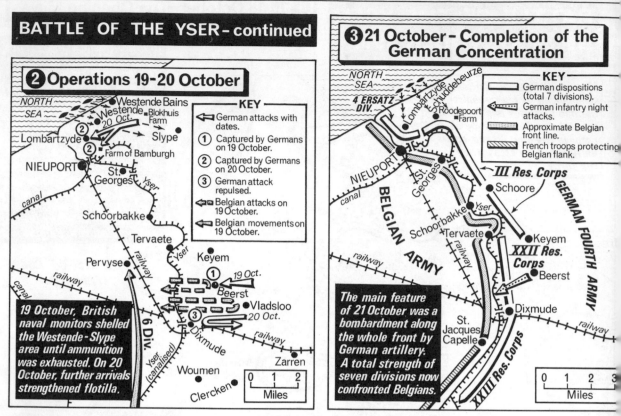

② Operations 19-20 October

NORTH SEA

Westende Bains
Westende 20 Oct.
Blokhuis Farm
② ②
Lombartzyde
① Slype
② ②
Farm of Bamburgh
NIEUPORT
St. Georges
canal
Yser
Schoorbakke
Tervaete
Yser
Keyem
railway
Pervyse
① 19 Oct.
Beerst
6 Div.
Vladsloo
② 20 Oct.
③
Dixmude
Yser (canalised)
railway
Woumen
Zarren
Clercken

KEY
← German attacks with dates.
① Captured by Germans on 19 October.
② Captured by Germans on 20 October.
③ German attack repulsed.
⇐⇐ Belgian attacks on 19 October.
⇐ Belgian movements on 19 October.

19 October, British naval monitors shelled the Westende-Slype area until ammunition was exhausted. On 20 October, further arrivals strengthened flotilla.

0 1 2
Miles

③ 21 October – Completion of the German Concentration

NORTH SEA
4 ERSATZ DIV.
Lombartzyde
Schuddebeurze
Roodepoort Farm
NIEUPORT
BELGIAN ARMY
St. Georges
canal
Yser
III Res. Corps
Schoore
Schoorbakke
Yser
Tervaete
Keyem
XXII Res. Corps
railway
Beerst
GERMAN FOURTH ARMY
St. Jacques Capelle
Dixmude
railway
XXIII Res. Corps

KEY
☐ German dispositions (total 7 divisions).
⇐ German infantry night attacks.
▨ Approximate Belgian front line.
▨ French troops protecting Belgian flank.

The main feature of 21 October was a bombardment along the whole front by German artillery. A total strength of seven divisions now confronted Belgians.

0 1 2 3
Miles

④ Naval Operations: Evening 21 October – Morning 31 October

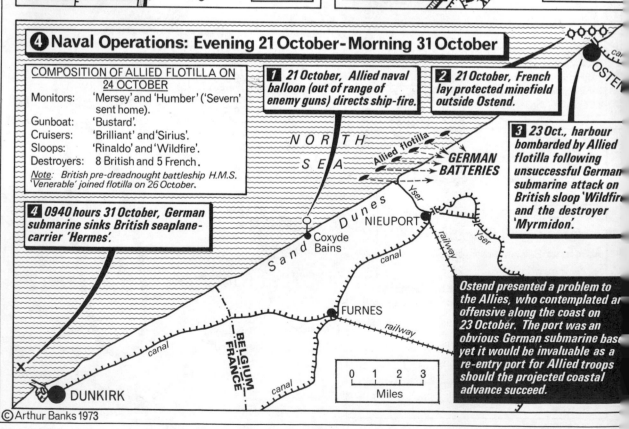

COMPOSITION OF ALLIED FLOTILLA ON 24 OCTOBER

Monitors: 'Mersey' and 'Humber' ('Severn' sent home).
Gunboat: 'Bustard'.
Cruisers: 'Brilliant' and 'Sirius'.
Sloops: 'Rinaldo' and 'Wildfire'.
Destroyers: 8 British and 5 French.

Note: British pre-dreadnought battleship H.M.S. 'Venerable' joined flotilla on 26 October.

④ 0940 hours 31 October, German submarine sinks British seaplane-carrier 'Hermes'.

① 21 October, Allied naval balloon (out of range of enemy guns) directs ship-fire.

② 21 October, French lay protected minefield outside Ostend.

OSTEND

③ 23 Oct., harbour bombarded by Allied flotilla following unsuccessful German submarine attack on British sloop 'Wildfire' and the destroyer 'Myrmidon'.

NORTH SEA

Allied flotilla

GERMAN BATTERIES

Sand Dunes
Yser
Coxyde Bains
NIEUPORT
canal
railway
Yser

FURNES
railway

BELGIUM FRANCE
canal

X
DUNKIRK
canal

Ostend presented a problem to the Allies, who contemplated an offensive along the coast on 23 October. The port was an obvious German submarine base, yet it would be invaluable as a re-entry port for Allied troops should the projected coastal advance succeed.

0 1 2 3
Miles

© Arthur Banks 1973

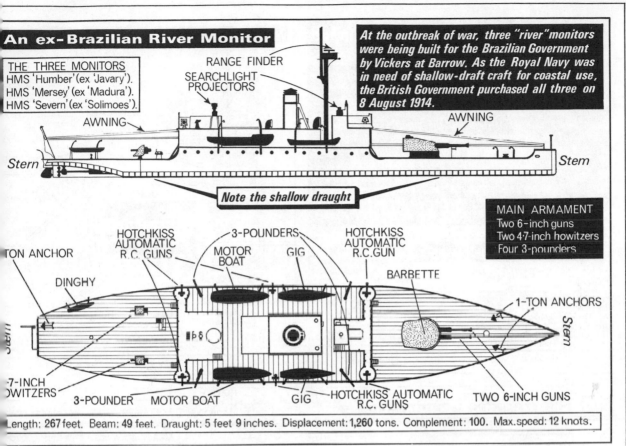

An ex-Brazilian River Monitor

THE THREE MONITORS
HMS 'Humber' (ex 'Javary').
HMS 'Mersey' (ex 'Madura').
HMS 'Severn' (ex 'Solimoes').

RANGE FINDER

SEARCHLIGHT PROJECTORS

AWNING

AWNING

Stern

Stem

Note the shallow draught

At the outbreak of war, three "river" monitors were being built for the Brazilian Government by Vickers at Barrow. As the Royal Navy was in need of shallow-draft craft for coastal use, the British Government purchased all three on 8 August 1914.

MAIN ARMAMENT
Two 6-inch guns
Two 4·7-inch howitzers
Four 3-pounders

1-TON ANCHOR

DINGHY

HOTCHKISS AUTOMATIC R.C. GUNS

MOTOR BOAT

3-POUNDERS

GIG

HOTCHKISS AUTOMATIC R.C. GUN

BARBETTE

1-TON ANCHORS

Stern

4·7-INCH HOWITZERS

3-POUNDER

MOTOR BOAT

GIG

HOTCHKISS AUTOMATIC R.C. GUNS

TWO 6-INCH GUNS

Length: 267 feet. Beam: 49 feet. Draught: 5 feet 9 inches. Displacement: 1,260 tons. Complement: 100. Max. speed: 12 knots.

HMS "VENERABLE" "London" Class of three ships

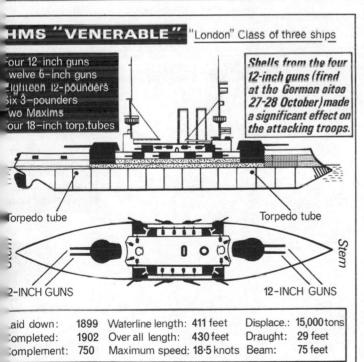

Four 12-inch guns
Twelve 6-inch guns
Eighteen 12-pounders
Six 3-pounders
Two Maxims
Four 18-inch torp. tubes

Shells from the four 12-inch guns (fired at the German oitoo 27-28 October) made a significant effect on the attacking troops.

Torpedo tube

Torpedo tube

Stern

12-INCH GUNS

12-INCH GUNS

Laid down:	1899	Waterline length:	411 feet	Displace.:	15,000 tons
Completed:	1902	Over all length:	430 feet	Draught:	29 feet
Complement:	750	Maximum speed:	18·5 knots	Beam:	75 feet

⑤ Military Operations 22-23 October

④ 22 October, Belgian attacks.

③ 22 October, German attack repulsed by 4 Line Regiment.

Lombartzyde
Farm of Bamburgh
canal

NIEUPORT

St. Georges

Heavy fire from German artillery.

⑤ 23 October, arrival of French 42 Division.

One Bde. (French 42 Div.)

Schoorbakke

Yser

② 22 October, Belgian counter-attack fails to dislodge German units.

Tervaete

① Night 21/22 October, Germans establish footing on west bank of Yser. They deploy infantry and guns.

0   1
Mile

BATTLE OF THE YSER – continued

By 24 October, Belgian resistance was deteriorating due to exhaustion of troops, lack of ammunition, and only a few reinforcements arriving (French 42 Division). However, as the whole area was intersected by canals and ditches, a possibility existed of flooding the countryside to a depth sufficient to render the attacking Germans unoperational. Stated briefly, this entailed damming 22 culverts under the Nieuport – Dixmude railway embankment to contain the rising waters in the east, followed by opening the Nieuport sluices to admit the sea. This manœuvre was accomplished successfully and by 30 October the drive by the Germans along the coast was virtually at an end.

NIEUPORT'S SLUICES AND CHANNELS

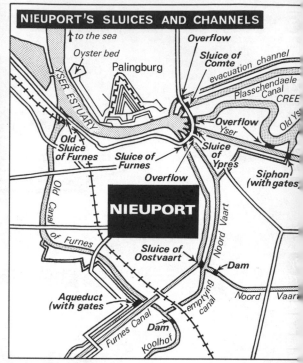

THE OLD SLUICE OF FURNES

On 26 October, efforts to manipulate doors failed due to inadequate housing.

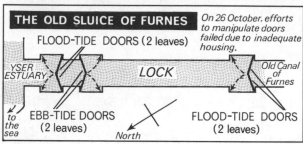

FLOOD-TIDE DOORS (2 leaves)

YSER ESTUARY

LOCK

Old Canal of Furnes

to the sea

EBB-TIDE DOORS (2 leaves)

North

FLOOD-TIDE DOORS (2 leaves)

❻ The Irrigated Countryside

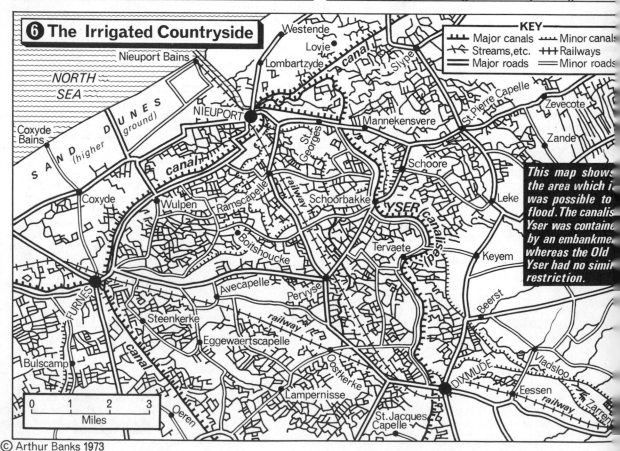

KEY
- ╫ Major canals
- ⫫ Minor canals
- ⋇ Streams, etc.
- ┼┼┼ Railways
- ── Major roads
- ═══ Minor roads

This map shows the area which it was possible to flood. The canalis Yser was containe by an embankme whereas the Old Yser had no simil restriction.

0 1 2 3
Miles

❼ Military Operations 24-30 October

KEY
- ⬅ Belgian retreats on 24 October.
- ⬅ German attacks on 24 October.
- ⬅ Franco-Belgian attack on 25 October.
- ⬅ Allied withdrawals on 26 October.
- ⬅ German attacks on 30 October.

24 October, a heavy German bombardment.

30 October, German attacks repulsed.

By 26 October, Belgian artillery ammunition was down to 100 rounds per gun.

24 October, a heavy German bombardment.

15 SEPARATE ATTACKS

26 October, two Senegalese battalions arrive here.

NIEUPORT · St.Georges · Ramscapelle · Pervyse · Tervaete · Oud-Stuyvekenskerke · DIXMUDE

canal · YSER · Noord Vaart · Beverdyk · railway

Mile 0 — 1

BELGIAN ENGINEERING OPERATIONS AT NIEUPORT

The operational procedures were extremely complex, depending for success upon tides from the North Sea being propitious, force and direction of winds being correct, plus the actual manipulation of sluice gates being feasible. At the old sluice of Furnes, the two sets of flood-tide doors needed to be held open permanently with the one set of ebb-tide doors freed from their racks so that they opened and closed according to the water pressure from rising and receding tides. At other sluices, doors and gates required to be operated manually for each manœuvre; that is, opened at high tides and closed before low tides. *(The full moon of 29 October assisted operations by causing a very high tide).*

21 October. 1100 hours, Old Yser's overflow is opened; water rapidly inundates creek; Noord Vaart-Old Yser siphon closed to avoid flooding 2 Division's established position.

25 October. Foch contemplates flooding area east of Dunkirk, but delays plan temporarily.

26 October. Attempt fails at old sluice of Furnes.

28 October. Second try succeeds; waters rise.

29 October. 1930 hours, gates of N.Vaart opened.

30 October. Manœuvre repeated; floods spread.

---

❽ The Inundated Countryside

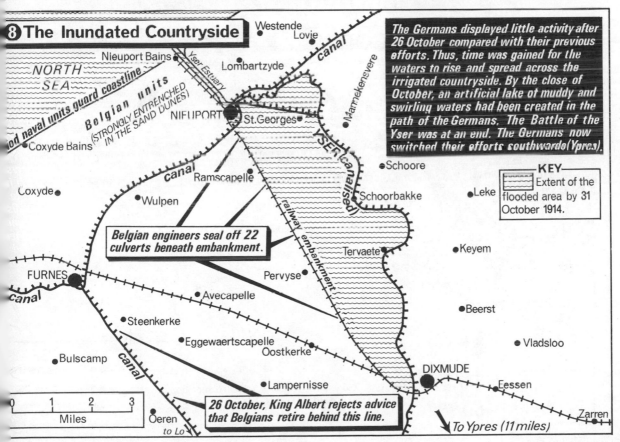

The Germans displayed little activity after 26 October compared with their previous efforts. Thus, time was gained for the waters to rise and spread across the irrigated countryside. By the close of October, an artificial lake of muddy and swirling waters had been created in the path of the Germans. The Battle of the Yser was at an end. The Germans now switched their efforts southwards (Ypres).

KEY
░ Extent of the flooded area by 31 October 1914.

NORTH SEA

Allied naval units guard coastline

Belgian units (STRONGLY ENTRENCHED IN THE SAND DUNES)

Westende · Lovie · Nieuport Bains · Lombartzyde · Coxyde Bains · Coxyde · Wulpen · Ramscapelle · NIEUPORT · St.Georges · Mannekensvere · Schoore · Leke · Schoorbakke · Tervaete · Keyem · Pervyse · FURNES · Avecapelle · Steenkerke · Beerst · Eggewaertscapelle · Oostkerke · Vladsloo · Bulscamp · Lampernisse · DIXMUDE · Eessen · Oeren to Lo · Zarren

Yser Estuary · canal · YSER (canalised) · railway embankment · canal

Belgian engineers seal off 22 culverts beneath embankment.

26 October, King Albert rejects advice that Belgians retire behind this line.

To Ypres (11 miles)

Miles 0 — 1 — 2 — 3

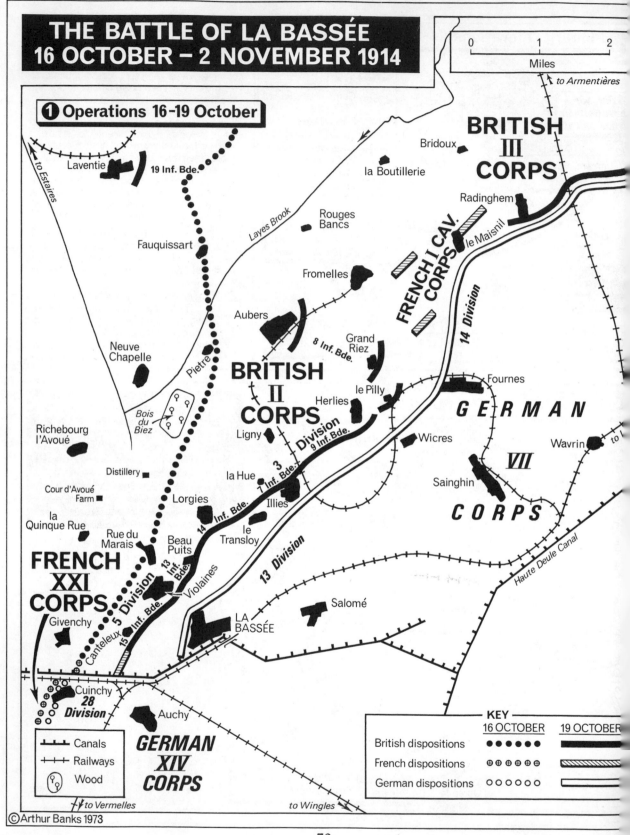

THE BATTLE OF LA BASSÉE
16 OCTOBER – 2 NOVEMBER 1914

❶ Operations 16-19 October

0   1   2

Miles

to Armentières

BRITISH III CORPS

Bridoux

la Boutillerie

Radinghem

le Maisnil

FRENCH I CAV. CORPS

14 Division

to Estaires

Laventie

19 Inf. Bde.

Fauquissart

Layes Brook

Rouges Bancs

Fromelles

Aubers

Grand Riez

8 Inf. Bde.

Neuve Chapelle

Pietre

BRITISH II CORPS

Herlies

le Pilly

Fournes

GERMAN

Richebourg l'Avoué

Bois du Biez

Ligny

Division

9 Inf. Bde.

Wicres

Wavrin

to

VII

Distillery

la Hue

3 Inf. Bde.

Illies

Sainghin

CORPS

Cour d'Avoué Farm

Lorgies

7 Inf. Bde.

la Quinque Rue

Rue du Marais

Beau Puits

14 Inf. Bde.

le Transloy

13 Division

FRENCH XXI CORPS

5 Division

13 Inf. Bde.

Violaines

Haute Deule Canal

Givenchy

Canteleux

15 Inf. Bde.

LA BASSÉE

Salomé

Cuinchy

28 Division

Auchy

GERMAN XIV CORPS

to Vermelles

to Wingles

| Canals |
| Railways |
| Wood |

KEY

	16 OCTOBER	19 OCTOBER
British dispositions	••••••	▬▬▬
French dispositions	⊕⊕⊕⊕⊕	▨▨▨
German dispositions	○○○○○	▭▭▭

© Arthur Banks 1973

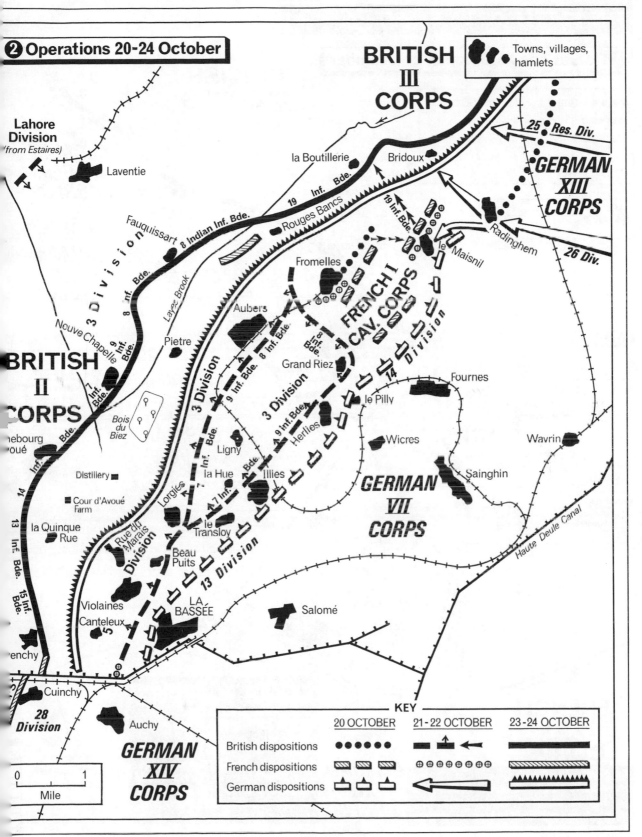

❷ Operations 20-24 October

Towns, villages, hamlets

BRITISH
III
CORPS

Lahore
Division
(from Estaires)

Laventie

la Boutillerie

Bridoux

25 Res. Div.

GERMAN
XIII
CORPS

19 Inf. Bde.

Fauquissart   8 Indian Inf. Bde.

Rouges Bancs

19 Inf. Bde.

Radinghem

26 Div.

le Maisnil

Fromelles

FRENCH I
CAV CORPS

Aubers

8 Inf. Bde.

Neuve Chapelle

3 Division

8 Inf. Bde.

Layes Brook

Pietre

3 Division

8 Inf. Bde.

9 Inf. Bde.   8 Inf. Bde.

Grand Riez

Division

14

Fournes

BRITISH
II
CORPS

Inf. Bde.

Inf. Bde.

Bois
du
Biez

3 Division

9 Inf Bde.

Herlies

le Pilly

Inf. Bde.

Ligny

la Hue

Illies

Wicres

Wavrin

nebourg
oué

Distillery

Inf. Bde.

Bde.

Sainghin

GERMAN
VII
CORPS

Cour d'Avoué
Farm

Lorgies

7 Inf.

14

13

Inf. Bde.

la Quinque
Rue

Rue du
Marais

Division

le
Transloy

13 Division

Beau
Puits

Haute Deule Canal

15 Inf.
Bde.

Division

Violaines

LA
BASSÉE

Salomé

Canteleux

5

rency

Cuinchy

28
Division

Auchy

GERMAN
XIV
CORPS

0   1
Mile

KEY

	20 OCTOBER	21-22 OCTOBER	23-24 OCTOBER
British dispositions	●●●●●●	▬ ↑ ←	▬▬▬
French dispositions	▨▨▨	⊕⊕⊕⊕⊕⊕	▨▨
German dispositions	⊔⊔⊔	⬅	▲▲▲▲

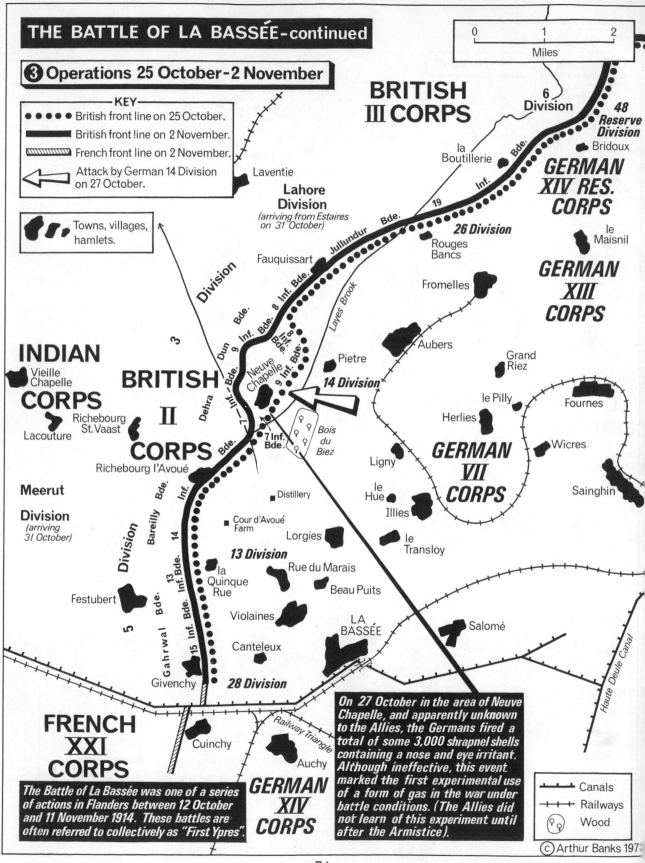

THE BATTLE OF LA BASSÉE—continued

③ Operations 25 October–2 November

KEY
- • • • • • British front line on 25 October.
- ▬▬▬ British front line on 2 November.
- ░░░ French front line on 2 November.
- ⬅ Attack by German 14 Division on 27 October.

Towns, villages, hamlets.

0   1   2 Miles

BRITISH III CORPS

6 Division

48 Reserve Division

la Boutillerie

Bridoux

GERMAN XIV RES. CORPS

Lahore Division *(arriving from Estaires on 31 October)*

Laventie

Inf. Bde.

19 Bde.

26 Division

Jullundur Bde.

Rouges Bancs

le Maisnil

GERMAN XIII CORPS

Fauquissart

Layes Brook

Fromelles

Aubers

Grand Riez

le Pilly

Fournes

Pietre

Herlies

Wicres

GERMAN VII CORPS

3 Division

Dun Bde.

9 Inf. Bde.

8 Inf. Bde.

Neuve Chapelle

14 Division

Ligny

le Hue

INDIAN CORPS

Vieille Chapelle

BRITISH II CORPS

Dehra Bde.

Illies

Lacouture

Richebourg St. Vaast

7 Inf. Bde.

Bois du Biez

le Transloy

Richebourg l'Avoué

Meerut Division *(arriving 31 October)*

Inf. Bde.

Bareilly Bde.

14 Bde.

Distillery

Cour d'Avoué Farm

Lorgies

13 Division

Rue du Marais

Division

13 Inf. Bde.

la Quinque Rue

Beau Puits

5

Gahrwal Bde.

15 Inf. Bde.

Violaines

LA BASSÉE

Salomé

Festubert

Canteleux

Givenchy

28 Division

FRENCH XXI CORPS

Cuinchy

Railway Triangle

Auchy

GERMAN XIV CORPS

Haute Deule Canal

The Battle of La Bassée was one of a series of actions in Flanders between 12 October and 11 November 1914. These battles are often referred to collectively as "First Ypres".

On 27 October in the area of Neuve Chapelle, and apparently unknown to the Allies, the Germans fired a total of some 3,000 shrapnel shells containing a nose and eye irritant. Although ineffective, this event marked the first experimental use of a form of gas in the war under battle conditions. (The Allies did not learn of this experiment until after the Armistice).

— Canals
┼┼┼ Railways
🌳 Wood

© Arthur Banks 197

74

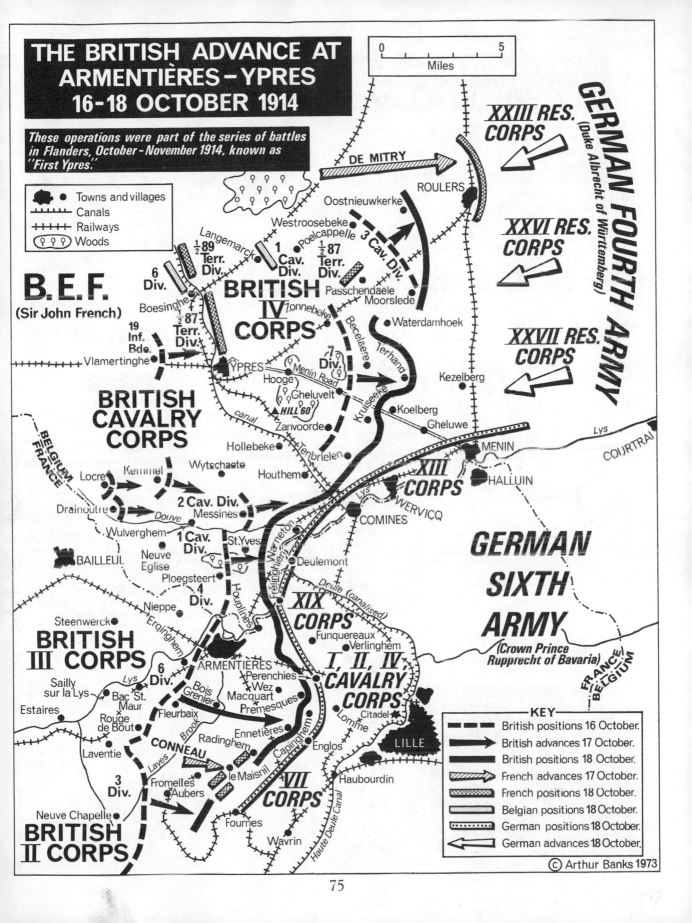

THE BRITISH ADVANCE AT ARMENTIÈRES – YPRES 16-18 OCTOBER 1914

These operations were part of the series of battles in Flanders, October – November 1914, known as "First Ypres."

Towns and villages
Canals
Railways
Woods

B.E.F.
(Sir John French)

XXIII RES. CORPS

GERMAN FOURTH ARMY
(Duke Albrecht of Württemberg)

DE MITRY

ROULERS

Oostnieuwkerke

Westroosebeke

Langemarck
½ 89 Terr. Div.

1 Cav. Div.

Poelcappelle
½ 87 Terr. Div.

3 Cav. Div.

XXVI RES. CORPS

6 Div.

Boesinghe

BRITISH IV CORPS

Passchendaele
Moorslede

½ 87 Terr. Div.

Zonnebeke

Waterdamhoek

19 Inf. Bde.

Becelaere

Terhand

XXVII RES. CORPS

Vlamertinghe

YPRES

7 Div.

Menin Road

Kezelberg

Hooge

Gheluvelt

▲ HILL 60

Kruiseecke

Koelberg

Gheluwe

Lys

COURTRAI

BRITISH CAVALRY CORPS

canal

Zanvoorde

Hollebeke

Tenbrielen

MENIN

HALLUIN

Wytschaete

Houthem

XIII CORPS

WERVICQ

Locre

Kemmel

Drainoutre

Douve

2 Cav. Div.
Messines

Lys

COMINES

GERMAN SIXTH ARMY
(Crown Prince Rupprecht of Bavaria)

Wulverghem

1 Cav. Div.

St. Yves

Warneton

Deulemont

BAILLEUL

Neuve Eglise

Ploegsteert

Frelinghien

Deule (canalised)

Houplines

4 Div.

XIX CORPS

Nieppe

Steenwerck

Erquinghem

Funquereaux
Verlinghem

FRANCE
BELGIUM

BRITISH III CORPS

6 Div.

ARMENTIÈRES

Perenchies
Wez
Macquart

I, II, IV, CAVALRY CORPS

Sailly sur la Lys

Lys

Bois Grenier

Premesques

Lomme

Citadel

KEY

Estaires

Bac St. Maur

Rouge de Bout

Fleurbaix

Ennetières

Radinghem

Capinghem

Englos

LILLE

- - - British positions 16 October.
→ British advances 17 October.
▬▬ British positions 18 October.
⟶ French advances 17 October.
▤ French positions 18 October.
▥ Belgian positions 18 October.
···· German positions 18 October.
⟵ German advances 18 October.

Laventie

CONNEAU

Layes

3 Div.

le Maisnil

VII CORPS

Haubourdin

Fromelles
Aubers

Neuve Chapelle

Fournes

Wavrin

BRITISH II CORPS

© Arthur Banks 1973

75

THE BATTLE OF ARMENTIÈRES
19 OCTOBER – 2 NOVEMBER 1914

KEY
- British positions 19-20 October.
- British positions 21-22 October.
- British front line on 2 November.
- French positions (Conneau) on 19 October.
- French positions 22-24 October, with dates.
- German attacks 19-20 October.
- German attacks 21 October.
- German attacks 22-29 October, with dates.

B. E. F.
(Sir John French)

BELGIUM
FRANCE

le Bizet

to Bailleul

Nieppe

Pont de Nieppe

Lys

ARMENTIÈRES

Chapelle d'Armentières

Erquinghem

BRITISH III CORPS
(Pulteney)

Bac St. Maur

Sailly sur la Lys

Fleurbaix

6 Division

Bois Grenier

Lys

Estaires

Lahore Division
23 Oct.

Croix Maréchal

Touquet

16 Inf. Bde.

16

to Aire

19 Inf. Bde.
19 Oct.

Rouge de Bout

Layes Brook

la Boutillerie

Bde.

Bridoux

22-24 Oct.

Laventie

Inf.

48 Res. Div.

29 Oct.

Bacquart

BRITISH II CORPS
(Smith-Dorrien)

3 Division

Fauquissart

Jullundur

Bde.

19

GERMAN XIV RES. CORPS
(Loden)

le Maisnil

Lahore Division
24 Oct.

8 Inf. Bde.

Rouges Bancs

20 Oct.

19 Inf. Bde.

19 Inf. Bde.

The main area of operations during this period was more to the north where the Germans were attacking in great strength near Ypres. However, at this time, important actions took place at Armentières and La Bassée, influencing moves and dispositions in the Ypres area. This map is intended to illustrate operations to the west of the "open town" of Lille, virtually undefended.

23-24 Oct.

Fromelles

22-23 Oct.

23 Oct.

Bas Flandre

Neuve Chapelle

Aubers

Pietre

8 Inf. Bde.
19 Oct.

Grand Riez

8 Inf. Bde.

© Arthur Banks 1973

14 Division
27 Oct.

to Fournes

le Pilly

Fournes

76

to Comines
& Menin

40 Division

Frélinghien

Lys

le Ruage

Houplines

4 Division

Epinette

Rue du Bois

Int. 17 — taken over by 4 Div. 23-24 Oct.

23-24 Oct.

24 Division

20 Oct.

17 Inf. Bde.

17 Inf. Bde.

Wez Macquart

Premesques

18 Inf. Bde.

22-24 Oct.

Paradis
20 Oct.

18 Inf. Bde.

le Quesne
22-24 Oct.

22-24 Oct.
le Touquet

Ennetières

la Vallée

18 Inf. Bde.

nghem

16 Inf. Bde.

Division

26 Division

Englos

Escobecques

Erquinghem le Sec

Beaucamps

GERMAN VII CORPS

(Claer)

to La Bassée

Haute Deule Canal

GERMAN XIX CORPS

(Laffert)

Funquereau

Verlinghem

Deule (canalised)

Perenchies

SENARMONT BATTERY

Mont de Premesques

Capinghem

25 Reserve Division

★ **Fort d'Englos**

GERMAN XIII CORPS

(Fabeck)

Lomme

Citadel

Haubourdin

Loos

GERMAN SIXTH ARMY

(Crown Prince Rupprecht of Bavaria)

Fort Carnot ★

★ Fort de Bondues

These operations formed part of the series of battles fought in Flanders in 1914 known as "First Ypres".

LILLE
Occupied by Germans on 12 October

0   1   2
Miles

Towns, villages, hamlets   ╞ Bridges   +++ Railways   ┴┴┴ Canals

to Comines

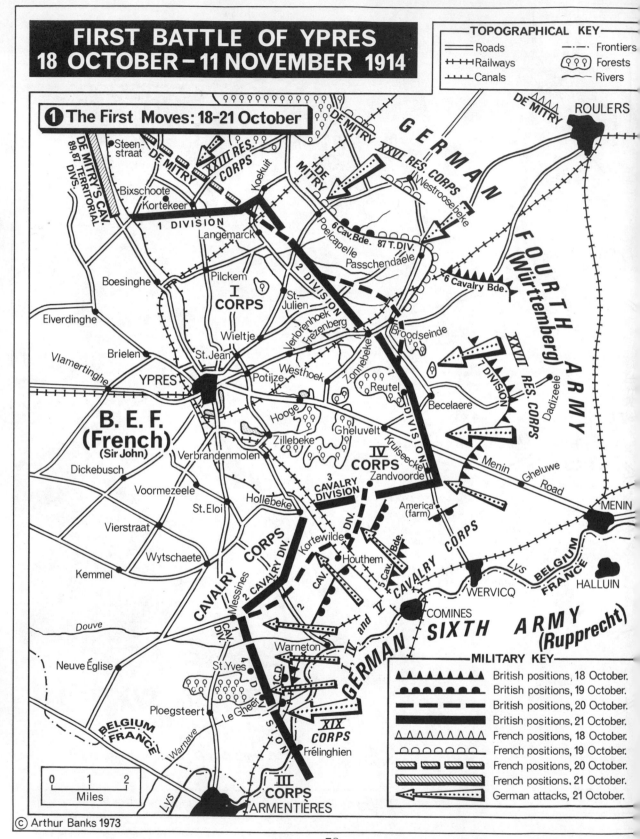

FIRST BATTLE OF YPRES 18 OCTOBER – 11 NOVEMBER 1914

TOPOGRAPHICAL KEY
- Roads
- Railways
- Canals
- Frontiers
- Forests
- Rivers

① The First Moves: 18–21 October

ROULERS

Steen-straat
DE MITRY
DE MITRY
XXIII RES. CORPS
Koekuit
DE MITRY
XXVII RES. CORPS
Westroosebeke
GERMAN
DE MITRY
Bixschoote
89,87 TERRITORIAL 89,87 DIVS.
DE MITRY'S CAV.
Kortekeer
1 DIVISION
6 Cav. Bde. 87 T. DIV.
Langemarck
Poelcapelle
Passchendaele
6 Cavalry Bde.
FOURTH ARMY (Württemberg)
Boesinghe
Pilckem
I CORPS
St. Julien
2 DIVISION
Elverdinghe
Wieltje
Verlorenhoek Frezenberg
Broodseinde
Brielen
St. Jean
Westhoek
Zonnebeke
XXVII RES. CORPS
Vlamertinghe
YPRES
Potijze
Reutel
1 DIVISION
Dadizeele
B.E.F. (French) (Sir John)
Hooge
Becelaere
Dickebusch
Zillebeke
Gheluvelt
Kruiseecke
Menin
Gheluwe Road
MENIN
Verbrandenmolen
IV CORPS
Voormezeele
St. Eloi
Hollebeke
3 CAVALRY DIVISION
Zandvoorde
America (farm)
Vierstraat
Kortewilde
DIV.
CAVALRY CORPS
HALLUIN
Wytschaete
CAVALRY CORPS
Houthem
5 Cav. Bde.
Lys
BELGIUM FRANCE
Kemmel
Messines
2 CAVALRY DIV.
CAV.
WERVICQ
Douve
CAV.
2
I., IV., and V. CAVALRY CORPS
COMINES
GERMAN SIXTH ARMY (Rupprecht)
Neuve Église
Warneton
DIVISION
MILITARY KEY
St. Yves
CAV. D.
XIX CORPS
Ploegsteert
Le Gheer
BELGIUM FRANCE
Warnave
Frélinghien
Lys
III CORPS
ARMENTIÈRES

▲▲▲▲▲▲	British positions, 18 October.
●●●●●●	British positions, 19 October.
▬ ▬ ▬	British positions, 20 October.
▬▬▬▬	British positions, 21 October.
△△△△△△	French positions, 18 October.
◠◠◠◠◠◠	French positions, 19 October.
▱▱▱▱	French positions, 20 October.
▨▨▨▨	French positions, 21 October.
⬅	German attacks, 21 October.

0   1   2
Miles

© Arthur Banks 1973

78

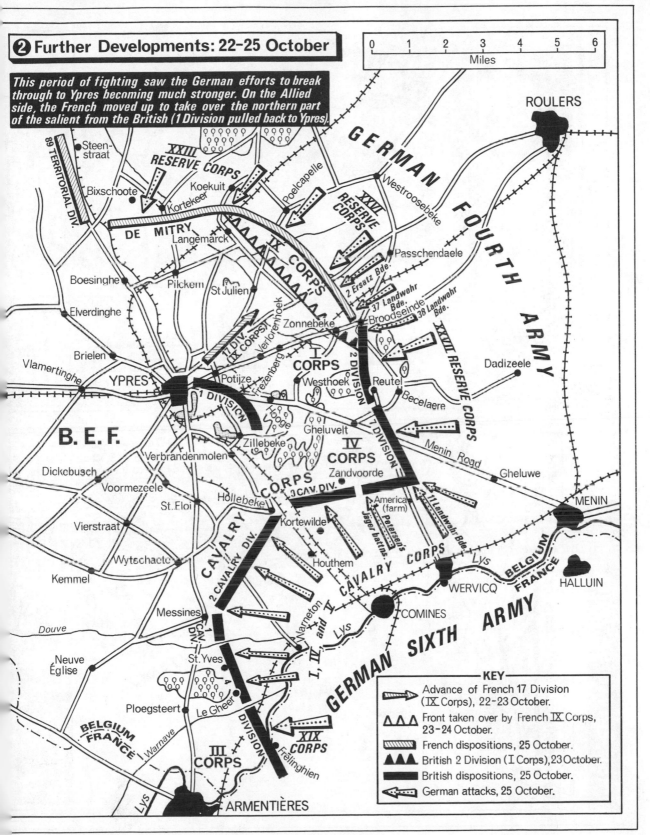

❷ Further Developments: 22–25 October

This period of fighting saw the German efforts to break through to Ypres becoming much stronger. On the Allied side, the French moved up to take over the northern part of the salient from the British (1 Division pulled back to Ypres).

0 1 2 3 4 5 6
Miles

ROULERS

GERMAN FOURTH ARMY

89 TERRITORIAL DIV.

Steenstraat

XXIII RESERVE CORPS

Bixschoote

Koekuit

Kortekeer

DE MITRY

Langemarck

Poelcapelle

Westroosebeke

XXVI RESERVE CORPS

Passchendaele

IX CORPS

Boesinghe

Pilckem

St Julien

2 Ersatz Bde.

2 Landwehr Bde.

37 Landwehr Bde.

Broodseinde

38 Landwehr Bde.

Elverdinghe

17 DIV. (IX CORPS)

Verlorenhoek

Zonnebeke

Brielen

I CORPS

2 DIVISION

Reutel

XXIII RESERVE CORPS

Dadizeele

Vlamertinghe

YPRES

Potijze

Frezenberg

Westhoek

Becelaere

1 DIVISION

Hooge

Gheluvelt

7 DIVISION

B. E. F.

Zillebeke

IV CORPS

Menin Road

Gheluwe

Verbrandenmolen

Dickebusch

Zandvoorde

MENIN

Voormezeele

St. Eloi

Hollebeke

3 CAV. DIV.

America (farm)

11 Landwehr Bde.

CORPS

Vierstraat

CAVALRY DIV.

Kortewilde

Petersen's Jäger battns.

CAVALRY CORPS

BELGIUM FRANCE

HALLUIN

Wytschaete

2 CAVALRY DIV.

Houthem

Lys

Kemmel

Messines

1 CAV. DIV.

Warneton

I, II, and V

Lys

WERVICQ

COMINES

GERMAN SIXTH ARMY

Douve

Neuve Église

St. Yves

4

GERMAN SIXTH ARMY

Ploegsteert

Le Gheer

XIX CORPS

BELGIUM FRANCE

Warnave

DIVISION

III CORPS

Frelinghien

LYS

ARMENTIÈRES

— KEY —

Advance of French 17 Division (IX Corps), 22–23 October.

Front taken over by French IX Corps, 23–24 October.

French dispositions, 25 October.

British 2 Division (I Corps), 23 October.

British dispositions, 25 October.

German attacks, 25 October.

79

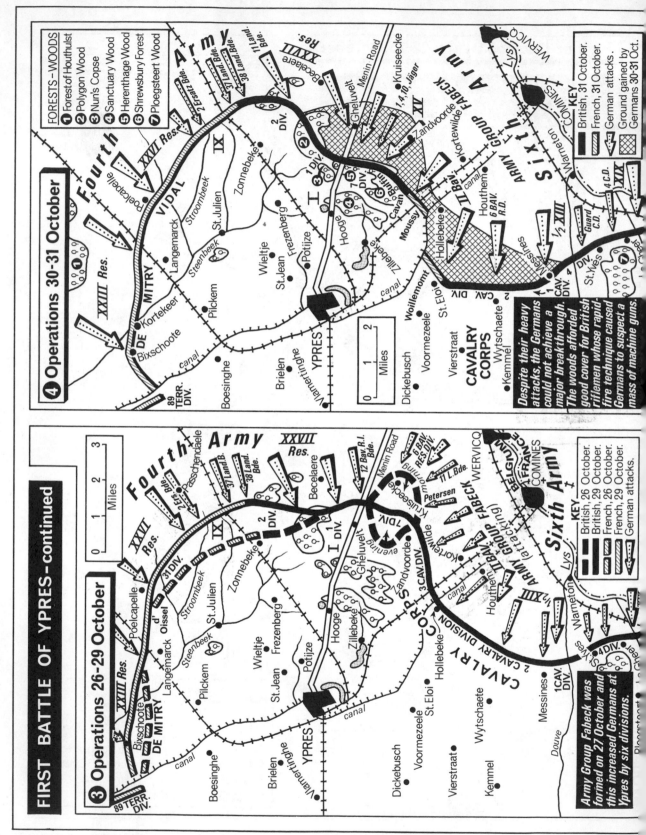

FIRST BATTLE OF YPRES—continued

④ Operations 30-31 October

FORESTS-WOODS
1. Forest of Houthulst
2. Polygon Wood
3. Nun's Copse
4. Sanctuary Wood
5. Herenthage Wood
6. Shrewsbury Forest
7. Ploegsteert Wood

Fourth Army

XXVII Res.
2 Ersatz Bde.
37 Land. Bde.
38 Land. Bde.
11 Land. Bde.
XXVI Res.
XXIII Res.
IX

VIDAL
DE MITRY
89 TERR. DIV.

Poelcapelle
Bixschoote
Kortekeer
Langemarck
St. Julien
Zonnebeke
Steenbeek
Stroombeek
Pilckem
Wieltje
St. Jean
Frezenberg
Potijze
Hooge
Zillebeke
Becelaere
Gheluvelt
Zandvoorde
Kortewilde
Kruiseecke

I
IX
2 DIV.
1 DIV.
3
7
5
4
2 DIV.

Cavan
Moussy
Hollebeke
Houthem
Wytschaete
Messines
Warneton
St. Yves

II Bav.
ARMY GROUP FABECK
6 BAV. R.D.
2 CAV. DIV.
1 CAV. DIV.
XV
XIX
Guard C.D.
4 C.D.
½ XIII
DIV.
St. Yves

Sixth Army

WERVICQ
COMINES
Woillemont
Voormezeele
Vierstraat
Kemmel
Dickebusch
Brielen
Boesinghe
Vlamertinghe
YPRES

CAVALRY CORPS

1, 4, 10, Jäger
Kruiseecke
Menin Road
Lys
canal

Miles 0 1 2

KEY
British, 31 October.
French, 31 October.
German attacks.
Ground gained by Germans 30-31 Oct.

Despite their heavy attacks, the Germans could not achieve a major breakthrough. The woods afforded good cover for British riflemen whose rapid-fire technique caused Germans to suspect a mass of machine guns.

③ Operations 26-29 October

Fourth Army

XXVII Res.
2 Ers Bde.
37 Land. B.
38 Land. Bde.
12 Bav. R.I. Bde.
6 BAV. RES. DIV.
11 L Bde.
XXVI Res.
XXIII Res.

d' Oissel
DE MITRY
89 TERR. DIV.
31 DIV.
IX
2 DIV.
I DIV.
1 DIV.
7 DIV.
3 CAV. DIV.

Poelcapelle
Bixschoote
Langemarck
St. Julien
Zonnebeke
Steenbeek
Stroombeek
Pilckem
Wieltje
St. Jean
Frezenberg
Potijze
Hooge
Zillebeke
Gheluvelt
Zandvoorde
Kortewilde
Kruiseecke
Passchendaele
Becelaere

Petersen
(II BAV. ARMY GROUP FABECK)
Houthem
Hollebeke
Messines
Wytschaete
Warneton
St. Eloi
Voormezeele
Vierstraat
Kemmel
Dickebusch
Brielen
Boesinghe
Vlamertinghe
YPRES

CAVALRY CORPS
2 CAVALRY DIVISION
1 CAV. DIV.

Zandvoorde (evening)
(attack) (morning)
4 DIV.
St. Yves
Warneton
½ XIII
Lys
Douve
canal

WERVICQ
COMINES
BELGIUM
FRANCE

Sixth Army

KEY
British, 26 October.
British, 29 October.
French, 26 October.
French, 29 October.
German attacks.

Army Group Fabeck was formed on 27 October and this increased Germans at Ypres by six divisions.

Miles 0 1 2 3

80

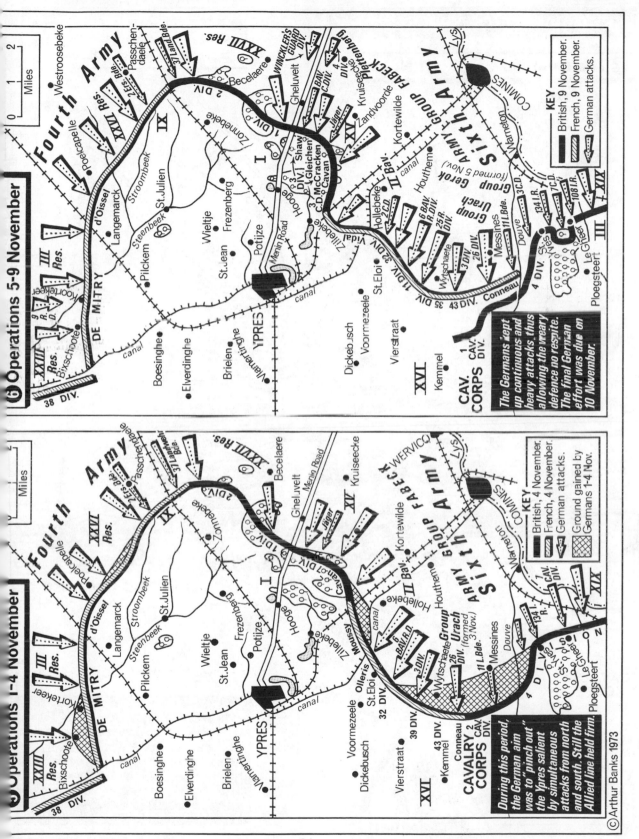

(6) Operations 5-9 November

KEY
British, 9 November.
French, 9 November.
German attacks.

(5) Operations 1-4 November

KEY
British, 4 November.
French, 4 November.
German attacks.
Ground gained by Germans 1-4 Nov.

© Arthur Banks 1973

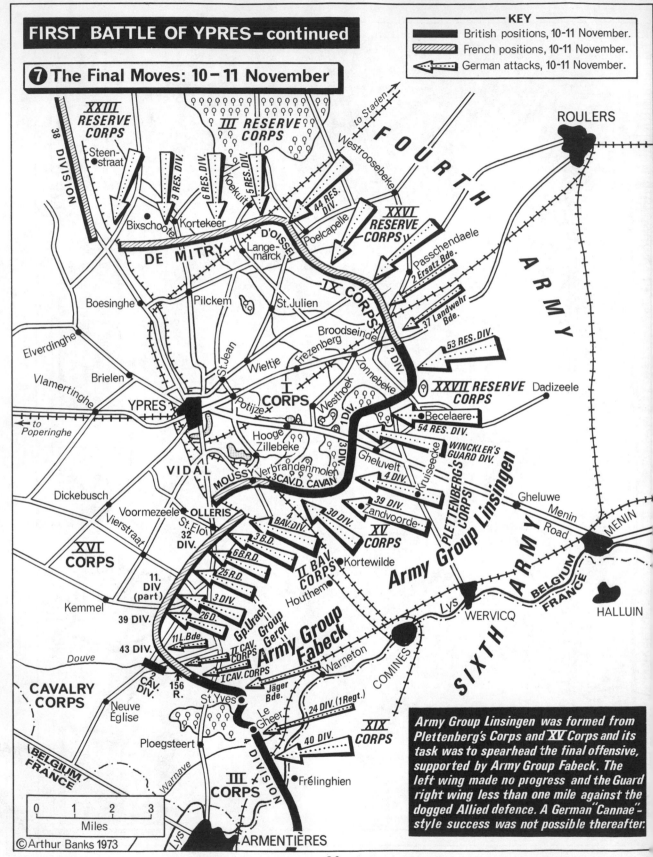

FIRST BATTLE OF YPRES—continued

7 The Final Moves: 10–11 November

ROULERS

to Staden

FOURTH ARMY

XXIII RESERVE CORPS

38 DIVISION

III RESERVE CORPS

Steen-straat

9 RES. DIV.

6 RES. DIV.

5 RES. DIV.

Koekuit

Westroosebeke

Bixschoote

Kortekeer

44 RES. DIV.

XXVI RESERVE CORPS

D'OISSEL

DE MITRY

Langemarck

Poelcapelle

Passchendaele

2 Ersatz Bde.

Boesinghe

Pilckem

St. Julien

37 Landwehr Bde.

Broodseinde

IX CORPS

53 RES. DIV.

Elverdinghe

St. Jean

Wieltje

Frezenberg

Zonnebeke

2 DIV.

XXVII RESERVE CORPS

Dadizeele

Vlamertinghe

Brielen

YPRES

Potijze

I CORPS

Westhoek

1 DIV.

Becelaere

54 RES. DIV.

to Poperinghe

Hooge

Zillebeke

3 DIV.

Gheluvelt

WINCKLER'S GUARD DIV.

Verbrandenmolen

4 DIV.

Kruiseecke

Gheluwe

VIDAL

MOUSSY

3 CAV. D. CAVAN

39 DIV.

Zandvoorde

PLETTENBERG'S CORPS

Menin Road

Menin

Dickebusch

Voormezeele

OLLERIS

St. Eloi

4 BAV. DIV.

30 DIV.

XV CORPS

Army Group Linsingen

SIXTH ARMY

Vierstraat

32 DIV.

3 B.D.

HALLUIN

XVI CORPS

11. DIV. (part)

6 B.R.D.

II BAV. CORPS

Kortewilde

BELGIUM FRANCE

25 R.D.

Houthem

Kemmel

3 DIV.

39 DIV.

26 D.

Gp. Urach

Group Gerok

Army Group Fabeck

Lys

WERVICQ

43 DIV.

11 L. Bde.

II CAV. CORPS

I CAV. CORPS

Warneton

COMINES

Douve

156 R.

Jäger Bde.

24 DIV. (1 Regt.)

XIX CORPS

CAVALRY CORPS

2 CAV. DIV.

St. Yves

Le Gheer

Neuve Église

40 DIV.

Ploegsteert

BELGIUM FRANCE

Warnave

4 DIVISION

III CORPS

Frélinghien

Lys

ARMENTIÈRES

Army Group Linsingen was formed from Plettenberg's Corps and XV Corps and its task was to spearhead the final offensive, supported by Army Group Fabeck. The left wing made no progress and the Guard right wing less than one mile against the dogged Allied defence. A German "Cannae"-style success was not possible thereafter.

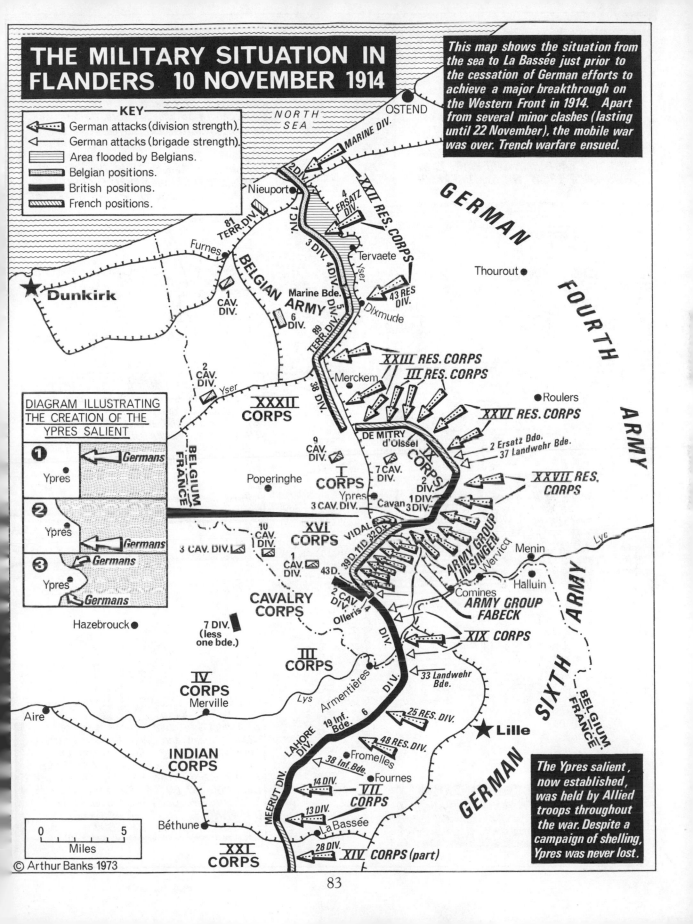

THE MILITARY SITUATION IN FLANDERS 10 NOVEMBER 1914

This map shows the situation from the sea to La Bassée just prior to the cessation of German efforts to achieve a major breakthrough on the Western Front in 1914. Apart from several minor clashes (lasting until 22 November), the mobile war was over. Trench warfare ensued.

KEY
- German attacks (division strength).
- German attacks (brigade strength).
- Area flooded by Belgians.
- Belgian positions.
- British positions.
- French positions.

NORTH SEA

OSTEND

MARINE DIV.

2 DIV.

Nieuport

1 DIV.

XXII RES. CORPS

4 ERSATZ DIV.

81 TERR. DIV.

3 DIV. 4 DIV.

Tervaete

Yser

GERMAN

FOURTH ARMY

Thourout

Furnes

BELGIAN ARMY

Marine Bde.

5

43 RES. DIV.

Dixmude

★ Dunkirk

1 CAV. DIV.

6 DIV.

89 TERR. DIV.

DIAGRAM ILLUSTRATING THE CREATION OF THE YPRES SALIENT

❶ Ypres — Germans

❷ Ypres — Germans

❸ Ypres — Germans / Germans

2 CAV. DIV.

Yser

38 DIV.

Merckem

XXIII RES. CORPS
III RES. CORPS

Roulers

XXXII CORPS

9 CAV. DIV.

DE MITRY d'Olssel

XXVI RES. CORPS

2 Ersatz Ddo.
37 Landwehr Bde.

BELGIUM
FRANCE

Poperinghe

I CORPS

7 CAV. DIV.

IX CORPS

2 DIV.
1 DIV.
3 DIV.

XXVII RES. CORPS

Ypres

3 CAV. DIV.

Cavan

VIDAL

39 D. 11 D. 32 D.

ARMY GROUP LINSINGEN

Wervicq

Lye

Menin

10 CAV. DIV.

XVI CORPS

3 CAV. DIV.

1 CAV. DIV.

43 D.

DIV.

Halluin

Hazebrouck

7 DIV. (less one bde.)

CAVALRY CORPS

2 CAV. DIV.

Olleris

Comines

ARMY GROUP FABECK

III CORPS

DIV.

XIX CORPS

IV CORPS

Merville

Lys

Armentières

6

33 Landwehr Bde.

Aire

INDIAN CORPS

MEERUT DIV.

LAHORE DIV.

19 Inf. Bde.

25 RES. DIV.

48 RES. DIV.

★ Lille

GERMAN

SIXTH ARMY

BELGIUM
FRANCE

38 Inf. Bde.

Fromelles

Fournes

14 DIV.

VII CORPS

13 DIV.

La Bassée

Béthune

28 DIV.   XIV CORPS (part)

XXI CORPS

0 — 5 Miles

The Ypres salient, now established, was held by Allied troops throughout the war. Despite a campaign of shelling, Ypres was never lost.

© Arthur Banks 1973

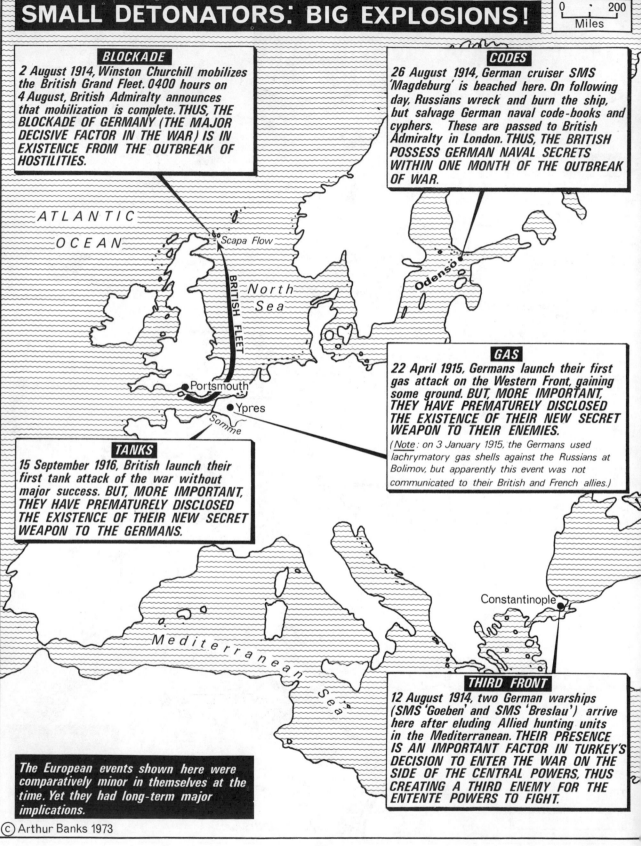

SMALL DETONATORS: BIG EXPLOSIONS!

0 · 200
Miles

BLOCKADE

2 August 1914, Winston Churchill mobilizes the British Grand Fleet. 0400 hours on 4 August, British Admiralty announces that mobilization is complete. THUS, THE BLOCKADE OF GERMANY (THE MAJOR DECISIVE FACTOR IN THE WAR) IS IN EXISTENCE FROM THE OUTBREAK OF HOSTILITIES.

CODES

26 August 1914, German cruiser SMS 'Magdeburg' is beached here. On following day, Russians wreck and burn the ship, but salvage German naval code-books and cyphers. These are passed to British Admiralty in London. THUS, THE BRITISH POSSESS GERMAN NAVAL SECRETS WITHIN ONE MONTH OF THE OUTBREAK OF WAR.

ATLANTIC
OCEAN

Scapa Flow

BRITISH FLEET

North
Sea

Odensö

Portsmouth

Ypres

Somme

GAS

22 April 1915, Germans launch their first gas attack on the Western Front, gaining some ground. BUT, MORE IMPORTANT, THEY HAVE PREMATURELY DISCLOSED THE EXISTENCE OF THEIR NEW SECRET WEAPON TO THEIR ENEMIES.

(Note: on 3 January 1915, the Germans used lachrymatory gas shells against the Russians at Bolimov, but apparently this event was not communicated to their British and French allies.)

TANKS

15 September 1916, British launch their first tank attack of the war without major success. BUT, MORE IMPORTANT, THEY HAVE PREMATURELY DISCLOSED THE EXISTENCE OF THEIR NEW SECRET WEAPON TO THE GERMANS.

Mediterranean Sea

Constantinople

THIRD FRONT

12 August 1914, two German warships (SMS 'Goeben' and SMS 'Breslau') arrive here after eluding Allied hunting units in the Mediterranean. THEIR PRESENCE IS AN IMPORTANT FACTOR IN TURKEY'S DECISION TO ENTER THE WAR ON THE SIDE OF THE CENTRAL POWERS, THUS CREATING A THIRD ENEMY FOR THE ENTENTE POWERS TO FIGHT.

The European events shown here were comparatively minor in themselves at the time. Yet they had long-term major implications.

© Arthur Banks 1973

84

THE WAR ON THE EASTERN FRONT

There were four other theatres of war in Europe during the autumn of 1914. Eight hundred miles to the east of the Belgian cockpit, Russian and German armies clashed in the marchlands of East Prussia while to their south other forces manoeuvred for position in the great plains of the Vistulan Basin. The principal Austrian army was concentrated at the outbreak of war in Galicia, with the well-forested range of the Carpathians in its rear, an admirable position for withstanding any Russian onslaught (compare pages 24 and 32). Farther south still, nearly four hundred miles across the Austro-Hungarian empire, another quarter of a million soldiers from Franz Josef's multinational empire were assigned the duty of 'punishing' Serbia. The commander of this Balkan Army was the former Governor of Bosnia, General Potiorek, who had been sitting in front of Archduke Franz Ferdinand on that fateful day in Sarajevo. But Potiorek, like all other Austro-Hungarian commanders, was subordinate to General Conrad von Hötzendorf, the Austrian Chief of Staff, who established his first headquarters in the reputedly impregnable Galician fortress town of Przemysl.

Although Conrad had hoped to cut off the Russians in Poland by joint Austro-German operations uniting the commands in East Prussia and Galicia, there was in fact little co-ordination between the various eastern European armies. The first shots in the whole war were fired by two monitors of the Austro-Hungarian Danube flotilla, which bombarded Belgrade on 29 July, five days before the opening of hostilities in western Europe. But thereafter all was peaceful until the middle of the second week in August when Conrad sent his First and Fourth armies northward into Russian Poland, while the first units of the Russian 1st Army invaded East Prussia, and Potiorek's troops crossed the river Sava and seized the Serbian town of Sabac.

The most dramatic of these undertakings was the Russian incursion towards the historic Prussian coronation city, Königsberg, some ninety miles from the frontier. The Schlieffen Plan had anticipated a German holding operation against Russia for some six or seven weeks, before the full weight of German arms was shifted to the West. On paper, there was no reason for

German alarm, even though the invaders had a numerical superiority of more than four to one. But on 20 August three German army corps clashed with Rennenkampf's Russian First Army at Gumbinnen and did not distinguish themselves (pages 88–89). The German commander, Prittwitz, was worried by news that the Russian Second Army, under Samsonov, was threatening his southern flank, and sent alarming messages to Moltke's headquarters in the West. The situation was saved by one of Prittwitz's staff officers, Lieutenant-Colonel Max von Hoffmann, who knew there was a deep personal vendetta between Samsonov and Rennenkampf. Hoffmann proposed that the Germans should concentrate against Samsonov, leaving the route towards Königsberg apparently open for Rennenkampf (who would not resist this bait simply to aid the rival he so detested). Thus began the deployment for the battle of Tannenberg, three days of agony for the Russians, in which the Second Army was destroyed and its commander shot himself in despair.

Tannenberg, like the Marne, became a legendary victory. The discovery of a Russian staff officer's body on the battlefield, with detailed military directives in his pocket, helped the Germans considerably; and so did the incredible folly of the three Russian headquarters in sending unciphered operations orders by wireless, with the Germans able to note down every word (see page 98). The ease of their victory made the Germans despise their Russian opponents and they therefore suffered heavy casualties in rash frontal assaults on Rennenkampf's army, which was caught at the Masurian Lakes in the first week of September. But the Masurian Lakes completed the triumph of Tannenberg: the Russians, after nibbling at the edge of East Prussia for twenty-eight days, were thrown back across the frontier, broken and demoralised. No Russian army penetrated German territory again until 1945.

The twin victories enabled the German people to find a heroic father-figure to idolise for the remainder of the War and beyond. Paul von Hindenburg was six weeks short of his sixty-seventh birthday when, on 22 August, he was summoned from obscure retirement to replace Prittwitz on the Eastern Front. Hindenburg had been decorated for bravery both in the 1866 war with Austria and the 1870 war with France and he had witnessed the proclamation of the German Empire at Versailles in 1871. No one could describe him as a strategic genius. His greatest asset was his rocklike imperturbability. The brain behind his triumphs belonged to his deputy, Ludendorff, who had already distinguished himself in reducing the Liége forts (page 41); and, at least on the Eastern Front, Ludendorff owed much to Hoffmann, who understood the Russian military mind. But, in Germany, sentiment and propaganda combined to turn Hindenburg into a colossus of victory.

Austria-Hungary discovered no such idol. Conrad's decision to send the First and Fourth armies northwards from Galicia was based upon a false assumption. He thought that the Russian commander-in-chief, Grand Duke Nicholas, had ordered the commander of the South-Western Army Group, General Ivanov, to concentrate around Lublin. In reality the Russians were farther south-east, threatening Lemberg (Lvov) where Ivanov had, in his turn, wrongly assumed the main Austrian forces to be. There was, in consequence, a curious week of shadow-boxing before Conrad turned to meet the challenge to his flank from Ivanov (see pages 100–101). Conrad made the mistake of opening up a gap in the north which was filled by the Russian Fifth Army. Fearing he might be encircled, Conrad ordered a general retreat on 11 September, and found it impossible to stabilise the Front until the Russians had penetrated over a hundred miles, reaching the Carpathian passes into Hungary. The Austrians thus sustained a humiliating defeat, with the Russians capturing two provincial capitals, Lemberg (the fourth largest city in Austria-Hungary) and Czernowitz, as well as beseiging Przemsyl. The Slav contingents in the Austro-Hungarian Army (particularly the Czechs) had little heart for a war against 'Mother Russia', but large-scale desertions did not begin until the spring of 1915, and it is clear that the disaster reflects as much on Conrad and his staff as on the quality of the troops they commanded. Eventually the Austrians were saved by an offensive mounted by Hindenburg in central Poland and threatening Warsaw. An abortive Russian counter-offensive in Poland at the end of October threatened Silesia but brought down a massive German response from the north, when Mackensen's Ninth Army fell on the Russians at Lodz and as winter set in, destroyed all prospects of avenging Tannenberg. Though the Russians had triumphed in Galicia, the first four months of fighting against the Germans had proved disastrous and left the Russian artillery desperately short of shells.

Yet the strangest development of the war was in Serbia. For Putnik, the Serbian commander-in-chief, had successfully repelled Potiorek's first incursion across the river Sava, and nipped another offensive (across the river Drina) in the bud. At the end of November Potiorek tried again and captured Belgrade on 2 December, sweeping the Serbs back into the mountain heart of the Kingdom. Yet, though short of men and munitions, the Serbs made a surprise counter-attack and within eleven days had recovered their capital. 'On the whole territory of the Serbian Government there remains not one free enemy soldier', ran a proud communiqué on 15 December. Austria's humiliation was complete. Small wonder the German High Command began privately to wonder if they were allied to a living Empire or a corpse.

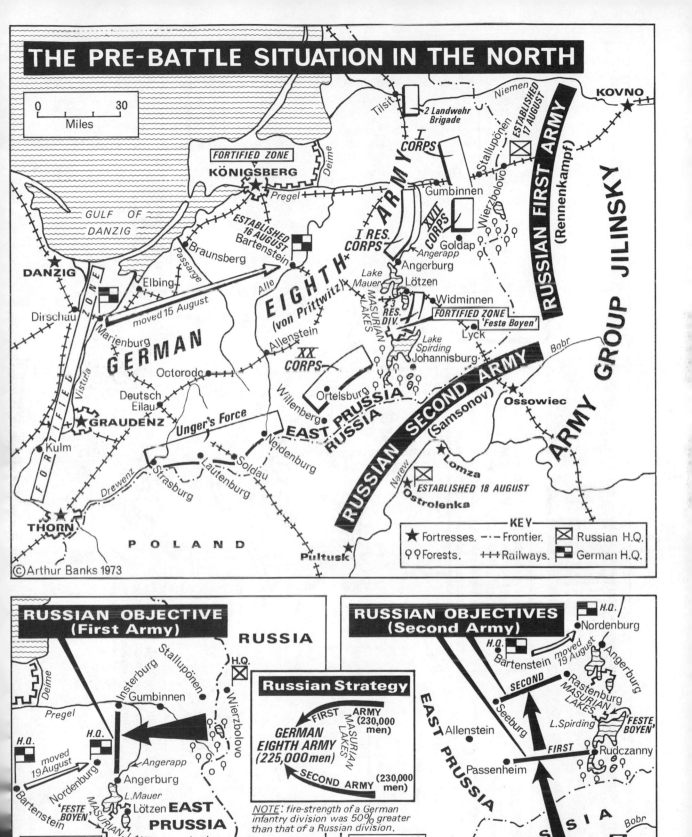

THE PRE-BATTLE SITUATION IN THE NORTH

0 — 30
Miles

KOVNO

Niemen

Tilsit
2 Landwehr Brigade

I CORPS

ESTABLISHED 17 AUGUST

Stallupönen

RUSSIAN FIRST ARMY (Rennenkampf)

FORTIFIED ZONE
KÖNIGSBERG

Deime

Pregel

Gumbinnen

Wierzbolovo

ARMY GROUP JILINSKY

GULF OF DANZIG

ESTABLISHED 16 AUGUST
Bartenstein

Braunsberg

DANZIG

Elbing

passarge

Dirschau

Alle

Marienburg

FORTIFIED ZONE

GERMAN

EIGHTH
(von Prittwitz)

I RES. CORPS

XVII CORPS

Goldap

Angerapp

Angerburg

Lötzen

Widminnen

FORTIFIED ZONE
'Feste Boyen'

Lyck

Lake Mauer

MASURIAN LAKES

23 RES. DIV.

moved 15 August

Allenstein

XX CORPS

Lake Spirding

Johannisburg

Bobr

RUSSIAN SECOND ARMY (Samsonov)

Osterode

Vistula

Deutsch Eilau

GRAUDENZ

Unger's Force

Willenberg

Ortelsburg

EAST PRUSSIA
RUSSIA

Ossowiec

FORTIFIED ZONE

Kulm

Drewenz

Strasburg

Lautenburg

Soldau

Neidenburg

EAST PRUSSIA

Narew

Lomza

ESTABLISHED 18 AUGUST

THORN

POLAND

Ostrolenka

Pultusk

KEY
★ Fortresses. –·–·– Frontier. ⊠ Russian H.Q.
♀♀ Forests. +++ Railways. ▦ German H.Q.

© Arthur Banks 1973

RUSSIAN OBJECTIVE (First Army)

RUSSIA

Stallupönen

Insterburg

Gumbinnen

H.Q.

Wierzbolovo

Deime

Pregel

H.Q.

H.Q.

moved 19 August

Nordenburg

Bartenstein

Angerapp

Angerburg

'FESTE BOYEN'

L.Mauer

Lötzen **EAST PRUSSIA**

MASURIAN LAKES

Lyck

L. Spirding

RUSSIA

0 — 20
Miles

Russian Strategy

FIRST ARMY (230,000 men)

GERMAN EIGHTH ARMY (225,000 men)

MASURIAN LAKES

SECOND ARMY (230,000 men)

NOTE: fire-strength of a German infantry division was 50% greater than that of a Russian division.

RUSSIAN OBJECTIVES (Second Army)

H.Q.

Nordenburg

H.Q.

Bartenstein

moved 19 August

Angerburg

SECOND

Rastenburg

MASURIAN LAKES

'FESTE BOYEN'

Seeburg

L.Spirding

EAST PRUSSIA

Allenstein

FIRST

Rudczanny

Passenheim

RUSSIA

Bobr

H.Q.

Ostrolenka ★

0 — 20
Miles

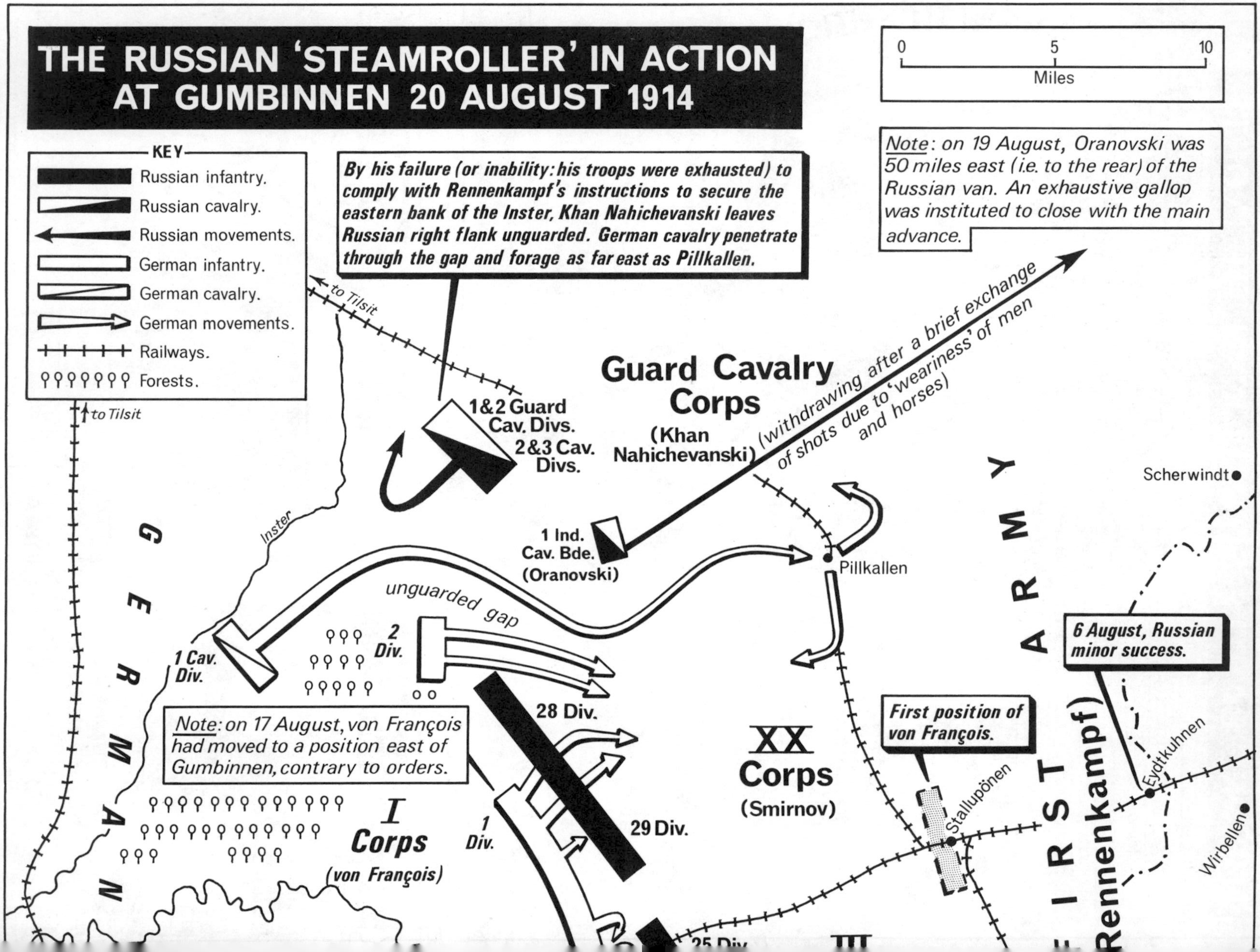

THE RUSSIAN 'STEAMROLLER' IN ACTION AT GUMBINNEN 20 AUGUST 1914
KEY
Russian infantry.
Russian cavalry.
Russian movements.
German infantry.
German cavalry.
German movements.
Railways.
Forests.
0
5
10
Miles
By his failure (or inability: his troops were exhausted) to comply with Rennenkampf's instructions to secure the eastern bank of the Inster, Khan Nahichevanski leaves Russian right flank unguarded. German cavalry penetrate through the gap and forage as far east as Pillkallen.
Note: on 19 August, Oranovski was 50 miles east (i.e. to the rear) of the Russian van. An exhaustive gallop was instituted to close with the main advance.
to Tilsit
to Tilsit
1&2 Guard Cav. Divs.
2&3 Cav. Divs.
Guard Cavalry Corps
(Khan Nahichevanski)
(withdrawing after a brief exchange of shots due to 'weariness' of men and horses)
Scherwindt
Inster
1 Ind. Cav. Bde.
(Oranovski)
Pillkallen
unguarded gap
1 Cav. Div.
2 Div.
28 Div.
29 Div.
1 Div.
Note: on 17 August, von François had moved to a position east of Gumbinnen, contrary to orders.
I Corps
(von François)
XX Corps
(Smirnov)
First position of von François.
6 August, Russian minor success.
Stallupönen
Eydtkuhnen
Wirbellen
FIRST ARMY
(Rennenkampf)
GERMAN
25 Div.

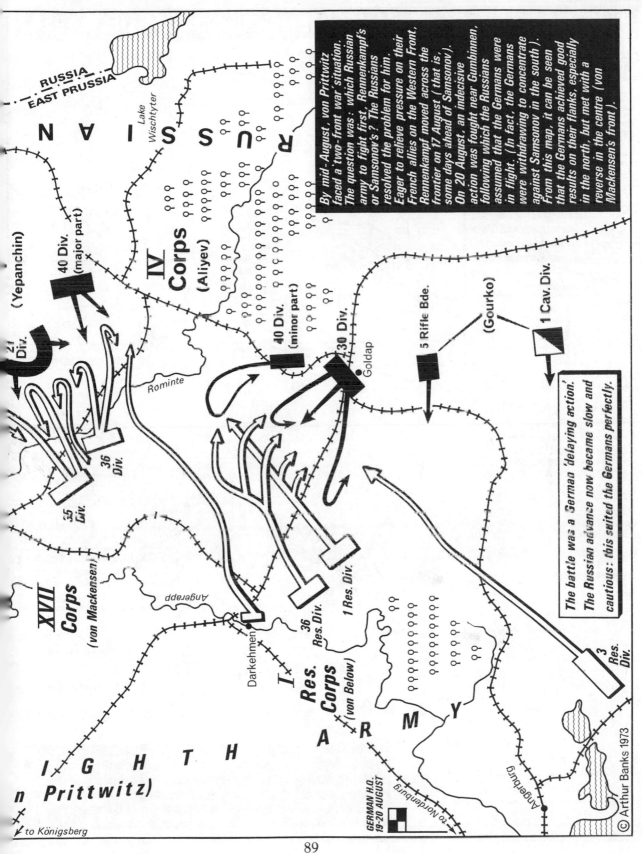

RUSSIA
·—··—··
EAST PRUSSIA

N A I S S U R

Lake
Wischtyter

(Yepanchin)

40 Div.
(major part)

41
Div.

IV
Corps
(Aliyev)

40 Div.
(minor part)

30 Div.

● Goldap

5 Rifle Bde.

(Gourko)

1 Cav. Div.

Rominte

36
Div.

35
Div.

XVII
Corps
(von Mackensen)

Angerapp

Darkehmen ●

36
Res. Div.

1 Res. Div.

I
Res.
Corps
(von Below)

A R M Y

3
Res.
Div.

By mid-August, von Prittwitz faced a 'two-front war' situation. The question was: which Russian army to fight first, Rennenkampf's or Samsonov's? The Russians resolved the problem for him. Eager to relieve pressure on their French allies on the Western Front, Rennenkampf moved across the frontier on 17 August (that is, some days ahead of Samsonov). On 20 August, an indecisive action was fought near Gumbinnen, following which the Russians assumed that the Germans were in flight. (In fact, the Germans were withdrawing to concentrate against Samsonov in the south). From this map, it can be seen that the Germans achieved good results on their flanks, especially in the north, but met with a reverse in the centre (von Mackensen's front).

The battle was a German 'delaying action'. The Russian advance now became slow and cautious: this suited the Germans perfectly.

I G H T H

n Prittwitz)

to Königsberg

GERMAN H.Q.
19-20 AUGUST

to Nordenburg

Angerburg

© Arthur Banks 1973

89

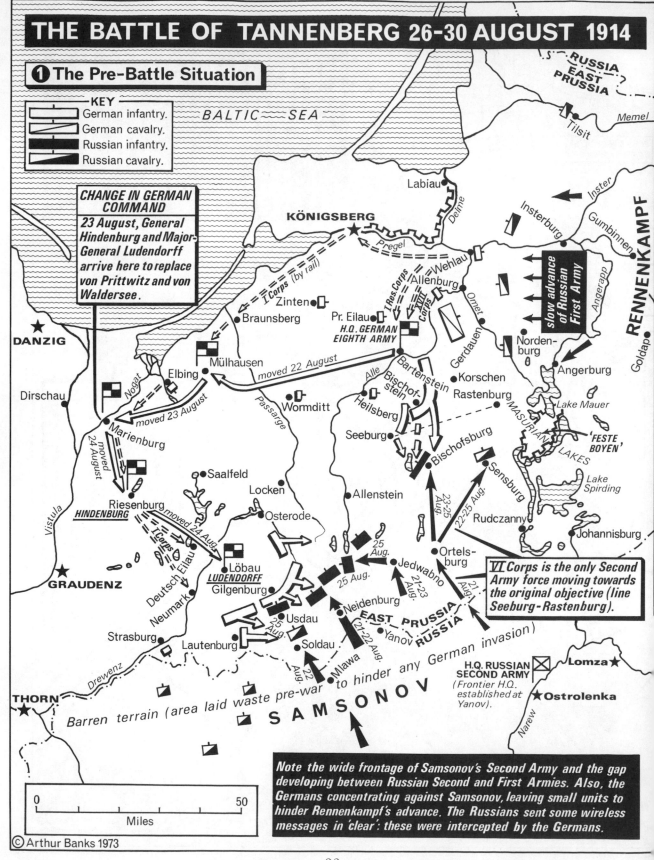

THE BATTLE OF TANNENBERG 26-30 AUGUST 1914

❶ The Pre-Battle Situation

KEY
- German infantry.
- German cavalry.
- Russian infantry.
- Russian cavalry.

BALTIC SEA

RUSSIA
EAST
PRUSSIA

Memel

Tilsit

Inster

RENNENKAMPF

CHANGE IN GERMAN COMMAND
23 August, General Hindenburg and Major-General Ludendorff arrive here to replace von Prittwitz and von Waldersee.

Labiau

Insterburg

Gumbinnen

KÖNIGSBERG

Wehlau

Allenburg

Pregel

Delme

Angerapp

slow advance of Russian First Army

Omet

Nordenburg

Goldap

I Corps (by rail)

Zinten

Braunsberg

Pr. Eilau
H.Q. GERMAN EIGHTH ARMY

I Res. Corps

XVII Corps

Gerdauen

Angerburg

Lake Mauer

DANZIG

Mülhausen

Elbing

moved 22 August

Bartenstein

Bischofstein

Korschen

Rastenburg

MASURIAN LAKES

'FESTE BOYEN'

Dirschau

Nogat

Wormditt

Alle

Heilsberg

Lake Spirding

moved 23 August

Marienburg

Passarge

Seeburg

Bischofsburg

moved 24 August

Saalfeld

Locken

Allenstein

Sensburg

23-25 Aug.

22-25 Aug.

Rudczanny

Johannisburg

Riesenburg
HINDENBURG

Osterode

25 Aug.

Ortelsburg

Vistula

I Corps *moved 24 Aug.*

Löbau

LUDENDORFF

Gilgenburg

25 Aug.

Jedwabno

21-23 Aug.

VI Corps is the only Second Army force moving towards the original objective (line Seeburg-Rastenburg).

GRAUDENZ

Deutsch Eilau

Neumark

Usdau

25 Aug.

Neidenburg

EAST PRUSSIA

Yanov

21 Aug.

Strasburg

Lautenburg

Soldau

21-22 Aug.

RUSSIA

H.Q. RUSSIAN SECOND ARMY
(Frontier H.Q. established at Yanov).

Lomza

Drewenz

Mlawa

22 Aug.

to hinder any German invasion)

SAMSONOV

Ostrolenka

THORN

Barren terrain (area laid waste pre-war

Narew

0   50
Miles

Note the wide frontage of Samsonov's Second Army and the gap developing between Russian Second and First Armies. Also, the Germans concentrating against Samsonov, leaving small units to hinder Rennenkampf's advance. The Russians sent some wireless messages in 'clear': these were intercepted by the Germans.

© Arthur Banks 1973

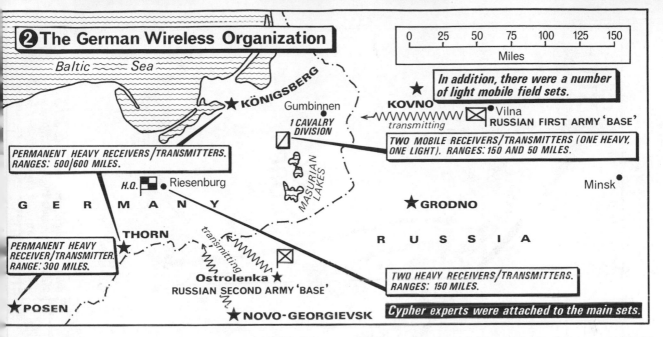

❷ The German Wireless Organization

Baltic — Sea

★ KÖNIGSBERG

Gumbinnen

1 CAVALRY DIVISION

KOVNO ★

In addition, there were a number of light mobile field sets.

〜〜〜〜〜〜 Vilna
transmitting ⊠ **RUSSIAN FIRST ARMY 'BASE'**

PERMANENT HEAVY RECEIVERS/TRANSMITTERS. RANGES: 500/600 MILES.

TWO MOBILE RECEIVERS/TRANSMITTERS (ONE HEAVY, ONE LIGHT). RANGES: 150 AND 50 MILES.

0 25 50 75 100 125 150
Miles

H.Q. ⚑ ▪ Riesenburg

MASURIAN LAKES

Minsk ▪

G E R M A N Y

★ **GRODNO**

PERMANENT HEAVY RECEIVER/TRANSMITTER. RANGE: 300 MILES.

THORN ▪

transmitting 〜〜〜〜

R U S S I A

⊠

★ **POSEN**

Ostrolenka ★
RUSSIAN SECOND ARMY 'BASE'

TWO HEAVY RECEIVERS/TRANSMITTERS. RANGES: 150 MILES.

★ **NOVO-GEORGIEVSK**

Cypher experts were attached to the main sets.

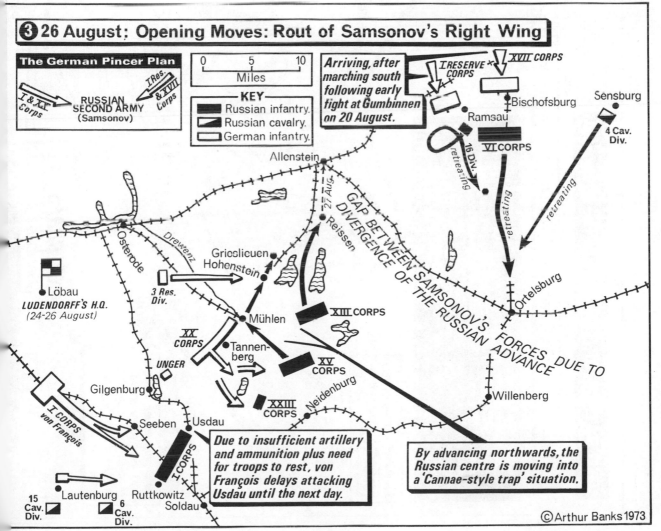

❸ 26 August: Opening Moves: Rout of Samsonov's Right Wing

The German Pincer Plan

I & XX Corps
RUSSIAN SECOND ARMY (Samsonov)
I Res. & XVII Corps

0 5 10
Miles

KEY
▰ Russian infantry.
◤ Russian cavalry.
▱ German infantry.

Arriving, after marching south following early fight at Gumbinnen on 20 August.

I RESERVE CORPS ★   XVII CORPS

Bischofsburg   Sensburg ▪

Ramsau

16 DIV. retreating   **VI CORPS**   4 Cav. Div.

Allenstein

27 Aug.

Reissen

GAP BETWEEN SAMSONOV'S FORCES DUE TO DIVERGENCE OF THE RUSSIAN ADVANCE

Grieslicuen
Hohenstein

▪ Löbau
LUDENDORFF'S H.Q. (24-26 August)

Osterode

Drewenz

3 Res. Div.

Mühlen

XIII CORPS

Ortelsburg

XX CORPS

Tannenberg

XV CORPS

UNGER

Gilgenburg ▪

XXIII CORPS

Neidenburg

Willenberg ▪

I CORPS von François

Seeben   Usdau

I CORPS

Due to insufficient artillery and ammunition plus need for troops to rest, von François delays attacking Usdau until the next day.

By advancing northwards, the Russian centre is moving into a 'Cannae-style trap' situation.

15 Cav. Div.   Lautenburg   6 Cav. Div.

Ruttkowitz   Soldau

©Arthur Banks 1973

91

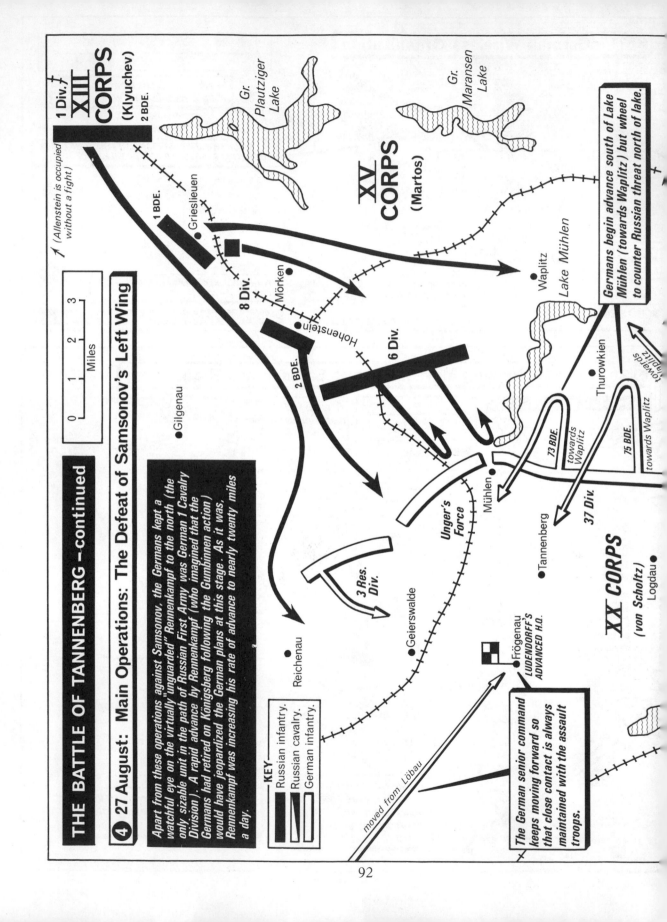

THE BATTLE OF TANNENBERG – continued

④ 27 August: Main Operations: The Defeat of Samsonov's Left Wing

Apart from these operations against Samsonov, the Germans kept a watchful eye on the virtually "unguarded" Rennenkampf to the north (the only sizable unit in the path of Russian First Army was German 1 Cavalry Division). A rapid advance by Rennenkampf (who imagined that the Germans had retired on Königsberg following the Gumbinnen action) would have jeopardized the German plans at this stage. As it was, Rennenkampf was increasing his rate of advance to nearly twenty miles a day.

KEY
- Russian infantry.
- Russian cavalry.
- German infantry.

0 1 2 3
Miles

XIII CORPS (Klyuchev)
1 Div.
2 BDE.

↑ *(Allenstein is occupied without a fight)*

Gr. Plautziger Lake

Gr. Maransen Lake

XV CORPS (Martos)

1 BDE.
Grieslieuen

8 Div.
Mörken

2 BDE.
Hohenstein

6 Div.

Waplitz
Lake Mühlen

Thurowkien

towards Waplitz

73 BDE.
towards Waplitz

75 BDE.
towards Waplitz

37 Div.

Germans begin advance south of Lake Mühlen (towards Waplitz) but wheel to counter Russian threat north of lake.

•Gilgenau

Unger's Force

Mühlen•

Tannenberg•

•Reichenau

3 Res. Div.

•Geierswalde

Frögenau
LUDENDORFF'S ADVANCED H.Q.

XX CORPS (von Scholtz)
Logdau•

moved from Löbau

The German senior command keeps moving forward so that close contact is always maintained with the assault troops.

92

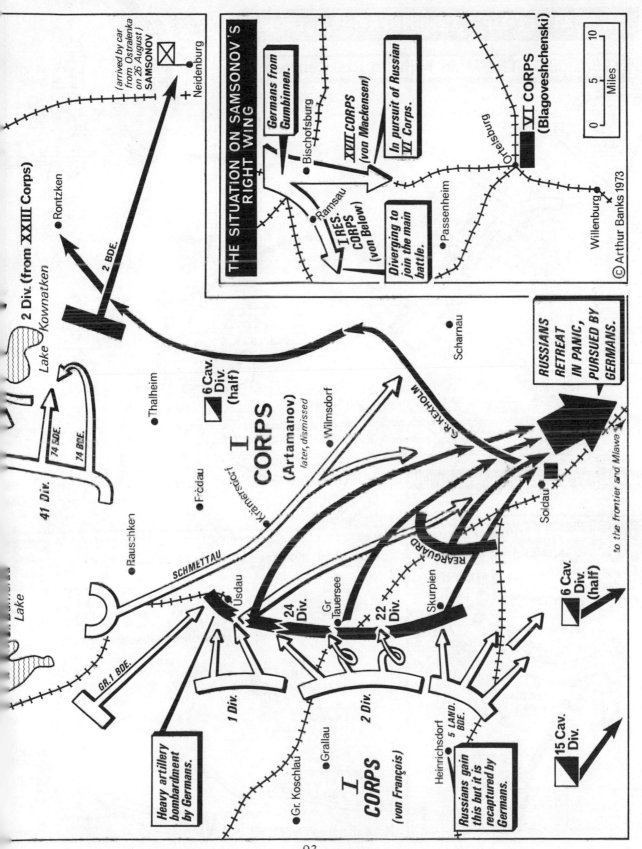

THE SITUATION ON SAMSONOV'S RIGHT WING

Germans from Gumbinnen.

Bischofsburg

XVII CORPS (von Mackensen)

In pursuit of Russian VI Corps.

VI CORPS (Blagoveshchenski)

Ortelsburg

Ramsau

I RES. CORPS (von Below)

Passenheim

Willenburg

Diverging to join the main battle.

© Arthur Banks 1973

Miles
0   5   10

(arrived by car from Ostralenka on 26 August) SAMSONOV

Neidenburg

Rontzken

2 BDE.

2 Div. (from XXIII Corps)

Lake Kownatken

41 Div.

74 SBDE.

74 BDE.

Thalheim

6 Cav. Div. (half)

later, dismissed

I CORPS (Artamanov)

Wilmsdorf

Scharnau

GR. KEKHOLM

RUSSIANS RETREAT IN PANIC, PURSUED BY GERMANS.

Fr.dau

Kränerstdorf

Pauschken

SCHMETTAU

GR. 1 BDE.

Usdau

24 Div.

Gr Tauersee

22 Div.

Skurpien

REARGUARD

Soldau

to the frontier and Mlawa

6 Cav. Div. (half)

Lake

1 Div.

2 Div.

5 LAND. BDE.

15 Cav. Div.

Heavy artillery bombardment by Germans.

Grallau

Gr. Koschlau

I CORPS (von François)

Heinrichsdorf

Russians gain this but it is recaptured by Germans.

93

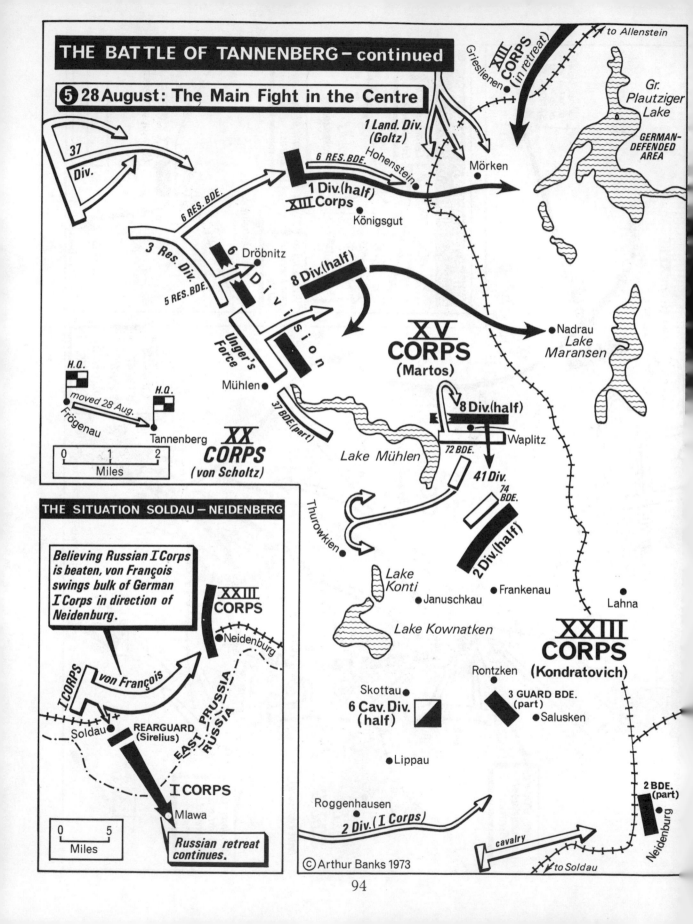

THE BATTLE OF TANNENBERG – continued

⑤ 28 August: The Main Fight in the Centre

37 Div.

to Allenstein

XIII CORPS (in retreat)

Grieslienen

Gr. Plautziger Lake

GERMAN-DEFENDED AREA

1 Land. Div. (Goltz)

6 RES. BDE.

Hohenstein

Mörken

6 RES. BDE.

3 Res. Div.

5 RES. BDE.

1 Div. (half)
XIII Corps

Königsgut

6 Dröbnitz

8 Div. (half)

D i v i s i o n

Nadrau
Lake Maransen

Unger's Force

XV CORPS (Martos)

Mühlen

8 Div. (half)

37 BDE. (part)

72 BDE.

Waplitz

H.Q.

moved 28 Aug.

Frögenau

H.Q.

Tannenberg

XX CORPS (von Scholtz)

Lake Mühlen

41 Div.

74 BDE.

2 Div. (half)

Thurowkien

0 1 2
Miles

Lake Konti

Januschkau

Frankenau

Lahna

Lake Kownatken

XXIII CORPS (Kondratovich)

Rontzken

THE SITUATION SOLDAU – NEIDENBERG

Believing Russian I Corps is beaten, von François swings bulk of German I Corps in direction of Neidenburg.

XXIII CORPS

Neidenburg

I CORPS

von François

EAST PRUSSIA
RUSSIA

Soldau

REARGUARD (Sirelius)

I CORPS

Mlawa

0 5
Miles

Russian retreat continues.

Skottau

6 Cav. Div. (half)

3 GUARD BDE. (part)

Salusken

Lippau

Roggenhausen

2 Div. (I Corps)

cavalry

2 BDE. (part)

Neidenburg

to Soldau

© Arthur Banks 1973

94

6 28 August: The Strategic Situation

This map shows the broad scene on the third day of the battle. In the south, the German pincers were beginning to close on Samsonov. In the north, Rennenkampf (his sight focused on Königsberg) was groping forward seeking a virtually non-existent foe. Meanwhile, Jilinsky (days too late) was intent on closing the gap between his two armies.

0 — Miles — 30

MAIN RESERVE

Deime

Pregel

Insterburg

Inster

Pregel

Gumbinnen

Königsberg

Zinten

Braunsberg

Allenburg

Friedland

III CORPS

XX CORPS

RENNENKAMPF

Angerapp

Pr. Eylau

Bartenstein

Landsberg

Alle

Heilsberg

Zaine

IV CORPS

II CORPS

Korschen

Rastenburg

1 Cav. Div.

Lötzen

'barrier'

Wormditt

Lautern

von Mackensen is ordered to close with the main fight.

Guttstadt

'FESTE BOYEN'

Masurian Lakes

L U D E N D O R F F

Allenstein

XVII CORPS

J I L I N S K Y

XIII CORPS

I RES. CORPS

small units

(RUSSIAN ARMY GROUP COMMANDER) UNAWARE OF SAMSONOV'S *URGENT NEED* FOR ASSISTANCE

arriving from Schleswig-Holstein by rail

1 Land.Div. (Goltz)

Osterode

Hohenstein

Passenheim

COMPLETE LACK OF CO-ORDINATED POLICY (PERSONAL ENMITY?)

Ortelsburg

VI CORPS

XX CORPS

XV CORPS

Waplitz

XXIII CORPS

Löbau

Tannenberg

S A M S O N O V

J

Willenberg

EAST PRUSSIA

R U S S I A

Gilgenburg

Neidenburg

Usdau

I CORPS

small units

Soldau

I CORPS

Mlawa

This retreating force, although in disorder, is not to be disregarded.

KEY

▮ Russian infantry.	▭ German infantry.
▱ Russian cavalry.	▨ German cavalry.
← Russian movements.	⬅ German movements.
⇨ Possible escape routes.	⌁ German fortifications.

NO MAJOR GERMAN FORCE IN THIS AREA

© Arthur Banks 1973

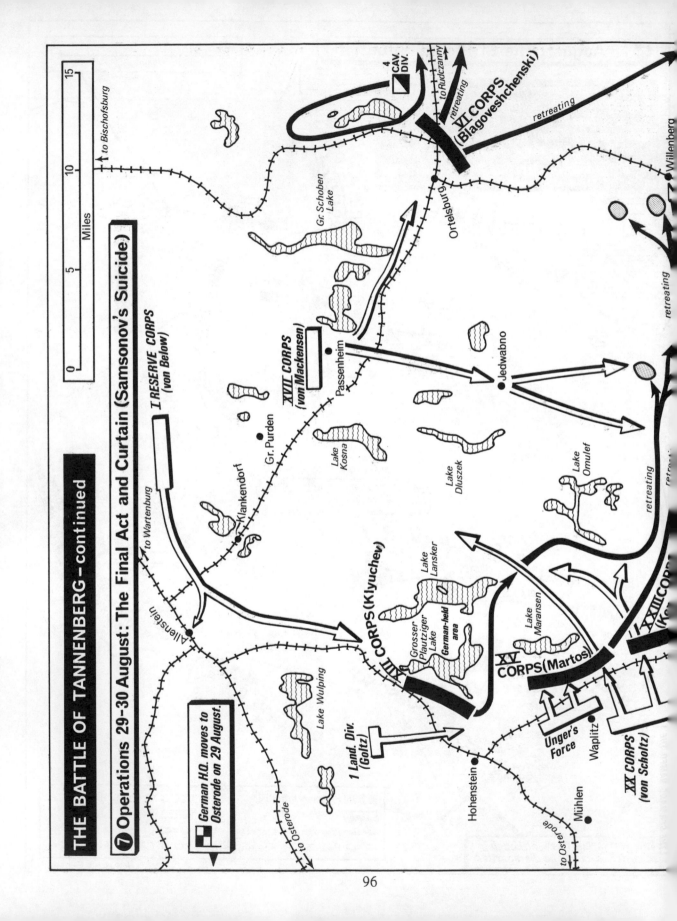

THE BATTLE OF TANNENBERG – continued

⑦ Operations 29–30 August: The Final Act and Curtain (Samsonov's Suicide)

Miles
0 5 10 15

← to Bischofsburg

4 CAV. DIV.

to Rudczanny →

VI CORPS (Blagoveshchenski)

retreating

retreating

Gr. Schoben Lake

Ortelsburg

Willenberg

retreating

I RESERVE CORPS (von Below)

XVII CORPS (von Mackensen)

Passenheim

Gr. Purden

Klankendorf

→ to Wartenburg

Jedwabno

Lake Kosna

Lake Dluszek

Lake Omulef

retreating

retreating

Allenstein

Lake Lansker

Grosser Plautziger Lake

German-held area

XIII CORPS (Klyuchev)

XV CORPS (Martos)

Lake Maransen

XXIII CORPS (Kondratovich)

German H.Q. moves to Osterode on 29 August.

1 Land. Div. (Goltz)

Lake Wulping

Unger's Force

Waplitz

XX CORPS (von Scholtz)

Hohenstein

Mühlen

to Osterode ↓

← to Osterode

96

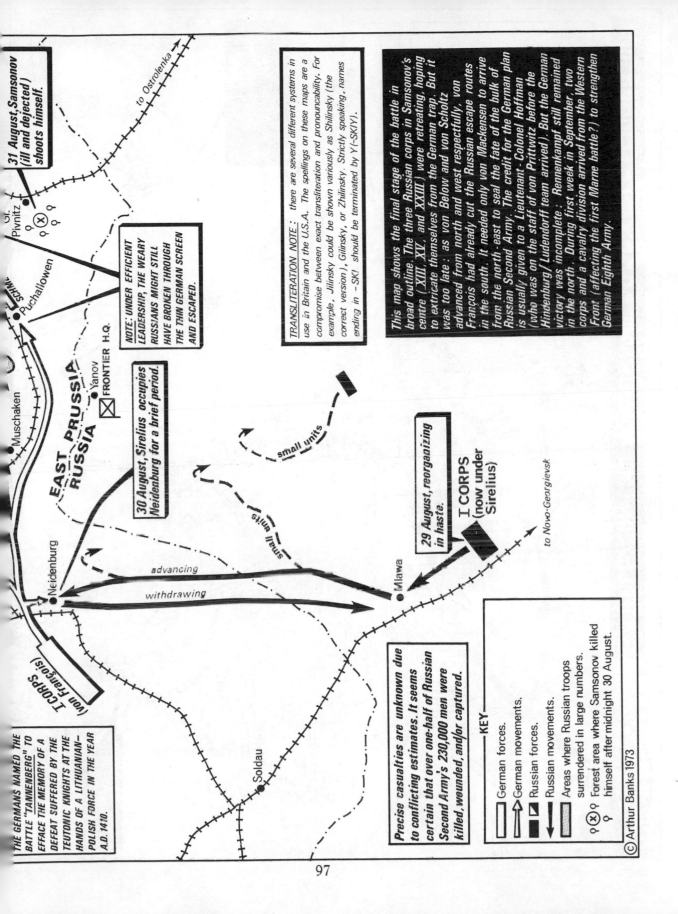

THE GERMANS NAMED THE BATTLE "TANNENBERG" TO EFFACE THE MEMORY OF A DEFEAT SUFFERED BY THE TEUTONIC KNIGHTS AT THE HANDS OF A LITHUANIAN–POLISH FORCE IN THE YEAR A.D. 1410.

I CORPS (von François)

NOTE: UNDER EFFICIENT LEADERSHIP, THE WEARY RUSSIANS MIGHT STILL HAVE BROKEN THROUGH THE THIN GERMAN SCREEN AND ESCAPED.

31 August, Samsonov (ill and dejected) shoots himself.

Gt. Pivnitz

Puchallowen

SCHN...

EAST PRUSSIA
RUSSIA

Muschaken

Yanov
FRONTIER H.Q.

TRANSLITERATION NOTE: there are several different systems in use in Britain and the U.S.A. The spellings on these maps are a compromise between exact transliteration and pronounceability. For example, Jilinsky could be shown variously as Shilinsky (the correct version), Gilinsky, or Zhilinsky. Strictly speaking, names ending in -SKI should be terminated by Y(-SKIY).

This map shows the final stage of the battle in broad outline. The three Russian corps in Samsonov's centre (XIII, XV, and XXIII) were retreating, hoping to extricate themselves from the German trap. But it was too late: as von Below and von Scholtz advanced from north and west respectively, von François had already cut the Russian escape routes in the south. It needed only von Mackensen to arrive from the north-east to seal the fate of the bulk of Russian Second Army. The credit for the German plan is usually given to a Lieutenant-Colonel Hoffman (who was on the staff of von Prittwitz before the Hindenburg/Ludendorff team arrived). But the German victory was incomplete: Rennenkampf still remained in the north. During first week in September, two corps and a cavalry division arrived from the Western Front (affecting the first Marne battle?) to strengthen German Eighth Army.

30 August, Sirelius occupies Meidenburg for a brief period.

small units

small units

Neidenburg

advancing

withdrawing

29 August, reorganizing in haste.

I CORPS (now under Sirelius)

Mlawa

to Novo-Georgievsk

to Ostrolenka

Soldau

Precise casualties are unknown due to conflicting estimates. It seems certain that over one-half of Russian Second Army's 230,000 men were killed, wounded, and/or captured.

KEY

German forces.

German movements.

Russian forces.

Russian movements.

Areas where Russian troops surrendered in large numbers.

Forest area where Samsonov killed himself after midnight 30 August.

© Arthur Banks 1973

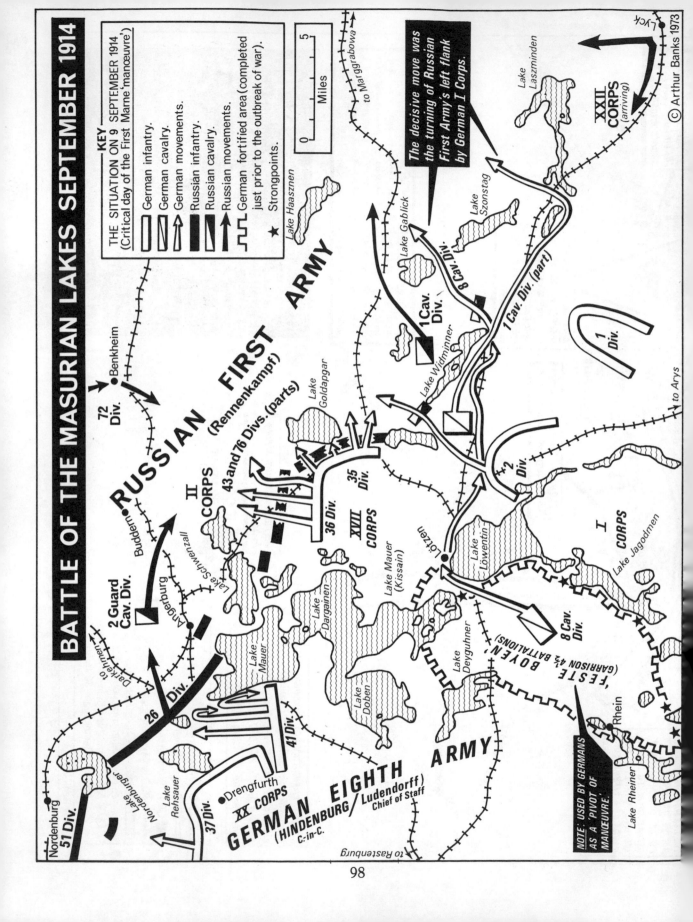

BATTLE OF THE MASURIAN LAKES SEPTEMBER 1914

KEY

THE SITUATION ON 9 SEPTEMBER 1914
(Critical day of the First Marne 'manoeuvre')

German infantry.
German cavalry.
German movements.
Russian infantry.
Russian cavalry.
Russian movements.
German fortified area (completed just prior to the outbreak of war).
Strongpoints.

© Arthur Banks 1973

to Marggrabowa

Lyck

XXII CORPS (arriving)

Lake Lasminden

The decisive move was the turning of Russian First Army's left flank by German I Corps.

Lake Szonstag

8 Cav. Div.

Lake Gablick

1 Cav. Div. (part)

1 Div.

to Arys

1 Cav. Div.

Lake Widminnen

2 Div.

RUSSIAN FIRST ARMY
(Rennenkampf)

Lake Haasznen

Benkheim

72 Div.

Lake Goldapgar

43 and 76 Divs. (parts)

II CORPS

36 Div.

35 Div.

XVII CORPS

Buddern

Lake Schwenzall

2 Guard Cav. Div.

Angerburg

Lötzen

Lake Mauer (Kissain)

I CORPS

Lake Löwentin

Lake Jagodmen

26 Div.

to Dar̃hmen

Lake Dargainen

Lake Mauer

Lake Doben

8 Cav. Div.

Lake Deyguhner

'FESTE BOYEN'
(GARRISON 4½ BATTALIONS)

Norakenbürg

51 Div.

Nordenburg

Lake Rehsauer

37 Div.

41 Div.

Drengfurth

XX CORPS

GERMAN EIGHTH ARMY
(HINDENBURG/Ludendorff)
C.-in-C.   Chief of Staff

Rhein

Lake Rheiner

NOTE: USED BY GERMANS AS A 'PIVOT OF MANOEUVRE'.

to Rastenburg

0   5
Miles

98

SERBIA IN TRAVAIL AND TRIUMPH 1914

*Punitive expedition: so-called by the Austrians *after* it had failed.

① Serbia's Strategic Position

Anti-Serbia: hence pro-Central Powers.

GERMANY
Berlin
Poland
Vienna
AUSTRIA-HUNGARY
AREA OF OPERATIONS IN 1914
ITALY
SERBIA
BULGARIA
GREECE
TURKEY
RUSSIA
RUMANIA
Constantinople

Berlin-Baghdad railway project

0 100 200 Miles

Railway link runs through Serbia.

② Austria's "Strafexpedition"*

12-24 AUGUST
AUSTRIAN SECOND ARMY

ONLY PART SECOND ARMY ENGAGED. (some units diverted to Galicia)

Sava
Shabatz
BELGRADE
Danube
Serbian units guarding Belgrade
AUSTRIAN FIFTH ARMY
VIII CORPS
VII CORPS
Jadar
Kolubara
SERBIAN MAIN FORCE
Dring
Valjevo (Putnik's H.Q.)
AUSTRIAN SIXTH ARMY
Uzhitse
SERBIAN UZHITSE (UŽICE) GROUP

STRENGTHS	
Austrians:	190,000
Serbians:	180,000
CASUALTIES	
Austrians:	38,000
Serbians:	18,000

③ Serbia the Bastion

0 20 Miles

AUSTRIAN ADVANCE (NOVEMBER)

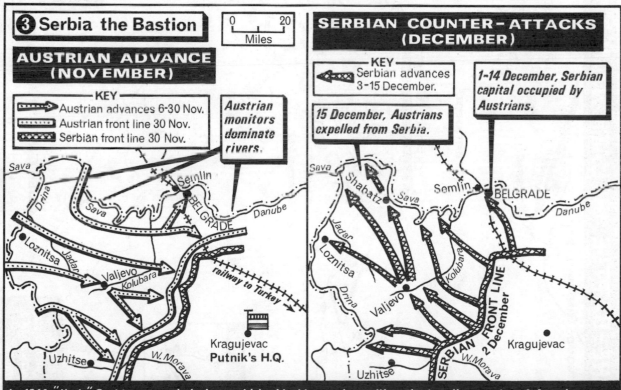

KEY
▭▭▶ Austrian advances 6-30 Nov.
▭▭▭ Austrian front line 30 Nov.
⬤⬤⬤ Serbian front line 30 Nov.

Austrian monitors dominate rivers.

Sava
Drina
Sava
Semlin
BELGRADE
Danube
Loznitsa
Jadar
Valjevo
Kolubara
railway to Turkey
Uzhitse
W. Morava
Kragujevac
Putnik's H.Q.

SERBIAN COUNTER-ATTACKS (DECEMBER)

KEY
◀◀◀ Serbian advances 3-15 December.

15 December, Austrians expelled from Serbia.

1-14 December, Serbian capital occupied by Austrians.

Sava
Shabatz
Sava
Semlin
BELGRADE
Danube
Jadar
Loznitsa
Drina
Valjevo
Kolubara
SERBIAN FRONT LINE 2 December
W. Morava
Kragujevac
Uzhitse

In 1914, "little" Serbia astounded the world by blocking and repelling the invading armies of Austria-Hungary. German reaction was derisive: "Allies? We are shackled to a corpse." It is important to note that part only of Austrian Second Army was engaged in August, and these units were gradually withdrawn to fight on the Galician front. However, a Serbian Army equalled little more than an Austrian corps.

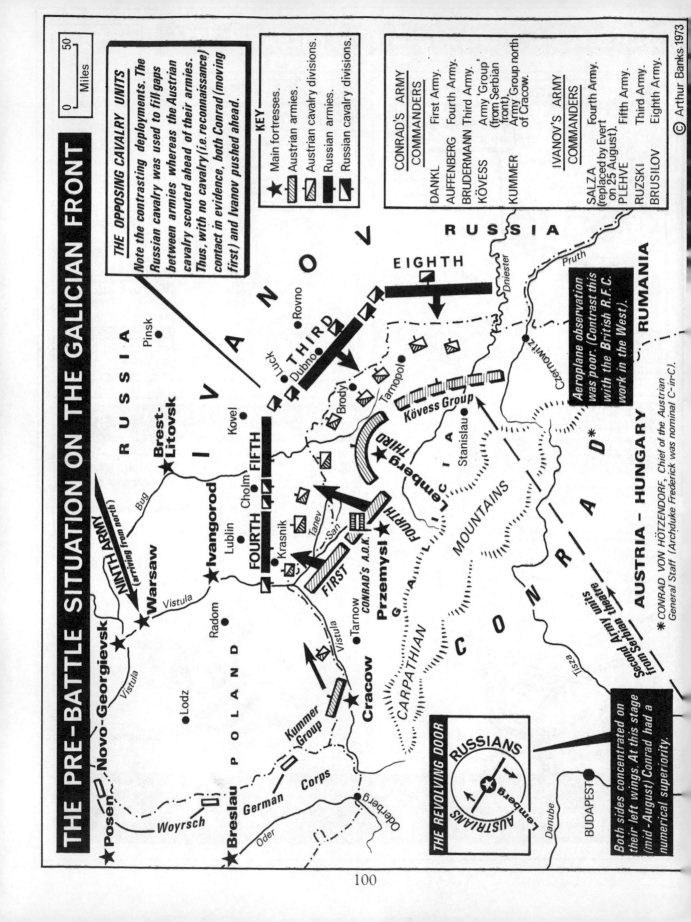

THE PRE-BATTLE SITUATION ON THE GALICIAN FRONT

0 [____] 50 Miles

THE OPPOSING CAVALRY UNITS

Note the contrasting deployments. The Russian cavalry was used to fill gaps between armies whereas the Austrian cavalry scouted ahead of their armies. Thus, with no cavalry (i.e. reconnaissance) contact in evidence, both Conrad (moving first) and Ivanov pushed ahead.

KEY

★ Main fortresses.
▨ Austrian armies.
▨ Austrian cavalry divisions.
■ Russian armies.
◧ Russian cavalry divisions.

CONRAD'S ARMY COMMANDERS

DANKL — First Army.
AUFFENBERG — Fourth Army.
BRUDERMANN — Third Army.
KÖVESS — Army 'Group' (from Serbian front).
KUMMER — Army Group north of Cracow.

IVANOV'S ARMY COMMANDERS

SALZA (replaced by Evert on 25 August). — Fourth Army.
PLEHVE — Fifth Army.
RUZSKI — Third Army.
BRUSILOV — Eighth Army.

© Arthur Banks 1973

Aeroplane observation was poor. (Contrast this with the British R.F.C. work in the West).

* CONRAD VON HÖTZENDORF, Chief of the Austrian General Staff (Archduke Frederick was nominal C-in-C).

RUSSIA

Pinsk
Rovno
Luck
Dubno
Brody
Tarnopol
Kövess Group
Stanislau
Czernowitz
Pruth
Dniester

EIGHTH
THIRD

Brest-Litovsk
Kovel
Cholm
FIFTH
Lemberg THIRD
G A L I C I A
FOURTH
CONRAD'S A.O.K.
Przemysl
FIRST
Krasnik
Tanev
San
FOURTH
Lublin
Ivangorod
Radom
Vistula
Bug
Vistula

NINTH ARMY (arriving from north)

Warsaw
Novo-Georgievsk
Posen

Lodz

P O L A N D

Tarnow
Cracow
Kummer Group
CARPATHIAN MOUNTAINS
C O N R A D*
AUSTRIA – HUNGARY

German Corps
Woyrsch
Breslau
Oderberg
Oder

Second Army units from Serbian theatre

Tisza
Danube
BUDAPEST
RUMANIA

I V A N O V

THE REVOLVING DOOR

RUSSIANS
Lemberg
AUSTRIANS

Both sides concentrated on their left wings. At this stage (mid-August) Conrad had a numerical superiority.

100

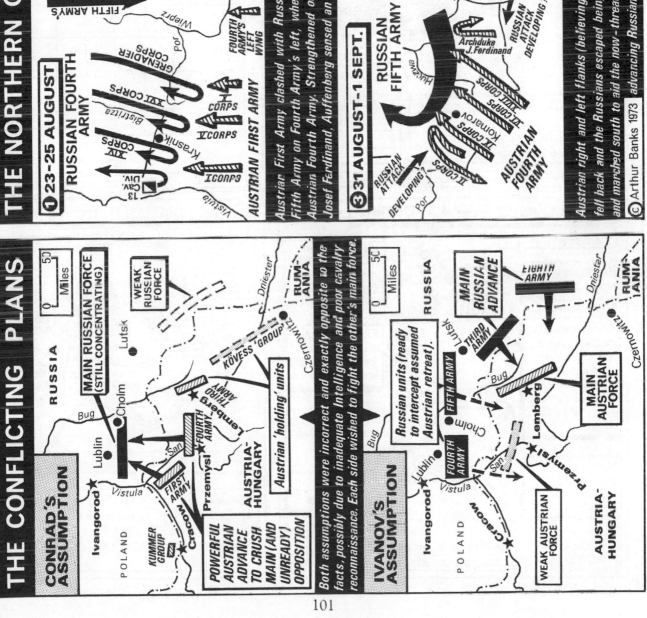

THE NORTHERN CLASH

② 26-30 AUGUST

RUSSIAN FIFTH ARMY

Bug

Sop

XXV CORPS

XIX CORPS

V CORPS

XVII CORPS

Komarov

THREE DIVISIONS FROM THIRD ARMY, PLUS CAVALRY.

XVII CORPS

Sokolive

II CORPS

IX CORPS

II CORPS

Por

Wieprz

FIRST ARMY'S RIGHT WING

AUSTRIAN FOURTH ARMY (Auffenberg)

① 23-25 AUGUST

RUSSIAN FOURTH ARMY

FIFTH ARMY'S RIGHT WING

Wieprz

GRENADIER CORPS

XVII CORPS

Bistritza

I CORPS

V CORPS

XIV CORPS

Krasnik

13 Cav. Div.

GRDS CORPS

I CORPS

FOURTH ARMY'S LEFT WING

Por

Vistula

AUSTRIAN FIRST ARMY

Austrian First Army clashed with Russian Fourth Army which withdrew. Russian Fifth Army on Fourth Army's left, wheeled right thus exposing its left flank to the Austrian Fourth Army. Strengthened on his right by divisions under Archduke Josef Ferdinand, Auffenberg sensed an opportunity to envelop the Russians.

④ 2 SEPTEMBER

RUSSIAN FIFTH ARMY (Plehve)

AUSTRIAN FOURTH ARMY

RUSSIAN THIRD ARMY

③ 31 AUGUST-1 SEPT.

RUSSIAN FIFTH ARMY

Bug

RUSSIAN ATTACK DEVELOPING?

Archduke J. Ferdinand

Hukawa

XVII CORPS

II CORPS

IX CORPS

Komarov

RUSSIAN ATTACK DEVELOPING?

II CORPS

Por

AUSTRIAN FOURTH ARMY

Austrian right and left flanks (believing enemy units to be moving towards their rears) fell back and the Russians escaped being encircled. Auffenberg reversed his main force and marched south to aid the now-threatened Austrian Third Army (see next page). The advancing Russian Third Army swung north-west to aid Plehve.

© Arthur Banks 1973

THE CONFLICTING PLANS

CONRAD'S ASSUMPTION

0 50 Miles

RUSSIA

Lutsk

MAIN RUSSIAN FORCE (STILL CONCENTRATING)

WEAK RUSSIAN FORCE

Dniester

RUM-ANIA

Czernowitz

KÖVESS 'GROUP'

Cholm

Bug

Lublin

Lemberg

THIRD ARMY

Vistula

Ivangorod

Przemysl

FOURTH ARMY

FIRST ARMY

San

Austrian 'holding' units

AUSTRIA-HUNGARY

POLAND

Cracow

KUMMER GROUP

POWERFUL AUSTRIAN ADVANCE TO CRUSH MAIN (AND UNREADY) OPPOSITION

Both assumptions were incorrect and exactly opposite to the facts, possibly due to inadequate Intelligence and poor cavalry reconnaissance. Each side wished to fight the other's main force.

IVANOV'S ASSUMPTION

0 50 Miles

RUSSIA

MAIN RUSSIAN ADVANCE

EIGHTH ARMY

Lutsk

THIRD ARMY

Dniester

RUM-ANIA

Czernowitz

Russian units (ready to intercept assumed Austrian retreat).

FIFTH ARMY

Bug

Cholm

Lublin

Lemberg

Vistula

Ivangorod

FOURTH ARMY

San

Przemysl

MAIN AUSTRIAN FORCE

Cracow

WEAK AUSTRIAN FORCE

POLAND

AUSTRIA-HUNGARY

101

LEMBERG-PRZEMYSL OPERATIONS

The Austro-Hungarian armies were multi-racial: the graph below gives a broad guide to their heterogenous make-up.

❶ The Russian Advance on Lemberg

26-31 AUGUST

RUSSIAN THIRD ARMY (Ruzski)

AUSTRIAN THIRD ARMY (Brudermann)

Cavalry

Lemberg

Dniester

KÖVESS "GROUP" part SECOND ARMY (rest confronting Serbia)

Brzezany

Złota Lipa

G. Lipa

RUSSIAN EIGHTH ARMY (Brusilov)

Halicz

Dniester

KEY
- ◀ Russian attacks (corps shown).
- —x— Russian army boundary.
- ▨ Austrian line 26 August.
- ◀ Austrian retreat (in disorder).

0 10 20 30
Miles

(Senior officers largely of German race)

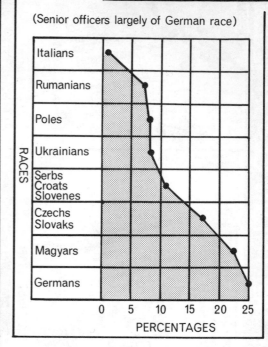

RACES		PERCENTAGES
Italians		
Rumanians		
Poles		
Ukrainians		
Serbs Croats Slovenes		
Czechs Slovaks		
Magyars		
Germans		

0 5 10 15 20 25
PERCENTAGES

❷ The Overall Scene in Outline

3-11 SEPTEMBER

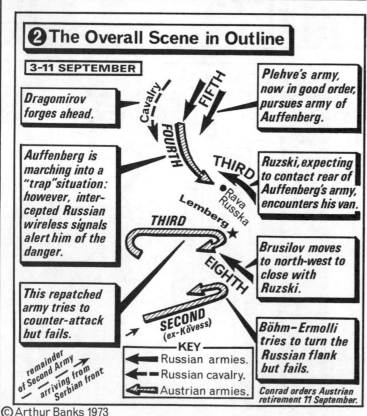

Dragomirov forges ahead.

Auffenberg is marching into a "trap" situation: however, intercepted Russian wireless signals alert him of the danger.

This repatched army tries to counter-attack but fails.

remainder of Second Army arriving from Serbian front

Cavalry

FIFTH

FOURTH

THIRD

Lemberg

Rava Russka

THIRD

EIGHTH

SECOND (ex-Kövess)

Plehve's army, now in good order, pursues army of Auffenberg.

Ruzski, expecting to contact rear of Auffenberg's army, encounters his van.

Brusilov moves to north-west to close with Ruzski.

Böhm-Ermolli tries to turn the Russian flank but fails.

Conrad orders Austrian retirement 11 September.

KEY
- ◀ Russian armies.
- ◀- - Russian cavalry.
- ◁ Austrian armies.

❸ The Austrian Retreat

11 SEPT.- 3 OCT.

Fresh army arriving.

Vistula

Ivangorod

Lublin

NINTH

FOURTH

FIFTH

FIRST

FIRST

FOURTH

San

THIRD

Rava Russka

Lemberg

Cracow

Vistula

Tarnow

Dunajetz

Przemysl

Gorlice

THIRD

SECOND

EIGHTH

Dniester

0 20
Miles

Invested by Russians 24 Sept.- 9 Oct.

KEY
- ◀ Russian armies (attacking).
- ▨ Austrian line 11 September.
- ◀ Austrian armies (retreating).
- ▲▲▲ Austrian line (3 October).
- ✂ Fierce clash.

© Arthur Banks 1973

THE DISCORDANT VIEWS OF CONRAD & MOLTKE

Four double-gauge railway lines running west to east across Germany form the basis of her military mobility. (Two corps west→east Sept.).

BELGIUM
WESTERN FRONT
FRANCE

E. PRUSSIA
EASTERN FRONT
POLAND

GERMANY
Berlin
"NEGLECTED" RAILWAY

RUSSIA

Vienna
AUSTRIA-HUNGARY

SERBIA

MOLTKE

This commander's attention is fixed upon the Western Front: he desires a quick victory over France so that he can switch Germany's military might against Russia. He is irritated by Conrad's exhortations for aid, regarding them as a distraction from the main task in hand.

14 September 1914, von Falkenhayn replaces Moltke (who has bungled application of amended Schlieffen Plan). The new Chief of the German General Staff recognizes Conrad's plight but is adamant that any German aid to Austria must come from East Prussia, not the Western Front.

Moltke's irritation with Conrad turns to disdain when Austria fails to defeat "little" Serbia in August and the Serbs raid Hungary (Sept.).

CONRAD

This commander expects German aid from the outset (it was implied rather than promised): he feels betrayed and snubbed. (Austria's main foe is Russia, not France).

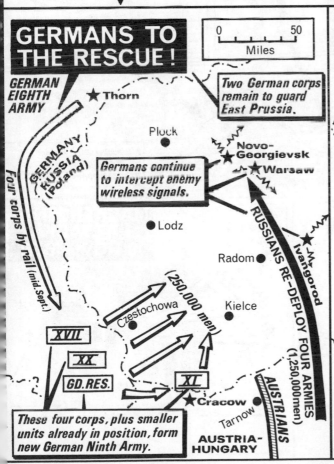

GERMANS TO THE RESCUE!

0 — 50 Miles

GERMAN EIGHTH ARMY

★ Thorn

Plock •

Novo-Georgievsk ★

★ Warsaw

Two German corps remain to guard East Prussia.

Germans continue to intercept enemy wireless signals.

GERMANY (RUSSIA (Poland)

Four corps by rail (mid. Sept.)

Lodz •

Radom •

★ Ivangorod

RUSSIANS RE-DEPLOY FOUR ARMIES (1,250,000 men)

(250,000 men)

Czestochowa
Kielce •

XVII

XX

GD. RES.

XI

★ Cracow
Tarnow •

AUSTRIANS

AUSTRIA-HUNGARY

These four corps, plus smaller units already in position, form new German Ninth Army.

CENTRAL POWERS ON THE MOVE

0 — 20 Miles

Vistula
Plock •

② Novo-Georgievsk ★
★ Warsaw
⑤

RUSSIA

④

G E R M A N Y

Lodz •

P O L A N D

GERMANS

GERMANS

Radom
Hindenburg

⑨ Ivangorod

San

Czestochowa •

AUSTRIANS

Vistula

AUSTRIA-HUNGARY

★ Cracow

KEY

GER. AUS.
Central Powers' line 28 September (start of advance).
Central Powers' line 17 October (limit of advance).
Central Powers' drives.
● Russian armies.

© Arthur Banks 1973

103

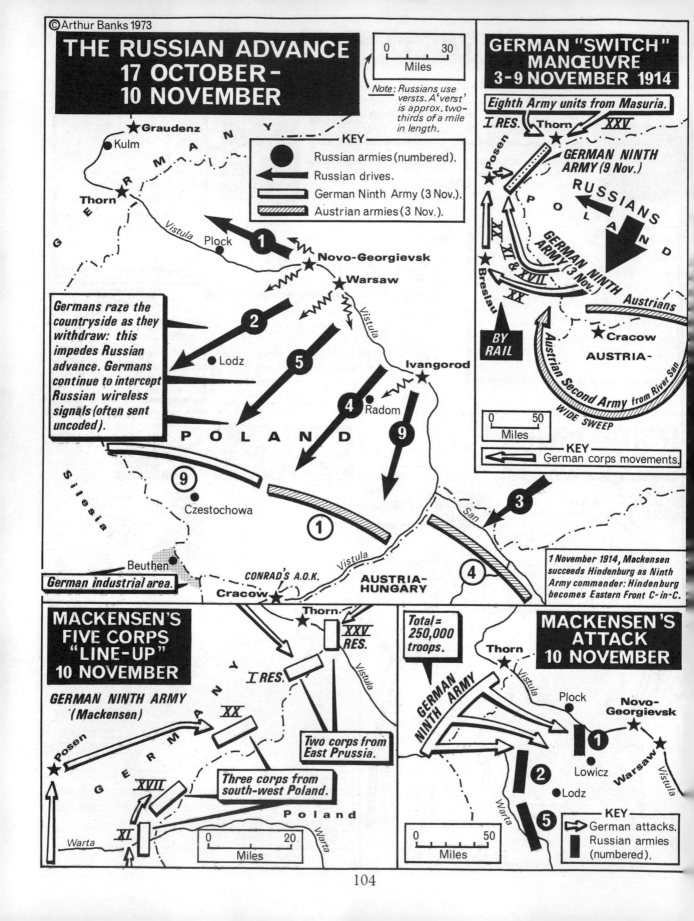

© Arthur Banks 1973

THE RUSSIAN ADVANCE 17 OCTOBER – 10 NOVEMBER

0 — 30 Miles

Note: Russians use versts. A 'verst' is approx. two-thirds of a mile in length.

KEY
● Russian armies (numbered).
← Russian drives.
▭ German Ninth Army (3 Nov.).
▨ Austrian armies (3 Nov.).

Graudenz
Kulm
G E R M A N Y
Thorn
Vistula
Plock
1
Novo-Georgievsk
Warsaw
Vistula

Germans raze the countryside as they withdraw: this impedes Russian advance. Germans continue to intercept Russian wireless signals (often sent uncoded).

2
Lodz
5
Ivangorod
4 Radom
9

Silesia
9
Czestochowa
①
P O L A N D
San
3
Beuthen
German industrial area.
CONRAD'S A.O.K.
Vistula
AUSTRIA-HUNGARY
Cracow
④

GERMAN "SWITCH" MANŒUVRE 3–9 NOVEMBER 1914

Eighth Army units from Masuria.
I RES. Thorn XXV
Posen
GERMAN NINTH ARMY (9 Nov.)
R U S S I A N S
P O L A N D
Breslau
XX
XI & XVII
XX
GERMAN NINTH ARMY (3 Nov.)
BY RAIL
Austrian Second Army from River San
WIDE SWEEP
Cracow
AUSTRIA-
Austrians

0 — 50 Miles

KEY
← German corps movements.

1 November 1914, Mackensen succeeds Hindenburg as Ninth Army commander: Hindenburg becomes Eastern Front C-in-C.

MACKENSEN'S FIVE CORPS "LINE-UP" 10 NOVEMBER

GERMAN NINTH ARMY *(Mackensen)*
Thorn
XXV RES.
I RES.
Posen
G E R M A N Y
XX
XVII
XI
Warta
P o l a n d
Warta

Two corps from East Prussia.
Three corps from south-west Poland.

0 — 20 Miles

MACKENSEN'S ATTACK 10 NOVEMBER

Total = 250,000 troops.

Thorn
Vistula
Plock
Novo-Georgievsk
1
GERMAN NINTH ARMY
Lowicz
Warsaw
Vistula
2
Lodz
Warta
5

KEY
⇨ German attacks.
■ Russian armies (numbered).

0 — 50 Miles

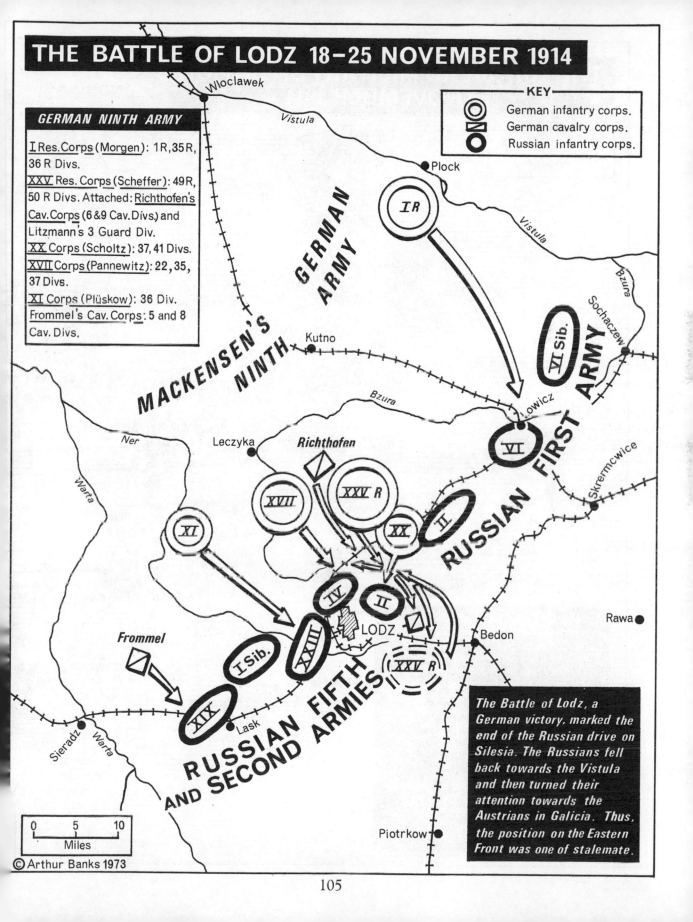

THE BATTLE OF LODZ 18–25 NOVEMBER 1914

KEY
- German infantry corps.
- German cavalry corps.
- Russian infantry corps.

GERMAN NINTH ARMY

<u>I</u> Res. Corps (Morgen): 1R, 35R, 36 R Divs.

<u>XXV</u> Res. Corps (Scheffer): 49R, 50 R Divs. Attached: <u>Richthofen's</u> Cav. Corps (6 & 9 Cav. Divs.) and Litzmann's 3 Guard Div.

<u>XX</u> Corps (Scholtz): 37, 41 Divs.

<u>XVII</u> Corps (Pannewitz): 22, 35, 37 Divs.

<u>XI</u> Corps (Plüskow): 36 Div.
<u>Frommel's Cav. Corps</u>: 5 and 8 Cav. Divs.

Wloclawek

Vistula

Plock

GERMAN ARMY

MACKENSEN'S NINTH

Kutno

Leczyka

Richthofen

Ner

Warta

Frommel

Sieradz

Warta

Lask

Bzura

Vistula

Sochaczew

VI Sib.

Lowicz

VI

RUSSIAN FIRST ARMY

Skrermcwice

XVII

XXV R

XI

XX

II

IV

II

XXIII

I Sib.

LODZ

XXV R

Bedon

Rawa

XIX

RUSSIAN FIFTH AND SECOND ARMIES

Piotrkow

The Battle of Lodz, a German victory, marked the end of the Russian drive on Silesia. The Russians fell back towards the Vistula and then turned their attention towards the Austrians in Galicia. Thus, the position on the Eastern Front was one of stalemate.

| 0 | 5 | 10 |
Miles

© Arthur Banks 1973

105

THE EUROPEAN MILITARY SITUATION
30 NOVEMBER 1914

0   200
Miles

NORWAY
CHRISTIANIA

SWEDEN

Skagerrak

Kattegat

DENMARK

COPENH

Glasgow

Edinburgh

NORTH SEA

Kiel Canal

HELIGOLAND

Kiel

Hamburg

IRELAND
Dublin

Bremen

Elbe

BERL

Manchester

THE HAGUE

Amsterdam

G E R M A

BRITAIN

Antwerp

BRUSSELS

BELGIUM

Liège

Rhine

Dresden

LONDON

Southampton

Rouen

LUX.

Frankfurt

ATLANTIC

English Channel

Aisne

Pra

OCEAN

Brest

PARIS

Marne

Seine

> 2 August, occupied
> by Germans.

Munich

Danu

Loire

Belfort

BERNE

Innsbruck

Bay of Biscay

SWITZ.

F R A N C E

Rhône

Milan

Venice

Tri

Po

Bordeaux

Turin

Genoa

AU

Marseilles

Florence

I T A L

SPAIN

Barcelona

CORSICA

ROM

BALEARIC ISLANDS

SARDINIA

TYRRHEN SEA

Paler

MEDITERRANEAN

Towards the end of November 1914 the initial
energetic thrusts of the Central Powers had
exhausted themselves. After four months
of activity (the Central Powers meeting with
determined resistance on both the Eastern
and Western Fronts), the war had reached
a position of stalemate. This map depicts
the "de facto" situation that existed at this
stage of operations. As opposed to large-
scale movements, the campaign settled
into a localised trench-warfare situation,
each side testing the other, rather than
initiating a definite major advance.
Consequently the mobile war switched to
other areas (e.g. the war at sea, in the air,
the Dardanelles, Mesopotamia, etc.) in the
hope of achieving "side-show" breakthroughs
that would affect the main battle fronts.

Oran

ALGIERS

Bône

Bizerta

TUNIS

© Arthur Banks 1973

106

KEY

- The Entente Powers and associates on 30 November 1914.
- The Central Powers on 30 November 1914. *Note:* Britain declared war on Turkey on 5 November 1914.
- Neutral states on 30 November 1914.
- The Western and Eastern fronts on 30 November 1914.

Gulf of Bothnia

FINLAND

PETROGRAD

Reval

STOCKHOLM

Moscow

Riga

Gulf of Finland

Libau

Smolensk

BALTIC SEA

Kovno

Gumbinnen

Vilna

Königsberg

Minsk

R U S S I A

Danzig

Grodno

Tannenberg

Brest-Litovsk

Vistula

Lodz

Warsaw

sen

Oder

POLAND

Kiev

Dnieper

Lemberg

Dniester

Pressburg

Ticza

Odessa

ENNA

Budapest

Pruth

AUSTRIA – HUNGARY

29 November, vacated by Serbs.

RUMANIA

BLACK SEA

Drava

DUCHAREST

Sava

BELGRADE

Danube

Frontier operations.

BULGARIA

SERBIA

SOFIA

MONTE-NEGRO

ALBANIA

Salonika

Constantinople

Angora

Brindisi

GREECE

Dardanelles

OTTOMAN EMPIRE [TURKEY]

ATHENS

AEGEAN SEA

Smyrna

IONIAN SEA

RHODES

5 November, annexed by Britain.

CYPRUS

Messina

SICILY

SEA

CRETE

THE SITUATION AT THE END OF THE YEAR 1914

By the end of the year 1914 there was deadlock over every battlefront in Europe. From the Swiss frontier northwards fortified lines ran by way of the Vosges, the hills of the Meuse, the Argonne and the Chemin des Dames to the Aisne and up to Armentières and the Ypres Salient, reaching down to the inundated fields around Dixmude and so to the sand dunes of the North Sea. A tenth of metropolitan France, including the main French coalfields, and almost the whole of Belgium were behind the German trenches, and remained so throughout the war. The line of the Western Front did not move as much as ten miles in either direction for the following two and a half years. In the East, stalemate had come only through the onset of winter and there were no continuous systems of entrenchment to rule out a war movement. Yet there seemed little prospect of a decisive victory, and both sides had by now abandoned all hope of a short war.

Both the British and the German public were surprised by what was happening in the war at sea. After more than a decade of naval rivalry it was assumed there would be a naval battle between the great capital ships at an early date. But the Kaiser personally vetoed an engagement which might have destroyed his battle fleet until after the enemy fleet had been weakened by other means. The Germans accordingly made extensive use of their submarines (see page 246) and of minefields, although there was a sharp clash between cruisers and destroyers in Heligoland Bight at the end of August (see pages 242–245) and twice the German battle-cruisers took advantage of the long winter nights to cross the North Sea and bombard the East coast of England (see page 255). It was accepted in Britain that the days of isolation were over, a point emphasised on Christmas Eve when the first aerial bombs were dropped on English soil, at Dover.

The main clashes of sea power were, however, on the oceans. Vice-Admiral von Spee's squadron caused havoc in the Pacific and won a naval victory off Coronel before being defeated at the Falkland Islands early in December (pages 238, 240–241). The German cruiser *Emden* effectively disrupted trade in the East Indies (page 239), but by the end of the year, the British had reasserted their naval supremacy, clearing the seas of surface raiders and virtually destroying Germany's overseas commerce. Japanese, Australian and New Zealand forces mopped up Germany's island possessions in the Pacific, and British and Japanese troops occupied Kiaochow (the small German protectorate on the coast of China) in November. General von Lettow-Vorbeck retained firm control of German East Africa (pages 216–218) and the South Africans were in some difficulty in German South-West Africa but Togoland had surrendered and there was minimal resistance in the interior of the Cameroons.

The attention of the British outside Europe was from now on primarily concentrated on the Ottoman Empire. Turkey, long under the influence of Germany militarily, entered the War early in November, hoping to gain territory from Russia in the Caucasus and to recover, with German backing, her influence in the Balkans. The handing over by Germany to Turkey of the battle-cruiser *Goeben* and the cruiser *Breslau* (page 237) finally decided Turkey's course of action. Militarily Turkey was a distraction both to Britain and Russia, but her entry into the war suggested a possible alternative strategy—of toppling Germany, not on the main battlefronts, but by destroying her supports and entering Central Europe by the back door. It seemed the only way to make the war once more fluid. From such ideas developed the Dardanelles and Gallipoli campaigns, and belatedly the expedition to Salonika.

THE GALLIPOLI CAMPAIGN

The attempt to force the Dardanelles and gain control of Constantinople and the Straits was the first strategically imaginative project of the war. Its origins lie in a proposal made by Churchill to the War Council of 25 November 1914. He argued that 'the ideal method of defending Egypt' and the Suez Canal from an invading Turkish army 'was by an attack on the Gallipoli Peninsula' which, if successful, would enable the Allies to 'dictate terms at Constantinople'. Subsequently the possibilities of using British naval power to open up a new front against the enemy appealed to other members of the War Council, including Lloyd George, Admiral Sir John Fisher and the Secretary of the Council, Colonel Hankey. There was much debate over the best place for a landing, Lloyd George urging the occupation of Salonika and the transportation by rail of an army to aid Serbia against Austria-Hungary, and this plan was favoured by two leading French Generals, Gallieni and Franchet d'Espèrey. The Dardanelles project had, however, three major advantages: it appeared to be primarily a naval operation; it would rally Turkey's traditional enemies among the Balkan nations to the Allied side; and it would open up a short warm-water route for supplies to Russia. It was this third consideration which was decisive: for at the end of December gloomy reports were received from Petrograd, indicating an acute shortage of munitions and appealing for British help in relieving Turkish pressure on the Russian armies in the Caucasus. The War Council agreed on a naval expedition 'with Constantinople as its objective' on 15 January 1915.

The Gallipoli enterprise falls into four distinctive phases (which may be studied in pages 110–129, supplemented for naval and submaritime operations by pages 252–254). Naval bombardments on 19 and 26 February were followed by nearly three weeks of abortive mine-sweeping before the principal attempt by capital ships to force the passage of the Dardanelles on 18 March. Preparations were then made for using British, Australian and New Zealand troops for a series of landings on the Gallipoli peninsula while a French army corps temporarily occupied Kum Kale on the mainland and made a feint assault on Besika Bay. These landings were carried out on 25 April in an atmosphere of almost crusading ardour, but without proper landing craft and with no real training in amphibious operations. The Anzacs established themselves in a cove of steep cliffs and backed by a gorge covered in scrub, where it was difficult to penetrate more than half a mile inland. The British made more headway at Cape Helles, but suffered appalling casualties. Further landings in early August came near to success, but by the end of the summer the troops on the peninsula were as effectively pinned down in a network of trenches as the armies in France and Flanders; four thousand men died in seeking to secure four hundred yards on a mile front. Kitchener went out to investigate in November and accepted the inevitability of evacuation. The final phase, the withdrawal from Anzac and Suvla in December and from Helles a fortnight later, was the most successful aspect of the campaign.

The expedition failed because of confused leadership, insufficient co-ordination, inadequate planning, and sheer lack of troops and firepower; perhaps, too, it failed because the landings were made at the tip of the peninsula rather than at its neck, where there would have been greater freedom of manouvere. Failure at the Dardanelles cost Churchill his predominant position in the War Council; it deprived the Allies of a grand Balkan alliance against Berlin; above all, it completed the isolation of Russia. Gallipoli, with its high hopes twice nearly realised, was a tragic disappointment which discredited imaginative strategic thought in London for many years ahead.

TURKISH DEFENCES AT THE DARDANELLES 1915

This map depicts the Turkish defences guarding the Dardanelles prior to the Allied naval attacks during February and March 1915. Following a Russian request to the Western Allies at the end of 1914 for a "second front" to be created against Turkey to ease pressure on the Russian forces in the Caucasus, British naval authorities devised a three-point plan to force the Dardanelles passage. First, a naval bombardment of the entrance forts; secondly, a minefield-clearing operation; thirdly, a naval force to sail right through the Dardanelles to the Sea of Marmara, and thence on to the Turkish capital of Constantinople.

Vice-Admiral Carden, commander of the British squadron in the Aegean, considered that he would require the following units to successfully force the Dardanelles passage: 12 battleships, 3 battlecruisers, 3 light cruisers, 16 destroyers, 6 submarines, 4 seaplanes, 12 minesweepers, and a plentiful supply of ammunition.

KEY TO MINEFIELDS

1 – 26 February 1915.
3 – 5 November 1914 - 19 February 1915.
4 – 5 November 1914 - 15 February 1915.
7 – 5 November 1914 - 15 February 1915.
8 – 5 November 1914 - 19 February 1915.
11 – 8 March 1915 (laid by 'Nousret').

Note: The correct name for Achi Baba was Alchi Tepe; this was due to a spelling error on British maps, but Achi Baba became the accepted name.

Note: spellings are those used on British maps in 1915. For example, Chanak Kale is used instead of the Turkish name Çanakkale. The modern romanized spelling of Turkish was not introduced until 1925; prior to that, Turkish map names were shown in Arabic characters.

REVOLUTION UPON ALLIED FLEET'S ARRIVAL? TURKEY TO MAKE PEACE?

BULGARIA (INTERESTED OBSERVER)

Black Sea

Bosporus

Constantinople (Turkish capital)

Sea of Marmara

EUROPEAN TURKEY

DARDANELLES

ASIATIC TURKEY

Aegean Sea

Boghali

Koja Dere

KOJA CHEMEN TEPE (971 ft.)
BESIM TEPE (900 ft.)
CHUNUK BAIR (850 ft.)
Sari Bair Ridge
Battleship Ridge

Ari Burnu

Gaba Tepe

Maidos

Derma Burnu

Kilid Bahr

Namazieh

Hamidieh

Rumili Medjidieh

Yildiz

Hauslar

Entrance to Sea of Marmara

Nagara

Nagara Burnu

Abydos Pt.

Anadolu Mejidieh

Medjidieh Avan

Chanak Kale

Chemenlik Fort

THE NARROWS

AEGEAN

Gun emplacements

Two 26-cm. L/22 Krupp
Five 24-cm. L/22 Krupp
Five 15-cm. L/26 Krupp

Three 28-cm. L/22 Krupp
Four 26-cm. L/22 Krupp
Two 24-cm. L/22 Krupp
Two 21-cm. L/22 Krupp
Three 15-cm. L/22 Krupp

Six 21-cm. mortars

One 35·5-cm. L/35 Krupp
One 35·5-cm. L/22 Krupp
One 24-cm. L/35 Krupp
Two 21-cm. L/35 Krupp
Four 15-cm. howitzers

Two 35·5-cm. L/35 Krupp

Six 24-cm. L/22 Krupp

One 28-cm. L/22 Krupp
One 26-cm. L/22 Krupp
Nine 24-cm. L/22 Krupp
Two 24-cm. L/35 Krupp
Three 21-cm. L/22 Krupp
Three 15-cm. howitzers

Two 35·5-cm. L/35 Krupp

Two 28-cm. L/22 Krupp
Four 24-cm. L/35 Krupp

Six 15-cm. L/26 Krupp

Four 12-cm. siege guns

Six 4·7-cm. howitzers

Four 7·5-cm. L/30 quick-firers

Minefields
53 mines
29
26
39
2 mines
3
5

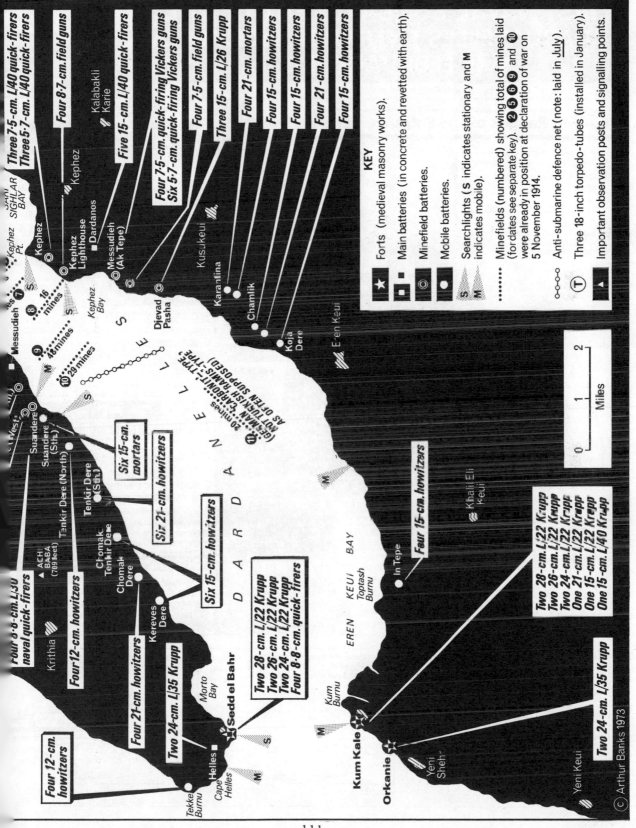

Three 7·5-cm. L/40 quick-firers
Three 5·7-cm. L/40 quick-firers

Four 8·7-cm. field guns

Kalabakli
Karie

Five 15-cm. L/40 quick-firers

Four 7·5-cm. quick-firing Vickers guns
Six 5·7-cm. quick-firing Vickers guns

Four 7·5-cm. field guns

Three 15-cm. L/26 Krupp

Four 21-cm. mortars

Four 15-cm. howitzers

Four 15-cm. howitzers

Four 21-cm. howitzers

Four 15-cm. howitzers

SARI
SIGHLAR
BAY

Kephez

Kephez

Kephez Pt.

Kephez
Lighthouse   Dardanos
Messudieh
(Ak Tepe)

Kusukeui

Karanlina

Chamlik

Djevad
Pasha

Kephez
Bay

Koja
Dere

E'en Keui

Messudieh ⑦ S
⑧ 16
mines
S

⑨ 48 mines

M

⑩ 29 mines

West

Suandere

Suandere
(Sth)

Tenkir Dere (North)

......20 mines
(GERMAN 'CARBONIT'-TYPE
AND TURKISH 'RAMIS'-TYPE:
AS OFTEN SUPPOSED)

D A R D A N E L L E S

Six 15-cm. mortars

Tenkir Dere
(Sth.)

Six 21-cm. howitzers

Six 15-cm. howitzers

Four 15-cm. howitzers

Khalil Eli
Keui

Two 28-cm. L/22 Krupp
Two 26-cm. L/22 Krupp
Two 24-cm. L/22 Krupp
One 21-cm. L/22 Krupp
One 15-cm. L/22 Krupp
One 15-cm. L/40 Krupp

In Tepe

EREN   KEUI   BAY

Toptash
Burnu

Two 24-cm. L/35 Krupp

Four 6·5-cm. L/30
naval quick-firers

Krithia

Four 12-cm. howitzers

ACHI
BABA
(709 feet)

Chomak
Tenkir Dere

Chomak
Dere

Four 21-cm. howitzers

Kereves
Dere

Two 24-cm. L/35 Krupp

Morto
Bay

Sedd el Bahr

Six 15-cm. howitzers

Two 28-cm. L/22 Krupp
Two 26-cm. L/22 Krupp
Two 24-cm. L/22 Krupp
Four 8·8-cm. quick-firers

Kum
Burnu

EREN KEUI BAY

Kum Kale

Orkanie

Yeni
Sheh-

Yeni Keui

Four 12-cm.
howitzers

Helles

Cape
Helles

M

Tekke
Burnu

© Arthur Banks 1973

0   1   2

Miles

111

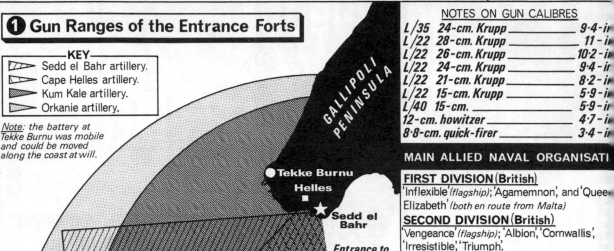

FIRST NAVAL BOMBARDMENT OF THE DARDANELLES ENTRANCE WORKS 19 FEBRUARY 1915

GUN RANGES OF TURKIS[H] ENTRANCE WORKS

Allied estimated maximum ranges of the main guns :
L/35..........12,000 ya[rds]
L/22..........10,000 yar[ds]
(effective ranges rather le[ss])

✱ Note: on 3 November 1914, four Allied warships had bombarded Sedd el Bahr and Kum Kale using 12-inch guns.

❶ Gun Ranges of the Entrance Forts

KEY
- Sedd el Bahr artillery.
- Cape Helles artillery.
- Kum Kale artillery.
- Orkanie artillery.

Note: the battery at Tekke Burnu was mobile and could be moved along the coast at will.

GALLIPOLI PENINSULA

● Tekke Burnu
■ Helles
★ Sedd el Bahr

Entrance to Dardanelles passage

★ Kum Kale
★ Orkanie

ASIATIC TURKEY

0   1   2
Nautical Miles

NOTES ON GUN CALIBRES

L/35	24-cm. Krupp	9·4-in
L/22	28-cm. Krupp	11-in
L/22	26-cm. Krupp	10·2-in
L/22	24-cm. Krupp	9·4-in
L/22	21-cm. Krupp	8·2-in
L/22	15-cm. Krupp	5·9-in
L/40	15-cm.	5·9-in
	12-cm. howitzer	4·7-in
	8·8-cm. quick-firer	3·4-in

MAIN ALLIED NAVAL ORGANISATI[ON]

FIRST DIVISION (British)
'Inflexible' *(flagship)*; 'Agamemnon', and 'Quee[n] Elizabeth' *(both en route from Malta)*

SECOND DIVISION (British)
'Vengeance' *(flagship)*; 'Albion', 'Cornwallis', 'Irresistible', 'Triumph'.

THIRD DIVISION (French)
'Suffren' *(flagship)*; 'Bouvet', 'Charlemagne', 'Gaulois'.

THE ALLIED PLAN

1. **Long-range bombardment.** (This stag[e] commenced at 0951 hours).
2. **Medium-range bombardment.** (This st[age] commenced at 1400 hours).
3. **Short-range bombardment.** (This sta[ge] never materialised).

Note: Main armament of warships to be emplo[yed] for Stage 1, secondary armament for Stage 2, [and] main armament again for Stage 3 (to complete[ly] obliterate the forts and defence remnants, if [...])

TARGETS OF SHIPS (STAGE ON[E])

'Inflexible'	⟶ Sedd el B[ahr]
'Triumph'	⟶ Helles
'Cornwallis'	⟶ Orkanie
'Suffren'	⟶ Kum Kal[e]

('Bouvet' spotting; 'Gaulois' patrolling off Besika[...])

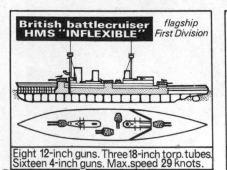

British battlecruiser HMS "INFLEXIBLE" *flagship First Division*

Eight 12-inch guns. Three 18-inch torp. tubes. Sixteen 4-inch guns. Max. speed 29 knots.

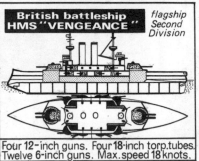

British battleship HMS "VENGEANCE" *flagship Second Division*

Four 12-inch guns. Four 18-inch torp. tubes. Twelve 6-inch guns. Max. speed 18 knots.

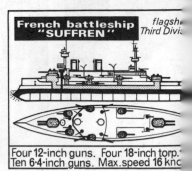

French battleship "SUFFREN" *flagsh[ip] Third Divis[ion]*

Four 12-inch guns. Four 18-inch torp. [tubes.] Ten 6·4-inch guns. Max. speed 16 kno[ts.]

© Arthur Banks 1973

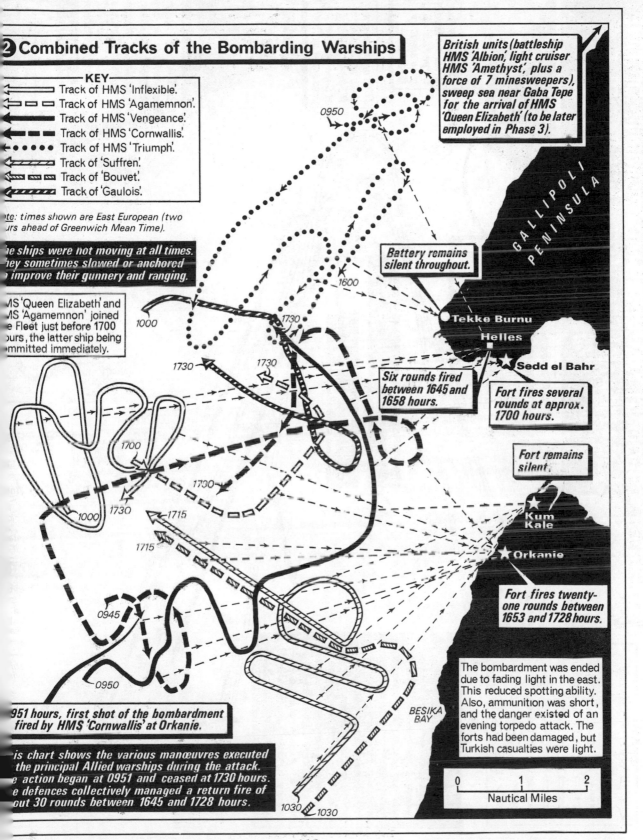

❷ Combined Tracks of the Bombarding Warships

KEY
- ▭ Track of HMS 'Inflexible'.
- ▭ Track of HMS 'Agamemnon'.
- ◄ Track of HMS 'Vengeance'.
- ◄ Track of HMS 'Cornwallis'.
- •••• Track of HMS 'Triumph'.
- ▭ Track of 'Suffren'.
- ▭ Track of 'Bouvet'.
- ▭ Track of 'Gaulois'.

Note: times shown are East European (two hours ahead of Greenwich Mean Time).

The ships were not moving at all times. They sometimes slowed or anchored to improve their gunnery and ranging.

HMS 'Queen Elizabeth' and HMS 'Agamemnon' joined the Fleet just before 1700 hours, the latter ship being committed immediately.

British units (battleship HMS 'Albion', light cruiser HMS 'Amethyst', plus a force of 7 minesweepers), sweep sea near Gaba Tepe for the arrival of HMS 'Queen Elizabeth' (to be later employed in Phase 3).

0950

1600

1730

1000

1730

1730

1700

1730

1000

1730

1715

1715

0945

0950

Battery remains silent throughout.

GALLIPOLI PENINSULA

○ Tekke Burnu

■ Helles

★ Sedd el Bahr

Six rounds fired between 1645 and 1658 hours.

Fort fires several rounds at approx. 1700 hours.

Fort remains silent.

★ Kum Kale

★ Orkanie

Fort fires twenty-one rounds between 1653 and 1728 hours.

BESIKA BAY

The bombardment was ended due to fading light in the east. This reduced spotting ability. Also, ammunition was short, and the danger existed of an evening torpedo attack. The forts had been damaged, but Turkish casualties were light.

1030   1030

951 hours, first shot of the bombardment fired by HMS 'Cornwallis' at Orkanie.

is chart shows the various manœuvres executed the principal Allied warships during the attack. e action began at 0951 and ceased at 1730 hours. e defences collectively managed a return fire of ut 30 rounds between 1645 and 1728 hours.

0	1	2

Nautical Miles

113

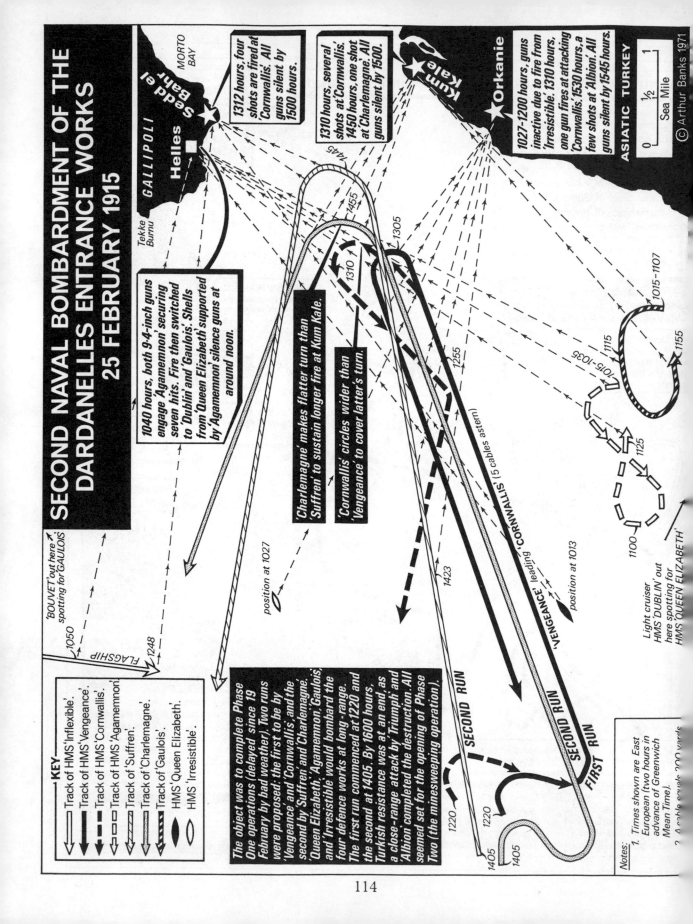

SECOND NAVAL BOMBARDMENT OF THE DARDANELLES ENTRANCE WORKS 25 FEBRUARY 1915

© Arthur Banks 1971

ASIATIC TURKEY

Sea Mile
0   ½   1

MORTO BAY

Sedd el Bahr

GALLIPOLI

Helles

Tekke Burnu

Kum Kale

Orkanie

1312 hours, four shots are fired at 'Cornwallis'. All guns silent by 1500 hours.

1310 hours, several shots at 'Cornwallis'. 1450 hours, one shot at 'Charlemagne'. All guns silent by 1500.

1027-1200 hours, guns inactive due to fire from 'Irresistible'. 1310 hours, one gun fires at attacking 'Cornwallis'. 1530 hours, a few shots at 'Albion'. All guns silent by 1545 hours.

1040 hours, both 9·4-inch guns engage 'Agamemnon' securing seven hits. Fire then switched to 'Dublin' and 'Gaulois'. Shells from Queen Elizabeth supported by Agamemnon silence guns at around noon.

'Charlemagne' makes flatter turn than 'Suffren' to sustain longer fire at Kum Kale.

'Cornwallis' circles wider than 'Vengeance' to cover latter's turn.

'BOUVET' out here spotting for 'GAULOIS'.

1050

1248

FLAGSHIP

position at 1027

'VENGEANCE' leading 'CORNWALLIS' (5 cables astern)

position at 1013

Light cruiser HMS 'DUBLIN' out here spotting for HMS 'QUEEN ELIZABETH'.

1445
1455
1305
1310
1255
1115
1015-1038
1155
1125
1100
1015-1107

1405
1405
1220
1220
1423

FIRST RUN
SECOND RUN
FIRST RUN
SECOND RUN

The object was to complete Phase One operations (delayed since 19 February by bad weather). Two runs were proposed: the first to be by 'Vengeance' and 'Cornwallis'; and the second by 'Suffren' and 'Charlemagne'. 'Queen Elizabeth', 'Agamemnon', 'Gaulois', and 'Irresistible' would bombard the four defence works at long-range. The first run commenced at 1220 and the second at 1405. By 1600 hours, Turkish resistance was at an end, as a close-range attack by 'Triumph' and 'Albion' completed the destruction. All seemed set for the opening of Phase Two (the minesweeping operation).

KEY

→ Track of HMS 'Inflexible'.
⟶ Track of HMS 'Vengeance'.
– ∙ – Track of HMS 'Cornwallis'.
▭▭▭ Track of HMS 'Agamemnon'.
⟍⟍⟍ Track of 'Suffren'.
⟶ Track of 'Charlemagne'.
⇨ Track of 'Gaulois'.
◆ HMS 'Queen Elizabeth'.
◇ HMS 'Irresistible'.

Notes:

1. Times shown are East European (two hours in advance of Greenwich Mean Time).

2. A cable equals 200 yards

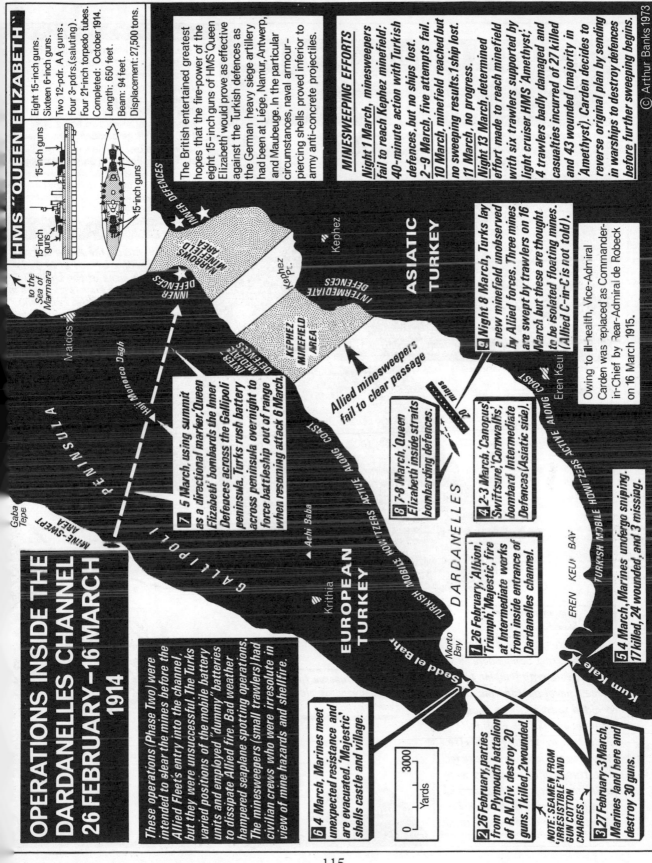

OPERATIONS INSIDE THE DARDANELLES CHANNEL 26 FEBRUARY–16 MARCH 1914

© Arthur Banks 1973

HMS "QUEEN ELIZABETH"

Eight 15-inch guns.
Sixteen 6-inch guns.
Two 12-pdr. AA guns.
Four 3-pdrs.(saluting).
Four 21-inch torpedo tubes.
Completed: October 1914.
Length: 650 feet.
Beam: 94 feet.
Displacement: 27,500 tons.

The British entertained greatest hopes that the fire-power of the eight 15-inch guns of HMS 'Queen Elizabeth' would prove as effective against the Turkish defences as the German heavy siege artillery had been at Liége, Namur, Antwerp, and Maubeuge. In the particular circumstances, naval armour-piercing shells proved inferior to army anti-concrete projectiles.

MINESWEEPING EFFORTS

Night 1 March, minesweepers fail to reach Kephez minefield: 40-minute action with Turkish defences, but no ships lost.
2–9 March, five attempts fail.
10 March, minefield reached but no sweeping results. 1 ship lost.
11 March, no progress.
Night 13 March, determined effort made to reach minefield with six trawlers supported by light cruiser HMS 'Amethyst'. 4 trawlers badly damaged and casualties incurred of 27 killed and 43 wounded (majority in 'Amethyst'). Carden decides to reverse original plan by sending in warships to destroy defences before further sweeping begins.

9 Night 8 March, Turks lay a new minefield unobserved by Allied forces. Three mines are swept by trawlers on 16 March but these are thought to be isolated floating mines. (Allied C-in-C is not told).

Owing to ill-health, Vice-Admiral Carden was replaced as Commander-in-Chief by Rear-Admiral de Robeck on 16 March 1915.

These operations (Phase Two) were intended to clear the mines before the Allied Fleet's entry into the channel, but they were unsuccessful. The Turks varied positions of the mobile battery units and employed "dummy" batteries to dissipate Allied fire. Bad weather hampered seaplane spotting operations. The minesweepers (small trawlers) had civilian crews who were irresolute in view of mine hazards and shellfire.

7 5 March, using summit as a directional marker,'Queen Elizabeth' bombards the Inner Defences across the Gallipoli peninsula. Turks rush battery across peninsula overnight to force battleship out of range when resuming attack 6 March.

8 7–8 March, 'Queen Elizabeth' inside straits bombarding defences.

Allied minesweepers fail to clear passage

4 2–3 March, 'Canopus','Swiftsure','Cornwallis', bombard Intermediate Defences (Asiatic side).

6 4 March, Marines meet unexpected resistance and are evacuated. 'Majestic' shells castle and village.

1 26 February, 'Albion','Triumph','Majestic', fire at Intermediate works from inside entrance of Dardanelles channel.

5 4 March, Marines undergo sniping. 17 killed, 24 wounded, and 3 missing.

2 26 February, parties from Plymouth battalion of R.N.Div. destroy 20 guns. 1 killed, 2 wounded.

NOTE: SEAMEN FROM 'IRRESISTIBLE' LAND GUN COTTON CHARGES.

3 27 February–3 March, Marines land here and destroy 30 guns.

to the Sea of Marmara

GALLIPOLI PENINSULA

Gaba Tepe

MINE-SWEPT AREA

Maidos

Hali Monoico Dagh

Achi Baba

Krithia

EUROPEAN TURKEY

Sedd el Bahr

Morto Bay

INNER DEFENCES

NARROWS MINEFIELD AREA

Kephez Pt.

Kephez

INTERMEDIATE DEFENCES

KEPHEZ MINEFIELD AREA

ASIATIC TURKEY

DARDANELLES

EREN KEUI BAY

TURKISH MOBILE HOWITZERS ACTIVE ALONG COAST

Eren Keui

Kum Kale

0   3000
Yards

THE ALLIED FAILURE TO FORCE THE DARDANELLES PASSAGE 18 MARCH 1915

1030 hours, preceded by destroyers, the Allied fleet of 17 battleships and 1 battlecruiser entered the straits and advanced to allotted positions. Line 'A' opened fire at 1130 and Line 'B' was advanced at 1206. By 1345, the defences were inactive; consequently the minesweepers were ordered up supported by Second Division (to relieve Line 'B'). Moving out, 'Bouvet' was mined at 1355, then capsized and sank in two minutes. 1610 'Irresistible' was mined; 1614 'Inflexible' suffered a similar fate. At 1715 'Gaulois' was badly holed and had to beached. 1805 'Ocean' was mined and abandoned. Thus one-third of the capital ships were either sunk or incapacitated and the naval attempt to force the Dardanelles was called off. Prematurely? By 16 April, a British destroyer-minesweeping "fast" force was in existence ("Beagle"-class ships). This fact is not generally appreciated.

The attack of 18 March was intended to break the stalemate situation of Phase Two in whi the minesweeper crews were reluctant to pursue their operations until the capital ship had silenced the Turkish main batteries. Th Allied plan allowed for the trawlers to begin sweeping operations two hours after start of the long-range bombardment, whereupo they were to clear a channel 900 yards broa past Kephez Point into Sari Sighlar Bay.
(It should be noted that the Allied comman was unaware of the full extent of the Turkish mi fields despite detailed Intelligence reports which had not been passed on).

Prior to the attack, the Allies worried over the alleged existence of torpedo-tubes on both sides of the channel. In fact, there were only three tubes in position, all at Kilid Bahr. Each tube was equipped with two torpedoes, but only one tube could fire right across the width of the Narrows, the others less than halfway across.

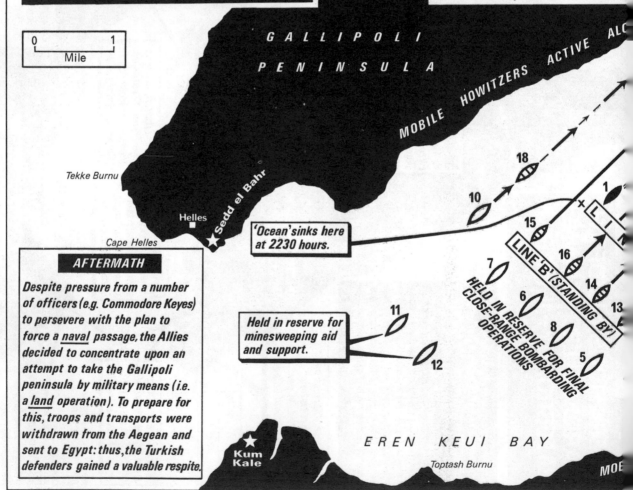

SARI TEPE

KRITHIA

GALLIPOLI

PENINSULA

MOBILE HOWITZERS ACTIVE ALC

0 — 1 Mile

Tekke Burnu

Helles

Sedd el Bahr

Cape Helles

'Ocean' sinks here at 2230 hours.

LINE 'B'(STANDING BY)

HELD IN RESERVE FOR FINAL CLOSE-RANGE BOMBARDING OPERATIONS

Held in reserve for minesweeping aid and support.

AFTERMATH

Despite pressure from a number of officers (e.g. Commodore Keyes) to persevere with the plan to force a naval passage, the Allies decided to concentrate upon an attempt to take the Gallipoli peninsula by military means (i.e. a land operation). To prepare for this, troops and transports were withdrawn from the Aegean and sent to Egypt: thus, the Turkish defenders gained a valuable respite.

Kum Kale

EREN KEUI BAY

Toptash Burnu

MOE

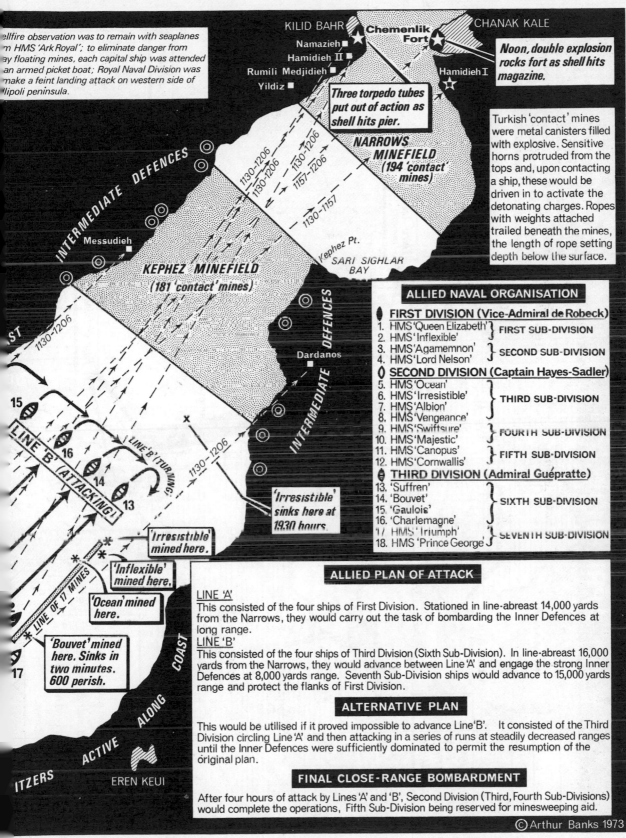

ellfire observation was to remain with seaplanes
m HMS 'Ark Royal'; to eliminate danger from
ay floating mines, each capital ship was attended
an armed picket boat; Royal Naval Division was
make a feint landing attack on western side of
lipoli peninsula.

KILID BAHR   CHANAK KALE

Chemenlik Fort

Namazieh ■
Hamidieh II ■
Rumili Medjidieh ■
Yildiz ■

Hamidieh I ☆

Noon, double explosion rocks fort as shell hits magazine.

Three torpedo tubes put out of action as shell hits pier.

NARROWS MINEFIELD (194 'contact' mines)

1130–1206
1130–1206
1130–1206
1157–1206
1130–1157

Kephez Pt.
SARI SIGHLAR BAY

Turkish 'contact' mines were metal canisters filled with explosive. Sensitive horns protruded from the tops and, upon contacting a ship, these would be driven in to activate the detonating charges. Ropes with weights attached trailed beneath the mines, the length of rope setting depth below the surface.

INTERMEDIATE DEFENCES

Messudieh ■

KEPHEZ MINEFIELD (181 'contact' mines)

1130–1206

Dardanos ■

INTERMEDIATE DEFENCES

ST

15

16

14

13

LINE 'B' (ATTACKING)

LINE 'B' (TURNING)

1130–1206

×

1130–1206

'Irresistible' sinks here at 19.30 hours.

'Irresistible' mined here.

'Inflexible' mined here.

'Ocean' mined here.

LINE OF 17 MINES

'Bouvet' mined here. Sinks in two minutes. 600 perish.

17

ITZERS   ACTIVE   ALONG   COAST

EREN KEUI

ALLIED NAVAL ORGANISATION

FIRST DIVISION (Vice-Admiral de Robeck)
1. HMS 'Queen Elizabeth' } FIRST SUB-DIVISION
2. HMS 'Inflexible'
3. HMS 'Agamemnon' } SECOND SUB-DIVISION
4. HMS 'Lord Nelson'

SECOND DIVISION (Captain Hayes-Sadler)
5. HMS 'Ocean'
6. HMS 'Irresistible' } THIRD SUB-DIVISION
7. HMS 'Albion'
8. HMS 'Vengeance'
9. HMS 'Swiftsure' } FOURTH SUB-DIVISION
10. HMS 'Majestic'
11. HMS 'Canopus' } FIFTH SUB-DIVISION
12. HMS 'Cornwallis'

THIRD DIVISION (Admiral Guépratte)
13. 'Suffren'
14. 'Bouvet' } SIXTH SUB-DIVISION
15. 'Gaulois'
16. 'Charlemagne'
17. HMS 'Triumph' } SEVENTH SUB-DIVISION
18. HMS 'Prince George'

ALLIED PLAN OF ATTACK

LINE 'A'
This consisted of the four ships of First Division. Stationed in line-abreast 14,000 yards from the Narrows, they would carry out the task of bombarding the Inner Defences at long range.

LINE 'B'
This consisted of the four ships of Third Division (Sixth Sub-Division). In line-abreast 16,000 yards from the Narrows, they would advance between Line 'A' and engage the strong Inner Defences at 8,000 yards range. Seventh Sub-Division ships would advance to 15,000 yards range and protect the flanks of First Division.

ALTERNATIVE PLAN

This would be utilised if it proved impossible to advance Line 'B'. It consisted of the Third Division circling Line 'A' and then attacking in a series of runs at steadily decreased ranges until the Inner Defences were sufficiently dominated to permit the resumption of the original plan.

FINAL CLOSE-RANGE BOMBARDMENT

After four hours of attack by Lines 'A' and 'B', Second Division (Third, Fourth Sub-Divisions) would complete the operations, Fifth Sub-Division being reserved for minesweeping aid.

ⓒ Arthur Banks 1973

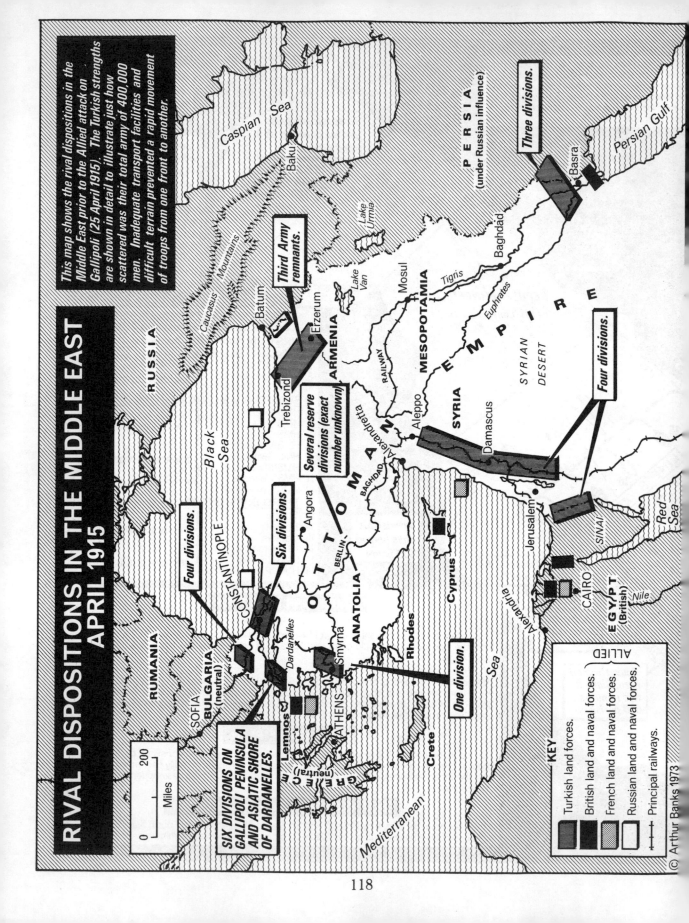

RIVAL DISPOSITIONS IN THE MIDDLE EAST
APRIL 1915

This map shows the rival dispositions in the Middle East prior to the Allied attack on Gallipoli (25 April 1915). The Turkish strengths are shown in detail to illustrate just how scattered was their total army of 400,000 men. Inadequate transport facilities and difficult terrain prevented a rapid movement of troops from one front to another.

Three divisions.

Four divisions.

Third Army remnants.

Several reserve divisions (exact number unknown).

Four divisions.

Six divisions.

One division.

SIX DIVISIONS ON GALLIPOLI PENINSULA AND ASIATIC SHORE OF DARDANELLES.

KEY

Turkish land forces.	
British land and naval forces.	ALLIED
French land and naval forces.	
Russian land and naval forces.	
Principal railways.	

PERSIA (under Russian influence)

Persian Gulf

Basra

Baghdad

Mosul

Tigris

Euphrates

MESOPOTAMIA

SYRIAN DESERT

EMPIRE

SYRIA

Damascus

Aleppo

Alexandretta

Jerusalem

SINAI

Red Sea

Nile

EGYPT (British)

CAIRO

Alexandria

Cyprus

Rhodes

Crete

Mediterranean Sea

Lemnos

ATHENS

GREECE (neutral)

Smyrna

ANATOLIA

Dardanelles

CONSTANTINOPLE

Angora

BERLIN-BAGHDAD

OTTOMAN

Black Sea

SOFIA

BULGARIA (neutral)

RUMANIA

RUSSIA

Caspian Sea

Baku

Batum

Trebizond

Erzerum

ARMENIA

Lake Van

Lake Urmia

Caucasus Mountains

RAILWAY

Miles

0   200

© Arthur Banks 1973

118

GALLIPOLI PENINSULA: PHYSICAL FEATURES

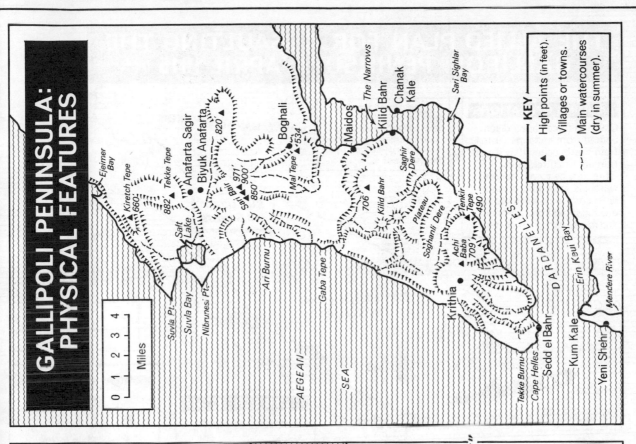

Miles
0 1 2 3 4

KEY
▲ High points (in feet).
● Villages or towns.
〰 Main watercourses (dry in summer).

Ejelmer Bay
Kiretch Tepe 660'
Tekke Tepe 882'
Salt Lake
Suvla Pt.
Suvla Bay
Nibrunesi Pt.
Ari Burnu
Gaba Tepe
Anafarta Sagir
Biyuk Anafarta
Boghali
Sari Bair 971'
850'
900'
534'
820'
Mal Tepe
Maidos
Saghir Dere
Kilid Bahr
The Narrows
Kilid Bahr
Chanak Kale
Sari Sighlar Bay
706'
Soghanli Dere
Plateau
Krithia
Achi Baba 709'
Tenkir Tepe 490'
DARDANELLES
Kum Kale
Sedd el Bahr
Cape Helles
Tekke Burnu
Erin Keui Bay
Yeni Shehr
Mendere River
AEGEAN SEA

TURKISH DISPOSITIONS AT THE DARDANELLES 24 APRIL 1915

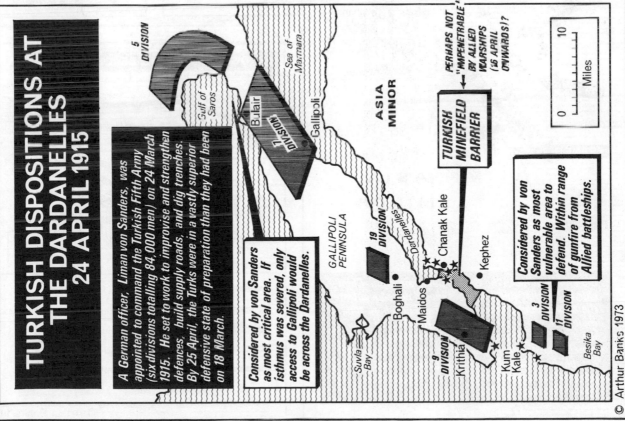

A German officer, Liman von Sanders, was appointed to command the Turkish Fifth Army (six divisions totalling 84,000 men) on 24 March 1915. He set to work to improvise and strengthen defences, build supply roads, and dig trenches. By 25 April, the Turks were in a vastly superior defensive state of preparation than they had been on 18 March.

Considered by von Sanders as most critical area. If isthmus was severed, only access to Gallipoli would be across the Dardanelles.

5 DIVISION
Gulf of Saros
Bulair
7 DIVISION
Sea of Marmara
Gallipoli
ASIA MINOR

PERHAPS NOT "IMPENETRABLE" BY ALLIED WARSHIPS (16 April onwards)?

TURKISH MINEFIELD BARRIER

Considered by von Sanders as most vulnerable area to defend. Within range of gunfire from Allied battleships.

19 DIVISION
GALLIPOLI PENINSULA
Boghali
Maidos
Dardanelles
Chanak Kale
Kephez
9 DIVISION
Krithia
Kum Kale
3 DIVISION
11 DIVISION
Suvla Bay
Besika Bay

Miles
0 10

© Arthur Banks 1973

119

THE ALLIED PLAN FOR ASSAULTING THE GALLIPOLI PENINSULA APRIL 1915

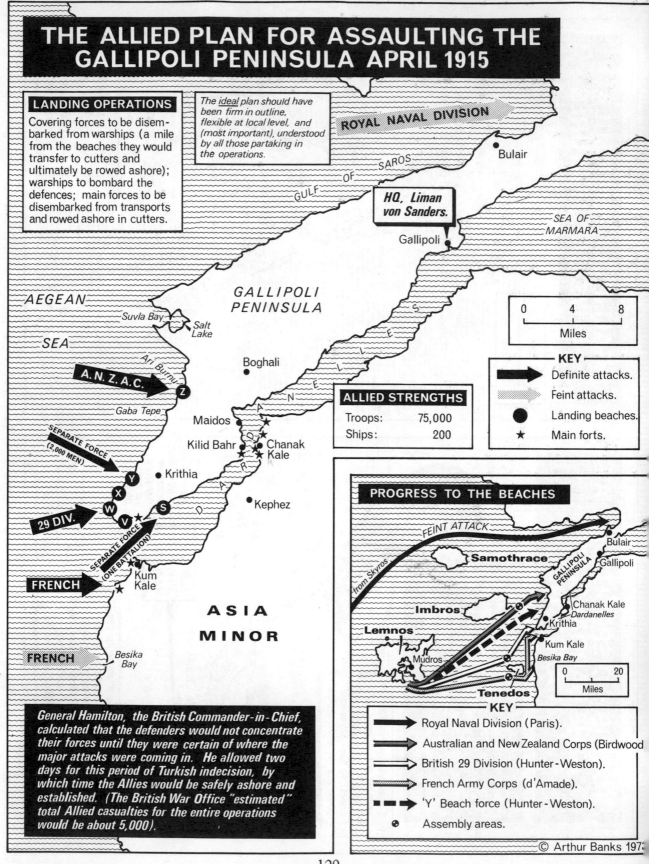

LANDING OPERATIONS

Covering forces to be disembarked from warships (a mile from the beaches they would transfer to cutters and ultimately be rowed ashore); warships to bombard the defences; main forces to be disembarked from transports and rowed ashore in cutters.

The ideal plan should have been firm in outline, flexible at local level, and (most important), understood by all those partaking in the operations.

ROYAL NAVAL DIVISION

GULF OF SAROS

Bulair

HQ, Liman von Sanders.

SEA OF MARMARA

Gallipoli

AEGEAN

SEA

Suvla Bay
Salt Lake

GALLIPOLI PENINSULA

Ari Burnu

A.N.Z.A.C.

Z

Gaba Tepe

Boghali

DARDANELLES

SEPARATE FORCE (2,000 MEN)

Maidos

Kilid Bahr

Chanak Kale

29 DIV.

Y

X

W

V

S

Krithia

Kephez

SEPARATE FORCE (ONE BATTALION)

FRENCH

Kum Kale

ALLIED STRENGTHS

| Troops: | 75,000 |
| Ships: | 200 |

KEY	
→	Definite attacks.
⇒	Feint attacks.
●	Landing beaches.
★	Main forts.

ASIA MINOR

FRENCH

Besika Bay

General Hamilton, the British Commander-in-Chief, calculated that the defenders would not concentrate their forces until they were certain of where the major attacks were coming in. He allowed two days for this period of Turkish indecision, by which time the Allies would be safely ashore and established. (The British War Office "estimated" total Allied casualties for the entire operations would be about 5,000).

PROGRESS TO THE BEACHES

FEINT ATTACK

from Skyros

Samothrace

Imbros

Lemnos

Mudros

Tenedos

GALLIPOLI PENINSULA

Bulair

Gallipoli

Chanak Kale
Dardanelles

Krithia

Kum Kale

Besika Bay

0		20
	Miles	

KEY	
→	Royal Naval Division (Paris).
⇒	Australian and New Zealand Corps (Birdwood
⇒	British 29 Division (Hunter-Weston).
⇒	French Army Corps (d'Amade).
▬ ▬ ▶	'Y' Beach force (Hunter-Weston).
⊕	Assembly areas.

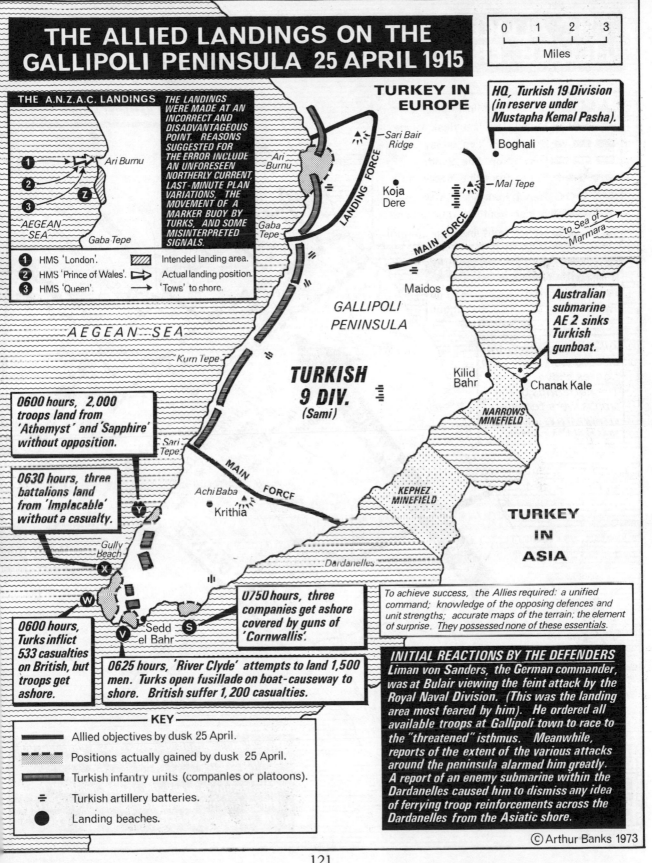

THE ALLIED LANDINGS ON THE GALLIPOLI PENINSULA 25 APRIL 1915

0 1 2 3
Miles

THE A.N.Z.A.C. LANDINGS

THE LANDINGS WERE MADE AT AN INCORRECT AND DISADVANTAGEOUS POINT. REASONS SUGGESTED FOR THE ERROR INCLUDE AN UNFORESEEN NORTHERLY CURRENT, LAST-MINUTE PLAN VARIATIONS, THE MOVEMENT OF A MARKER BUOY BY TURKS, AND SOME MISINTERPRETED SIGNALS.

1. HMS 'London'.
2. HMS 'Prince of Wales'.
3. HMS 'Queen'.

Intended landing area.
Actual landing position.
'Tows' to shore.

Ari Burnu
Z
AEGEAN SEA
Gaba Tepe

TURKEY IN EUROPE

Sari Bair Ridge
Ari Burnu
Koja Dere
Mal Tepe
Boghali

HQ, Turkish 19 Division (in reserve under Mustapha Kemal Pasha).

LANDING FORCE
MAIN FORCE
Gaba Tepe

to Sea of Marmara

Maidos

Australian submarine AE 2 sinks Turkish gunboat.

GALLIPOLI PENINSULA

AEGEAN SEA

Kilid Bahr
Chanak Kale

Kum Tepe

TURKISH 9 DIV. (Sami)

NARROWS MINEFIELD

0600 hours, 2,000 troops land from 'Athemyst' and 'Sapphire' without opposition.

Sari Tepe

0630 hours, three battalions land from 'Implacable' without a casualty.

Y

KEPHEZ MINEFIELD

TURKEY IN ASIA

MAIN FORCE
Achi Baba
Krithia

Gully Beach
X

Dardanelles

W

0600 hours, Turks inflict 533 casualties on British, but troops get ashore.

Sedd el Bahr
V
S

0750 hours, three companies get ashore covered by guns of 'Cornwallis'.

0625 hours, 'River Clyde' attempts to land 1,500 men. Turks open fusillade on boat-causeway to shore. British suffer 1,200 casualties.

To achieve success, the Allies required: a unified command; knowledge of the opposing defences and unit strengths; accurate maps of the terrain; the element of surprise. *They possessed none of these essentials.*

INITIAL REACTIONS BY THE DEFENDERS

Liman von Sanders, the German commander, was at Bulair viewing the feint attack by the Royal Naval Division. (This was the landing area most feared by him). He ordered all available troops at Gallipoli town to race to the "threatened" isthmus. Meanwhile, reports of the extent of the various attacks around the peninsula alarmed him greatly. A report of an enemy submarine within the Dardanelles caused him to dismiss any idea of ferrying troop reinforcements across the Dardanelles from the Asiatic shore.

KEY

Allied objectives by dusk 25 April.
Positions actually gained by dusk 25 April.
Turkish infantry units (companies or platoons).
Turkish artillery batteries.
Landing beaches.

© Arthur Banks 1973

121

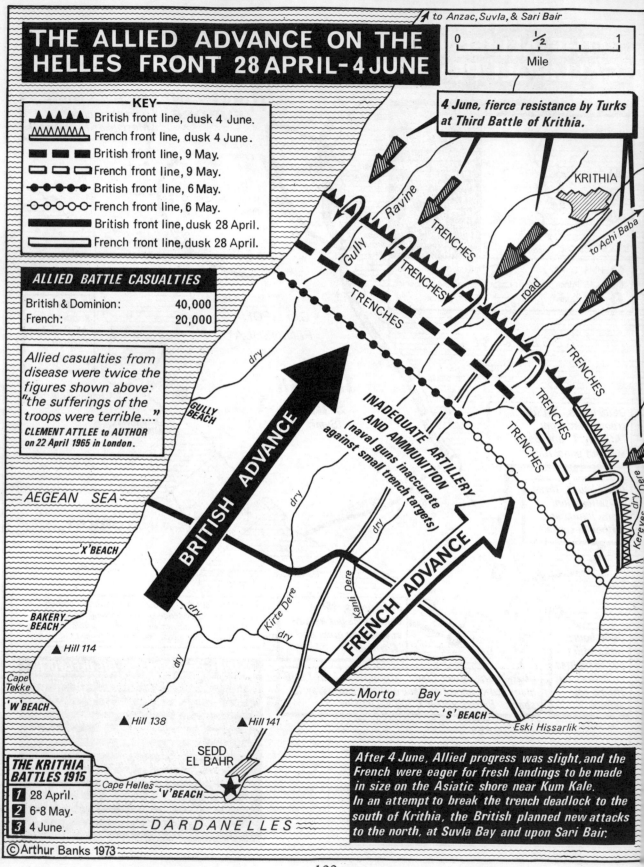

THE ALLIED ADVANCE ON THE HELLES FRONT 28 APRIL – 4 JUNE

0   ½   1
Mile

KEY
- ▲▲▲▲ British front line, dusk 4 June.
- ∧∧∧∧ French front line, dusk 4 June.
- ■▬■▬■ British front line, 9 May.
- ▭▬▭▬▭ French front line, 9 May.
- ●━●━● British front line, 6 May.
- ○━○━○ French front line, 6 May.
- ▬▬▬ British front line, dusk 28 April.
- ▭▭▭ French front line, dusk 28 April.

ALLIED BATTLE CASUALTIES
British & Dominion:	40,000
French:	20,000

Allied casualties from disease were twice the figures shown above: "the sufferings of the troops were terrible...."
CLEMENT ATTLEE to AUTHOR on 22 April 1965 in London.

to Anzac, Suvla, & Sari Bair

4 June, fierce resistance by Turks at Third Battle of Krithia.

KRITHIA

to Achi Baba

Gully Ravine

TRENCHES

TRENCHES

road

TRENCHES

TRENCHES

TRENCHES

TRENCHES

TRENCHES

Kereves dry Dere

AEGEAN SEA

GULLY BEACH

dry

INADEQUATE ARTILLERY AND AMMUNITION (naval guns inaccurate against small trench targets)

BRITISH ADVANCE

FRENCH ADVANCE

'X' BEACH

dry

BAKERY BEACH

dry

Kirte Dere

Kanli Dere

dry

dry

▲ Hill 114

Cape Tekke

'W' BEACH

Morto   Bay

'S' BEACH

Eski Hissarlik

▲ Hill 138

▲ Hill 141

SEDD EL BAHR

Cape Helles 'V' BEACH

DARDANELLES

THE KRITHIA BATTLES 1915
- 1 28 April.
- 2 6-8 May.
- 3 4 June.

After 4 June, Allied progress was slight, and the French were eager for fresh landings to be made in size on the Asiatic shore near Kum Kale. In an attempt to break the trench deadlock to the south of Krithia, the British planned new attacks to the north, at Suvla Bay and upon Sari Bair.

© Arthur Banks 1973

122

FRESH BRITISH LANDINGS 1915

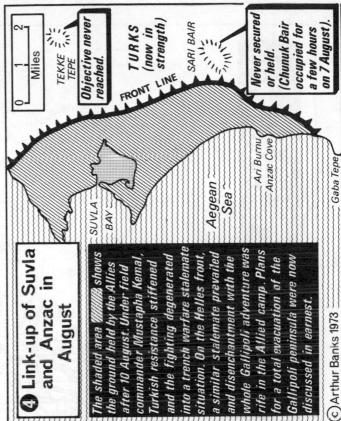

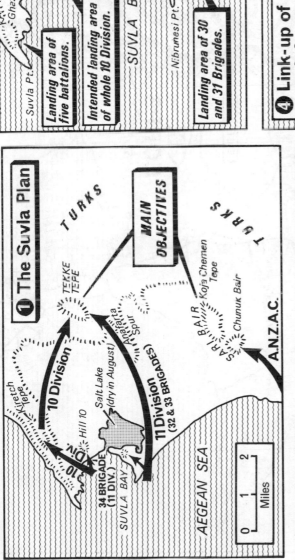

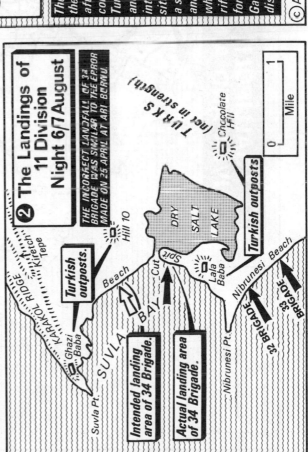

© Arthur Banks 1973

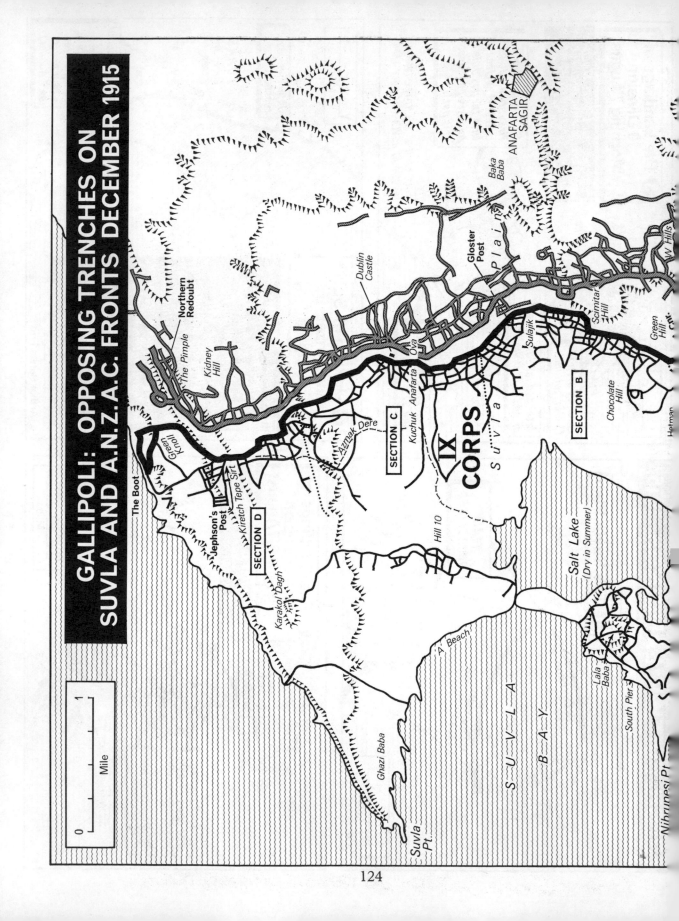

GALLIPOLI: OPPOSING TRENCHES ON SUVLA AND A.N.Z.A.C. FRONTS DECEMBER 1915

0   1

Mile

ANAFARTA SAGIR

Baka Baba

Dublin Castle

Gloster Post

Plain

Scimitar Hill

Green Hill

Northern Redoubt

The Pimple

Kidney Hill

Oya

Kuchuk Anafarta

Sulajik

SECTION B

Chocolate Hill

Herman

Green Knoll

Azmak Dere

SECTION C

IX CORPS

Suvla

The Boot

Jephson's Post

Kiretch Tepe Sirt

SECTION D

Karakol Dagh

Hill 10

Salt Lake
(Dry in Summer)

Ghazi Baba

'A' Beach

S - U - V - L - A

B - A - Y

Lala Baba

South Pier

Suvla Pt.

Nibrunesi Pt.

W. Hills

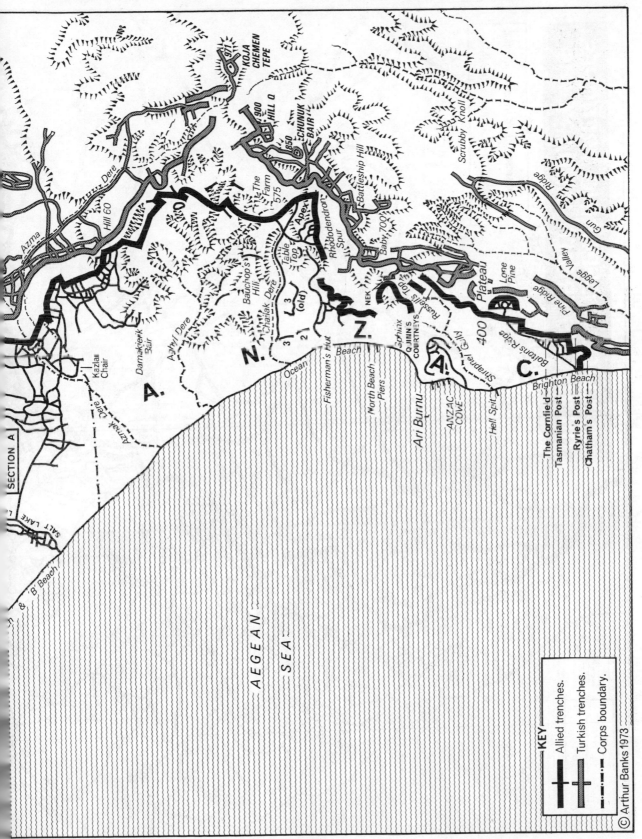

KEY

Allied trenches.

Turkish trenches.

Corps boundary.

© Arthur Banks 1973

125

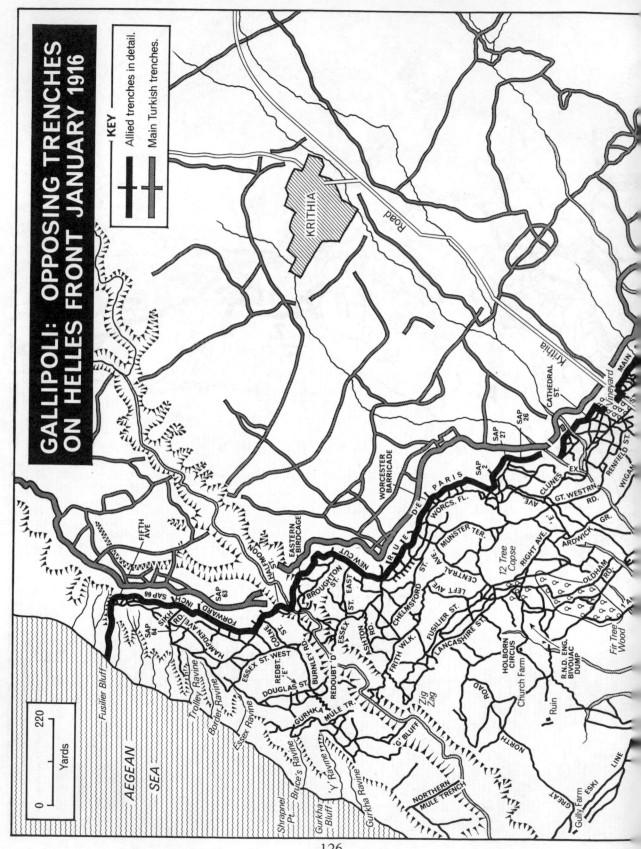

GALLIPOLI: OPPOSING TRENCHES ON HELLES FRONT JANUARY 1916

KEY

Allied trenches in detail.
Main Turkish trenches.

KRITHIA

Road

Krithia

MAIN

Vineyard

ST.

CATHEDRAL ST.

EX

RENFIELD ST.

SAP 27

SAP 26

SAP 2

CLUNES

WIGAN

DE PARIS

WORCS. FL.

GT. WESTRN. RD.

WORCESTER BARRICADE

EASTERN BIRDCAGE

NEW CUT

MUNSTER TER.

'E' AVE.

ARDWICK GR.

B L U E

FIFTH AVE

HALFMOON ST.

BROUGHTON ST.

CENTRAL AVE.

LEFT AVE.

FUSILIER ST.

12 Tree Copse

RIGHT AVE.

OLDHAM RD.

SAP 63

EAST ST.

CHELMSFORD

ST. COLNE

ESSEX ST.

ASHTON RD.

FRITH WLK.

LANCASHIRE ST.

Fir Tree Wood

FORWARD INCH RD.

SAP 66

HAMPDEN AVE.

BURNLEY RD.

ESSEX ST. WEST

REDBT. 'E'

REDOUBT 'D'

HOLBORN CIRCUS

Church Farm

R.N.D. ENG. BIVOUAC DUMP

SAP 64

DOUGLAS ST.

GURKHA

MULE TR.

Zig Zag

Ruin

Fusilier Bluff

Trolley Ravine

Border Ravine

Essex Ravine

'Y' Ravine

Gurkha Ravine

'G' BLUFF

NORTH ROAD

0   220

Yards

AEGEAN SEA

Shrapnel Pt.

Bruce's Ravine

Gurkha Bluff

NORTHERN MULE TRENCH

GREAT

Gully Farm

ESKI LINE

126

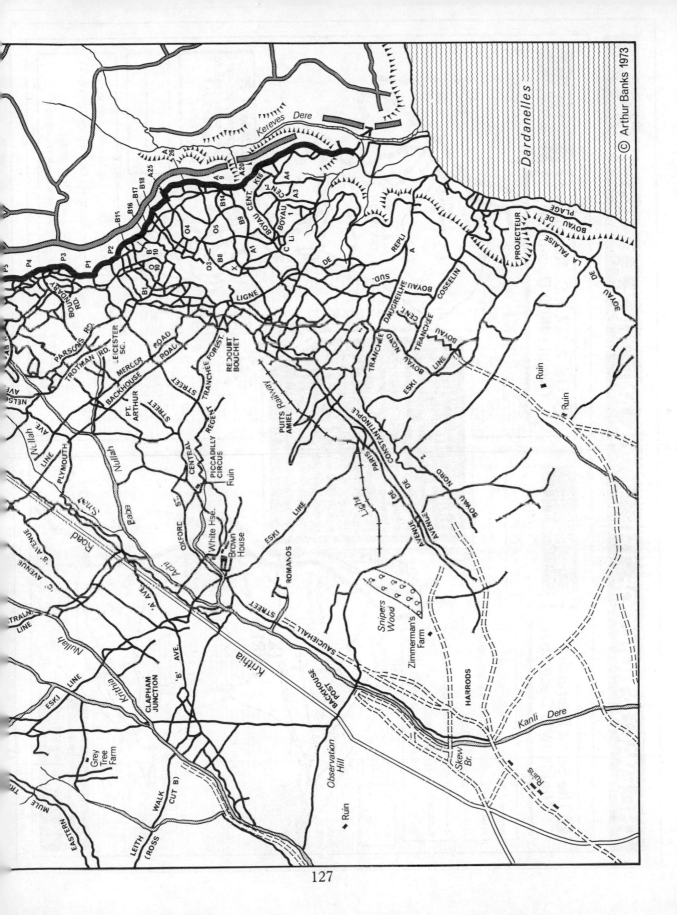

© Arthur Banks 1973

Dardanelles

Kereves Dere

LA FALAISE

BOYAU DE PLAGE

PROJECTEUR

REPLI

A

SUD.

BOYAU COSSELIN

TRANCHÉE CENT.

BOYAU NORD GIXON DAUGREILHE

TRANCHÉE SUD.

LIGNE

ESKI

BOYAU NORD

2

A4
A3
BOYAU 1
CENT. K16
BOYAU CENT.
C Li
A1
DE

A 26
A 25
B18 B17
B16 B15
B14
B9
B8
O4 O5
O3
B10 B
O
B1
P1 P2 P3 P4 P5
BOUNDARY RD.

LIGNE

REDOUBT BOUCHET
TRANCHÉE FOREST
REGENT STREET
PICCADILLY CIRCUS
Ruin
ROAD
ROAD
MERCER STREET
LEICESTER SC.
PARSONS RD.
TROTMAN RD.
BACKHOUSE STREET
PT. ARTHUR
CENTRAL S.
OXFORD S.

PUITS AMIEL Railway
PARIS DE CONSTANTINOPLE
Light Rly

AVENUE NORD

AVENUE DE PARIS

Ruin
Ruin
Ruin

NELSON AVE.
Nullah Line
PLYMOUTH AVE.
Nullah
Eski
Road
Achi
White Hse.
Brown House
ESKI LINE
ROMANOS STREET
SAUCIEHALL STREET

Sniper's Wood

Zimmerman's Farm

HARRODS

Kanli Dere

'A' AVENUE
'B' AVENUE
'C' AVENUE
AUSTRALIAN LINE
MULE TR
EASTERN
ESKI LINE
Krithia Nullah
Krithia
'B' AVE.
CLAPHAM JUNCTION
'B' AVE.
BACKHOUSE POST

Ruins

Skew Br.

Grey Tree Farm

LEITH (ROSS
WALK CUT B)

Observation Hill

Ruin

127

THE EVACUATIONS OF THE SUVLA AND A.N.Z.A.C. POSITIONS

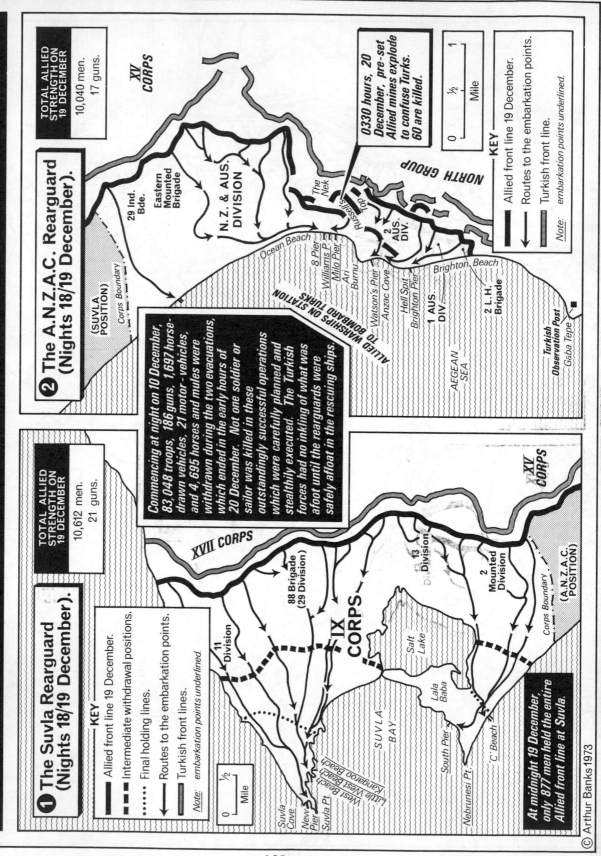

❷ The A.N.Z.A.C. Rearguard (Nights 18/19 December).

XV CORPS

TOTAL ALLIED STRENGTH ON 19 DECEMBER	10,040 men. 17 guns.

0330 hours, 20 December, pre-set Allied mines explode to confuse Turks. 60 are killed.

29 Ind. Bde.

Eastern Mounted Brigade

N.Z. & AUS. DIVISION

NORTH GROUP

The Nek

Russell's Top

2 AUS. DIV.

(SUVLA POSITION)

Corps Boundary

Ocean Beach

8 Pier
Williams P.
Milo Pier
Watson's Pier
Ari Burnu
Anzac Cove
Hell Spit
Brighton Pier
Brighton Beach

1 AUS. DIV.

2 L.H. Brigade

ALLIED WARSHIPS ON STATION TO BOMBARD TURKS

AEGEAN SEA

Turkish Observation Post
Gaba Tepe

Commencing at night on 10 December, 83,048 troops, 186 guns, 1,697 horse-drawn vehicles, 21 motor-vehicles, and 4,695 horses and mules were withdrawn during the two evacuations, which ended in the early hours of 20 December. Not one soldier or sailor was killed in these outstandingly successful operations which were carefully planned and stealthily executed. The Turkish forces had no inkling of what was afoot until the rearguards were safely afloat in the rescuing ships.

KEY
▬▬ Allied front line 19 December.
→ Routes to the embarkation points.
▨▨▨ Turkish front line.
Note: *embarkation points underlined.*

0 ½ 1
Mile

❶ The Suvla Rearguard (Nights 18/19 December).

TOTAL ALLIED STRENGTH ON 19 DECEMBER	10,612 men. 21 guns.

KEY
▬▬ Allied front line 19 December.
▬ ▬ Intermediate withdrawal positions.
•••• Final holding lines.
→ Routes to the embarkation points.
▨▨▨ Turkish front lines.
Note: *embarkation points underlined.*

0 ½
Mile

XVII CORPS

11 Division

88 Brigade (29 Division)

IX CORPS

13 Division

2 Mounted Division

Corps Boundary

(A.N.Z.A.C. POSITION)

Salt Lake

Lala Baba

SUVLA BAY

South Pier

'C' Beach

Nebrunesi Pt.

Suvla Cove
New Pier
Suvla Pt.
West Beach
Little West Beach
Kangaroo Beach

At midnight 19 December, only 877 men held the entire Allied front line at Suvla.

© Arthur Banks 1973

128

THE EVACUATION OF THE HELLES POSITION

The Final Withdrawals (Night 8/9 January 1916).

KEY
- ▬▬▬ Allied front line 8 January.
- ••••••• Beach defence lines.
- ◀━━ Lines of retirement.
- **R** Divisional rendezvous.
- **F** Forming-up places.
- ▨▨▨ Turkish front line.

ALLIED EMBARKATIONS

'V' Beach	7,600 men
'W' Beach	8,912 men
Gully Beach	400 men

37 guns were embarked

ALLIED WARSHIPS BOMBARD TURKS (7 JANUARY)

7 January, Turks launch offensive which is stubbornly repulsed by British.

XIV CORPS

KRITHIA

V CORPS

Y Beach

13 DIVISION

RD.

Ravine

Gulley

JENNET

GT.

NORTH

MULE

TRENCH

ROAD

29 DIVISION

EASTERN

Krithia Nullah

Gully Beach

13 DIV.

Pink Farm

MULE TRENCH

52 DIVISION

CENTRAL ST.

REGENT ST.

Kereves Dere

AEGEAN SEA

29 DIV.

VIII CORPS

Observation Hill

SAYICH-IEHALL ST.

AVENUE OF PARIS

ROYAL NAVAL DIVISION

'X' Beach

29 DIV.

Zimmerman's Farm

HARRODS

BOYAU NORD?

Kirte Dere

Kanli Dere

Fme. Vermerch

CEN.

BOYAU

Bakery Beach

Hill 114

F

F

R.N.D.

Morto Bay

52 DIV.

R

Hill 141

Hill 138

sunken wreck

'MARIA DELLE VITTORIE'

'VICENZO FLORIO'

Cape Helles

'SAGHALIEN'

'MASSENA'

'RIVER CLYDE'

Dredger

Sedd el Bahr

DARDANELLES

In the week up to the final withdrawals on the night 8/9 January, 35, 268 troops, 3,689 horses and mules, 328 vehicles, 127 guns and 1,600 tons of stores were evacuated. As at Suvla and A.N.Z.A.C. positions, the operations were at night and completed with stealth and thoroughness. Again, the Turks had no inkling of the Allied intentions until the operations were completed.

© Arthur Banks 1973

129

THE WAR IN 1915

The Dardanelles and Gallipoli dominated the minds of the political leaders in Whitehall during the opening months of 1915. But Sir John French and his generals across the Channel bitterly opposed any plans which might divert troops from the Western Front, and Joffre agreed with them. French and his principal subordinate, Haig, wished to attack the Germans in Belgium as soon as the weather was favourable. Joffre had hopes of a two-pronged thrust later in the spring in Artois and Champagne, intended to break through the German lines and sweep across Belgium west of the Ardennes. Reality fell short of expectation that year on every sector of the Western Front: the British gained the town of Neuve Chapelle at the cost of heavy casualties in March (pages 136–137); the German offensive in the West during April sought to eliminate the Ypres Salient, but, despite the use of poison gas, their success was limited to a few villages; and later frontal assaults by the British and the French in Artois, at Loos, and in Champagne, though shaking the vertebrae of the German defensive system, failed to crack the spinal cord. The newspapers continued to carry long casualty lists which, together with the frustrations of Gallipoli, emphasised the terrible burden of the War on families far from the battlefronts. The first Zeppelin raids (pages 286–290) brought a new terror to English homes.

The news from other fronts was no more encouraging. At first it seemed that the Russians would make some progress on the southern sector of the Eastern Front, for they at last captured the fortress of Przemysl on 22 March. But Falkenhayn, unlike Moltke in the previous year, was prepared to co-ordinate strategy with Conrad. In May a massive Austro-German offensive began in Galicia, breaking through four lines of Russian defences at Gorlice and forcing a general withdrawal from the Carpathians. The Russians were driven out of Przemysl, out of Galicia, and out of Poland as well. When the campaign ended, half a million Russians were in prisoner-of-war cages. Nor was this the limit of Falkenhayn's success. In October Mackensen, the victor of Gorlice, set up his headquarters in southern Hungary and took command of a joint Austro–Germano–Bulgarian army which overran Serbia (page 160) and gave Germany control of a continuous railway route from Berlin to Constantinople and the Middle East. The Allied response to Bulgaria's alliance with Germany was, at last, to establish a base at Salonika, but no effective aid could be given to Serbia.

Bulgaria's entry into the German camp was preceded by Italy's adhesion to the Allied cause in May 1915. But, though it was hoped in London and Paris that Italy would pose a new threat to Austria-Hungary, this Front, too, was soon paralysed by defensive trench warfare (page 200–201). Briefly it seemed possible that the German U-Boat campaign, and especially the sinking of the Cunard liner *Lusitania* with the loss of 128 American lives on 6 May, would bring the United States into the War, but the Germans gave informal assurances that passenger ships would not be sunk without warning, and America maintained her neutrality.

By the end of the year the war seemed as rapacious of lives and material as ever, and there was no prospect of peace. Among the Allies, and especially in Britain, indignation mounted at the lack of munitions. On both sides governments began to take unprecedented measures to organise their economy for a long war. The task was to prove too great for Tsarist Russia.

GERMAN CARTOGRAPHIC PROPAGANDA 1915

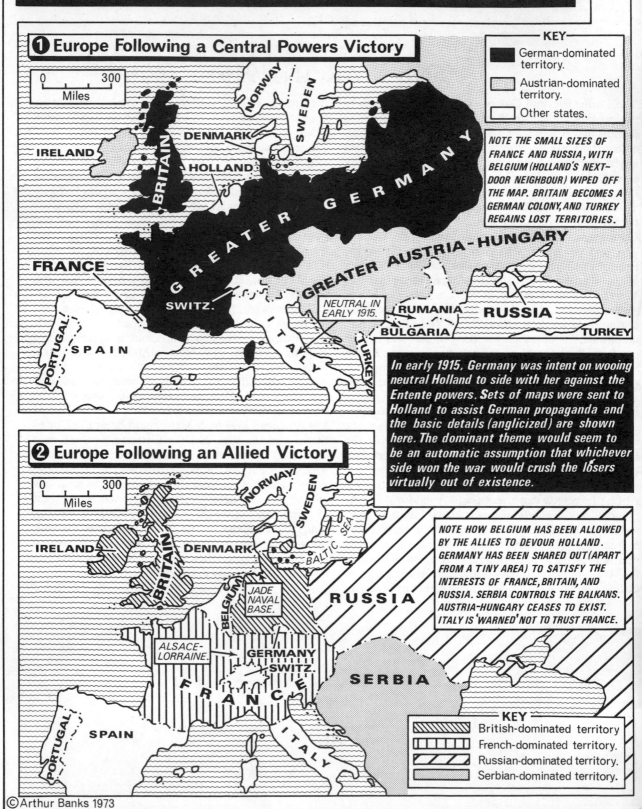

① Europe Following a Central Powers Victory

0 — 300
Miles

KEY
- German-dominated territory.
- Austrian-dominated territory.
- Other states.

IRELAND

NORWAY

SWEDEN

DENMARK

BRITAIN

HOLLAND

GREATER GERMANY

GREATER AUSTRIA-HUNGARY

RUSSIA

FRANCE

SWITZ.

ITALY

NEUTRAL IN EARLY 1915.

RUMANIA

BULGARIA

TURKEY

PORTUGAL

SPAIN

NOTE THE SMALL SIZES OF FRANCE AND RUSSIA, WITH BELGIUM (HOLLAND'S NEXT-DOOR NEIGHBOUR) WIPED OFF THE MAP. BRITAIN BECOMES A GERMAN COLONY, AND TURKEY REGAINS LOST TERRITORIES.

In early 1915, Germany was intent on wooing neutral Holland to side with her against the Entente powers. Sets of maps were sent to Holland to assist German propaganda and the basic details (anglicized) are shown here. The dominant theme would seem to be an automatic assumption that whichever side won the war would crush the losers virtually out of existence.

② Europe Following an Allied Victory

0 — 300
Miles

IRELAND

NORWAY

SWEDEN

BALTIC SEA

DENMARK

BRITAIN

BELGIUM

JADE NAVAL BASE.

RUSSIA

ALSACE-LORRAINE.

GERMANY

SWITZ.

FRANCE

SERBIA

ITALY

PORTUGAL

SPAIN

NOTE HOW BELGIUM HAS BEEN ALLOWED BY THE ALLIES TO DEVOUR HOLLAND. GERMANY HAS BEEN SHARED OUT (APART FROM A TINY AREA) TO SATISFY THE INTERESTS OF FRANCE, BRITAIN, AND RUSSIA. SERBIA CONTROLS THE BALKANS. AUSTRIA-HUNGARY CEASES TO EXIST. ITALY IS 'WARNED' NOT TO TRUST FRANCE.

KEY
- British-dominated territory
- French-dominated territory.
- Russian-dominated territory.
- Serbian-dominated territory.

© Arthur Banks 1973

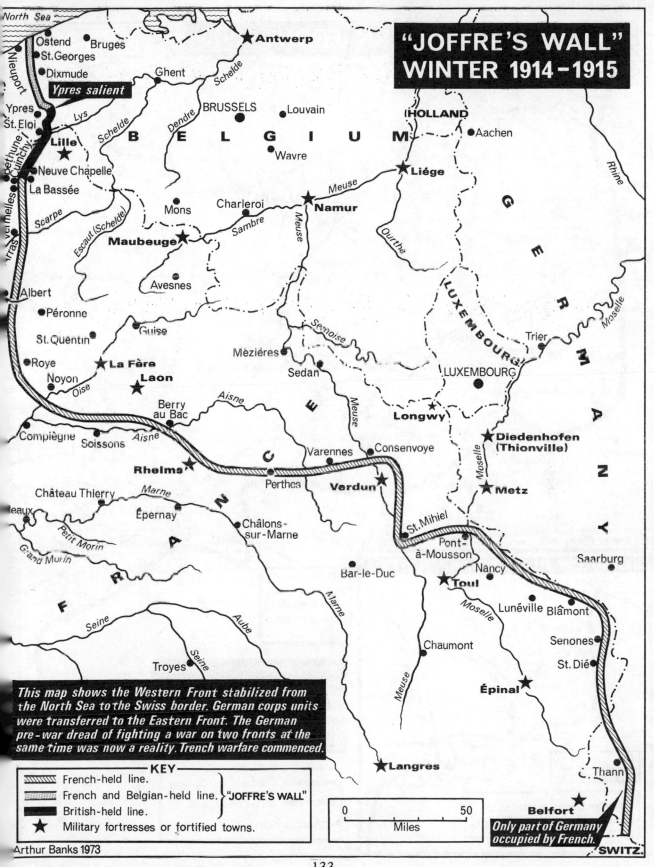

"JOFFRE'S WALL"
WINTER 1914 – 1915

North Sea

Ostend
Bruges
Antwerp
St.Georges
Dixmude
Ghent
Ypres salient
Nieuport
HOLLAND
Ypres
Schelde
Dendre
BRUSSELS
Louvain
Aachen
St.Eloi
Lys
Schelde
Lille
B E L G I U M
Wavre
Liége
Bethune
Meuse
Neuve Chapelle
Mons
Charleroi
Namur
Quinchy
La Bassée
Sambre
Meuse
G
Ourthe
Vermelles
Scarpe
Escaut (Schelde)
Maubeuge
Rhine
E
Arras
Avesnes
Albert
Péronne
Guise
Mézières
Semoise
R
LUXEMBOURG
Trier
Moselle
St.Quentin
Roye
La Fère
Sedan
Noyon
Laon
Oise
LUXEMBOURG
M
Aisne
Meuse
Longwy
Berry au Bac
Compiègne
Soissons
Aisne
Varennes
Consenvoye
Diedenhofen (Thionville)
Rheims
Perthes
Verdun
A
Metz
N
Château Thierry
Marne
Moselle
Meaux
Épernay
Châlons-sur-Marne
St.Mihiel
Y
Petit Morin
Pont-à-Mousson
Saarburg
Grand Morin
F
R
Bar-le-Duc
Nancy
Toul
Marne
Lunéville
Blâmont
Seine
Aube
Moselle
Senones
Chaumont
St.Dié
Troyes
Seine
Meuse
Épinal

This map shows the Western Front stabilized from the North Sea to the Swiss border. German corps units were transferred to the Eastern Front. The German pre-war dread of fighting a war on two fronts at the same time was now a reality. Trench warfare commenced.

Langres
Thann
Belfort

KEY
///// French-held line.
::::: French and Belgian-held line. } **"JOFFRE'S WALL"**
▬▬▬ British-held line.
★ Military fortresses or fortified towns.

Arthur Banks 1973

0 _____ 50
Miles

Only part of Germany occupied by French.
SWITZ.

133

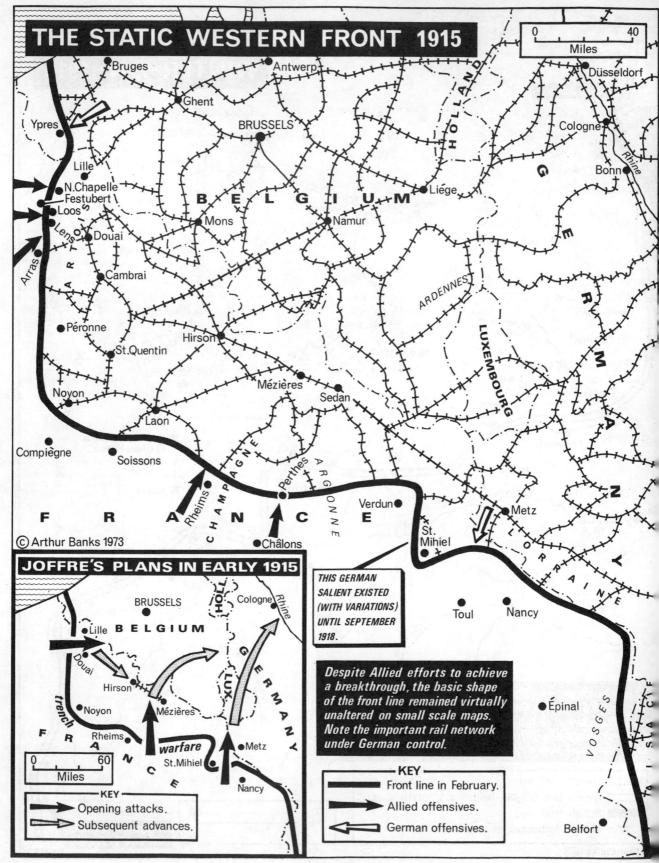

THE STATIC WESTERN FRONT 1915

0 _____ 40
Miles

Bruges
Antwerp
Düsseldorf
Ghent
Cologne
Ypres
BRUSSELS
HOLLAND
Bonn
Lille
Rhine
N.Chapelle
Liége
B E L G I U M
Festubert
G
Loos
Mons
Namur
Lens
Douai
Cambrai
E
ARDENNES
Péronne
R
St.Quentin
Hirson
LUXEMBOURG
Noyon
Mézières
M
Laon
Sedan
Compiègne
Soissons
Perthes
A
N
© Arthur Banks 1973
Rheims
CHAMPAGNE
R
Verdun
Metz
F R A N C E
Châlons
ARGONNE
St. Mihiel
Y
LORRAINE

THIS GERMAN SALIENT EXISTED (WITH VARIATIONS) UNTIL SEPTEMBER 1918.

Toul
Nancy

Despite Allied efforts to achieve a breakthrough, the basic shape of the front line remained virtually unaltered on small scale maps. Note the important rail network under German control.

Épinal

V
O
S
G
E
S

A
L
S

JOFFRE'S PLANS IN EARLY 1915

BRUSSELS
HOLLAND
Cologne
Rhine
Lille
B E L G I U M
Douai
G
Hirson
Noyon
Mézières
E
R
trench
M
Rheims
A
Metz
N
warfare
Y
St.Mihiel
F R A N C E
Nancy

0 _____ 60
Miles

KEY
→ Opening attacks.
⟹ Subsequent advances.

KEY
▬▬ Front line in February.
➤ Allied offensives.
⟸ German offensives.

Belfort

134

THE MOBILE EASTERN FRONT 1915

0   50   100
Miles

Riga

Libau
Fell on 8 May.

Memel

Not captured by Germans.

Dvina

Dvinsk ★

Stormed by Germans 17-18 August.

BALTIC SEA

Kovno ★

Germany's aim was to make the Eastern Front safe and passive so that she could switch her main assault to the Western Front (she did not hope to completely defeat Russia). Rather than instituting an "enveloping" operation, she decided to attempt a "breakthrough" attack between Gorlice and Tarnow. This commenced on 2 May 1915, in concert with the Austrians. This front contrasts sharply with the Western Front during 1915.

Königsberg ★

Danzig ★

E A S T
P R U S S I A

Vistula

Graudenz ★

MASURIAN LAKES

Niemen

Grodno ★

Fell on 2 September.

R U S S I A

Thorn ★

Vistula

Narew

Capitulated on 20 August.

North of this position, the front line remained as shown (with minor variations) until the end of 1917.

Entered by Germans on 5 August.

Novo-Georgievsk ★
Warsaw ★

Bug

Brest-Litovsk ★

Surrendered on 26 August.

P O L A N D

Vistula

Ivangorod ★

Pripet

South of this position, the front line remained as shown (with minor variations) until June 1916.

Fell on 5 August.

San

Evacuated by Russians on 22 June.

Vistula

Cracow ★

Tarnow

G A L I C I A

Lemberg ★

GERMAN ELEVENTH ARMY

2 MAY 1915

Przemysl

Gorlice

Fell on 3 June.

C A R P A T H I A N
M O U N T A I N S

Dniester

Tisza

Pruth

KEY

⇨ Opening assault by German and Austrian armies.

⇨ Advances by German and Austrian armies.

······· Front line, 2 May.

——— Front line, 1 June.

▬▬▬ Front line, 16 July.

▭▭▭ Front line, 15 August.

– – – Front line, 1 September.

▲▲▲ Front line, winter 1915.

© Arthur Banks 1973

135

THE BATTLE OF NEUVE CHAPELLE 10-12 MARCH 1915

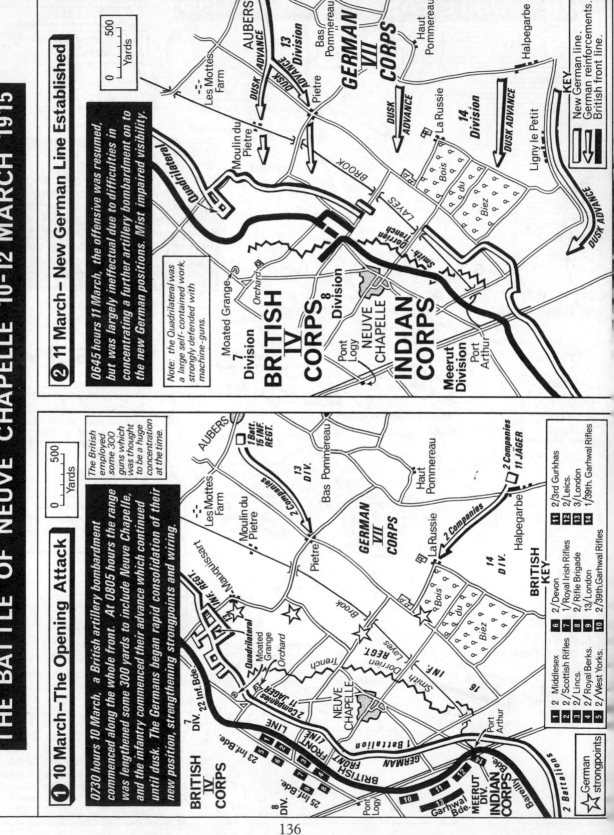

2 11 March – New German Line Established

0645 hours 11 March, the offensive was resumed, but was largely ineffectual due to difficulties in concentrating a further artillery bombardment on to the new German positions. Mist impaired visibility.

Note: the Quadrilateral was a large self-contained work, strongly defended with machine-guns.

KEY
New German line.
German reinforcements.
British front line.

1 10 March – The Opening Attack

0730 hours 10 March, a British artillery bombardment commenced along the whole front. At 0805 hours the range was lengthened some 300 yards to include Neuve Chapelle, and the infantry commenced their advance which continued until dusk. The Germans began rapid consolidation of their new position, strengthening strongpoints and wiring.

The British employed some 300 guns which was thought to be a huge concentration at the time.

BRITISH KEY

1	2/Middlesex	6	2/Devon
2	2/Scottish Rifles	7	1/Royal Irish Rifles
3	2/Lincs.	8	2/Rifle Brigade
4	2/Royal Berks.	9	13/London
5	2/West Yorks.	10	2/39th.Garhwal Rifles

11	2/3rd Gurkhas
12	2/Leics.
13	3/London
14	1/39th. Garhwal Rifles

☆ German strongpoints

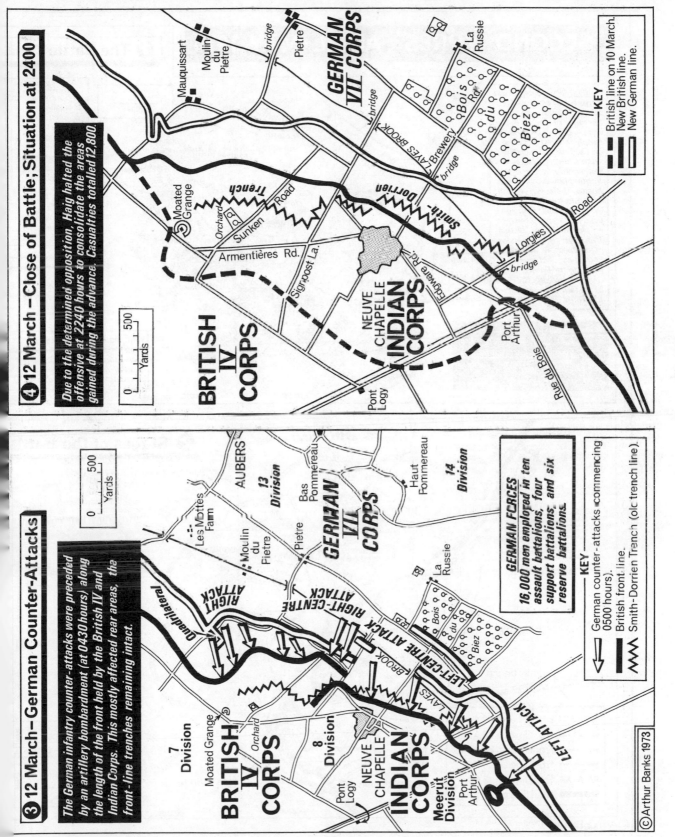

④ 12 March – Close of Battle; Situation at 2400

Due to the determined opposition, Haig halted the offensive at 2240 hours to consolidate the areas gained during the advance. Casualties totalled 12,800.

KEY

▮▮ British line on 10 March.
▬▬ New British line.
▭▭ New German line.

0 — 500
Yards

GERMAN VII CORPS

Mauquissart
Moulin du Pietre
bridge
Pietre
La Russie
Bois du Biez
Brewery
LAYES BROOK
bridge
bridge

Moated Grange
Orchard
Sunken Road
Trench
Smith-Dorrien
Armentières Rd.
Sighoost La.
Lorgies
bridge
Edgware Rd.
Road

BRITISH IV CORPS

NEUVE CHAPELLE
INDIAN CORPS

Port Arthur
Pont Logy
Rue du Bois

---

③ 12 March – German Counter-Attacks

The German infantry counter-attacks were preceded by an artillery bombardment (at 0430 hours) along the length of the front held by the British IV and Indian Corps. This mostly affected rear areas, the front-line trenches remaining intact.

0 — 500
Yards

AUBERS
Les Mottes Farm
13 Division
Bas Pommereau
Moulin du Fietre
Pietre
GERMAN VII CORPS
Haut Pommereau
14 Division

KEY

GERMAN FORCES
16,000 men employed in ten assault battalions, four support battalions, and six reserve battalions.

⇩ German counter-attacks (commencing 0500 hours).
▬▬ British front line.
ᴧᴧᴧ Smith-Dorrien Trench (old trench line).

© Arthur Banks 1973

Quadrilateral
RIGHT ATTACK
RIGHT-CENTRE ATTACK
LEFT-CENTRE ATTACK
LAYES BROOK
LEFT ATTACK

7 Division
Moated Grange
Orchard

BRITISH IV CORPS

8 Division
NEUVE CHAPELLE
Pont Logy
INDIAN CORPS
Meerut Division
Port Arthur
La Russie
Bois du Biez

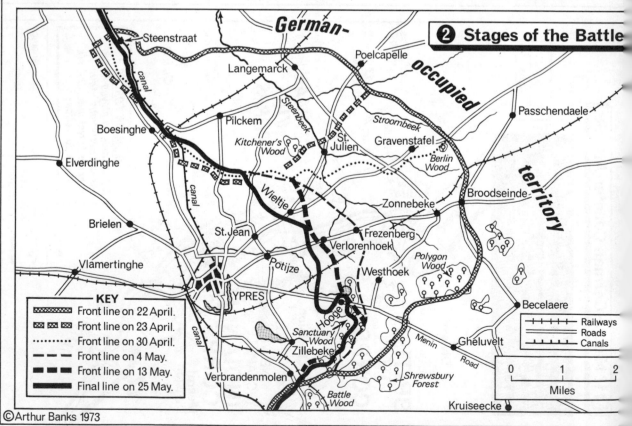

"SECOND YPRES" APRIL-MAY 1915

① The Battle Area

Note on farm names: most farms were not named on military maps in use at this stage of the war in the vicinity of Ypres, and were simply referred to by the grid square in which they were situated. This caused some confusion, and the fighting powers began to bestow their own versions of names to various farms. On these maps, British-used names have been employed. Using 'Mouse Trap Farm' (British version) as an example, it was known as 'Chateau du Nord' to the French and Belgians, 'Wieltje Chateau' to the Germans, and 'Shell Trap Farm' to the Canadians.

Note on ridges: these have been emphasised solely for clarity. In reality, they are low gradual spurs with gradients rarely exceeding 1 in 20. Highest points about 250 feet.

FARMS
1. South Zwaanhof
2. Fusilier
3. Turco
4. Welch
5. Canadian
6. Oblong
7. Vanheule
8. Mouse Trap
9. Hampshire
10. Foch
11. Belle Alliance
12. Boetleer's
13. Bellewaarde
14. Château
15. White Château

● Villages
■ Farms
🌳🌳 Woods

With the exception of Langemarck (population 7,500) and Boesinghe (population 2,500), the villages around Ypres were small, and the populations were less than 1,000.

0 ——— 1 Mile

Steenstraat · Poelcapelle · Langemarck · Lekkerboterbeek · Stroombeek Ridge · Passchendaele · Boesinghe · Pilckem · Pilckem Ridge · Steenbeek · Gravenstafel Ridge · St. Julien · Gravenstafel · Mauser Ridge · Haanebeek · Brielen · Hill Top Ridge · Wieltje · Zonnebeke Ridge · Broodseinde · Zonnebeke · Frezenberg · St. Jean Ridge · St. Jean · Verlorenhoek · RIDGE · Potijze · Westhoek · Becelaere · YPRES · Zillebeke · Bellewaarde Ridge · Hooge · Zillebeke Lake · Zillebeke · YPRES Ridge · Gheluvelt · Verbrandenmolen · Hill 60 · Kruiseecke

② Stages of the Battle

German-occupied territory

Steenstraat · Poelcapelle · Langemarck · Passchendaele · Pilckem · Steenbeek · St. Julien · Stroombeek · Gravenstafel · Boesinghe · Kitchener's Wood · Berlin Wood · Broodseinde · Elverdinghe · Wieltje · Zonnebeke · Brielen · St. Jean · Frezenberg · Verlorenhoek · Polygon Wood · Potijze · Westhoek · Becelaere · YPRES · Hooge · Sanctuary Wood · Gheluvelt · Zillebeke · Menin Road · Verbrandenmolen · Battle Wood · Shrewsbury Forest · Kruiseecke

KEY
▨▨▨ Front line on 22 April.
▨ ▨ ▨ Front line on 23 April.
⋯⋯⋯ Front line on 30 April.
— — — Front line on 4 May.
▬ ▬ ▬ Front line on 13 May.
▬▬▬ Final line on 25 May.

+++ Railways
——— Roads
+—+ Canals

0 ——— 1 ——— 2 Miles

© Arthur Banks 1973

138

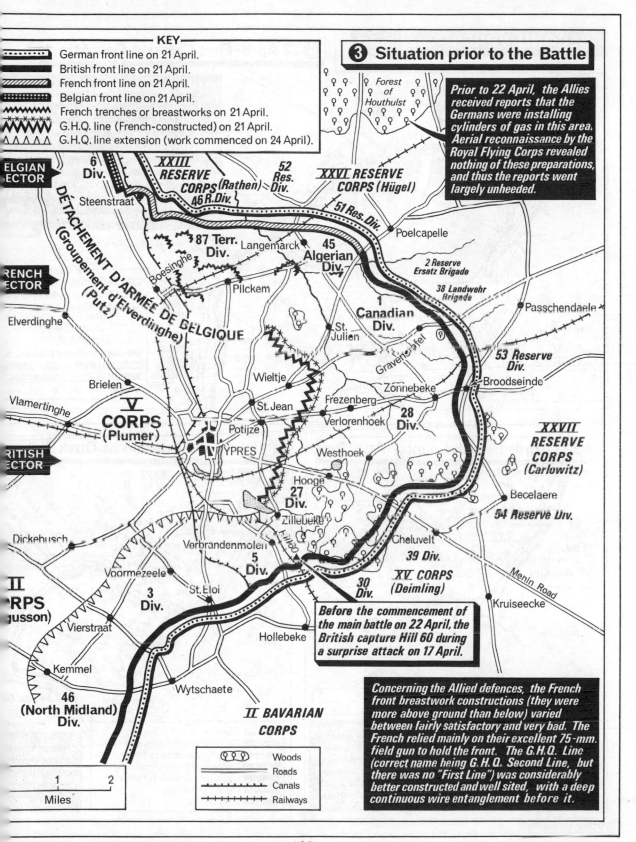

KEY

- German front line on 21 April.
- British front line on 21 April.
- French front line on 21 April.
- Belgian front line on 21 April.
- French trenches or breastworks on 21 April.
- G.H.Q. line (French-constructed) on 21 April.
- G.H.Q. line extension (work commenced on 24 April).

3 Situation prior to the Battle

Prior to 22 April, the Allies received reports that the Germans were installing cylinders of gas in this area. Aerial reconnaissance by the Royal Flying Corps revealed nothing of these preparations, and thus the reports went largely unheeded.

Forest of Houthulst

BELGIAN SECTOR

6 Div.

XXIII RESERVE CORPS (Rathen) 46 R.Div.

52 Res. Div.

XXVI RESERVE CORPS (Hügel)

51 Res. Div.

Steenstraat

DÉTACHEMENT D'ARMÉE DE BELGIQUE (Groupement d'Elverdinghe) (Putz)

FRENCH SECTOR

87 Terr. Div.

Boesinghe

Langemarck

Pilckem

45 Algerian Div.

Poelcapelle

2 Reserve Ersatz Brigade

38 Landwehr Brigade

Passchendaele

Elverdinghe

St. Julien

1 Canadian Div.

Gravenstafel

53 Reserve Div.

Broodseinde

Brielen

Wieltje

Zonnebeke

V CORPS (Plumer)

St. Jean

Frezenberg

Verlorenhoek

28 Div.

XXVII RESERVE CORPS (Carlowitz)

Vlamertinghe

Potijze

YPRES

Westhoek

Becelaere

BRITISH SECTOR

Hooge

54 Reserve Div.

27 Div.

Zillebeke

Cheluvelt

Dickebusch

Verbrandenmolen

39 Div.

Menin Road

II CORPS (Fergusson)

Voormezeele

5 Div.

Hill 60

30 Div.

XV CORPS (Deimling)

Kruiseecke

3 Div.

St. Eloi

Before the commencement of the main battle on 22 April, the British capture Hill 60 during a surprise attack on 17 April.

Vierstraat

Hollebeke

Kemmel

Wytschaete

46 (North Midland) Div.

II BAVARIAN CORPS

Concerning the Allied defences, the French front breastwork constructions (they were more above ground than below) varied between fairly satisfactory and very bad. The French relied mainly on their excellent 75-mm. field gun to hold the front. The G.H.Q. Line (correct name being G.H.Q. Second Line, but there was no "First Line") was considerably better constructed and well sited, with a deep continuous wire entanglement before it.

	Woods
	Roads
	Canals
	Railways

1 2
Miles

"SECOND YPRES" - continued

④ 22 April – First Chlorine Gas Attack

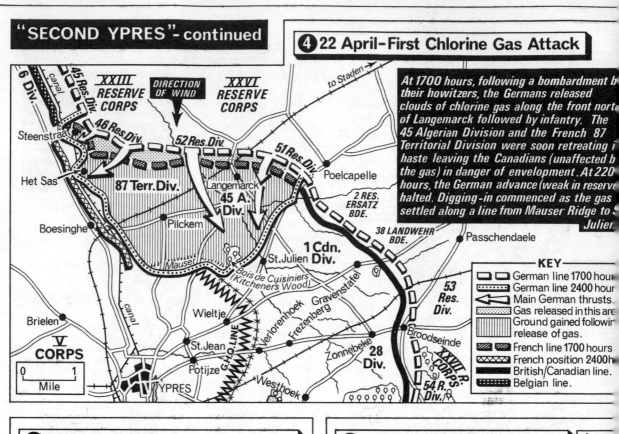

At 1700 hours, following a bombardment by their howitzers, the Germans released clouds of chlorine gas along the front north of Langemarck followed by infantry. The 45 Algerian Division and the French 87 Territorial Division were soon retreating in haste leaving the Canadians (unaffected by the gas) in danger of envelopment. At 2200 hours, the German advance (weak in reserves) halted. Digging-in commenced as the gas settled along a line from Mauser Ridge to St. Julien.

KEY
- German line 1700 hours.
- German line 2400 hours.
- Main German thrusts.
- Gas released in this area.
- Ground gained following release of gas.
- French line 1700 hours.
- French position 2400 hours.
- British/Canadian line.
- Belgian line.

⑤ 23 April – British Counter-Attacks

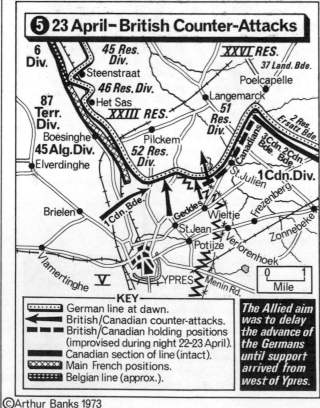

KEY
- German line at dawn.
- British/Canadian counter-attacks.
- British/Canadian holding positions (improvised during night 22-23 April).
- Canadian section of line (intact).
- Main French positions.
- Belgian line (approx.).

The Allied aim was to delay the advance of the Germans until support arrived from west of Ypres.

⑥ 23 April – Situation at Dusk

KEY
- German line at dusk.
- German attacks (developing).
- British advances to front.
- Canadian/British holding units.
- Canadian/British firm line.
- French positions.
- Belgian line.

By dusk, despite German artillery superiority, the gap in the Allied line north of had been filled.

© Arthur Banks 1973

140

7 24 April-Battle of St. Julien

0 1 Mile

0130 hours, Germans occupy Lizerne. Belgians stem further progress.

37 Land. Bde.

46 Res. Div.

XXVI RES.

XXIII RES.

Lizerne

102 Res. Bde.

4 Marine Bde.

2 Res. Ersatz Bde.

Composite Bde. (53 Res. Bde.)

51 R. Div.

G

38 Land. Bde.

52 R. Div.

French Attack

1330 hrs.

St. Julien

Zonnebeke

Passchendaele

Fierce house-to-house fighting.

53 Res. Div.

St. Jean

Frezenberg

Hooge

Westhoek

XXVII R.

54 Res. Div.

YPRES

V CORPS

Potijze

Zillebeke

Gheluvelt

KEY

······· German line at dawn.

⬅ Main German thrusts.

▦ Ground gained by Germans.

Gas released at **G** (0400 hours).

Allied units have been omitted for clarity. German artillery batteries dominated area.

8 25 April-Situation at Dusk

0 1 Mile

Throughout the day, the German artillery shelled Allied units and positions in the salient.

Steenstraat

XXIII RES.

XXVI RES.

Poelcapelle

Langemarck

51 R. Div.

Pilckem

52 R. Div.

Taken and held by Germans.

Passchendaele

Boesinghe

St. Julien

Brielen

St. Jean

Wieltje

Frezenberg

53 Res. Div.

Potijze

Westhoek

Zonnebeke

XXVII RES.

V YPRES

Hooge

54 R. Div.

Zillebeke

Gheluvelt

Noon, Lahore Division (Indian) concentrates at Ouderdom, five miles south-west of Ypres.

During the evening, the bulk of the Canadian Division was pulled back into reserve. Its casualties since 22 April: 1,700 dead and 2,500 wounded.

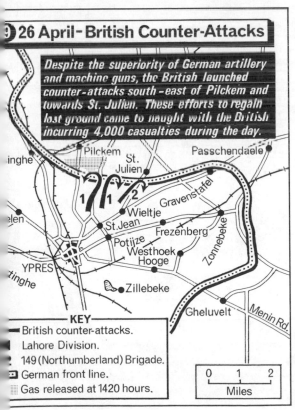

9 26 April-British Counter-Attacks

Despite the superiority of German artillery and machine guns, the British launched counter-attacks south-east of Pilckem and towards St. Julien. These efforts to regain lost ground came to naught with the British incurring 4,000 casualties during the day.

-inghe

Pilckem

St. Julien

Passchendaele

1 1 2

Gravenstafel

Wieltje

St. Jean

Frezenberg

Zonnebeke

-elen

Potijze

Westhoek

Hooge

YPRES

-tinghe

Zillebeke

Gheluvelt

Menin Rd.

KEY

━ British counter-attacks.

Lahore Division.

1 149 (Northumberland) Brigade.

▣ German front line.

▦ Gas released at 1420 hours.

0 1 2 Miles

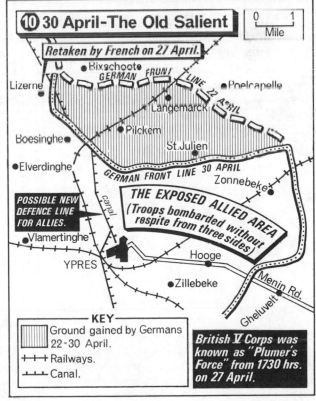

10 30 April-The Old Salient

0 1 Mile

Retaken by French on 27 April.

Bixschoote

GERMAN FRONT

LINE 22 APRIL

Lizerne

Poelcapelle

Langemarck

Boesinghe

Pilckem

St. Julien

Elverdinghe

GERMAN FRONT LINE 30 APRIL

Zonnebeke

POSSIBLE NEW DEFENCE LINE FOR ALLIES.

canal

THE EXPOSED ALLIED AREA (Troops bombarded without respite from three sides)

Vlamertinghe

YPRES

Hooge

Zillebeke

Gheluvelt

Menin Rd.

KEY

▦ Ground gained by Germans 22-30 April.

+++ Railways.

┷┷┷ Canal.

British V Corps was known as "Plumer's Force" from 1730 hrs. on 27 April.

141

"SECOND YPRES"- continued

⑪ 4 May-The New Salient

0 — 1 Mile

Langemarck

Boesinghe   Pilckem

Between 1 and 4 May, British units retired to new positions to shorten their lines of defence.

Zonnebeke

G.H.Q. Line defences are strengthened and extended at speed.

Vlamertinghe   YPRES   Hooge   Menin Road

Zillebeke   Gheluvelt

HILL 60

KEY
- Ground relinquished by British, 1-4 May.
- British front line, 1 May.
- British front line, 4 May.
- French front line, 4 May.

1 May, British defeat a German gas-assisted attack for first time.

⑫ 8 May-Battle of Frezenberg Ridge

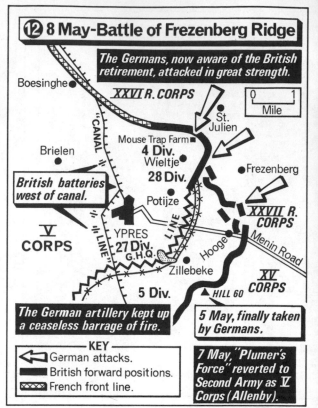

The Germans, now aware of the British retirement, attacked in great strength.

Boesinghe

XXVI R. CORPS

0 — 1 Mile

St. Julien

Mouse Trap Farm

Brielen   **4 Div.**   Wieltje   Frezenberg

28 Div.

British batteries west of canal.   Potijze

V CORPS   YPRES   **27 Div.**   G.H.Q.   Hooge   *XXVII R. CORPS*

Zillebeke   *XV CORPS*

5 Div.   ▲ HILL 60

The German artillery kept up a ceaseless barrage of fire.

5 May, finally taken by Germans.

KEY
- German attacks.
- British forward positions.
- French front line.

7 May, "Plumer's Force" reverted to Second Army as V Corps (Allenby).

⑬ 13 May-Final Moves at Frezenberg

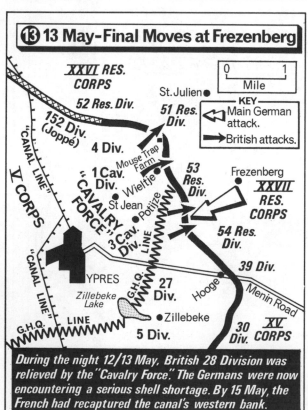

XXVI RES. CORPS

52 Res. Div.

St. Julien

152 Div. (Joppé)   **51 Res. Div.**

0 — 1 Mile

KEY
- Main German attack.
- British attacks.

4 Div.

1 Cav. Div.   Mouse Trap Farm   **53 Res. Div.**   Frezenberg

V CORPS   "CAVALRY FORCE"   Wieltje   *XXVII RES. CORPS*

St Jean   Potijze

3 Cav. Div.   **54 Res. Div.**

YPRES   G.H.Q.   Hooge   **39 Div.**   Menin Road

Zillebeke Lake   **27 Div.**   Zillebeke

5 Div.   **30 Div.**   *XV CORPS*

"CANAL LINE"   "CANAL LINE"   G.H.Q. LINE

During the night 12/13 May, British 28 Division was relieved by the "Cavalry Force". The Germans were now encountering a serious shell shortage. By 15 May, the French had recaptured the canal's western bank.

⑭ 24 May-Battle of Bellewaarde Ridge

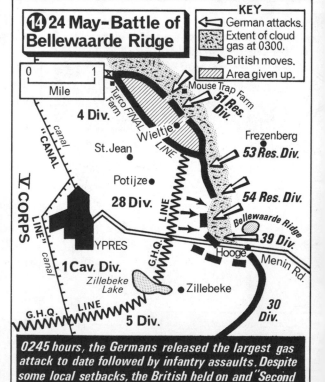

KEY
- German attacks.
- Extent of cloud gas at 0300.
- British moves.
- Area given up.

0 — 1 Mile

Turco Farm   Mouse Trap Farm   **51 Res. Div.**

4 Div.   Wieltje   FINAL LINE

canal "CANAL LINE"   St. Jean   Frezenberg

53 Res. Div.

V CORPS   Potijze   **28 Div.**

54 Res. Div.

G.H.Q. LINE   Bellewaarde Ridge

YPRES   **1 Cav. Div.**   **39 Div.**

Zillebeke Lake   Hooge   Menin Rd.

G.H.Q. LINE   Zillebeke   **30 Div.**

5 Div.

0245 hours, the Germans released the largest gas attack to date followed by infantry assaults. Despite some local setbacks, the British held on and "Second Ypres" dwindled out. British 4 Division retired at 2000.

© Arthur Banks 1973

142

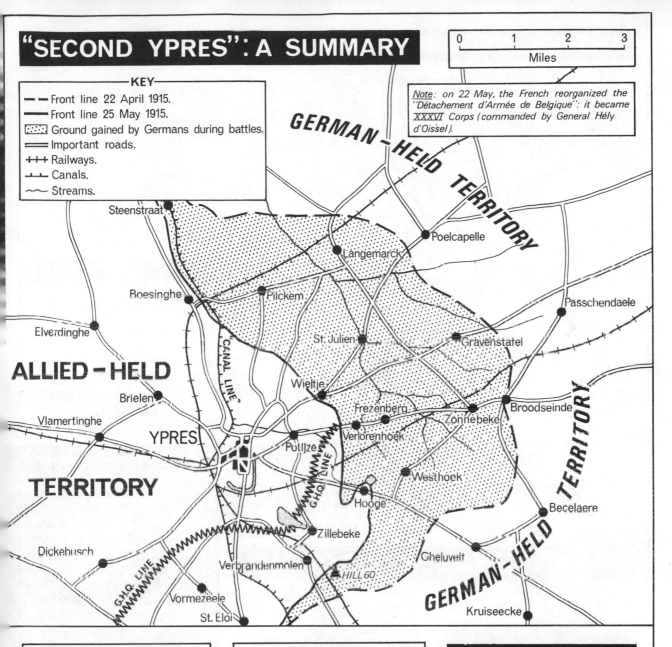

"SECOND YPRES": A SUMMARY

0 1 2 3
Miles

KEY

- **– –** Front line 22 April 1915.
- **——** Front line 25 May 1915.
- Ground gained by Germans during battles.
- **═══** Important roads.
- **+++** Railways.
- **⊥⊥⊥** Canals.
- **∿∿** Streams.

Note: on 22 May, the French reorganized the 'Détachement d'Armée de Belgique': it became XXXVI Corps (commanded by General Hély d'Oissel).

GERMAN-HELD TERRITORY

Steenstraat
Poelcapelle
Langemarck
Boesinghe
Pilckem
Passchendaele
Elverdinghe

ALLIED-HELD
St. Julien
Gravenstafel
Brielen
Wieltje
Vlamertinghe
Frezenberg
Zonnebeke
Broodseinde
YPRES
Verlorenhoek
Pollize
TERRITORY
Westhoek
Hooge
Becelaere
Dickebusch
Zillebeke
Gheluvelt
Verbrandenmolen
HILL 60
Vormezeele
GERMAN-HELD TERRITORY
St. Eloi
Kruiseecke

"CANAL LINE"
G.H.Q. LINE

TERRITORY

BRITISH CASUALTIES (59,275)	
1 Cavalry Division :	1,203
2 Cavalry Division :	244
3 Cavalry Division :	1,618
4 Division :	10,859
5 Division :	7,994
27 Division :	7,263
28 Division :	15,533
50 Division :	5,204
1 Canadian Division :	5,469
Lahore Division :	3,888

GERMAN CASUALTIES (34,933)	
XXIII Reserve Corps :	10,592
XXVI Reserve Corps :	12,845
XXVII Reserve Corps :	8,652
XV Corps :	2,844

FRENCH CASUALTIES
(10,000)
→ ESTIMATE   *Precise figs. unknown*

BELGIAN CASUALTIES
(1,530)

BY THE CLOSE OF "SECOND YPRES", THE GERMANS HAD GAINED SOME GROUND BUT THE SALIENT STILL REMAINED, ALBEIT REDUCED IN SIZE. MORE IMPORTANT FOR THE FUTURE, THEY HAD DISCLOSED THEIR SECRET WEAPON (GAS) PREMATURELY, AS THEY WERE NOT SUFFICIENTLY EQUIPPED TO EXPLOIT THEIR INITIAL SUCCESS OF 22 APRIL. ON THE BRITISH SIDE, THE BATTLES WERE MARKED BY INDECISION AMONG THE HIGHER RANKS AS TO THE CORRECT DEFENSIVE ACTION TO EMPLOY, AND GENERAL SMITH-DORRIEN (2 ARMY COMMANDER) WAS DISMISSED ON 6 MAY AS A RESULT OF DISSENSION BETWEEN HIMSELF AND THE COMMANDER-IN-CHIEF, FIELD-MARSHAL SIR JOHN FRENCH.

© Arthur Banks 1973

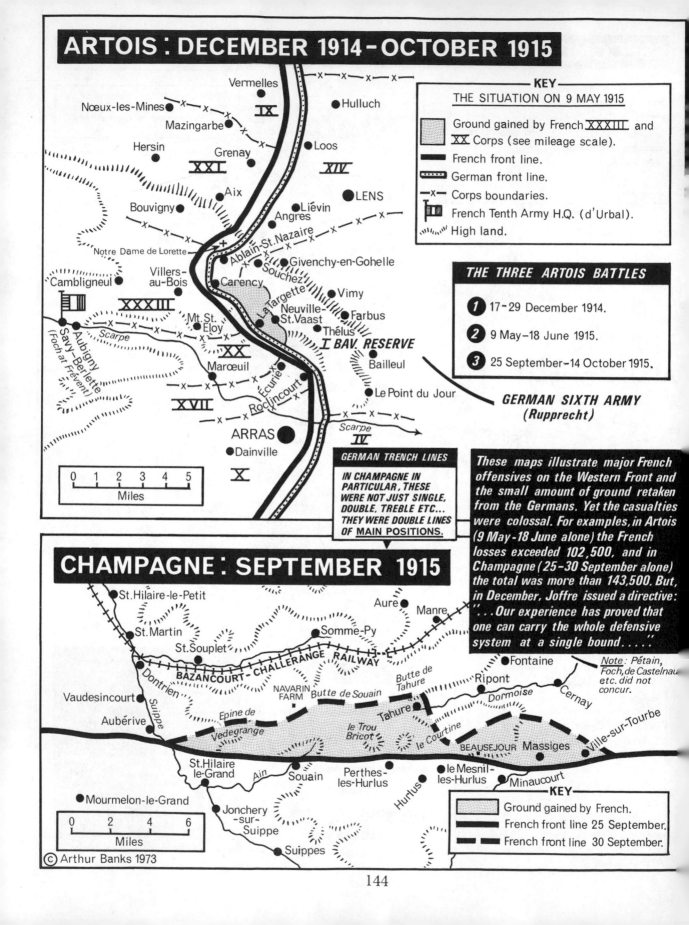

ARTOIS : DECEMBER 1914 – OCTOBER 1915

KEY

THE SITUATION ON 9 MAY 1915

Ground gained by French XXXIII and XX Corps (see mileage scale).

——— French front line.

▥▥▥ German front line.

–x–x– Corps boundaries.

🚩 French Tenth Army H.Q. (d'Urbal).

ⱮⱮⱮ High land.

Vermelles

Nœux-les-Mines

Hulluch

Mazingarbe

IX

Hersin

Grenay

Loos

XXI

XIV

Aix

Bouvigny

Liévin

LENS

Angres

Notre Dame de Lorette

Ablain-St.Nazaire

Givenchy-en-Gohelle

Villers-au-Bois

Souchez

Cambligneul

Carency

la Targette

Vimy

Neuville-St.Vaast

Farbus

Mt.St. Eloy

Thélus

Aubigny Savy-Berlette (Foch at Frévent)

Scarpe

I BAV. RESERVE

XXXIII

XX

Bailleul

Marœuil

Ecurie

Roclincourt

Le Point du Jour

XVII

ARRAS

Scarpe

IV

Dainville

X

```
0  1  2  3  4  5
Miles
```

THE THREE ARTOIS BATTLES

1 17–29 December 1914.

2 9 May–18 June 1915.

3 25 September–14 October 1915.

GERMAN SIXTH ARMY
(Rupprecht)

GERMAN TRENCH LINES

IN CHAMPAGNE IN PARTICULAR, THESE WERE NOT JUST SINGLE, DOUBLE, TREBLE ETC... THEY WERE DOUBLE LINES OF **MAIN POSITIONS**.

These maps illustrate major French offensives on the Western Front and the small amount of ground retaken from the Germans. Yet the casualties were colossal. For examples, in Artois (9 May–18 June alone) the French losses exceeded 102,500, and in Champagne (25–30 September alone) the total was more than 143,500. But, in December, Joffre issued a directive: "...Our experience has proved that one can carry the whole defensive system at a single bound...."

Note: Pétain, Foch, de Castelnau etc. did not concur.

CHAMPAGNE : SEPTEMBER 1915

St.Hilaire-le-Petit

Aure

Manre

St.Martin

Somme-Py

St.Souplet

BAZANCOURT–CHALLERANGE RAILWAY

Fontaine

Vaudesincourt

Dontrien

NAVARIN FARM

Butte de Souain

Butte de Tahure

Ripont

Dormoise

Cernay

Aubérive

Suippe

Epine de Vedegrange

le Trou Bricot

Tahure

le Courtine

BEAUSEJOUR

Massiges

Ville-sur-Tourbe

St.Hilaire le-Grand

Ain

Souain

Perthes-les-Hurlus

le Mesnil-les-Hurlus

Minaucourt

Mourmelon-le-Grand

Jonchery -sur- Suippe

Hurlus

KEY

Ground gained by French.

——— French front line 25 September.

▬ ▬ French front line 30 September.

```
0    2    4    6
Miles
```

© Arthur Banks 1973

Suippes

144

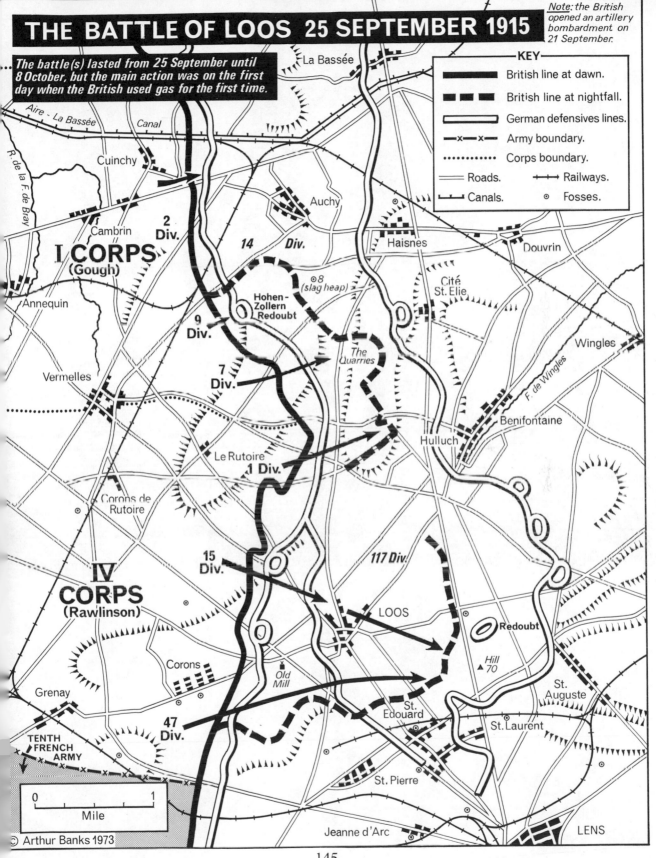

THE BATTLE OF LOOS 25 SEPTEMBER 1915

Note: the British opened an artillery bombardment on 21 September.

The battle(s) lasted from 25 September until 8 October, but the main action was on the first day when the British used gas for the first time.

KEY

▬▬▬▬	British line at dawn.
▬ ▬ ▬	British line at nightfall.
▭▭▭	German defensives lines.
×—×—×	Army boundary.
•••••••	Corps boundary.
——	Roads.
⊢⊢⊢⊢	Railways.
⊣⊢⊣⊢	Canals.
⊙	Fosses.

La Bassée

Aire - La Bassée   Canal

Cuinchy

Auchy

R. de la F. de Bray

Cambrin

2 Div.

I CORPS
(Gough)

14   Div.

Haisnes

Douvrin

Annequin

Hohen-Zollern Redoubt

⊙8 (slag heap)

Cité St. Elie

9 Div.

7 Div.

The Quarries

Wingles

Vermelles

F. de Wingles

Le Rutoire

1 Div.

Hulluch

Benifontaine

Corons de Rutoire

15 Div.

117 Div.

IV
CORPS
(Rawlinson)

LOOS

Redoubt

Corons

Old Mill

Hill ▲70

St. Auguste

Grenay

47 Div.

St. Edouard

St. Laurent

St. Pierre

TENTH FRENCH ARMY

0			1
	Mile		

Jeanne d'Arc

LENS

© Arthur Banks 1973

145

THE WAR IN 1916

The costly failures of 1915 had led to changes in command before the end of the year. In the autumn, against the advice of his ministers, Tsar Nicholas II assumed command on the Eastern Front, sending Grand Duke Nicholas to hold the Caucasus against the Turks (page 163). The heavy casualties at Loos discredited Sir John French who, in December, was replaced as British commander-in-chief by Sir Douglas Haig. At the same time Kitchener, though remaining War Minister, surrendered responsibility for operations to a new Chief of the Imperial General Staff, Sir William Robertson, an ex-footman who had enlisted as a private thirty-nine years before. Only in France did Joffre's supremacy pass unchallenged.

Haig and Robertson were a formidable partnership. They insisted that, after the frustrations of Gallipoli, the Western Front was to have priority over all other Fronts. This decision was endorsed by the Cabinet on 28 December 1915; it was welcomed by Joffre. His own plans for 1916 looked for wearing-down operations by his allies preparatory to a major offensive by the French later in the spring. But the initiative on the Western Front was seized by the Germans. Falkenhayn won the Kaiser's consent for a different concept of military operations: he proposed massive attack on a narrow sector where reasons of national sentiment would 'compel the French General Staff to throw in every man they have'. The sector he recommended for this attempt 'to bleed France white' (Falkenhayn's own expression) was Verdun, the historic city on the Meuse whose fall in 1792 precipitated the panic September massacres in revolutionary Paris.

The battle of Verdun, which began with a concentrated artillery barrage on 21 February 1916 and continued for 300 days, overshadowed—and to some extent predetermined—all other military events of the year. Verdun, like Ypres, never fell to the Germans; it consumed Joffre's reserves; it left the French Army permanently shell-shocked; but it also brought dis-illusionment to the Germans, who sustained a third of a million casualties in occupying a crater filled wasteland one-sixth the size of the Isle of Wight. Never again was morale steady, either in France or Germany.

Ultimately the defenders of Verdun were relieved by actions elsewhere. By midsummer Haig, supported by Foch's Sixth Army, was ready to attack on the Somme. 20,000 British soldiers perished on the first day of the battle, more than were killed in action during the five years of Wellington's Peninsular Campaign. Yet, despite the terrible losses, Haig continued to pound the German lines on the Somme, employing in September, for the first time, tanks to cross trenches and destroy machine gun nests. The Somme was a traumatic as Verdun.

Success in 1916 came on the south-west sector of the Eastern Front where General Brusilov convinced the Tsar that it was possible to break through the Austrian defences and, if assisted by an enveloping movement farther north, to knock Austria-Hungary out of the war. Brusilov forced the Austrians to fall back sixty or seventy miles in confusion: the Germans rushed divisions from the Western Front to plug the gap, the Austrians relaxed pressure on Italy, and even a Turkish Corps was hurried to Galicia. The northern attack never materialised, but Brusilov gained a remarkable triumph, sufficient to tempt Rumania into the war as an ally, although the Rumanians were speedily defeated (page 162). The victory over Rumania was won by Mackensen and Falkenhayn, who had been replaced as Chief of the German General Staff by Hindenburg when the Kaiser despaired of his Verdun policy at the end of August.

At sea, 1916 was the year of Jutland (pages 256–261), of intensified measures by the British to blockade Germany, and of a fifty per cent increase over the 1915 figures for the tonnage of Allied shipping sunk by U-boats. The outlook for 1917 was ominous.

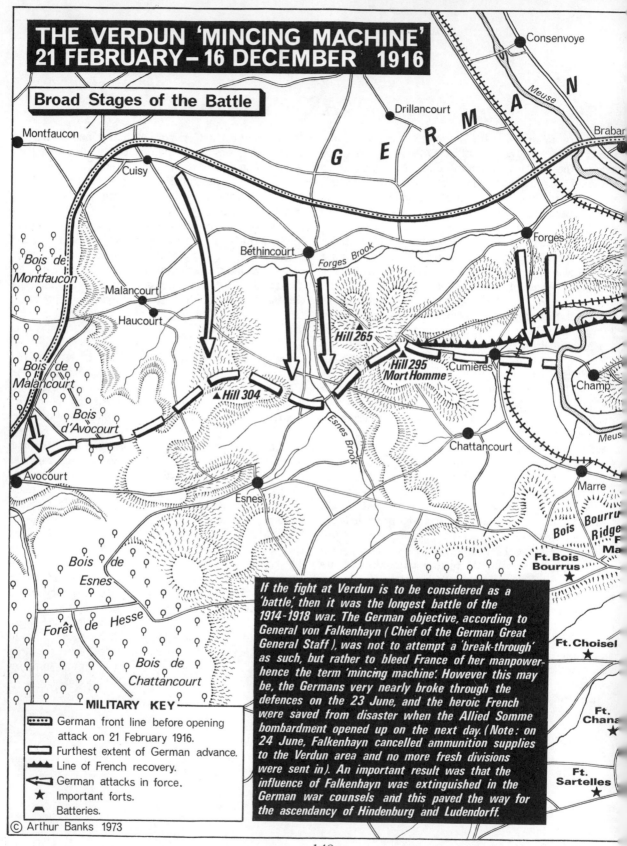

THE VERDUN 'MINCING MACHINE' 21 FEBRUARY – 16 DECEMBER 1916

Broad Stages of the Battle

Consenvoye

Drillancourt

G E R M A N

Montfaucon

Brabar

Cuisy

Meuse

Bois de Montfaucon

Béthincourt

Forges Brook

Forges

Malancourt

Hill 265

Haucourt

Hill 295
Mort Homme

Cumières

Bois de Malancourt

Hill 304

Champ

Bois d'Avocourt

Esnes Brook

Meus

Chattancourt

Avocourt

Marre

Esnes

Bois Bourru

Ridge
Ma

Ft. Bois
Bourrus ★

Bois de Esnes

Forêt de Hesse

Bois de Chattancourt

Ft. Choisel ★

MILITARY KEY

If the fight at Verdun is to be considered as a 'battle', then it was the longest battle of the 1914-1918 war. The German objective, according to General von Falkenhayn (Chief of the German Great General Staff), was not to attempt a 'break-through' as such, but rather to bleed France of her manpower- hence the term 'mincing machine'. However this may be, the Germans very nearly broke through the defences on the 23 June, and the heroic French were saved from disaster when the Allied Somme bombardment opened up on the next day. (Note: on 24 June, Falkenhayn cancelled ammunition supplies to the Verdun area and no more fresh divisions were sent in). An important result was that the influence of Falkenhayn was extinguished in the German war counsels and this paved the way for the ascendancy of Hindenburg and Ludendorff.

German front line before opening attack on 21 February 1916.

Furthest extent of German advance.

Line of French recovery.

German attacks in force.

★ Important forts.

▬ Batteries.

Ft.
Chana ★

Ft.
Sartelles ★

© Arthur Banks 1973

148

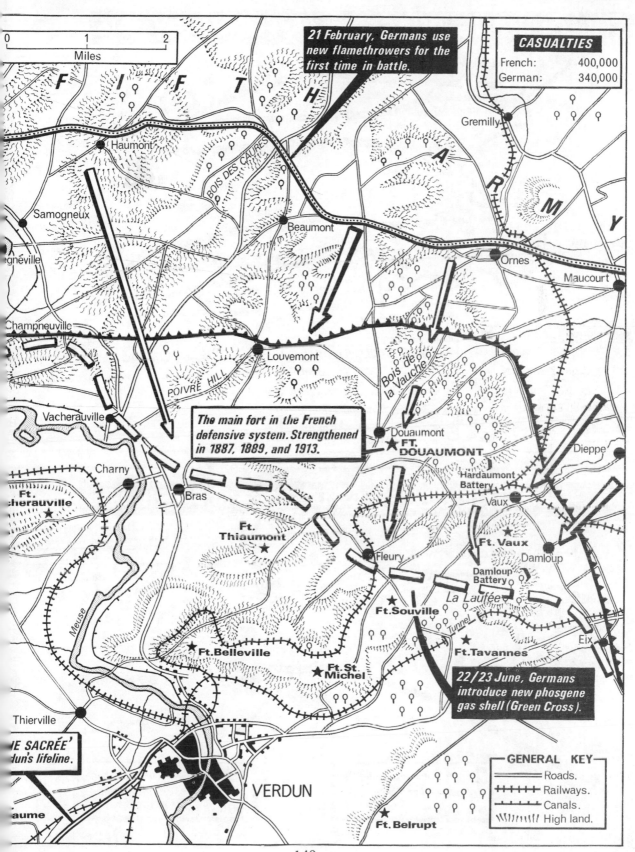

0   1   2
Miles

21 February, Germans use new flamethrowers for the first time in battle.

CASUALTIES

French:	400,000
German:	340,000

F I F T H   A R M Y

Gremilly

Haumont

BOIS DES CAURES

Samogneux

egnéville

Beaumont

Ornes

Maucourt

Champneuville

Louvemont

Bois de la Vauche

POIVRE HILL

The main fort in the French defensive system. Strengthened in 1887, 1889, and 1913.

Douaumont

Vacherauville

★ FT. DOUAUMONT

Dieppe

Charny

Hardaumont Battery

Ft. cherauville

Bras

Vaux

★

Ft. Thiaumont

★

Fleury

Ft. Vaux

★

Damloup

Damloup Battery

La Laufée

Meuse

Ft.Souville

★

Tunnel

Eix

Ft.Belleville

★

Ft.St. Michel

★

Ft.Tavannes

★

Thierville

22/23 June, Germans introduce new phosgene gas shell (Green Cross).

E SACRÉE'
dun's lifeline.

VERDUN

GENERAL KEY

════	Roads.
┼┼┼┼	Railways.
┴┴┴┴	Canals.
﹏﹏﹏	High land.

Ft.Belrupt

★

aume

149

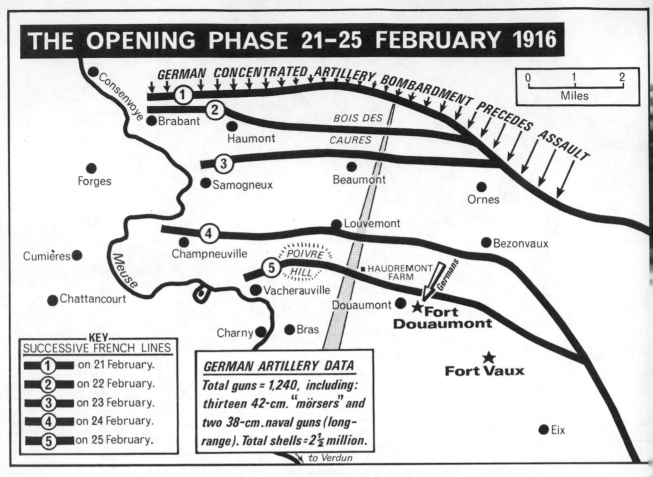

THE OPENING PHASE 21-25 FEBRUARY 1916

GERMAN CONCENTRATED ARTILLERY BOMBARDMENT PRECEDES ASSAULT

Consenvoye

Brabant

Haumont

BOIS DES CAURES

Forges

Samogneux

Beaumont

Ornes

Louvemont

Bezonvaux

Cumières

Champneuville

POIVRE HILL

HAUDREMONT FARM

Germans

Chattancourt

Vacherauville

Douaumont

★ **Fort Douaumont**

Charny

Bras

★ **Fort Vaux**

Meuse

Eix

0   1   2
Miles

KEY

SUCCESSIVE FRENCH LINES

① on 21 February.
② on 22 February.
③ on 23 February.
④ on 24 February.
⑤ on 25 February.

GERMAN ARTILLERY DATA
Total guns = 1,240, including:
thirteen 42-cm. "mörsers" and
two 38-cm. naval guns (long-
range). Total shells = 2½ million.

↙ *to Verdun*

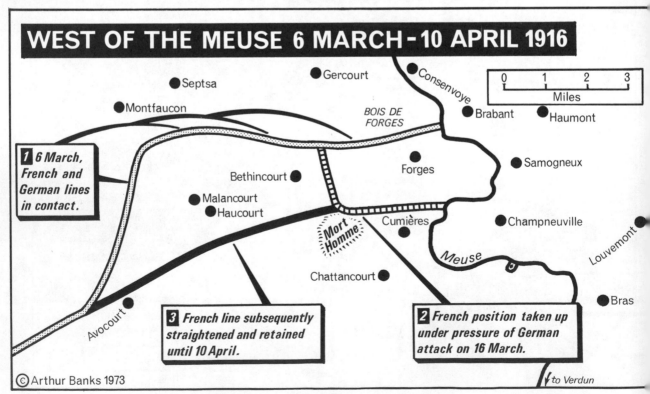

WEST OF THE MEUSE 6 MARCH-10 APRIL 1916

Septsa

Gercourt

Consenvoye

Montfaucon

BOIS DE FORGES

Brabant

Haumont

Forges

Samogneux

1 *6 March,*
French and
German lines
in contact.

Bethincourt

Malancourt

Haucourt

Cumières

Champneuville

Mort Homme

Meuse

Louvemont

Chattancourt

Bras

Avocourt

3 *French line subsequently*
straightened and retained
until 10 April.

2 *French position taken up*
under pressure of German
attack on 16 March.

0   1   2   3
Miles

© Arthur Banks 1973

↙ *to Verdun*

150

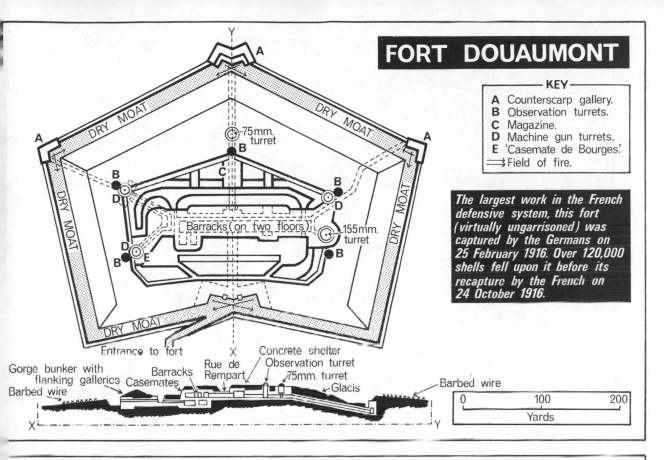

FORT DOUAUMONT

KEY
A Counterscarp gallery.
B Observation turrets.
C Magazine.
D Machine gun turrets.
E 'Casemate de Bourges.'
⇒ Field of fire.

The largest work in the French defensive system, this fort (virtually ungarrisoned) was captured by the Germans on 25 February 1916. Over 120,000 shells fell upon it before its recapture by the French on 24 October 1916.

75mm. turret

155mm. turret

Barracks (on two floors)

DRY MOAT

Entrance to fort

Gorge bunker with flanking galleries
Barbed wire
Barracks
Casemates
Rue de Rempart
Concrete shelter
Observation turret
75mm. turret
Glacis
Barbed wire

0   100   200
Yards

FORT VAUX

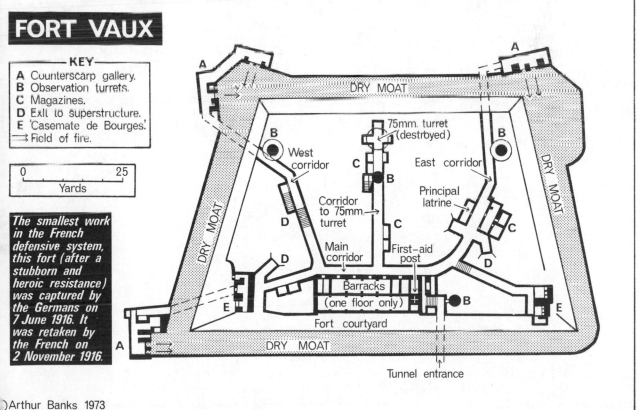

KEY
A Counterscarp gallery.
B Observation turrets.
C Magazines.
D Exit to superstructure.
E 'Casemate de Bourges.'
⇒ Field of fire.

0   25
Yards

The smallest work in the French defensive system, this fort (after a stubborn and heroic resistance) was captured by the Germans on 7 June 1916. It was retaken by the French on 2 November 1916.

DRY MOAT

75mm. turret (destroyed)

West corridor

East corridor

Principal latrine

Corridor to 75mm turret

Main corridor

First-aid post

Barracks (one floor only)

Fort courtyard

DRY MOAT

Tunnel entrance

© Arthur Banks 1973

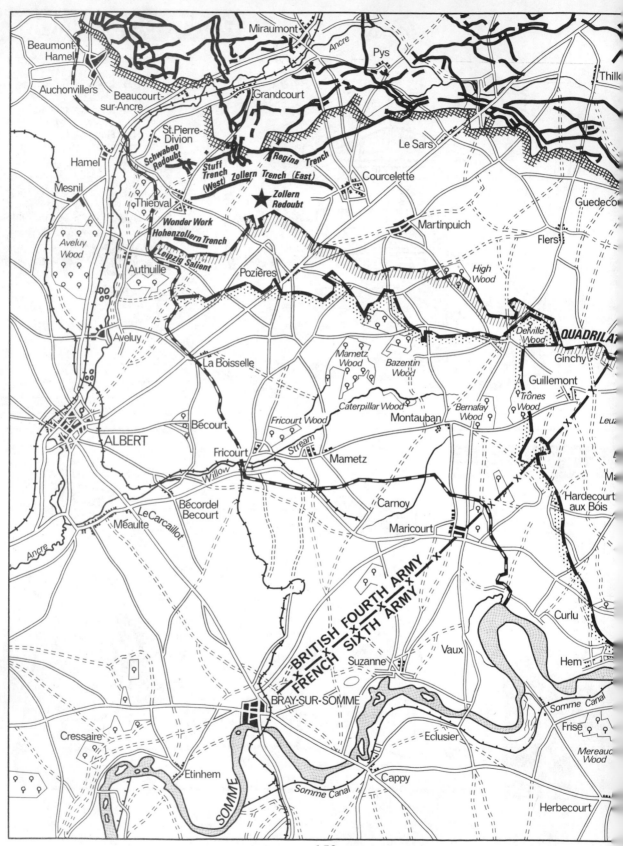

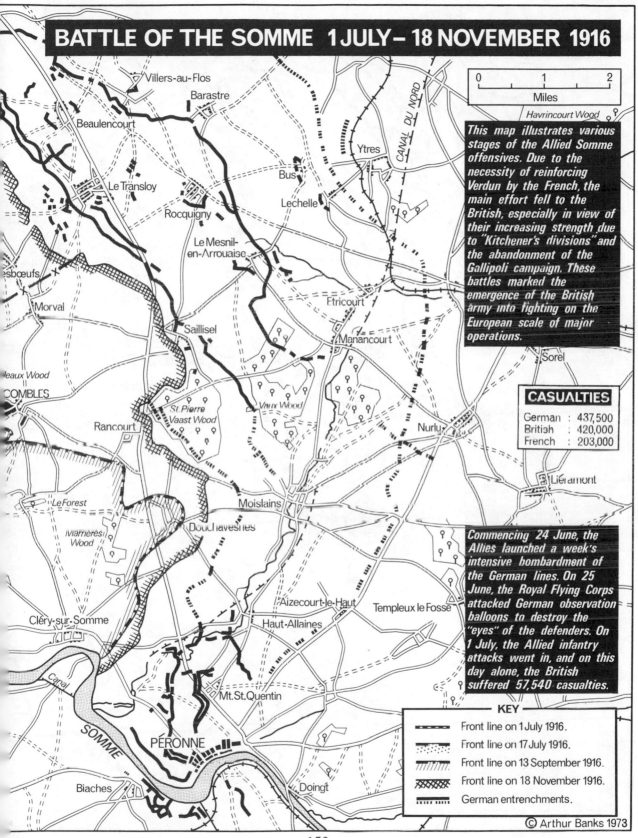

BATTLE OF THE SOMME 1 JULY – 18 NOVEMBER 1916

Villers-au-Flos
Barastre
Beaulencourt
Le Transloy
Rocquigny
Le Mesnil-en-Arrouaise
esbœufs
Morval
Saillisel
Rancourt
eaux Wood
COMBLES
St. Pierre Vaast Wood
Le Forest
Marrières Wood
Douchavesnes
Cléry-sur-Somme
Mt. St. Quentin
PÉRONNE
Biaches
Doingt

Ytres
Bus
Lechelle
Étricourt
Manancourt
Vaux Wood
Nurlu
Sorel
Lieramont
Moislains
Aizecourt-le-Haut
Templeux le Fosse
Haut-Allaines

CANAL DU NORD
Havrincourt Wood

SOMME
Canal

0 1 2
Miles

This map illustrates various stages of the Allied Somme offensives. Due to the necessity of reinforcing Verdun by the French, the main effort fell to the British, especially in view of their increasing strength due to "Kitchener's divisions" and the abandonment of the Gallipoli campaign. These battles marked the emergence of the British army into fighting on the European scale of major operations.

CASUALTIES

German : 437,500
British : 420,000
French : 203,000

Commencing 24 June, the Allies launched a week's intensive bombardment of the German lines. On 25 June, the Royal Flying Corps attacked German observation balloons to destroy the "eyes" of the defenders. On 1 July, the Allied infantry attacks went in, and on this day alone, the British suffered 57,540 casualties.

KEY

- Front line on 1 July 1916.
- Front line on 17 July 1916.
- Front line on 13 September 1916.
- Front line on 18 November 1916.
- German entrenchments.

© Arthur Banks 1973

Thiepval Wood

Thiepval

Moquet Farm

Pozières

Authuille Wood

Contalmaison Villa

Ovillers la Boisselle

Contalmaison Wood

Lower Wood

Pearl Wood

Mash Valley

Bailiff Wood

Contalmaison

Acid Drop Copse

Mametz Wood

la Boisselle

Peake Woods

Birch Tree Wood

The Quadrangle

Shelter Wood

Sausage Valley

Bottom Wood

Willow Stream

Lozenge Wood

Railway Copse

Bécourt

Fricourt Farm

Fricourt Wood

Bécourt Wood

FRICOURT

MAMETZ

Willow Stream

0   1000
Yards

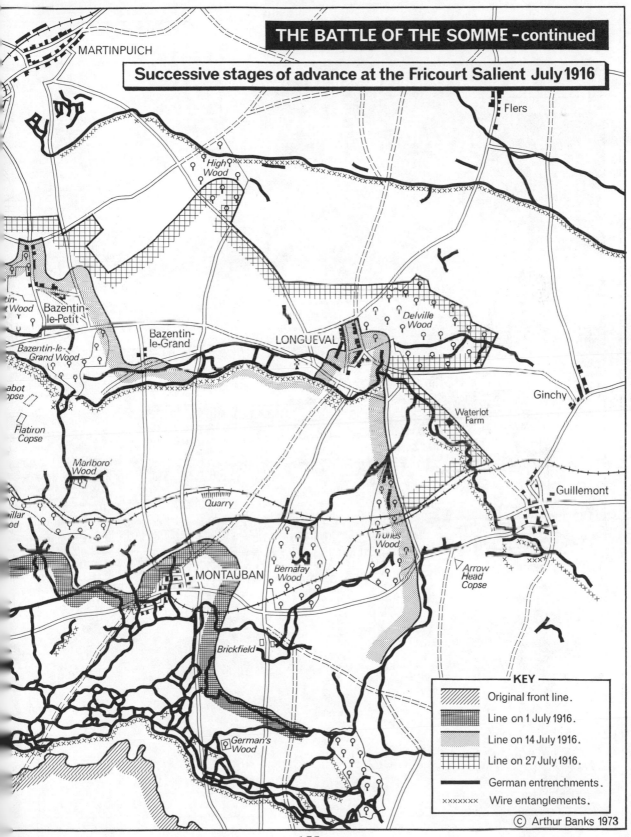

Successive stages of advance at the Fricourt Salient July 1916

MARTINPUICH

Flers

High Wood

Bazentin-le-Petit

Bazentin-le-Grand

LONGUEVAL

Delville Wood

Ginchy

Bazentin-le-Grand Wood

abot opse

Flatiron Copse

Waterlot Farm

Marlboro' Wood

Quarry

Guillemont

illar od

Trones Wood

MONTAUBAN

Bernafay Wood

Arrow Head Copse

Brickfield

German's Wood

KEY

- Original front line.
- Line on 1 July 1916.
- Line on 14 July 1916.
- Line on 27 July 1916.
- German entrenchments.
- xxxxxx Wire entanglements.

© Arthur Banks 1973

155

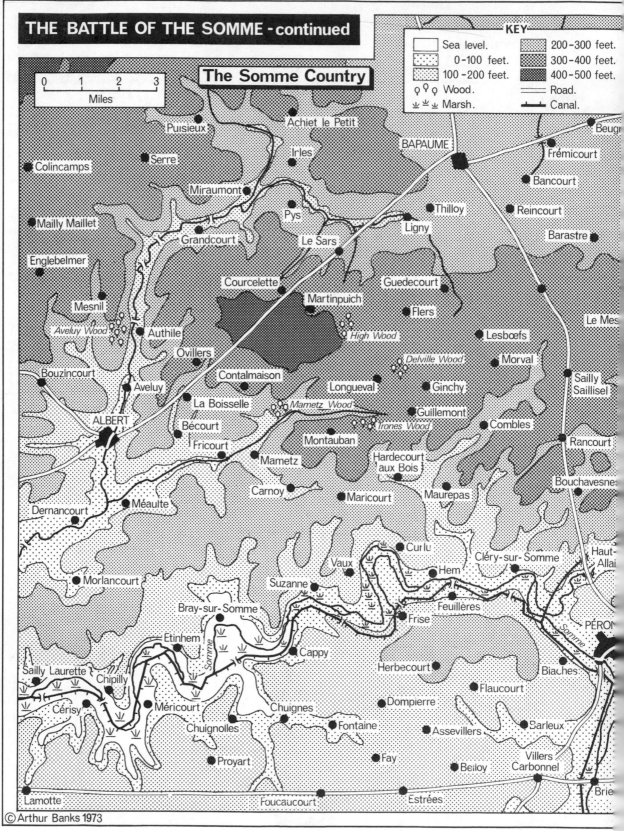

THE BATTLE OF THE SOMME - continued

The Somme Country

Miles
0 1 2 3

Puisieux

Achiet le Petit

BAPAUME

Beugn

Irles

Frémicourt

Serre

Colincamps

Bancourt

Miraumont

Reincourt

Pys

Thilloy

Mailly Maillet

Ligny

Barastre

Grandcourt

Le Sars

Englebelmer

Courcelette

Guedecourt

Le Mes

Martinpuich

Flers

Mesnil

Aveluy Wood

Authile

High Wood

Lesbœfs

Ovillers

Delville Wood

Morval

Bouzincourt

Contalmaison

Longueval

Ginchy

Sailly
Saillisel

Aveluy

Mametz Wood

Guillemont

Combles

La Boisselle

Bécourt

Trones Wood

ALBERT

Montauban

Rancourt

Fricourt

Hardecourt
aux Bois

Bouchavesne

Mametz

Carnoy

Maricourt

Maurepas

Dernancourt

Méaulte

Curlu

Cléry-sur-Somme

Haut-
Allai

Vaux

Hem

Morlancourt

Suzanne

Feuillères

PÉRON

Frise

Bray-sur-Somme

Etinhem

Somme

Cappy

Herbecourt

Biaches

Sailly Laurette

Chipilly

Flaucourt

Cérisy

Méricourt

Chuignes

Dompierre

Barleux

Chuignolles

Fontaine

Assevillers

Villers
Carbonnel

Proyart

Fay

Beiloy

Brie

Lamotte

Foucaucourt

Estrées

© Arthur Banks 1973

156

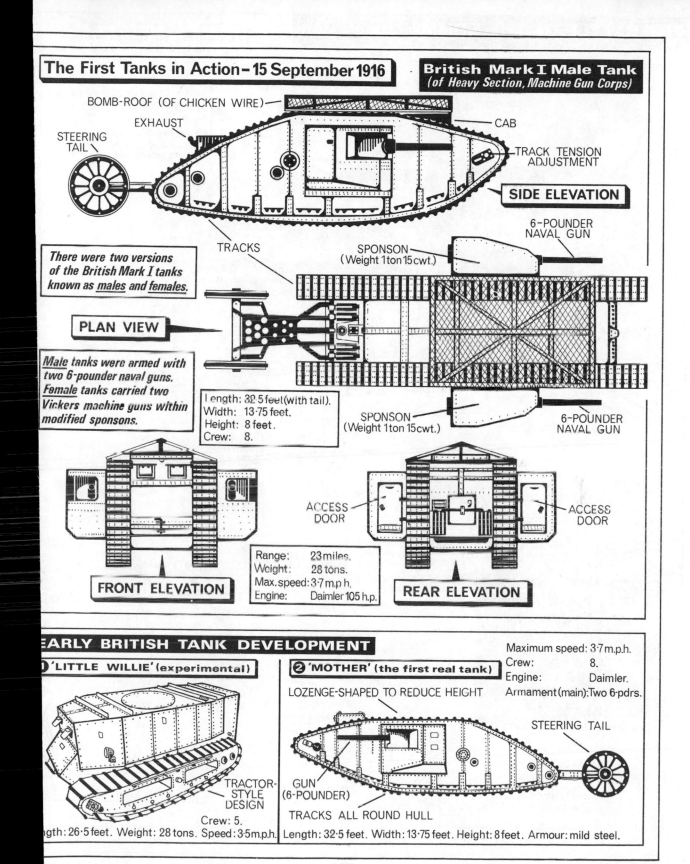

The First Tanks in Action – 15 September 1916

British Mark I Male Tank
(of Heavy Section, Machine Gun Corps)

SIDE ELEVATION

BOMB-ROOF (OF CHICKEN WIRE)

EXHAUST

STEERING TAIL

CAB

TRACK TENSION ADJUSTMENT

TRACKS

There were two versions of the British Mark I tanks known as males and females.

PLAN VIEW

Male tanks were armed with two 6-pounder naval guns. Female tanks carried two Vickers machine guns within modified sponsons.

6-POUNDER NAVAL GUN

SPONSON (Weight 1 ton 15 cwt.)

SPONSON (Weight 1 ton 15 cwt.)

6-POUNDER NAVAL GUN

Length: 32·5 feet (with tail).
Width: 13·75 feet.
Height: 8 feet.
Crew: 8.

FRONT ELEVATION

ACCESS DOOR

ACCESS DOOR

REAR ELEVATION

Range: 23 miles.
Weight: 28 tons.
Max. speed: 3·7 m.p.h.
Engine: Daimler 105 h.p.

EARLY BRITISH TANK DEVELOPMENT

1 'LITTLE WILLIE' (experimental)

TRACTOR-STYLE DESIGN

Crew: 5.
Length: 26·5 feet. Weight: 28 tons. Speed: 3·5 m.p.h.

2 'MOTHER' (the first real tank)

LOZENGE-SHAPED TO REDUCE HEIGHT

GUN (6-POUNDER)

TRACKS ALL ROUND HULL

STEERING TAIL

Maximum speed: 3·7 m.p.h.
Crew: 8.
Engine: Daimler.
Armament (main): Two 6-pdrs.

Length: 32·5 feet. Width: 13·75 feet. Height: 8 feet. Armour: mild steel.

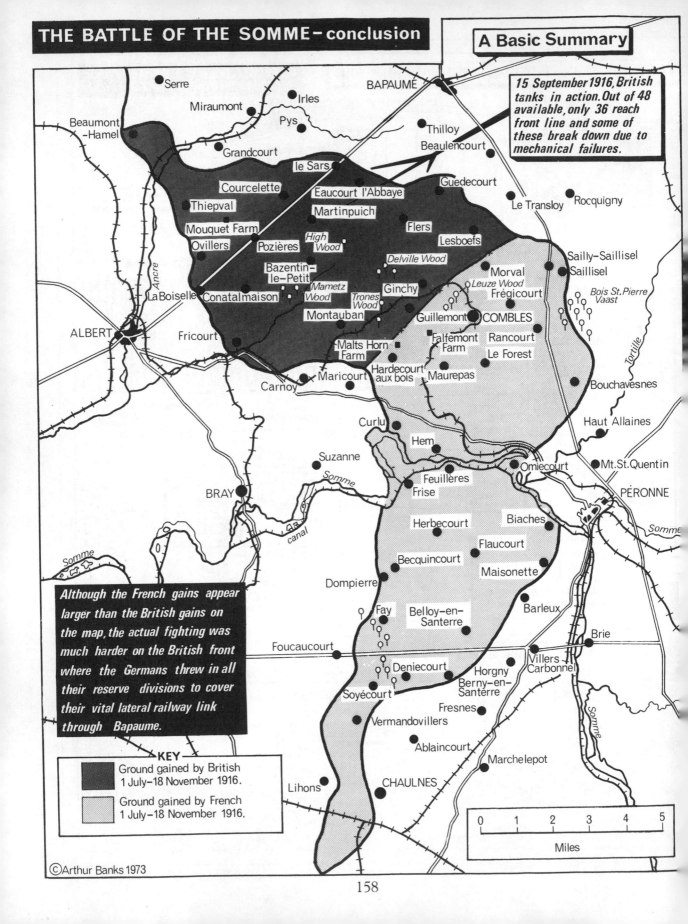

THE BATTLE OF THE SOMME – conclusion

A Basic Summary

15 September 1916, British tanks in action. Out of 48 available, only 36 reach front line and some of these break down due to mechanical failures.

Serre

Irles

Miraumont

Pys

BAPAUME

Beaumont-Hamel

Thilloy

Beaulencourt

Grandcourt

le Sars

Guedecourt

Courcelette

Eaucourt l'Abbaye

Le Transloy

Rocquigny

Thiepval

Martinpuich

Flers

Mouquet Farm

High Wood

Lesboefs

Sailly-Saillisel

Ovillers

Pozières

Saillisel

Bois St.Pierre Vaast

Bazentin-le-Petit

Delville Wood

Morval

Frégicourt

Leuze Wood

La Boiselle

Mametz Wood

Ginchy

COMBLES

Conatalmaison

Trones Wood

Guillemont

Rancourt

ALBERT

Montauban

Falfemont Farm

Le Forest

Fricourt

Malts Horn Farm

Bouchavesnes

Maricourt

Hardecourt aux bois

Maurepas

Carnoy

Haut Allaines

Curlu

Mt.St.Quentin

Hem

Suzanne

Omiecourt

Somme

Feuillères

PÉRONNE

BRAY

Frise

Biaches

Herbecourt

Somme

Flaucourt

canal

Becquincourt

Maisonette

Dompierre

Barleux

Somme

Fay

Belloy-en-Santerre

Brie

Foucaucourt

Villers Carbonnel

Deniecourt

Horgny

Berny-en-Santerre

Somme

Soyécourt

Fresnes

Vermandovillers

Lihons

Ablaincourt

Marchelepot

CHAULNES

Although the French gains appear larger than the British gains on the map, the actual fighting was much harder on the British front where the Germans threw in all their reserve divisions to cover their vital lateral railway link through Bapaume.

KEY

Ground gained by British 1 July–18 November 1916.

Ground gained by French 1 July–18 November 1916.

0 1 2 3 4 5

Miles

©Arthur Banks 1973

158

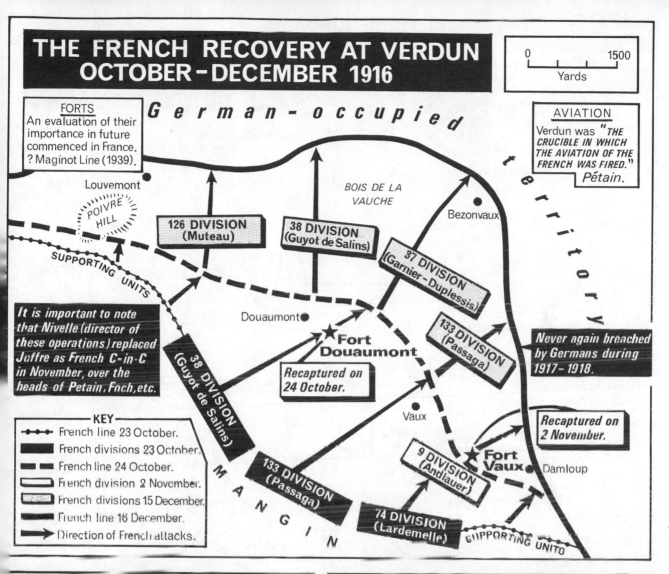

THE FRENCH RECOVERY AT VERDUN OCTOBER – DECEMBER 1916

0   1500
Yards

G e r m a n - o c c u p i e d

t e r r i t o r y

FORTS
An evaluation of their importance in future commenced in France. ? Maginot Line (1939).

AVIATION
Verdun was *"THE CRUCIBLE IN WHICH THE AVIATION OF THE FRENCH WAS FIRED."* Pétain.

Louvemont

POIVRE HILL

BOIS DE LA VAUCHE

Bezonvaux

126 DIVISION (Muteau)

38 DIVISION (Guyot de Salins)

37 DIVISION (Garnier - Duplessis)

SUPPORTING UNITS

It is important to note that Nivelle (director of these operations) replaced Joffre as French C-in-C in November, over the heads of Petain, Foch, etc.

Douaumont●

38 DIVISION (Guyot de Salins)

★ **Fort Douaumont**

133 DIVISION (Passaga)

Never again breached by Germans during 1917 - 1918.

Recaptured on 24 October.

● Vaux

Recaptured on 2 November.

—KEY—
- •–•–• French line 23 October.
- ▆▆ French divisions 23 October.
- ▬ ▬ French line 24 October.
- ▢ French division 2 November.
- ▨ French divisions 15 December.
- ▬ French line 16 December.
- → Direction of French attacks.

M A N G I N

133 DIVISION (Passaga)

9 DIVISION (Andlauer)

★ **Fort Vaux**

Damloup

74 DIVISION (Lardemelle)

SUPPORTING UNITS

159

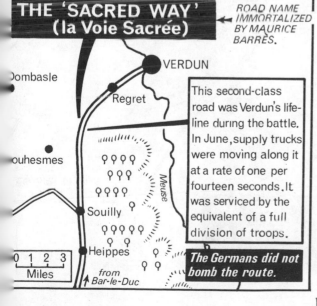

THE 'SACRED WAY' (la Voie Sacrée)

← *ROAD NAME IMMORTALIZED BY MAURICE BARRÈS.*

Dombasle

VERDUN

Regret

ouhesmes

Meuse

Souilly

Heippes

0 1 2 3
Miles

from Bar-le-Duc

This second-class road was Verdun's lifeline during the battle. In June, supply trucks were moving along it at a rate of one per fourteen seconds. It was serviced by the equivalent of a full division of troops.

The Germans did not bomb the route.

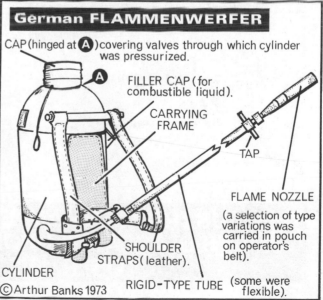

German FLAMMENWERFER

CAP (hinged at Ⓐ) covering valves through which cylinder was pressurized.

FILLER CAP (for combustible liquid).

CARRYING FRAME

TAP

FLAME NOZZLE
(a selection of type variations was carried in pouch on operator's belt).

SHOULDER STRAPS (leather).

CYLINDER

RIGID-TYPE TUBE (some were flexible).

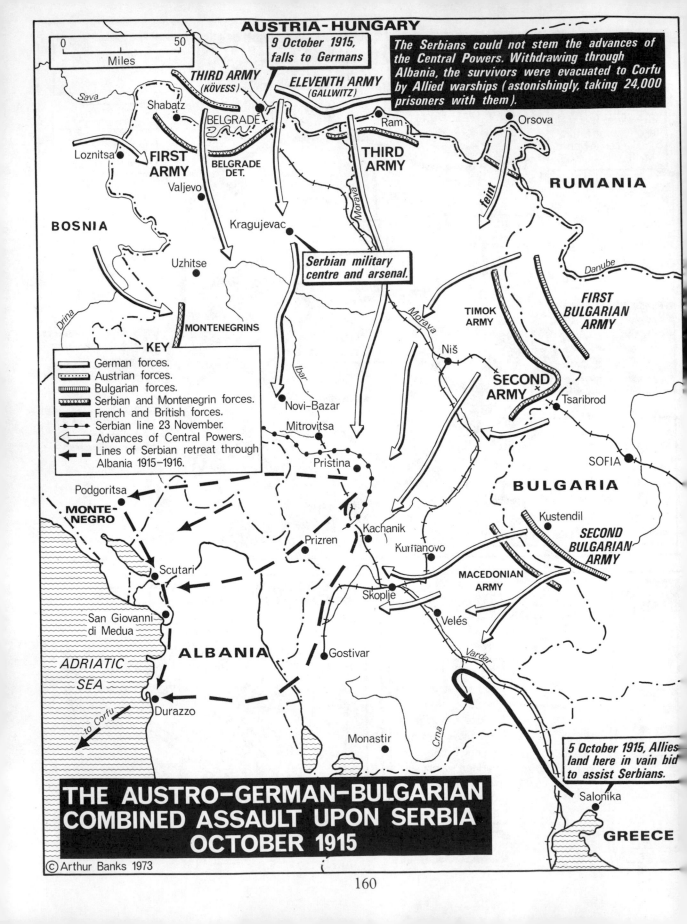

AUSTRIA-HUNGARY

9 October 1915, falls to Germans

The Serbians could not stem the advances of the Central Powers. Withdrawing through Albania, the survivors were evacuated to Corfu by Allied warships (astonishingly, taking 24,000 prisoners with them).

THIRD ARMY (KÖVESS)

ELEVENTH ARMY (GALLWITZ)

Sava

Shabatz

BELGRADE

Ram

Orsova

FIRST ARMY

Loznitsa

BELGRADE DET.

Valjevo

THIRD ARMY

RUMANIA

feint

BOSNIA

Kragujevac

Morava

Uzhitse

Serbian military centre and arsenal.

Danube

FIRST BULGARIAN ARMY

Drina

MONTENEGRINS

Morava

Ibar

TIMOK ARMY

Niš

SECOND ARMY

Tsaribrod

KEY

German forces.
Austrian forces.
Bulgarian forces.
Serbian and Montenegrin forces.
French and British forces.
Serbian line 23 November.
Advances of Central Powers.
Lines of Serbian retreat through Albania 1915–1916.

Novi-Bazar

Mitrovitsa

Pristina

SOFIA

BULGARIA

Podgoritsa

MONTE-NEGRO

Kustendil

SECOND BULGARIAN ARMY

Kachanik

Prizren

Kurñanovo

Scutari

Skoplje

MACEDONIAN ARMY

San Giovanni di Medua

Velés

ADRIATIC SEA

ALBANIA

Gostivar

Vardar

to Corfu

Durazzo

Monastir

Crna

5 October 1915, Allies land here in vain bid to assist Serbians.

Salonika

THE AUSTRO-GERMAN-BULGARIAN COMBINED ASSAULT UPON SERBIA OCTOBER 1915

GREECE

© Arthur Banks 1973

THE BRUSILOV OFFENSIVE JUNE–OCTOBER 1916

ABORTIVE ATTACKS 100 MILES TO NORTH (IN JUNE AND JULY)

RUSSIAN THIRD ARMY (Lesh)

EVERT (Commander: Russian Centre Army Group)

ARMY GROUP LINSINGEN (4 JUNE)

FOURTH AUSTRIAN ARMY (Archduke Josef Ferdinand)

FIRST AUSTRIAN ARMY (Pulhallo von Brlog)

SECOND AUSTRIAN ARMY (Böhm-Ermolli)

SOUTHERN 'GERMAN' ARMY (von Bothmer)

AUSTRIA-HUNGARY

SEVENTH AUSTRIAN ARMY (Pflanzer-Baltin)

TOTAL DIVISIONS 4 JUNE = 38.

HQ, RUSSIAN EIGHTH ARMY

BRUSILOV'S PLANS
To spread heavy pressure over the whole front simultaneously rather than to concentrate at fixed points, thus preventing the enemy switching reserves from point to point at will.

RUSSIA

RUSSIAN EIGHTH ARMY (Kaledin) (11 INF. & 4 CAV. DIVISIONS)

RUSSIAN ELEVENTH ARMY (Sakharov) (8 INF. & 1 CAV. DIVISIONS)

RUSSIAN SEVENTH ARMY (Shcherbachev) (7 INF. & 3½ CAV. DIVISIONS)

RUSSIAN NINTH ARMY (Lechitsky) (10 INF. & 4 CAV. DIVISIONS)

BRUSILOV'S G.H.Q.

ACTING IN CONCERT

BRUSILOV (Commander: Russian S.W. Army Group)

HQ RUSSIAN ELEVENTH ARMY

HQ RUSSIAN SEVENTH ARMY

HQ RUSSIAN NINTH ARMY

NOTE: BRUSILOV'S DIVISIONS 4 JUNE.

Places: Kovel, Lutsk, Krilov, Rovno, Dubno, Brody, Lemberg, Brzezany, Tarnopol, Volochisk, Gusyatin, Stanislau, Kolomea, Kamenets-Podolski, Kuty, Czernowitz, Kimpolung

Rivers: Pripet, Stokhod, Goryn, Styr, Sluch, Dniester, Pruth, Sereth

CARPATHIAN MTS.

RUMANIA

0 — 30 Miles

— KEY —
— Russian front line 4 June.
--- Russian front line 10 October.
▨ Ground gained by Russians.
← Main Russian advances.
+++ Double track railways.
⚜ Pripet marshes.
⊠ Russian Army H.Q.
⊠ Russian Army Group G.H.Q.

© Arthur Banks 1973

DIVISIONAL COMPARISONS. Most Russian divisions had 16 battalions, the remainder 12. Austrian divisions had 12 battalions: German had 9.

The Brusilov Offensive was the most competent Russian operation of the war. It weakened the offensives of the Central Powers at Verdun and in Italy, and without German assistance being forthcoming, Austria probably would have collapsed. It was a direct cause of the Habsburg Empire's disintegration. On both sides casualties were colossal, over two million men being involved. The offensive halted through sheer exhaustion on the Russian side, and discontent in the rear areas eventually led to the Russian Revolution.

THE RUMANIAN CAMPAIGN 1916

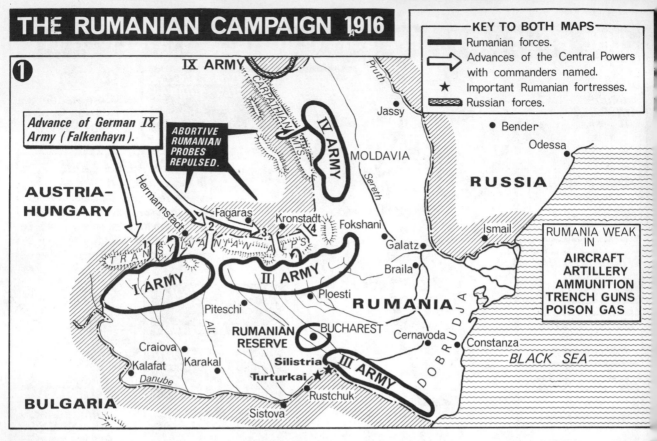

①

IX ARMY

Advance of German IX Army (Falkenhayn).

ABORTIVE RUMANIAN PROBES REPULSED.

IV ARMY

Jassy

Bender

Odessa

AUSTRIA-HUNGARY

Hermannstadt

Fagaras

Kronstadt

Fokshani

MOLDAVIA

RUSSIA

Sereth

TRANSYLVANIAN ALPS

1 2 3 4

I ARMY

II ARMY

Galatz

Braila

Ismail

RUMANIA WEAK IN
AIRCRAFT
ARTILLERY
AMMUNITION
TRENCH GUNS
POISON GAS

Piteschi

Ploesti

RUMANIAN RESERVE

BUCHAREST

Cernavoda

Constanza

Craiova

Karakal

Silistria

Turturkai

III ARMY

DOBRUDJA

BLACK SEA

Kalafat

Danube

Rustchuk

BULGARIA

Sistova

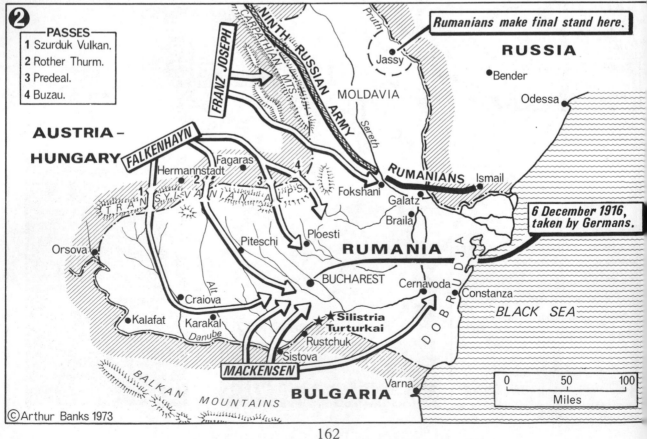

②

PASSES
1 Szurduk Vulkan.
2 Rother Thurm.
3 Predeal.
4 Buzau.

FRANZ JOSEPH

NINTH RUSSIAN ARMY

CARPATHIAN MTS.

Pruth

Rumanians make final stand here.

Jassy

RUSSIA

Bender

Odessa

MOLDAVIA

Sereth

AUSTRIA-HUNGARY

FALKENHAYN

Hermannstadt

Fagaras

TRANSYLVANIAN ALPS

1 2 3 4

Fokshani

RUMANIANS

Ismail

Galatz

Braila

6 December 1916, taken by Germans.

Orsova

Piteschi

Ploesti

RUMANIA

Craiova

BUCHAREST

Cernavoda

Constanza

BLACK SEA

Kalafat

Karakal

Silistria
Turturkai

DOBRUDJA

Alt

Danube

Rustchuk

Sistova

MACKENSEN

BALKAN MOUNTAINS

BULGARIA

Varna

0   50   100
Miles

© Arthur Banks 1973

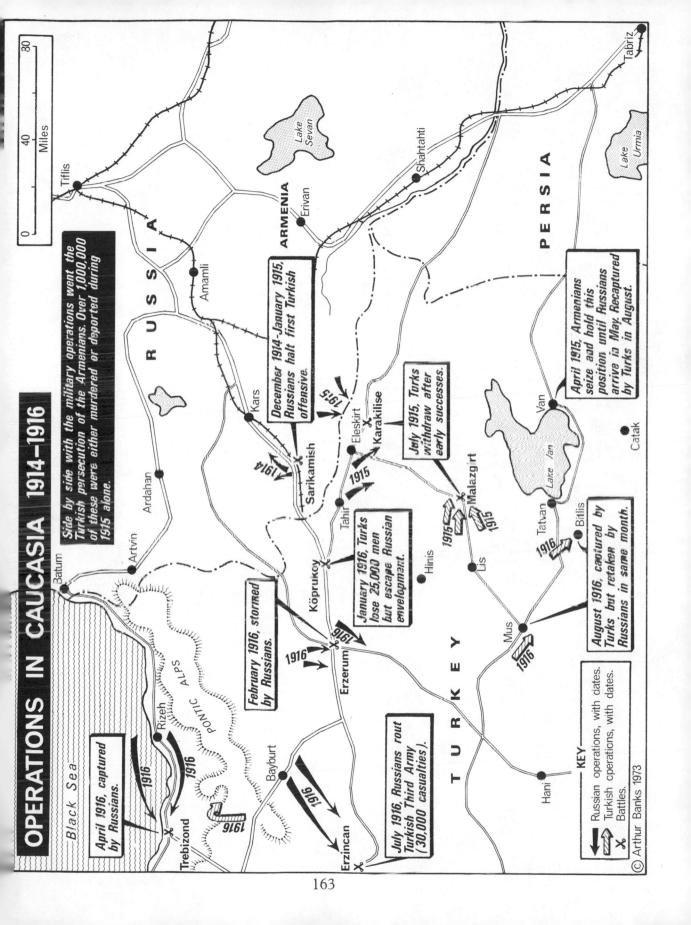

OPERATIONS IN CAUCASIA 1914–1916

Black Sea

Side by side with the military operations went the Turkish persecution of the Armenians. Over 1,000,000 of these were either murdered or deported during 1915 alone.

December 1914–January 1915, Russians halt first Turkish offensive.

July 1915, Turks withdraw after early successes.

April 1915, Armenians seize and hold this position until Russians arrive in May. Recaptured by Turks in August.

January 1916, Turks lose 25,000 men but escape Russian envelopment.

February 1916, stormed by Russians.

August 1916, captured by Turks but retaken by Russians in same month.

July 1916, Russians rout Turkish Third Army (30,000 casualties).

April 1916, captured by Russians.

RUSSIA

ARMENIA

PERSIA

TURKEY

Tiflis

Lake Sevan

Shahtahti

Lake Urmia

Tabriz

Erivan

Amamli

Kars

Eleskirt

Karakilise

Van

Catak

Lake Tan

Malazgirt

Bitlis

Tatvan

Ardahan

Sarikamish

Tahir

Hinis

Lis

Artvin

Köprukoy

Erzerum

Mus

Hani

Batum

Rizeh

PONTIC ALPS

Trebizond

Bayburt

Erzincan

1914
1915
1916

KEY

→ Russian operations, with dates.
⇨ Turkish operations, with dates.
✕ Battles.

© Arthur Banks 1973

163

THE WAR IN 1917

The wasteful slaughter of 1916 was followed by a year of astonishing political change and upheaval. When, on 1 February 1917, the Germans announced a resumption of unrestricted U-Boat warfare, they knew that they ran the risk of bringing America into the conflict, but they calculated that they could eliminate Russia and France on land and starve the British into surrender before the effects of American belligerency were felt in Europe. In the event, the United States was finally brought to declare war on Germany in April 1917 as much by evidence of German intrigues in Mexico (the Zimmermann telegram) as by the submarine (see page 214). The fall of the Tsarist autocracy and the establishment of a democratic Provisional Government in Russia (page 177) made it easier for Congress to accept the idea of war; but British and French hopes that the Provisional Government would purge corruption and make Russia again an efficient military partner proved ill-founded. The so-called Kerensky Offensive of July 1917 soon petered out (page 176); the Russian people were apathetic and anxious only for 'peace and bread'. When in the first week of November Lenin's Bolsheviks seized power in Petrograd, Russia virtually withdrew from the war, opened negotiations with Germany and her allies, and concluded a separate peace (the Treaty of Brest-Litovsk, March 1918) by which Russia surrendered Poland, the Ukraine, the Baltic provinces, Finland and much of the Caucasus (see page 178).

Bolshevik propaganda contributed to unrest elsewhere in the Allied camp, notably among the French and Russians in Macedonia (page 204) and among mutinous French units on the Western Front (page 168). Although there was disaffection among the Austro-Hungarian forces, their morale was strengthened by the combined Austro-German victory over the Italians at Caporetto (page 202), in which the rout was only halted by the arrival of British and French reinforcements. The principal successes of the Allies during 1917 were in Asia. The Tigris port of Kut (where the first British expedition of Mesopotamia had been forced to surrender to the Turks in the spring of 1916) was retaken in February and Baghdad captured a fortnight later. The most dramatic victory was won by Allenby in Palestine, enabling the British to enter Jerusalem at the beginning of December. (For Mesopotamia see pages 206–210 and for Palestine see pages 211–213.)

On the Western Front Nivelle had succeeded Joffre in the second week of December 1916. The new commander-in-chief planned an offensive towards Laon, and persisted in his project even when the Germans withdrew to stronger defensive positions. The offensive was a disaster; Nivelle was replaced by Pétain, who with great skill gradually restored the confidence of the French soldiery. But there was little the French Army could do for the remainder of the year. Haig hoped to defeat the Germans in Flanders, a policy which appealed to the British naval chiefs, since it would have eliminated the U-boat bases on the Belgian coast. Heavy bombardments and rain made the ground impassable, and the 'third battle of Ypres' came to a disastrous halt in the mud of Passchendaele. Earlier in the year the Canadians gained a striking success at Vimy Ridge, north-east of Arras, and the British Second Army (which included an Australian and New Zealand Corps) won a comprehensive local victory at Messines, south of Ypres. Potentially the most significant military development of the year was the breakthrough by massed British tanks at Cambrai in November, but Haig by now did not have sufficient reserves to consolidate the gains made by the tanks, and the Germans recovered much of the land they had lost in a counter-attack ten days later.

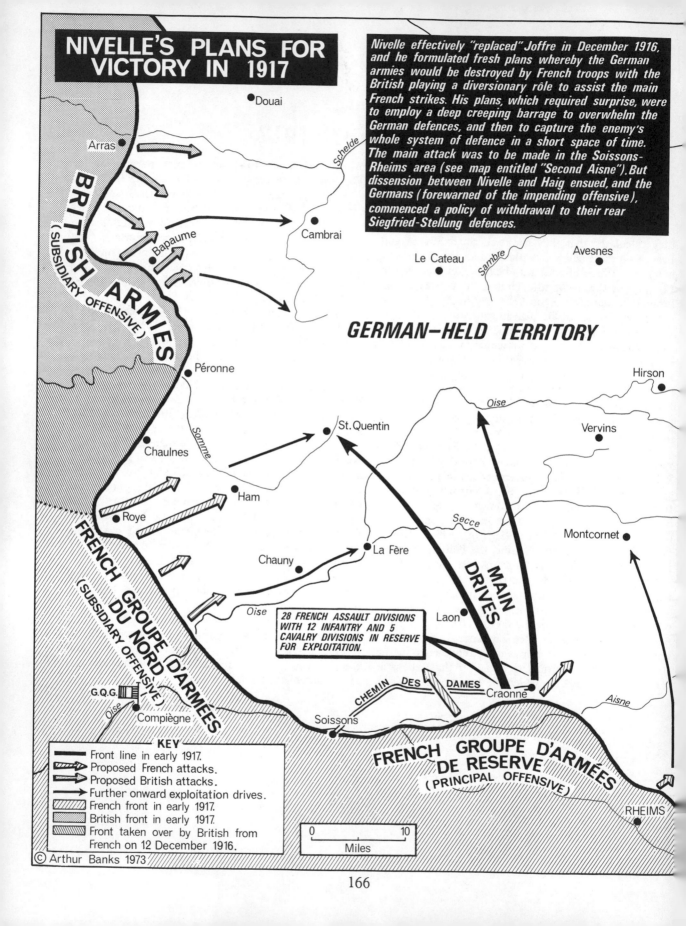

NIVELLE'S PLANS FOR VICTORY IN 1917

Nivelle effectively "replaced" Joffre in December 1916, and he formulated fresh plans whereby the German armies would be destroyed by French troops with the British playing a diversionary rôle to assist the main French strikes. His plans, which required surprise, were to employ a deep creeping barrage to overwhelm the German defences, and then to capture the enemy's whole system of defence in a short space of time. The main attack was to be made in the Soissons-Rheims area (see map entitled "Second Aisne"). But dissension between Nivelle and Haig ensued, and the Germans (forewarned of the impending offensive), commenced a policy of withdrawal to their rear Siegfried-Stellung defences.

Douai

Arras

Schelde

Cambrai

BRITISH ARMIES (SUBSIDIARY OFFENSIVE)

Bapaume

GERMAN–HELD TERRITORY

Le Cateau

Sambre

Avesnes

Péronne

Hirson

Oise

Vervins

Chaulnes

Somme

St. Quentin

Roye

Ham

Secce

Montcornet

FRENCH GROUPE DU NORD D'ARMÉES (SUBSIDIARY OFFENSIVE)

Chauny

La Fère

Oise

MAIN DRIVES

Laon

28 FRENCH ASSAULT DIVISIONS WITH 12 INFANTRY AND 5 CAVALRY DIVISIONS IN RESERVE FOR EXPLOITATION.

G.Q.G.

Oise

Compiègne

CHEMIN DES DAMES

Craonne

Aisne

Soissons

FRENCH GROUPE D'ARMÉES DE RESERVE (PRINCIPAL OFFENSIVE)

KEY
- Front line in early 1917.
- Proposed French attacks.
- Proposed British attacks.
- Further onward exploitation drives.
- French front in early 1917.
- British front in early 1917.
- Front taken over by British from French on 12 December 1916.

RHEIMS

0   10
Miles

© Arthur Banks 1973

THE GERMAN WITHDRAWAL FEBRUARY–APRIL 1917

0 10 Miles

In early 1917, German strategy on the Western Front was defensive (in contrast to her U-boat naval offensive), and she decided to shorten her line by a planned withdrawal to a new prepared position (Siegfried-Stellung). The area evacuated was devastated, towns and villages razed, roads destroyed, woods levelled, and water sources poisoned.

THE GERMAN CODE-NAME FOR THIS OPERATION WAS "ALBERICH" (THE DECEITFUL DWARF OF THE NIBELUNG LEGEND).

Note: through a misunderstanding of a German deserter's statement by Allied Intelligence, the Siegfried-Stellung was misnamed "The Hindenburg Line".

Arras
Neuville Vitasse
Scarpe
Cambrai
Schelde
Bapaume
Le Catelet
Ancre
Somme
Péronne
Vermand
Omignon
St. Quentin
Avre
Oise
Ham
Serre
Roye
La Fère
Chauny
Noyon
Oise
Laon
Allemant Filain Cerny
Laffaux
Vailly
Aisne
Missy
Soissons

KEY
– – – German front line 25 February 1917
▲▲▲ German front line 5 April 1917.
▓ Area evacuated by Germans.

"SECOND AISNE" APRIL–MAY 1917

0 6 Miles

This offensive achieved little but lowered French morale, leading to the army mutinies at the end of May.

Vauxaillon Allemant
Filain
Cerny
Craonne Juvincourt
Laffaux Guignicourt
Jouy CHEMIN DES
Braye DAMES
Vailly Soupir
Condé Bourg Berry
Aisne
Aisne
Soissons
Loivre
Betheny
Fismes Vesle
RHEIMS

KEY
– – – French line on 16 April 1917.
——— French line on 8 May 1917.
▨ Ground gained by French.

© Arthur Banks 1973

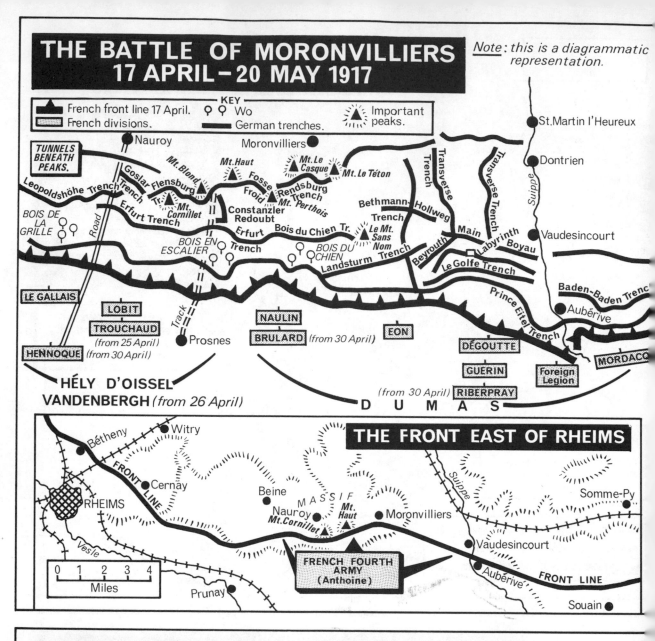

THE BATTLE OF MORONVILLIERS
17 APRIL – 20 MAY 1917

Note: this is a diagrammatic representation.

KEY
- ▲ French front line 17 April.
- ▦ French divisions.
- ♀ ♀ Wo
- ▬ German trenches.
- ▲ Important peaks.

St.Martin l'Heureux

Nauroy · Moronvilliers

Dontrien

TUNNELS BENEATH PEAKS.

Mt.Le Casque · Mt.Le Téton

Transverse Trench

Transverse Trench

Suippe

Mt.Haut

Goslar Trench · Flensburg · Fosse

Mt.Blond · Froid · Rendsburg Trench

Vaudesincourt

Leopoldshöhe Trench · Erfurt Trench · Tr. · Mt.Cornillet · Mt.Perthois

Bethmann-Hollweg Trench

BOIS DE LA GRILLE

Road

Constanzler Redoubt

Erfurt Trench · Bois du Chien Tr. · Le Mt. Sans Nom

Main Boyau

Labyrinth

BOIS EN ESCALIER

BOIS DU CHIEN

Landsturm Trench

Beyrouth · Le Golfe Trench

Baden-Baden Trench

Prince Eitel Trench

Aubérive

LE GALLAIS

LOBIT

Track

NAULIN

EON

DÉGOUTTE

MORDACQ

TROUCHAUD *(from 25 April)*

Prosnes

BRULARD *(from 30 April)*

GUERIN

Foreign Legion

HENNOQUE *(from 30 April)*

HÉLY D'OISSEL

VANDENBERGH *(from 26 April)*

(from 30 April) **RIBERPRAY**

D U M A S

THE FRONT EAST OF RHEIMS

Bétheny · Witry

FRONT LINE

Cernay

RHEIMS

Beine

M A S S I F

Nauroy · Mt.Haut

Mt.Cornillet

Moronvilliers

Somme-Py

Suippe

Vesle

FRENCH FOURTH ARMY (Anthoine)

Vaudesincourt

Aubérive

FRONT LINE

0 1 2 3 4 Miles

Prunay

Souain

THE FRENCH MUTINIES MAY–JUNE 1917

✱ *Main period. Acts of disobedience lasted into September.*

French G.Q.G. · Compiègne

GERMANS FRONT LINE

Soissons

Rheims

APPROX. 70 MILES

On 4 June, only two reliable divisions stand between the Germans and Paris.

PARIS

© Arthur Banks 1973

MAIN AREA AFFECTED

CHEMIN DES DAMES

Aisne · Soissons · Missy · Aisne

Cœuvres · Longueval

Villers-Cotterets

Vesle · Prouilly

Fere-en-Tardenois

Note: Russian brigades (inspired by the Revolution) mutinied at La Courtine, 200 miles south of Paris.

Following the failure of Nivelle's offensive, many French units refused to go up to the front (54 divisions were involved). The situation was alarming and pressure mounted on the British to distract German attention. Many court-martials were held in secret and ringleaders executed by firing-squad.

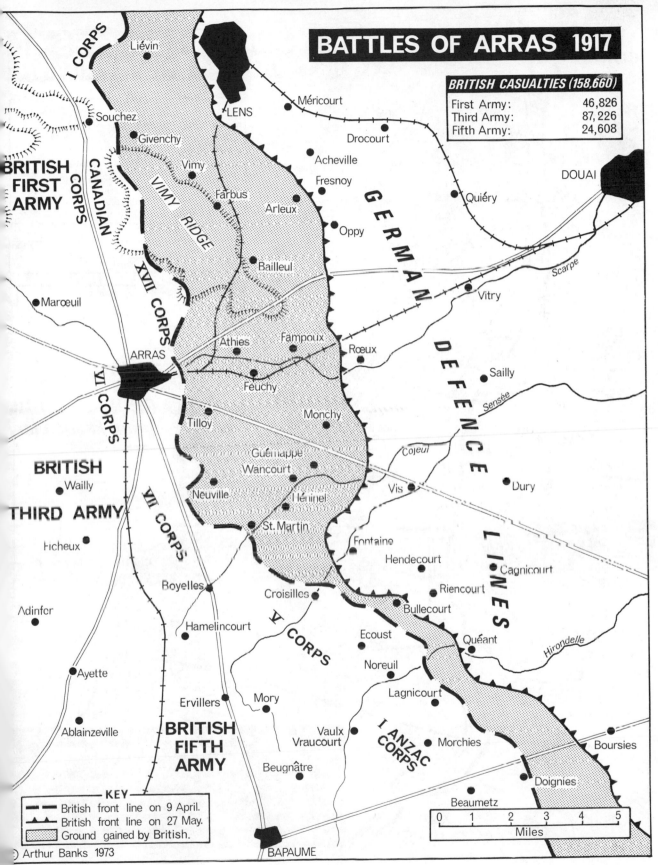

BATTLES OF ARRAS 1917

BRITISH CASUALTIES (158,660)

First Army:	46,826
Third Army:	87,226
Fifth Army:	24,608

I CORPS

Liévin

LENS

Méricourt

Souchez

Givenchy

Drocourt

BRITISH FIRST ARMY

CANADIAN CORPS

Vimy

Acheville

Fresnoy

DOUAI

VIMY RIDGE

Farbus

Arleux

Quiéry

Marœuil

XVII CORPS

Bailleul

Oppy

G E R M A N

Vitry

ARRAS

Athies

Fampoux

Rœux

Scarpe

VI CORPS

Feuchy

Sailly

Tilloy

Monchy

Sensée

BRITISH

Wailly

VII CORPS

Guémappe
Wancourt

Cojeul

Vis

Dury

THIRD ARMY

Neuville

Héninel

D E F E N C E

Ficheux

St. Martin

Fontaine

Hendecourt

Cagnicourt

Adinfer

Boyelles

Croisilles

Bullecourt

Riencourt

L I N E S

Hamelincourt

V CORPS

Ecoust

Quéant

Hirondelle

Ayette

Noreuil

Mory

Lagnicourt

Ervillers

BRITISH

Ablainzeville

FIFTH

Vaulx
Vraucourt

I ANZAC CORPS

Morchies

Boursies

ARMY

Beugnâtre

Doignies

Beaumetz

— **KEY** —

- - - British front line on 9 April.
- ▲▲▲ British front line on 27 May.
- ░░░ Ground gained by British.

0	1	2	3	4	5

Miles

© Arthur Banks 1973

BAPAUME

169

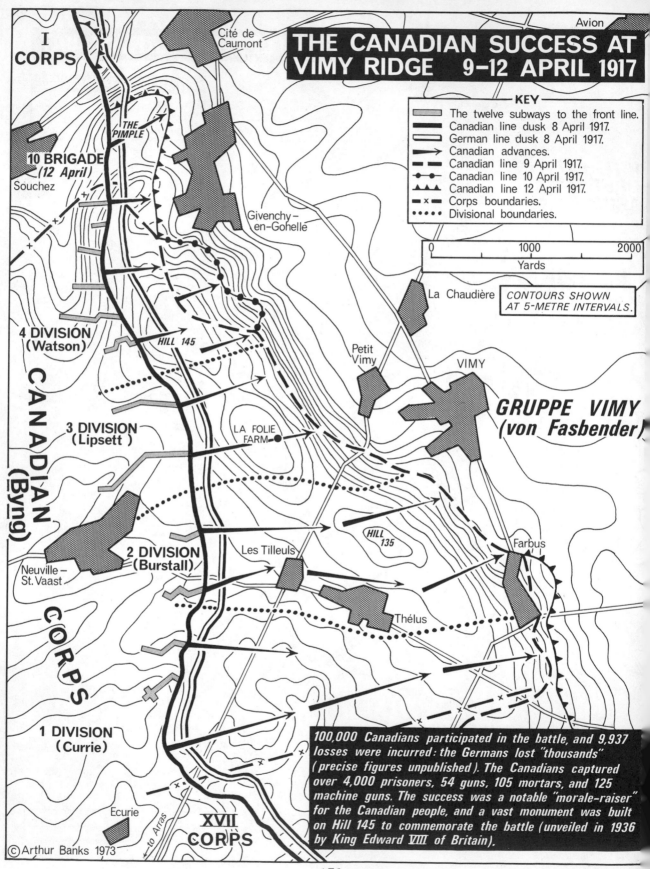

THE CANADIAN SUCCESS AT VIMY RIDGE 9–12 APRIL 1917

I CORPS

Avion

Cité de Caumont

THE PIMPLE

10 BRIGADE *(12 April)*

Souchez

Givenchy-en-Gohelle

4 DIVISION (Watson)

HILL 145

3 DIVISION (Lipsett)

LA FOLIE FARM

2 DIVISION (Burstall)

Neuville–St. Vaast

Les Tilleuls

HILL 135

Thélus

CANADIAN (Byng) **CORPS**

La Chaudière

Petit Vimy

VIMY

GRUPPE VIMY (von Fasbender)

Farbus

1 DIVISION (Currie)

Ecurie

to Arras

XVII CORPS

© Arthur Banks 1973

KEY

- The twelve subways to the front line.
- Canadian line dusk 8 April 1917.
- German line dusk 8 April 1917.
- Canadian advances.
- Canadian line 9 April 1917.
- Canadian line 10 April 1917.
- Canadian line 12 April 1917.
- Corps boundaries.
- Divisional boundaries.

0   1000   2000
Yards

CONTOURS SHOWN AT 5-METRE INTERVALS.

100,000 Canadians participated in the battle, and 9,937 losses were incurred: the Germans lost "thousands" (precise figures unpublished). The Canadians captured over 4,000 prisoners, 54 guns, 105 mortars, and 125 machine guns. The success was a notable "morale-raiser" for the Canadian people, and a vast monument was built on Hill 145 to commemorate the battle (unveiled in 1936 by King Edward VIII of Britain).

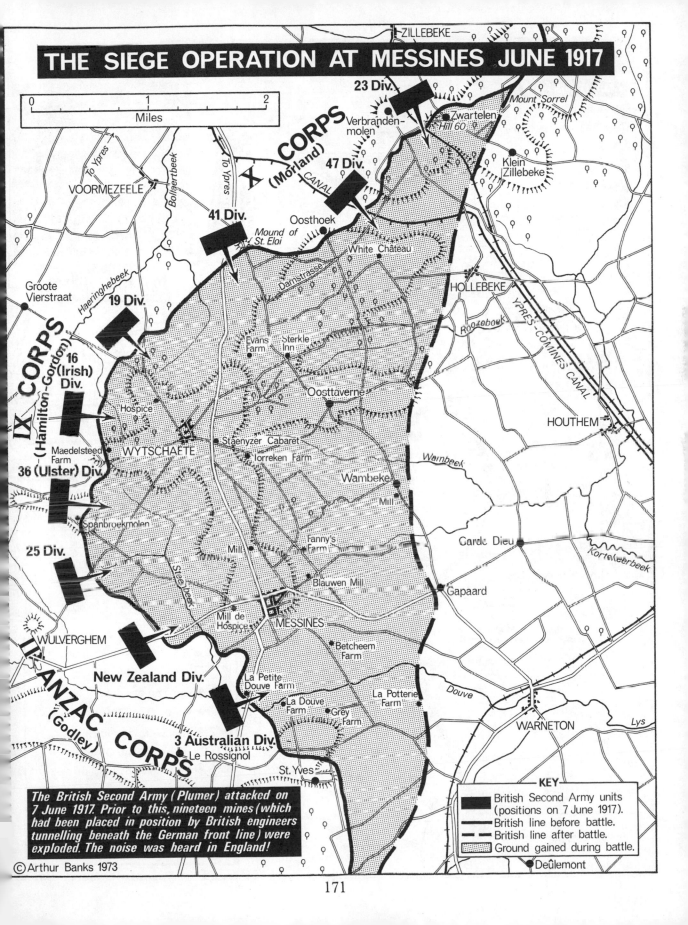

THE SIEGE OPERATION AT MESSINES JUNE 1917

0 1 2
Miles

ZILLEBEKE

23 Div.

Mount Sorrel

Verbranden-molen

Zwartelen

Hill 60

X CORPS (Morland)

47 Div.

CANAL

Klein Zillebeke

To Ypres

VOORMEZEELE

Bollaertbeek

To Ypres

41 Div.

Oosthoek

Mound of St. Eloi

White Château

HOLLEBEKE

Damstrasse

Rooiebeek

YPRES-COMINES CANAL

Groote Vierstraat

Haeringhebeek

19 Div.

HOUTHEM

IX CORPS (Hamilton-Gordon)

16 (Irish) Div.

Evans Farm

Sterkle Inn

Oosttaverne

Hospice

Warnbeek

Staenyzer Cabaret

WYTSCHAETE

Maedelsteed Farm

Torreken Farm

36 (Ulster) Div.

Wambeke

Mill

Spanbroekmolen

Garde Dieu

Korteleerbeek

25 Div.

Mill

Fanny's Farm

Steenbeek

Blauwen Mill

Gapaard

Mill de Hospice

MESSINES

II ANZAC (Godley) CORPS

WULVERGHEM

Betcheem Farm

Douve

New Zealand Div.

La Petite Douve Farm

La Potterie Farm

WARNETON

Lys

3 Australian Div.

La Douve Farm

Grey Farm

Le Rossignol

St. Yves

The British Second Army (Plumer) attacked on 7 June 1917. Prior to this, nineteen mines (which had been placed in position by British engineers tunnelling beneath the German front line) were exploded. The noise was heard in England!

© Arthur Banks 1973

KEY

British Second Army units (positions on 7 June 1917).

British line before battle.

British line after battle.

Ground gained during battle.

Deûlemont

171

BRITISH PLANS FOR "WIPERS THREE" 1917

ALLIED DISPOSITIONS

- **N** Allied naval forces.
- **4** British Fourth Army.
- **B** Belgians.
- **F** French.
- **5** British Fifth Army.
- **2** British Second Army.

NORTH SEA

NOTE: *IN FACT, THESE WERE SHORT-RANGE CRAFT.*

Haig (secretly under intense French pressure to distract German attention from their mutinous sectors) outlined these plans to a meeting of the Cabinet Committee on War Policy in London on 21 June. Jellicoe stressed the German U-boat threat: Haig stated that Bruges was his main objective.

U-BOATS

ZEEBRUGGE

U-BOATS

U-BOATS

OSTEND

U-BOATS

③ BRUGES

GERMAN FLANDERS SUBMARINE BASE.

U-BOATS

DUNES

Middelkerke

FEN COUNTRY

STRATEGIC

DUNES

Nieuport

Yser (canalised)

4

B

F

Couckelaere

②

Thourout
Cortemarck

To Ghent (possible Fourth Objective).

Aeltre

Thielt

Dixmude

Yser

Staden

ROULERS

RAILWAY

Lys

LINE

Passchendaele

①

RIDGE

YPRES

Hooge

STIRLING CASTLE (chateau)

Gheluvelt

Menin

COURTRAI

5

Known to British troops as "Wipers."

Wytschaete

Messines

Comines

Warneton

2

Lys

Armentières

TOURCOING

ROUBAIX

LILLE

KEY

▬▬	Allied front line 21 June.
▒	Allied-held territory.
①➤	Opening assault.
▬ ▬	Haig's First Objective.
②➤	"Follow-up" assault.
▥▥	Haig's Second Objective.
③➤	Main concentrated attack.
▨	Haig's Third (Main) Objective.
▱➤	Flankguards along River Lys.
⟵	German U-boat routes to sea.
┴┴┴	Canals (note Bruges area).

0   5   10
Miles

© Arthur Banks 1973

172

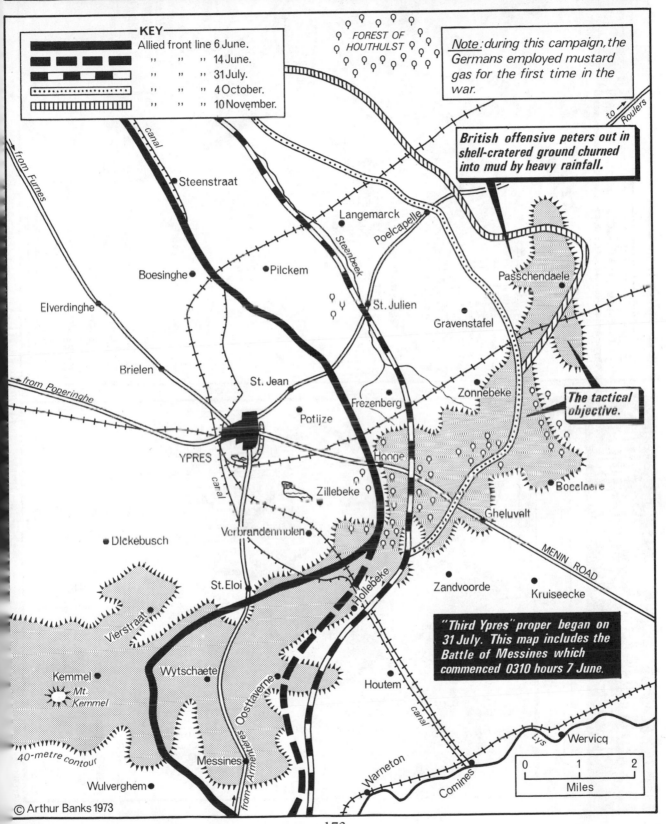

"THIRD YPRES" (PASSCHENDAELE): JULY – NOVEMBER 1917

KEY

Allied front line 6 June.
,, ,, ,, 14 June.
,, ,, ,, 31 July.
,, ,, ,, 4 October.
,, ,, ,, 10 November.

FOREST OF HOUTHULST

Note: during this campaign, the Germans employed mustard gas for the first time in the war.

British offensive peters out in shell-cratered ground churned into mud by heavy rainfall.

to Roulers

Steenstraat

canal

Langemarck
Poelcapelle

Passchendaele

Boesinghe

Pilckem

Steenbeek

St. Julien

Gravenstafel

Elverdinghe

from Furnes

Brielen

St. Jean

Frezenberg

Zonnebeke

The tactical objective.

from Poperinghe

Potijze

Hooge

Becelaere

YPRES

canal

Zillebeke

Gheluvelt

Verbrandenmolen

MENIN ROAD

Dickebusch

St. Eloi

Hollebeke

Zandvoorde

Kruiseecke

Vierstraat

Wytschaete

Oosttaverne

Houtem

canal

"Third Ypres" proper began on 31 July. This map includes the Battle of Messines which commenced 0310 hours 7 June.

Kemmel

Mt. Kemmel

from Armentières

Lys

Wervicq

40-metre contour

Messines

Warneton

Comines

0   1   2

Miles

Wulverghem

© Arthur Banks 1973

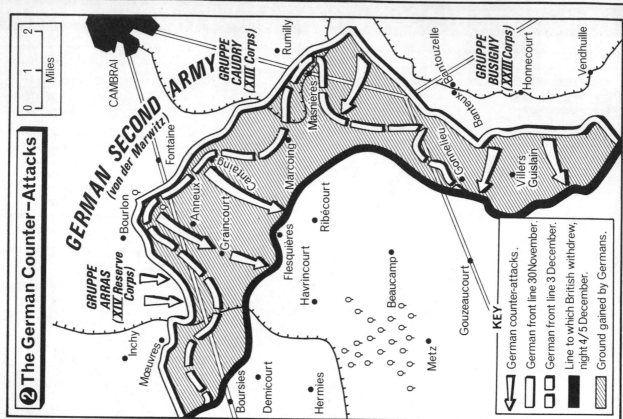

② The German Counter–Attacks

GERMAN SECOND ARMY (von der Marwitz)

GRUPPE CAUDRY (XIII Corps)

GRUPPE BUSIGNY (XXIII Corps)

GRUPPE ARRAS (XIV Reserve Corps)

CAMBRAI

Rumilly · Bantouzelle · Banteux · Honnecourt · Vendhuille

Fontaine · Bourlon · Anneux · Graincourt · Cantaing · Marcoing · Masnières · Gonnelieu · Villers Guislain

Ribécourt · Flesquières · Havrincourt · Beaucamp · Gouzeaucourt · Metz

Inchy · Mœuvres · Boursies · Demicourt · Hermies

KEY

German counter-attacks.	
German front line 30 November.	
German front line 3 December.	
Line to which British withdrew, night 4/5 December.	
Ground gained by Germans.	

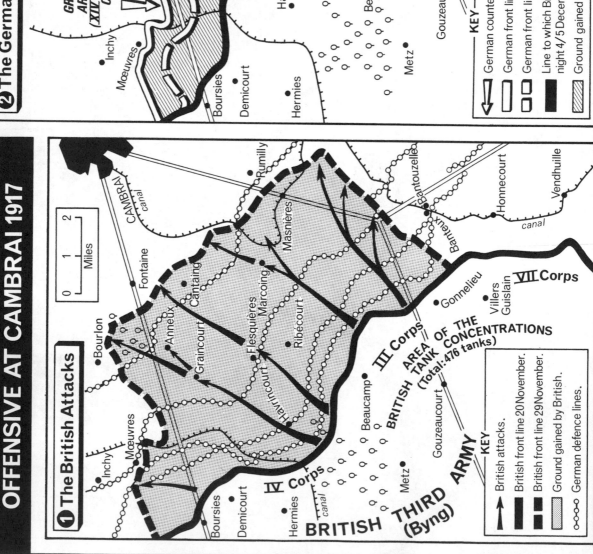

THE BRITISH TANK–SPEARHEADED OFFENSIVE AT CAMBRAI 1917

① The British Attacks

CAMBRAI · canal

Rumilly · Bantouzelle · Banteux · Honnecourt · Vendhuille · canal

Fontaine · Bourlon · Anneux · Cantaing · Masnières · Marcoing · Flesquières · Ribécourt

Gonnelieu · Villers Guislain

VII Corps

III Corps

AREA OF THE BRITISH TANK CONCENTRATIONS (Total : 476 tanks)

Inchy · Mœuvres · Boursies · Demicourt · Hermies · canal

Havrincourt · Graincourt

Beaucamp · Gouzeaucourt · Metz

IV Corps

BRITISH THIRD ARMY (Byng)

KEY

British attacks.	
British front line 20 November.	
British front line 29 November.	
Ground gained by British.	
German defence lines.	

© Arthur Banks 1973

174

TRENCH WARFARE : A TYPICAL SECTION OF FRONT SOUTH-EAST OF ARRAS FEBRUARY 1917

KEY
- German trenches.
- British trenches.
- x x x x x Barbed wire entanglements.
- Railway.
- Road.

ARRAS

BRITISH LINES

NO MAN'S LAND

GERMAN LINES

to Douai

to Cambrai

Gosport Trench
Gloucester Terrace
Gosford Terrace
Gourock Trench
Hermes Trench
Glenarm Lane
Glenelg Lane
Guildford Trench
Hertford Trench
Henley Lane
Hove Trench
Glengarry Trench
Havant Lane
Gillingham Trench
Glasgow Trench
Hornsea Lane
Hastings Lane
Gairloch Trench
Gateshead Trench
Harfleur Trench
Galway Trench

Iron St.
Income Tax
Inns of Court
Ivory St.
Interpreter St.
Islington St.
Islington St.
Cemetery Tr.
Ivy St.
Ivy St.
Ings Ave.
Infantry Road
Ink Trench
Imp St.
Idiot Ct.
Italy Trench
Idiot St.
India Lane
Inverness Lane
Ink Trench
Idle St.
Iris St.
India Lane
Imperial St.
Iodine
Twenty St.
Hunter St.
Iceland St.
Nineteen St.
Ice St.
Eighteen St.
Hooge St.
Halifax St.
Horace St.
Hunter St.
Hazebrouck
Halstead St.
Hooge St.

Note the consecutive lines of defence on the German side with "switch" trenches incorporated to compartment any Allied intrusion. By comparison, the British system was simpler and somewhat haphazard. British names for German trenches are utilized on this map.

0   500   1000
Yards

© Arthur Banks 1973

175

RUSSIA'S FINAL EFFORT IN 1917

② Central Powers' Backlash 19 July – 4 August

Despite some early success the Russian offensive petered-out by 16 July. The troops were war-weary and supplies failed to arrive. The Germans brought reinforcements (via their railways) from the west and began a counter-offensive on 19 July. The Russians collapsed under the onslaught and fled back to the River Zbrucz. Only insufficient reserves and logistical factors halted the German advance.

R U S S I A N S

Khotin

Zbrucz

Sereth

Dniester

Czernowitz

Pruth

Kolomea

Stanislau

Halicz

Kalusz

Zlota   Lipa

Brzezany

Zloczow

Strypa

Tarnopol

Dniester

★ Lemberg

C E N T R A L   POWERS

GERMAN RIGA OFFENSIVE 1–5 SEPTEMBER 1917

KEY

0 5 10 15 Miles	

German advances.

Russian defences.

German tactics: assault troops by-pass strongpoint which is reduced by the "follow-up" units.

RUSSIAN ESCAPE ROUTE.

road

Dvina

RIGA

GULF OF RIGA

marsh

GERMAN EIGHTH ARMY (Von Hutier)

① The Kerensky Offensive 1–16 July

OR "SECOND BRUSILOV"

R U S S I A

RUSSIAN UNUSED ARMY

ELEVENTH ARMY (Erdelli)

Tarnopol

BRUSILOV'S H.Q.

SEVENTH ARMY (Belkovitch)

1 July

Zbrucz

Sereth

Dniester

Strypa

Zlota   Lipa

Brzezany

Brody

Zloczow

SÜDARMEE (4 German, 3 Austrian, 1 Turkish div.)

G A L I C I A

Lemberg

Russian objective.

AUSTRIAN SECOND ARMY

Dniester

AUSTRIAN THIRD ARMY

AUSTRIAN SEVENTH ARMY

A U S T R I A – H U N G A R Y

Halicz

Jezupol

Stanislau

Kalusz

EIGHTH ARMY (Kornilov)

6 July

Kolomea

Pruth

Czernowitz

RUMANIA

Turning flank move.

KEY

0 30 Miles	

Russian armies.

Russian advances.

Extent of main Russian advance 16 July.

Extent of Russian retreat 4 August.

Armies of Central Powers.

Counter-drives of Central Powers.

© Arthur Banks 1973

176

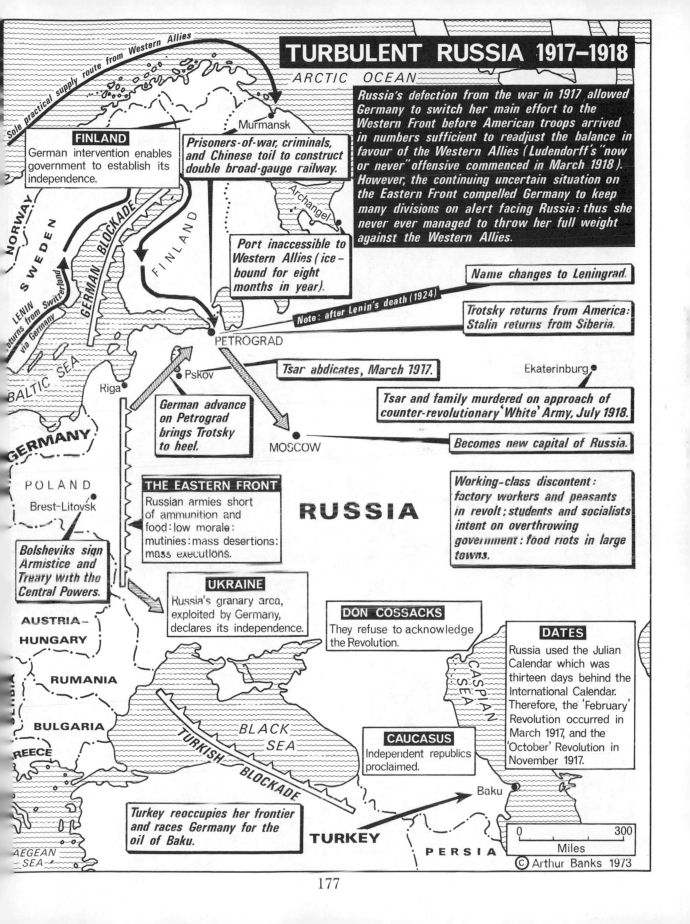

TURBULENT RUSSIA 1917–1918

ARCTIC OCEAN

Sole practical supply route from Western Allies

FINLAND
German intervention enables government to establish its independence.

Prisoners-of-war, criminals, and Chinese toil to construct double broad-gauge railway.

Russia's defection from the war in 1917 allowed Germany to switch her main effort to the Western Front before American troops arrived in numbers sufficient to readjust the balance in favour of the Western Allies (Ludendorff's "now or never" offensive commenced in March 1918). However, the continuing uncertain situation on the Eastern Front compelled Germany to keep many divisions on alert facing Russia: thus she never ever managed to throw her full weight against the Western Allies.

Murmansk

Archangel

Port inaccessible to Western Allies (ice-bound for eight months in year).

Name changes to Leningrad.

Note: after Lenin's death (1924)

Trotsky returns from America: Stalin returns from Siberia.

PETROGRAD

LENIN returns from Switzerland via Germany

Tsar abdicates, March 1917.

Ekaterinburg

Riga

Pskov

German advance on Petrograd brings Trotsky to heel.

Tsar and family murdered on approach of counter-revolutionary 'White' Army, July 1918.

MOSCOW

Becomes new capital of Russia.

GERMANY

POLAND
Brest-Litovsk

THE EASTERN FRONT
Russian armies short of ammunition and food: low morale: mutinies: mass desertions: mass executions.

RUSSIA

Working-class discontent: factory workers and peasants in revolt: students and socialists intent on overthrowing government: food riots in large towns.

Bolsheviks sign Armistice and Treaty with the Central Powers.

UKRAINE
Russia's granary area, exploited by Germany, declares its independence.

DON COSSACKS
They refuse to acknowledge the Revolution.

AUSTRIA–HUNGARY

RUMANIA

BULGARIA

GREECE

BLACK SEA

TURKISH BLOCKADE

CAUCASUS
Independent republics proclaimed.

CASPIAN SEA

DATES
Russia used the Julian Calendar which was thirteen days behind the International Calendar. Therefore, the 'February' Revolution occurred in March 1917, and the 'October' Revolution in November 1917.

Baku

Turkey reoccupies her frontier and races Germany for the oil of Baku.

TURKEY

PERSIA

AEGEAN SEA

| 0 | | 300 |
Miles

© Arthur Banks 1973

177

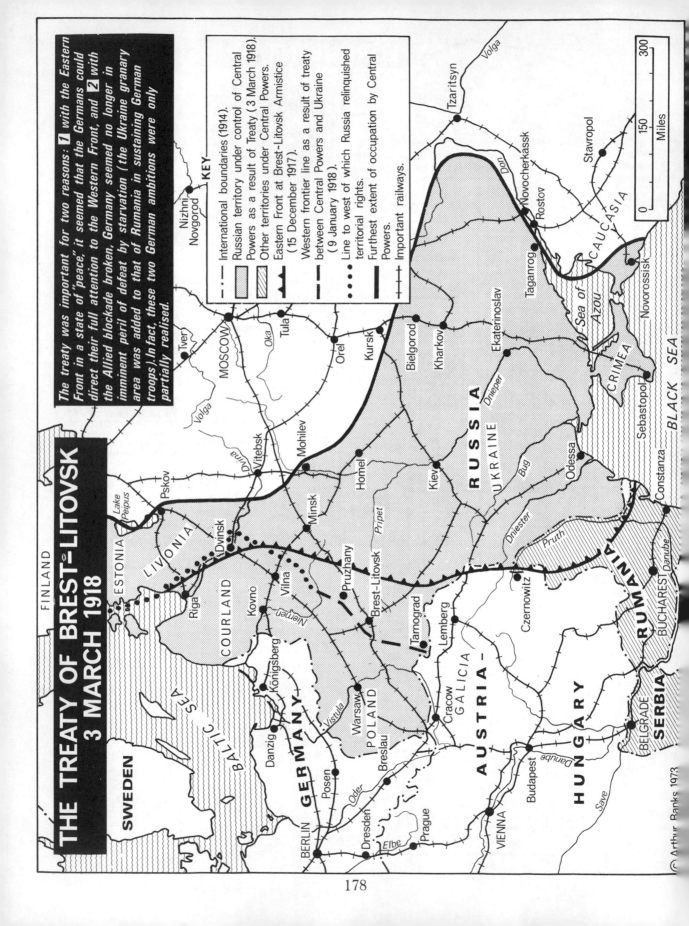

THE TREATY OF BREST-LITOVSK 3 MARCH 1918

*The treaty was important for two reasons: **1** with the Eastern Front in a state of "peace," it seemed that the Germans could direct their full attention to the Western Front, and **2** with the Allied blockade broken, Germany seemed no longer in imminent peril of defeat by starvation (the Ukraine granary area was added to that of Rumania in sustaining German troops). In fact, these two German ambitions were only partially realised.*

KEY

International boundaries (1914).	
Russian territory under control of Central Powers as a result of Treaty (3 March 1918).	
Other territories under Central Powers.	
Eastern Front at Brest-Litovsk Armistice (15 December 1917).	
Western frontier line as a result of treaty between Central Powers and Ukraine (9 January 1918).	
Line to west of which Russia relinquished territorial rights.	
Furthest extent of occupation by Central Powers.	
Important railways.	

© Arthur Banks 1973

THE WAR IN 1918

The war weariness which had assailed the Russian people at the start of winter in 1917–1918 threatened to spread to other countries which had been subjected to many years of heavy casualties and short rations. The German home front was hard-pressed by the British blockade while the British themselves had come close to disaster during the worst month of sinkings by U-boat, April 1917. There was widespread disaffection in Austria-Hungary, accentuated by conflicts between the nationalities within the Empire, and an extensive peace movement in Bulgaria, while desertions from the Turkish army in Palestine began to increase sharply. It was therefore essential for Hindenburg and Ludendorff to achieve a rapid military victory on the Western Front, using reinforcements from the East to defeat the British and French armies in the field before the Americans flooded in. In March 1917 there were three Allied soldiers to every two Germans in France and Belgium: a year later, the troop trains from Russia had changed the balance to four Germans to every three Allies.

The French and British prime ministers, Clemenceau and Lloyd George, anticipated a hard thrust by Germany; but no one believed it possible for Ludendorff to have achieved such concentration of firepower as the Germans mounted in March 1918. Within a week the Germans penetrated the Allied line to a depth of forty miles, although the Germans caused problems to themselves by outrunning their supplies. In April they struck farther north, penetrating a section of the Flanders Front held by inexperienced Portuguese troops; and in May Ludendorff succeeded in bringing the campaign back to the Marne and threatening Paris. His last great stroke, around Rheims on 15 July, was checked by astute defensive positioning on the part of Pétain. The German drive was brought to a standstill, with an exhausted army exposing the flanks of a series of salients to counter-attack.

The Allies had at last accepted the principle of unified command, entrusting Foch with the task of throwing back the Germans. American troops, disembarking in France at the rate of a quarter of a million each month, replenished the Allied armies. On 18 July tanks (as at Cambrai) provided the spearhead for Foch's counter-offensive although it was the German break in morale on 8 August which convinced Ludendorff Germany could not win the War. In September the Allied attacks seemed to lose impetus, but the British at last penetrated the Hindenburg Line on 29 September. At the same time news reached Supreme German Headquarters of collapse elsewhere: Bulgaria capitulated, after Franchet d'Espèrey's Salonika armies broke through on the Macedonian Front (page 204); Allenby and Lawrence's Arab Legion entered Damascus (3 October), and the Turks began to seek peace; at the end of October the Italians, with British and French support, launched a furious offensive on the Piave and induced Austria-Hungary to seek terms (page 203). Lloyd George, who had long believed in 'knocking away the props from under Germany', found his policy vindicated.

Hindenburg accepted the need for peace on 3 October, but he became more optimistic once he saw the Allies were themselves tiring. It was, in the end, bread riots, revolution and a mutiny of the fleet which convinced the German High Command the war was over. The tightening grip of the blockade prevented any hopes of further resistance, while a mass influenza epidemic lowered the morale of the civilian population. A German armistice delegation set out from Berlin on 6 November. The Armistice became effective five days later.

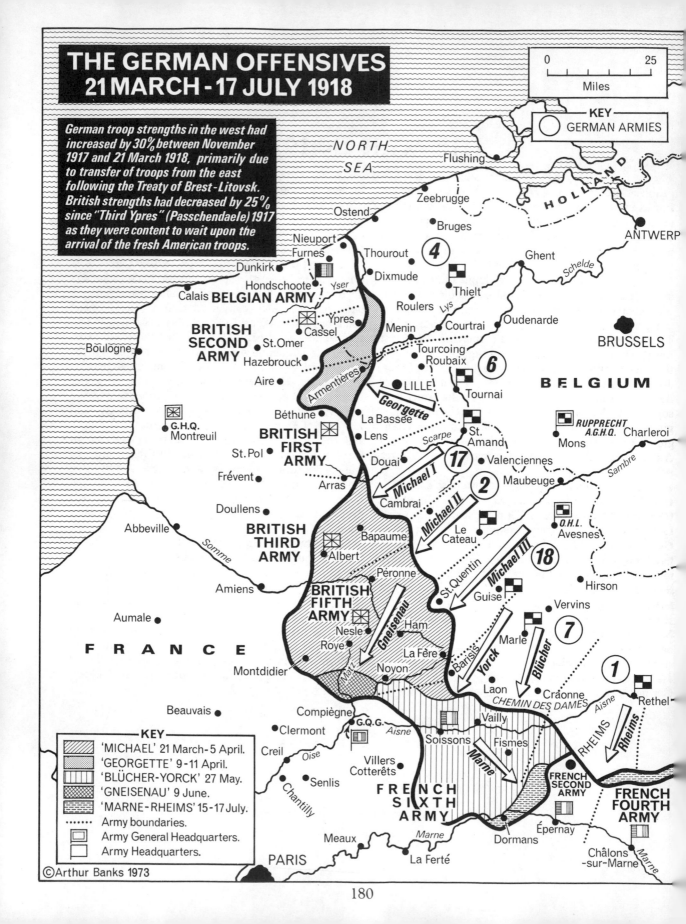

THE GERMAN OFFENSIVES 21 MARCH - 17 JULY 1918

0 — 25
Miles

KEY
GERMAN ARMIES

German troop strengths in the west had increased by 30% between November 1917 and 21 March 1918, primarily due to transfer of troops from the east following the Treaty of Brest-Litovsk. British strengths had decreased by 25% since "Third Ypres" (Passchendaele) 1917 as they were content to wait upon the arrival of the fresh American troops.

NORTH SEA

Flushing

HOLLAND

ANTWERP

Zeebrugge

Bruges

Ostend

Ghent

Schelde

④

Nieuport

Furnes

Thourout

Dixmude

Thielt

BRUSSELS

Dunkirk

Hondschoote

Yser

BELGIAN ARMY

Roulers

Menin

Courtrai

Oudenarde

Lys

Calais

Ypres

BRITISH SECOND ARMY

Cassel

St.Omer

Hazebrouck

Aire

Armentières

Tourcoing

Roubaix

⑥

Tournai

BELGIUM

Boulogne

Georgette

LILLE

Béthune

La Bassée

St. Amand

RUPPRECHT A.G.H.Q.

Charleroi

G.H.Q. Montreuil

BRITISH FIRST ARMY

Lens

Scarpe

Mons

St. Pol

Douai

Michael I

⑰

Valenciennes

Maubeuge

Sambre

Frévent

Arras

Cambrai

Michael II

②

Le Cateau

O.H.L. Avesnes

Doullens

BRITISH THIRD ARMY

Bapaume

Michael III

⑱

Abbeville

Somme

Albert

Péronne

St. Quentin

Guise

Hirson

Amiens

BRITISH FIFTH ARMY

Gneisenau

Ham

La Fère

Vervins

⑦

Aumale

Nesle

Roye

Barisis

Marle

Blücher

Yorck

FRANCE

Montdidier

Matz

Noyon

Laon

Craonne

①

Rethel

Beauvais

Compiègne

G.Q.G.

Aisne

Vailly

CHEMIN DES DAMES

Aisne

Rheims

Clermont

Soissons

Fismes

RHEIMS

Creil

Oise

Marne

FRENCH SECOND ARMY

Senlis

Villers Cotterêts

FRENCH SIXTH ARMY

Épernay

FRENCH FOURTH ARMY

Chantilly

Marne

Dormans

Châlons -sur-Marne

Marne

Meaux

La Ferté

PARIS

KEY

'MICHAEL' 21 March-5 April.
'GEORGETTE' 9-11 April.
'BLÜCHER-YORCK' 27 May.
'GNEISENAU' 9 June.
'MARNE-RHEIMS' 15-17 July.
Army boundaries.
Army General Headquarters.
Army Headquarters.

© Arthur Banks 1973

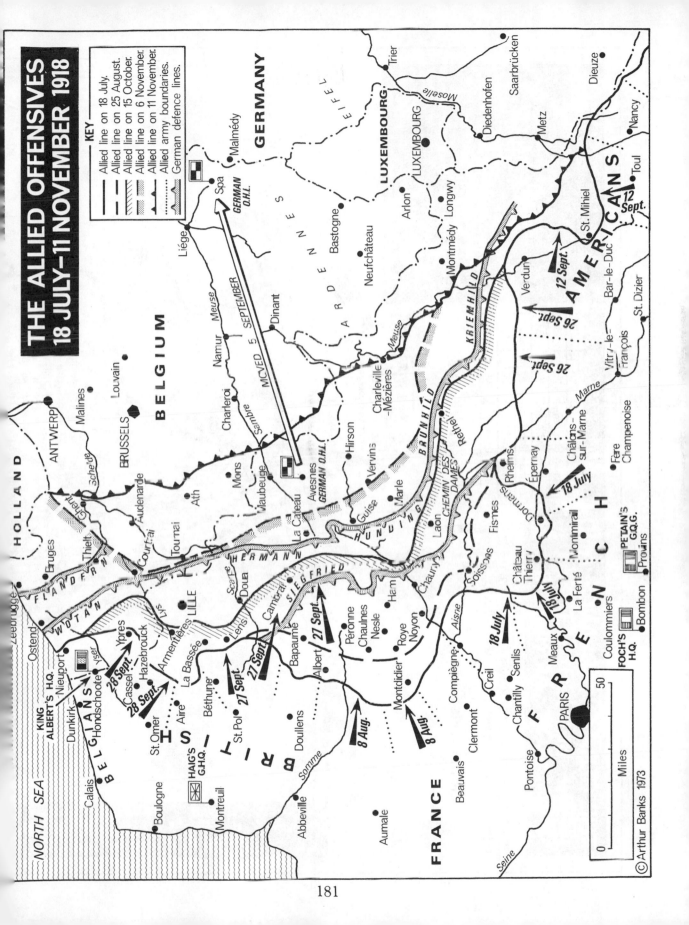

THE ALLIED OFFENSIVES
18 JULY–11 NOVEMBER 1918

KEY
Allied line on 18 July.
Allied line on 25 August.
Allied line on 15 October.
Allied line on 6 November.
Allied line on 11 November.
Allied army boundaries.
German defence lines.

NORTH SEA

HOLLAND

GERMANY

EIFEL

GERMAN O.H.L.

Spa

Liége

Malmédy

Trier

Saarbrücken

Dieuze

Diedenhofen

Metz

Nancy

Toul

LUXEMBOURG

LUXEMBOURG

Arlon

Longwy

Montmédy

Bastogne

Neufchâteau

A R D E N N E S

St. Mihiel

12 Sept.

A M E R I C A N S

Bar-le-Duc

St. Dizier

Verdun

12 Sept.

26 Sept.

26 Sept.

Vitry-le-François

KRIEMHILD

BRUNHILD

CHEMIN DES DAMES

Rethel

Charleville
-Mézières

Dinant

Namur

Meuse

Charleroi

Sambre

5 SEPTEMBER

MEUSE

Avesnes

GERMAN O.H.L.

La Cateau

Hirson

Vervins

Guise

Marle

Laon

Chaury

Soissons

Aisne

Fismes

Rheims

Épernay

Dormans

Châlons-
sur-Marne

Fère
Champenoise

Marne

18 July

BELGIUM

BRUSSELS

Louvain

Malines

ANTWERP

Bruges

Ghent

Sche de

Audenarde

Ath

Mons

Maubeuge

Tournai

Courtrai

Thielt

FLANDERN

WOTAN

HERMANN

Scarpe

Douai

Cambrai

SIEGFRIED

Péronne

Chaulnes

Nesle

Roye

Noyon

Ham

27 Sept.

27 Sept.

27 Sept.

Bapaume

Albert

Montdidier

8 Aug.

8 Aug.

Compiègne

Clermont

Creil

Senlis

Chantilly

Beauvais

HUNDING

Château
Thierry

La Ferté

Coulommiers

Montmirail

PETAIN'S G.Q.G.

Provins

Bombon

FOCH'S H.Q.

18 July

18 July

18 July

Meaux

PARIS

F R E N C H

F R A N C E

Zeebrugge

Ostend

Nieuport

Dunkirk

Calais

Boulogne

Ypres

Hazebrouck

Cassel

Hondschoote

St. Omer

Aire

Béthune

La Bassée

Armentières

LILLE

Lens

St. Pol

Doullens

Abbeville

Aumale

Montreuil

HAIG'S G.H.Q.

KING
ALBERT'S H.Q.

BELGIANS

B R I T I S H

Somme

Lys

Yser

28 Sept.

28 Sept.

27 Sept.

Seine

Pontoise

Chaury

Vitry-le-
François

Miles

0   50

© Arthur Banks 1973

181

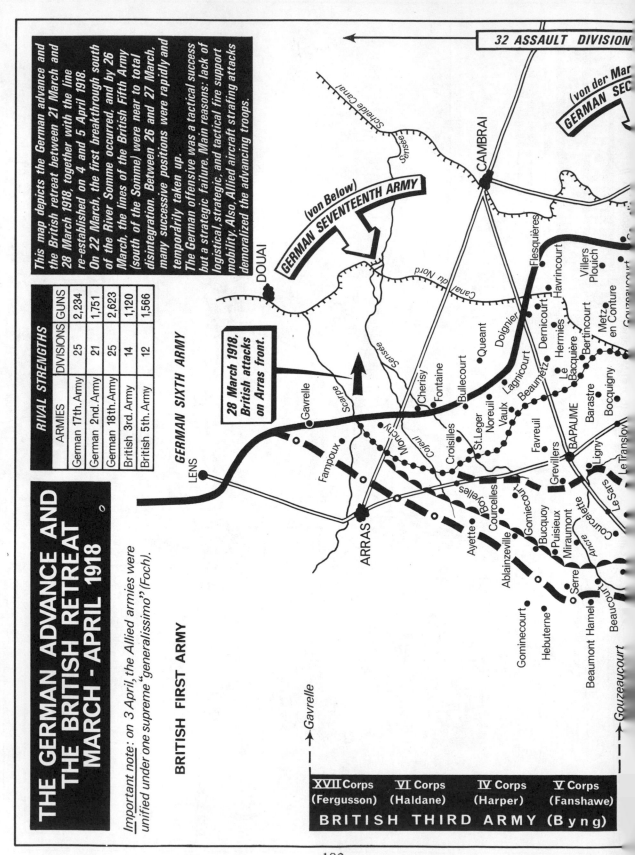

THE GERMAN ADVANCE AND THE BRITISH RETREAT MARCH - APRIL 1918

Important note: on 3 April, the Allied armies were unified under one supreme "generalissimo" (Foch).

This map depicts the German advance and the British retreat between 21 March and 28 March 1918, together with the line re-established on 4 and 5 April 1918. On 22 March, the first breakthrough south of the River Somme occurred, and by 26 March, the lines of the British Fifth Army (south of the Somme) were near to total disintegration. Between 26 and 27 March, many successive positions were rapidly and temporarily taken up.

The German offensive was a tactical success but a strategic failure. Main reasons: lack of logistical, strategic, and tactical fire support mobility. Also, Allied aircraft strafing attacks demoralized the advancing troops.

RIVAL STRENGTHS

ARMIES	DIVISIONS	GUNS
German 17th. Army	25	2,234
German 2nd. Army	21	1,751
German 18th. Army	25	2,623
British 3rd. Army	14	1,120
British 5th. Army	12	1,566

28 March 1918, British attacks on Arras front.

32 ASSAULT DIVISION

(von der Mar

GERMAN SEC

GERMAN SEVENTEENTH ARMY (von Below)

GERMAN SIXTH ARMY

BRITISH FIRST ARMY

CAMBRAI

DOUAI

LENS

ARRAS

BAPAUME

| XVII Corps (Fergusson) | VI Corps (Haldane) | IV Corps (Harper) | V Corps (Fanshawe) |

BRITISH THIRD ARMY (Byng)

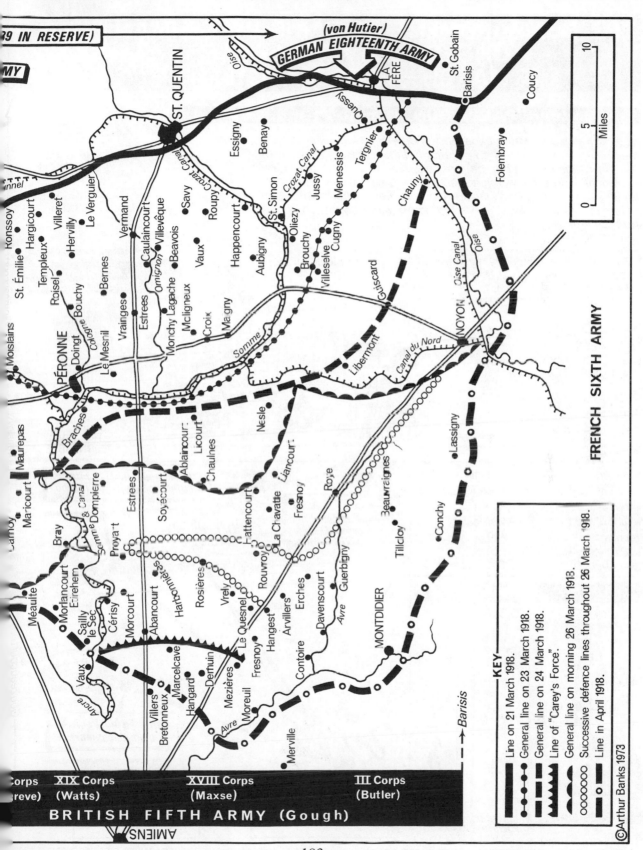

(89 IN RESERVE)

...MY

(von Hutier)
GERMAN EIGHTEENTH ARMY

ST. QUENTIN

Oise
LA FÈRE
St. Gobain
Barisis
Coucy

Essigny
Benay
Crozat Canal
Folembray

Quessy

Tergnier

Jussy
Menessis

Savy
St. Simon
Roupy
Happencourt
Oliezy
Brouchy
Cugny

Essign·y
Beauvois
Vaux
Aubigny
Villeseve
Chauny

Le Verguier
Villeret
Villeveque
Magny
Croix

Vermand
Caulaincourt
Estrees
Monchy Lagache
Guiscard

Hervilly
Omignon
Oise Canal

St. Émilie
Hargicourt
Vrainges
Somme
Libermont

Templeux
Bernes
Roisel
Le Mesnil
NOYON
Canal du Nord

Konssoy
Bouchy
Cologne
Doingt

Moislains
PÉRONNE
Nesle
Lassigny

Maurepas
Braches
Ablaincourt
Licourt
Chaulnes
Liancourt
Roye
Conchy

Carnoy
Maricourt
Estrees
Soyécourt
Fresnoy
Beauvraignes

Bray
Somme & Canal
Proyart
Harbonnières
Le Chavatie
Rouvroy
Guerbigny
Tilloy

Méaulte
Morlancourt
Etrehem
Morcourt
Abancourt
Rosières
Vrely
Le Quesnel
Erches
Davenscourt
MONTDIDIER

Vaux
Sailly
le Sec
Cérisy
Proya·t
Hangest
Arvillers
Contoire
Avre

Villers
Bretonneux
Marcelcave
Hangard
Derhuin
Mezières
Fresnoy

Ancre
Moreuil
Merville

Avre

Barisis

FRENCH SIXTH ARMY

KEY

▬▬▬	Line on 21 March 1918.
••••••	General line on 23 March 1918.
┴┴┴┴	General line on 24 March 1918.
▲▲▲▲	Line of "Carey's Force".
⌒⌒⌒⌒	General line on morning 26 March 1918.
○○○○○	Successive defence lines throughout 26 March 1918.
▬ ▬ ▬	Line in April 1918.

©Arthur Banks 1973

...orps   **XIX** Corps   **XVIII** Corps   **III** Corps
...reve)   (Watts)   (Maxse)   (Butler)

BRITISH FIFTH ARMY (Gough)

AMIENS

THE BOMBARDMENT OF PARIS BY GERMAN LONG-RANGE ARTILLERY 23 MARCH – 9 AUGUST 1918

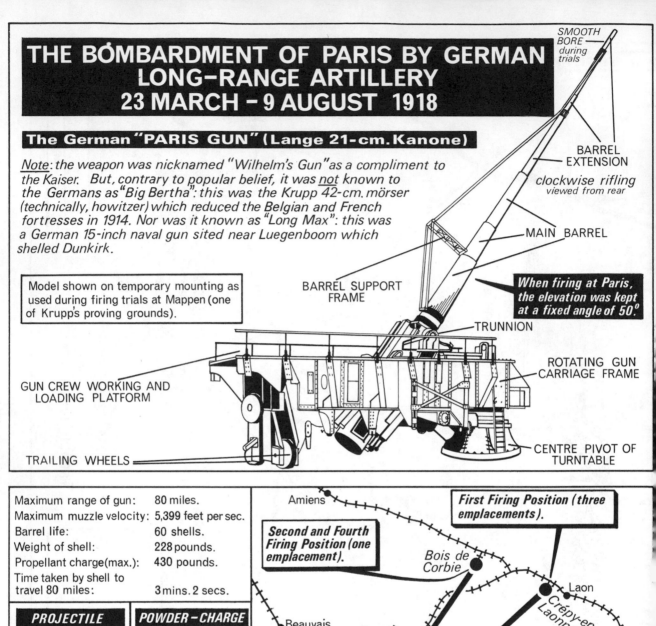

The German "PARIS GUN" (Lange 21-cm. Kanone)

Note: the weapon was nicknamed "Wilhelm's Gun" as a compliment to the Kaiser. But, contrary to popular belief, it was not known to the Germans as "Big Bertha": this was the Krupp 42-cm. mörser (technically, howitzer) which reduced the Belgian and French fortresses in 1914. Nor was it known as "Long Max": this was a German 15-inch naval gun sited near Luegenboom which shelled Dunkirk.

SMOOTH BORE *during trials*

BARREL EXTENSION

clockwise rifling viewed from rear

MAIN BARREL

BARREL SUPPORT FRAME

Model shown on temporary mounting as used during firing trials at Mappen (one of Krupp's proving grounds).

When firing at Paris, the elevation was kept at a fixed angle of 50.°

TRUNNION

ROTATING GUN CARRIAGE FRAME

GUN CREW WORKING AND LOADING PLATFORM

CENTRE PIVOT OF TURNTABLE

TRAILING WHEELS

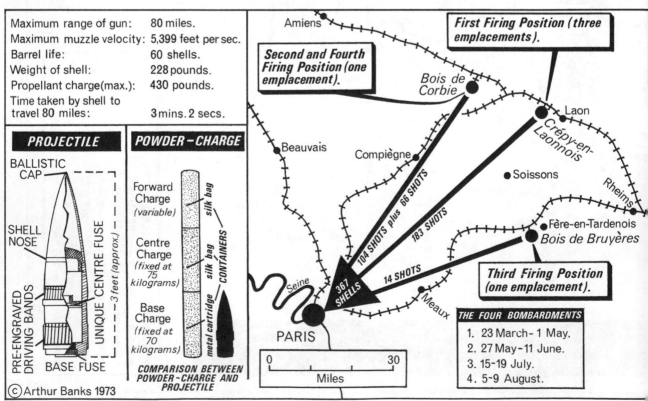

Maximum range of gun:	80 miles.
Maximum muzzle velocity:	5,399 feet per sec.
Barrel life:	60 shells.
Weight of shell:	228 pounds.
Propellant charge (max.):	430 pounds.
Time taken by shell to travel 80 miles:	3 mins. 2 secs.

PROJECTILE

BALLISTIC CAP

SHELL NOSE

PRE-ENGRAVED DRIVING BANDS

BASE FUSE

UNIQUE CENTRE FUSE

-- 3 feet (approx.) --

POWDER-CHARGE

Forward Charge *(variable)*

Centre Charge *(fixed at 75 kilograms)*

Base Charge *(fixed at 70 kilograms)*

silk bag

silk bag

metal cartridge

CONTAINERS

COMPARISON BETWEEN POWDER-CHARGE AND PROJECTILE

© Arthur Banks 1973

Amiens

First Firing Position (three emplacements).

Second and Fourth Firing Position (one emplacement).

Bois de Corbie

Laon

Crépy-en-Laonnois

Beauvais

Compiègne

Soissons

Rheims

104 SHOTS plus 66 SHOTS

183 SHOTS

Fère-en-Tardenois

Bois de Bruyères

Seine

367 SHELLS

14 SHOTS

Third Firing Position (one emplacement).

Meaux

PARIS

0 — 30 Miles

THE FOUR BOMBARDMENTS
1. 23 March – 1 May.
2. 27 May – 11 June.
3. 15-19 July.
4. 5-9 August.

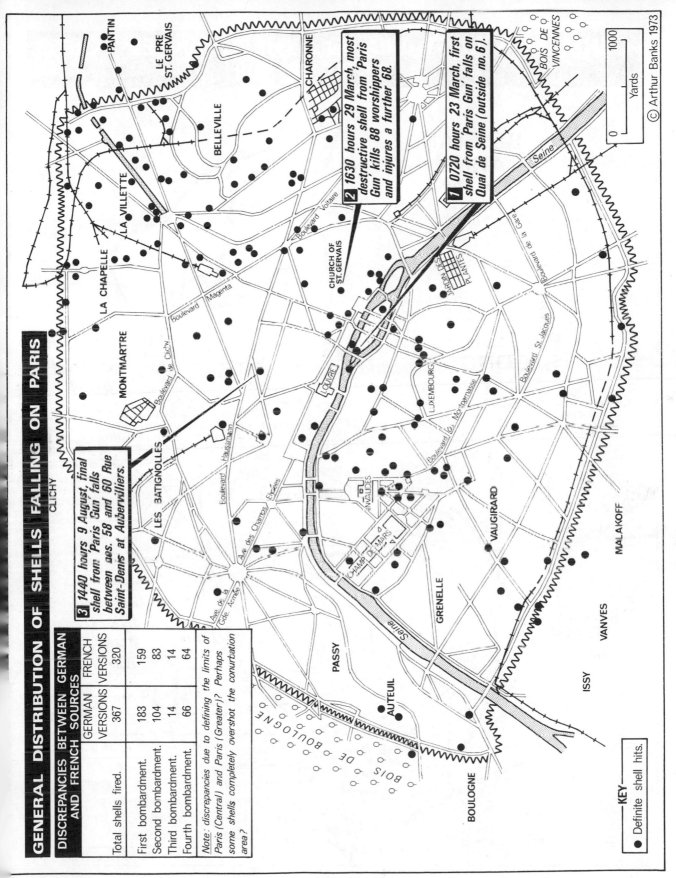

GENERAL DISTRIBUTION OF SHELLS FALLING ON PARIS

DISCREPANCIES BETWEEN GERMAN AND FRENCH SOURCES

	GERMAN VERSIONS	GERMAN VERSIONS	FRENCH VERSIONS	FRENCH VERSIONS
Total shells fired.	367		320	
First bombardment.	183		159	
Second bombardment.	104		83	
Third bombardment.	14		14	
Fourth bombardment.	66		64	

Note: discrepancies due to defining the limits of Paris (Central) and Paris (Greater)? Perhaps some shells completely overshot the conurbation area?

1 *0720 hours 23 March, first shell from 'Paris Gun' falls on Quai de Seine (outside no. 6).*

2 *1630 hours 29 March, most destructive shell from 'Paris Gun' kills 88 worshippers and injures a further 68.*

3 *1440 hours 9 August, final shell from 'Paris Gun' falls between nos. 58 and 60 Rue Saint-Denis at Aubervilliers.*

© Arthur Banks 1973

1000

0

Yards

KEY

● Definite shell hits.

185

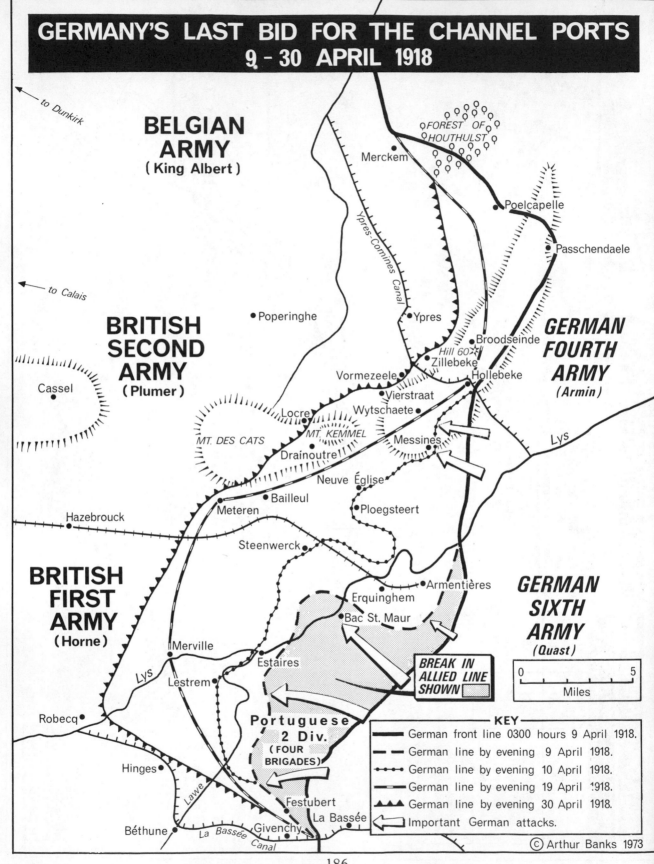

GERMANY'S LAST BID FOR THE CHANNEL PORTS
9 - 30 APRIL 1918

to Dunkirk

BELGIAN ARMY
(King Albert)

FOREST OF HOUTHULST

Merckem

Poelcapelle

Passchendaele

to Calais

BRITISH SECOND ARMY
(Plumer)

Poperinghe

Ypres

Broodseinde

Hill 60

Zillebeke

Hollebeke

GERMAN FOURTH ARMY
(Armin)

Cassel

Vormezeele

Vierstraat

Wytschaete

MT. DES CATS

Locre

MT. KEMMEL

Messines

Lys

Drainoutre

Neuve Église

Bailleul

Ploegsteert

Hazebrouck

Meteren

Steenwerck

Armentières

BRITISH FIRST ARMY
(Horne)

Erquinghem

Bac St. Maur

GERMAN SIXTH ARMY
(Quast)

Merville

Estaires

Lestrem

BREAK IN ALLIED LINE SHOWN

Lys

Robecq

Portuguese 2 Div.
(FOUR BRIGADES)

Hinges

0 — 5
Miles

Lawe

Festubert

La Bassée

Béthune

Givenchy

La Bassée Canal

KEY

▬▬▬	German front line 0300 hours 9 April 1918.
▬ ▬ ▬	German line by evening 9 April 1918.
••••••	German line by evening 10 April 1918.
‒‒‒‒‒	German line by evening 19 April 1918.
▲▲▲▲	German line by evening 30 April 1918.
⇦	Important German attacks.

© Arthur Banks 1973

186

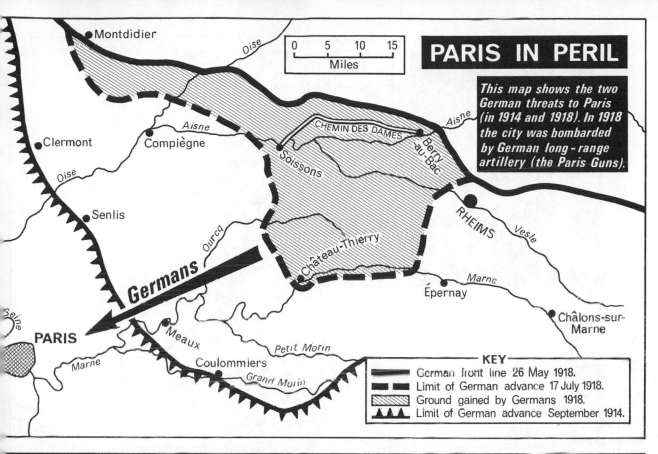

PARIS IN PERIL

This map shows the two German threats to Paris (in 1914 and 1918). In 1918 the city was bombarded by German long-range artillery (the Paris Guns).

Montdidier

Oise

0 5 10 15
Miles

Clermont

Aisne
Compiègne

CHEMIN DES DAMES

Soissons

Berry-au-Bac

Aisne

RHEIMS

Vesle

Senlis

Oise

Ourcq

Germans

Château-Thierry

Épernay

Marne

Châlons-sur-Marne

Seine

PARIS

Meaux

Marne

Coulommiers

Petit Morin

Grand Morin

KEY

German front line 26 May 1918.
Limit of German advance 17 July 1918.
Ground gained by Germans 1918.
Limit of German advance September 1914.

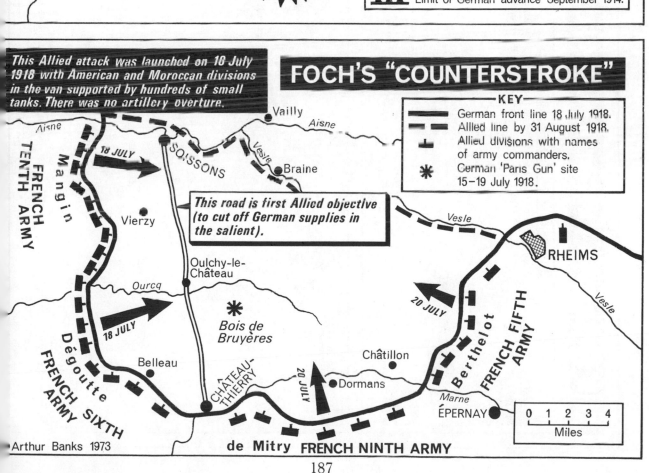

This Allied attack was launched on 18 July 1918 with American and Moroccan divisions in the van supported by hundreds of small tanks. There was no artillery overture.

FOCH'S "COUNTERSTROKE"

KEY

German front line 18 July 1918.
Allied line by 31 August 1918.
Allied divisions with names of army commanders.
German 'Paris Gun' site 15–19 July 1918.

Aisne

Vailly

Aisne

FRENCH TENTH ARMY

Mangin

18 JULY

SOISSONS

Vesle

Braine

Vierzy

This road is first Allied objective (to cut off German supplies in the salient).

Vesle

RHEIMS

Oulchy-le-Château

Ourcq

18 JULY

*

Bois de Bruyères

20 JULY

Berthelot **FRENCH FIFTH ARMY**

Vesle

Belleau

Châtillon

Dégoutte **FRENCH SIXTH ARMY**

CHÂTEAU-THIERRY

20 JULY

Dormans

Marne

ÉPERNAY

0 1 2 3 4
Miles

Arthur Banks 1973

de Mitry FRENCH NINTH ARMY

THE AMERICAN EXPEDITIONARY FORCE IN EUROPE 1918

Note: the United States lost more soldiers from illness than it lost from all battles combined.

The United States declared war on Germany on 6 April 1917, and against Austria-Hungary on 7 December 1917. General John Joseph Pershing was appointed commander of the American Expeditionary Force to Europe, and a vast training and camp-building programme was commenced. By May 1918, there were over 500,000 U.S. troops in France, and by mid-July, over 1,000,000 men had arrived in Europe.

NUMBERS OF UNITED STATES TROOPS

EMBARKED FOR EUROPE AT:	
New York	1,656,000 men
Newport News	288,000 men
Boston	46,000 men
Philadelphia	35,000 men
Portland	6,000 men
Baltimore	4,000 men

PLUS 45,000 TROOPS EMBARKED AT CANADIAN PORTS

Montreal	32,000 men
Quebec	11,000 men
Halifax	5,000 men
St. John's	1,000 men
	2,084,000 men

DISEMBARKED IN EUROPE AT:	
Liverpool (including 4,000 at Manchester)	848,000 men
Brest	791,000 men
St. Nazaire	198,000 men
London	62,000 men
Southampton	57,000 men
Bassens (including Bordeaux)	50,000 men
Glasgow	45,000 men
Le Havre	13,000 men
Bristol	11,000 men
La Pallice (including La Rochelle)	4,000 men
Cherbourg	2,000 men
Marseilles	1,000 men
Plymouth	1,000 men
Falmouth	1,000 men
	2,08 ,000 men

Precise figs. 71 men were lost in Atlantic crossings.

Arrival in Europe

KEY
Disembarkation ports shown ●
KEY TO BRITISH DISEMBARKATION PORTS

Mobilization

KEY
■ National Guard camps.
□ National Army camps.

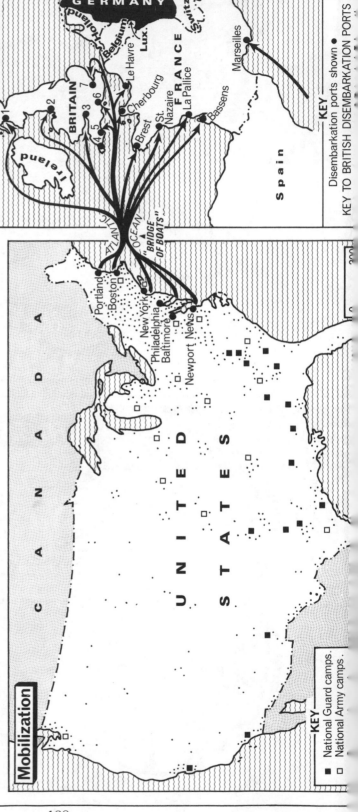

188

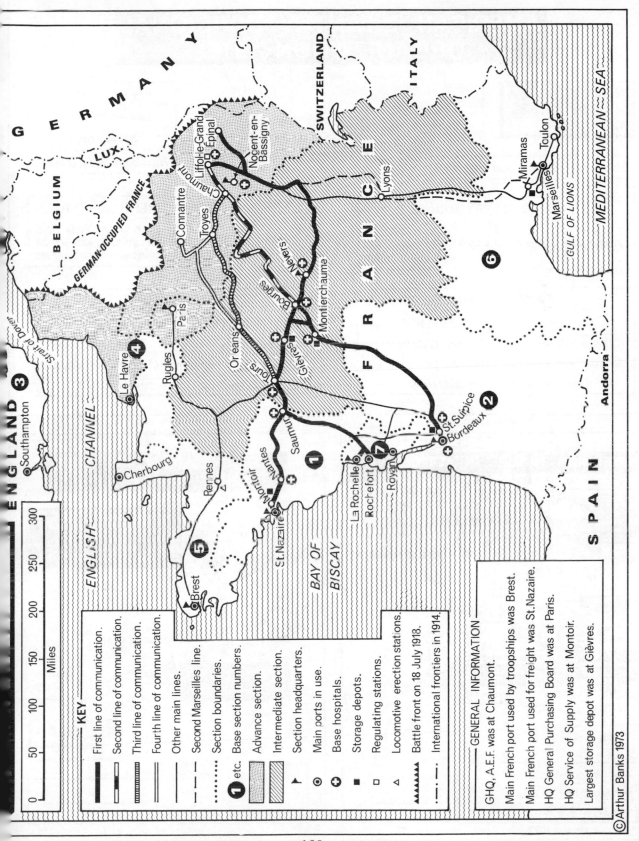

KEY

— First line of communication.
▮ Second line of communication.
▨ Third line of communication.
▨ Fourth line of communication.
— Other main lines.
--- Second Marseilles line.
⋯⋯ Section boundaries.
①etc. Base section numbers.
▨ Advance section.
▨ Intermediate section.
⋯⋯ Section headquarters.
▲ Main ports in use.
⊙ Base hospitals.
✚ Storage depots.
▪ Regulating stations.
□ Locomotive erection stations.
△
▲▲▲▲ Battle front on 18 July 1918.
—··— International frontiers in 1914.

GENERAL INFORMATION
GHQ, A.E.F. was at Chaumont.
Main French port used by troopships was Brest.
Main French port used for freight was St.Nazaire.
HQ General Purchasing Board was at Paris.
HQ Service of Supply was at Montoir.
Largest storage depot was at Gièvres.

© Arthur Banks 1973

189

AMERICAN INFANTRY DIVISIONAL ORGANIZATION 1918

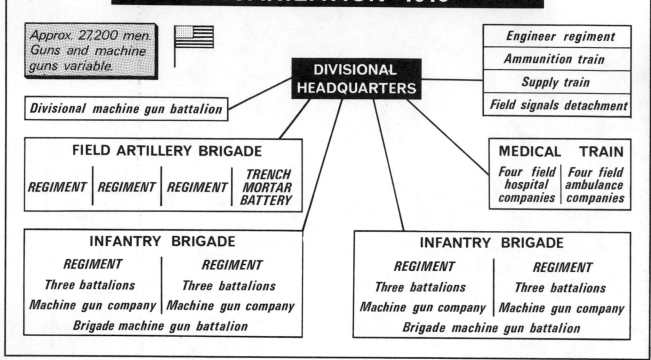

Approx. 27,200 men. Guns and machine guns variable

DIVISIONAL HEADQUARTERS

Engineer regiment

Ammunition train

Supply train

Field signals detachment

Divisional machine gun battalion

FIELD ARTILLERY BRIGADE

REGIMENT	REGIMENT	REGIMENT	TRENCH MORTAR BATTERY

MEDICAL TRAIN

Four field hospital companies	Four field ambulance companies

INFANTRY BRIGADE

REGIMENT	REGIMENT
Three battalions	Three battalions
Machine gun company	Machine gun company
Brigade machine gun battalion	

INFANTRY BRIGADE

REGIMENT	REGIMENT
Three battalions	Three battalions
Machine gun company	Machine gun company
Brigade machine gun battalion	

AMERICAN TROOPS IN ACTION 1918

HOLLAND

BELGIUM

• BRUSSELS

GERMANY

YPRES-LYS

• Lille

Armentières

Mons •

Namur •

Meuse

Rhine

Lys

Cambrai

SOMME

Oise

Somme

Amiens •

Cantigny •

Noyon

Laon

Sedan •

LUX.

Montdidier •

Aisne

AISNE-MARNE

Rheims •

Metz •

OISE-AISNE

MEUSE-ARGONNE

PARIS •

Marne

Château-Thierry

St.Mihiel •

Strassburg •

Seine

ST. MIHIEL

Rhine

FRANCE

KEY
➝ American attacks.
--- Front line 18 July.
— Armistice line 11 November.

0 — 50
Miles

© Arthur Banks 1973

THE FIGHT AT BELLEAU WOOD
4 JUNE – 10 JULY 1918

THE U.S. MARINE BRIGADE OF SECOND DIVISION FOUGHT FOUR GERMAN DIVISIONS. THE FRONT HELD, AND THE ROAD TO PARIS REMAINED SECURE.

Torcy •

Givry
Belleau •

Belleau Wood

Marigny •

Champillon •

Bouresches •

HQ. U.S. 2 Div.

Lucy-le-Bocage •

Château-Thierry

U.S. SECOND DIVISION

Vaux •

Monneaux •

Marne

Coupru •

← to Paris

U.S. THIRD DIVISION

KEY
➝ American attacks.
--- Front line 4 June.
— Front line 10 July.

0 — 1 — 2
Miles

190

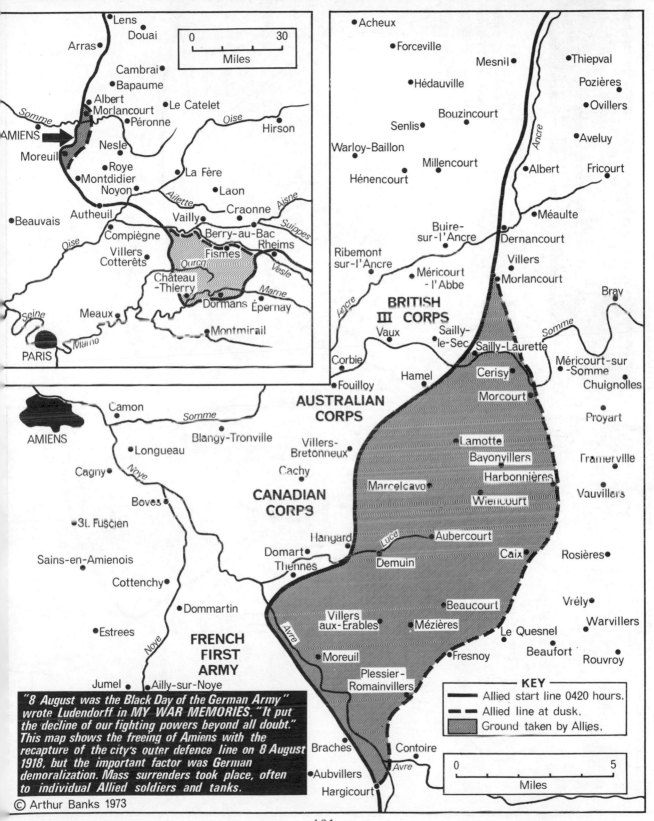

"BLACK DAY OF THE GERMAN ARMY" 8 AUGUST 1918

Inset map (upper left):

0 — 30
Miles

Lens
Douai
Arras
Cambrai
Bapaume
Albert
Morlancourt
Le Catelet
Péronne
Somme
Oise
Hirson
AMIENS
Nesle
Moreuil
Roye
La Fère
Montdidier
Noyon
Ailette
Laon
Aisne
Beauvais
Autheuil
Craonne
Vailly
Suippes
Oise
Compiègne
Berry-au-Bac
Rheims
Villers
Cotterêts
Fismes
Vesle
Ourcq
Château-Thierry
Marne
Dormans
Épernay
Seine
Meaux
Marne
Montmirail
PARIS

Main map:

Acheux
Forceville
Mesnil
Thiepval
Hédauville
Pozières
Ovillers
Bouzincourt
Senlis
Aveluy
Warloy-Baillon
Millencourt
Albert
Fricourt
Hénencourt
Ancre
Méaulte
Buire-sur-l'Ancre
Dernancourt
Ribemont sur-l'Ancre
Villers
Morlancourt
Méricourt-l'Abbé
Bray

BRITISH III CORPS

Ancre
Vaux
Sailly-le-Sec
Sailly-Laurette
Somme
Méricourt-sur-Somme
Corbie
Cerisy
Chuignolles
Hamel
Morcourt
Fouilloy
Proyart

AUSTRALIAN CORPS

Camon
Somme
Blangy-Tronville
AMIENS
Villers-Bretonneux
Lamotte
Bayonvillers
Framerville
Longueau
Cachy
Harbonnières
Cagny
Noye
Marcelcave
Wiencourt
Vauvillers

CANADIAN CORPS

Boves
St. Fuscien
Luce
Hangard
Aubercourt
Sains-en-Amienois
Domart
Thennes
Demuin
Caix
Rosières
Cottenchy
Vrély
Dommartin
Beaucourt
Warvillers
Estrees
Villers aux-Erables
Mézières
Le Quesnel
Beaufort
Rouvroy
Avre
Noye
Moreuil
Fresnoy

FRENCH FIRST ARMY

Plessier-Romainvillers
Jumel
Ailly-sur-Noye
Braches
Contoire
Avre
Aubvillers
Hargicourt

KEY
— Allied start line 0420 hours.
– – Allied line at dusk.
▨ Ground taken by Allies.

0 — 5
Miles

*"8 August was the Black Day of the German Army"
wrote Ludendorff in MY WAR MEMORIES. "It put
the decline of our fighting powers beyond all doubt."
This map shows the freeing of Amiens with the
recapture of the city's outer defence line on 8 August
1918, but the important factor was German
demoralization. Mass surrenders took place, often
to individual Allied soldiers and tanks.*

© Arthur Banks 1973

191

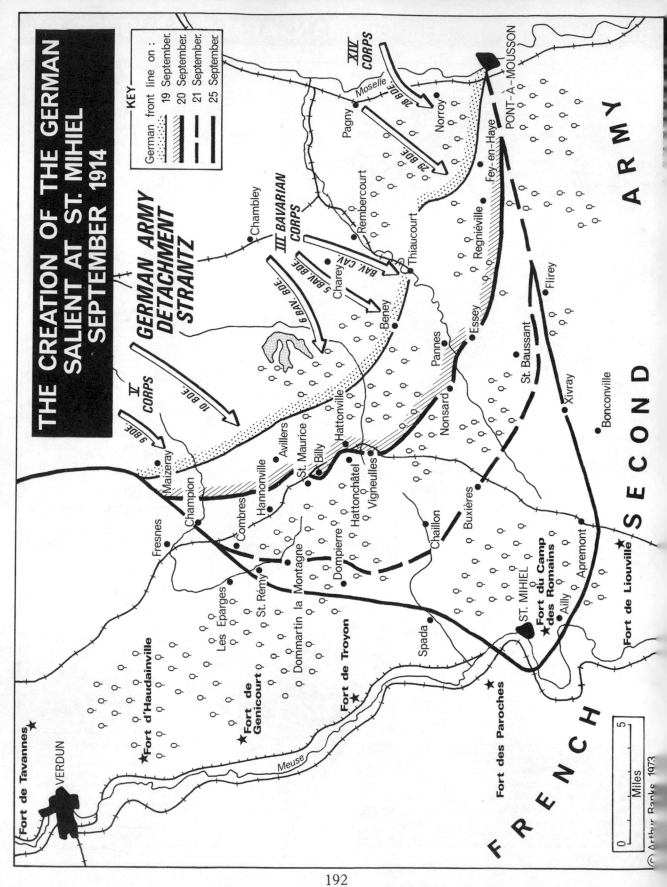

THE CREATION OF THE GERMAN SALIENT AT ST. MIHIEL SEPTEMBER 1914

KEY

German front line on:
.... 19 September.
|||||||||| 20 September.
— — — 21 September.
———— 25 September.

XIV CORPS

Moselle

PONT-À-MOUSSON

28 BDE.

29 BDE.

Pagny

Norroy

Fey-en-Haye

S E C O N D   A R M Y

GERMAN ARMY DETACHMENT STRANTZ

III BAVARIAN CORPS

Chambley

Rembercourt

Regniéville

Thiaucourt

Essey

5 BAV. BDE.

BAV. CAV.

Charey

Beney

Flirey

6 BAV. BDE.

Pannes

St. Baussant

V CORPS

10 BDE.

Nonsard

Xivray

Bonconville

9 BDE.

Maizeray

Hattonville

Champion

Avillers

St. Maurice

Billy

Hattonchâtel

Vigneulles

Buxières

Apremont

Fresnes

Combres

Hannonville

Chaillon

Fort de Liouville

Les Eparges

St. Rémy

Dompierre

Fort du Camp des Romains

Ailly

Fort d'Haudainville

Dommartin la Montagne

ST. MIHIEL

Fort de Genicourt

Fort de Troyon

Spada

Fort des Paroches

VERDUN

Fort de Tavannes,

Meuse

F R E N C H

0   Miles   5

© Arthur Banks 1973

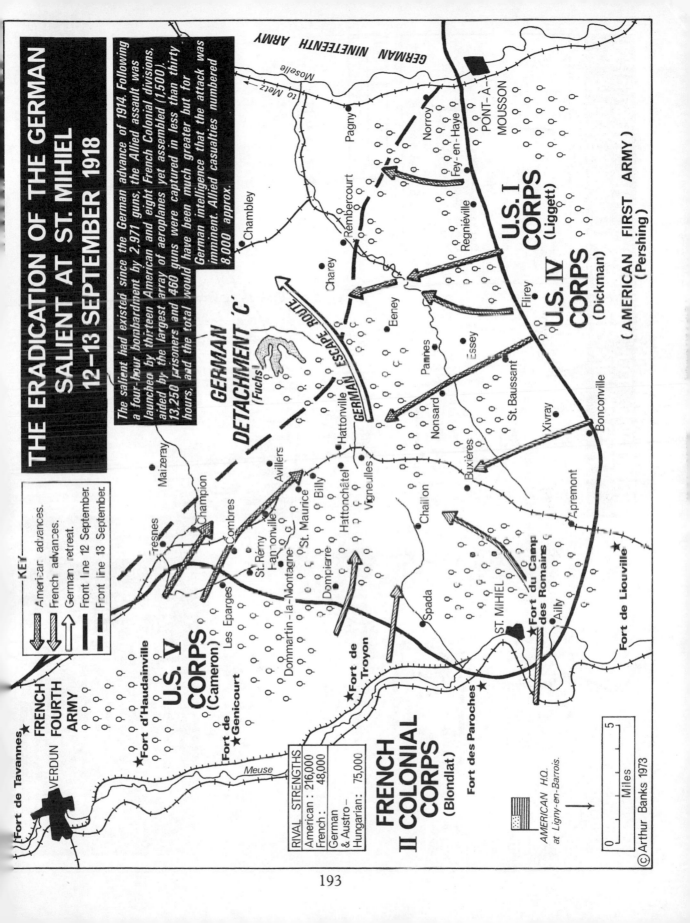

THE ERADICATION OF THE GERMAN SALIENT AT ST. MIHIEL 12–13 SEPTEMBER 1918

The salient had existed since the German advance of 1914. Following a four-hour bombardment by 2,971 guns, the Allied assault was launched by thirteen American and eight French Colonial divisions, aided by the largest array of aeroplanes yet assembled (1,500). 13,250 prisoners and 460 guns were captured in less than thirty hours, and the total would have been much greater but for German intelligence that the attack was imminent. Allied casualties numbered 8,000 approx.

GERMAN NINETEENTH ARMY

to Metz

Moselle

PONT-À-MOUSSON

Pagny

Norroy

Fey-en-Haye

Chambley

Rembercourt

Regniéville

U.S. I CORPS (Liggett)

Charey

Eeney

Flirey

U.S. IV CORPS (Dickman)

(AMERICAN FIRST ARMY) (Pershing)

GERMAN DETACHMENT 'C' (Fuchs)

Pannes

Essey

GERMAN ESCAPE ROUTE

Hattonville

Nonsard

St. Baussant

Bonconville

Maizeray

Avillers

Buxières

Xivray

Apremont

Champion

Hattonchâtel

Vigneulles

Chaillon

Fresnes

Combres

St. Rémy

Hannonville

St. Maurice

Billy

Dompierre-la-Montagne

Les Eparges

Dommartin-la-Montagne

Spada

Ailly

ST. MIHIEL

Fort du Camp des Romains

Fort de Liouville

U.S. V CORPS (Cameron)

Fort d'Haudainville

Fort de Genicourt

Fort de Troyon

Fort des Paroches

Meuse

VERDUN

FRENCH FOURTH ARMY

Fort de Tavannes

FRENCH II COLONIAL CORPS (Blondlat)

RIVAL STRENGTHS	
American :	216,000
French :	48,000
German & Austro-Hungarian :	75,000

AMERICAN H.Q. at Ligny-en-Barrois.

KEY

	American advances.
	French advances.
	German retreat.
	Front line 12 September.
	Front line 13 September.

Miles	
0	5

© Arthur Banks 1973

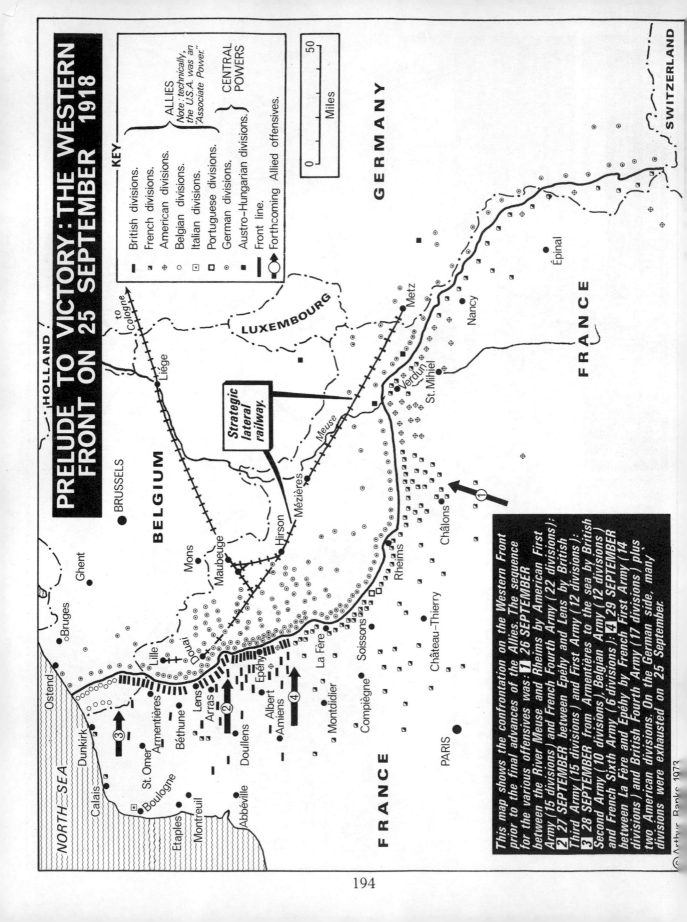

PRELUDE TO VICTORY: THE WESTERN FRONT ON 25 SEPTEMBER 1918

KEY

- British divisions.
- French divisions.
- American divisions.
- Belgian divisions.
- Italian divisions.
- Portuguese divisions.
- German divisions.
- Austro-Hungarian divisions.
- Front line.
- Forthcoming Allied offensives.

ALLIES
Note: technically, the U.S.A. was an "Associate Power."

CENTRAL POWERS

50 — 0 Miles

Strategic lateral railway.

HOLLAND

BELGIUM

LUXEMBOURG

GERMANY

SWITZERLAND

FRANCE

NORTH SEA

This map shows the confrontation on the Western Front prior to the final advances of the Allies. The sequence for the various offensives was: **1** *26 SEPTEMBER between the River Meuse and Rheims by American First Army (15 divisions) and French Fourth Army (22 divisions);* **2** *27 SEPTEMBER between Epéhy and Lens by British Third Army (15 divisions) and First Army (12 divisions);* **3** *28 SEPTEMBER from Armentières to the sea by British Second Army (10 divisions), Belgian Army (12 divisions) and French Sixth Army (6 divisions);* **4** *29 SEPTEMBER between La Fère and Epéhy by French First Army (14 divisions) and British Fourth Army (17 divisions) plus two American divisions. On the German side, many divisions were exhausted on 25 September.*

© Arthur Banks 1973

Brussels, Ghent, Bruges, Liége, Mons, Maubeuge, Hirson, Mézières, Lille, Douai, Lens, Arras, Epéhy, La Fère, Soissons, Compiègne, Château-Thierry, Rheims, Châlons, Verdun, St. Mihiel, Metz, Nancy, Épinal, Ostend, Dunkirk, Calais, Boulogne, Étaples, Montreuil, Abbéville, St. Omer, Armentières, Béthune, Albert, Amiens, Doullens, Montdidier, PARIS, to Cologne, Meuse

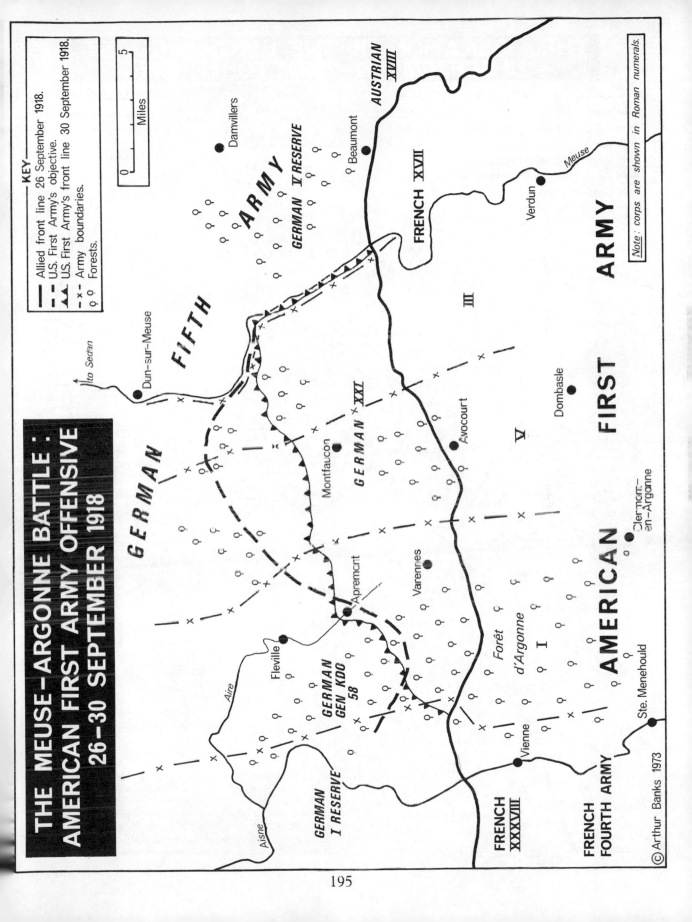

THE MEUSE–ARGONNE BATTLE:
AMERICAN FIRST ARMY OFFENSIVE
26–30 SEPTEMBER 1918

KEY
Allied front line 26 September 1918.
U.S. First Army's objective.
U.S. First Army's front line 30 September 1918.
Army boundaries.
Forests.

Miles
0   5

Note: corps are shown in Roman numerals.

to Sedan

Dun-sur-Meuse

FIFTH   ARMY

GERMAN   V RESERVE

Damvillers

Beaumont

AUSTRIAN XVIII

Meuse

Verdun

GERMAN

Montfaucon

GERMAN XXI

Avocourt

FRENCH XVII

III

Dombasle

V

FIRST

ARMY

Apremont

Varennes

Forêt
d'Argonne

I

AMERICAN

Clermont–
en–Argonne

Fleville

Aire

GERMAN
GEN KDO
58

GERMAN
I RESERVE

Aisne

Vienne

Ste. Menehould

FRENCH
XXXXVIII

FRENCH FOURTH ARMY

© Arthur Banks 1973

195

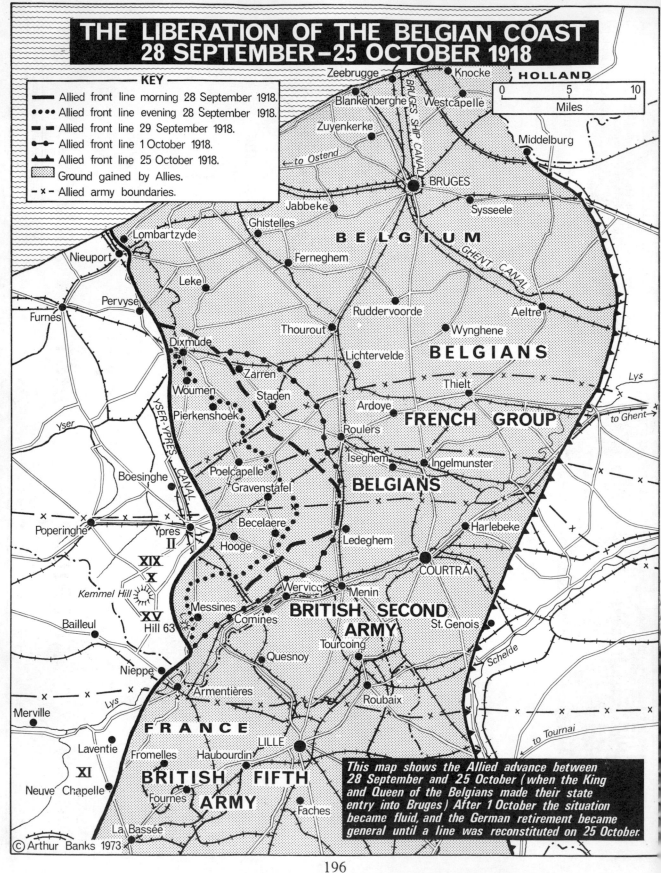

THE LIBERATION OF THE BELGIAN COAST
28 SEPTEMBER–25 OCTOBER 1918

KEY
— Allied front line morning 28 September 1918.
••• Allied front line evening 28 September 1918.
— — Allied front line 29 September 1918.
•–•–• Allied front line 1 October 1918.
▲▲▲ Allied front line 25 October 1918.
▨ Ground gained by Allies.
–×– Allied army boundaries.

HOLLAND

0   5   10
Miles

Zeebrugge
Knocke
Blankenberghe
Westcapelle
Zuyenkerke
Middelburg
BRUGES SHIP CANAL
BRUGES
Jabbeke
Sysseele
← to Ostend
BELGIUM
Ghistelles
GHENT CANAL
Lombartzyde
Ferneghem
Nieuport
Leke
Pervyse
Ruddervoorde
Aeltre
Furnes
Thourout
Wynghene
BELGIANS
Dixmude
Lichtervelde
Lys
Zarren
Thielt
Yser
Woumen
Staden
Ardoye
FRENCH GROUP
Pierkenshoek
Roulers
to Ghent →
YSER-YPRES CANAL
Boesinghe
Poelcapelle
Iseghem
Ingelmunster
Gravenstafel
BELGIANS
Poperinghe
Ypres
Becelaere
Harlebeke
II
Ledeghem
XIX
Hooge
X
COURTRAI
Kemmel Hill
Wervicq
Bailleul
Messines
Menin
XV
Comines
St. Genois
Hill 63
BRITISH SECOND
ARMY
Schelde
Nieppe
Tourcoing
Quesnoy
Armentières
Roubaix
Merville
Lys
to Tournai
FRANCE
LILLE
Laventie
Fromelles
Haubourdin
XI
BRITISH FIFTH
Neuve Chapelle
Fournes
ARMY
Faches
La Bassée
© Arthur Banks 1973

This map shows the Allied advance between 28 September and 25 October (when the King and Queen of the Belgians made their state entry into Bruges) After 1 October the situation became fluid, and the German retirement became general until a line was reconstituted on 25 October.

FINALE ON THE WESTERN FRONT
8 AUGUST — 11 NOVEMBER 1918

NORTH SEA

Ostend
Nieuport
Dunkirk
Calais
St.Omer

Bruges Ecloo
Thourout
Dixmude
Roulers
Isegham   Oudenarde
Courtrai
Roubaix
LILLE   Tournai
Lens St. Amand Condé Mons
Douai   Binche
Arras Valenciennes
Cambrai   Aulnoy   Beaumont
Bapaume Le Cateau   Chimay
Péronne Landrecies
La Capelle
Roye Guise Hirson
Ham St. Quentin   Liart
La Fère
Montdidier Noyon   Rethel
Laon Craonne   Buzancy
Rethondes   Grandpré
Soissons
RHEIMS
Epernay   Châlons

Ghent
Termonde
ANTWERP
Louvain
BRUSSELS
Grammont
Ath Soignies
Charleroi
Givet

Roermond

HOLLAND
Maastricht
Aachen
(Aix la Chapelle)
LIÉGE
Spa
GERMAN O.H.L.

KAISER

STILL NOT INVADED.

BELGIUM

GERMANY

LUXEMBOURG

Mézières
Sedan
Donchery
Mauzon
Montmédy
Stenay
Dun
Longuyon
Azannes
Briey
Conflans METZ
Pagny
Verdun
Pont-à-Mousson

Armistice signed here.

0 ——— 50
Miles

KEY
———— Allied front line on 8 August 1918.
— — — Allied front line on 11 November 1918.
▨▨▨▨ Ground gained by Allies.

FRANCE

Yser
Lys
Somme
Aisne
Oise
Aisne
Marne
Aisne
Aire
Schelde
Demer
Meuse
Namur
Sambre
Meuse
Moselle

Since 18 July, when Foch sent Mangin and Dégoutte to open the Allied attack, the following prisoners had been taken: 188,000 (by the British), 140,000 (by the French), 44,000, (by the Americans), and 14,000 (by the Belgians). Plus some 7,000 guns captured. If German killed and wounded are added, it is plain that the German armies could not continue to fight on effectively.

On 10 November, the Kaiser fled to Holland, followed by the Crown Prince. The basic Armistice terms signed at 1100 hours on 11 November were: immediate cessation of hostilities: German evacuation of invaded territory and of Alsace – Lorraine: repatriation of Allied citizens and prisoners of war: surrender of war materials and weapons: evacuation of the Rhine's left bank and bridgeheads: surrender of U–boats: internment of German surface warships: a declaration that the Treaties of Bucharest and Brest – Litovsk were null and void.

© Arthur Banks 1973

NOTE: MONS (FROM WHICH THE BRITISH RETREAT HAD BEGUN IN 1914) WAS RETAKEN BY THE CANADIANS A FEW HOURS PRIOR TO THE ARMISTICE.

THE PERIPHERAL CAMPAIGNS

Throughout the War most military leaders in Britain and France were 'Westerners'; they believed the principal task of their armies was to defeat the enemy in the theatre of operations which the Germans had themselves selected for their main effort. All other campaigns were dangerous 'sideshows', eating up men and munitions; and it was not until the final months of the war that a resolute effort was made to gain victories against Germany's allies in northern Italy, the Balkans, and the Middle East.

In practice these peripheral campaigns fall strategically into three categories. Some were intended, at least originally, as offensive thrusts against the central bloc from new points of the compass: the Italian and Macedonian Fronts, for example. Others were forced on the allies by Turkey's adhesion to the Germano-Austrian side: the need to defend the Suez lifeline by a campaign in Palestine, and to secure Anglo-Persian oil supplies by an offensive up the Shatt-el-Arab. Finally there was the fighting in Africa, and notably in German East Africa, where General von Lettow-Vorbeck waged colonial warfare throughout the four years of the European conflict, eventually surrendering a fortnight after the Armistice in France.

The character of several of these campaigns changed as the war dragged on: thus operations to safeguard oil refineries and counter intrigues in the Middle East developed into a lengthy campaign in Mesopotamia, with the possibility of a strike against the interior of Turkey. Conversely, the Italian Front, where it was hoped in 1915 that Austria-Hungary would drain away her last resources, became a burden for Italy's allies, although the Italian troops fought at first with fiercely whipped-up patriotic courage. They suffered from inadequate supplies of munitions and artillery, from poor training, and from the assumption that frontal assaults were the sole method of achieving victory. The Italians sustained 600,000 casualties in eleven offensives along the river Isonzo from mid-June 1915 to mid-

September 1917; and after all this terrible fighting, they succeeded in advancing the front line only seven miles. The twelfth Isonzo battle, the combined German and Austrian offensive at Caporetto in October 1917, pushed the Italians back fifty miles to the river Piave. Eventually, on the first anniversary of Caporetto, the Italians launched an attack on the Austrian positions which cost them 25,000 casualties in sixty hours of grim combat, before the Austrians lost their headquarters at Vittorio Veneto and sued for peace.

The Salonika Front, originating with the Austro–German–Bulgarian offensive against Serbia (page 160) was for long quiescent, although joint operations by Serbs, Italians, Russians and French liberated Serbian Monastir in November 1916 and the British were heavily engaged with the Bulgarians around Lake Doiran and the River Struma in the spring of 1917. Disease, especially malaria, caused the heaviest casualties in Macedonia. The final offensive of 1918 involved an initial assault by the French and the Serbs on a formless ridge known as the Dobropolje, more than 7,000 feet above sea-level. Subsequently Franchet d'Espèrey's army made the swiftest long advance of the war, sweeping up to the Danube and the plains of Hungary, and preparing to march on Berlin by way of Budapest and Dresden.

In Palestine General Allenby, with elaborate deception and imaginative use of cavalry pushed the Turks (and the German 'Asia Corps') rapidly northwards into the Lebanon and Syria in the autumn of 1918. His advanced cavalry reached Aleppo before Turkish delegates concluded an armistice at Mudros on 30 October, with the commander-in-chief of the British Mediterranean Fleet. Both Allenby in Palestine and Franchet d'Espèrey in Salonika had shown the need for unconventional commanders filled with offensive spirit in the fringe theatres of war. So, indeed, did Lettow-Vorbeck in East Africa.

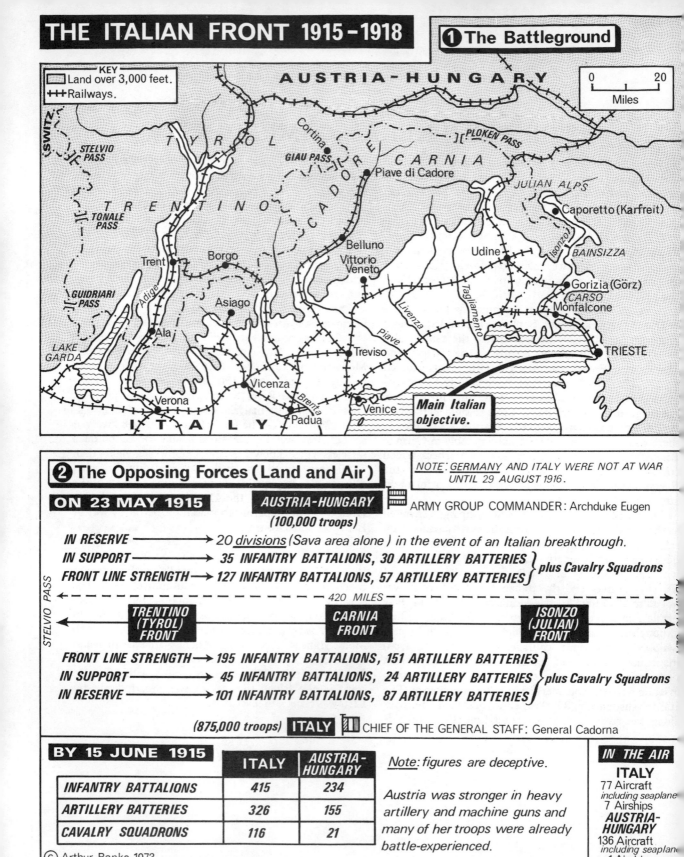

THE ITALIAN FRONT 1915-1918

① The Battleground

KEY
- Land over 3,000 feet.
- +++ Railways.

0 — 20 Miles

SWITZ.

AUSTRIA-HUNGARY

STELVIO PASS

TYROL

TONALE PASS

TRENTINO

GUIDRIARI PASS

Trent

Borgo

Ala

LAKE GARDA

Verona

Vicenza

Brenta

Padua

ITALY

Asiago

Treviso

Venice

Main Italian objective.

CADORE

Cortina

GIAU PASS

Piave di Cadore

Belluno

Vittorio Veneto

Piave

Livenza

Adige

PLOKEN PASS

CARNIA

Tagliamento

Udine

JULIAN ALPS

Caporetto (Karfreit)

Isonzo

BAINSIZZA

Gorizia (Görz)

CARSO

Monfalcone

TRIESTE

---

② The Opposing Forces (Land and Air)

NOTE: *GERMANY AND ITALY WERE NOT AT WAR UNTIL 29 AUGUST 1916.*

ON 23 MAY 1915

AUSTRIA-HUNGARY
(100,000 troops)

ARMY GROUP COMMANDER: Archduke Eugen

IN RESERVE ⟶ 20 <u>divisions</u> (Sava area alone) in the event of an Italian breakthrough.

IN SUPPORT ⟶ 35 INFANTRY BATTALIONS, 30 ARTILLERY BATTERIES ⎫

FRONT LINE STRENGTH ⟶ 127 INFANTRY BATTALIONS, 57 ARTILLERY BATTERIES ⎬ *plus Cavalry Squadrons*

STELVIO PASS

←------------------------ 420 MILES ------------------------→

| TRENTINO (TYROL) FRONT | CARNIA FRONT | ISONZO (JULIAN) FRONT |

FRONT LINE STRENGTH ⟶ 195 INFANTRY BATTALIONS, 151 ARTILLERY BATTERIES ⎫

IN SUPPORT ⟶ 45 INFANTRY BATTALIONS, 24 ARTILLERY BATTERIES ⎬ *plus Cavalry Squadrons*

IN RESERVE ⟶ 101 INFANTRY BATTALIONS, 87 ARTILLERY BATTERIES ⎭

(875,000 troops) **ITALY** CHIEF OF THE GENERAL STAFF: General Cadorna

BY 15 JUNE 1915

	ITALY	AUSTRIA-HUNGARY
INFANTRY BATTALIONS	415	234
ARTILLERY BATTERIES	326	155
CAVALRY SQUADRONS	116	21

Note: figures are deceptive.

Austria was stronger in heavy artillery and machine guns and many of her troops were already battle-experienced.

IN THE AIR

ITALY
77 Aircraft *including seaplane*
7 Airships

AUSTRIA-HUNGARY
136 Aircraft *including seaplane*
1 Airship

© Arthur Banks 1973

200

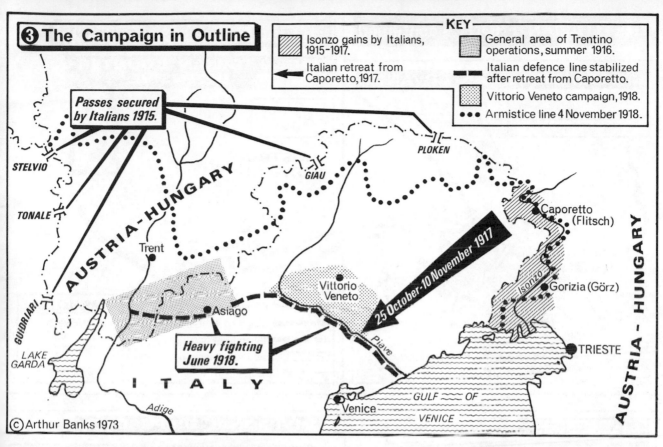

3 The Campaign in Outline

KEY

- ▨ Isonzo gains by Italians, 1915-1917.
- ← Italian retreat from Caporetto, 1917.
- ▒ General area of Trentino operations, summer 1916.
- ━ ━ Italian defence line stabilized after retreat from Caporetto.
- ░ Vittorio Veneto campaign, 1918.
- •••• Armistice line 4 November 1918.

Passes secured by Italians 1915.

STELVIO

TONALE

GUIDRIARI

LAKE GARDA

AUSTRIA-HUNGARY

Trent

GIAU

PLOKEN

Caporetto (Flitsch)

Isonzo

Gorizia (Görz)

25 October–10 November 1917

Vittorio Veneto

Asiago

Heavy fighting June 1918.

Plave

ITALY

Adige

Venice

GULF — OF — VENICE

TRIESTE

AUSTRIA – HUNGARY

© Arthur Banks 1973

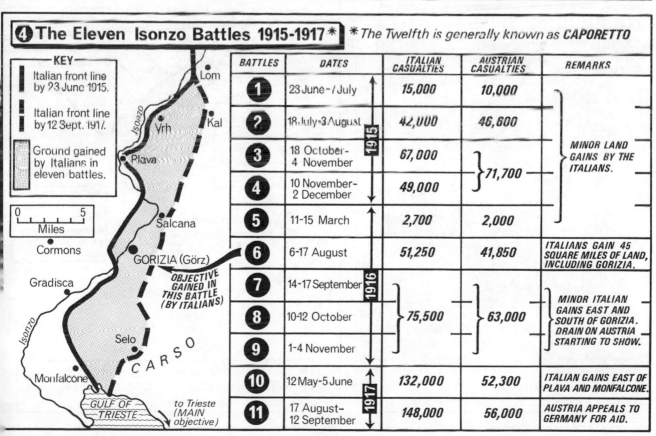

4 The Eleven Isonzo Battles 1915-1917 * * The Twelfth is generally known as CAPORETTO

KEY

- ▮ Italian front line by 23 June 1915.
- ▮ Italian front line by 12 Sept. 1917.
- ▨ Ground gained by Italians in eleven battles.

0 — 5 Miles

Lom

Isonzo

Vrh

Kal

Plava

Salcana

Cormons

GORIZIA (Görz)

OBJECTIVE GAINED IN THIS BATTLE (BY ITALIANS)

Gradisca

Selo

C A R S O

Monfalcone

GULF OF TRIESTE

to Trieste (MAIN objective)

BATTLES	DATES	ITALIAN CASUALTIES	AUSTRIAN CASUALTIES	REMARKS
1	23 June – 7 July	15,000	10,000	MINOR LAND GAINS BY THE ITALIANS.
2	18 July – 3 August	42,000	46,600	
3	18 October – 4 November	67,000	} 71,700	
4	10 November – 2 December	49,000		
5	11-15 March	2,700	2,000	
6	6-17 August	51,250	41,850	ITALIANS GAIN 45 SQUARE MILES OF LAND, INCLUDING GORIZIA.
7	14-17 September	} 75,500	} 63,000	MINOR ITALIAN GAINS EAST AND SOUTH OF GORIZIA. DRAIN ON AUSTRIA STARTING TO SHOW.
8	10-12 October			
9	1-4 November			
10	12 May – 5 June	132,000	52,300	ITALIAN GAINS EAST OF PLAVA AND MONFALCONE.
11	17 August – 12 September	148,000	56,000	AUSTRIA APPEALS TO GERMANY FOR AID.

(1915 spans battles 1-5; 1916 spans battles 6-9; 1917 spans battles 10-11)

201

STAGE 1. AUSTRIAN ADVANCE

0 — 30
Miles

Bolzano

T R E N T I N O

Adige

AUSTRIAN ELEVENTH and THIRD ARMIES

Trent

Arco

Adige

LAKE GARDA

ITALIAN

Arsiero

Asiago

FIRST ARMY

Feltre

Mt. Grappa

KEY
— Austrian front line 14 May.
⟹ Austrian drives.
- - - Austrian front line 16 June.
▨ Ground gained.

⑤ Austrian Trentino Offensive 1916

STAGE 2. ITALIAN COUNTER-OFFENSIVE

0 — 5
Miles

AUSTRIA-HUNGARY

pass

pass

Roama   Asiago

Arsiero

ITALY

KEY
— Italian front line 17 June.
← Italian counter-attacks.
- - - Italian front line 1 July.
▨ Ground regained by Italians.
-·-·- Frontier.

CASUALTIES
AUSTRIAN
180,000
(estimate)
ITALIAN
286,000

⑥ Eve of Caporetto: 23 Oct. 1917

THE RIVAL ARMIES

0 — 5
Miles

ITALIAN CARNIA GROUP

AUSTRIAN TENTH ARMY

Plezzo

Saga

Caporetto

Tolmino

GERMAN FOURTEENTH ARMY (INCLUDING TWO AUSTRIAN CORPS)

ITALIAN SECOND ARMY

Cividale

●UDINE

Auzza
Vrh
Plava

Isonzo

AUSTRIAN SECOND ISONZO ARMY

Cormons

Gradisca

GORIZIA

Vipacco

ITALIAN THIRD ARMY

Monfalcone

AUSTRIAN FIRST ISONZO ARMY

KEY
— Front line.   ·•·•·•· Army boundaries.
▨ Italian-held territory.
▨ Austro-Hungarian/German-held territory.

DIVISIONAL DISPOSITIONS

(INCLUDING 500 24-cm. MORTARS)

Note heavy **German** concentrations in contrast with the Italians on this section of front.

Plezzo
Saga

1,485 GUNS

Caporetto

Italian commanders vascillate over the defensive posture to adopt in this region.

Tolmino

Cividale
UDINE

Vrh
Plava

Auzza

RESERVE DIVS.

Cormons

THE WEATHER. Poor visibility due to rain mist and snow (on high ground) assists German preparations rather than Italian.

Gradisca

GORIZIA

Vipacco

Monfalcone

KEY
■ Italian infantry divisions.   ⊕ German gas battery.
Ⓖ German infantry divisions.   ⌒ Italian reserve areas.
Ⓐ Austro-Hungarian infantry divisions.

© Arthur Banks 1973

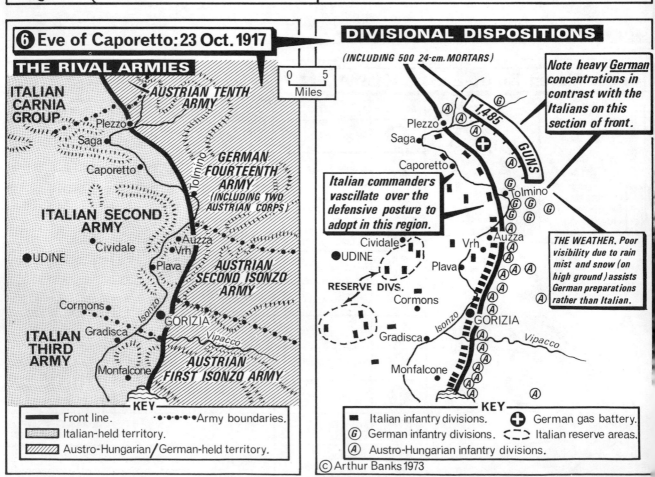

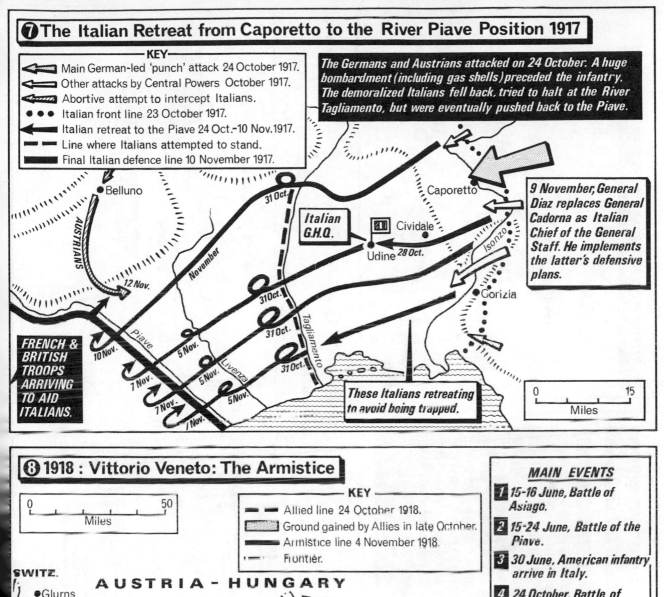

7 The Italian Retreat from Caporetto to the River Piave Position 1917

KEY

- ◄══ Main German-led 'punch' attack 24 October 1917.
- ◄── Other attacks by Central Powers October 1917.
- ◄╍╍ Abortive attempt to intercept Italians.
- • • • Italian front line 23 October 1917.
- ◄── Italian retreat to the Piave 24 Oct.-10 Nov. 1917.
- ─ ─ Line where Italians attempted to stand.
- ▬▬ Final Italian defence line 10 November 1917.

The Germans and Austrians attacked on 24 October. A huge bombardment (including gas shells) preceded the infantry. The demoralized Italians fell back, tried to halt at the River Tagliamento, but were eventually pushed back to the Piave.

9 November, General Diaz replaces General Cadorna as Italian Chief of the General Staff. He implements the latter's defensive plans.

Belluno

AUSTRIANS

31 Oct.

Italian G.H.Q.

411 Cividale

Udine 28 Oct.

Isonzo

Gorizia

November

31 Oct.

31 Oct.

31 Oct.

Tagliamento

12 Nov.

Piave

10 Nov.

5 Nov.

Livenza

FRENCH & BRITISH TROOPS ARRIVING TO AID ITALIANS.

7 Nov.

5 Nov.

7 Nov.

5 Nov.

7 Nov.

These Italians retreating to avoid being trapped.

0 ─────── 15
Miles

8 1918 : Vittorio Veneto: The Armistice

0 ─────── 50
Miles

KEY

- ─ ─ Allied line 24 October 1918.
- ▒▒ Ground gained by Allies in late October.
- ▬▬ Armistice line 4 November 1918.
- ·─·─ Frontier.

MAIN EVENTS

1 15-16 June, Battle of Asiago.

2 15-24 June, Battle of the Piave.

3 30 June, American infantry arrive in Italy.

4 24 October, Battle of Vittorio Veneto opens. British take Papadopoli.

5 27 October, Austria asks Italy for armistice.

6 2 November, Hungarians ordered to disarm.

7 3 November, armistice signed near Padua: takes effect 1500 hours 4 Nov.

SWITZ.
• Glurns

AUSTRIA - HUNGARY

• Bolzano

Piave di Cadore

• Tolmezzo

Caporetto

Piave

• Trent

I T A L Y

• Belluno

Udine •

• Vittorio Veneto

Gorizia

Asiago

Papadopoli Island

Heavy fighting in June 1918.

• Treviso

Piave

TRIESTE

LAKE GARDA

• Vicenza

• Verona

• Padua

VENICE

3 November 1918, Italian landing party is received by the Yugoslav National Council which has taken over the port.

© Arthur Banks 1973

203

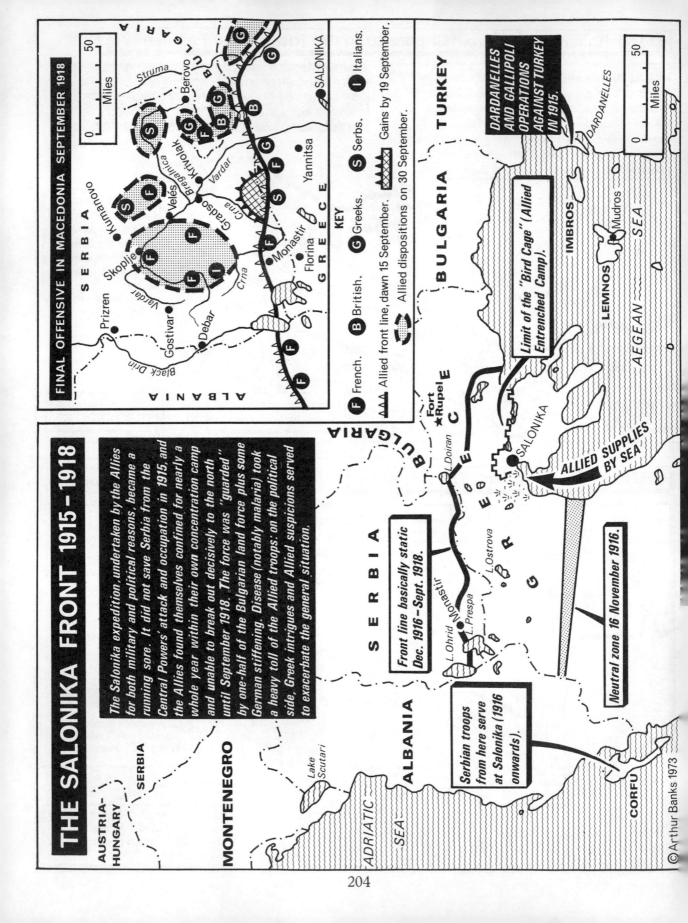

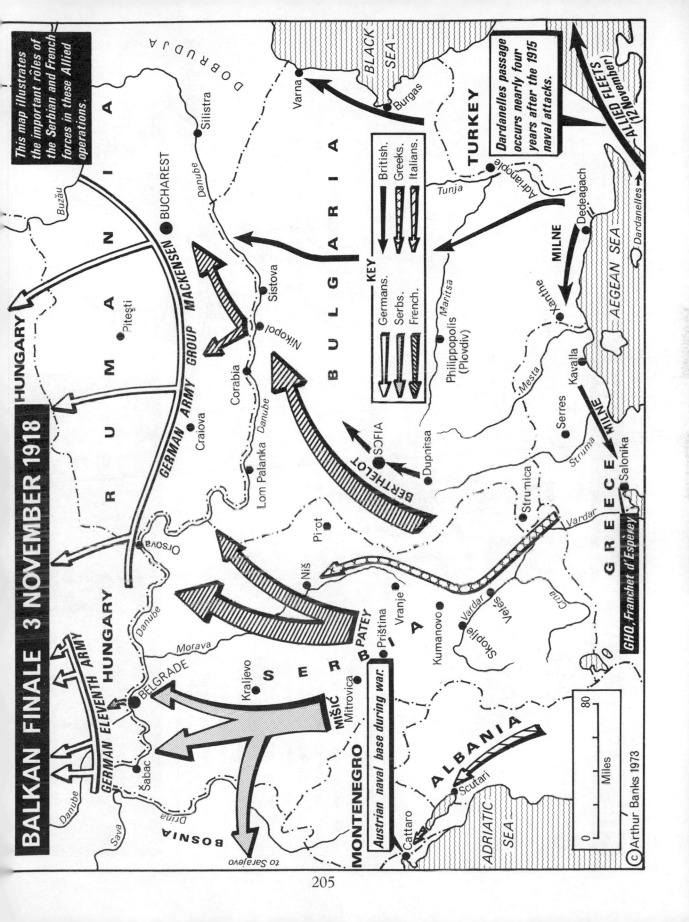

BALKAN FINALE 3 NOVEMBER 1918

This map illustrates the important rôles of the Serbian and French forces in these Allied operations.

KEY

British. Greeks. Italians.

Germans. Serbs. French.

Dardanelles passage occurs nearly four years after the 1915 naval attacks.

ALLIED FLEETS (12 November)

BLACK SEA

DOBRUDJA

ROUMANIA

HUNGARY

Varna
Burgas
Silistra
BUCHAREST
Buzău
Pitești
Danube
Sistova
Nikopol
Corabia
Craiova
Lom Palanka
Danube
Orsova
Morava

GERMAN ARMY GROUP MACKENSEN

TURKEY
Adrianople
Tunja
Dedeagach
Dardanelles
AEGEAN SEA
MILNE
Xanthe
Maritsa
Philippopolis (Plovdiv)
Mesta
Kavalla
Serres
Struma

BULGARIA

SOFIA
Dupnitsa

BERTHELOT

GREECE
Salonika
GHQ. Franchet d'Espèrey
Vardar
Strumica
Veles
Vardar
Crna
Kumanovo
Skoplje
Vranje
Priština
Niš
Pirot

MILNE

SERBIA

PATEY

BOSNIA
HUNGARY
GERMAN ELEVENTH ARMY
Danube
Morava
BELGRADE
Kraljevo
Mitrovica
Šabac
Sava
Drina
Danube

MIŠIĆ

Austrian naval base during war.

MONTENEGRO
Cattaro
to Sarajevo

ALBANIA
Scutari
ADRIATIC SEA

0   80
Miles

© Arthur Banks 1973

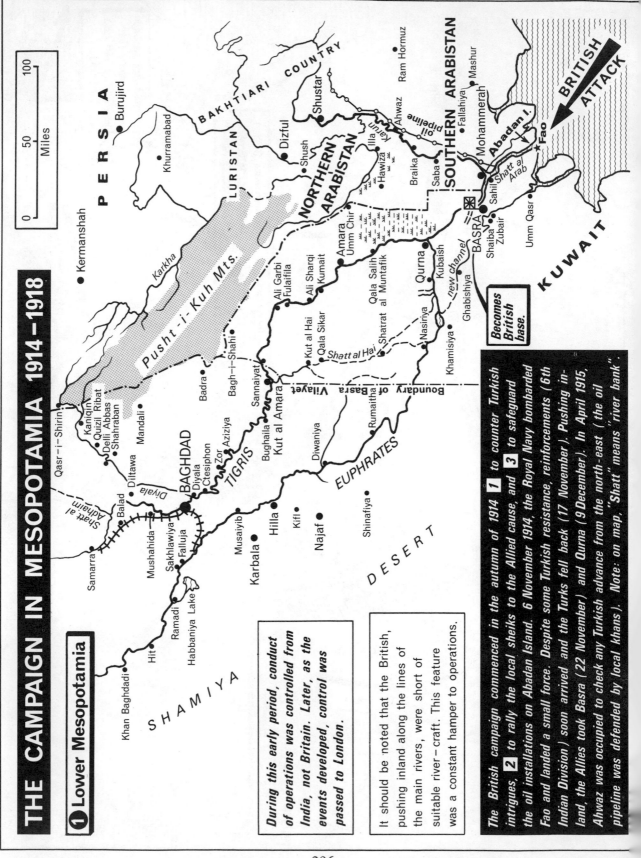

THE CAMPAIGN IN MESOPOTAMIA 1914–1918

1 Lower Mesopotamia

During this early period, conduct of operations was controlled from India, not Britain. Later, as the events developed, control was passed to London.

It should be noted that the British, pushing inland along the lines of the main rivers, were short of suitable river-craft. This feature was a constant hamper to operations.

The British campaign commenced in the autumn of 1914 1 to counter Turkish intrigues, 2 to rally the local sheiks to the Allied cause, and 3 to safeguard the oil installations on Abadan Island. 6 November 1914, the Royal Navy bombarded Fao and landed a small force. Despite some Turkish resistance, reinforcements (6th Indian Division) soon arrived and the Turks fell back (17 November). Pushing inland, the Allies took Basra (22 November) and Qurna (9 December). In April 1915, Ahwaz was occupied to check any Turkish advance from the north-east (the oil pipeline was defended by local khans). Note: on map, "Shatt" means "river bank".

PERSIA

BAKHTIARI COUNTRY

LURISTAN

NORTHERN ARABISTAN

SOUTHERN ARABISTAN

KUWAIT

BRITISH ATTACK

Pusht-i-Kuh Mts.

Becomes British base.

Boundary of Basra Vilayet

DESERT

SHAMIYA

TIGRIS

EUPHRATES

Shatt al Adhaim

Shatt al Ha'i

Shatt al Arab

new channel

oil pipeline

Kermanshah
Burujird
Khurramabad
Dizful
Shush
Shustar
Ram Hormuz
Mashur
Fallahiya
Ahwaz
Mohammerah
Abadan I.
Fao
Illa
Hawiza
Braika
Saba
Sahil
Shaiba
Umm Qasr
Zubair
BASRA
Ghabishiya
Kubaish
Nasiriya
Khamisiya
Rumaithia
Amara
Umm Chir
Qala Salih
Sharrat al Muntafik
Qurna
Ali Garbi
Fulaifila
Ali Sharqi
Kumait
Kut al Hai
Qala Sikar
Diwaniya
Shinafiya
Sannaiyat
Bughaila
Kut al Amara
Aziziya
Zor
Ctesiphon
Diyala
BAGHDAD
Badra
Bagh-i-Shahi
Mandali
Shahraban
Delli Abbas
Quizil Ribat
Kaniqin
Qasr-i-Shirin
Diltawa
Balad
Samarra
Mushahida
Sakhlawiya
Falluja
Musaiyib
Hilla
Kifl
Najaf
Karbala
Habbaniya Lake
Ramadi
Hit
Khan Baghdadi
Karkha
Karun

0 50 100
Miles

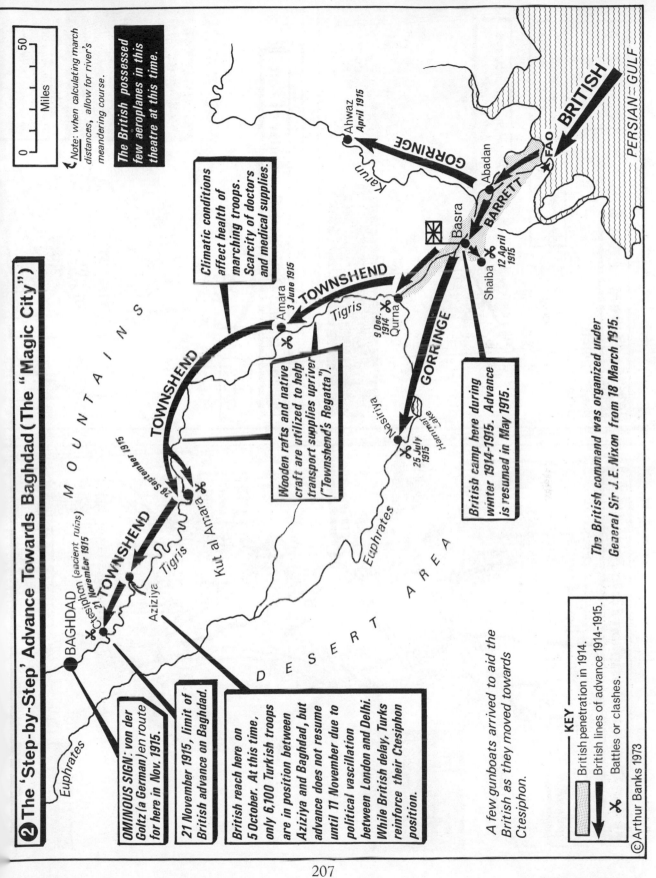

② The 'Step-by-Step' Advance Towards Baghdad (The "Magic City")

PERSIAN GULF

BRITISH

FAO

Abadan

BARRETT

Basra

Shaiba
12 April
1915

GORRINGE

Ahwaz
April 1915

Karun

Climatic conditions affect health of marching troops. Scarcity of doctors and medical supplies.

Amara
3 June 1915

TOWNSHEND

Tigris

Qurna
9 Dec.
1914

GORRINGE

Wooden rafts and native craft are utilized to help transport supplies upriver ("Townshend's Regatta").

Nasiriya

Hammar Lake
25 July
1915

British camp here during winter 1914-1915. Advance is resumed in May 1915.

M O U N T A I N S

28 September 1915

TOWNSHEND

Ctesiphon
21 November 1915

BAGHDAD (ancient ruins)

Aziziya

Tigris

Kut al Amara

TOWNSHEND

Euphrates

D E S E R T   A R E A

Euphrates

OMINOUS SIGN: von der Goltz (a German) en route for here in Nov. 1915.

21 November 1915, limit of British advance on Baghdad.

British reach here on 5 October. At this time, only 6,100 Turkish troops are in position between Aziziya and Baghdad, but advance does not resume until 11 November due to political vascillation between London and Delhi. While British delay, Turks reinforce their Ctesiphon position.

A few gunboats arrived to aid the British as they moved towards Ctesiphon.

The British command was organized under General Sir J.E. Nixon from 18 March 1915.

---- **KEY** ----

British penetration in 1914.

British lines of advance 1914-1915.

Battles or clashes.

© Arthur Banks 1973

Note: when calculating march distances, allow for river's meandering course.

The British possessed few aeroplanes in this theatre at this time.

0   50
Miles

207

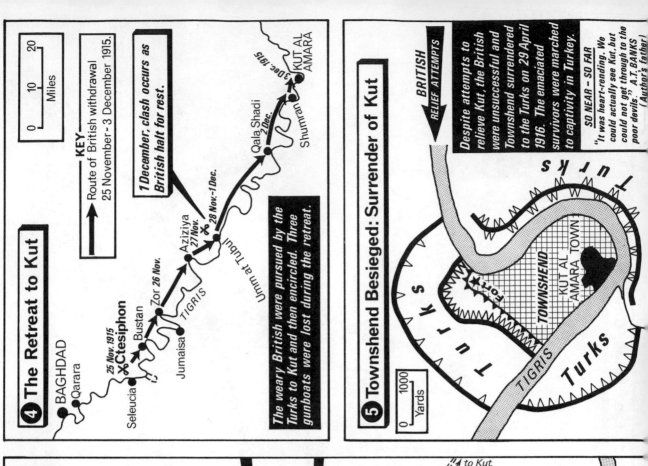

4 The Retreat to Kut

KEY

→ Route of British withdrawal 25 November - 3 December 1915.

1 December, clash occurs as British halt for rest.

KUT AL AMARA
3 Dec. 1915

Shumran

Qala Shadi 2 Dec.

28 Nov.-1 Dec.

Umm at Tubul

Aziziya 27 Nov.

Zor 26 Nov.

Bustan

Jumaisa

TIGRIS

25 Nov. 1915
Ctesiphon

Seleucia

BAGHDAD

Qarara

Miles 0 10 20

The weary British were pursued by the Turks to Kut and then encircled. Three gunboats were lost during the retreat.

5 Townshend Besieged: Surrender of Kut

BRITISH
RELIEF ATTEMPTS

Despite attempts to relieve Kut, the British were unsuccessful and Townshend surrendered to the Turks on 29 April 1916. The emaciated survivors were marched to captivity in Turkey.

SO NEAR – SO FAR
"It was heart-rending. We could actually see Kut, but could not get through to the poor devils." A.T. BANKS
(Author's father)

T u r k s

Turks

Turks

TIGRIS

Fort

TOWNSHEND

KUT AL AMARA TOWN

Yards 0 1000

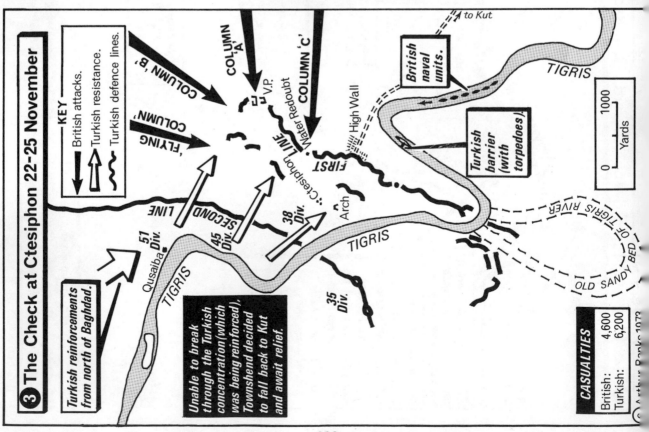

3 The Check at Ctesiphon 22-25 November

KEY

→ British attacks.

⇧ Turkish resistance.

〰 Turkish defence lines.

Turkish reinforcements from north of Baghdad.

COLUMN 'A'

COLUMN 'B'

COLUMN 'C'

'FLYING' COLUMN

V.P.

Water Redoubt

High Wall

FIRST LINE

'Ctesiphon'

Arch

SECOND LINE

38 Div.

45 Div.

51 Div.

35 Div.

Qusaiba

TIGRIS

TIGRIS

Unable to break through the Turkish concentration (which was being reinforced), Townshend decided to fall back to Kut and await relief.

A to Kut

British naval units.

TIGRIS

Turkish barrier (with torpedoes).

OLD SANDY BED OF TIGRIS RIVER

Yards 0 1000

CASUALTIES
British: 4,600
Turkish: 6,200

© Arthur Banks 1973

208

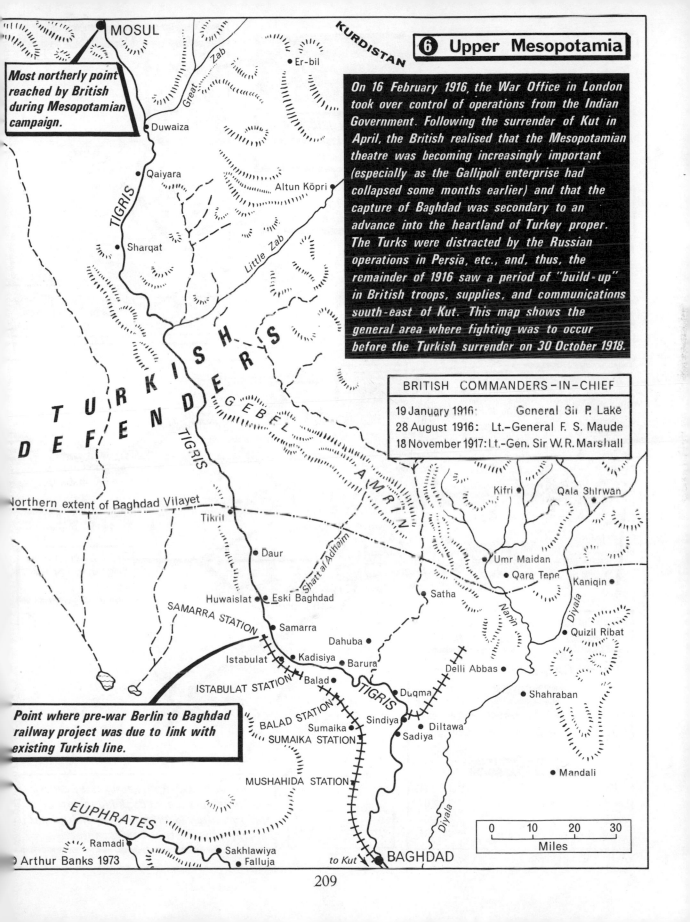

MOSUL

KURDISTAN

6 Upper Mesopotamia

Most northerly point reached by British during Mesopotamian campaign.

• Er-bil

• Duwaiza

Great Zab

TIGRIS

• Qaiyara

• Altun Köpri

Little Zab

• Sharqat

On 16 February 1916, the War Office in London took over control of operations from the Indian Government. Following the surrender of Kut in April, the British realised that the Mesopotamian theatre was becoming increasingly important (especially as the Gallipoli enterprise had collapsed some months earlier) and that the capture of Baghdad was secondary to an advance into the heartland of Turkey proper. The Turks were distracted by the Russian operations in Persia, etc., and, thus, the remainder of 1916 saw a period of "build-up" in British troops, supplies, and communications south-east of Kut. This map shows the general area where fighting was to occur before the Turkish surrender on 30 October 1918.

T U R K I S H
D E F E N D E R S

GEBEL HAMRIN

BRITISH COMMANDERS–IN–CHIEF

19 January 1916: General Sir P. Lake
28 August 1916: Lt.-General F. S. Maude
18 November 1917: Lt.-Gen. Sir W. R. Marshall

• Kifri   • Qala Shirwan

Northern extent of Baghdad Vilayet

TIGRIS

• Tikrit

• Daur

• Umr Maidan
• Qara Tepe

Kaniqin

Diyala

Shatt al Adhaim

Huwaislat • • Eski Baghdad

SAMARRA STATION

• Samarra

• Satha

Narin

• Quizil Ribat

• Dahuba

Istabulat • • Kadisiya

• Barura

• Delli Abbas

Point where pre-war Berlin to Baghdad railway project was due to link with existing Turkish line.

ISTABULAT STATION • Balad

TIGRIS

• Duqma

• Shahraban

BALAD STATION

• Sumaika

• Sindiya

• Diltawa

SUMAIKA STATION

• Sadiya

MUSHAHIDA STATION

• Mandali

EUPHRATES

Diyala

0   10   20   30
Miles

• Ramadi

© Arthur Banks 1973

• Sakhlawiya
• Falluja

to Kut   **BAGHDAD**

209

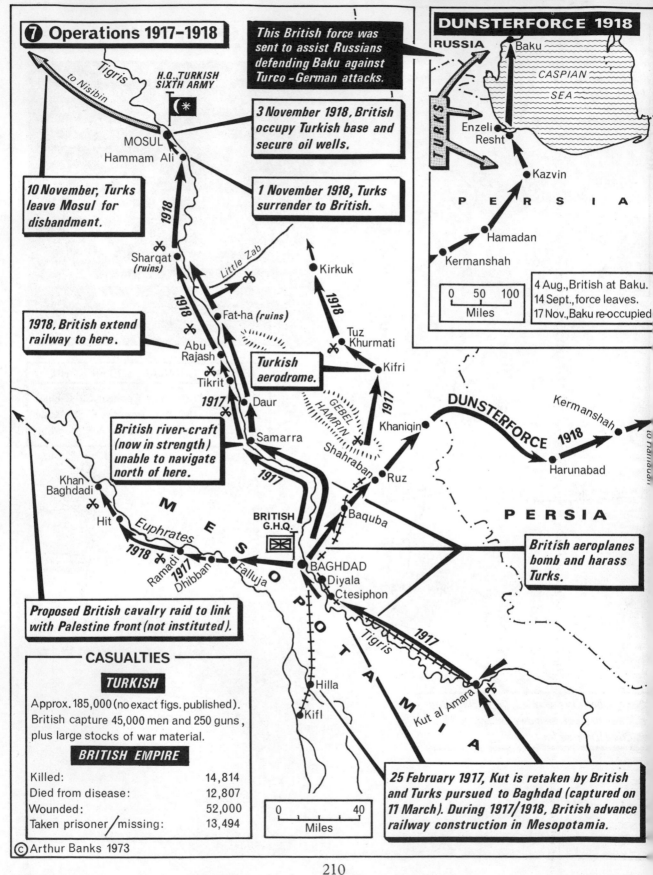

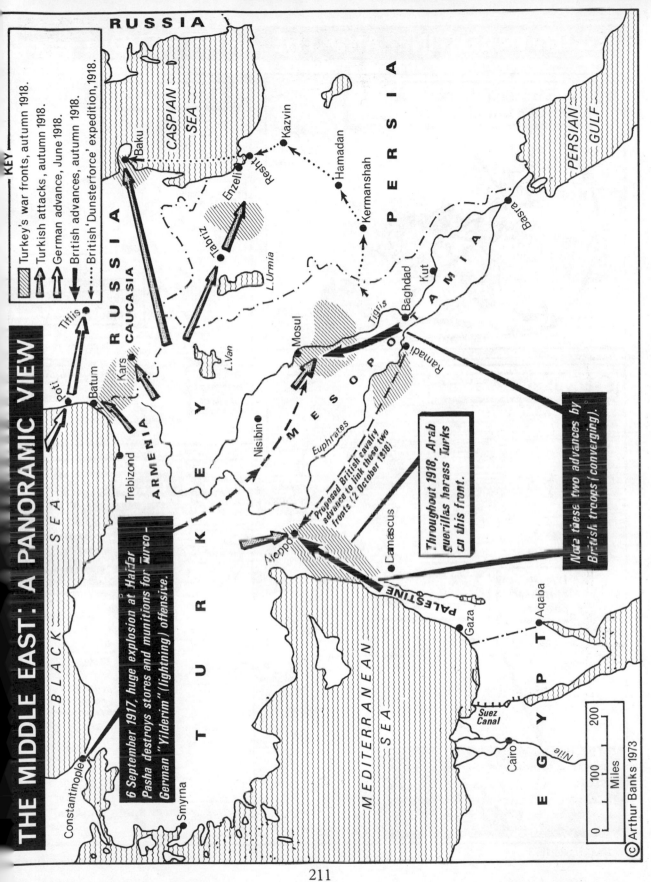

THE MIDDLE EAST: A PANORAMIC VIEW

Turkey's war fronts, autumn 1918.

Turkish attacks, autumn 1918.

German advance, June 1918.

British advances, autumn 1918.

British 'Dunsterforce' expedition, 1918.

RUSSIA

Tiflis

CAUCASIA

Poti

Batum

Kars

Trebizond

ARMENIA

L. Van

BLACK SEA

CASPIAN SEA

Baku

Tabriz

L. Urmia

Enzeli

Rasht

Kazvin

Hamadan

Kermanshah

PERSIA

Basra

PERSIAN GULF

Mosul

Tigris

Baghdad

Kut

Ramadi

MESOPOTAMIA

Euphrates

Nisibin

T U R K E Y

Aleppo

Damascus

6 September 1917, huge explosion at Haifar Pasha destroys stores and munitions for Turco-German "Yilderim" (lightning) offensive.

Proposed British cavalry advance to link these two fronts (2 October 1918)

Throughout 1918, Arab guerillas harass Turks on this front.

Note these two advances by British troops (converging).

PALESTINE

Gaza

Aqaba

Suez Canal

Nile

Cairo

E G Y P T

MEDITERRANEAN SEA

Constantinople

Smyrna

0   100   200

Miles

© Arthur Banks 1973

EGYPT, PALESTINE, AND THE ARAB REVOLT

The canal was opened in 1869.

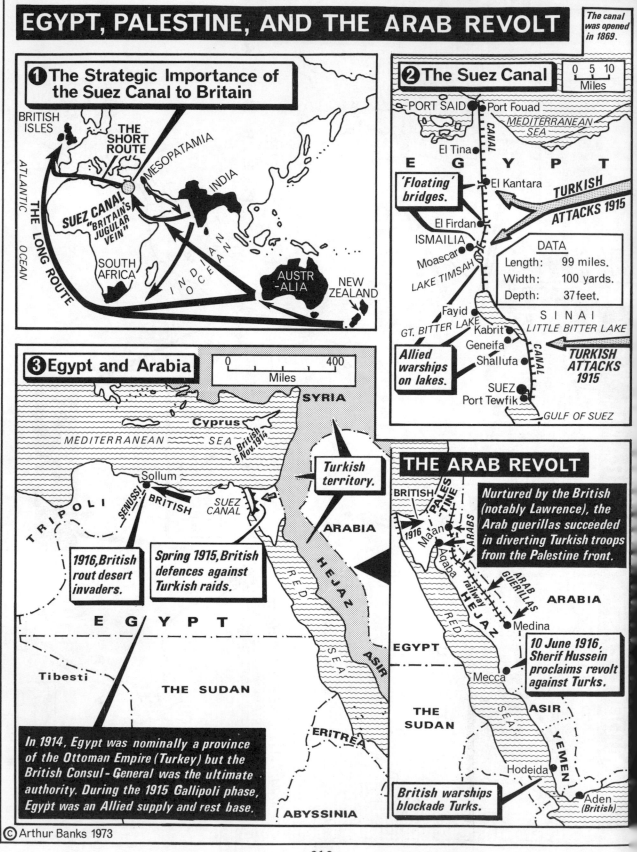

❶ The Strategic Importance of the Suez Canal to Britain

BRITISH ISLES
THE SHORT ROUTE
MESOPATAMIA
INDIA
ATLANTIC OCEAN
THE LONG ROUTE
SUEZ CANAL "BRITAIN'S JUGULAR VEIN"
SOUTH AFRICA
INDIAN OCEAN
AUSTR-ALIA
NEW ZEALAND

❷ The Suez Canal

0 5 10 Miles

PORT SAID — Port Fouad
MEDITERRANEAN SEA
El Tina
CANAL
E G Y P T
El Kantara
TURKISH ATTACKS 1915
'Floating' bridges.
El Firdan
ISMAILIA
Moascar
LAKE TIMSAH

DATA
Length: 99 miles.
Width: 100 yards.
Depth: 37 feet.

Fayid
GT. BITTER LAKE
Kabrit
Geneifa
Shallufa
Allied warships on lakes.
SUEZ
Port Tewfik
S I N A I
LITTLE BITTER LAKE
CANAL
TURKISH ATTACKS 1915
GULF OF SUEZ

❸ Egypt and Arabia

0 400 Miles

SYRIA
Cyprus
MEDITERRANEAN SEA
British 5 Nov 1914
Sollum
SENUSSI
BRITISH
SUEZ CANAL
Turkish territory.
ARABIA
TRIPOLI
HEJAZ
1916, British rout desert invaders.
Spring 1915, British defences against Turkish raids.
E G Y P T
RED SEA
ASIR
Tibesti
THE SUDAN
ERITREA
ABYSSINIA

In 1914, Egypt was nominally a province of the Ottoman Empire (Turkey) but the British Consul-General was the ultimate authority. During the 1915 Gallipoli phase, Egypt was an Allied supply and rest base.

THE ARAB REVOLT

Nurtured by the British (notably Lawrence), the Arab guerillas succeeded in diverting Turkish troops from the Palestine front.

BRITISH
PALESTINE
1916
Maan
ARABS
Aqaba
ABAB GUERILLAS
HEJAZ
railway
ARABIA
Medina
RED SEA
EGYPT
Mecca
ASIR
THE SUDAN
YEMEN
Hodeida
Aden (British)

10 June 1916, Sherif Hussein proclaims revolt against Turks.

British warships blockade Turks.

212

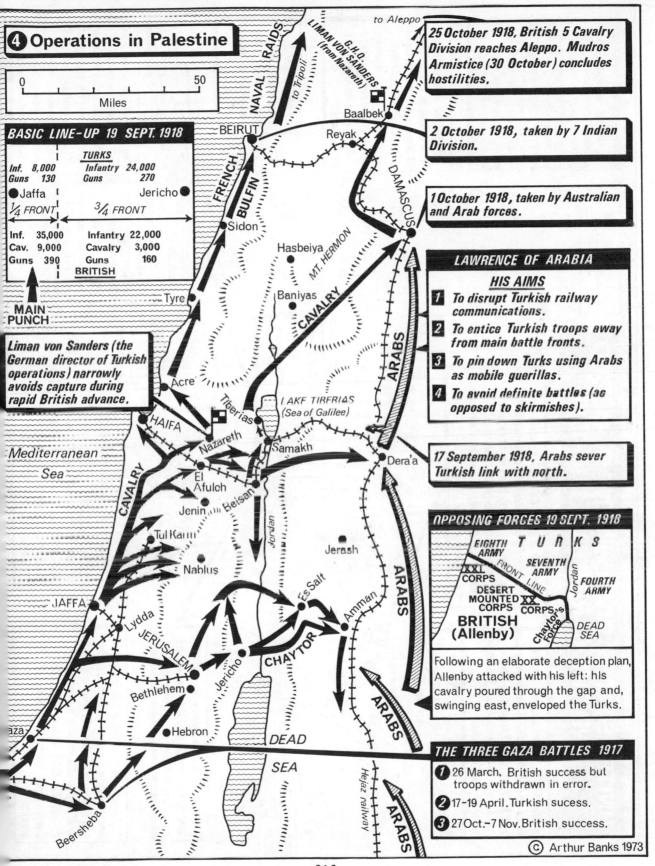

④ Operations in Palestine

0 — 50 Miles (scale bar)

BASIC LINE-UP 19 SEPT. 1918

	TURKS	
Inf. 8,000	Infantry 24,000	
Guns 130	Guns 270	
● Jaffa	Jericho ●	
¼ FRONT	¾ FRONT	
Inf. 35,000	Infantry 22,000	
Cav. 9,000	Cavalry 3,000	
Guns 390	Guns 160	
	BRITISH	

MAIN PUNCH

Liman von Sanders (the German director of Turkish operations) narrowly avoids capture during rapid British advance.

25 October 1918, British 5 Cavalry Division reaches Aleppo. Mudros Armistice (30 October) concludes hostilities.

2 October 1918, taken by 7 Indian Division.

1 October 1918, taken by Australian and Arab forces.

LAWRENCE OF ARABIA

HIS AIMS

1. To disrupt Turkish railway communications.
2. To entice Turkish troops away from main battle fronts.
3. To pin down Turks using Arabs as mobile guerillas.
4. To avoid definite battles (as opposed to skirmishes).

17 September 1918, Arabs sever Turkish link with north.

OPPOSING FORCES 19 SEPT. 1918

T U R K S — EIGHTH ARMY, SEVENTH ARMY, FOURTH ARMY, FRONT LINE, Jordan

XXI CORPS, DESERT MOUNTED CORPS, XX CORPS, Chaytor's Force

BRITISH (Allenby)

DEAD SEA

Following an elaborate deception plan, Allenby attacked with his left: his cavalry poured through the gap and, swinging east, enveloped the Turks.

THE THREE GAZA BATTLES 1917

1. 26 March, British success but troops withdrawn in error.
2. 17–19 April. Turkish success.
3. 27 Oct.–7 Nov. British success.

© Arthur Banks 1973

Map labels: NAVAL RAIDS, LIMAN VON SANDERS (from Nazareth), G.H.Q., to Aleppo, to Tripoli, Baalbek, BEIRUT, Reyak, FRENCH, BULFIN, Sidon, Hasbeiya, MT. HERMON, Baniyas, DAMASCUS, CAVALRY, ARABS, Tyre, Acre, Tiberias, LAKE TIBERIAS (Sea of Galilee), HAIFA, Nazareth, Samakh, Dera'a, Mediterranean Sea, CAVALRY, El Afuleh, Jenin, Beisan, Jordan, Jerash, Tul Karm, Nablus, JAFFA, Lydda, JERUSALEM, Jericho, Bethlehem, Hebron, Es Salt, Amman, CHAYTOR, ARABS, DEAD SEA, Hejaz railway, ARABS, Gaza, Beersheba

213

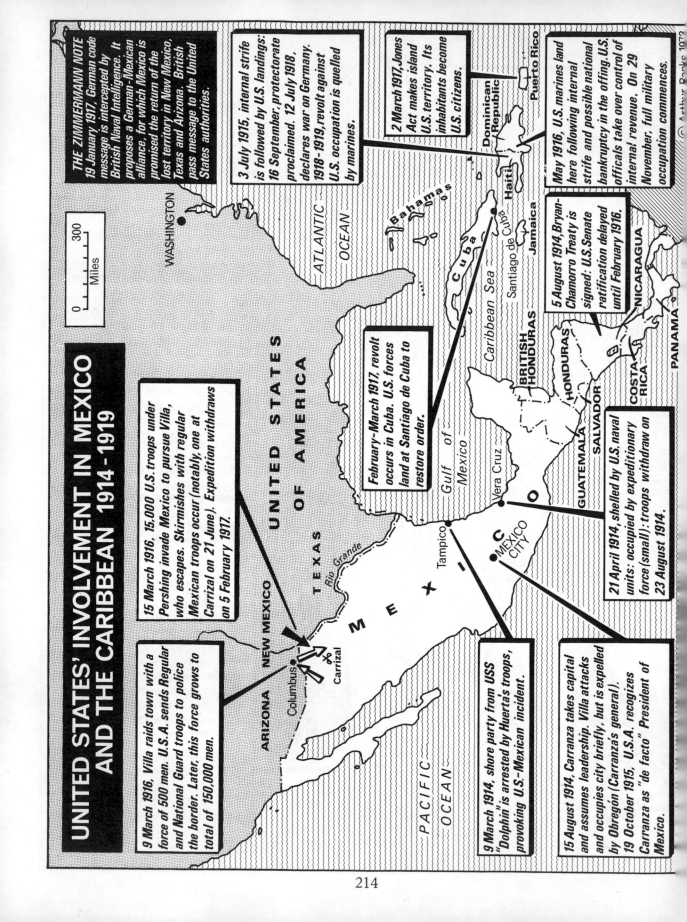

UNITED STATES' INVOLVEMENT IN MEXICO AND THE CARIBBEAN 1914-1919

THE ZIMMERMANN NOTE 19 January 1917, German code message is intercepted by British Naval Intelligence. It proposes a German-Mexican alliance, for which Mexico is promised the return of the lost territory in New Mexico, Texas and Arizona. British pass message to the United States authorities.

3 July 1915, internal strife is followed by U.S. landings: 16 September, protectorate proclaimed. 12 July 1918, declares war on Germany. 1918-1919, revolt against U.S. occupation is quelled by marines.

2 March 1917, Jones Act makes island U.S. territory. Its inhabitants become U.S. citizens.

May 1916, U.S. marines land here following internal strife and possible national bankruptcy in the offing. U.S. officals take over control of internal revenue. On 29 November, full military occupation commences.

5 August 1914, Bryan-Chamorro Treaty is signed: U.S. Senate ratification delayed until February 1916.

February-March 1917, revolt occurs in Cuba. U.S. forces land at Santiago de Cuba to restore order.

15 March 1916, 15,000 U.S. troops under Pershing invade Mexico to pursue Villa, who escapes. Skirmishes with regular Mexican troops occur (notably, one at Carrizal on 21 June). Expedition withdraws on 5 February 1917.

9 March 1916, Villa raids town with a force of 500 men. U.S.A. sends Regular and National Guard troops to police the border. Later, this force grows to total of 150,000 men.

21 April 1914, shelled by U.S. naval units: occupied by expeditionary force (small): troops withdraw on 23 August 1914.

9 March 1914, shore party from USS "Dolphin" is arrested by Huerta's troops, provoking U.S.-Mexican incident.

15 August 1914, Carranza takes capital and assumes leadership. Villa attacks and occupies city briefly, but is expelled by Obregón (Carranza's general). 19 October 1915, U.S.A. recogizes Carranza as "de facto" President of Mexico.

© Arthur Banks 1973

214

SOUTH AMERICA 1914-1918

KEY

- At war against the Central Powers 1917-1918.
- Neutral states.
- British territory.
- French territory.
- Track of SMS 'Dresden' from 8 December 1914 to 14 March 1915.

0 — 500 Miles

PACIFIC OCEAN

VENEZUELA

COLOMBIA

ECUADOR

BRITISH GUIANA

DUTCH GUIANA

FRENCH GUIANA

Panama Canal

PERU

B R A Z I L

BOLIVIA

PARAGUAY

URUGUAY

CHILE

ARGENTINA

ATLANTIC OCEAN

Buenos Aires

Coronel

Juan Fernandez Islands

HUNTED BY BRITISH WARSHIPS

Falkland Islands

> April 1917, the 'Paranã' is sunk by a German submarine.
> 11 April 1917, Brazil severs her relations with Germany and on 1 June 1917, revokes neutrality in favour of the Allies.
> 26 October 1917, Brazil declares war upon the Central Powers.

> 1914, revolt led by Benavides ends in the overthrow of President Billinghurst. Pardo is president from 1914 to 1919; breaks off diplomatic relations with Germany in 1917.

> 14 March 1915, SMS 'Dresden' is destroyed following action with HMS 'Glasgow' and 'Kent'.

> 1 November 1914, naval battle.

> 1917, three Argentinian ships are sunk by German submarines. After secret diplomatic exchanges, the German minister is withdrawn from Buenos Aires.

> German cruiser SMS 'Dresden' is the sole survivor from the Falkland Islands naval battle.

> Brazil was the sole Latin American state at war with the Central Powers. In 1918, a Brazilian squadron served for nine months with the Allies off the African coast, and on 10 November 1918, Brazilian warships entered the Mediterranean Sea for further duty with the Allies.

> 'Dresden' hides in this area from 11 December 1914 to 8 February 1915.

> 8 December 1914, naval battle.

© Arthur Banks 1973

215

THE WAR IN AFRICA 1914–1918

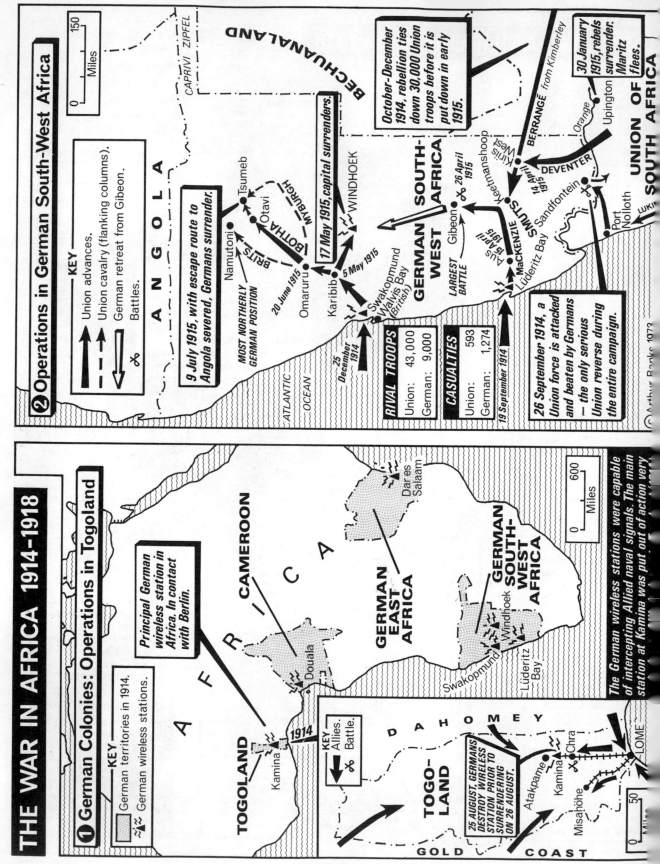

① German Colonies: Operations in Togoland

KEY
German territories in 1914.
German wireless stations.

Principal German wireless station in Africa. In contact with Berlin.

A F R I C A

CAMEROON

GERMAN EAST AFRICA

Dar es Salaam

GERMAN SOUTH-WEST AFRICA

Windhoek

Swakopmund

Lüderitz Bay

Douala

TOGOLAND

Kamina

1914

KEY
Allies.
Battle.

DAHOMEY

TOGO-LAND

25 AUGUST, GERMANS DESTROY WIRELESS STATION PRIOR TO SURRENDERING ON 26 AUGUST.

Atakpame

Kamina

Chra

LOME

Misahöhe

GOLD   COAST

0   600 Miles

0   50 Miles

The German wireless stations were capable of intercepting Allied naval signals. The main station at Kamina was put out of action very...

② Operations in German South-West Africa

KEY
Union advances.
Union cavalry (flanking columns).
German retreat from Gibeon.
Battles.

ANGOLA

CAPRIVI ZIPFEL

BECHUANALAND

October–December 1914, rebellion ties down 30,000 Union troops before it is put down in early 1915.

30 January 1915, rebels surrender. Maritz flees.

BERRANGÉ from Kimberley

Orange

Upington

UNION OF SOUTH AFRICA

DEVENTER

14 April 1915

Keetmanshoop

Kiris West

⚔ 26 April 1915

SMUTS

Sandfontein

Port Nolloth

LUKI

Gibeon

LARGEST BATTLE

Aus 1 April 1915

MacKENZIE

Lüderitz Bay

26 September 1914, a Union force is attacked and beaten by Germans — the only serious Union reverse during the entire campaign.

RIVAL TROOPS
Union: 43,000
German: 9,000

CASUALTIES
Union: 593
German: 1,274

19 September 1914

GERMAN SOUTH-WEST AFRICA

WINDHOEK

17 May 1915, capital surrenders.

5 May 1915

Swakopmund

Walvis Bay (British)

ATLANTIC OCEAN

25 December 1914

Karibib

Omaruru

20 June 1915

BOTHA

MYBURGH

BRITS

Namutoni

MOST NORTHERLY GERMAN POSITION

Otavi

Tsumeb

9 July 1915, with escape route to Angola severed, Germans surrender.

0   150 Miles

© Arthur Banks 1072

216

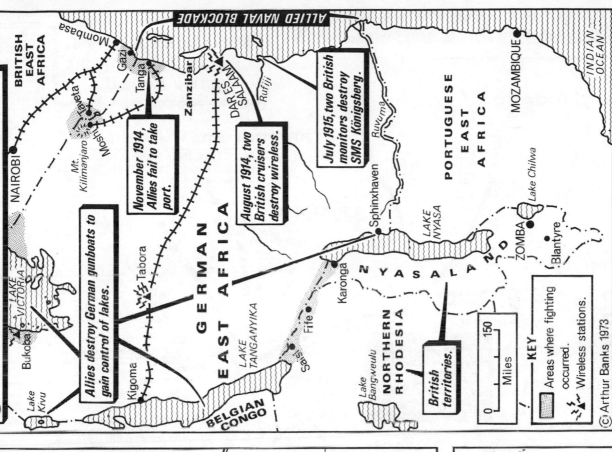

4 The Main Theatre: East Africa 1914-1915

ALLIED NAVAL BLOCKADE

BRITISH EAST AFRICA

Mombasa
Gazi
Tanga
Taveta
Moshi
Mt. Kilimanjaro
NAIROBI

November 1914, Allies fail to take port.

Zanzibar

DAR ES SALAAM

Rufiji

August 1914, two British cruisers destroy wireless.

July 1915, two British monitors destroy SMS Königsberg.

GERMAN EAST AFRICA

Allies destroy German gunboats to gain control of lakes.

Tabora
Bukoba
LAKE VICTORIA
Lake Kivu
Kigoma
LAKE TANGANYIKA

BELGIAN CONGO

Sphinxhaven
LAKE NYASA
Karonga
Fife
Saisi

PORTUGUESE EAST AFRICA

MOZAMBIQUE

Lake Chilwa
ZOMBA
Blantyre
N Y A S A L A N D

NORTHERN RHODESIA

Lake Bangweulu

British territories.

INDIAN OCEAN

KEY

Miles
0   150

Areas where fighting occurred.
Wireless stations.

© Arthur Banks 1973

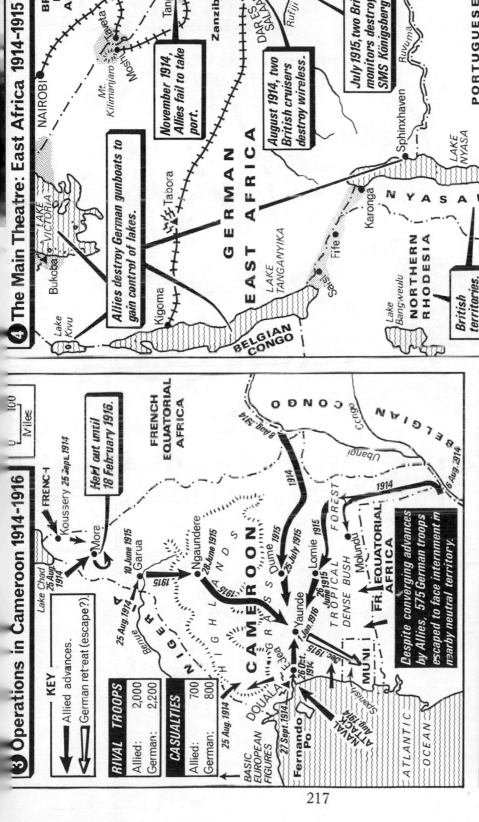

3 Operations in Cameroon 1914-1916

KEY

Allied advances.
German retreat (escape?).

Miles
0   100

RIVAL TROOPS	
Allied:	2,000
German:	2,200

CASUALTIES	
Allied:	700
German:	800

BASIC EUROPEAN FIGURES

FRENCH EQUATORIAL AFRICA

Lake Chad
FRENCH
Koussery 25 Sept.1914
Held out until 18 February 1916.
Mora
25 Aug. 1914
10 June 1915 Garua
Benue
N I G E R I A
H I G H L A N D S
Ngaundere
28 June 1915
1915
Dume 1915
25 July 1915
Lomie 1915
26 June 1915
Yaunde
1 Jan.1916
Dec. 1915
Esea
DOUALA
26 Oct. 1914
27 Sept.1914
Fernando Po
NAVAL ATTACK
Aug.1914
Spanish
MUNI
FR. EQUATORIAL AFRICA
TROPICAL DENSE BUSH
Molundu
EQUATORIAL FOREST
8 Aug. 1914
Ubangi
Congo
C O N G O
B E L G I A N
16 Aug. 1914
1914

Despite converging advances by Allies, 575 German troops escaped to face internment in nearby neutral territory.

ATLANTIC OCEAN

STRENGTHS AND CASUALTIES

These cannot be given precise you maps as a detailed analysis of each total is necessary. For example, the German force which surrendered at Abercorn on 25 November 1918, included 30 German officers, 125 other Europeans, Askari, porters, headmen, natives, and women.

SMS 'KÖNIGSBERG'

The German light cruiser 'Königsberg' sank HMS 'Pegasus' in Zanzibar harbour in September 1914 but later was blockaded in the Rufiji river. She was destroyed on 11 July 1915 after an action with British monitors and two aircraft, but her guns were salvaged and used by the Germans in east Africa.

THE WAR IN AFRICA – continued

⑤ East Africa 1916-1918: von Lettow-Vorbeck's Fighting Retreat

0 — 50 Miles

UGANDA (British)

LAKE VICTORIA

Lake Kivu

BELGIAN CONGO

1916

GERMAN

Kigoma Ujiji

1916

Tabora 19 Sept. 1916

LAKE TANGANYIKA

EAST

Sept. 1916

BRITISH EAST AFRICA

ALLIED COMMANDERS
SMUTS (Feb. 1916) HOSKINS (Jan. 1917)
DEVENTER (June 1917).

Mt. Kilimanjaro Moshi

Aug. 1916

Tanga

Mombasa

Pemba

Aug. 1916

Zanzibar

1916

AFRICA

Kilosa

> 25 November 1918, the German surrender included 155 Europeans, 4,275 natives, 1 field gun, 24 Maxims, and 14 Lewis guns.

29 Aug. 1916 Iringa

1916

24 July 1916 Malangali

Abercorn Fifé

1916

DAR ES SALAAM

Kitope

Mahenge

Mpepo

> 4 September 1916, capital falls to Allies without opposition.

1916

Kilwa

1916

Lindi

Liwale

Oct. 1918

Aug. 1916

Gumbiro

Kasama Nov. 1918

Songea

Newala

> 13 November 1918, von Lettow-Vorbeck learns of the Armistice. German force later moves to Abercorn to surrender formally.

BELGIAN CONGO

1918

N Y A S A L A N D (British)

LAKE NYASA

Ruvuma

Ngomano

28 Sept. 1918

12 Dec. 1917

Nanguari

March 1918 Mesa

> 4 December 1917, Germans cross into Portuguese East Africa.

1918

Porto Amelia

Mwembe March 1918

Nanungu May 1918

NORTHERN RHODESIA (British)

1917

PORTUGUESE

EAST **AFRICA**

Lioma Muanhupa

MOZAMBIQUE

Aug. 1918 Nyamirue Chalaua 1918

Regone

July 1918

INDIAN

OCEAN

Kokosani 1918

KEY

✗ Area of heavy fighting 1916-1917 where Germans made their main stand.

← Allied advances and landings.

⇐ Retreat of von Lettow-Vorbeck 1917-1918.

© Arthur Banks 1973

218

WEAPONS

During the half century preceding the First World War military science had taken note of technological developments but had not appreciated the extent to which they revolutionised traditional concepts of warfare. French infantrymen armed with the *chassepot* breech-loading rifle had wrought havoc with the German attackers in 1870 and convinced military authorities that rifles would henceforth strengthen the defensive position of troops, especially if they were also supported by artillery. But because the original French machine guns —the *mitrailleuses*—of 1870 had proved ineffectual, the potentialities of this weapon were ignored. The trench fighting of the Russo-Japanese War (1905–1905) should have awakened an interest in the machine gun, for Maxim's water-cooled weapon of 1884, firing 2,000 rounds in three minutes, was very different from the prototypes of the Franco-Prussian campaign; and it was eventually the German Maxim which proved so terribly effective on the first day of the Somme (compare pages 152–153 and page 224). Without well-sited machine guns and barbed-wire entanglements, there would have been no war of stalemate on the Western Front.

At first it was assumed that mobility could be restored to warfare by artillery power. This, at least, had been a lesson of the Russo-Japanese War, and in the ten years before Sarajevo much attention was given to the development of howitzers, the heaviest models being used to reduce the Belgian fortifications in 1914 (pages 33 and 62). The most effective field gun was the French 75-mm (page 33), with a buffer recoil system which allowed a fire rate of 20/30 rounds a minute. By contrast, the British 18-pounder had a rate of fire of only 8 rounds a minute, and this was faster than the best German and Austrian guns. During the First World War three-quarters of the wounds caused by guns came from shells, high explosive or shrapnel, rather than from bullets.

The experience of the long barrages used as preparation for offensives in 1915 showed that artillery was a less decisive weapon in the field than the experts had anticipated. Concrete pill-boxes stood up against most normal field artillery, while the barrages ruled out all element of surprise and made soft ground impassable to heavily encumbered infantry. It was partly to overcome these problems that petrol driven armoured vehicles with caterpillar tracks were introduced, first as 'tanks' in the British army and then into the armies of other countries. No commander, however, felt sufficiently confident to develop the tank as a revolutionary weapon in its own right. On the Somme in 1916 tanks suffered as much as infantry from shell craters, and at Cambrai in 1917 (page 174) no attempt was made to follow penetration by exploitation with vehicles mounted on caterpillar tracks. Moreover, although use was made of armoured cars, lorries (notably at Verdun), and the famous Paris taxis (page 55), the value of the internal combustion engine was only slowly perceived.

This hardly is surprising: military minds did not rapidly assimilate the changed patterns of daily life. Thus, although the transport of armies by rail from one war zone to another dates from 1862–1863 (both Confederate and Union forces in the American Civil War), it was not until the outbreak of the First World War that the smooth running of a railway transport system was recognised as an essential prerequisite for offensive operations. General Groener, who succeeded Ludendorff as virtual field commander in the last days of the War, was the first military leader to have 'graduated' as a railway specialist.

By contrast, trench warfare brought new forms of old weapons: clubs, knives, canisters of burning oil, pistols and revolvers. The greatest innovations of all, however, were in the skies and under the waves.

219

British 4·5-inch howitzer

Length of gun (overall):	13 feet, 6 inches.
Weight of gun in action:	3,004 pounds.
Range:	7,000 yards.
Elevation:	−5 to +45 degs.
Barrel length:	13·33 calibres.
Weight of shell:	35 pounds.
Muzzle velocity:	1,010 ft./sec.
Rate of fire:	4 rds. per min.

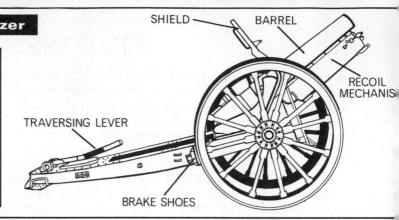

SHIELD BARREL

RECOIL MECHANIS

TRAVERSING LEVER

BRAKE SHOES

British 60-pounder field gun

Length of gun (overall):	21 feet, 7 inches.
Weight of gun in action:	11,705 pounds.
Range:	10,300 yards.
Elevation:	21°30′.
Barrel length:	33·61 calibres.
Weight of shell:	60 pounds.
Muzzle velocity:	2,149 ft./sec.
Rate of fire:	2 rds. per min.
Traverse:	4° left / 4° right.
Calibre:	5 inches.

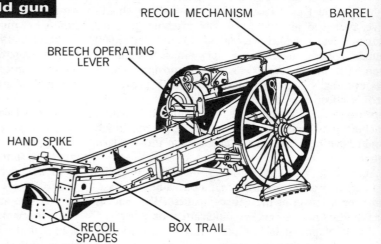

RECOIL MECHANISM BARREL

BREECH OPERATING LEVER

HAND SPIKE

RECOIL SPADES BOX TRAIL

British 9·2-inch (Mark I) howitzer

Length of gun (overall):	11 feet, 15 inches.
Weight of gun in action:	25,906 pounds.
Range:	10,000 yards.
Elevation:	55°.
Barrel length:	14·5 calibres.
Weight of shell:	290 pounds.
Muzzle velocity:	1,187 ft./sec.
Rate of fire:	2 rds. per min.
Traverse:	30° left / 30° right.
Height:	8 feet, 6 inches.

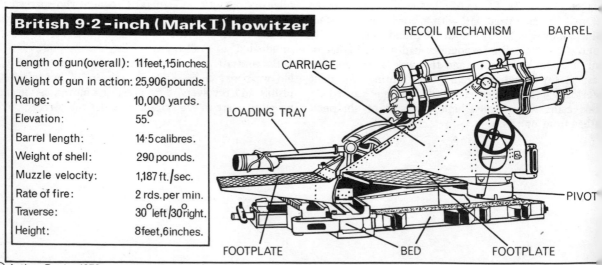

RECOIL MECHANISM BARREL

CARRIAGE

LOADING TRAY

PIVOT

FOOTPLATE BED FOOTPLATE

© Arthur Banks 1973

German 10·5-cm. howitzer 1916

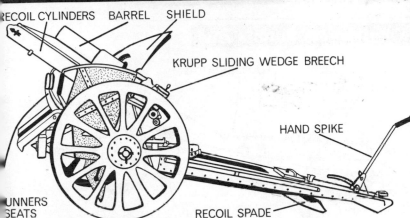

RECOIL CYLINDERS   BARREL   SHIELD

KRUPP SLIDING WEDGE BREECH

HAND SPIKE

GUNNERS SEATS

RECOIL SPADE

Length of gun (overall):	12 feet.
Weight of gun in action:	3,036 pounds.
Range:	6,250 yards.
Elevation:	40°.
Barrel length:	22 calibres.
Weight of shell:	34·5 pounds.
Muzzle velocity:	1,400 ft./sec.
Rate of fire:	4 rds. per min.
Traverse:	4° left/4° right.

(note: unusual nine increment cartridge).

German 13-cm. (Model 1913) field gun

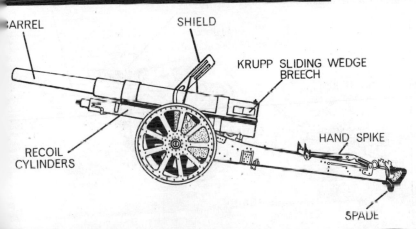

BARREL   SHIELD

KRUPP SLIDING WEDGE BREECH

HAND SPIKE

RECOIL CYLINDERS

SPADE

Length of gun (overall):	22 feet.
Weight of gun in action:	12,768 pounds.
Range:	15,750 yards.
Elevation:	26°.
Barrel length:	35 calibres.
Weight of shell:	89 pounds.
Muzzle velocity:	2,280 ft./sec.
Rate of fire:	2 rds. per min.
Traverse:	2° left/2° right.

(note: shrapnel shell contains 1,170 lead bullets).

German 21-cm. "mörser"

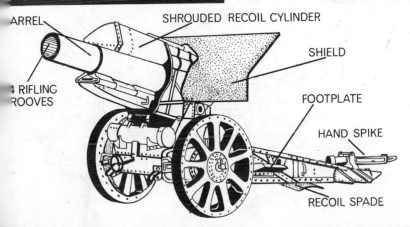

BARREL   SHROUDED RECOIL CYLINDER

SHIELD

FOOTPLATE

HAND SPIKE

4 RIFLING GROOVES

RECOIL SPADE

Length of gun (overall):	20 feet.
Weight of gun in action:	9,828 pounds.
Range:	10,280 yards.
Elevation:	70°.
Barrel length:	12 calibres.
Weight of shell:	184 pounds.
Muzzle velocity:	1,203 ft./sec.
Rate of fire:	2 rds. per min.
Traverse:	2° left/2° right.

(note: H.E. shell contains 17 pounds of amatol).

French 155-mm. Grande Puissance Filloux gun

Length of gun (overall):	29 feet, 7 inches.
Weight of gun in action:	24,640 pounds.
Range:	19,650 yards.
Elevation:	35°.
Barrel length:	38·2 calibres.
Weight of shell:	97 pounds.
Muzzle velocity:	2,339 ft./sec.
Rate of fire:	2 rds. per min.

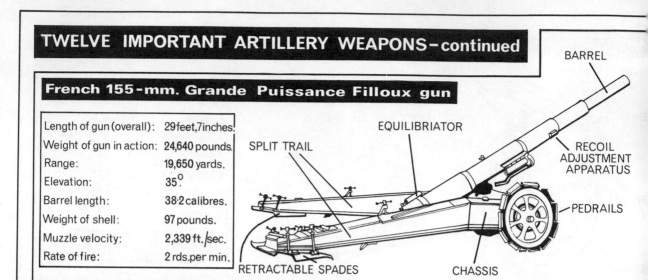

BARREL

EQUILIBRIATOR

SPLIT TRAIL

RECOIL ADJUSTMENT APPARATUS

PEDRAILS

RETRACTABLE SPADES

CHASSIS

British 18-pounder (Mark I) field gun

Length of gun (overall):	13 feet, 8 inches.
Weight of gun in action:	2,904 pounds.
Range:	7,000 yards.
Calibre:	3·3 inches.
Elevation:	−5 to +6 degs.
Barrel length:	28 calibres.
Weight of shell:	18 pounds.
Muzzle velocity:	1,614 ft./sec.
Rate of fire:	8 rds. per min.

(note: developed from the lessons of the Boer War).

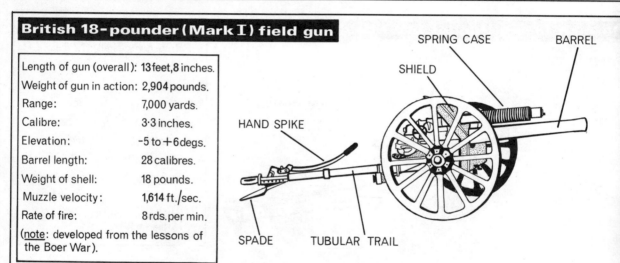

SPRING CASE

BARREL

SHIELD

HAND SPIKE

SPADE

TUBULAR TRAIL

British 12-inch (Mark III) railway howitzer

Length of mounting:	41 feet, 3 inches.
Weight of gun in action:	76 tons.
Range:	14,300 yards.
Elevation:	40°.
Barrel length:	17·3 calibres.
Weight of shell:	750 pounds.
Muzzle velocity:	1,474 ft./sec.
Rate of fire:	1 rd. per min.
Traverse:	5° left/5° right.

(note: most used British railway howitzer).

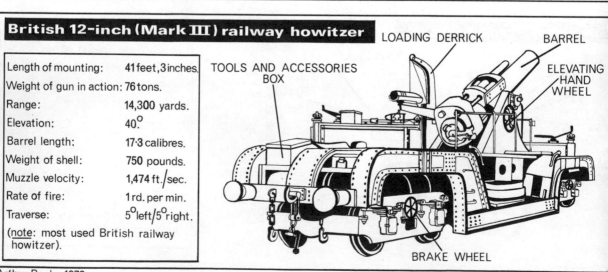

LOADING DERRICK

BARREL

TOOLS AND ACCESSORIES BOX

ELEVATING HAND WHEEL

BRAKE WHEEL

German 10-cm. (Model 1917) field gun

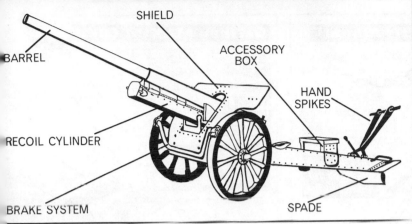

BARREL

SHIELD

ACCESSORY BOX

HAND SPIKES

RECOIL CYLINDER

BRAKE SYSTEM

SPADE

Length of gun (overall):	20 feet.
Weight of gun in action:	6,104 pounds.
Range:	12,085 yards.
Elevation:	-5 to +30 degs.
Barrel length:	35 calibres.
Weight of shell:	39·5 pounds.
Muzzle velocity:	1,923 ft./sec.
Rate of fire:	2 rds. per min.
Traverse:	2° left/2° right.

(note: smallest high-velocity gun in field use during 1914–1918 war).

Austrian 10·4-cm. field gun M.14

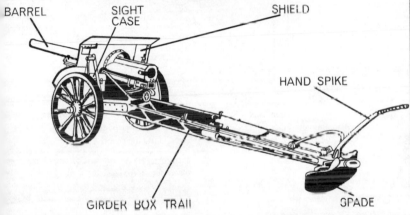

BARREL

SIGHT CASE

SHIELD

HAND SPIKE

GIRDER BOX TRAIL

SPADE

Length of gun (overall):	14 feet.
Weight of gun in action:	5,040 pounds.
Range:	13,670 yards.
Elevation:	-10 to +30 degs.
Barrel length:	35 calibres.
Weight of shell:	38·5 pounds.
Muzzle velocity:	2,230 ft./sec.
Rate of fire:	4 rds. per min.
Traverse:	3° left/3° right.

(note: first Austrian steel field gun: previous guns were bronze).

French 370-mm. mortar

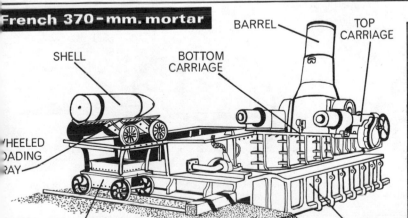

BARREL

TOP CARRIAGE

SHELL

BOTTOM CARRIAGE

WHEELED LOADING TRAY

AMMUNITION TRUCK

BED

Length of gun:	13 feet.
Weight of gun in action:	30 tons.
Range:	8,820 yards.
Elevation:	60°.
Barrel length:	8 calibres.
Weight of shell:	1,076 pounds.
Muzzle velocity:	1,230 ft./sec.
Rate of fire:	1 rd. per 2 mins.
Traverse:	Nil.

(note: shell contains 262 pounds of high explosive).

SIX IMPORTANT MACHINE GUNS 1914-1918

French HOTCHKISS (1914 Model)

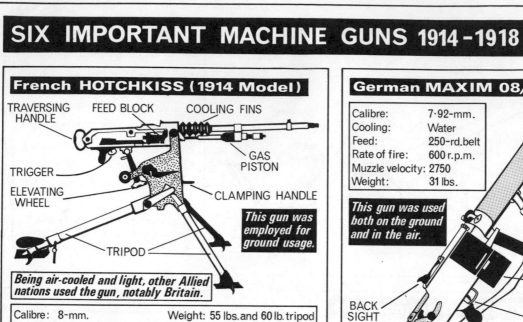

TRAVERSING HANDLE
FEED BLOCK
COOLING FINS
GAS PISTON
TRIGGER
ELEVATING WHEEL
CLAMPING HANDLE
TRIPOD

This gun was employed for ground usage.

Being air-cooled and light, other Allied nations used the gun, notably Britain.

Calibre:	8-mm.	Weight:	55 lbs. and 60 lb. tripod
Cooling:	Air	Rate of fire:	600 r.p.m.
Feed:	30-round strip	Muzzle velocity:	2291

German MAXIM 08/15

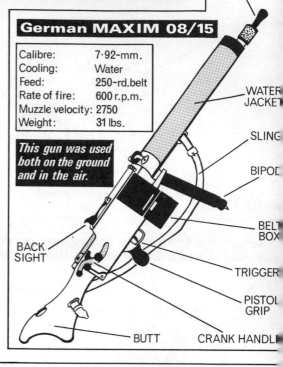

FLASH HIDER

Calibre:	7·92-mm.
Cooling:	Water
Feed:	250-rd. belt
Rate of fire:	600 r.p.m.
Muzzle velocity:	2750
Weight:	31 lbs.

This gun was used both on the ground and in the air.

WATER JACKET
SLING
BIPOD
BELT BOX
BACK SIGHT
TRIGGER
PISTOL GRIP
BUTT
CRANK HANDLE

German MAXIM 08

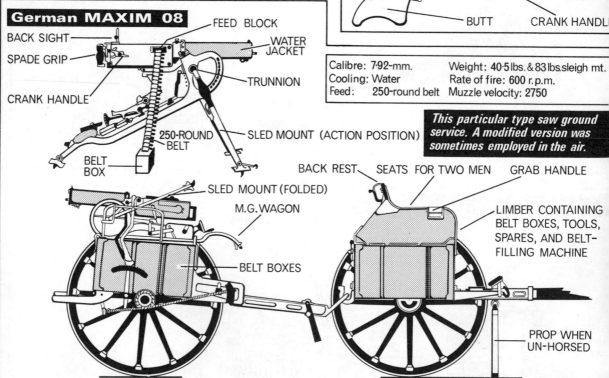

BACK SIGHT
FEED BLOCK
SPADE GRIP
WATER JACKET
CRANK HANDLE
TRUNNION
250-ROUND BELT
SLED MOUNT (ACTION POSITION)
BELT BOX

Calibre: 7·92-mm.	Weight:	40·5 lbs. & 83 lbs. sleigh mt.
Cooling: Water	Rate of fire:	600 r.p.m.
Feed: 250-round belt	Muzzle velocity:	2750

This particular type saw ground service. A modified version was sometimes employed in the air.

SLED MOUNT (FOLDED)
M.G. WAGON
BELT BOXES
BACK REST
SEATS FOR TWO MEN
GRAB HANDLE
LIMBER CONTAINING BELT BOXES, TOOLS, SPARES, AND BELT-FILLING MACHINE
PROP WHEN UN-HORSED

This gun was the "slayer" of 1 July 1916, the opening day of the Allied infantry offensive at the Battle of the Somme. Its devastating fire-power accounted for 90% of the 60,000 Allied casualties (mainly British) incurred on that one day.

© Arthur Banks 1973

224

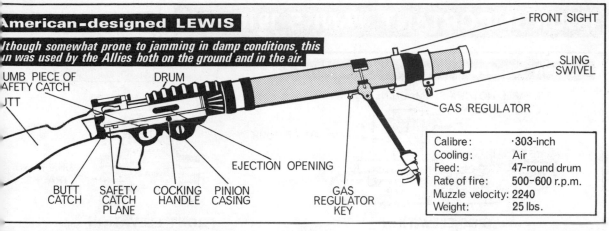

Although somewhat prone to jamming in damp conditions, this gun was used by the Allies both on the ground and in the air.

THUMB PIECE OF
SAFETY CATCH

BUTT

DRUM

FRONT SIGHT

SLING
SWIVEL

GAS REGULATOR

EJECTION OPENING

BUTT
CATCH

SAFETY
CATCH
PLANE

COCKING
HANDLE

PINION
CASING

GAS
REGULATOR
KEY

Calibre:	·303-inch
Cooling:	Air
Feed:	47-round drum
Rate of fire:	500–600 r.p.m.
Muzzle velocity:	2240
Weight:	25 lbs.

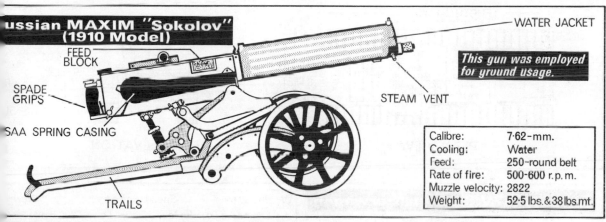

**Russian MAXIM "Sokolov"
(1910 Model)**

FEED
BLOCK

WATER JACKET

*This gun was employed
for ground usage.*

SPADE
GRIPS

SAA SPRING CASING

STEAM VENT

TRAILS

Calibre:	7·62-mm.
Cooling:	Water
Feed:	250-round belt
Rate of fire:	500–600 r.p.m.
Muzzle velocity:	2822
Weight:	52·5 lbs. & 38 lbs. mt.

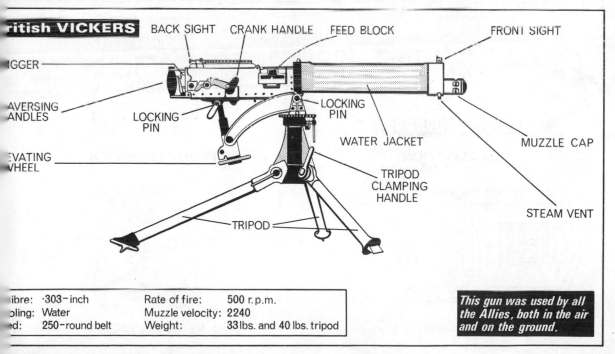

British VICKERS

TRIGGER

BACK SIGHT

CRANK HANDLE

FEED BLOCK

FRONT SIGHT

TRAVERSING
HANDLES

LOCKING
PIN

LOCKING
PIN

MUZZLE CAP

ELEVATING
WHEEL

WATER JACKET

TRIPOD
CLAMPING
HANDLE

STEAM VENT

TRIPOD

Calibre:	·303-inch	Rate of fire:	500 r.p.m.
Cooling:	Water	Muzzle velocity:	2240
Feed:	250-round belt	Weight:	33 lbs. and 40 lbs. tripod

*This gun was used by all
the Allies, both in the air
and on the ground.*

FOUR IMPORTANT TANKS 1916-1918

Weight:	14 tons.
Speed:	8·3 m.p.h.
Range:	80 miles.
Crew:	3.
Engines:	2 Tylor (total: 90 h.p.)

British Medium Mark A "Whippet"

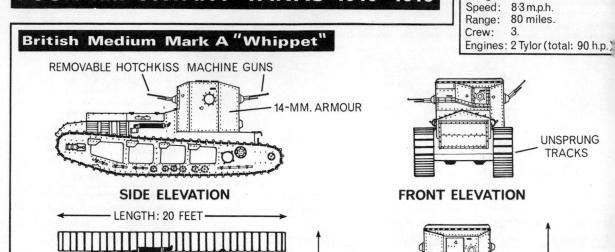

REMOVABLE HOTCHKISS MACHINE GUNS

14-MM. ARMOUR

SIDE ELEVATION

UNSPRUNG TRACKS

FRONT ELEVATION

LENGTH: 20 FEET

WIDTH: 8 FEET, 7 INCHES

PLAN VIEW

HEIGHT: 9 FEET

REAR ELEVATION

German A7V Sturmpanzerwagen

| Weight: 30 tons. | Speed: 8 m.p.h. | Crew: |
| Engines: 2 Daimler four-cylinder (total: 200 h.p.). | | |

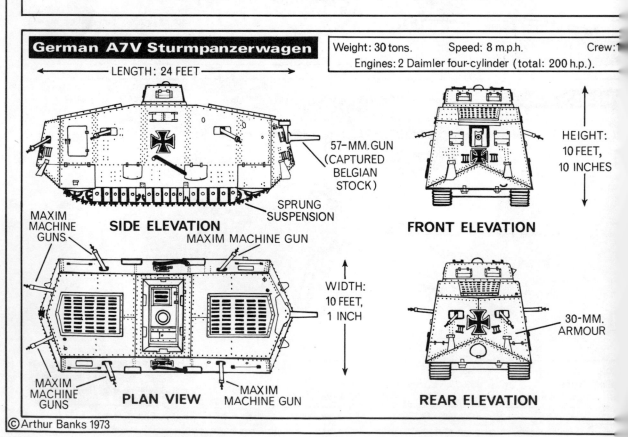

LENGTH: 24 FEET

57-MM. GUN (CAPTURED BELGIAN STOCK)

SPRUNG SUSPENSION

SIDE ELEVATION

MAXIM MACHINE GUNS

HEIGHT: 10 FEET, 10 INCHES

FRONT ELEVATION

MAXIM MACHINE GUN

WIDTH: 10 FEET, 1 INCH

MAXIM MACHINE GUNS

MAXIM MACHINE GUN

PLAN VIEW

30-MM. ARMOUR

REAR ELEVATION

© Arthur Banks 1973

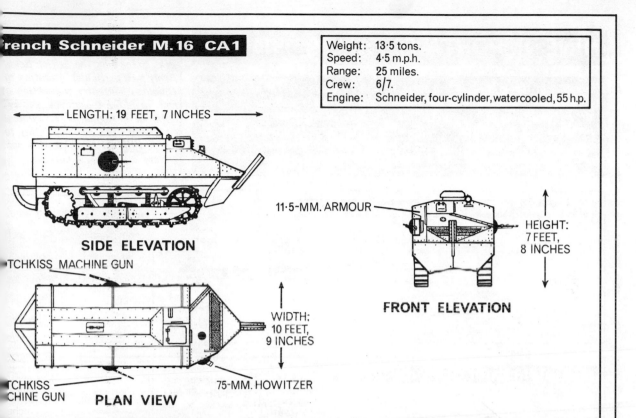

French Schneider M.16 CA1

Weight:	13·5 tons.
Speed:	4·5 m.p.h.
Range:	25 miles.
Crew:	6/7.
Engine:	Schneider, four-cylinder, watercooled, 55 h.p.

LENGTH: 19 FEET, 7 INCHES

SIDE ELEVATION

11·5-MM. ARMOUR

HEIGHT: 7 FEET, 8 INCHES

FRONT ELEVATION

HOTCHKISS MACHINE GUN

WIDTH: 10 FEET, 9 INCHES

HOTCHKISS MACHINE GUN

PLAN VIEW

75-MM. HOWITZER

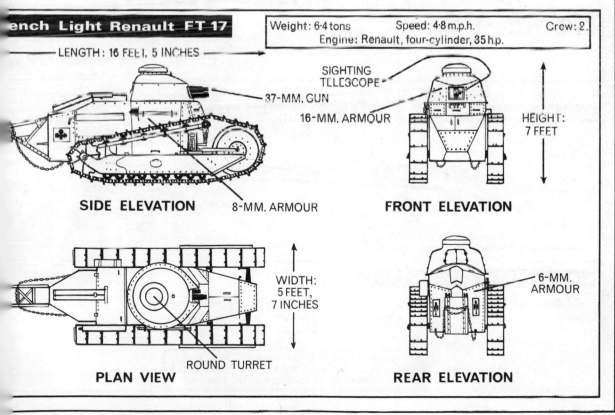

French Light Renault FT 17

Weight: 6·4 tons	Speed: 4·8 m.p.h.	Crew: 2.
Engine: Renault, four-cylinder, 35 h.p.		

LENGTH: 16 FEET, 5 INCHES

SIGHTING TELESCOPE

37-MM. GUN

16-MM. ARMOUR

HEIGHT: 7 FEET

SIDE ELEVATION

8-MM. ARMOUR

FRONT ELEVATION

WIDTH: 5 FEET, 7 INCHES

6-MM. ARMOUR

ROUND TURRET

PLAN VIEW

REAR ELEVATION

NINE IMPORTANT RIFLES 1914-1918

The rifles of the 1914–1918 war were basically similar in performance. All incorporated hand–operated bolt actions, some straight pull, others turn–bolt. Reliability varied somewhat, but no single rifle had any outstanding advantage over the others. In 1918, efforts were made to produce rifles of a self–loading nature, but only one type saw some limited service. The vast majority of rifles used were of the basic types shown on these pages.

THE BRITISH REGULAR ARM

Prior to the war, the British Regul Army paid particular attention to training its infantry in marksmansh and "rapid fire" techniques and by outbreak in August 1914, regiment contained riflemen with ability to fire at rates of 15-20 rounds per minute with great accuracy.

German "MAUSER" (Model 1898)

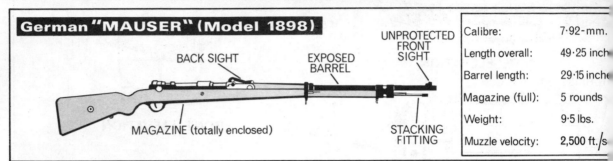

BACK SIGHT — EXPOSED BARREL — UNPROTECTED FRONT SIGHT

MAGAZINE (totally enclosed) — STACKING FITTING

Calibre:	7·92-mm.
Length overall:	49·25 inch
Barrel length:	29·15 inche
Magazine (full):	5 rounds
Weight:	9·5 lbs.
Muzzle velocity:	2,500 ft./s

French "LEBEL" (Model 1916)

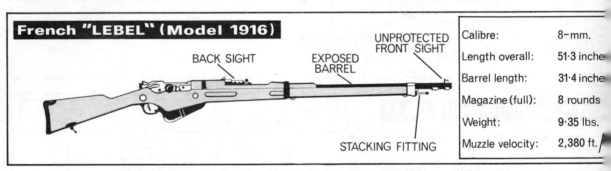

BACK SIGHT — EXPOSED BARREL — UNPROTECTED FRONT SIGHT

STACKING FITTING

Calibre:	8-mm.
Length overall:	51·3 inche
Barrel length:	31·4 inche
Magazine (full):	8 rounds
Weight:	9·35 lbs.
Muzzle velocity:	2,380 ft. /

United States "SPRINGFIELD" (Model 1903)

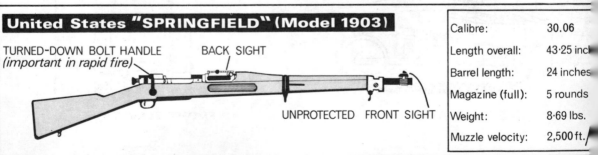

TURNED-DOWN BOLT HANDLE *(important in rapid fire)* — BACK SIGHT

UNPROTECTED FRONT SIGHT

Calibre:	30.06
Length overall:	43·25 inch
Barrel length:	24 inches
Magazine (full):	5 rounds
Weight:	8·69 lbs.
Muzzle velocity:	2,500 ft. /

United States (Model 1917)

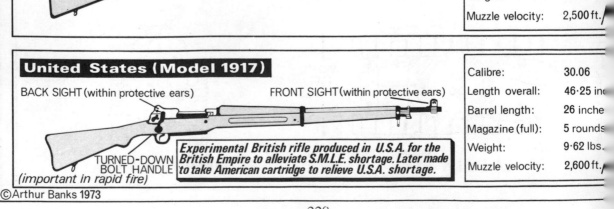

BACK SIGHT (within protective ears) — FRONT SIGHT (within protective ears)

TURNED-DOWN BOLT HANDLE *(important in rapid fire)*

Experimental British rifle produced in U.S.A. for the British Empire to alleviate S.M.L.E. shortage. Later made to take American cartridge to relieve U.S.A. shortage.

Calibre:	30.06
Length overall:	46·25 in
Barrel length:	26 inche
Magazine (full):	5 rounds
Weight:	9·62 lbs.
Muzzle velocity:	2,600 ft. /

© Arthur Banks 1973

British SHORT MAGAZINE "LEE-ENFIELD" Mark III

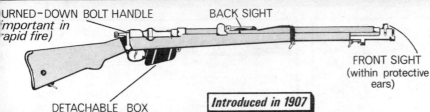

TURNED-DOWN BOLT HANDLE (important in rapid fire)

BACK SIGHT

FRONT SIGHT (within protective ears)

DETACHABLE BOX

Introduced in 1907

Calibre:	·303-inch
Length overall:	44·5 inches
Barrel length:	25·19 inches
Magazine (full):	10 rounds
Weight:	8·12 lbs.
Muzzle velocity:	2,060 ft./sec.

Canadian "ROSS" Mark III B

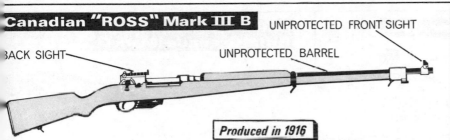

UNPROTECTED FRONT SIGHT

UNPROTECTED BARREL

BACK SIGHT

Produced in 1916

Calibre:	·303-inch
Length overall:	50·5 inches
Barrel length:	30·5 inches
Magazine (full):	5 rounds
Weight:	9·75 lbs.
Muzzle velocity:	2,060 ft./sec.

Russian "MOISIN-NAGANT" (Model 1891)

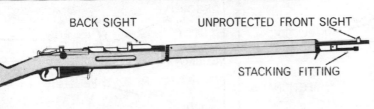

BACK SIGHT

UNPROTECTED FRONT SIGHT

STACKING FITTING

Calibre:	7·62-mm.
Length overall:	51·37 inches
Barrel length:	31·6 inches
Magazine (full):	5 rounds
Weight:	9·62 lbs.
Muzzle velocity:	2,660 ft./sec.

Austrian "MÄNNLICHER" (Model 1895)

Diagram and main details refer to the long version

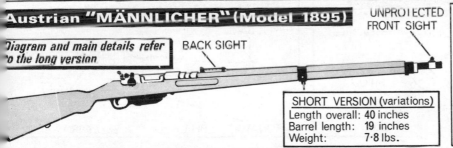

UNPROTECTED FRONT SIGHT

BACK SIGHT

SHORT VERSION (variations)
Length overall: 40 inches
Barrel length: 19 inches
Weight: 7·8 lbs.

Calibre:	8-mm.
Length overall:	50 inches
Barrel length:	30 inches
Magazine (full):	5 rounds
Weight:	8·4 lbs.
Muzzle velocity:	2,030 ft./sec.

Italian "MÄNNLICHER-CARCANO" (Model 1891)

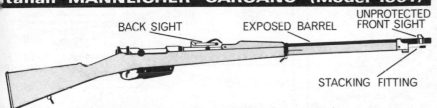

BACK SIGHT

EXPOSED BARREL

UNPROTECTED FRONT SIGHT

STACKING FITTING

Calibre:	6·5-mm.
Length overall:	50·75 inches
Barrel length:	30·7 inches
Magazine (full):	6 rounds
Weight:	9 lbs.
Muzzle velocity:	2,200 ft./sec.

TWENTY TRENCH WEAPONS AND MUNITIONS

German 240-mm. old style Minenwerfer "Iko"

BARREL
ELEVATING GEAR
SECTIONAL PLATFORM
EARTH

British "Jam Tin" Bomb

BICKFORD SAFETY FUSE
AMMONAL
ASSORTED SCRAP
PROTECTIVE CAP
CASE (TIN CAN)

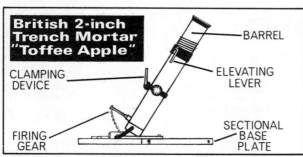

German 75-mm. new style Minenwerfer

RECOIL CYLINDER
REAR SIGHT
ELEVATING LEVER
TRAVERSING LEVER
BARREL
RECOIL SPADE
EARTH

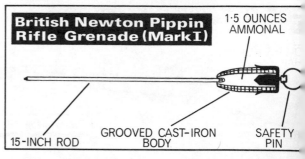

British Newton Pippin Rifle Grenade (Mark I)

1·5 OUNCES AMMONAL
15-INCH ROD
GROOVED CAST-IRON BODY
SAFETY PIN

British 2-inch Trench Mortar "Toffee Apple"

BARREL
CLAMPING DEVICE
ELEVATING LEVER
FIRING GEAR
SECTIONAL BASE PLATE

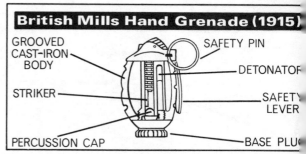

British Mills Hand Grenade (1915)

GROOVED CAST-IRON BODY
SAFETY PIN
DETONATOR
STRIKER
SAFETY LEVER
PERCUSSION CAP
BASE PLUG

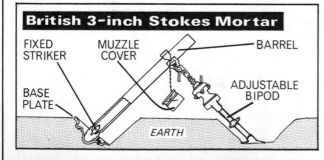

British 3-inch Stokes Mortar

FIXED STRIKER
MUZZLE COVER
BARREL
ADJUSTABLE BIPOD
BASE PLATE
EARTH

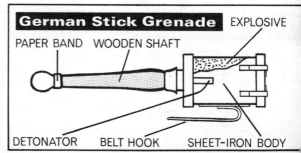

German Stick Grenade

EXPLOSIVE
PAPER BAND
WOODEN SHAFT
DETONATOR
BELT HOOK
SHEET-IRON BODY

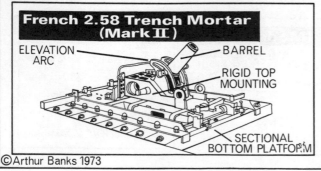

French 2.58 Trench Mortar (Mark II)

ELEVATION ARC
BARREL
RIGID TOP MOUNTING
SECTIONAL BOTTOM PLATFORM

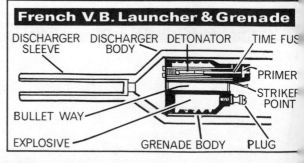

French V.B. Launcher & Grenade

DISCHARGER SLEEVE
DISCHARGER BODY
DETONATOR
TIME FUSE
PRIMER
STRIKER POINT
BULLET WAY
EXPLOSIVE
GRENADE BODY
PLUG

© Arthur Banks 1973

230

Typical High Explosive Shell

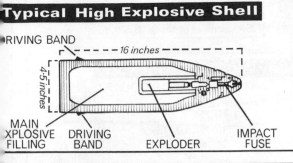

DRIVING BAND
16 inches
4·5 inches
MAIN EXPLOSIVE FILLING
DRIVING BAND
EXPLODER
IMPACT FUSE

German 76-mm. Minenwerfer Message Shell

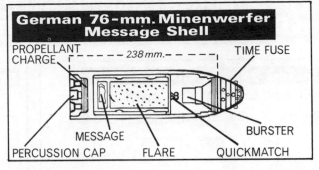

PROPELLANT CHARGE
238 mm.
TIME FUSE
MESSAGE
BURSTER
PERCUSSION CAP
FLARE
QUICKMATCH

Typical Shrapnel Shell

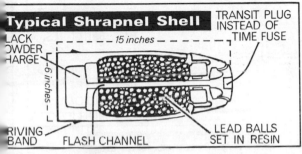

BLACK POWDER CHARGE
TRANSIT PLUG INSTEAD OF TIME FUSE
15 inches
6 inches
DRIVING BAND
FLASH CHANNEL
LEAD BALLS SET IN RESIN

Trench Club

IMPROVISED IN THE TRENCHES

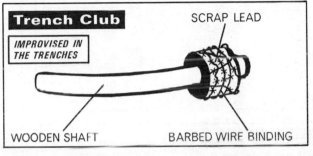

SCRAP LEAD
WOODEN SHAFT
BARBED WIRE BINDING

Typical Gas Shell

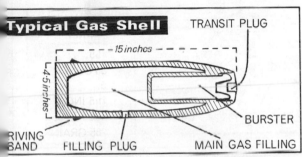

TRANSIT PLUG
15 inches
4·5 inches
DRIVING BAND
FILLING PLUG
MAIN GAS FILLING
BURSTER

Old Welsh Knife

TRADITIONAL FROM DAYS OF THE LONGBOW

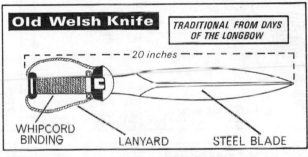

20 inches
WHIPCORD BINDING
LANYARD
STEEL BLADE

Typical Semi Armour-Piercing Shell

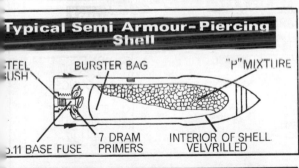

STEEL BUSH
BURSTER BAG
"P" MIXTURE
No. 11 BASE FUSE
7 DRAM PRIMERS
INTERIOR OF SHELL VELVRILLED

Knuckleduster Knife

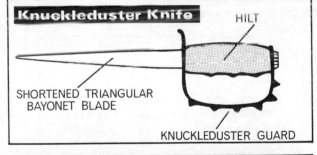

HILT
SHORTENED TRIANGULAR BAYONET BLADE
KNUCKLEDUSTER GUARD

Typical Incendiary (Thermite) Shell

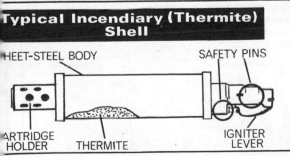

SHEET-STEEL BODY
SAFETY PINS
CARTRIDGE HOLDER
THERMITE
IGNITER LEVER

British Webley (Mark VI) Stock & Bayonet

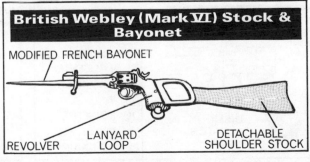

MODIFIED FRENCH BAYONET
REVOLVER
LANYARD LOOP
DETACHABLE SHOULDER STOCK

EIGHT IMPORTANT PISTOLS AND REVOLVERS 1914 – 1918

United States COLT M 1917

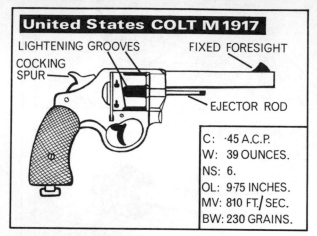

LIGHTENING GROOVES
FIXED FORESIGHT
COCKING SPUR
EJECTOR ROD

C: ·45 A.C.P.
W: 39 OUNCES.
NS: 6.
OL: 9·75 INCHES.
MV: 810 FT./SEC.
BW: 230 GRAINS.

British WEBLEY Mark VI

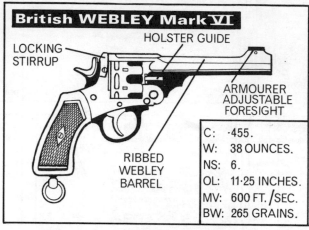

LOCKING STIRRUP
HOLSTER GUIDE
ARMOURER ADJUSTABLE FORESIGHT
RIBBED WEBLEY BARREL

C: ·455.
W: 38 OUNCES.
NS: 6.
OL: 11·25 INCHES.
MV: 600 FT./SEC.
BW: 265 GRAINS.

British COLT

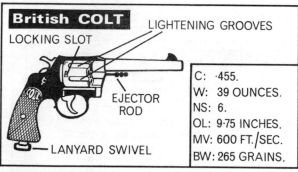

LOCKING SLOT
LIGHTENING GROOVES
EJECTOR ROD
LANYARD SWIVEL

C: ·455.
W: 39 OUNCES.
NS: 6.
OL: 9·75 INCHES.
MV: 600 FT./SEC.
BW: 265 GRAINS.

British WEBLEY-FOSBERY

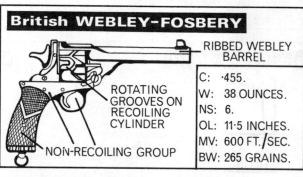

RIBBED WEBLEY BARREL
ROTATING GROOVES ON RECOILING CYLINDER
NON-RECOILING GROUP

C: ·455.
W: 38 OUNCES.
NS: 6.
OL: 11·5 INCHES.
MV: 600 FT./SEC.
BW: 265 GRAINS.

German MAUSER

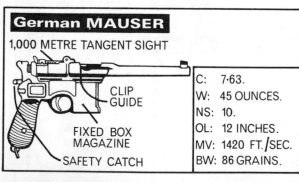

1,000 METRE TANGENT SIGHT
CLIP GUIDE
FIXED BOX MAGAZINE
SAFETY CATCH

C: 7·63.
W: 45 OUNCES.
NS: 10.
OL: 12 INCHES.
MV: 1420 FT./SEC.
BW: 86 GRAINS.

German LUGER (Parabellum)

LANYARD LOOP TOGGLE LINK
FINGER GRIPS ON MAGAZINE

C: 9 PARABELLUM.
W: 30 OUNCES.
NS: 7.
OL: 8·75 INCHES.
MV: 1,150 FT./SEC.
BW: 125 GRAINS.

Italian GLISENTI

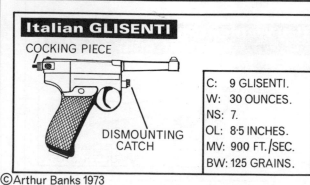

COCKING PIECE
DISMOUNTING CATCH

C: 9 GLISENTI.
W: 30 OUNCES.
NS: 7.
OL: 8·5 INCHES.
MV: 900 FT./SEC.
BW: 125 GRAINS.

Japanese NAMBU

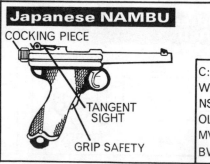

COCKING PIECE
TANGENT SIGHT
GRIP SAFETY

C: 8 NAMBU.
W: 30 OUNCES.
NS: 8.
OL: 10 INCHES.
MV: 950 FT./SEC.
BW: 102 GRAINS.

FIVE IMPORTANT ANTI-AIRCRAFT GUNS 1914-1918

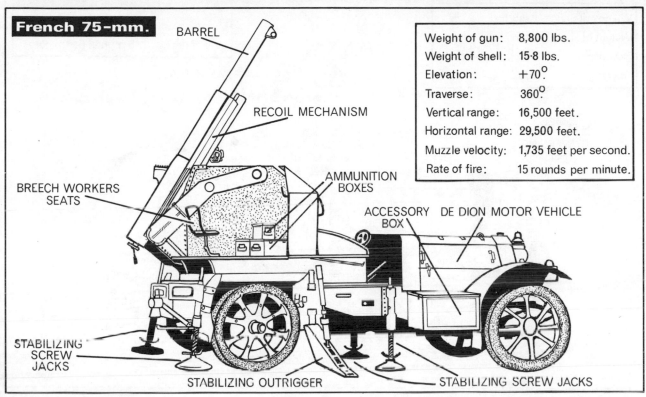

French 75-mm.

BARREL

RECOIL MECHANISM

BREECH WORKERS SEATS

AMMUNITION BOXES

ACCESSORY BOX

DE DION MOTOR VEHICLE

STABILIZING SCREW JACKS

STABILIZING OUTRIGGER

STABILIZING SCREW JACKS

Weight of gun:	8,800 lbs.
Weight of shell:	15·8 lbs.
Elevation:	+70°.
Traverse:	360°
Vertical range:	16,500 feet.
Horizontal range:	29,500 feet.
Muzzle velocity:	1,735 feet per second.
Rate of fire:	15 rounds per minute.

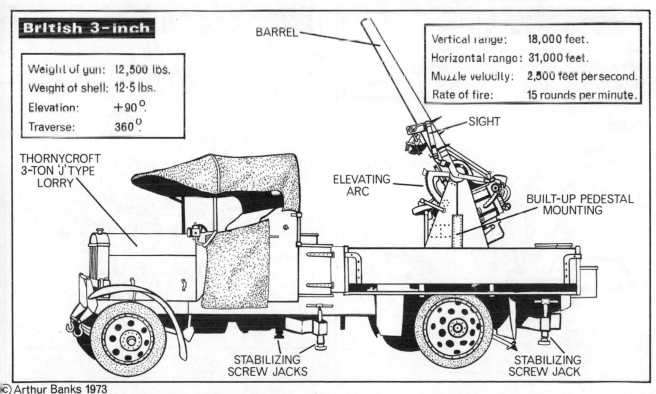

British 3-inch

Weight of gun:	12,500 lbs.
Weight of shell:	12·5 lbs.
Elevation:	+90°.
Traverse:	360°

BARREL

Vertical range:	18,000 feet.
Horizontal range:	31,000 feet.
Muzzle velocity:	2,500 feet per second.
Rate of fire:	15 rounds per minute.

SIGHT

THORNYCROFT 3-TON 'J' TYPE LORRY

ELEVATING ARC

BUILT-UP PEDESTAL MOUNTING

STABILIZING SCREW JACKS

STABILIZING SCREW JACK

British 13-pounder

Weight of gun: 2,150 lbs.
Weight of shell: 13 lbs.
Elevation: +80°.
Traverse: 360°.

Vertical range: 13,000 feet.
Horizontal range: 24,500 feet.
Muzzle velocity: 1,700 feet per second.
Rate of fire: 8 rounds per minute.

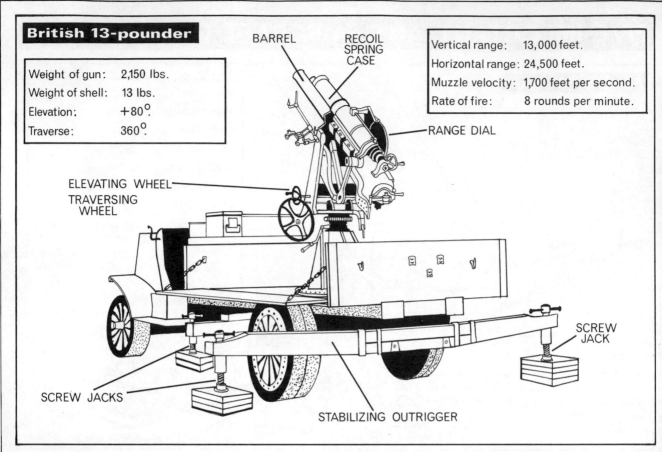

BARREL
RECOIL SPRING CASE
RANGE DIAL
ELEVATING WHEEL
TRAVERSING WHEEL
SCREW JACK
SCREW JACKS
STABILIZING OUTRIGGER

German 8·8-cm.

Elevation: +70°
Traverse: 360°.

Weight of gun: 6,700 lbs.
Weight of shell: 21 lbs.
Vert. range: 12,500 feet.
Horiz. range: 35,500 feet.

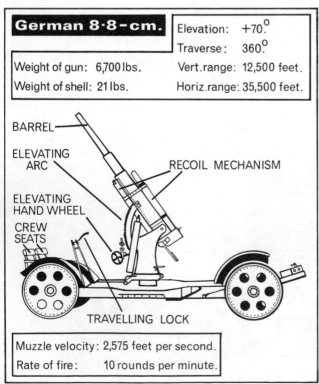

BARREL
ELEVATING ARC
RECOIL MECHANISM
ELEVATING HAND WHEEL
CREW SEATS
TRAVELLING LOCK

Muzzle velocity: 2,575 feet per second.
Rate of fire: 10 rounds per minute.

German 7·7-cm.

Weight of shell: 15 lbs.
Vertical range: 14,000 ft.
Weight of gun: 3,675 lbs.
Horiz. range: 26,000 ft.

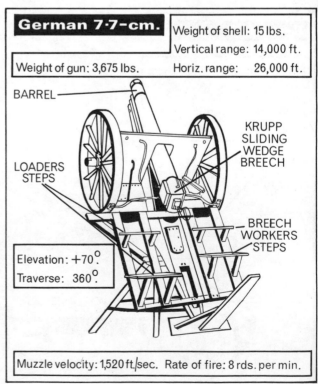

BARREL
KRUPP SLIDING WEDGE BREECH
LOADERS STEPS
BREECH WORKERS STEPS
Elevation: +70°.
Traverse: 360°.

Muzzle velocity: 1,520 ft./sec. Rate of fire: 8 rds. per min.

THE WAR AT SEA

During the first decade of the century a radical change in warship construction led to the development of 'all big gun' battleships. The first British vessel of this type was H.M.S. *Dreadnought* (ten 12-inch guns and a speed of 21 knots), laid down in October 1905, launched February 1906, at sea by October 1906. The Dreadnoughts could outrange and outpace all previous battleships, which were soon made obsolete. Other countries followed Britain's lead: a German dreadnought, the *Nassau*, was launched in 1907. The Royal Navy in 1914 had twenty dreadnoughts or 'super-dreadnoughts' based in home waters: Germany, the second largest naval power in Europe, had fifteen. Everyone awaited a dreadnought Trafalgar. A difference in concepts of naval strategy postponed the clash. The Germans hoped to offset their numerical inferiority by splitting the British Grand Fleet by a feint, enabling their battle squadrons to fall on the enemy a portion at a time; the British, on the other hand, were content to use dreadnoughts as a distant deterrent, exercising naval supremacy in home waters from Scapa Flow, in the Orkneys. The prospect of a great naval battle receded.

Meanwhile, the British, French, Russian and Japanese navies were confronted with the problem of German cruisers in distant seas. The battle-cruiser *Goeben* and the cruiser *Breslau* succeeded in evading pursuit in the Mediterranean and took refuge at Constantinople, where their transference to the Turkish fleet played a considerable part in inducing the Turks to enter the war. The German Pacific Squadron (Spee) inflicted, off Coronel, the first defeat sustained by the Royal Navy since the 1812 War with America, sinking an outdated armoured cruiser and a light cruiser. Coronel was avenged at the Falkland Islands five weeks later, while the lone raider *Emden* was tracked down by the Australian cruiser *Sydney* in the Indian Ocean. The chivalrous seamanship of the commanders of the German surface vessels won high regard; but the development by the Germans of submarine warfare, and especially the increasing number of underwater attacks on merchantmen and passenger liners, aroused anger and resentment in Britain and the United States. On the other hand, the Americans also resented the British imposition of a naval blockade on Germany and her allies. British submarine activity was especially effective in the Sea of Marmara, off Constantinople, and in the Baltic.

In January 1915 the battle-cruisers of the Grand Fleet, under Beatty, intercepted Admiral Hipper's 'scouting group' off the Dogger Bank and pursued the Germans but lost contact after Beatty's flagship was immobilised. The German armoured cruiser *Blücher* was sunk, and the Germans concentrated for the remainder of the year on U-boat activity. In February 1916 Admiral Scheer took command of the High Seas Fleet at Wilhelmshaven, and planned to tempt Beatty into another battle-cruiser engagement, with a pack of U-boats waiting to intercept the dreadnoughts of the Grand Fleet (Jellicoe) as they moved south. Surface, submarine and Zeppelin activity was, however, not as co-ordinated as Scheer wished. The British were remarkably well-informed of German movements (by wireless interception), and were prepared for a major battle in May 1916.

Jutland, the largest naval action in world history, was essentially a battle of feints and manoeuvres. It involved 151 British warships and 99 German vessels although the dreadnoughts themselves (28 British, 16 German) were in action against each other for only twenty minutes during the evening of 31 May. Beatty, realising the German cruisers were seeking to draw his squadron towards the heavy guns of the High Seas Fleet, himself tried to lure the Germans towards Jellicoe's squadron. The British battle-cruisers suffered heavily from accurate German fire, but tactically trapped Scheer into allowing the Grand Fleet to get between his vessels and his home port. Jellicoe hoped to bring Scheer to battle next morning, but the Germans evaded him at night, partly through sheer speed and partly through better training for a running battle by night. British casualties and losses were far higher than those of the Germans at Jutland; but it was harder for the Germans to fill the gaps in their fleet. Strategically Jutland was a British victory, for it reinforced the Kaiser's inclination to preserve his navy intact, rather than risk another encounter with the Grand Fleet.

After Jutland there was little surface conflict between rival warships. The Austro-Hungarian fleet made a number of sorties on the barrage which the Allies sought to establish across the Strait of Otranto, so as to seal off the Adriatic from the Mediterranean; and there were occasional alarms in the Black Sea, where the Russian and Turkish fleets had already clashed briefly off the southern tip of the Crimea in November 1914. It is often said that the German High Seas Fleet remained inactive off Heligoland and Kiel for the remainder of the War until a break in morale led to mutiny in 1918. Yet, though the Kaiser was opposed to offensive action, Scheer took the Fleet to sea again in the third week of August 1916 and, for the last time, in April 1918. These sweeps seem, however, to have been intended as diversions rather than as preliminaries to another battle, and no contact was made with British surface vessels. It should, of course, be noted (page 276) that the rival fleets were increasingly hemmed in by minefields.

Both the British and German Admiralties had anticipated that attempts would be made in any war to strangle the economy of a country, and cut off its food supply, by means of a blockade. The British system (for which a separate Government department, the Ministry of Blockade, was eventually established early in 1916) was basically an extension of the controversial rights exercised during the Napoleonic Wars: an Order in Council of March 1915 authorising the seizure by British warships of goods destined for Germany by way of a neutral port provoked similar hostility to the notorious Orders in Council of 1807, although German submarine ruthlessness assuaged the wrath of some neutral countries. Neither the British nor the Germans had worked out the implications of using the submarine as a destroyer of commerce; but by the spring of 1916 the U-boat was recognised in Berlin as the most effective of all naval weapons. Attempts were made later that summer to counter the U-boat menace with new minefields, increased defensive nets and disguised 'mystery ships' (Q-ships). Yet the tonnage of merchant shipping sunk by U-boat averaged 300,000 a month in the last quarter of 1916 and rose dramatically in February when the Germans began unrestricted submarine warfare. Over half a million tons of British merchant shipping was lost in April 1917, one in four vessels leaving British ports never returning there again. Corn supplies in England were down to six weeks.

The U-boat menace was mastered by a return to the eighteenth century concept of convoys, imposed on a reluctant Admiralty by the Prime Minister Lloyd George, in May 1917 (see page 266). The addition of American naval strength to Atlantic patrols helped ensure the effectiveness of convoying. At the same time, new anti-submarine techniques were perfected, notably the depth-charge. The Admiralty remained concerned over the use which the Germans made of the Belgian ports as U-boat bases. In April 1918 a raid was made on Zeebrugge—the prototype of amphibious commando raids in the Second World War—which sought to block the canal to Bruges, where there were docking facilities for destroyers and as many as 30 U-boats. An attempt was also made on the Bruges–Ostend Canal. The Zeebrugge Raid (for which eight Victoria Crosses were awarded) was only partially successful and the accompanying raid on Ostend (which won another three Victoria Crosses) was so disappointing that a second assault had to be made a fortnight later. It, too, proved largely abortive. But the Zeebrugge-Ostend operations sealed off the U-boats and destroyers at Bruges, even if the shallow-draught boats were soon able to move again out to sea. The chief effect of the raids was as a fillip to lagging morale in Britain.

A final plan to challenge the Grand Fleet in the hopes of securing better Armistice terms in 1918 came to nothing when the German naval ratings mutinied, first at the fleet anchorage off Wilhelmshaven on 29 October and later at Kiel. It was the beginning of the revolution which, within a fortnight, turned Germany from an autocracy to a republic.

THE PURSUIT AND ESCAPE OF SMS 'GOEBEN' AND 'BRESLAU', AUGUST 1914

The safe arrival of the two German warships strongly influenced Turkey's decision to join the Central Powers.

Black Sea

Odessa · Crimea · Constantinople · Bosporus · Dardanelles

TURKEY · RUMANIA · BULGARIA · SERBIA · MONTE-NEGRO · ALBANIA · AUSTRIA - HUNGARY · GREECE

Salonika · Athens · Valona · Brindisi · Taranto · Rome

AEGEAN SEA

Lemnos · Imbros · Denusa · CRETE

Goeben & Breslau

1700, 10 Aug. · 1200, 11 Aug. · 1630, 7 Aug. · 1630, 7 Aug. · 8-10 Aug.

MEDITERRANEAN SEA

FRANCE · ITALY · SARDINIA · CORSICA

Toulon · Marseilles

Messina · SICILY · Malta · Bizerta · Bone · Philippeville · TUNISIA · ALGERIA

0500, 5 Aug to 1700, 6 Aug. · 1905, 4 Aug. · 2100, 3 Aug. · 1100, 4 Aug. · 1400, 6 Aug. · 1530, 3 Aug. · Malta 0300, 8 Aug. · 0300, 8 Aug.

0855, 7 Aug. · 0200, 7 Aug. · 0400, 7 Aug. · 1020, 7 Aug. · 1530, 6 Aug. · 1010, 7 Aug. · 0001, 9 Aug. · 1430, 8 Aug.

Adriatic Sea

10 AUGUST, BRITISH BATTLECRUISERS ON PATROL IN THIS AREA

KEY

- ⟶ Track of HMS 'Gloucester.'
- - - Track of HMS 'Dublin'.
- ······ Track of Battlecruisers.
- | Track of First Cruiser Squadron.
- ⟹ Track of SMS 'Goeben'.
- ⇦⇨ Track of SMS. 'Breslau'.

Scale: 0 — 200 Miles

Note: to avoid any possible confusion, times on tracks are based on the 24-hour clock system.

BRITISH SHIPS IN THE HUNT

- 3 Battlecruisers
- 4 Armoured cruisers
- 4 Light cruisers
- 16 Destroyers

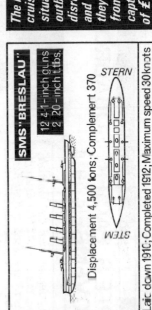

The battlecruiser 'Goeben' and the light cruiser 'Breslau', were German warships situated in the Mediterranean area at the outbreak of the war. After attempting to disrupt French troop convoys between Africa and France by bombarding Algerian ports, they were hunted by British naval units from Messina to the Dardanelles. To escape capture, they were sold to Turkey for a sum of £3,800,000, and then used against Russia.

SMS "BRESLAU"

- 12 4.1-inch guns
- 2 20-inch t.tbs.

STERN · STEM

Displacement 4,500 tons; Complement 370

Laid down 1910; Completed 1912; Maximum speed 30 knots

SMS "GOEBEN"

- 10 11-in. guns
- 12 6-in. guns
- 12 24-pd's.
- 4 20-in. t.tbs.

STERN · STEM

Displacement 23,000 tons; Complement 1,107

Laid down 1909; Completed 1912; Maximum speed 28 knots

© Arthur Banks 1973

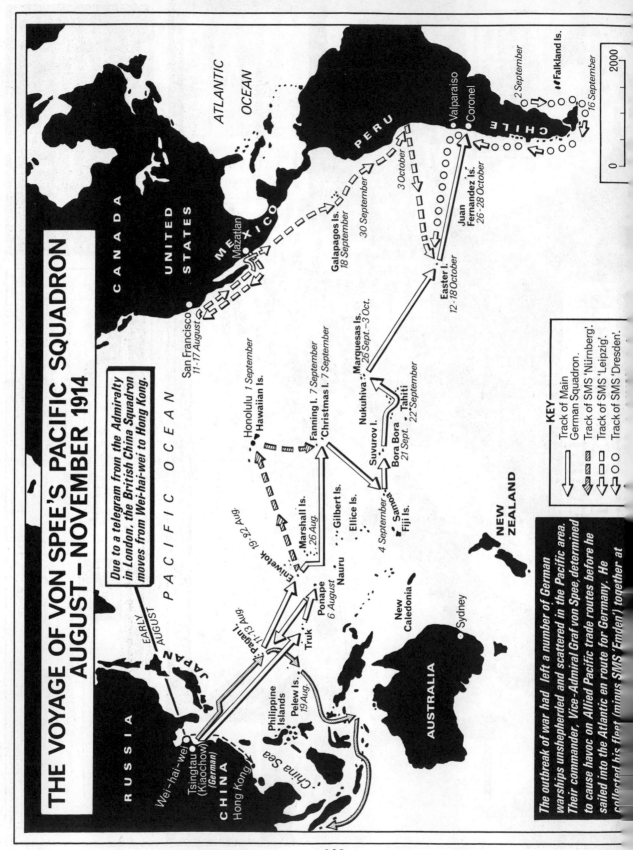

THE VOYAGE OF VON SPEE'S PACIFIC SQUADRON AUGUST–NOVEMBER 1914

Due to a telegram from the Admiralty in London, the British China Squadron moves from Wei-hai-wei to Hong Kong.

ATLANTIC OCEAN

PACIFIC OCEAN

KEY

Track of Main German Squadron.

Track of SMS 'Nürnberg'.

Track of SMS 'Leipzig'.

Track of SMS 'Dresden'.

The outbreak of war had left a number of German warships unshepherded and scattered in the Pacific area. Their commander, Vice-Admiral Graf von Spee, determined to cause havoc on Allied Pacific trade routes before he sailed into the Atlantic en route for Germany. He collected his fleet (minus SMS 'Emden') together at

2000

0

CANADA

UNITED STATES

MEXICO

PERU

CHILE

Mazatlan

San Francisco
11-17 August

Honolulu *1 September*
Hawaiian Is.

Fanning I. *7 September*
Christmas I. *7 September*

Galapagos Is.
18 September

30 September

3 October

Valparaiso

Coronel

2 September

Falkland Is.

16 September

Juan Fernandez Is.
26-28 October

Easter I.
12-18 October

Marquesas Is.
26 Sept.–3 Oct.

Nukuhiva

Suvurov I.

Bora Bora
21 Sept.

Tahiti
22 September

4 September

Samoa
Fiji Is.

Marshall Is.
26 Aug.

Gilbert Is.

Ellice Is.

Eniwetok *19–28 Aug.*

Nauru

Ponape
6 August

Truk

Pagan I. *17–13 Aug.*

Pelew Is.
19 Aug.

Philippine Islands

China Sea

Wei-hai-wei

Tsingtau (Kiaochow)
(German)

Hong Kong

RUSSIA

JAPAN

CHINA

EARLY AUGUST

NEW ZEALAND

New Caledonia

Sydney

AUSTRALIA

238

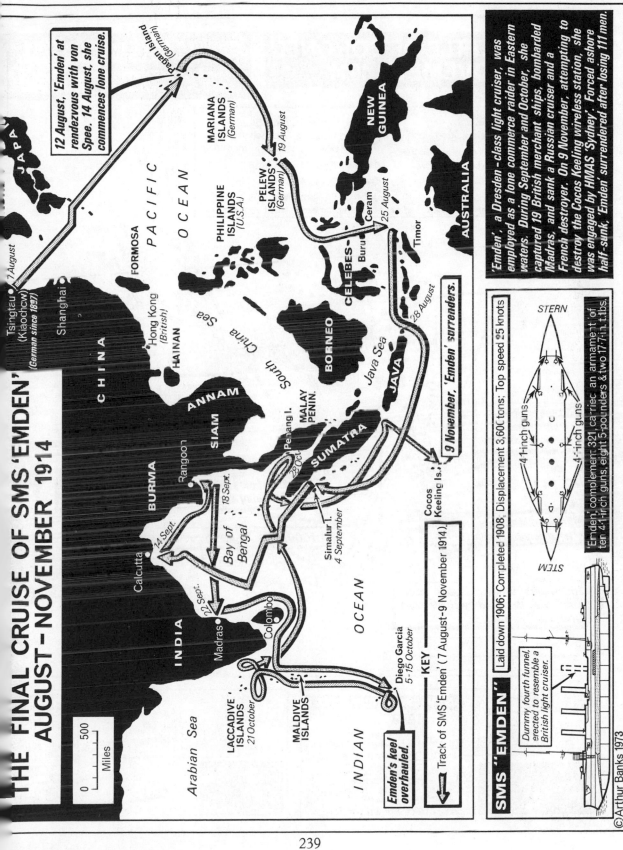

THE FINAL CRUISE OF SMS 'EMDEN' AUGUST–NOVEMBER 1914

12 August, 'Emden' at rendezvous with von Spee. 14 August, she commences lone cruise.

Pagan Island (German)

Tsingtau 7 August (Kiaochow) (German since 1897)

Shanghai

JAPAN

CHINA

FORMOSA

Hong Kong (British)

HAINAN

South China Sea

ANNAM

SIAM

BURMA

Rangoon

Calcutta

14 Sept.
18 Sept.
22 Sept.

INDIA

Madras

Colombo

Bay of Bengal

Penang I.

MALAY PENIN.

28 Oct.

SUMATRA

Simalur I. 4 September

Diego Garcia 5–15 October

LACCADIVE ISLANDS 21 October

MALDIVE ISLANDS

Arabian Sea

INDIAN OCEAN

Emden's keel overhauled.

PACIFIC OCEAN

MARIANA ISLANDS (German)

PHILIPPINE ISLANDS (U.S.A.)

PELEW ISLANDS (German)

19 August

25 August

CELEBES

Buru Ceram

BORNEO

Java Sea

JAVA

Timor

NEW GUINEA

AUSTRALIA

28 August

9 November, 'Emden' surrenders.

Cocos Keeling Is.

KEY
Track of SMS 'Emden' (7 August–9 November 1914).

'Emden', a Dresden-class light cruiser, was employed as a lone commerce raider in Eastern waters. During September and October, she captured 19 British merchant ships, bombarded Madras, and sank a Russian cruiser and a French destroyer. On 9 November, attempting to destroy the Cocos Keeling wireless station, she was engaged by HMAS 'Sydney'. Forced ashore half-sunk, 'Emden' surrendered after losing 111 men.

STERN

4-inch guns

4-inch guns

STEM

'Emden', complement 321, carried an armament of ten 4.1-inch guns, eight 5-pounders & two 17.7-in. t.tbs.

SMS "EMDEN"
Laid down 1906; Completed 1908; Displacement 3,600 tons; Top speed 25 knots

Dummy fourth funnel, erected to resemble a British light cruiser.

© Arthur Banks 1973

239

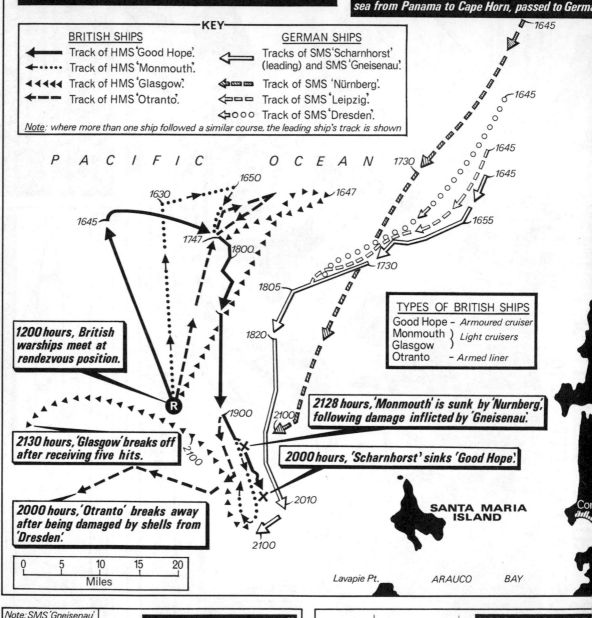

THE BATTLE OF CORONEL 1 NOVEMBER 1914

The Battle of Coronel resulted in a German victory. It was the first major British naval reverse for over a century, and command of the sea from Panama to Cape Horn, passed to German

— KEY —

BRITISH SHIPS
- Track of HMS 'Good Hope'.
- Track of HMS 'Monmouth'.
- Track of HMS 'Glasgow'.
- Track of HMS 'Otranto'.

GERMAN SHIPS
- Tracks of SMS 'Scharnhorst' (leading) and SMS 'Gneisenau'.
- Track of SMS 'Nürnberg'.
- Track of SMS 'Leipzig'.
- Track of SMS 'Dresden'.

Note: where more than one ship followed a similar course, the leading ship's track is shown

P A C I F I C   O C E A N

1630 1650 1647
1645
1747
1800
1805
1820
1730
1745

1200 hours, British warships meet at rendezvous position.

2130 hours, 'Glasgow' breaks off after receiving five hits.

2000 hours, 'Otranto' breaks away after being damaged by shells from 'Dresden'.

1900
2100
2010
2100

2128 hours, 'Monmouth' is sunk by 'Nurnberg', following damage inflicted by 'Gneisenau'.

2000 hours, 'Scharnhorst' sinks 'Good Hope'.

TYPES OF BRITISH SHIPS
Good Hope	Armoured cruiser
Monmouth Glasgow	Light cruisers
Otranto	Armed liner

SANTA MARIA ISLAND

Cor

1645 1645
1645
1645
1655

0	5	10	15	20
Miles

Lavapie Pt.   ARAUCO   BAY

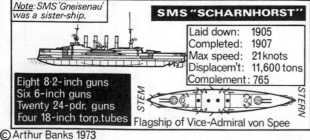

Note: SMS 'Gneisenau' was a sister-ship.

SMS "SCHARNHORST"

Laid down:	1905
Completed:	1907
Max speed:	21 knots
Displacem't:	11,600 tons
Complement:	765

Eight 8·2-inch guns
Six 6-inch guns
Twenty 24-pdr. guns
Four 18-inch torp.tubes

STEM   STERN

Flagship of Vice-Admiral von Spee

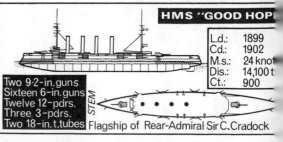

HMS "GOOD HOP[E]

L.d.:	1899
Cd.:	1902
M.s.:	24 knot
Dis.:	14,100 t
Ct.:	900

Two 9·2-in.guns
Sixteen 6-in.guns
Twelve 12-pdrs.
Three 3-pdrs.
Two 18-in.t.tubes

STEM   STERN

Flagship of Rear-Admiral Sir C. Cradock

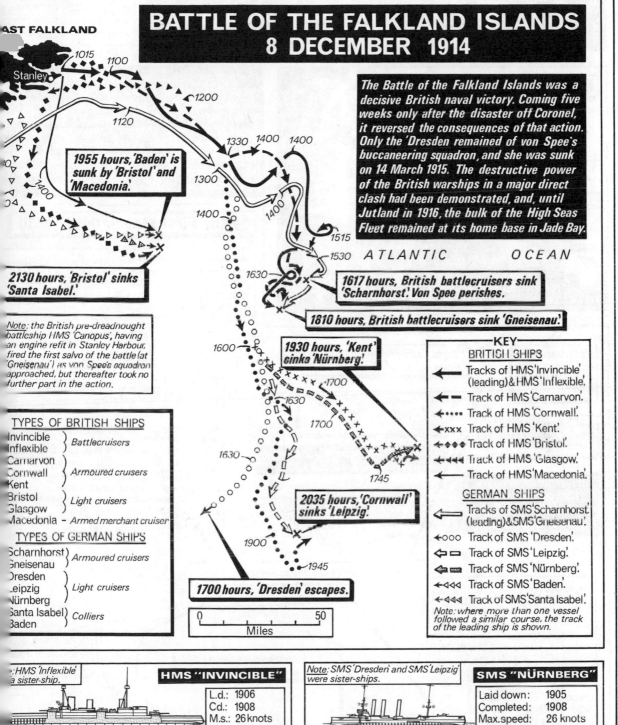

BATTLE OF THE FALKLAND ISLANDS
8 DECEMBER 1914

AST FALKLAND

Stanley

1015
1100
1200
1120
1330 1400 1400
1300
1400 1400
1515
1530

The Battle of the Falkland Islands was a decisive British naval victory. Coming five weeks only after the disaster off Coronel, it reversed the consequences of that action. Only the 'Dresden' remained of von Spee's buccaneering squadron, and she was sunk on 14 March 1915. The destructive power of the British warships in a major direct clash had been demonstrated, and, until Jutland in 1916, the bulk of the High Seas Fleet remained at its home base in Jade Bay.

1955 hours, 'Baden' is sunk by 'Bristol' and 'Macedonia'.

1400

2130 hours, 'Bristol' sinks 'Santa Isabel'.

Note: the British pre-dreadnought battleship HMS 'Canopus', having an engine refit in Stanley Harbour, fired the first salvo of the battle (at 'Gneisenau') as von Spee's squadron approached, but thereafter took no further part in the action.

1630

ATLANTIC OCEAN

1617 hours, British battlecruisers sink 'Scharnhorst'. Von Spee perishes.

1810 hours, British battlecruisers sink 'Gneisenau'.

1600

1930 hours, 'Kent' sinks 'Nürnberg'.

1700
1630
1700
1630

1745

2035 hours, 'Cornwall' sinks 'Leipzig'.

1900

1945

1700 hours, 'Dresden' escapes.

TYPES OF BRITISH SHIPS

Invincible Inflexible	} Battlecruisers
Carnarvon Cornwall	} Armoured cruisers
Kent Bristol Glasgow	} Light cruisers
Macedonia	– Armed merchant cruiser

TYPES OF GERMAN SHIPS

Scharnhorst Gneisenau	} Armoured cruisers
Dresden Leipzig Nürnberg	} Light cruisers
Santa Isabel Baden	} Colliers

KEY
BRITISH SHIPS
← Tracks of HMS 'Invincible' (leading) & HMS 'Inflexible'.
←- - Track of HMS 'Carnarvon'.
←•••• Track of HMS 'Cornwall'.
←xxx Track of HMS 'Kent'.
←♦♦♦ Track of HMS 'Bristol'.
←◄◄◄ Track of HMS 'Glasgow'.
← Track of HMS 'Macedonia'.

GERMAN SHIPS
⇐ Tracks of SMS 'Scharnhorst' (leading) & SMS 'Gneisenau'.
←ooo Track of SMS 'Dresden'.
⇐▢ Track of SMS 'Leipzig'.
⇐▰ Track of SMS 'Nürnberg'.
←◄◄◄ Track of SMS 'Baden'.
←◄◄◄ Track of SMS 'Santa Isabel'.

Note: where more than one vessel followed a similar course, the track of the leading ship is shown.

0 _____ 50
Miles

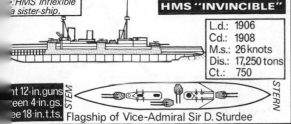

Note: HMS 'Inflexible' is a sister-ship.

HMS "INVINCIBLE"

L.d.:	1906
Cd.:	1908
M.s.:	26 knots
Dis.:	17,250 tons
Ct.:	750

STEM ... STERN

nt 12-in.guns
een 4-in.gs.
ee 18-in.t.t.s. **Flagship of Vice-Admiral Sir D. Sturdee**

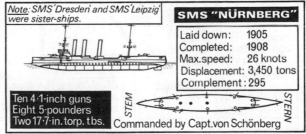

Note: SMS 'Dresden' and SMS 'Leipzig' were sister-ships.

SMS "NÜRNBERG"

Laid down:	1905
Completed:	1908
Max.speed:	26 knots
Displacement:	3,450 tons
Complement:	295

Ten 4·1-inch guns
Eight 5-pounders
Two 17·7-in. torp. tbs. **Commanded by Capt. von Schönberg**

THE BATTLE OF HELIGOLAND BIGHT 28 AUGUST 1914

NOTE: GREENWICH MEAN TIME HAS BEEN ADOPTED FOR TRACK CALCULATIONS

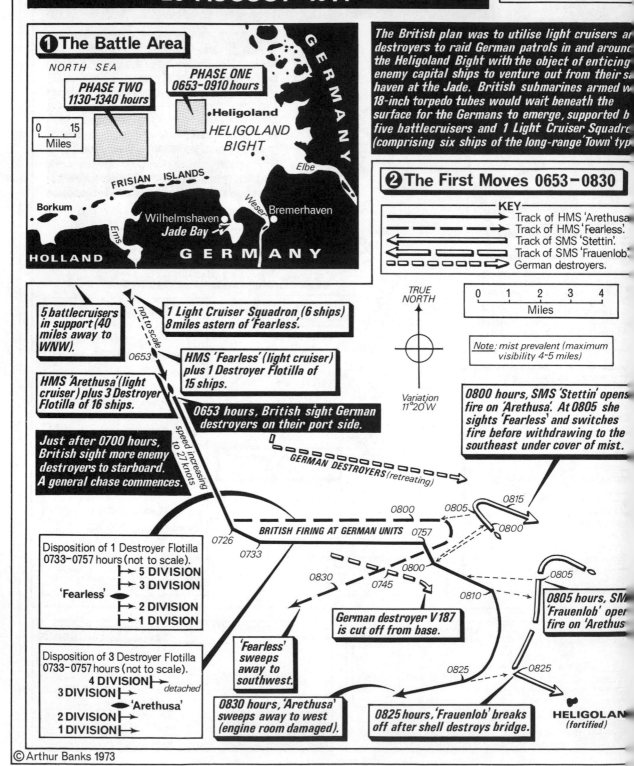

① The Battle Area

NORTH SEA

GERMANY

PHASE TWO 1130-1340 hours

PHASE ONE 0653-0910 hours

• Heligoland

HELIGOLAND BIGHT

0 — 15
Miles

Elbe

FRISIAN ISLANDS

Weser

Borkum

Wilhelmshaven ●
Jade Bay

Bremerhaven ●

Ems

HOLLAND

G E R M A N Y

The British plan was to utilise light cruisers and destroyers to raid German patrols in and around the Heligoland Bight with the object of enticing enemy capital ships to venture out from their safe haven at the Jade. British submarines armed with 18-inch torpedo tubes would wait beneath the surface for the Germans to emerge, supported by five battlecruisers and 1 Light Cruiser Squadron (comprising six ships of the long-range 'Town' type.

② The First Moves 0653-0830

KEY
- Track of HMS 'Arethusa'.
- Track of HMS 'Fearless'.
- Track of SMS 'Stettin'.
- Track of SMS 'Frauenlob'.
- German destroyers.

TRUE NORTH

0 1 2 3 4
Miles

Variation 11°20'W

Note: mist prevalent (maximum visibility 4-5 miles)

5 battlecruisers in support (40 miles away to WNW).

not to scale

0653

1 Light Cruiser Squadron (6 ships) 8 miles astern of 'Fearless'.

HMS 'Fearless' (light cruiser) plus 1 Destroyer Flotilla of 15 ships.

HMS 'Arethusa' (light cruiser) plus 3 Destroyer Flotilla of 16 ships.

0653 hours, British sight German destroyers on their port side.

speed increasing to 27 knots

Just after 0700 hours, British sight more enemy destroyers to starboard. A general chase commences.

0800 hours, SMS 'Stettin' opens fire on 'Arethusa'. At 0805 she sights 'Fearless' and switches fire before withdrawing to the southeast under cover of mist.

GERMAN DESTROYERS (retreating)

0800   0805   0815
0800

BRITISH FIRING AT GERMAN UNITS   0757

0726
0733

Disposition of 1 Destroyer Flotilla 0733-0757 hours (not to scale).
→ 5 DIVISION
→ 3 DIVISION
'Fearless' ●
→ 2 DIVISION
→ 1 DIVISION

0830   0745   0800   0810   0805

German destroyer V 187 is cut off from base.

0805 hours, SMS 'Frauenlob' opens fire on 'Arethusa'.

Disposition of 3 Destroyer Flotilla 0733-0757 hours (not to scale).
4 DIVISION → detached
3 DIVISION →
● 'Arethusa'
2 DIVISION →
1 DIVISION →

'Fearless' sweeps away to southwest.

0825   0825

0830 hours, 'Arethusa' sweeps away to west (engine room damaged).

0825 hours, 'Frauenlob' breaks off after shell destroys bridge.

HELIGOLAND (fortified)

© Arthur Banks 1973

The Sinking of German Destroyer V 187

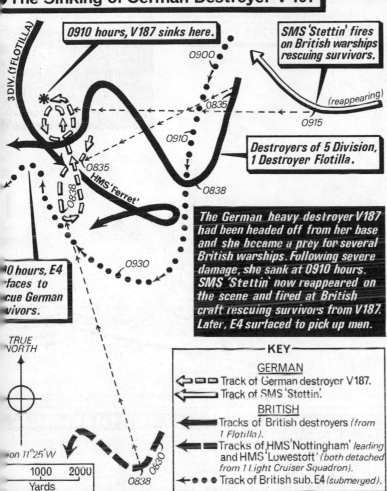

0910 hours, V 187 sinks here.

0900

SMS 'Stettin' fires on British warships rescuing survivors.

3 DIV. (1 FLOTILLA)

0835

(reappearing)

0915

0910

0835

Destroyers of 5 Division, 1 Destroyer Flotilla.

HMS 'Ferret'

0838

0838

0930

0 hours, E4 faces to cue German vivors.

The German heavy destroyer V 187 had been headed off from her base and she became a prey for several British warships. Following severe damage, she sank at 0910 hours. SMS 'Stettin' now reappeared on the scene and fired at British craft rescuing survivors from V 187. Later, E4 surfaced to pick up men.

TRUE NORTH

ion 11°25'W

1000   2000
Yards

0630

0838

KEY

GERMAN
⇦▭▭ Track of German destroyer V 187.
⬅ Track of SMS 'Stettin'.

BRITISH
⬅ Tracks of British destroyers (from 1 Flotilla).
⬅ Tracks of HMS 'Nottingham' leading and HMS 'Lowestoft' (both detached from 1 Light Cruiser Squadron).
◄••• Track of British sub. E4 (submerged).

SMS 'STETTIN'

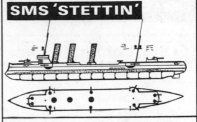

Ten 4·1-in. guns.	Laid down: 1905.
Eight 5-pdrs.	Completed: 1908.
Length: 360 feet.	Complement: 320.
Beam: 44 feet.	Displacement: 3,450 tons.

SMS 'FRAUENLOB'

Ten 4·1-in. guns.	Laid down: 1900.
Ten 1-pdrs.	Completed: 1903.
Length: 330 feet.	Complement: 265.
Beam: 40 feet.	Displacement: 2,715 tons.

V 187

Note: the letter 'V' referred to the Vulkan construction yard at Stettin.

Two 24-pdr. guns.	Complement: 84.
Three 18-in. torp. tbs.	Max. speed: 35 knots.

E4

Built by Vickers at Chatham, the 'E' referred to the class. The serial no. was 84.

Five 18-in. torp. tubes.	One 12-pdr. gun.
Displacement: 700 tons.	Length: 181 feet.
Complement: 30.	Beam: 22·5 feet.

MS 'ARETHUSA'

Light cruiser of 'Arethusa' class.

Laid down:	1912.	Two 6-inch guns (as built; later a third was added, replacing part of 4-inch armament).
Completed:	1914.	
Length:	450 feet.	
Beam:	39 feet.	Six 4-inch guns.
Complement:	319.	Two 3-inch guns.
Displacement:	3,512 tons.	Eight 21-inch torp. tbs.
Max. speed:	29 knots.	(four above water).

MS 'FEARLESS'

Scout light cruiser of 'Active' class.

Laid down:	1911.	Ten 4-inch guns.
Completed:	1913.	Four 3-pounder guns.
Length:	385 feet.	Two 21-inch torp. tbs.
Beam:	41·5 feet.	Armour: nil.
Complement:	320.	(double skin amidships).
Displacement:	3,440 tons.	Mean draught: 14 feet.
Max. speed:	26 knots.	H.P. 18,000.

The German battlecruisers were "trapped" behind the sand bar at the Jade and could not move out until high tide. Meanwhile, several cruisers were despatched at full speed to engage the enemy (unaware of the British battlecruisers being near at hand). SMS 'Strassburg' and SMS 'Mainz' were the first arrivals.

0   10,0...
Yards

❹ Start of Phase Two: Operations 1130–1200 hours

Note: mist and haze prevalent.

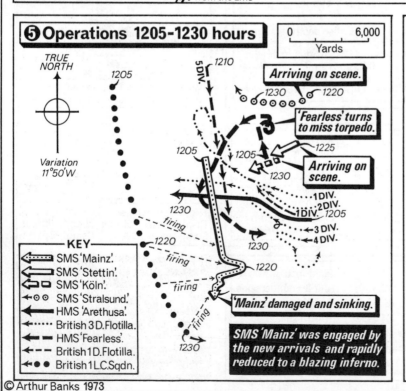

1150

1200

1150

1200

1155

1200

2 & 3 DIVS.

5 DIV.

1150

1150

1200

1155

1150

1145

1200

1 DIVISION

1145

1140

firing

firing

firing

1140

1140

1130

2 DIVISION

1125

1145

1130

1130

3 DIVISION

1135

1130

1135

5 DIVISION

1200

1140

firing

TRUE NORTH

Variation 11°45′W

1140

1 DIVIS
2 DIVIS
3 DIVIS
4 DIVIS

1130

SMS 'Mainz' turns to south after spotting approach of British 1 Light Cruiser Squadron.

1DIV.
2DIV.

1200

1145

1130

KEY
←	HMS 'Arethusa'.
←····	British 3 Dest. Flotilla.
← ―	HMS 'Fearless'.
← – –	British 1 Dest. Flotilla.
←••••	British 1 Lt. Cruiser Sqdn.
⟸▭▭	SMS 'Mainz'.
⟸▭▭	SMS 'Strassburg'.

↑ from the Ems

❺ Operations 1205–1230 hours

0   6,000
Yards

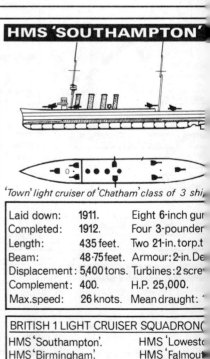

TRUE NORTH

Variation 11°50′W

1205

1210

5 DIV.

1230

1220

Arriving on scene.

'Fearless' turns to miss torpedo.

1225

1205

1205

1230

Arriving on scene.

1DIV.
2DIV.
1205

1DIV.

3 DIV.

4 DIV.

1230

1230

1220

firing

1220

firing

1220

firing

1230

firing

'Mainz' damaged and sinking.

SMS 'Mainz' was engaged by the new arrivals and rapidly reduced to a blazing inferno.

KEY
⟸▭▭	SMS 'Mainz'.
⟸▭	SMS 'Stettin'.
⟸▭	SMS 'Köln'.
←⊙⊙	SMS 'Stralsund'.
←	HMS 'Arethusa'.
←····	British 3 D. Flotilla.
← ―	HMS 'Fearless'.
← – –	British 1 D. Flotilla.
←•••	British 1 L.C. Sqdn.

© Arthur Banks 1973

HMS 'SOUTHAMPTON'

'Town' light cruiser of 'Chatham' class of 3 shi...

Laid down:	1911.	Eight 6-inch gu...
Completed:	1912.	Four 3-pounder...
Length:	435 feet.	Two 21-in. torp.t...
Beam:	48·75 feet.	Armour: 2-in. De...
Displacement:	5,400 tons.	Turbines: 2 scre...
Complement:	400.	H.P. 25,000.
Max. speed:	26 knots.	Mean draught: 1...

BRITISH 1 LIGHT CRUISER SQUADRON
HMS 'Southampton'.	HMS 'Lowest...
HMS 'Birmingham'.	HMS 'Falmout...
HMS 'Nottingham'.	HMS 'Liverpo...

The Final Moves: 1230-1340 hours

[R]ealizing that sizable German reinforcements were arriving on [th]e scene, the British battlecruisers were called into action. [Th]eir fire-power proved decisive: SMS 'Köln' was sunk and SMS [Ar]iadne' severely damaged (sinking later). Only the mist shroud [pr]evented the remaining German ships from suffering like fates.

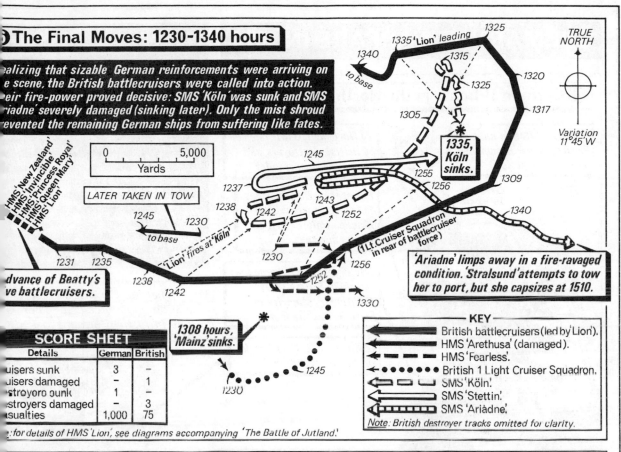

1335 'Lion' leading

TRUE NORTH

1325

1340 to base

1315

1320

1305

1325

1317

1309

1335, Köln sinks.

Variation 11°45'W

1245

1255

1256

1340

1237

1238

1243

1252

1242

1256

(1 Lt.Cruiser Squadron in rear of battlecruiser force)

'Lion' fires at 'Köln'

1245

1230

1230

1252

1330

'Ariadne' limps away in a fire-ravaged condition. 'Stralsund' attempts to tow her to port, but she capsizes at 1510.

0 — 5,000
Yards

LATER TAKEN IN TOW

1245

1230

to base

1231 1235

1238

1242

[A]dvance of Beatty's [fi]ve battlecruisers.

1308 hours, 'Mainz' sinks.

1245

1230

KEY

◀━━━	British battlecruisers (led by 'Lion').
◀━━	HMS 'Arethusa' (damaged).
◀- - -	HMS 'Fearless'.
◀••••••	British 1 Light Cruiser Squadron.
◁▭▭▭	SMS 'Köln'.
◁━━━	SMS 'Stettin'.
◁▦▦▦	SMS 'Ariadne'.

Note: British destroyer tracks omitted for clarity.

SCORE SHEET

Details	German	British
[Cr]uisers sunk	3	–
[Cr]uisers damaged	–	1
[De]stroyers sunk	1	–
[De]stroyers damaged	–	3
[Ca]sualties	1,000	75

[Note]: for details of HMS 'Lion', see diagrams accompanying 'The Battle of Jutland'.

[S]MS 'MAINZ' & SMS 'KÖLN'

Note: both ships were light cruisers of the 'Kolberg' class.

Laid down:	1907 } 'Mainz'	Twelve 4·1-inch guns.	
Completed:	1909	Four 5-pounder guns.	
Laid down:	1908 } 'Köln'	Four machine guns.	
Completed:	1910	Two 18-inch torpedo tubes.	
Length:	428 feet.	Complement:	375.
Beam:	46 feet.	Max. speed:	27 knots.
Displacement:	4,350 tons.	Max. draught:	10 feet.

[S]MS 'ARIADNE'

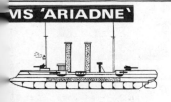

Protected cruiser of 'Nymphe' class.

Laid down:	1899.	Ten 4·1-inch guns.	
Completed:	1901.	Fourteen 1-pounder guns.	
Length:	328 feet.	Four machine guns.	
Beam:	40 feet.	Two 17·7-inch torp. tubes.	
Complement:	265.	Max. draught: 17·25 feet.	
Displacement:	2,670 tons.	Armour: 2-in. Deck (amid.).	
Max. speed:	21 knots.	" 1-in. Deck (ends).	

[S]MS 'STRASSBURG'

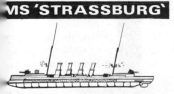

Note: SMS 'Stralsund' was a sister-ship. (Similar details, including later armament alterations).

Light cruiser of 'Breslau' class.

Laid down:	1910.	Twelve 4·1-inch guns.
Completed:	1912.	(*Note*: later altered to seven 5·9-inch and two 3·4-inch A.A. guns).
Length:	445 feet.	
Beam:	43 feet.	
Complement:	370.	Two 20-inch torp. tubes.
Displacement:	4,550 tons.	Mean draught: 16·5 feet.
Max. speed:	28 knots.	Armour: 2-in. Deck (amid.).

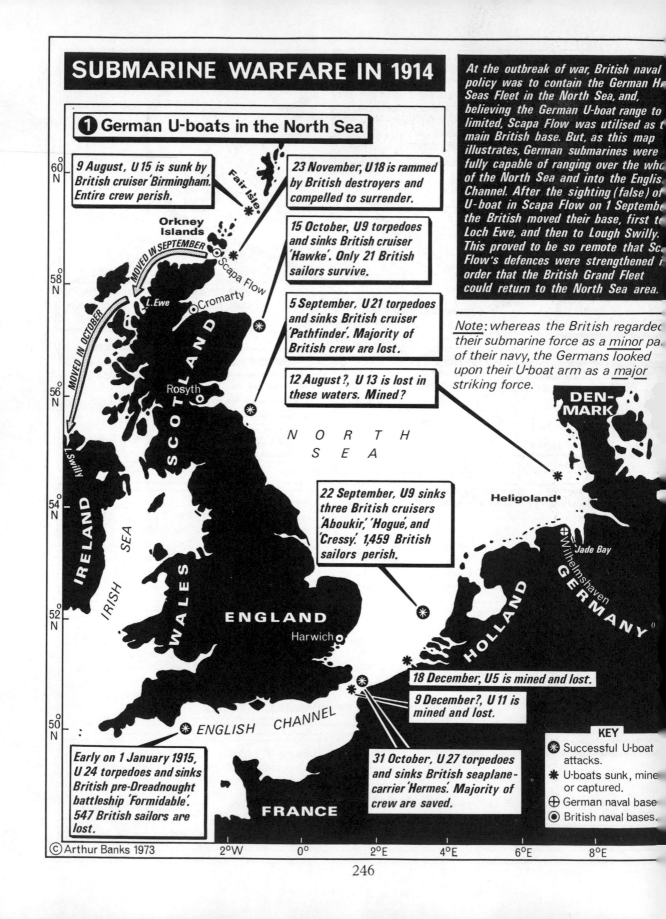

SUBMARINE WARFARE IN 1914

① German U-boats in the North Sea

At the outbreak of war, British naval policy was to contain the German H Seas Fleet in the North Sea, and, believing the German U-boat range to limited, Scapa Flow was utilised as t main British base. But, as this map illustrates, German submarines were fully capable of ranging over the whc of the North Sea and into the Englis Channel. After the sighting (false) of U-boat in Scapa Flow on 1 Septembe the British moved their base, first to Loch Ewe, and then to Lough Swilly. This proved to be so remote that Sca Flow's defences were strengthened i order that the British Grand Fleet could return to the North Sea area.

Note: whereas the British regarded their submarine force as a _minor_ pa of their navy, the Germans looked upon their U-boat arm as a _major_ striking force.

9 August, U 15 is sunk by British cruiser 'Birmingham'. Entire crew perish.

23 November, U 18 is rammed by British destroyers and compelled to surrender.

15 October, U 9 torpedoes and sinks British cruiser 'Hawke'. Only 21 British sailors survive.

5 September, U 21 torpedoes and sinks British cruiser 'Pathfinder'. Majority of British crew are lost.

12 August?, U 13 is lost in these waters. Mined?

22 September, U 9 sinks three British cruisers 'Aboukir', 'Hogue', and 'Cressy'. 1,459 British sailors perish.

Early on 1 January 1915, U 24 torpedoes and sinks British pre-Dreadnought battleship 'Formidable'. 547 British sailors are lost.

31 October, U 27 torpedoes and sinks British seaplane-carrier 'Hermes'. Majority of crew are saved.

18 December, U 5 is mined and lost.

9 December?, U 11 is mined and lost.

Fair Isle

Orkney Islands

MOVED IN SEPTEMBER

Scapa Flow

L. Ewe · Cromarty

MOVED IN OCTOBER

Rosyth

SCOTLAND

IRELAND

IRISH SEA

SWILLY?

WALES

ENGLAND

Harwich

WALES

N O R T H   S E A

DEN-MARK

Heligoland•

Jade Bay

Wilhelmshaven

GERMANY

HOLLAND

ENGLISH   CHANNEL

FRANCE

© Arthur Banks 1973

KEY

✸ Successful U-boat attacks.
✱ U-boats sunk, mine or captured.
⊕ German naval base
◉ British naval bases.

60° N · 58° N · 56° N · 54° N · 52° N · 50° N

2°W · 0° · 2°E · 4°E · 6°E · 8°E

246

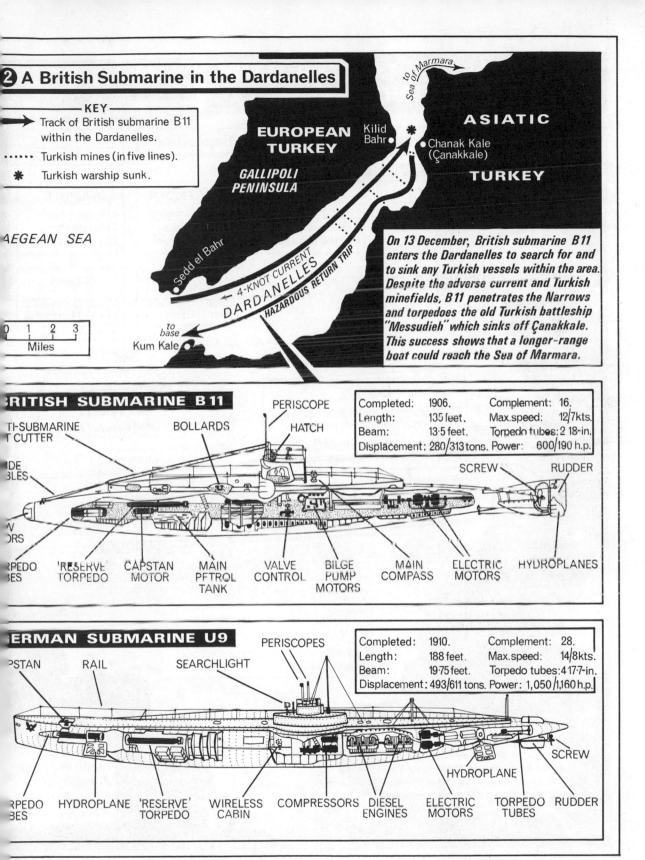

② A British Submarine in the Dardanelles

KEY
- ➤ Track of British submarine B 11 within the Dardanelles.
- ····· Turkish mines (in five lines).
- ✱ Turkish warship sunk.

AEGEAN SEA

EUROPEAN TURKEY

GALLIPOLI PENINSULA

Kilid Bahr

Chanak Kale (Çanakkale)

ASIATIC TURKEY

to Sea of Marmara

Sedd el Bahr

4-KNOT CURRENT

DARDANELLES

HAZARDOUS RETURN TRIP

to base
Kum Kale

Miles
0 1 2 3

On 13 December, British submarine B 11 enters the Dardanelles to search for and to sink any Turkish vessels within the area. Despite the adverse current and Turkish minefields, B 11 penetrates the Narrows and torpedoes the old Turkish battleship "Messudieh" which sinks off Çanakkale. This success shows that a longer-range boat could reach the Sea of Marmara.

BRITISH SUBMARINE B 11

Completed:	1906.	Complement:	16.
Length:	135 feet.	Max. speed:	12/7 kts.
Beam:	13·5 feet.	Torpedo tubes:	2 18-in.
Displacement:	280/313 tons.	Power:	600/190 h.p.

PERISCOPE · HATCH · BOLLARDS
ANTI-SUBMARINE NET CUTTER
SCREW · RUDDER

TORPEDO TUBES · 'RESERVE' TORPEDO · CAPSTAN MOTOR · MAIN PETROL TANK · VALVE CONTROL · BILGE PUMP MOTORS · MAIN COMPASS · ELECTRIC MOTORS · HYDROPLANES

GERMAN SUBMARINE U9

Completed:	1910.	Complement:	28.
Length:	188 feet.	Max. speed:	14/8 kts.
Beam:	19·75 feet.	Torpedo tubes:	4 17·7-in.
Displacement:	493/611 tons.	Power:	1,050/1,160 h.p.

PERISCOPES · SEARCHLIGHT · RAIL · CAPSTAN

TORPEDO TUBES · HYDROPLANE · 'RESERVE' TORPEDO · WIRELESS CABIN · COMPRESSORS · DIESEL ENGINES · ELECTRIC MOTORS · HYDROPLANE · TORPEDO TUBES · SCREW · RUDDER

BATTLE OF THE DOGGER BANK 24 JANUARY 1915

Note: in August 1914, SMS 'Magdeburg' (a German light cruiser of the 'Breslau' class) was lost in the Baltic. The Russians recovered its signal code book and passed them to the Admiralty in London. British cypher experts utilised these for decoding purposes.

① Eve of Battle: The Rival Commanders and Dispositions

0 — 80 Miles

Orkney Islands
Scapa Flow · Ronaldsay

Commander-in-Chief, BRITISH GRAND FLEET

JELLICOE
1 Battleship
1 Light Cruiser
1 Destroyer

BURNEY
1 Battle Squadron
7 Battleships
1 Light Cruiser

WARRENDER
2 Battle Squadron
6 Battleships
1 Light Cruiser

GAMBLE
4 Battle Squadron
7 Battleships
1 Light Cruiser

Cromarty Firth

GOUGH-CALTHORPE
2 Cruiser Squadron
3 Armoured Cruisers
PLUS
1 Light Cruiser } 4 DEST. FLOT.
21 Destroyers }

Peterhead ▲

ARBUTHNOT
1 Cruiser Squadron
3 Arm'd Cruisers

GRANT
6 Cruiser Squadron
3 Arm'd Cruisers

SCOTLAND

NORTH SEA

NAPIER
2 Light Cruiser Squadron
3 Light Cruisers
PLUS
1 Light Cruiser } 2 DEST. FLOT.
21 Destroyers }

Rosyth · Forth · May Island ▲

Beatty
1 Battlecruiser Squadron (**BEATTY**)
3 'fast' Battlecruisers *(M.Speed 29 ks.)*
2 Battlecruiser Squadron (**MOORE**)
2 'slow' Battlecruisers *(M.Speed 26 ks)*

Bamburgh ▲

PAKENHAM
3 Cruiser Squadron
3 Arm'd Cruisers

BRADFORD
3 Battle Squadron
6 Battleships
1 Light Cruiser

DOGGER BANK

GOODENOUGH
1 Light Cruiser Squadron
4 'Town' Light Cruisers

Sylt

Flamborough Head ▲

IRISH SEA

KEY
☐ British dispositions.
▒ German dispositions.
△ ▲ British directional wireless stations.
○ ● Naval bases.

Heligoland

ENGLAND

The Wash

WALES

Cypher experts at Admiralty (Room 40) decode German sailing signals which have been intercepted by the British directional wireless stations.

TYRWHITT
3 Light Cruisers
35 Destroyers

KEYES
2 Destroyers
4 Submarines

Zuyder Zee

Jade Bay

HIPPER
1 Scouting Group.
3 Battlecruisers
1 Armoured Cruiser
2 Scouting Group.
4 Light Cruisers
18 Destroyers

HOLLAND

Harwich
Thames

LONDON

Severn

BELGIUM

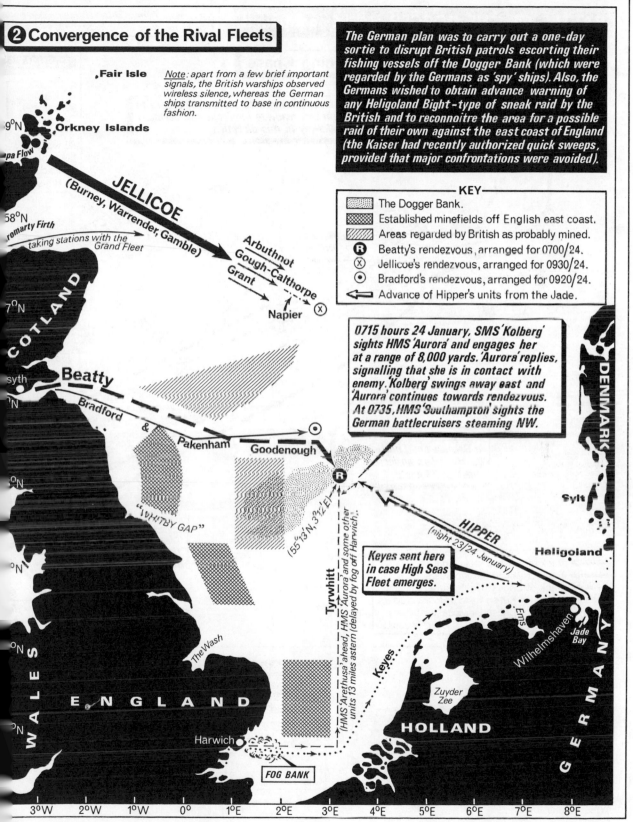

② Convergence of the Rival Fleets

Fair Isle

Note: apart from a few brief important signals, the British warships observed wireless silence, whereas the German ships transmitted to base in continuous fashion.

The German plan was to carry out a one-day sortie to disrupt British patrols escorting their fishing vessels off the Dogger Bank (which were regarded by the Germans as 'spy' ships). Also, the Germans wished to obtain advance warning of any Heligoland Bight-type of sneak raid by the British and to reconnoitre the area for a possible raid of their own against the east coast of England (the Kaiser had recently authorized quick sweeps, provided that major confrontations were avoided).

KEY
- The Dogger Bank.
- Established minefields off English east coast.
- Areas regarded by British as probably mined.
- ® Beatty's rendezvous, arranged for 0700/24.
- ⓧ Jellicoe's rendezvous, arranged for 0930/24.
- ⊙ Bradford's rendezvous, arranged for 0920/24.
- ⬅ Advance of Hipper's units from the Jade.

0715 hours 24 January, SMS 'Kolberg' sights HMS 'Aurora' and engages her at a range of 8,000 yards. 'Aurora' replies, signalling that she is in contact with enemy. 'Kolberg' swings away east and 'Aurora' continues towards rendezvous. At 0735, HMS 'Southampton' sights the German battlecruisers steaming NW.

Keyes sent here in case High Seas Fleet emerges.

Orkney Islands

9°N

Scapa Flow

JELLICOE
(Burney, Warrender, Gamble)

58°N Cromarty Firth

taking stations with the Grand Fleet

Arbuthnot
Gough-Calthorpe
Grant
Napier

7°N

COTLAND

Forsyth

Beatty

Bradford

Pakenham

Goodenough

& Bradford

"WHITBY GAP"

(55°13′N, 3½′E)

Tyrwhitt

(HMS 'Arethusa' ahead, HMS 'Aurora and some other units 13 miles astern (delayed by fog off Harwich)..

The Wash

WALES

E N G L A N D

Harwich

FOG BANK

HOLLAND

Zuyder Zee

Keyes

HIPPER

(night 23/24 January)

DENMARK

Sylt

Heligoland

Ems

Wilhelmshaven

Jade Bay

G E R M A N Y

3°W 2°W 1°W 0° 1°E 2°E 3°E 4°E 5°E 6°E 7°E 8°E

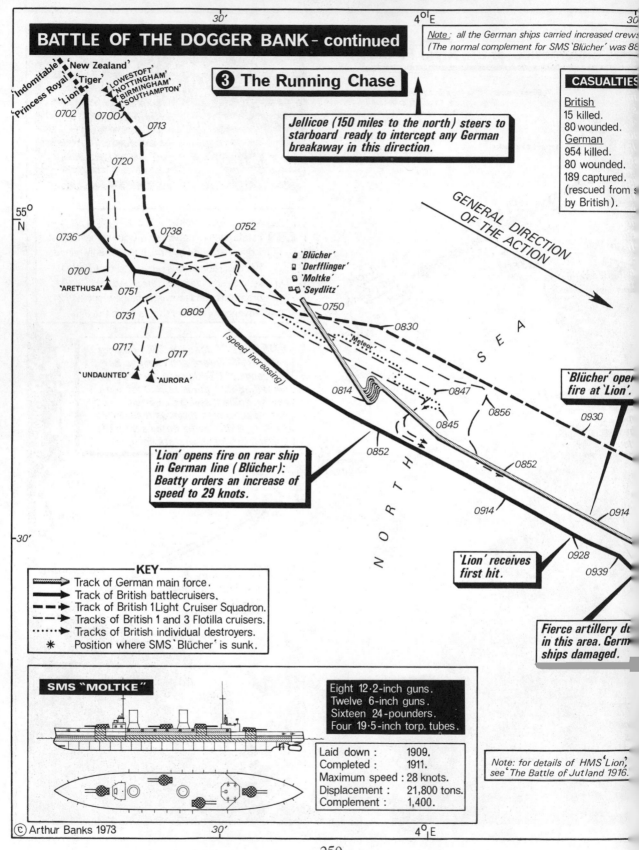

❸ The Running Chase

Note: all the German ships carried increased crews
(The normal complement for SMS 'Blücher' was 88

Jellicoe (150 miles to the north) steers to starboard ready to intercept any German breakaway in this direction.

GENERAL DIRECTION OF THE ACTION

CASUALTIES

British
15 killed.
80 wounded.
German
954 killed.
80 wounded.
189 captured.
(rescued from s
by British).

'Indomitable'
'New Zealand'
'Princess Royal' 'Tiger'
'Lion'
LOWESTOFT'
NOTTINGHAM'
BIRMINGHAM'
SOUTHAMPTON'

0702
0700
0713
0720
0736
0700
'ARETHUSA'
0751
0731
0717
'UNDAUNTED'
0717
'AURORA'
0738
0752
0809
(speed increasing)

🚩 'Blücher'
🚩 'Derfflinger'
🚩 'Moltke'
🚩🚩 'Seydlitz'

0750
'Meteor'
0830
0814
0847
0845
0856
0852
0852

55°
N

N O R T H   S E A

'Blücher' ope
fire at 'Lion'.

0930

'Lion' opens fire on rear ship in German line (Blücher): Beatty orders an increase of speed to 29 knots.

'Lion' receives first hit.

0914
0914
0928
0939

30'

Fierce artillery du
in this area. Germ
ships damaged.

KEY
- ▭▭▭▷ Track of German main force.
- ━━━▶ Track of British battlecruisers.
- ┅┅┅▶ Track of British 1 Light Cruiser Squadron.
- ╌╌╌▶ Tracks of British 1 and 3 Flotilla cruisers.
- ·······▶ Tracks of British individual destroyers.
- ✳ Position where SMS 'Blücher' is sunk.

SMS "MOLTKE"

Eight 12·2-inch guns.
Twelve 6-inch guns.
Sixteen 24-pounders.
Four 19·5-inch torp. tubes.

Laid down : 1909.
Completed : 1911.
Maximum speed : 28 knots.
Displacement : 21,800 tons.
Complement : 1,400.

Note: for details of HMS 'Lion',
see 'The Battle of Jutland 1916.'

Ⓒ Arthur Banks 1973

30'
4°E

250

is chart shows the 'running chase' th the Germans as the hare and e British as the hounds. During action, the 'Blücher' was sunk 'Seydlitz' and 'Derfflinger' badly maged. On the British side, 'Lion' s severely damaged but reached t safely. The action had portant results: the Germans lised the significance of cordite hes in turrets, but the British not (as the Jutland encounter 916 was to prove): ish signalling and nery were shown to be nting: the Germans saw a direct surface frontation with the British a hazardous venture, and centrated more attention their submarine force.

SMS "BLÜCHER"

Twelve 8·2-inch guns.
Eight 6-inch guns.
Sixteen 24-pounders.
Three torpedo tubes.

Laid down : 1906.
Completed : 1909.
Maximum speed : 26 knots.
Displacement : 15,500 tons.
Complement : 1,100.

SMS "SEYDLITZ"

Ten 11-inch guns.
Twelve 6-inch guns.
Twelve 24-pounders.
Four 14-pounders (A.A.)
Four 20-inch torp. tubes.

Laid down : 1911.
Completed : 1913.
Maximum speed : 29 knots.
Displacement : 24,610 tons.
Complement : 1,400.

Flagship of Rear-Admiral Hipper

55°N

man destroyers throw heavy smoke screen as lecruisers race for home.

'Seydlitz' is badly damaged in the aftermost turret.

The British were increasing speed as the chase developed, and a crushing victory appeared likely. However, from 1045 hours onwards, a series of misinterpreted signals from 'Lion' caused the British battlecruisers to concentrate on 'Blücher', thus enabling the remaining German ships to slip the net and escape.

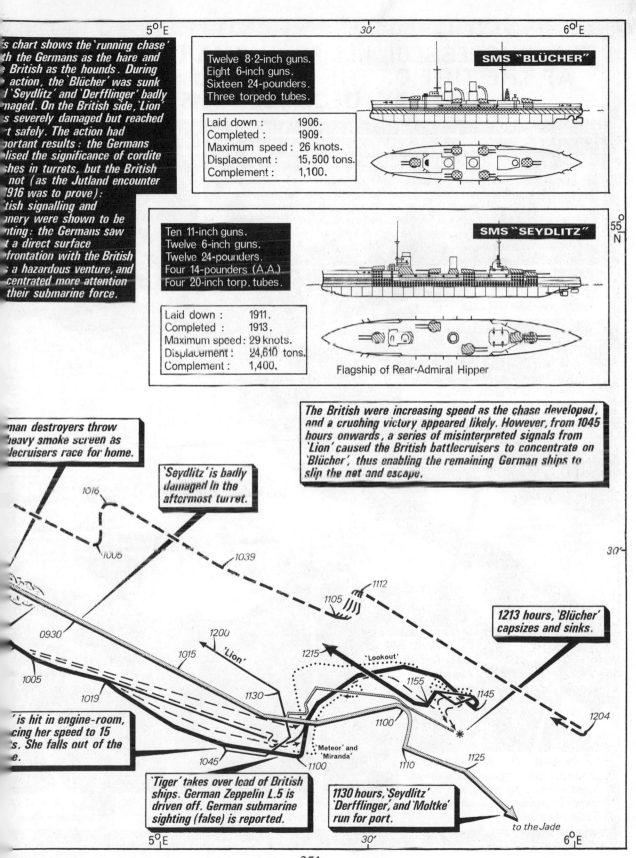

1016
1005
1039
1112
1105
0930
1015
1200
'Lion'
1215
'Lookout'
1005
1019
1130
1155
1145
1100
1045
1100
'Meteor' and 'Miranda'
1110
1125
1204

1213 hours, 'Blücher' capsizes and sinks.

30'

' is hit in engine-room, cing her speed to 15 s. She falls out of the e.

'Tiger' takes over lead of British ships. German Zeppelin L.5 is driven off. German submarine sighting (false) is reported.

1130 hours, 'Seydlitz' 'Derfflinger', and 'Moltke' run for port.

to the Jade

THE SUCCESSFUL ALLIED SUBMARINE CAMPAIGN AT THE TIME OF THE GALLIPOLI EXPEDITION MAY - DECEMBER 1915

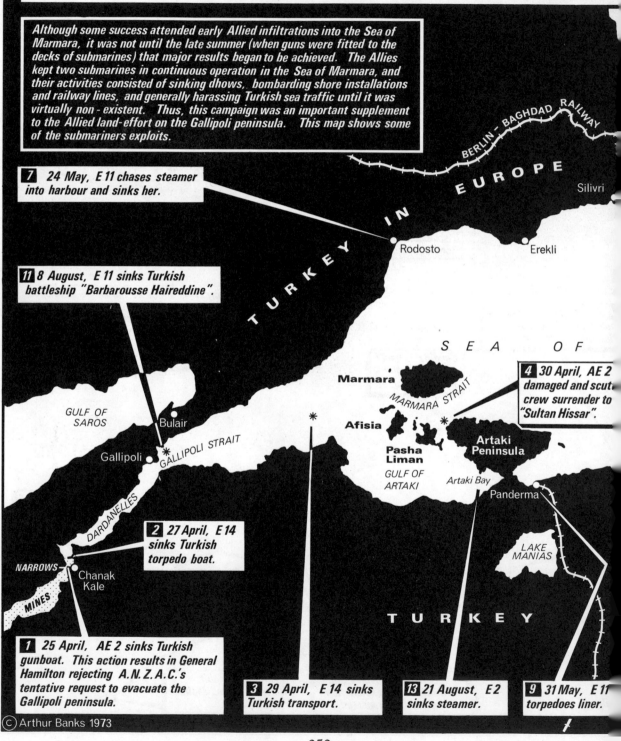

Although some success attended early Allied infiltrations into the Sea of Marmara, it was not until the late summer (when guns were fitted to the decks of submarines) that major results began to be achieved. The Allies kept two submarines in continuous operation in the Sea of Marmara, and their activities consisted of sinking dhows, bombarding shore installations and railway lines, and generally harassing Turkish sea traffic until it was virtually non - existent. Thus, this campaign was an important supplement to the Allied land-effort on the Gallipoli peninsula. This map shows some of the submariners exploits.

7 24 May, E 11 chases steamer into harbour and sinks her.

11 8 August, E 11 sinks Turkish battleship "Barbarousse Haireddine".

4 30 April, AE 2 damaged and scut... crew surrender to "Sultan Hissar".

2 27 April, E 14 sinks Turkish torpedo boat.

1 25 April, AE 2 sinks Turkish gunboat. This action results in General Hamilton rejecting A.N.Z.A.C.'s tentative request to evacuate the Gallipoli peninsula.

3 29 April, E 14 sinks Turkish transport.

13 21 August, E 2 sinks steamer.

9 31 May, E 11 torpedoes liner.

BERLIN - BAGHDAD RAILWAY

TURKEY IN EUROPE

Silivri

Rodosto

Erekli

SEA OF

Marmara

MARMARA STRAIT

Afisia

Pasha Liman

GULF OF ARTAKI

Artaki Peninsula

Artaki Bay

Panderma

LAKE MANIAS

GULF OF SAROS

Bulair

Gallipoli

GALLIPOLI STRAIT

DARDANELLES

NARROWS

Chanak Kale

MINES

TURKEY

© Arthur Banks 1973

252

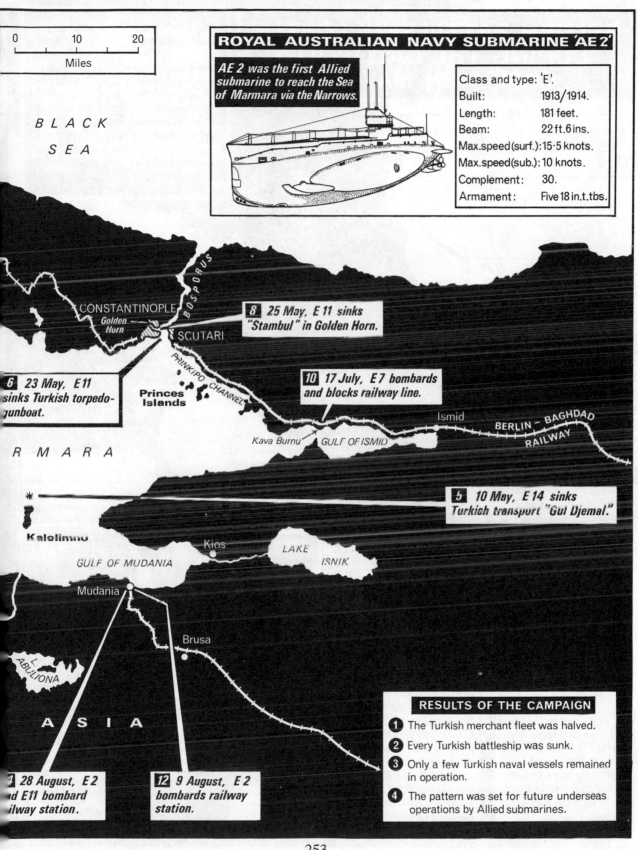

ROYAL AUSTRALIAN NAVY SUBMARINE 'AE 2'

AE 2 was the first Allied submarine to reach the Sea of Marmara via the Narrows.

Class and type: 'E'.
Built: 1913/1914.
Length: 181 feet.
Beam: 22 ft.6 ins.
Max.speed (surf.): 15·5 knots.
Max.speed (sub.): 10 knots.
Complement: 30.
Armament: Five 18 in.t.tbs.

BLACK SEA

BOSPORUS

CONSTANTINOPLE
Golden Horn
SCUTARI

8 25 May, E 11 sinks "Stambul" in Golden Horn.

6 23 May, E 11 sinks Turkish torpedo-gunboat.

PRINKIPO CHANNEL

Princes Islands

10 17 July, E 7 bombards and blocks railway line.

Ismid

BERLIN – BAGHDAD RAILWAY

Kava Burnu   GULF OF ISMID

MARMARA

5 10 May, E 14 sinks Turkish transport "Gul Djemal."

Kalolimno

Kios

LAKE ISNIK

GULF OF MUDANIA

Mudania

Brusa

L. ABULIONA

ASIA

RESULTS OF THE CAMPAIGN

1 The Turkish merchant fleet was halved.

2 Every Turkish battleship was sunk.

3 Only a few Turkish naval vessels remained in operation.

4 The pattern was set for future underseas operations by Allied submarines.

14 28 August, E 2 and E11 bombard railway station.

12 9 August, E 2 bombards railway station.

0   10   20
Miles

BRITISH BATTLESHIP LOSSES DURING THE GALLIPOLI CAMPAIGN MAY 1915

KEY
* ✳ Positions of the three British battleships when sunk during May.
* ★ Main forts.

On 12 May, HMS "Queen Elizabeth" was ordered home from the Aegean area to strengthen the British Grand Fleet. On 13 May, the British battleship HMS "Goliath" was sunk by a Turkish destroyer, and later in the month the U21 sank two more British battleships. The Allied heavy warships were withdrawn from the Gallipoli operations leaving the land troops with no large naval guns to support them until the new monitors arrived in August.

Boghali

Gaba Tepe

2 1225 hours 25 May, U 21 torpedoes HMS "Triumph" in full view of A.N.Z.A.C. troops. 3 British officers and 70 men are lost. De Robeck promptly recalls all large warships to Mudros: this causes a demoralizing effect upon the Allied troops on land. HMS "Majestic" is ordered to 'W' Beach on 26 May.

Maidos

GALLIPOLI PENINSULA

DARDANELLES

Kilid Bahr

Chanak Kale

AEGEAN SEA

Krithia

0 1 2 3
Miles

'W' Beach

Cape Helles

Morto Bay

Eski Hissarlik Pt.

1 0116 hours 13 May, HMS "Goliath" is sunk by Turkish destroyer "Muavenet-i-Miliet." Operating under cover of a thick mist, the destroyer fires three torpedoes. 570 British officers and men are lost. This is the largest single disaster suffered by the Royal Navy throughout the entire Dardanelles and Gallipoli campaign.

3 0645 hours 27 May, U 21 fires two torpedoes at HMS "Majestic". The "fish" penetrate the protecting torpedo-nets and British battleship sinks with the loss of 40 men.

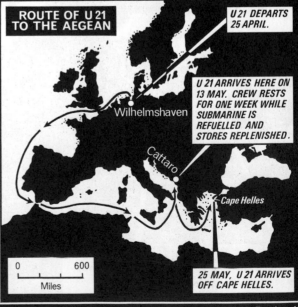

ROUTE OF U 21 TO THE AEGEAN

U 21 DEPARTS 25 APRIL.

U 21 ARRIVES HERE ON 13 MAY. CREW RESTS FOR ONE WEEK WHILE SUBMARINE IS REFUELLED AND STORES REPLENISHED.

Wilhelmshaven

Cattaro

Cape Helles

0 600
Miles

25 MAY, U 21 ARRIVES OFF CAPE HELLES.

© Arthur Banks 1973

254

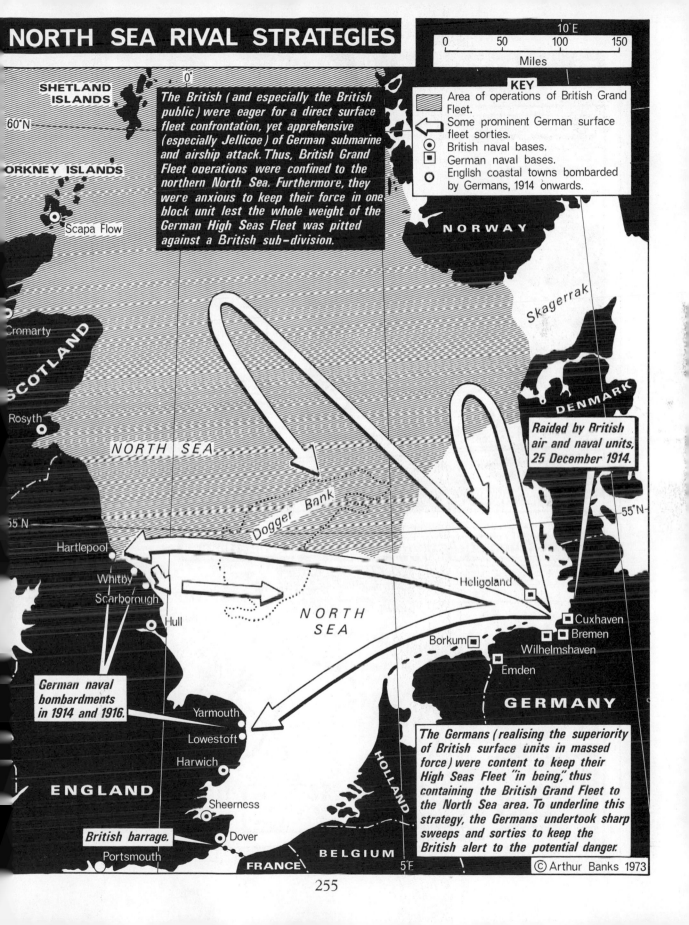

NORTH SEA RIVAL STRATEGIES

KEY

Area of operations of British Grand Fleet.

Some prominent German surface fleet sorties.

British naval bases.

German naval bases.

English coastal towns bombarded by Germans, 1914 onwards.

10°E

0 50 100 150
Miles

SHETLAND ISLANDS

60°N

ORKNEY ISLANDS

Scapa Flow

NORWAY

Cromarty

SCOTLAND

Rosyth

NORTH SEA

Skagerrak

DENMARK

The British (and especially the British public) were eager for a direct surface fleet confrontation, yet apprehensive (especially Jellicoe) of German submarine and airship attack. Thus, British Grand Fleet operations were confined to the northern North Sea. Furthermore, they were anxious to keep their force in one block unit lest the whole weight of the German High Seas Fleet was pitted against a British sub-division.

Raided by British air and naval units, 25 December 1914.

55°N

Dogger Bank

Hartlepool

Whitby

Scarborough

Hull

NORTH SEA

Heligoland

Cuxhaven

Bremen

Borkum

Wilhelmshaven

Emden

German naval bombardments in 1914 and 1916.

Yarmouth

Lowestoft

Harwich

ENGLAND

GERMANY

Sheerness

The Germans (realising the superiority of British surface units in massed force) were content to keep their High Seas Fleet "in being," thus containing the British Grand Fleet to the North Sea area. To underline this strategy, the Germans undertook sharp sweeps and sorties to keep the British alert to the potential danger.

British barrage.

Dover

Portsmouth

HOLLAND

BELGIUM

FRANCE

5°E

© Arthur Banks 1973

255

THE BATTLE OF JUTLAND 31 MAY 1916

Note: to avoid any poss
confusion, times are ba
on the 24-hour clock sys

❶ The advances of the British and German fleets to the scene of Jutlan

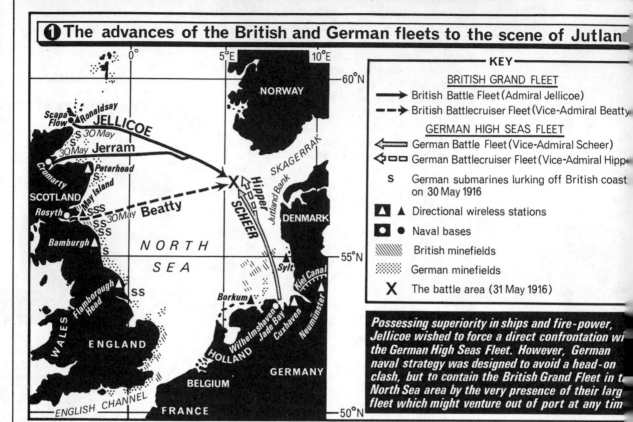

KEY

BRITISH GRAND FLEET
→ British Battle Fleet (Admiral Jellicoe)
⇢ British Battlecruiser Fleet (Vice-Admiral Beatty)

GERMAN HIGH SEAS FLEET
⇐ German Battle Fleet (Vice-Admiral Scheer)
⇐◻ German Battlecruiser Fleet (Vice-Admiral Hipp

S   German submarines lurking off British coast
on 30 May 1916

◼ ▲   Directional wireless stations

◼ ●   Naval bases

▨   British minefields

▒   German minefields

X   The battle area (31 May 1916)

*Possessing superiority in ships and fire-power,
Jellicoe wished to force a direct confrontation wi
the German High Seas Fleet. However, German
naval strategy was designed to avoid a head-on
clash, but to contain the British Grand Fleet in t
North Sea area by the very presence of their larg
fleet which might venture out of port at any tim*

❷ The Opening Action – clash of the battlecruisers

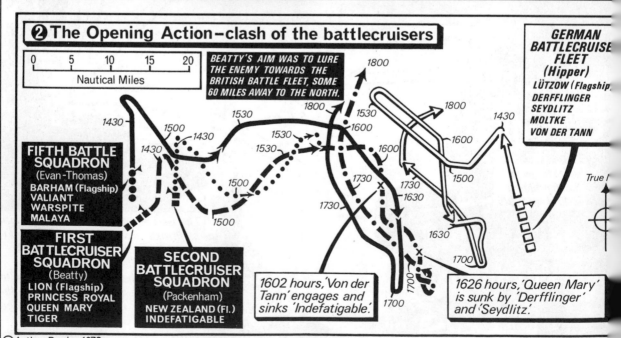

*BEATTY'S AIM WAS TO LURE
THE ENEMY TOWARDS THE
BRITISH BATTLE FLEET, SOME
60 MILES AWAY TO THE NORTH.*

Nautical Miles

**GERMAN
BATTLECRUISE
FLEET
(Hipper)**
LÜTZOW (Flagship
DERFFLINGER
SEYDLITZ
MOLTKE
VON DER TANN

**FIFTH BATTLE
SQUADRON**
(Evan-Thomas)
BARHAM (Flagship)
VALIANT
WARSPITE
MALAYA

**FIRST
BATTLECRUISER
SQUADRON**
(Beatty)
LION (Flagship)
PRINCESS ROYAL
QUEEN MARY
TIGER

**SECOND
BATTLECRUISER
SQUADRON**
(Packenham)
NEW ZEALAND (Fl.)
INDEFATIGABLE

*1602 hours, 'Von der
Tann' engages and
sinks 'Indefatigable'.*

*1626 hours, 'Queen Mary'
is sunk by 'Derfflinger'
and 'Seydlitz'.*

True

© Arthur Banks 1973

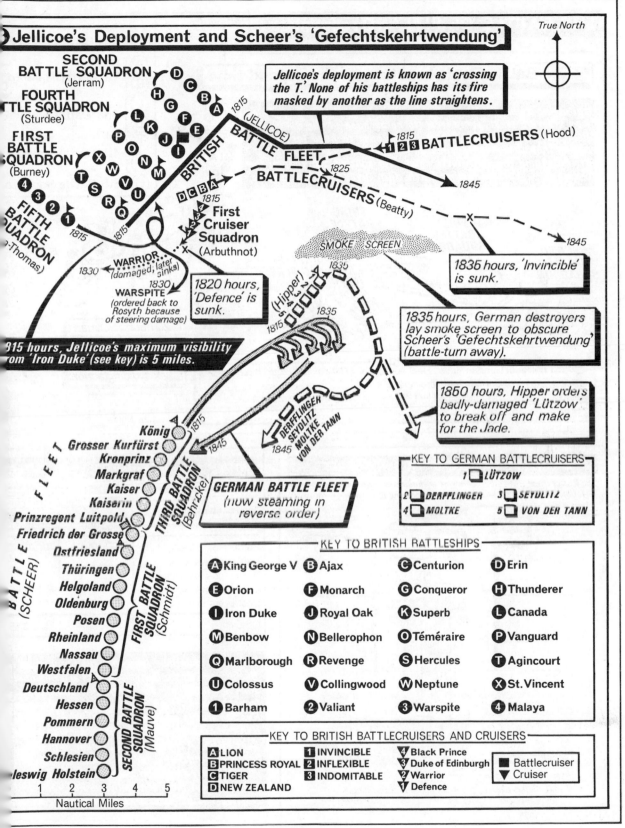

Jellicoe's Deployment and Scheer's 'Gefechtskehrtwendung'

True North

SECOND BATTLE SQUADRON (Jerram)

FOURTH BATTLE SQUADRON (Sturdee)

FIRST BATTLE SQUADRON (Burney)

FIFTH BATTLE SQUADRON (-Thomas)

Jellicoe's deployment is known as 'crossing the T.' None of his battleships has its fire masked by another as the line straightens.

1815 (JELLICOE)

BRITISH BATTLE FLEET

1815 **BATTLECRUISERS** (Hood)

1825 **BATTLECRUISERS** (Beatty)

1845

1845

First Cruiser Squadron (Arbuthnot)

1815

SMOKE SCREEN

1835 hours, 'Invincible' is sunk.

WARRIOR (damaged, later sinks)
1830

WARSPITE (ordered back to Rosyth because of steering damage)
1830

1820 hours, 'Defence' is sunk.

(Hipper)

1815 1835

1835 hours, German destroyers lay smoke screen to obscure Scheer's 'Gefechtskehrtwendung' (battle-turn away).

315 hours, Jellicoe's maximum visibility rom 'Iron Duke' (see key) is 5 miles.

1850 hours, Hipper orders badly-damaged 'Lützow' to break off and make for the Jade.

König 1815
Grosser Kurfürst
Kronprinz
Markgraf
Kaiser
Kaiserin
Prinzregent Luitpold
Friedrich der Grosse
Ostfriesland
Thüringen
Helgoland
Oldenburg
Posen
Rheinland
Nassau
Westfalen

THIRD BATTLE SQUADRON (Behncke)

1845

DERFFLINGER
SEYDLITZ
MOLTKE
VON DER TANN
1845

GERMAN BATTLE FLEET (now steaming in reverse order)

FIRST BATTLE SQUADRON (Schmidt)

KEY TO GERMAN BATTLECRUISERS
1 LÜTZOW
2 DERFFLINGER   3 SEYDLITZ
4 MOLTKE   5 VON DER TANN

Deutschland
Hessen
Pommern
Hannover
Schlesien
leswig Holstein

SECOND BATTLE SQUADRON (Mauve)

BATTLE FLEET (SCHEER)

KEY TO BRITISH BATTLESHIPS

A King George V	**B** Ajax	**C** Centurion	**D** Erin
E Orion	**F** Monarch	**G** Conqueror	**H** Thunderer
I Iron Duke	**J** Royal Oak	**K** Superb	**L** Canada
M Benbow	**N** Bellerophon	**O** Téméraire	**P** Vanguard
Q Marlborough	**R** Revenge	**S** Hercules	**T** Agincourt
U Colossus	**V** Collingwood	**W** Neptune	**X** St. Vincent
1 Barham	**2** Valiant	**3** Warspite	**4** Malaya

KEY TO BRITISH BATTLECRUISERS AND CRUISERS

A LION	**1** INVINCIBLE	**4** Black Prince	■ Battlecruiser
B PRINCESS ROYAL	**2** INFLEXIBLE	**3** Duke of Edinburgh	▼ Cruiser
C TIGER	**3** INDOMITABLE	**2** Warrior	
D NEW ZEALAND		**V** Defence	

1   2   3   4   5
Nautical Miles

257

THE BATTLE OF JUTLAND - continued

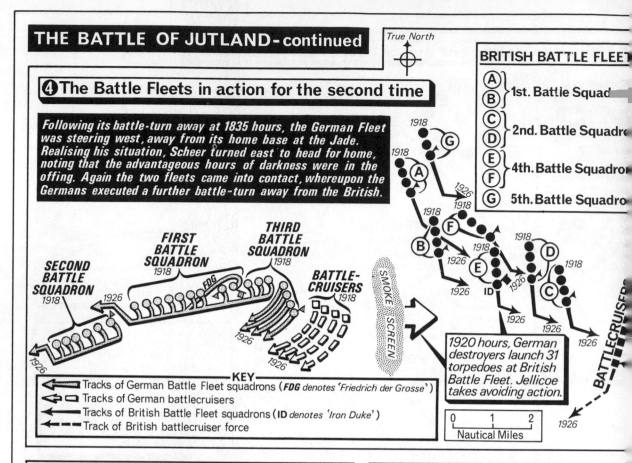

True North

④ The Battle Fleets in action for the second time

Following its battle-turn away at 1835 hours, the German Fleet was steering west, away from its home base at the Jade. Realising his situation, Scheer turned east to head for home, noting that the advantageous hours of darkness were in the offing. Again the two fleets came into contact, whereupon the Germans executed a further battle-turn away from the British.

BRITISH BATTLE FLEET

- Ⓐ
- Ⓑ 1st. Battle Squad...
- Ⓒ
- Ⓓ 2nd. Battle Squadro...
- Ⓔ
- Ⓕ 4th. Battle Squadro...
- Ⓖ 5th. Battle Squadro...

SECOND BATTLE SQUADRON 1918

FIRST BATTLE SQUADRON 1918

THIRD BATTLE SQUADRON 1918

BATTLE-CRUISERS 1918

FDG

SMOKE SCREEN

1920 hours, German destroyers launch 31 torpedoes at British Battle Fleet. Jellicoe takes avoiding action.

BATTLECRUISERS

KEY
- Tracks of German Battle Fleet squadrons (**FDG** denotes 'Friedrich der Grosse')
- Tracks of German battlecruisers
- Tracks of British Battle Fleet squadrons (**ID** denotes 'Iron Duke')
- Track of British battlecruiser force

0   1   2
Nautical Miles

A BRITISH BATTLECRUISER GUN TURRET

The loss of three British battlecruisers at Jutland was attributed to lack of adequate anti-flash screening between magazine and handling-room.

GUN HOUSE
GUN
RAMMER
MOUNTING
WORKING CHAMBER
RAMMERS
MAIN TRUNK
HANDLING ROOM
HANDLING ROOM
CORDITE CHARGES
MAGAZINE
CAGE
SHELL ROOM
SHELL ROOM

A shell exploding in the gun house of a turret could ignite a chain of charges down to the magazine section.

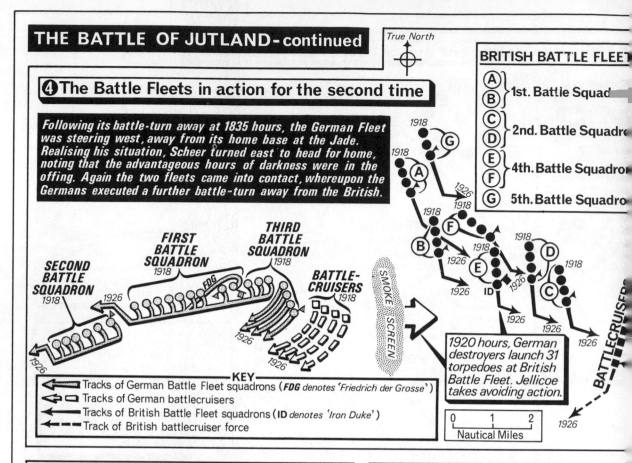

BRITISH AND GERMAN LOSSES AT JUTLA...

DETAILS	BRITISH	GERMA...
Total of ships engaged	151	9...
Total of men employed	60,000	36,00...
Battleships sunk	0	
Battlecruisers sunk	3	
Armoured cruisers sunk	3	
Light cruisers sunk	0	
Destroyers sunk	8	
Casualties	6,097	2,55...

The Battle of Jutland (known to the Germans as t... 'Skagerrak') was a German success in terms of sh... sunk and men lost, and contributed to Russia's e... from the war. Allied supplies to the hard-presse... Russian armies could not be guaranteed, as the ... Baltic approaches remained in possession of the ... Seas Fleet. A controversy commenced in Britai... apportion the blame for the result, and a Jellic... versus Beatty campaign ensued. Nevertheless, ... German Fleet had been badly mauled, and U-b... warfare against British commerce was a conse...

© Arthur Banks 1973

258

0 ——— 50
Miles

Throughout the hours of darkness, 31 May–1 June, there now followed a general chase towards the Jade, with the German warships intent on making their base with all haste, and the British warships bent on interposing themselves to block the various escape routes along the mine-swept channels. The bulk of the High Seas Fleet did, in fact, evade its pursuers, but arrived home in a severely battered condition, and unfit for further immediate service. The British squadrons re-formed, and, fearing a large submarine attack (German reconnaissance Zeppelin L11 had shadowed him since 0319 hours), Jellicoe ordered the Grand Fleet back to its bases. Within 48 hours, Jellicoe had his fleet at a state of instant readiness for a fresh encounter – indicating how he had really fared at Jutland Bank!

Note: during the night chase, the British Admiralty in London intercepted various German wireless signals stating Scheer's positions en route for the Jade. The use to which this valuable information was put by the British, is still undetermined.

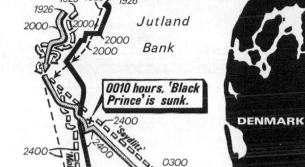

Unable to reach base, 'Lutzow' is sunk by German destroyer at 0145 hours.

Jutland Bank

1926 1926 1926
1926
2000 2000
2000
2000
2000

0010 hours, 'Black Prince' is sunk.

DENMARK

2400
'Seydlitz'
2400
2400
'Moltke'
0300
Light Vessel

0200

0300
0300

NORTH HELIGOLAND CHANNEL

0010 hours. 'Pommern' is sunk.

Horns Reef

AMRUM BANK CHANNEL

THE NIGHT ATTACKS BY BRITISH DESTROYERS

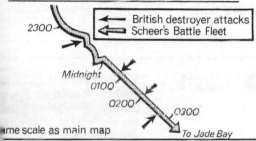

2300

→ British destroyer attacks
⇒ Scheer's Battle Fleet

Midnight
0100
0200
0300

Same scale as main map   To Jade Bay

N O R T H

S F A

H E L I G O L A N D

B I G H T

EMS CHANNEL

Frisian Islands

GERMANY

Elbe
Cuxhaven
Weser
Bremer-haven
Wilhelmshaven
Jade Bay
Emden
Ems

HOLLAND   GERMANY

KEY

——— Track of Jellicoe's Battle Fleet
- - - Track of Beatty's Battlecruisers
⩥⩥⩥ Track of Scheer's Battle Fleet
▭▭▭ Tracks of Hipper's Battlecruisers
⫟⫟⫟ British-laid minefields by 1 June, 1916
········ German-swept channels 1 June 1916

Smaller units were operating with the British and German Battle and Battlecruiser Fleets – these are listed below
Abbreviations:–   S = Squadron, F = Flotilla, AC = Armoured Cruiser, LC = Light Cruiser, D = Destroyer, SG = Scouting Group

BRITISH BATTLE FLEET		BRITISH BATTLECRUISER FLEET		GERMAN BATTLE FLEET		GERMAN BATTLECRUISER FLEET	
ACS	4 ships	1st. LCS	4 ships	4th. SG (LC)	5 ships	2nd. SG (LC)	4 ships
ACS	4 ships	2nd. LCS	4 ships	LC	1 ship	LC	1 ship
LCS	5 ships	3rd. LCS	4 ships	1st. DF (half)	4 ships	2nd. DF	10 ships
LCS (attached)	6 ships	1st. DF	10 ships	3rd. DF	7 ships	6th. DF	9 ships
DF	19 ships	9th. & 10th. DF (comb.)	8 ships	5th. DF	11 ships	9th. DF	11 ships
DF	16 ships	13th. DF	11 ships	7th. DF	9 ships		
DF	16 ships						
plus		plus					
layers	1 ship	Seaplane Carriers	1 ship				
enders	1 ship						

THE BATTLE OF JUTLAND – continued

HMS "IRON DUKE" (Flagship of Admiral Jellicoe)

ARMAMENT
Ten 13·5-inch guns
Twelve 6-inch guns
Four 3-pounder guns
Four 21-inch torpedo tubes

The 'Iron Duke' was a Dreadnought battleship, and the class was named after her. Sister-ships were 'Benbow', 'Emperor of India', and 'Marlborough'

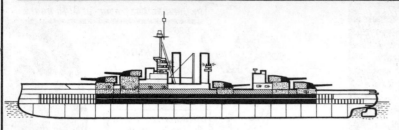

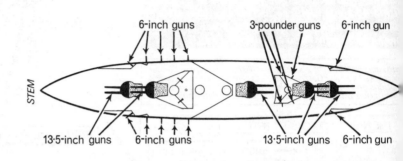

6-inch guns   3-pounder guns   6-inch gun

STEM

13·5-inch guns   6-inch guns   13·5-inch guns   6-inch gun

Laid down:	1912
Completed:	1914
Displacement:	25,000 tons
Waterline length:	620 feet
Maximum speed:	23 knots
Complement:	900

HMS "LION" (Flagship of Vice-Admiral Beatty)

ARMAMENT
Eight 13·5-inch guns
Sixteen 4-inch guns
Three 21-inch torpedo tubes

The 'Lion' was a battle-cruiser, and the class was named after her. There was one sister-ship, 'Princess Royal'.

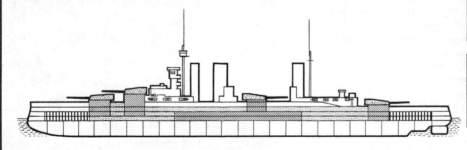

4-inch guns   13·5-inch guns

STEM

13·5-inch guns   4-inch guns   13·5-inch guns   4-inch guns

Laid down:	1909
Completed:	1912
Displacement:	26,350 tons
Waterline length:	675 feet
Maximum speed:	29 knots
Complement:	1,000

© Arthur Banks 1973

SMS "FRIEDRICH DER GROSSE" (Flagship of Vice-Admiral Scheer)

ARMAMENT
Ten 12-inch guns
Fourteen 6-inch guns
Twelve 24-pounder guns
Four 14-pounder anti-aerial guns
Five 20-inch torpedo tubes

The 'Friedrich der Grosse' was a Dreadnought battleship of the 'Kaiser' class. Sister-ships were 'Kaiser', 'Kaiserin', 'Prinzregent Luitpold', and 'König Albert'.

Laid down:	1909
Completed:	1912
Displacement:	24,700 tons
Waterline length:	564 feet
Maximum speed:	23 knots
Complement:	1,088

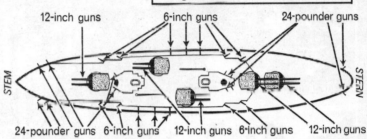

12-inch guns — 6-inch guns — 24-pounder guns
STEM — STERN
24-pounder guns — 6-inch guns — 12-inch guns — 6-inch guns — 12-inch guns

SMS "LÜTZOW" (Flagship of Vice-Admiral Hipper)

Note: during the battle, Hipper transferred his flag from the badly-damaged 'Lützow' to the 'Moltke'.

ARMAMENT
Eight 12-inch guns
Twelve 6-inch guns
Twelve 24-pounder guns
Five 22-inch torpedo tubes

The 'Lützow' was a battle-cruiser, and sister-ships were 'Derfflinger' and 'Ersatz Hertha'.

Laid down:	1912
Completed:	1915
Displacement:	28,000 tons
Waterline length:	590 feet
Maximum speed:	29 knots
Complement:	1,100

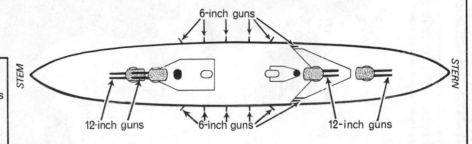

6-inch guns
STEM — STERN
12-inch guns — 6-inch guns — 12-inch guns

GERMAN AND AUSTRIAN SUBMARINE LOSSES 1914–1918

1 From 1914 to 1916

KEY

r Rammed.
g Sunk by gunfire.
m Mined.
n Lost in nets.
e Blown up in explosive sweep.

d Depth charged.
t Torpedoed.
u Unknown cause.
s Stranded.
o Lost through other causes.

German submarines lost in:
⬤ 1914.   ◉ 1915.
◯ 1916.

Austrian submarines lost in:
▣ 1915.   ☐ 1916.

A total of 307 German and 27 Austrian U–boats undertook wartime missions. Enemy mines accounted for 48 sinkings, depth charges for 30 sinkings, and gunfire for 20 sinkings. Other losses were due to rammings, torpedo attacks, sweeps, and unknown causes. Total U–boat losses amounted to 187.

ATLANTIC OCEAN

North Sea

Baltic Sea

Bay of Biscay

Mediterranean Sea

Adriatic Sea

Black Sea

sunk off Lapland

UC 7, UC 3, UB 13 in 1916
U5, U11 in 1914

262

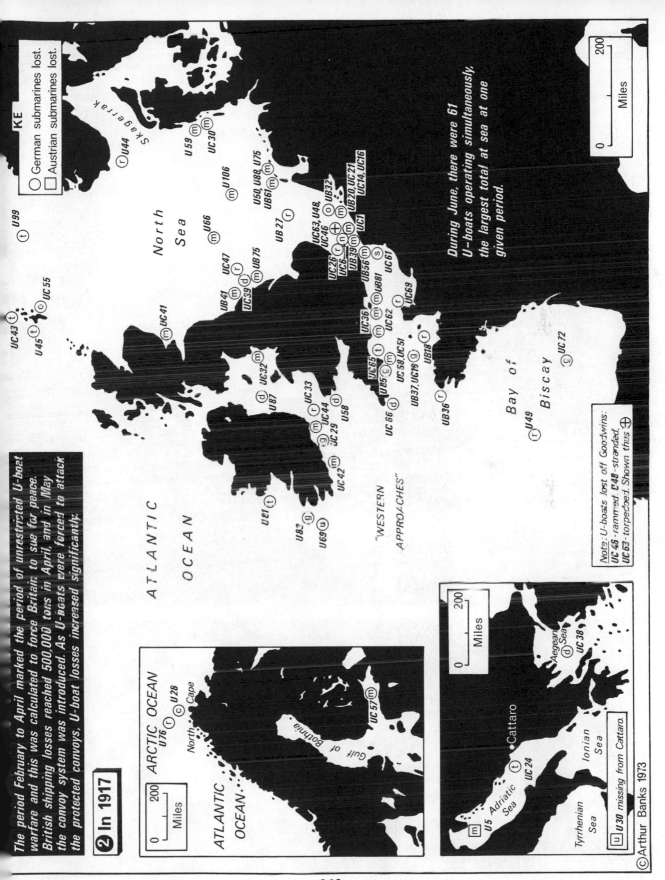

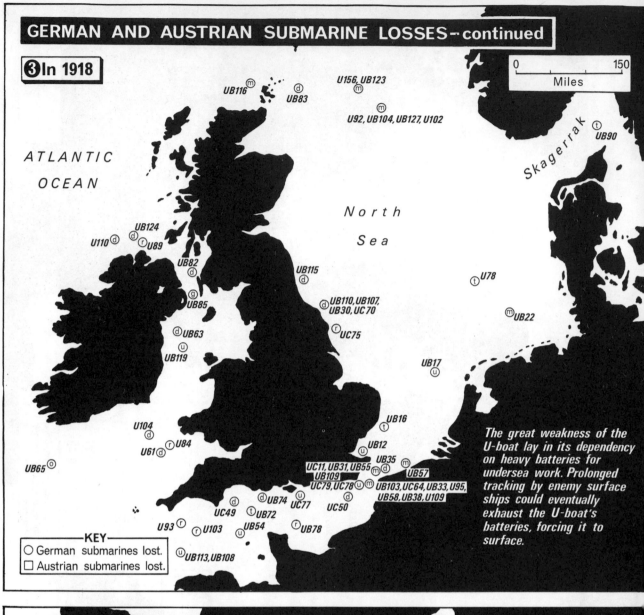

③ In 1918

0 ——— 150
Miles

ATLANTIC OCEAN

UB116 ⓜ

UB83 ⓓ

U156, UB123 ⓜ

U92, UB104, UB127, U102 ⓜ

ⓣ UB90

Skagerrak

North Sea

U110 ⓓ ⓡ U89
UB124 ⓓ

UB82 ⓓ

UB115 ⓓ

ⓖ UB85

ⓓ UB63

ⓤ UB119

ⓣ U78

ⓜ UB22

UB110, UB107, UB30, UC70 ⓓ

ⓡ UC75

UB17 ⓤ

UB16 ⓣ

U104 ⓓ

U61 ⓓ ⓡ U84

UB65 ⓞ

UB12 ⓤ

UB35 ⓜ ⓓ
UC11, UB31, UB55, UB109 ⓜ
UC79, UC78 ⓤ
UB57 ⓜ
UB103, UC64, UB33, U95, UB58, UB38, U109 ⓓ

ⓓ UB74
UC77 ⓤ
UC50 ⓓ

UC49 ⓓ
ⓣ UB72
U93 ⓡ
ⓡ U103
UB54 ⓤ
ⓡ UB78

ⓤ UB113, UB108

The great weakness of the U-boat lay in its dependency on heavy batteries for undersea work. Prolonged tracking by enemy surface ships could eventually exhaust the U-boat's batteries, forcing it to surface.

KEY
ⓞ German submarines lost.
▢ Austrian submarines lost.

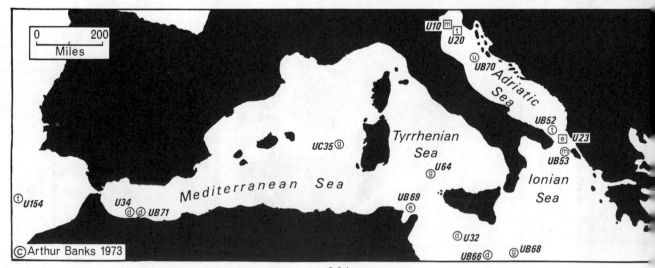

0 ——— 200
Miles

U10 ⓜ ⓣ
U20

ⓤ UB70

Adriatic Sea

UB52 ⓣ
ⓔ U23

ⓜ UB53

Tyrrhenian Sea

UC35 ⓖ

U64 ⓖ

Ionian Sea

ⓣ U154

U34 ⓓ ⓓ UB71

Mediterranean Sea

UB69 ⓔ

ⓓ U32

UB66 ⓓ ⓖ UB68

A SPECIALLY-CONSTRUCTED BRITISH 'Q'-SHIP: HMS "HYDERABAD"

Built by John I. Thorneycroft & Co. Ltd., in four months during 1917.

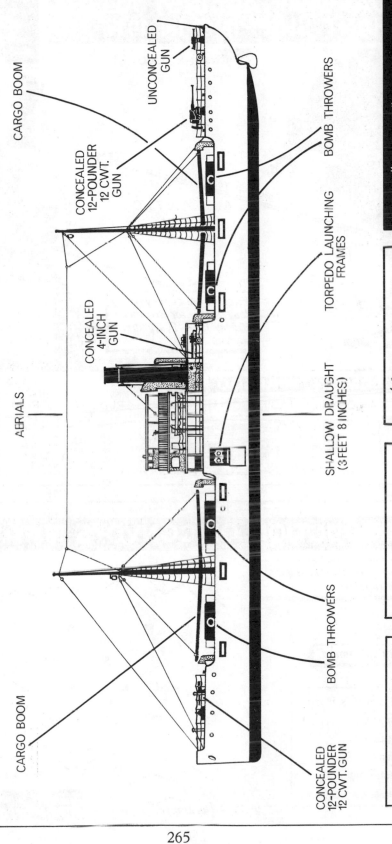

CARGO BOOM

UNCONCEALED GUN

CONCEALED 12-POUNDER 12 CWT. GUN

CONCEALED 4-INCH GUN

AERIALS

BOMB THROWERS

TORPEDO LAUNCHING FRAMES

SHALLOW DRAUGHT (3 FEET 8 INCHES)

BOMB THROWERS

CARGO BOOM

CONCEALED 12-POUNDER 12 CWT. GUN

On HMS "Hyderabad", funnel and masts were adjustable. The after compass pedestal and wheel collapsed to improve field of fire.

First 'Q'-ship to sink a U-boat was the "Prince Charles" on 24 July 1915.

The first 'Q'-ship in service was the "Victoria" in November 1914.

180 'Q'-ships were fitted out. 11 U-boats were sunk by them.

© Arthur Banks 1973

265

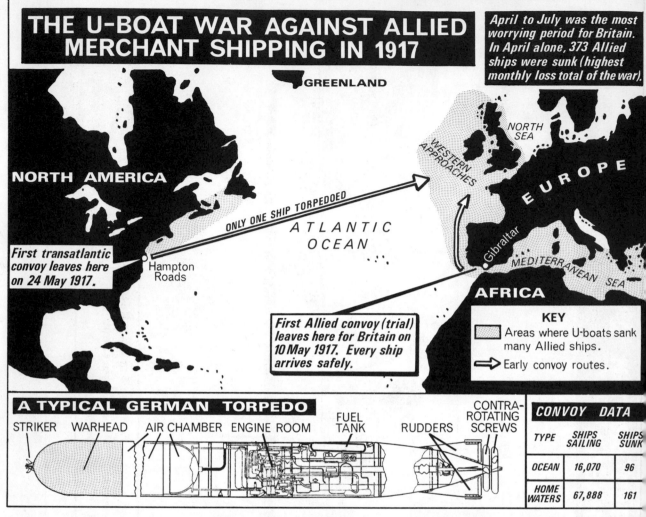

THE U-BOAT WAR AGAINST ALLIED MERCHANT SHIPPING IN 1917

April to July was the most worrying period for Britain. In April alone, 373 Allied ships were sunk (highest monthly loss total of the war).

GREENLAND

NORTH AMERICA

ONLY ONE SHIP TORPEDOED

ATLANTIC OCEAN

First transatlantic convoy leaves here on 24 May 1917.

Hampton Roads

First Allied convoy (trial) leaves here for Britain on 10 May 1917. Every ship arrives safely.

WESTERN APPROACHES

NORTH SEA

EUROPE

Gibraltar

MEDITERRANEAN SEA

AFRICA

KEY
Areas where U-boats sank many Allied ships.
Early convoy routes.

A TYPICAL GERMAN TORPEDO

STRIKER — WARHEAD — AIR CHAMBER — ENGINE ROOM — FUEL TANK — RUDDERS — CONTRA-ROTATING SCREWS

CONVOY DATA

TYPE	SHIPS SAILING	SHIPS SUNK
OCEAN	16,070	96
HOME WATERS	67,888	161

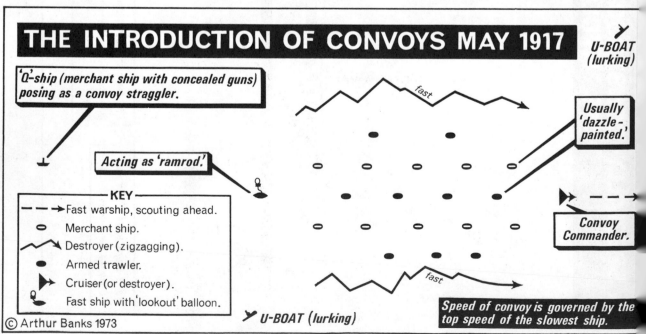

THE INTRODUCTION OF CONVOYS MAY 1917

'Q'-ship (merchant ship with concealed guns) posing as a convoy straggler.

U-BOAT (lurking)

fast

Usually 'dazzle-painted.'

Acting as 'ramrod.'

Convoy Commander.

KEY
- - -→ Fast warship, scouting ahead.
⬭ Merchant ship.
∿↘ Destroyer (zigzagging).
⬤ Armed trawler.
▶ Cruiser (or destroyer).
⚲ Fast ship with 'lookout' balloon.

fast

U-BOAT (lurking)

Speed of convoy is governed by the top speed of the slowest ship.

© Arthur Banks 1973

THE EFFECTIVENESS OF THE BRITISH CONVOY SYSTEM 1917–1918

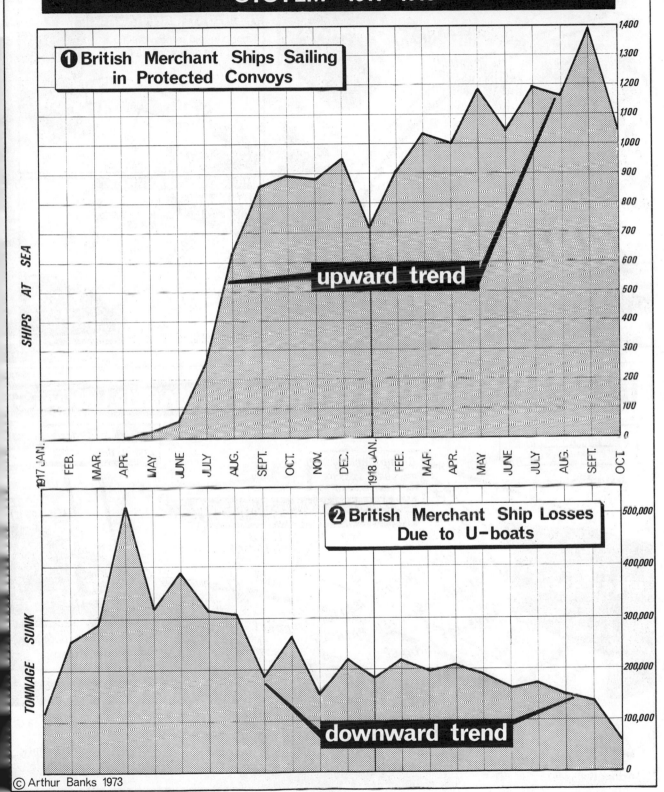

1 British Merchant Ships Sailing in Protected Convoys

upward trend

SHIPS AT SEA

2 British Merchant Ship Losses Due to U-boats

downward trend

TONNAGE SUNK

© Arthur Banks 1973

267

HAZARDS CONFRONTING GERMAN-BASED U-BOATS

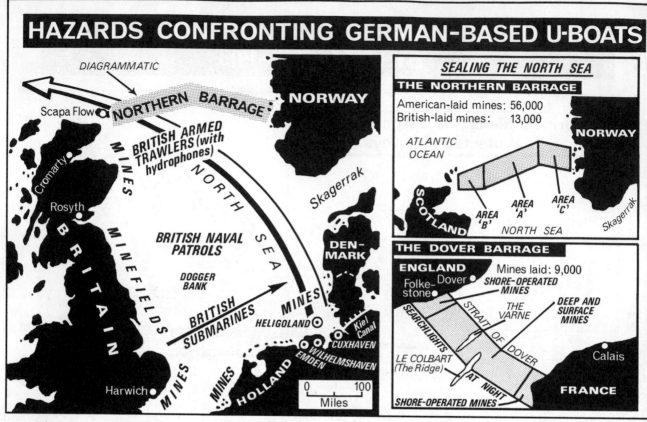

DIAGRAMMATIC

NORTHERN BARRAGE

NORWAY

Scapa Flow

BRITISH ARMED TRAWLERS (with hydrophones)

MINES

Cromarty

Rosyth

NORTH SEA

Skagerrak

BRITISH NAVAL PATROLS

MINEFIELDS

DOGGER BANK

DEN-MARK

BRITAIN

BRITISH SUBMARINES

MINES

HELIGOLAND

Kiel Canal

CUXHAVEN

WILHELMSHAVEN

EMDEN

MINES

Harwich

MINES

HOLLAND

0   100
Miles

SEALING THE NORTH SEA
THE NORTHERN BARRAGE

American-laid mines: 56,000
British-laid mines: 13,000

ATLANTIC OCEAN

NORWAY

SCOTLAND

AREA 'B'

AREA 'A'

AREA 'C'

NORTH SEA

Skagerrak

THE DOVER BARRAGE

ENGLAND   Mines laid: 9,000

Folkestone   Dover

SHORE-OPERATED MINES

THE VARNE

DEEP AND SURFACE MINES

SEARCHLIGHTS

STRAIT OF DOVER

Calais

LE COLBART (The Ridge)

AT NIGHT

FRANCE

SHORE-OPERATED MINES

HAZARDS CONFRONTING FLANDERS-BASED U-BOATS

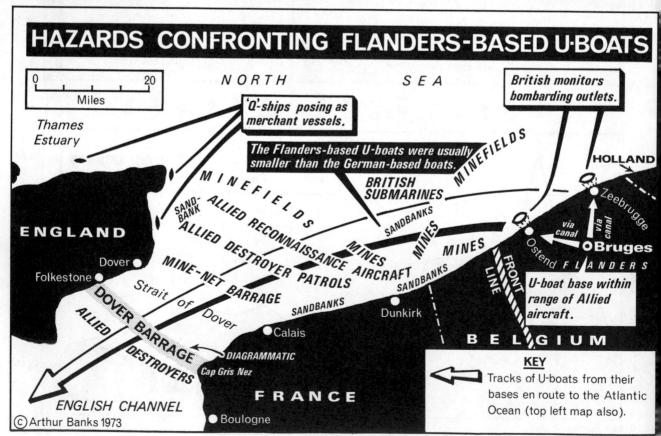

0   20
Miles

NORTH   SEA

'Q'-ships posing as merchant vessels.

British monitors bombarding outlets.

Thames Estuary

The Flanders-based U-boats were usually smaller than the German-based boats.

MINEFIELDS

MINEFIELDS

HOLLAND

BRITISH SUBMARINES

Zeebrugge

SAND-BANK

MINES

ALLIED RECONNAISSANCE AIRCRAFT

SANDBANKS

ENGLAND

ALLIED DESTROYER PATROLS

MINES

MINES

via canal

via canal

Bruges

Dover

MINE-NET BARRAGE

Ostend

FLANDERS

Folkestone

Strait of Dover

SANDBANKS

FRONT LINE

U-boat base within range of Allied aircraft.

DOVER BARRAGE

SANDBANKS

Dunkirk

ALLIED DESTROYERS

Calais

DIAGRAMMATIC

BELGIUM

Cap Gris Nez

FRANCE

KEY

Tracks of U-boats from their bases en route to the Atlantic Ocean (top left map also).

ENGLISH CHANNEL

© Arthur Banks 1973

Boulogne

268

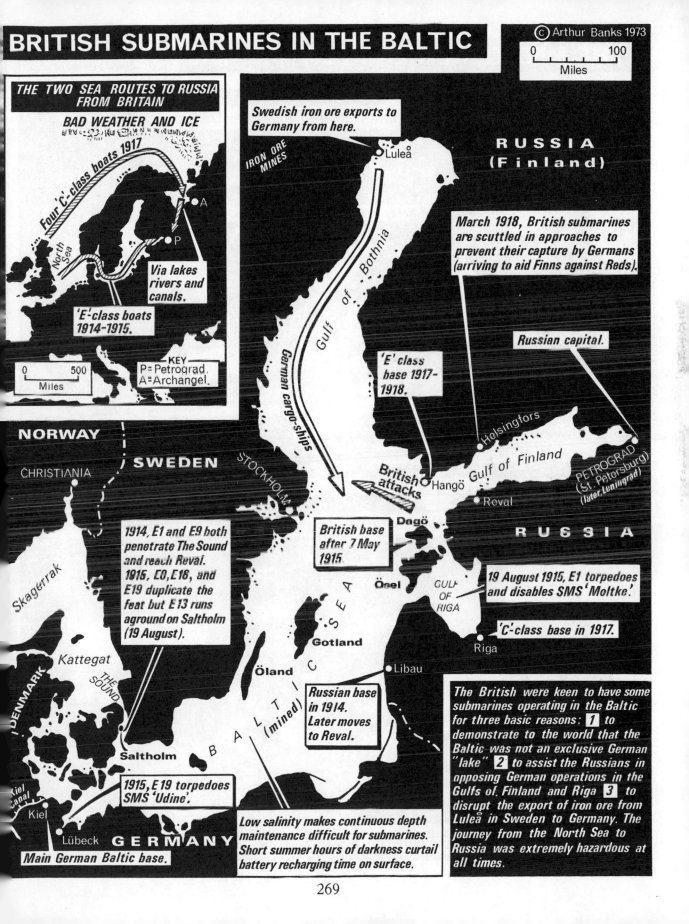

BRITISH SUBMARINES IN THE BALTIC

© Arthur Banks 1973

0 ———— 100
Miles

THE TWO SEA ROUTES TO RUSSIA FROM BRITAIN

BAD WEATHER AND ICE

Four 'C'-class boats 1917

North Sea

Via lakes rivers and canals.

'E'-class boats 1914-1915.

KEY
P = Petrograd.
A = Archangel.

0 ———— 500
Miles

Swedish iron ore exports to Germany from here.

IRON ORE MINES

Luleå

RUSSIA (Finland)

March 1918, British submarines are scuttled in approaches to prevent their capture by Germans (arriving to aid Finns against Reds).

Gulf of Bothnia

German cargo-ships

Russian capital.

'E' class base 1917-1918.

Helsingfors

Gulf of Finland

Hangö

PETROGRAD (St. Petersburg) (later, Leningrad)

British attacks

Reval

RUSSIA

NORWAY

SWEDEN

CHRISTIANIA

STOCKHOLM

Dagö

British base after 7 May 1915

Ösel

19 August 1915, E1 torpedoes and disables SMS 'Moltke'.

1914, E1 and E9 both penetrate The Sound and reach Reval. 1915, E0, E18, and E19 duplicate the feat but E13 runs aground on Saltholm (19 August).

Skagerrak

GULF OF RIGA

'C'-class base in 1917.

Gotland

Riga

Kattegat

THE SOUND

Öland

B A L T I C   S E A (mined)

Libau

Russian base in 1914. Later moves to Reval.

DENMARK

Saltholm

1915, E 19 torpedoes SMS 'Udine'.

Kiel Canal

Kiel

Lübeck

GERMANY

Main German Baltic base.

Low salinity makes continuous depth maintenance difficult for submarines. Short summer hours of darkness curtail battery recharging time on surface.

The British were keen to have some submarines operating in the Baltic for three basic reasons: **1** *to demonstrate to the world that the Baltic was not an exclusive German "lake"* **2** *to assist the Russians in opposing German operations in the Gulfs of Finland and Riga* **3** *to disrupt the export of iron ore from Luleå in Sweden to Germany. The journey from the North Sea to Russia was extremely hazardous at all times.*

THE MEDITERRANEAN SEA 1914–1918

During 1917 alone, nearly 900 Allied merchant ships were sunk.

❶ The U-boat Offensive Against Allied Merchant Shipping

Main bases of Mediterranean U-boats.

EUROPE

Cattaro

Constantinople

ASIA

FROM GERMANY

M E D I T E R R A N E A N S E A

A F R I C A

KEY
- U-boat routes into the Mediterranean Sea.
- ⊗ Minefields laid by U-boats.
- Areas where heavy Allied losses occurred.

0 400
Miles

❷ Allied Anti-U-boat Naval Patrol Zones

These zones were in use from early 1916 onwards.

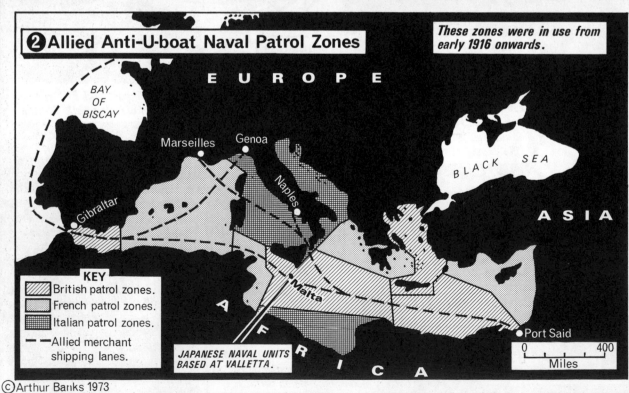

EUROPE

BAY OF BISCAY

Marseilles Genoa

Gibraltar

Naples

BLACK SEA

ASIA

Malta

A F R I C A

Port Said

KEY
- British patrol zones.
- French patrol zones.
- Italian patrol zones.
- Allied merchant shipping lanes.

JAPANESE NAVAL UNITS BASED AT VALLETTA.

0 400
Miles

© Arthur Banks 1973

270

THE ADRIATIC SEA 1914 – 1918

0 [___] 50
Miles

KEY

▨ Allied Otranto Barrage.
⊕ Italian naval base.
Ⓢ Italian seaplane base.
▨ Austro-Hungarian naval base.
✶ Naval action.
✳ Capital ship sunk.
⇨ U-boat routes from Adriatic to Mediterranean Sea.

Battle squadron, torpedo craft, etc.

Railway used to transport U-boats in sections from Germany to Pola.

Night 31 October 1918, an Italian miniature torpedo-style craft sinks Austrian battleship 'Viribus Unitis' in harbour.

Main Austrian surface fleet base.

ITALY

Venice · Trieste · Fiume

Pola

ADRIATIC SEA

AUSTRIA – HUNGARY

Ancona ●

Night 9 December 1917, Italian motor boat torpedoes and sinks Austrian battleship 'Wien'.

10 June 1918, Italian motor boat torpedoes Austrian battleship 'Szent Istvan'. 89 Austrian sailors are lost in sinking ship.

Main Austrian U-boat base and advance surface fleet anchorage.

Cattaro

Night 11 December 1916, Italian battleship 'Regina Margherita' hits mine and sinks.

Night 14/15 May 1917, Austrian cruisers raid Barrage and sink 14 Allied drifters.

ALBANIA
● Durazzo

ITALY

In use by British, French, and Italian ships.

Barrage is never 100% effective in containing U-boats in Adriatic Sea.

Valona

THE ALLIED ANTI–U-BOAT OTRANTO BARRAGE

1 Early 1015, British fishing vessels employed with 30-feet deep wire drift nets; Allied destroyers "on call": U-boats able to dive beneath nets.

2 Barrage weakened by drifters being transferred to assist in Salonika operations and Serbian evacuation to Corfu: remaining ships to port at night to avoid surface attacks.

3 Fixed net barrage commenced in April 1918: completed in September. Nets 150 feet deep, submerged 30 feet below surface, secured to moored buoys, mines attached. The whole complex patrolled by drifters with hydrophones, destroyers, sea-planes (from Otranto), American "sub-chasers" (based on Corfu).

© Arthur Banks 1973

Taranto ⊕

Brindisi

Otranto Ⓢ

Main Italian naval base.

Corfu

GREECE

21 December 1914, French battleship 'Jean Bart' is sunk by U-boat.

French naval base in the area.

The Austro-Hungarian surface fleet, locked in the Adriatic "lake" by Allied control of the Strait of Otranto, was restricted to hit-and-run sorties, whereas the U-boats were able to penetrate into the Mediterranean on numerous occasions to sink Allied shipping

SICILY

271

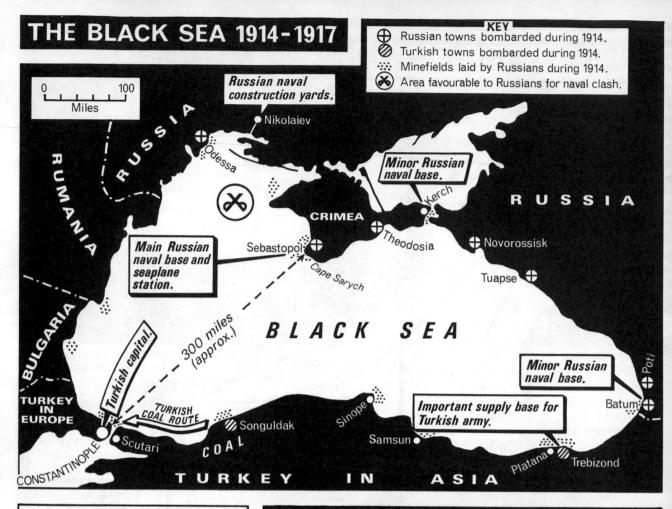

THE BLACK SEA 1914-1917

Russian naval construction yards.

Nikolaiev

RUSSIA

RUMANIA

Odessa

Minor Russian naval base.

Kerch

RUSSIA

CRIMEA

Theodosia

Novorossisk

Sebastopol

Main Russian naval base and seaplane station.

Cape Sarych

Tuapse

BULGARIA

Turkish capital.

300 miles (approx.)

BLACK SEA

Minor Russian naval base.

Poti

TURKEY IN EUROPE

TURKISH COAL ROUTE

Songuldak

Sinope

Important supply base for Turkish army.

Batum

CONSTANTINOPLE

Scutari

COAL

Samsun

Platana

Trebizond

TURKEY   IN   ASIA

RIVAL NAVAL STRENGTHS IN 1914

RUSSIAN FLEET

5 Pre-Dreadnought Battleships.

2 Cruisers.

4 Destroyers.

4 Submarines.

(3 Dreadnought Battleships and 2 Cruisers under construction)

TURKISH/GERMAN FLEET

1 Battlecruiser (SMS 'Goeben').

3 Pre-Dreadnought Battleships.

3 Cruisers (including SMS 'Breslau').

2 Destroyers.

The importance of the German warships must be stressed. SMS 'Goeben' was the most powerful warship in the area in 1914.

© Arthur Banks 1973

In 1914, the Black Sea naval scene was basically as follows: the Turkish/German fleet was intent on sorties from Constantinople to bombard Russian ports (spearheaded by SMS 'Goeben', the most powerful warship in the area). The Russians, eager to disrupt Turkish coal supplies by sea from Songuldak to Constantinople (there was no land railway link), yearned for a supply base on the Bulgarian coastline to shorten the distance between Sebastopol and Constantinople. They laid minefields off Turkish ports to impede enemy sorties, and entertained hopes that if a major naval confrontation occurred, it would take place between Odessa and Sebastopol, within range of Russian seaplanes.

THE NAVAL CLASH OFF CAPE SARYCH 18 NOVEMBER 1914

MIST

CLEAR WEATHER

SMS 'Breslau'

SMS 'GOEBEN'

firing

1221 hours

Russian cruisers

RUSSIAN BATTLE FLEET

This 14-minute action marked the first encounter between 'Goeben' and Russian capital ships. The old pre-dreadnoughts equalled the 'Goeben's' hit-rate of 10% from salvoes fired before the Germans broke off. There were 14 hits on 'Goeben' causing casualties of 115 killed and 59 wounded.

During 1915, two new dreadnoughts came into service with the Russian Black Sea fleet. These battleships, "Imperatritsa Maria" and "Ekaterina II," altered the naval balance of power, although the former was sunk at Sebastopol in the following year (27 October 1916): SMS "Goeben" made her final Black Sea sortie on 8 January 1916. In September 1915, U-boats appeared in the Black Sea, and in that year Bulgaria joined the Central Powers. Rumania became involved in 1916. There was no all-out naval clash, but several fights took place, sometimes involving Russian seaplanes. Russian troops were transported across the sea to fight on the Turkish shore. Trebizond was captured in April 1916 and used as a military port.

1915, BOMBARDED BY TURKISH/GERMAN FLEET AT TIME OF ALLIED OPERATIONS AT DARDANELLES AND GALLIPOLI TO DISTRACT AND DISRUPT RUSSIAN SUPPORT.

RUSSIAN EMBARKATION PORT FOR TROOPS. SAFE FROM ENEMY ATTACKS.

1915, BOMBARDED BY RUSSIANS.

MAY 1915, RUSSIANS LAND AND DESTROY POWER STATION.

THE UNSUCCESSFUL BRITISH AERIAL BID TO SINK SMS "GOEBEN" MAY-JULY 1916

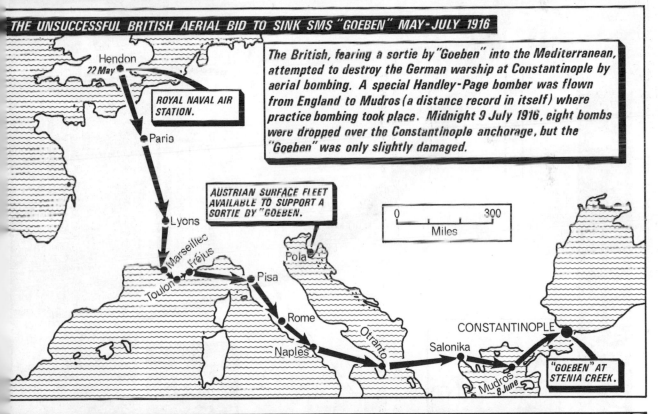

The British, fearing a sortie by "Goeben" into the Mediterranean, attempted to destroy the German warship at Constantinople by aerial bombing. A special Handley-Page bomber was flown from England to Mudros (a distance record in itself) where practice bombing took place. Midnight 9 July 1916, eight bombs were dropped over the Constantinople anchorage, but the "Goeben" was only slightly damaged.

ROYAL NAVAL AIR STATION.

AUSTRIAN SURFACE FLEET AVAILABLE TO SUPPORT A SORTIE BY "GOEBEN".

"GOEBEN" AT STENIA CREEK.

"GOEBEN" AND "BRESLAU" IN THE AEGEAN 20 JANUARY 1918

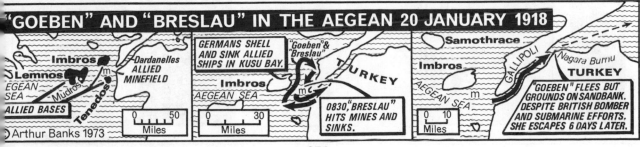

GERMANS SHELL AND SINK ALLIED SHIPS IN KUSU BAY.

0830, "BRESLAU" HITS MINES AND SINKS.

DARDANELLES ALLIED MINEFIELD

"GOEBEN" FLEES BUT GROUNDS ON SANDBANK. DESPITE BRITISH BOMBER AND SUBMARINE EFFORTS, SHE ESCAPES 6 DAYS LATER.

© Arthur Banks 1973

273

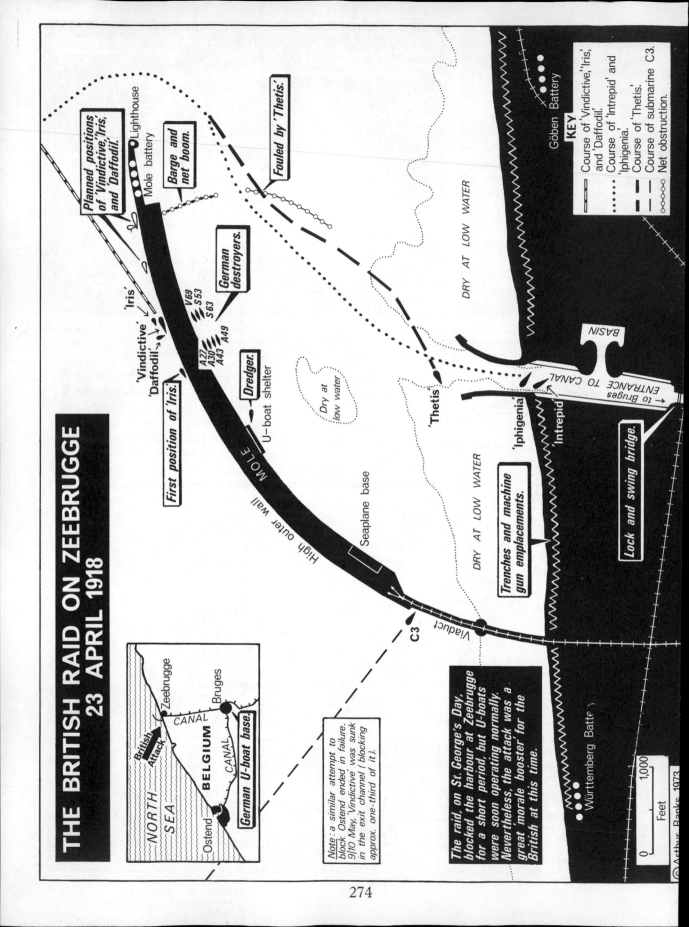

THE BRITISH RAID ON ZEEBRUGGE
23 APRIL 1918

Planned positions of 'Vindictive','Iris', and 'Daffodil'.

Lighthouse

Mole battery

Barge and net boom.

Fouled by 'Thetis'.

Göben Battery

KEY

- ▭▭▭ Course of 'Vindictive','Iris', and 'Daffodil'.
- ·········· Course of 'Intrepid' and 'Iphigenia.
- ▬ ▬ ▬ Course of 'Thetis'.
- — — — Course of submarine C.3.
- ○○○○○ Net obstruction.

'Iris'

'Vindictive' 'Daffodil'

German destroyers.

V69
S53
S63
A49
A27
A30
A43

First position of 'Iris'.

Dredger.

U–boat shelter

Dry at low water

DRY AT LOW WATER

BASIN

MOLE

High outer wall

Seaplane base

'Thetis'

← to Bruges ENTRANCE TO CANAL

'Iphigenia'

'Intrepid'

DRY AT LOW WATER

Trenches and machine gun emplacements.

Lock and swing bridge.

Viaduct

C.3

Württemberg Battery.

The raid, on St. George's Day, blocked the harbour at Zeebrugge for a short period; but U-boats were soon operating normally. Nevertheless, the attack was a great morale booster for the British at this time.

Note: a similar attempt to block Ostend ended in failure. 9/10 May, 'Vindictive' was sunk in the exit channel (blocking approx. one-third of it).

Inset map

NORTH SEA

Zeebrugge

British Attack

CANAL

Bruges

BELGIUM

CANAL

German U-boat base.

Ostend

0 1,000
Feet

© Arthur Banks 1973

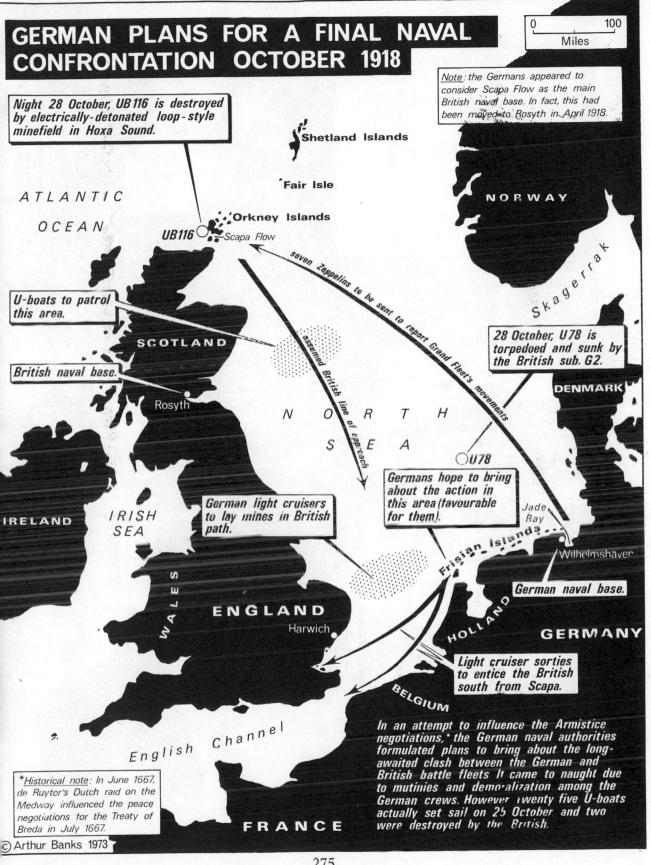

GERMAN PLANS FOR A FINAL NAVAL CONFRONTATION OCTOBER 1918

0 — 100 Miles

Note: the Germans appeared to consider Scapa Flow as the main British naval base. In fact, this had been moved to Rosyth in April 1918.

Night 28 October, UB 116 is destroyed by electrically-detonated loop-style minefield in Hoxa Sound.

Shetland Islands

Fair Isle

ATLANTIC OCEAN

NORWAY

Orkney Islands

UB116 · Scapa Flow

seven Zeppelins to be sent to report Grand Fleet's movements

Skagerrak

U-boats to patrol this area.

SCOTLAND

assumed British line of approach

28 October, U 78 is torpedoed and sunk by the British sub. G2.

DENMARK

British naval base.

Rosyth

N O R T H   S E A

○U78

Germans hope to bring about the action in this area (favourable for them).

Jade Bay

IRELAND

IRISH SEA

German light cruisers to lay mines in British path.

Frisian Islands

Wilhelmshaven

German naval base.

WALES

ENGLAND

Harwich

HOLLAND

GERMANY

Light cruiser sorties to entice the British south from Scapa.

BELGIUM

English Channel

In an attempt to influence the Armistice negotiations,* the German naval authorities formulated plans to bring about the long-awaited clash between the German and British battle fleets It came to naught due to mutinies and demoralization among the German crews. However twenty five U-boats actually set sail on 25 October and two were destroyed by the British.

*Historical note: In June 1667, de Ruyter's Dutch raid on the Medway influenced the peace negotiations for the Treaty of Breda in July 1667.

FRANCE

© Arthur Banks 1973

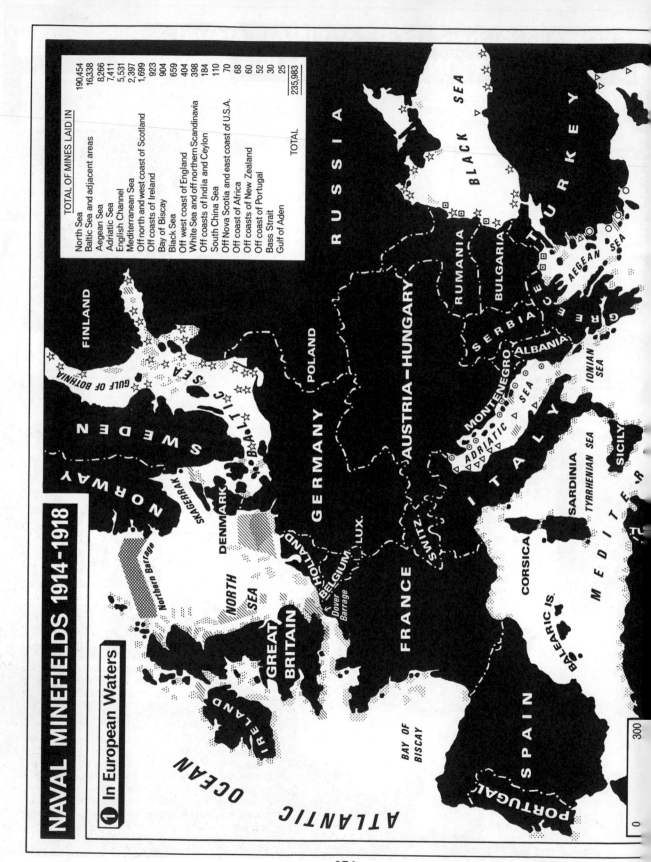

NAVAL MINEFIELDS 1914–1918

1 In European Waters

TOTAL OF MINES LAID IN	
North Sea	190,454
Baltic Sea and adjacent areas	16,338
Aegean Sea	8,266
Adriatic Sea	7,411
English Channel	5,531
Mediterranean Sea	2,397
Off north and west coast of Scotland	1,699
Off coasts of Ireland	923
Bay of Biscay	904
Black Sea	659
Off west coast of England	404
White Sea and off northern Scandinavia	398
Off coasts of India and Ceylon	184
South China Sea	110
Off Nova Scotia and east coast of U.S.A.	70
Off coast of Africa	68
Off coasts of New Zealand	60
Off coast of Portugal	52
Bass Strait	30
Gulf of Aden	25
TOTAL	**235,983**

ATLANTIC OCEAN

NORWAY

SWEDEN

FINLAND

GULF OF BOTHNIA

BALTIC SEA

SKAGERRAK

DENMARK

Northern Barrage

NORTH SEA

GREAT BRITAIN

IRELAND

HOLLAND

BELGIUM

Dover Barrage

LUX.

GERMANY

POLAND

RUSSIA

FRANCE

SWITZ.

AUSTRIA–HUNGARY

RUMANIA

BULGARIA

SERBIA

MONTENEGRO

ALBANIA

ADRIATIC SEA

ITALY

BAY OF BISCAY

SPAIN

PORTUGAL

BALEARIC IS.

CORSICA

SARDINIA

MEDITER

TYRRHENIAN SEA

SICILY

IONIAN SEA

GREECE

AEGEAN SEA

TURKEY

BLACK SEA

0   300

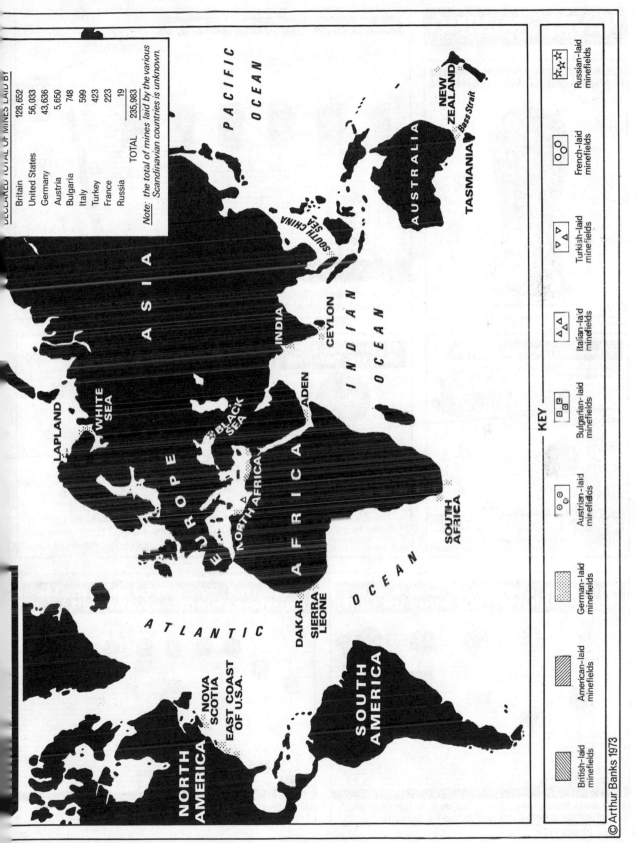

NAVAL MINING

German contact mine

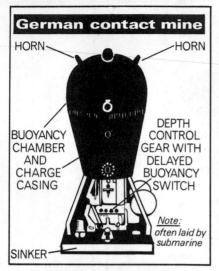

HORN — — HORN

BUOYANCY CHAMBER AND CHARGE CASING

DEPTH CONTROL GEAR WITH DELAYED BUOYANCY SWITCH

SINKER

Note: often laid by submarine

An Observation Minefield

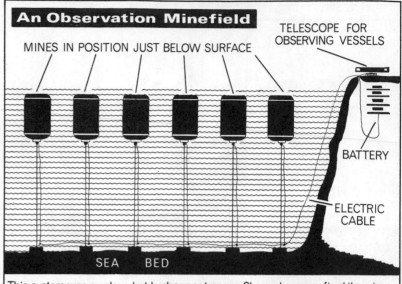

MINES IN POSITION JUST BELOW SURFACE

TELESCOPE FOR OBSERVING VESSELS

BATTERY

ELECTRIC CABLE

SEA BED

This system was employed at harbour entrances. Shore observers fired the mines by electrical methods at the moment when a hostile ship passed over the line.

The Antenna Mine

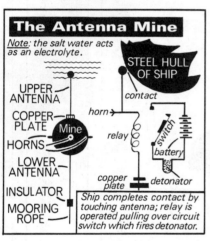

Note: the salt water acts as an electrolyte.

STEEL HULL OF SHIP

contact

UPPER ANTENNA

COPPER PLATE

horn

relay

switch

battery

Mine

HORNS

LOWER ANTENNA

INSULATOR

MOORING ROPE

copper plate

detonator

Ship completes contact by touching antenna; relay is operated pulling over circuit switch which fires detonator.

Hydrostatic depth-taking

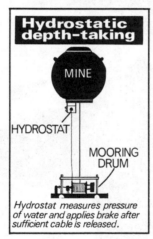

MINE

HYDROSTAT

MOORING DRUM

Hydrostat measures pressure of water and applies brake after sufficient cable is released.

The "HERZ" Horn

HORN BENT BY PASSING SHIP

UN-BENT LEAD HORNS

GLASS TUBES CONTAINING SOLUTION

PLATES

BROKEN GLASS TUBE

to detonator

The inside of the horn is similar to an electrical battery. A bichromate solution comes in contact with zinc and carbon plates, thus making voltage.

Plummet system of automatic depth-taking (non-buoyant unit)

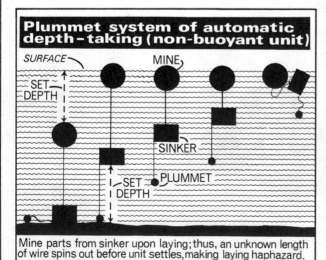

SURFACE

MINE

SET DEPTH

SINKER

SET DEPTH

PLUMMET

Mine parts from sinker upon laying; thus, an unknown length of wire spins out before unit settles, making laying haphazard.

Plummet system of automatic depth-taking (buoyant unit)

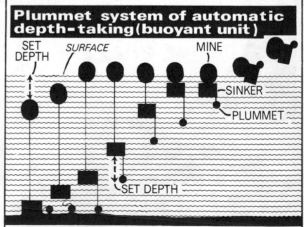

SET DEPTH

SURFACE

MINE

SINKER

PLUMMET

SET DEPTH

Mine stays with sinker until equilibrium is established. Thus, depth-taking with this system is more accurate and precise.

© Arthur Banks 1973

SEVEN IMPORTANT NAVAL MINES 1914 – 1918

TYPES OF MINE

CONTROLLED MINES (employed defensively, e.g. placed at harbour entrances). Fired from shore via electric wire.

INDEPENDENT MINES (employed both offensively and defensively in open sea, off coasts, etc. Types included moored, sea-bed, drifting, creeping, and oscillating.

British "SERVICE"

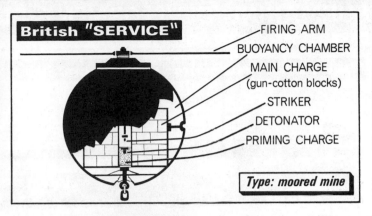

- FIRING ARM
- BUOYANCY CHAMBER
- MAIN CHARGE (gun-cotton blocks)
- STRIKER
- DETONATOR
- PRIMING CHARGE

Type: moored mine

British "H.2"

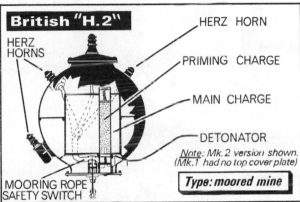

- HERZ HORNS
- HERZ HORN
- PRIMING CHARGE
- MAIN CHARGE
- DETONATOR
- MOORING ROPE SAFETY SWITCH

Note: Mk. 2 version shown. (Mk. 1 had no top cover plate)

Type: moored mine

British "ELIA"

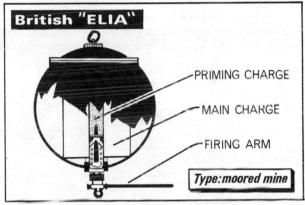

- PRIMING CHARGE
- MAIN CHARGE
- FIRING ARM

Type: moored mine

French "BREGUET"

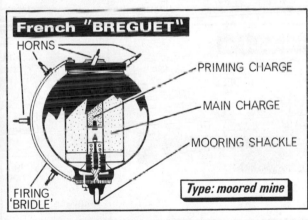

- HORNS
- PRIMING CHARGE
- MAIN CHARGE
- MOORING SHACKLE
- FIRING 'BRIDLE'

Type: moored mine

French "SAUTER–HARLÉ"

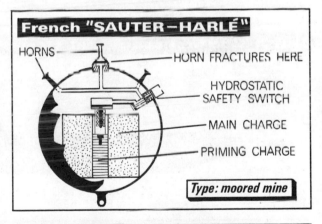

- HORNS
- HORN FRACTURES HERE
- HYDROSTATIC SAFETY SWITCH
- MAIN CHARGE
- PRIMING CHARGE

Type: moored mine

German "CARBONIT"

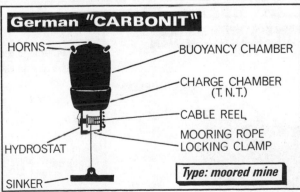

- HORNS
- BUOYANCY CHAMBER
- CHARGE CHAMBER (T. N. T.)
- CABLE REEL
- MOORING ROPE LOCKING CLAMP
- HYDROSTAT
- SINKER

Type: moored mine

Swedish–designed "LÉON"

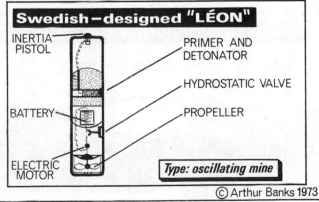

- INERTIA PISTOL
- PRIMER AND DETONATOR
- HYDROSTATIC VALVE
- PROPELLER
- BATTERY
- ELECTRIC MOTOR

Type: oscillating mine

SUBMARINE DEVELOPMENT DURING THE WAR

'DEUTSCHLAND' – first commercial boat

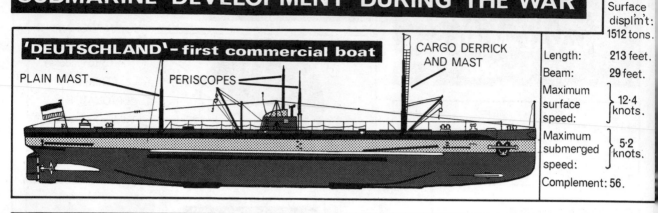

PLAIN MAST
PERISCOPES
CARGO DERRICK AND MAST

Surface displm't:	1512 tons.
Length:	213 feet.
Beam:	29 feet.
Maximum surface speed:	12·4 knots
Maximum submerged speed:	5·2 knots
Complement:	56.

British R.1 – first hunter killer submarine

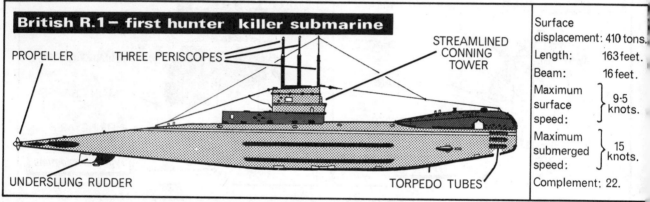

PROPELLER
THREE PERISCOPES
STREAMLINED CONNING TOWER
UNDERSLUNG RUDDER
TORPEDO TUBES

Surface displacement:	410 tons.
Length:	163 feet.
Beam:	16 feet.
Maximum surface speed:	9·5 knots.
Maximum submerged speed:	15 knots.
Complement:	22.

British K.3 – first successful steam submarine

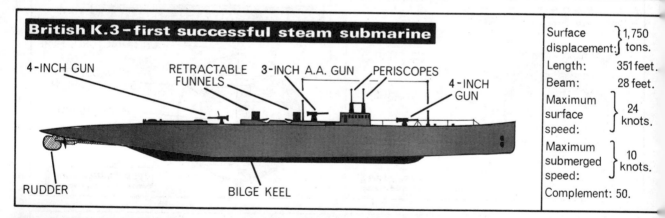

4-INCH GUN
RETRACTABLE FUNNELS
3-INCH A.A. GUN
PERISCOPES
4-INCH GUN
RUDDER
BILGE KEEL

Surface displacement:	1,750 tons.
Length:	351 feet.
Beam:	28 feet.
Maximum surface speed:	24 knots.
Maximum submerged speed:	10 knots.
Complement:	50.

Italian Class 'B' – first successful midget submarine

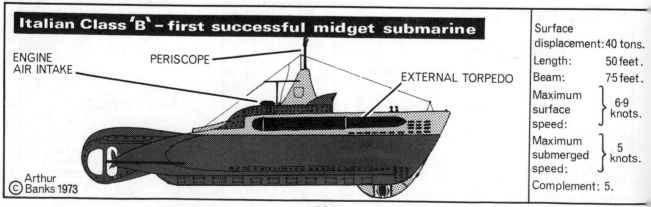

ENGINE AIR INTAKE
PERISCOPE
EXTERNAL TORPEDO

Arthur © Banks 1973

Surface displacement:	40 tons.
Length:	50 feet.
Beam:	7·5 feet.
Maximum surface speed:	6·9 knots.
Maximum submerged speed:	5 knots.
Complement:	5.

THE WAR IN THE AIR

On 1 November 1911 a primitive Italian aeroplane, supporting military operations in Libya, dropped four specially modified grenades on Turkish troops near Zuwarah. The pilot of the aircraft, Lieutenant Cavotti, was thus inaugurating a new and terrible phase of warfare, less than eight years since the first heavier-than-air machine had lifted off the ground. The French, German and American armies were already, in 1911, experimenting with aircraft, though they were uncertain how to use them. The British War Secretary, Haldane, took the lead in establishing a Royal Flying Corps in 1912, while at the Admiralty Churchill warmly supported the aeronautical enterprises (and himself took flying lessons). But by 1914 military and naval leaders, if not actively hostile to 'an air arm', saw in planes and airships little more than reconnaissance machines and gunnery spotters.

The only combatant possessing an aerial fleet of any significance was Germany, with eleven rigid airships, all except one manufactured by Count Zeppelin. During the early months of the war these craft bombed Liége, Antwerp and Warsaw. They proved, however, vulnerable to gunfire when used in close support of the army, and, at the beginning of 1915, it was decided that they would be most effective against targets in England, bringing 'terror to the people of London'. Navigational difficulties saved London from raids on several occasions (and similarly ruled out projected attacks on Petrograd), but the British capital was attacked by Zeppelins twelve times between May 1915 and October 1917. There were forty other raids on Britain, with bombs dropped in the Midlands, Liverpool, Newcastle and Hull as well as East Anglia and the Home Counties. Night bombing by Zeppelins interfered with efficiency in vital factories. Subsequently this role was assumed by aircraft, and the ten night raids of September-October 1917 (see page 296) had a particularly bad effect on civilian morale.

The Zeppelins which raided England in August 1915 were faster and bigger than the craft of a year earlier:
they carried twice the weight of bombs. Without these technological improvements, it would have been impossible to mount what was, in effect, a strategic air offensive against civilian and military targets. But improvements to airships were equalled by developments in aeroplane construction. The most revolutionary of these was Anthony Fokker's invention of an interrupter, a cam which could stop a machine gun firing when the propeller blade swept across the muzzle. This device made the fighter aircraft a weapon in itself. German Fokkers were able to check the mounting pressure by the French bombing planes, an arm in which Joffre himself had long been interested. The British developed DH 4s and DH 9s as light bombers to attack front line troops, and depended on the manoeuvrable Sopwith Camel and S.E. 5a as the principal fighters. The Royal Naval Air Service used seaplane carriers during the Dardanelles Operations and experimented with dropping torpedoes from aircraft, a technique which could be perfected only with more powerful engines, giving a greater impetus.

The 'dog fight', a new form of combat creating its own tactics, gave the opportunity for individualists to make themselves reputations as 'aces'. Yet by the spring of 1917 the most famous of these German aces, Richthofen, was himself perfecting a 'circus', a squadron which was standardising at a rate technical level the accumulated skills of air fighting. Nor were these developments limited to the German side.

By the last winter in the war the British Government had so far accepted the significance of air power that on 1 April 1918, it created a third military service, a Royal Air Force with an 'Air Staff', totally independent of army and navy. The light bombers of the R.A.F. played a prominent part in the final defeat of the Bulgarians in the Balkan mountains and of the Turks in the coastal plain of Palestine; but the authorities were more interested in the effects of strategic bombing on Germany's factories.

GERMAN AIRSHIPS

GERMAN AIRSHIP RAIDS ON BRITAIN 1915-1918

YEAR	NUMBER OF RAIDS	BOMBS DROPPED (All types)	CIVILIANS KILLED	CIVILIANS INJURED
1915	20	1,525	207	533
1916	22	3,458	293	691
1917	7	580	40	75
1918	4	188	16	59
TOTALS	53*	5,751	556	1,358

*Note: London was attacked on twelve occasions

NORTH-WEST GERMAN AIRSHIP BASES

NORTH SEA

BALTIC SEA

Tondern

Kiel

Nordholz

Fuhlsbüttel

Hage

Wittmundhaven

HOLLAND

GERMANY

Alhorn

Wildeshausen

HQ Naval Airship Division
14 Oct.1914 - 25 July.1917
10 Jan.1918 - 9 Nov.1918

HQ Naval Airship Division
25 July 1917 - 10 Jan.1918

L.3 — First Zeppelin to raid Britain

Complement: 16 men   ← GAS CELLS →   Maximum speed: 48 m.p.h.

PROPELLER   OPEN GONDOLAS   PROPELLER

Completed: 11 May 1914	Gas volume: 794,500 cubic ft.
Commissioned: 23 May 1914	Height: 60ft. 3ins.
Length: 518 ft. 2 ins.	Diameter: 48ft. 6ins.

Zeppelin "P" Type

Length: 536 ft. 5 ins.	Maximum speed: 59 m.p.h.	Gas volume: 1,126,400 cubic ft.	
Diameter: 61ft. 4 ins.	Complement: 16 men	Height: 79 ft. 4 ins.	

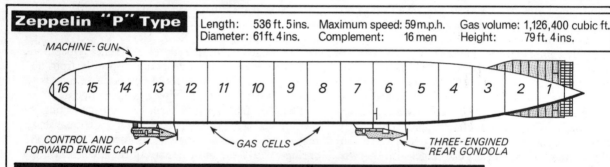

MACHINE-GUN

CONTROL AND FORWARD ENGINE CAR

GAS CELLS

THREE-ENGINED REAR GONDOLA

NAVAL NUMBER	COMMISSIONED	ACTUAL RAIDS	TOTAL FLIGHTS	TERMINATION OF SERVICE
L.10	17 May 1915	5	28	3 September 1915: destroyed off Neuwerk I.
L.11	8 June 1915	18	118	24 November 1917: dismantled at Hage.
L.12	22 June 1915	1	14	10 August 1915: burned at Ostend.
L.13	25 July 1915	17	159	11 December 1917: dismantled at Hage.
L.14	10 August 1915	17	127	23 June 1919: wrecked at Nordholz.
L.15	12 September 1915	3	36	1 April 1916: sank in sea at Knock Deep.
L.16	24 September 1915	16	132	19 October 1917: wrecked at Nordholz.
L.17	22 October 1915	11	73	28 December 1916: burned at Tondern.
L.18	6 November 1915	0	4	17 November 1915: burned at Tondern.
L.19	22 November 1915	1	14	2 February 1916: sank in North Sea.

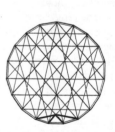

MAIN RING BRACING

THE THREE BASIC TYPES OF AIRSHIP

1. Non-rigid
A balloon, the shape of which was held by internal pressure.
2. Semi-rigid
A shaped balloon with a rigid girder to which the main weights were slung.
3. Rigid
A group of balloons inside a rigid frame with, usually, a fabric cover.

During the war, the Germans manufactured two main types of rigid airships, the Schütte-Lanz and the Zeppelin. The early S.L.'s were wooden-framed, and the Zeppelins metal-framed (the metal used was duralumin). Hydrogen was the gas employed, and Germany paid particular attention to purity to avoid explosions.

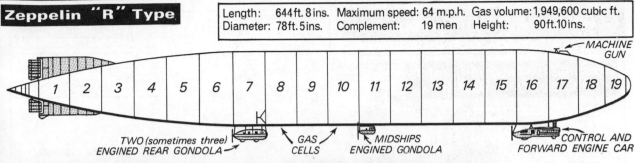

Zeppelin "R" Type

| Length: 644ft. 8ins. | Maximum speed: 64 m.p.h. | Gas volume: 1,949,600 cubic ft. |
| Diameter: 78ft. 5ins. | Complement: 19 men | Height: 90ft.10ins. |

MACHINE GUN

1 2 3 4 5 6 7 8 9 10 11 12 13 14 15 16 17 18 19

TWO (sometimes three) ENGINED REAR GONDOLA — *GAS CELLS* — *MIDSHIPS ENGINED GONDOLA* — *CONTROL AND FORWARD ENGINE CAR*

NAVAL NUMBER	COMMISSIONED	ACTUAL RAIDS	TOTAL FLIGHTS	TERMINATION OF SERVICE
L.30	30 May 1916	9	115	Broken up in 1920: parts to Belgium.
L.31	14 July 1916	8	19	2 October 1916: destroyed at Potters Bar.
L.32	7 August 1916	3	13	24 September 1916: destroyed at Gt. Burstead.
L.33	2 September 1916	1	10	24 Sept. 1916: captured at Little Wigborough.
L.34	22 September 1916	2	11	27 November 1916: destroyed off Hartlepool.
L.35	12 October 1916	5	54	September 1918: broken up at Jüterbog.
L.36	7 November 1916	1	20	7 February 1917: crashed on frozen River Aller.
L.37	27 November 1916	4	50 ?	Broken up in 1920: parts to Japan.
L.38	26 November 1916	1	10	29 December 1916: captured at Seemuppen.
L.39	18 December 1916	1	24	17 March 1917: destroyed at Compiègne.
L.40	7 January 1917	2	30	17 June 1917: dismantled at Nevenwald.
L.41	30 January 1917	4	36	23 June 1919: destroyed at Nordholz.
L.45	7 April 1917	3	27	20 October 1917: captured at Sisteron.
L.47	3 May 1917	4	44	5 January 1918: destroyed at Alhorn.
L.50	12 June 1917	2	19	20 October 1917: lost in Mediterranean.

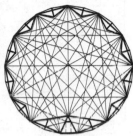

MAIN RING BRACING

Note: there were minor design variations in certain of the 'R'- type airships. Gondolas were altered here and there to improve the performance of engines and propellers.

GERMAN AIRSHIP BASES IN THE EASTERN BALTIC

On 26 January 1915, the German Naval Airship Division lost its first airship of the war when the Parseval Pl 19 set out from the Army shed near Königsberg to raid the Russian naval base at Libau. It crashed in the Baltic seven miles from the coast after severe icing which jammed a propellor and fractured an engine. Finally, the envelope buckled due to loss of pressure.

Wainoden (from 1916)
X Libau
Baltic Sea
RUSSIA
Memel
Telshi
Tilsit
GULF OF DANZIG
Königsberg
Seerappen
Seddin
EAST PRUSSIA
Danzig
Elbing

0 — 50 Miles

GERMANY Bases shown thus ◉

During the night of 21-22 March 1915, three German army airships attempted to raid Paris. The ZX and the LZ. 35 dropped seven high explosive and 45 incendiaries on Paris and its suburbs, killing one civilian and injuring a further eight. Hit by ground fire, the ZX was destroyed at St. Quentin on the return trip. Damaged by gunfire, the third airship (Schütte-Lanz SL.2) never reached the French capital, but distributed her bombs over Compiègne.

During the war, both the naval and the army airship services made unsuccessful attempts to raid the Russian capital of St. Petersburg (Petrograd). Distance alone prevented success during the early period, but the main problem throughout was bad weather. Ice and snow fouled engines and propellors, congealed oil, and made airships top-heavy and unstable.

Airships worked as scouts with the German navy and were present at a number of sea battles, such as Jutland and Dogger Bank. However, they were never used in conjunction with the U-boat offensive in the Atlantic.

© Arthur Banks 1973

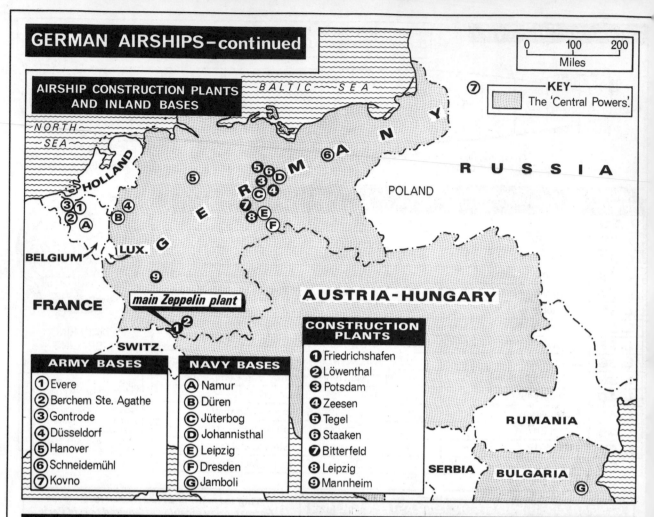

GERMAN AIRSHIPS–continued

AIRSHIP CONSTRUCTION PLANTS AND INLAND BASES

0 — 100 — 200
Miles

KEY
⑦ | The 'Central Powers'.

BALTIC SEA

NORTH SEA

HOLLAND

G E R M A N Y

RUSSIA

POLAND

BELGIUM

LUX.

FRANCE

SWITZ.

main Zeppelin plant

AUSTRIA-HUNGARY

RUMANIA

SERBIA | BULGARIA

ARMY BASES
① Evere
② Berchem Ste. Agathe
③ Gontrode
④ Düsseldorf
⑤ Hanover
⑥ Schneidemühl
⑦ Kovno

NAVY BASES
Ⓐ Namur
Ⓑ Düren
Ⓒ Jüterbog
Ⓓ Johannisthal
Ⓔ Leipzig
Ⓕ Dresden
Ⓖ Jamboli

CONSTRUCTION PLANTS
❶ Friedrichshafen
❷ Löwenthal
❸ Potsdam
❹ Zeesen
❺ Tegel
❻ Staaken
❼ Bitterfeld
❽ Leipzig
❾ Mannheim

On 5 January 1918, five German airships were destroyed in a sudden and still-unexplained fire at Alhorn. Zeppelins L.46, L.47, L.51, and L.58, plus the Schütte-Lanz SL.20, were involved and the German Naval Airship Division lost 10 men dead, 30 seriously injured, and 104 slightly injured. A further 4 civilian technicians were killed. The most widely held theory is that the blaze originated in the rear gondola of L.51 through the use of petroleum as a cleaning agent by civilian workmen. The German airship service never properly recovered from this disaster.

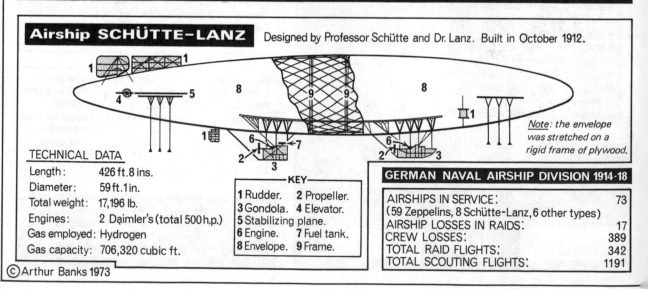

Airship SCHÜTTE-LANZ
Designed by Professor Schütte and Dr. Lanz. Built in October 1912.

Note: the envelope was stretched on a rigid frame of plywood.

TECHNICAL DATA
Length: 426 ft. 8 ins.
Diameter: 59 ft. 1 in.
Total weight: 17,196 lb.
Engines: 2 Daimler's (total 500 h.p.)
Gas employed: Hydrogen
Gas capacity: 706,320 cubic ft.

KEY
1 Rudder. 2 Propeller.
3 Gondola. 4 Elevator.
5 Stabilizing plane.
6 Engine. 7 Fuel tank.
8 Envelope. 9 Frame.

GERMAN NAVAL AIRSHIP DIVISION 1914-18

AIRSHIPS IN SERVICE:	73
(59 Zeppelins, 8 Schütte-Lanz, 6 other types)	
AIRSHIP LOSSES IN RAIDS:	17
CREW LOSSES:	389
TOTAL RAID FLIGHTS:	342
TOTAL SCOUTING FLIGHTS:	1191

© Arthur Banks 1973

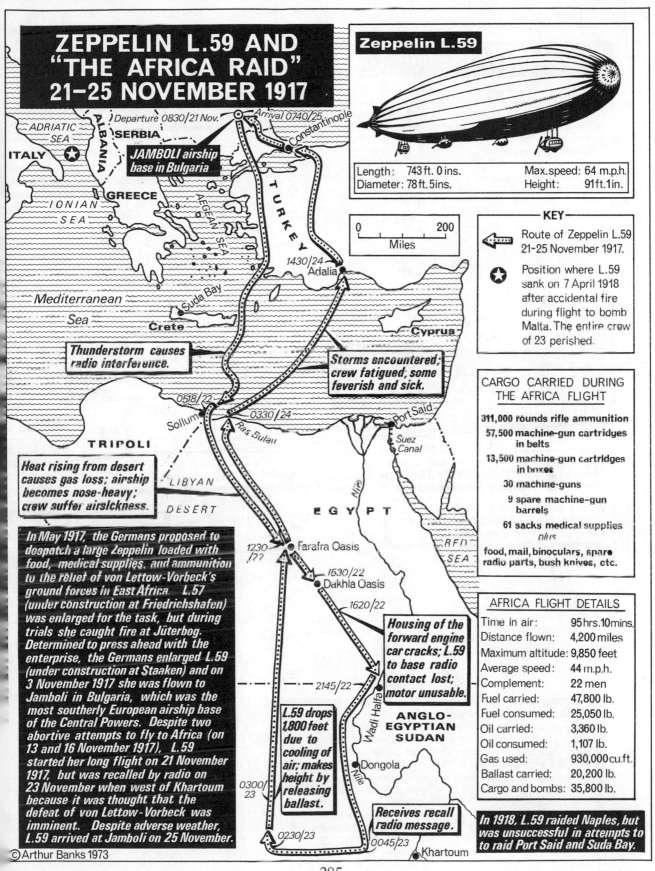

ZEPPELIN L.59 AND "THE AFRICA RAID" 21–25 NOVEMBER 1917

Zeppelin L.59

Length:	743 ft. 0 ins.	Max. speed:	64 m.p.h.
Diameter:	78 ft. 5 ins.	Height:	91 ft. 1 in.

KEY

Route of Zeppelin L.59 21–25 November 1917.

★ Position where L.59 sank on 7 April 1918 after accidental fire during flight to bomb Malta. The entire crew of 23 perished.

CARGO CARRIED DURING THE AFRICA FLIGHT

311,000 rounds rifle ammunition

57,500 machine-gun cartridges in belts

13,500 machine-gun cartridges in boxes

30 machine-guns

9 spare machine-gun barrels

61 sacks medical supplies plus

food, mail, binoculars, spare radio parts, bush knives, etc.

AFRICA FLIGHT DETAILS

Time in air:	95 hrs. 10 mins.
Distance flown:	4,200 miles
Maximum altitude:	9,850 feet
Average speed:	44 m.p.h.
Complement:	22 men
Fuel carried:	47,800 lb.
Fuel consumed:	25,050 lb.
Oil carried:	3,360 lb.
Oil consumed:	1,107 lb.
Gas used:	930,000 cu. ft.
Ballast carried:	20,200 lb.
Cargo and bombs:	35,800 lb.

Departure 0830/21 Nov.

Arrival 0740/25

Constantinople

JAMBOLI airship base in Bulgaria

ADRIATIC SEA

ITALY

ALBANIA

SERBIA

GREECE

IONIAN SEA

AEGEAN SEA

TURKEY

1430/24 Adalia

Mediterranean Sea

Suda Bay

Crete

Cyprus

Thunderstorm causes radio interference.

Storms encountered; crew fatigued; some feverish and sick.

0518/22

Sollum

0330/24

Ras Sulau

Port Said

Suez Canal

TRIPOLI

Heat rising from desert causes gas loss; airship becomes nose-heavy; crew suffer airsickness.

LIBYAN DESERT

EGYPT

Nile

RED SEA

1230/??

Farafra Oasis

1530/22 Dakhla Oasis

1620/22

Housing of the forward engine car cracks; L.59 to base radio contact lost; motor unusable.

In May 1917, the Germans proposed to despatch a large Zeppelin loaded with food, medical supplies, and ammunition to the relief of von Lettow-Vorbeck's ground forces in East Africa. L.57 (under construction at Friedrichshafen) was enlarged for the task, but during trials she caught fire at Jüterbog. Determined to press ahead with the enterprise, the Germans enlarged L.59 (under construction at Staaken) and on 3 November 1917 she was flown to Jamboli in Bulgaria, which was the most southerly European airship base of the Central Powers. Despite two abortive attempts to fly to Africa (on 13 and 16 November 1917), L.59 started her long flight on 21 November 1917, but was recalled by radio on 23 November when west of Khartoum because it was thought that the defeat of von Lettow-Vorbeck was imminent. Despite adverse weather, L.59 arrived at Jamboli on 25 November.

© Arthur Banks 1973

2145/22

ANGLO-EGYPTIAN SUDAN

Wadi Halfa

L.59 drops 1,800 feet due to cooling of air; makes height by releasing ballast.

Receives recall radio message.

Dongola

Nile

0300/23

0230/23

0045/23

Khartoum

In 1918, L.59 raided Naples, but was unsuccessful in attempts to to raid Port Said and Suda Bay.

0 200 Miles

GERMAN AIRSHIP RAIDS ON BRITAIN 1915–1918

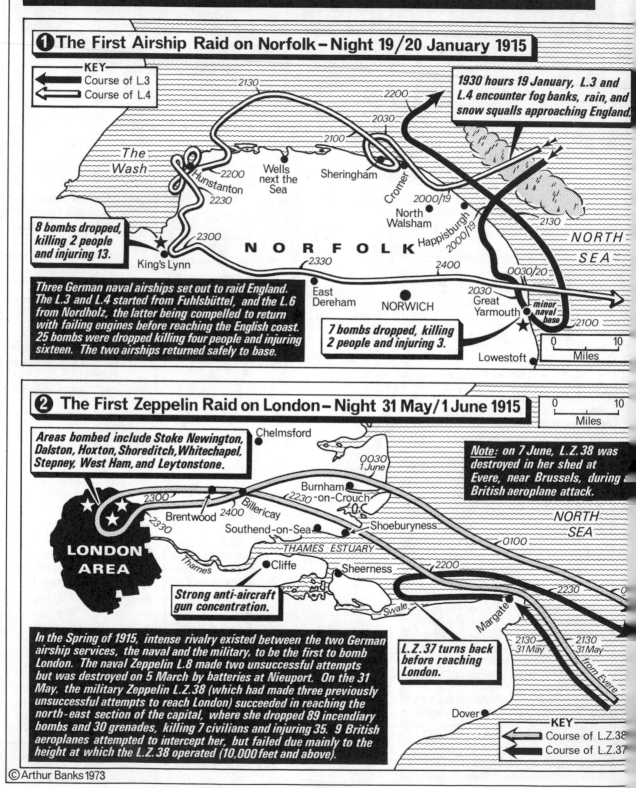

① The First Airship Raid on Norfolk – Night 19/20 January 1915

KEY
← Course of L.3
⇐ Course of L.4

1930 hours 19 January, L.3 and L.4 encounter fog banks, rain, and snow squalls approaching England.

2130
2200
2030
2100
The Wash
2200 — Hunstanton
2230
2300
Wells next the Sea
Sheringham
Cromer
2000/19
North Walsham
Happisburgh
2000/19
2130

8 bombs dropped, killing 2 people and injuring 13.

King's Lynn
2330
N O R F O L K
2400
0030/20

NORTH SEA

2030
Great Yarmouth
minor naval base
2100

Three German naval airships set out to raid England. The L.3 and L.4 started from Fuhlsbüttel, and the L.6 from Nordholz, the latter being compelled to return with failing engines before reaching the English coast. 25 bombs were dropped killing four people and injuring sixteen. The two airships returned safely to base.

East Dereham
NORWICH

7 bombs dropped, killing 2 people and injuring 3.

Lowestoft

0 — 10 Miles

② The First Zeppelin Raid on London – Night 31 May/1 June 1915

0 — 10 Miles

Areas bombed include Stoke Newington, Dalston, Hoxton, Shoreditch, Whitechapel, Stepney, West Ham, and Leytonstone.

Chelmsford

0030 1 June

Note: on 7 June, L.Z.38 was destroyed in her shed at Evere, near Brussels, during a British aeroplane attack.

2300
2330
2400
Brentwood
Billericay
Burnham-on-Crouch
2230

LONDON AREA

Southend-on-Sea
Shoeburyness
0100

NORTH SEA

Thames
THAMES ESTUARY
Cliffe
Sheerness
2200
2230

Strong anti-aircraft gun concentration.

Swale
Margate
from Evere

L.Z.37 turns back before reaching London.

In the Spring of 1915, intense rivalry existed between the two German airship services, the naval and the military, to be the first to bomb London. The naval Zeppelin L.8 made two unsuccessful attempts but was destroyed on 5 March by batteries at Nieuport. On the 31 May, the military Zeppelin L.Z.38 (which had made three previously unsuccessful attempts to reach London) succeeded in reaching the north-east section of the capital, where she dropped 89 incendiary bombs and 30 grenades, killing 7 civilians and injuring 35. 9 British aeroplanes attempted to intercept her, but failed due mainly to the height at which the L.Z.38 operated (10,000 feet and above).

2130 31 May
2130 31 May

Dover

KEY
← Course of L.Z.38
← Course of L.Z.37

© Arthur Banks 1973

286

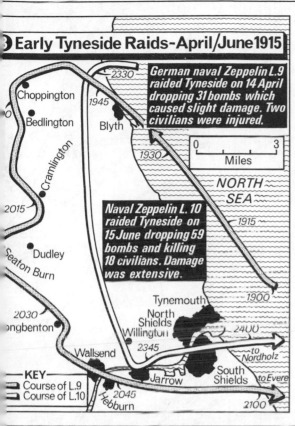

❸ Early Tyneside Raids - April/June 1915

German naval Zeppelin L.9 raided Tyneside on 14 April dropping 31 bombs which caused slight damage. Two civilians were injured.

Naval Zeppelin L.10 raided Tyneside on 15 June dropping 59 bombs and killing 18 civilians. Damage was extensive.

Choppington
Bedlington
Blyth
Cranlington
Dudley
Seaton Burn
Wallsend
Jarrow
Hebburn
Tynemouth
North Shields
Willington
South Shields
ongbenton

2330
1945
1930
2015
2030
2045
2345
2400
2100
2015
1915
1900

to Nordholz
to Evere

NORTH SEA

0   3
Miles

KEY
Course of L.9
Course of L.10

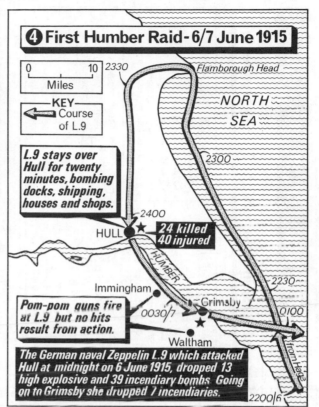

❹ First Humber Raid - 6/7 June 1915

0   10
Miles

KEY
Course of L.9

Flamborough Head

NORTH SEA

L.9 stays over Hull for twenty minutes, bombing docks, shipping, houses and shops.

HULL
2400

24 killed 40 injured

Immingham
Grimsby
Waltham

2330
2300
2230
0100
0030/7
2200/6

HUMBER

from Hage

Pom-pom guns fire at L.9 but no hits result from action.

The German naval Zeppelin L.9 which attacked Hull at midnight on 6 June 1915, dropped 13 high explosive and 39 incendiary bombs. Going on to Grimsby she dropped 7 incendiaries.

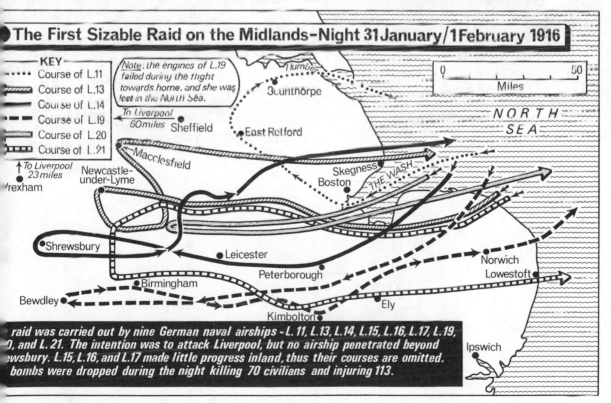

The First Sizable Raid on the Midlands - Night 31 January/1 February 1916

KEY
Course of L.11
Course of L.13
Course of L.14
Course of L.19
Course of L.20
Course of L.21

Note: the engines of L.19 failed during the flight towards home, and she was lost in the North Sea.

0   50
Miles

NORTH SEA

Humber
Scunthorpe
East Retford
To Liverpool 60 miles
Sheffield
Macclesfield
Skegness
Boston
THE WASH
Newcastle-under-Lyme
To Liverpool 23 miles
Wrexham
Shrewsbury
Leicester
Peterborough
Norwich
Lowestoft
Bewdley
Birmingham
Ely
Kimbolton
Ipswich

raid was carried out by nine German naval airships - L.11, L.13, L.14, L.15, L.16, L.17, L.19, L.20, and L.21. The intention was to attack Liverpool, but no airship penetrated beyond Shrewsbury. L.15, L.16, and L.17 made little progress inland, thus their courses are omitted. bombs were dropped during the night killing 70 civilians and injuring 113.

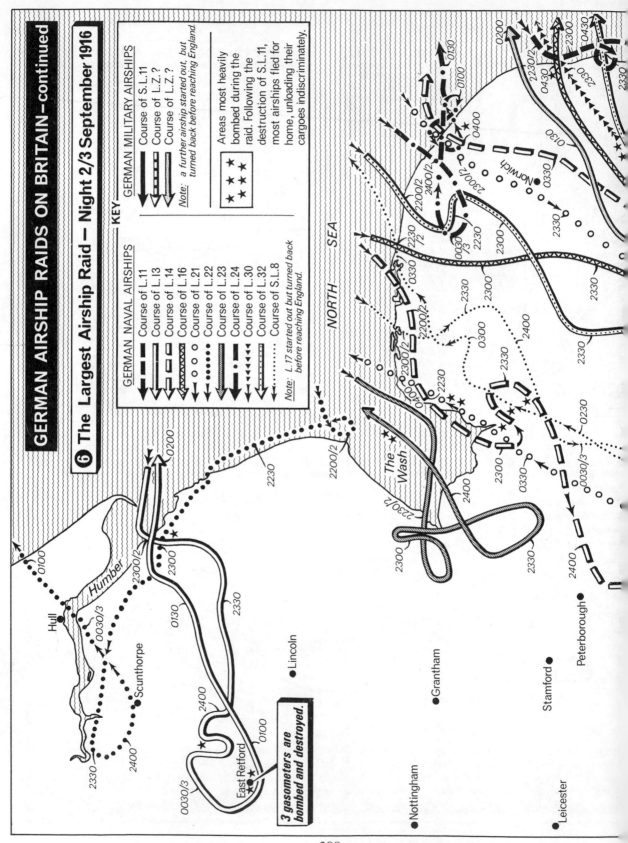

GERMAN AIRSHIP RAIDS ON BRITAIN—continued

6 The Largest Airship Raid – Night 2/3 September 1916

KEY

GERMAN NAVAL AIRSHIPS

Course of L.11
Course of L.13
Course of L.14
Course of L.16
Course of L.21
Course of L.22
Course of L.23
Course of L.24
Course of L.30
Course of L.32
Course of S.L.8

Note: L.17 started out but turned back before reaching England.

GERMAN MILITARY AIRSHIPS

Course of S.L.11
Course of L.Z. ?
Course of L.Z. ?

Note: a further airship started out, but turned back before reaching England.

Areas most heavily bombed during the raid. Following the destruction of S.L.11, most airships fled for home, unloading their cargoes indiscriminately.

3 gasometers are bombed and destroyed.

Hull

Scunthorpe

Humber

East Retford

Lincoln

Grantham

Nottingham

Stamford

Peterborough

Leicester

The Wash

Norwich

NORTH SEA

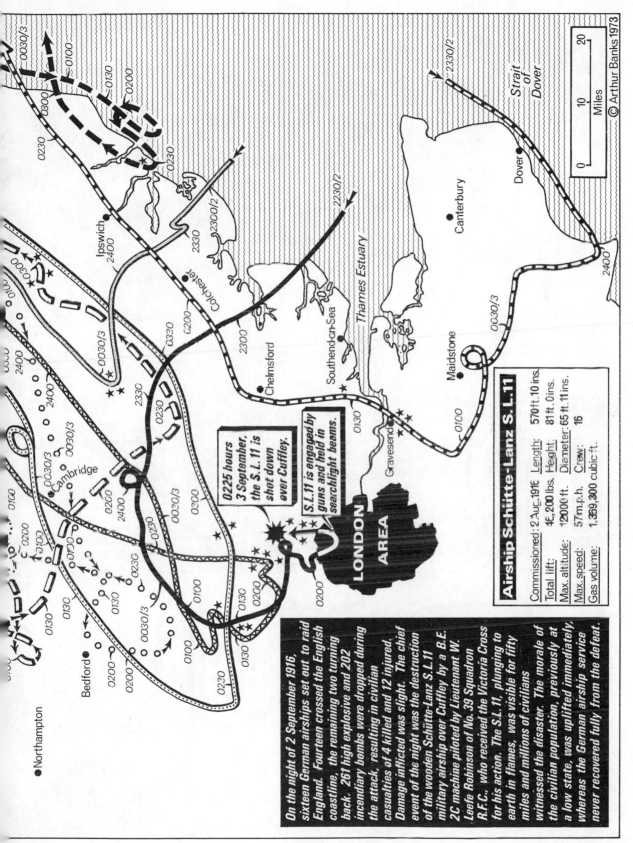

Airship Schütte-Lanz S.L.11

Commissioned:	2 Aug. 1916	Length:	570 ft. 10 ins.
Total lift:	46,200 lbs.	Height:	81 ft. 0 ins.
Max. altitude:	12000 ft.	Diameter:	65 ft. 11 ins.
Max. speed:	57 m.p.h.	Crew:	16
Gas volume:	1,359,300 cubic ft.		

0225 hours 3 September, the S. L. 11 is shot down over Cuffley.

S.L.11 is engaged by guns and held in searchlight beams.

LONDON AREA

On the night of 2 September 1916, sixteen German airships set out to raid England. Fourteen crossed the English coastline, the remaining two turning back. 261 high explosive and 202 incendiary bombs were dropped during the attack, resulting in civilian casualties of 4 killed and 12 injured. Damage inflicted was slight. The chief event of the night was the destruction of the wooden Schütte-Lanz S.L.11 military airship over Cuffley by a B.E. 2C machine piloted by Lieutenant W. Leefe Robinson of No.39 Squadron R.F.C., who received the Victoria Cross for his action. The S.L.11, plunging to earth in flames, was visible for fifty miles and millions of civilians witnessed the disaster. The morale of the civilian population, previously at a low state, was uplifted immediately, whereas the German airship service never recovered fully from the defeat.

Northampton
Bedford
Cambridge
Ipswich
Colchester
Chelmsford
Southend-on-Sea
Thames Estuary
Gravesend
Maidstone
Canterbury
Dover
Strait of Dover

© Arthur Banks 1973

Miles
0   10   20

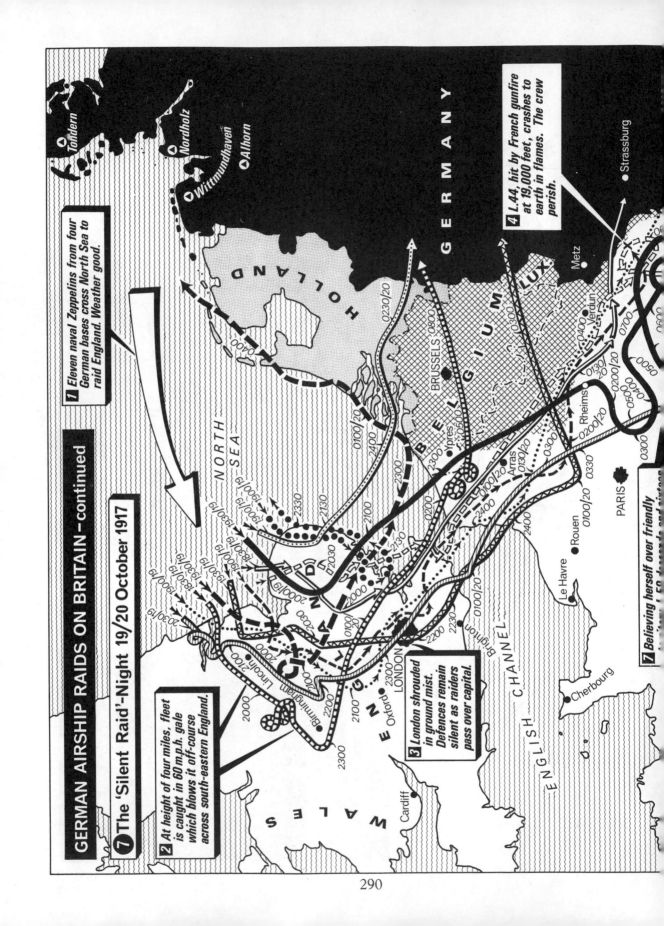

GERMAN AIRSHIP RAIDS ON BRITAIN – continued

7 The 'Silent Raid' – Night 19/20 October 1917

1 Eleven naval Zeppelins from four German bases cross North Sea to raid England. Weather good.

2 At height of four miles, fleet is caught in 60 m.p.h. gale which blows it off-course across south-eastern England.

3 London shrouded in ground mist. Defences remain silent as raiders pass over capital.

4 L.44, hit by French gunfire at 19,000 feet, crashes to earth in flames. The crew perish.

7 Believing herself over friendly

NORTH SEA

HOLLAND

GERMANY

BELGIUM

LUX.

ENGLAND

WALES

ENGLISH CHANNEL

Tondern
Nordholz
Wittmundhaven
Alhorn
Strassburg
Metz
Verdun
Rheims
Brussels
Ypres
Arras
Paris
Rouen
Le Havre
Cherbourg
Lincoln
Birmingham
Oxford
London
Brighton
Cardiff

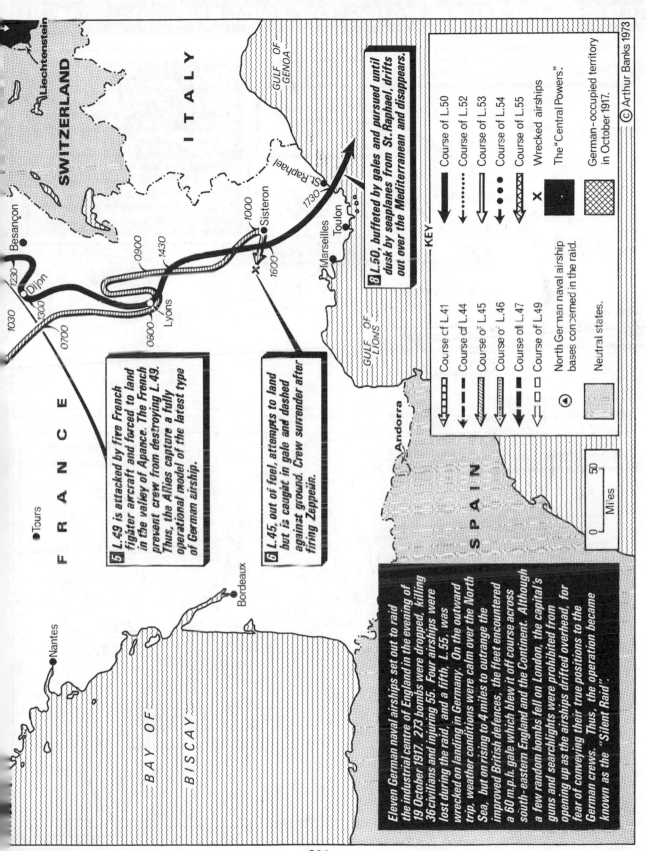

291

Eleven German naval airships set out to raid the industrial centre of England in the evening of 19 October 1917. 273 bombs were dropped, killing 36 civilians and injuring 55. Four airships were lost during the raid, and a fifth, L.55, was wrecked on landing in Germany. On the outward trip, weather conditions were calm over the North Sea, but on rising to 4 miles to outrange the improved British defences, the fleet encountered a 60 m.p.h. gale which blew it off course across south-eastern England and the Continent. Although a few random bombs fell on London, the capital's guns and searchlights were prohibited from opening up as the airships drifted overhead, for fear of conveying their true positions to the German crews. Thus, the operation became known as the "Silent Raid".

5 L.49 is attacked by five French fighter aircraft and forced to land in the valley of Apance. The French prevent crew from destroying L.49. Thus, the Allies capture a fully operational model of the latest type of German airship.

6 L.45, out of fuel, attempts to land but is caught in gale and dashed against ground. Crew surrender after firing Zeppelin.

8 L.50, buffeted by gales and pursued until dusk by seaplanes from St. Raphael, drifts out over the Mediterranean and disappears.

KEY

Course of L.41
Course of L.44
Course of L.45
Course of L.46
Course of L.47
Course of L.49

Course of L.50
Course of L.52
Course of L.53
Course of L.54
Course of L.55
X Wrecked airships
The "Central Powers".
German-occupied territory in October 1917.

North German naval airship bases concerned in the raid.

Neutral states.

0 50 Miles

© Arthur Banks 1973

GERMAN BOMBER RAIDS ON ENGLAND 1917-1918

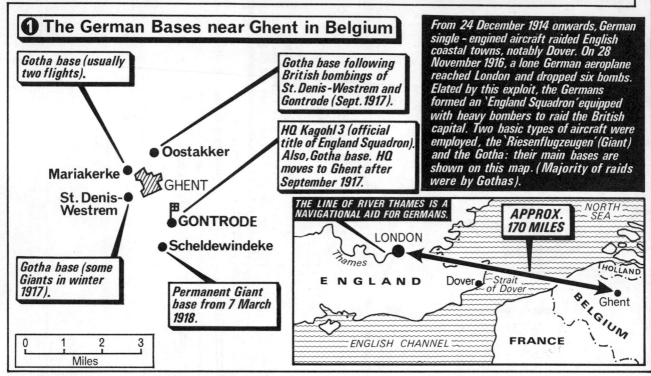

① The German Bases near Ghent in Belgium

Gotha base (usually two flights).

Gotha base following British bombings of St. Denis-Westrem and Gontrode (Sept. 1917).

HQ Kagohl 3 (official title of England Squadron). Also, Gotha base. HQ moves to Ghent after September 1917.

From 24 December 1914 onwards, German single-engined aircraft raided English coastal towns, notably Dover. On 28 November 1916, a lone German aeroplane reached London and dropped six bombs. Elated by this exploit, the Germans formed an 'England Squadron' equipped with heavy bombers to raid the British capital. Two basic types of aircraft were employed, the 'Riesenflugzeugen' (Giant) and the Gotha: their main bases are shown on this map. (Majority of raids were by Gothas).

● Oostakker

Mariakerke

St. Denis-Westrem

GHENT

⊞ GONTRODE

● Scheldewindeke

Gotha base (some Giants in winter 1917).

Permanent Giant base from 7 March 1918.

0 1 2 3 Miles

THE LINE OF RIVER THAMES IS A NAVIGATIONAL AID FOR GERMANS.

APPROX. 170 MILES

NORTH SEA

LONDON

Thames

ENGLAND

Dover — Strait of Dover

HOLLAND

Ghent

BELGIUM

ENGLISH CHANNEL

FRANCE

② The Main Target: LONDON

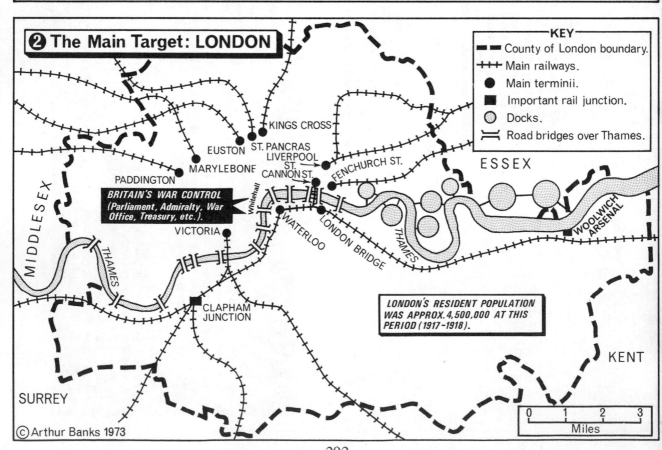

KEY
- – – County of London boundary.
- +++ Main railways.
- ● Main terminii.
- ■ Important rail junction.
- ◯ Docks.
- ⊔ Road bridges over Thames.

KINGS CROSS

EUSTON · ST. PANCRAS

MARYLEBONE

LIVERPOOL ST. · CANNON ST.

FENCHURCH ST.

ESSEX

PADDINGTON

BRITAIN'S WAR CONTROL (Parliament, Admiralty, War Office, Treasury, etc.).

Whitehall

VICTORIA

WATERLOO

LONDON BRIDGE

THAMES

WOOLWICH ARSENAL

MIDDLESEX

THAMES

CLAPHAM JUNCTION

LONDON'S RESIDENT POPULATION WAS APPROX. 4,500,000 AT THIS PERIOD (1917-1918).

KENT

SURREY

© Arthur Banks 1973

0 1 2 3 Miles

292

Employing Gotha bombers, the Germans made eight mass-attacks in daylight against England in 1917. 165 aircraft flights were involved and nearly 73,000 lbs. of bombs were dropped, killing or injuring 1,364 English civilians. Seventeen Gothas were destroyed during the period 25 May – 22 August 1917. Four of the attacks are shown below.

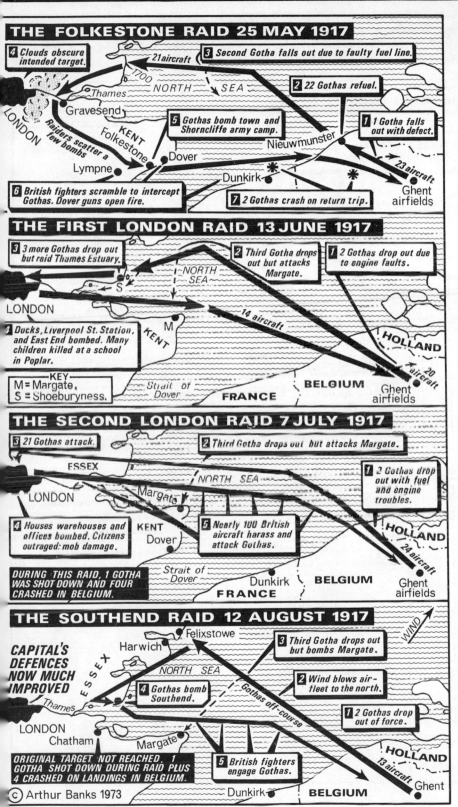

THE FOLKESTONE RAID 25 MAY 1917

4 Clouds obscure intended target.

3 Second Gotha falls out due to faulty fuel line.

21 aircraft

1700

NORTH SEA

2 22 Gothas refuel.

Thames

Gravesend

5 Gothas bomb town and Shorncliffe army camp.

KENT

Folkestone

Nieuwmunster

1 1 Gotha falls out with defect.

LONDON

Raiders scatter a few bombs

Dover

23 aircraft

Lympne

Dunkirk

Ghent airfields

6 British fighters scramble to intercept Gothas. Dover guns open fire.

7 2 Gothas crash on return trip.

THE FIRST LONDON RAID 13 JUNE 1917

3 3 more Gothas drop out but raid Thames Estuary.

2 Third Gotha drops out but attacks Margate.

1 2 Gothas drop out due to engine faults.

NORTH SEA

S

LONDON

14 aircraft

4 Docks, Liverpool St. Station, and East End bombed. Many children killed at a school in Poplar.

KENT

M

HOLLAND

20 aircraft

BELGIUM

Ghent airfields

KEY
M = Margate.
S = Shoeburyness.

Strait of Dover

FRANCE

THE SECOND LONDON RAID 7 JULY 1917

3 21 Gothas attack.

2 Third Gotha drops out but attacks Margate.

ESSEX

NORTH SEA

1 2 Gothas drop out with fuel and engine troubles.

LONDON

Margate

4 Houses warehouses and offices bombed. Citizens outraged: mob damage.

KENT

Dover

5 Nearly 100 British aircraft harass and attack Gothas.

HOLLAND

24 aircraft

Strait of Dover

Dunkirk

BELGIUM

Ghent airfields

FRANCE

DURING THIS RAID, 1 GOTHA WAS SHOT DOWN AND FOUR CRASHED IN BELGIUM.

THE SOUTHEND RAID 12 AUGUST 1917

CAPITAL'S DEFENCES NOW MUCH IMPROVED

Felixstowe

Harwich

WIND

3 Third Gotha drops out but bombs Margate.

ESSEX

NORTH SEA

Gothas off-course

2 Wind blows air-fleet to the north.

4 Gothas bomb Southend.

Thames

1 2 Gothas drop out of force.

LONDON

Chatham

Margate

HOLLAND

13 aircraft

ORIGINAL TARGET NOT REACHED, 1 GOTHA SHOT DOWN DURING RAID PLUS 4 CRASHED ON LANDINGS IN BELGIUM.

5 British fighters engage Gothas.

Dunkirk

BELGIUM

Ghent

© Arthur Banks 1973

THE EIGHT DAYLIGHT RAIDS

1 25 MAY 1917
Aircraft employed: 23.
Aircraft lost: 2.
Damage caused: £19,500.
Civilians killed: 95.

2 5 JUNE 1917
Aircraft employed: 22.
Aircraft lost: 1.
Damage caused: £5,000.
Civilians killed: 13.

3 13 JUNE 1917
Aircraft employed: 20.
Aircraft lost: Nil.
Damage caused: £129,500.
Civilians killed: 162.

4 4 JULY 1917
Aircraft employed: 25.
Aircraft lost: Nil.
Damage caused: £2,100.
Civilians killed: 17.

5 7 JULY 1917
Aircraft employed: 24.
Aircraft lost: 5.
Damage caused: £205,500.
Civilians killed: 57.

6 22 JULY 1917
Aircraft employed: 23.
Aircraft lost: 1.
Damage caused: £2,800.
Civilians killed: 13.

7 12 AUGUST 1917
Aircraft employed: 13.
Aircraft lost: 5.
Damage caused: £9,600.
Civilians killed: 32.

8 22 AUGUST 1917
Aircraft employed: 15.
Aircraft lost: 3.
Damage caused: £17,200.
Civilians killed: 12.

GERMAN BOMBER RAIDS ON ENGLAND*–continued

*TOTAL MASS RAIDS (1917-1918) = 27.

Because of the increasing efficiency of Britain's defences, the Germans switched from daylight to darkness for their attacks. 19 raids were carried out between 3 September 1917 and 20 May 1918 and often several towns were bombed during a single raid. At one period, 300,000 Londoners sought refuge at Underground stations.

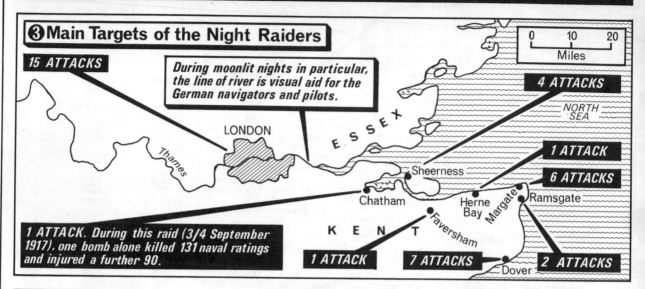

③ Main Targets of the Night Raiders

0   10   20
Miles

15 ATTACKS

During moonlit nights in particular, the line of river is visual aid for the German navigators and pilots.

4 ATTACKS

NORTH SEA

LONDON

Thames

ESSEX

1 ATTACK

Sheerness

6 ATTACKS

Chatham

Herne Bay

Margate

Ramsgate

1 ATTACK. During this raid (3/4 September 1917), one bomb alone killed 131 naval ratings and injured a further 90.

Faversham

KENT

1 ATTACK

7 ATTACKS

Dover

2 ATTACKS

THE 19 DARKNESS RAIDS

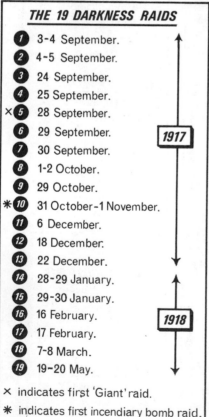

1   3-4 September.
2   4-5 September.
3   24 September.
4   25 September.
×5   28 September.
6   29 September.
7   30 September.
8   1-2 October.
9   29 October.
*10   31 October-1 November.
11   6 December.
12   18 December.
13   22 December.
14   28-29 January.
15   29-30 January.
16   16 February.
17   17 February.
18   7-8 March.
19   19-20 May.

1917

1918

× indicates first 'Giant' raid.

* indicates first incendiary bomb raid.

© Arthur Banks 1973

THE GERMAN 'ELEKTRON' BOMB (AUGUST 1918)

Weighing approx. one kilogram, this incendiary device ignited upon contact. Constructed of magnesium, its main feature was that when sprayed with water, the existing fire became even fiercer. The Germans planned to drop large numbers on London (and Paris), but the Allied offensives in the autumn of 1918 frustrated this idea.

GERMAN BOMBER LOSSES

43 Gothas (from 383 flights) } ALL ATTACKS, { shot down, crashed,
2 Giants (from 30 flights) } NIGHT AND DAY { missing, etc.

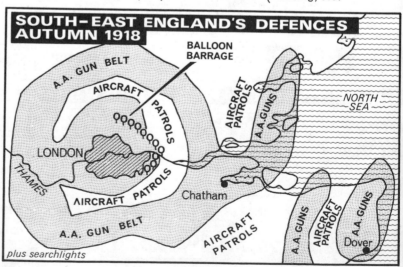

SOUTH-EAST ENGLAND'S DEFENCES AUTUMN 1918

BALLOON BARRAGE

A.A. GUN BELT

AIRCRAFT PATROLS

AIRCRAFT PATROLS

A.A. GUNS

NORTH SEA

LONDON

THAMES

AIRCRAFT PATROLS

Chatham

A.A. GUN BELT

AIRCRAFT PATROLS

A.A. GUNS

AIRCRAFT PATROLS

A.A. GUNS

Dover

plus searchlights

GERMAN Zeppelin-Staaken R.Ⅵ (Giant) Bomber

One R.Ⅵ, the R.39, delivered the greatest bomb-load of any single aeroplane during the war (26,000 kilograms in 20 raids). It dropped the only 3 1,000 kg. bombs to fall on Britain.

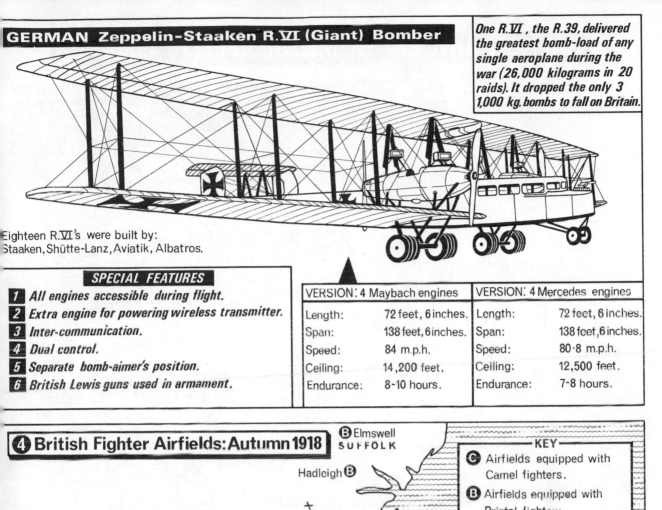

Eighteen R.Ⅵ's were built by:
Staaken, Shütte-Lanz, Aviatik, Albatros.

SPECIAL FEATURES

1. All engines accessible during flight.
2. Extra engine for powering wireless transmitter.
3. Inter-communication.
4. Dual control.
5. Separate bomb-aimer's position.
6. British Lewis guns used in armament.

VERSION: 4 Maybach engines		VERSION: 4 Mercedes engines	
Length:	72 feet, 6 inches.	Length:	72 feet, 6 inches.
Span:	138 feet, 6 inches.	Span:	138 feet, 6 inches.
Speed:	84 m.p.h.	Speed:	80·8 m.p.h.
Ceiling:	14,200 feet.	Ceiling:	12,500 feet.
Endurance:	8-10 hours.	Endurance:	7-8 hours.

④ British Fighter Airfields: Autumn 1918

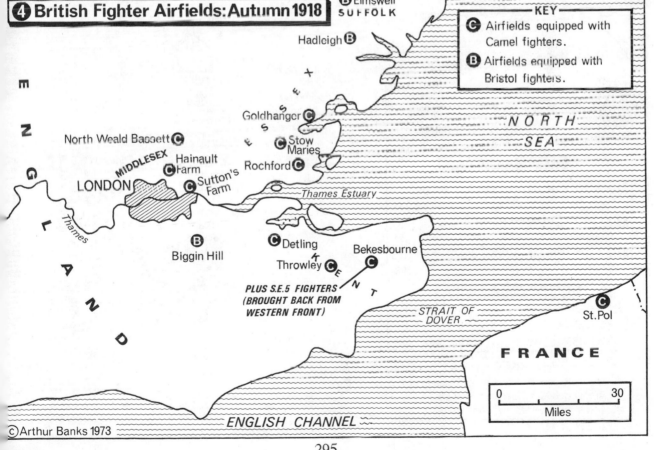

KEY
- **C** Airfields equipped with Camel fighters.
- **B** Airfields equipped with Bristol fighters.

Ⓑ Elmswell
SUFFOLK

Hadleigh Ⓑ

NORTH SEA

Goldhanger Ⓒ

ESSEX

North Weald Bassett Ⓒ

Stow Ⓒ Maries

Hainault Ⓒ Farm

MIDDLESEX

Rochford Ⓒ

LONDON

Sutton's Ⓒ Farm

Thames

Thames Estuary

Ⓑ
Biggin Hill

Ⓒ Detling

Bekesbourne

Throwley Ⓒ Ⓒ

KENT

PLUS S.E.5 FIGHTERS (BROUGHT BACK FROM WESTERN FRONT)

STRAIT OF DOVER

Ⓒ St. Pol

FRANCE

ENGLAND

0 — 30
Miles

ENGLISH CHANNEL

BRITAIN UNDER BOMBARDMENT 1914-1917

Between 16 December 1914 and 17 June 1917, there were 57 German aeroplane raids on Britain, 51 airship raids, and 12 naval bombardments from the North Sea. Total British casualties (civilian and military-naval) amounted to 5,620, 1,570 being killed and 4,050 injured. Damage amounted to over £3,500,000 (estimate based on 1914 values).

SCOTLAND

Berwick
Beal
Bedlington
Jarrow
South Shields
Newcastle
Sunderland
Seaham Harbour
Hartlepool
Bishop Auckland
Saltburn
Middlesbrough
Whitby
Whitehaven
Scarborough

ENGLAND

Isle of Man
York
Driffield
Beverley
Hornsea
IRISH SEA
Halifax
Leeds
Hull
NORTH SEA
Goole
Wakefield
Bolton
Rochdale
Grimsby
Wigan
Liverpool
Manchester
Sheffield
Anglesey
Warrington
Lincoln
Alford

WALES

Burslem
Newark
Hunstanton
Sheringham
Stoke
Sleaford
Derby
Nottingham
Norwich
Long Eaton
Burton
Loughborough
Wisbech
King's Lynn
Yarmouth
Walsall
Ashby
Stamford
March
Bungay
Tipton
Wednesbury
Thetford
Birmingham
Littleport
Bury St. Edmunds
Saxmundham
Coventry
Kettering
Newmarket
Woodbridge
Northampton
Haverhill
Ipswich
Felixstowe
Hitchin
Sudbury
Harwich
Luton
Braintree
Walton
Ware
Clacton
Chelmsford
LONDON
Southend
Sheerness
Thames
Margate
Croydon
Ramsgate
Deal
Ashford
Dover
Guildford
Hythe
Folkestone
Tunbridge Wells
Rye
Calais
Southampton

BRITISH CASUALTIES

1 DUE TO GERMAN AEROPLANE RAIDS
Total: 2,908

2 DUE TO GERMAN AIRSHIP RAIDS
Total: 1,914

3 DUE TO GERMAN NAVAL BOMBARDMENTS
Total: 798

ANALYSIS OF FIGURES

	Killed	Injured
1	857	2,051
2	556	1,358
3	157	641

KEY

- Areas raided by German aeroplanes.
- Areas raided by German airships.
- Areas bombarded by German naval units.

ENGLISH CHANNEL
Isle of Wight

0   50
Miles

© Arthur Banks 1973

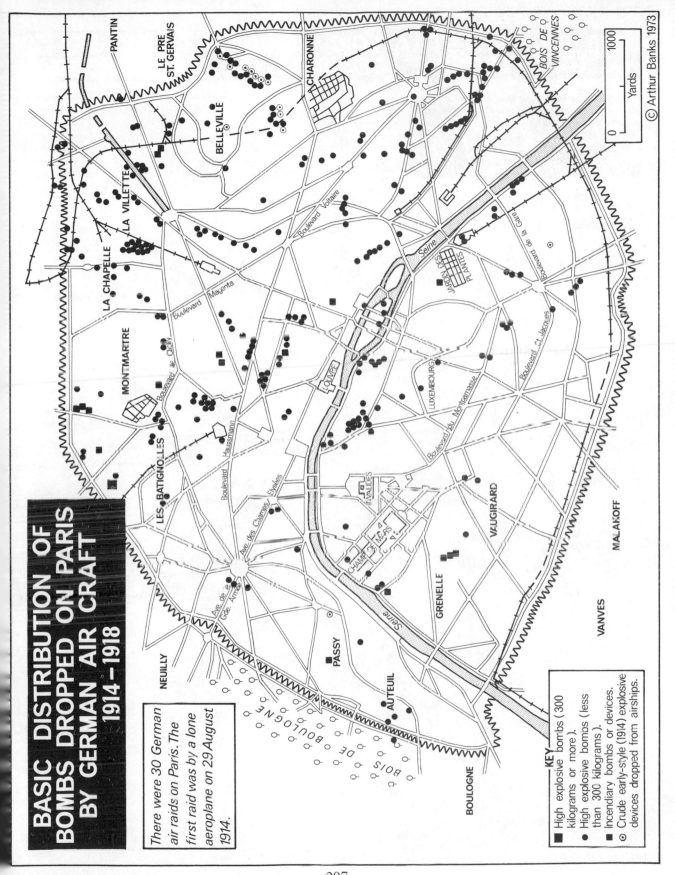

BASIC DISTRIBUTION OF BOMBS DROPPED ON PARIS BY GERMAN AIRCRAFT 1914–1918

There were 30 German air raids on Paris. The first raid was by a lone aeroplane on 29 August 1914.

© Arthur Banks 1973

KEY
- ■ High explosive bombs (300 kilograms or more).
- ● High explosive bombs (less than 300 kilograms).
- ■ Incendiary bombs or devices.
- ⊙ Crude early-style (1914) explosive devices dropped from airships.

0   1000 Yards

PANTIN

LE PRE ST. GERVAIS

CHARONNE

BOIS DE VINCENNES

BELLEVILLE

LA VILLETTE

LA CHAPELLE

Seine

Boulevard Voltaire

JARDIN DES PLANTES

Boulevard de la Gare

MONTMARTRE

Boulevard Magenta

Boulevard de Clichy

Boulevard Haussmann

LOUVRE

LUXEMBOURG

Boulevard St. Jacques

LES BATIGNOLLES

Boulevard du Montparnasse

Boulevard des Champs Elysées

Ave. des Champs

Ave de la Gde. Armée

INVALIDES

CHAMP DE MARS

VAUGIRARD

MALAKOFF

NEUILLY

GRENELLE

Seine

PASSY

VANVES

AUTEUIL

BOIS DE BOULOGNE

BOULOGNE

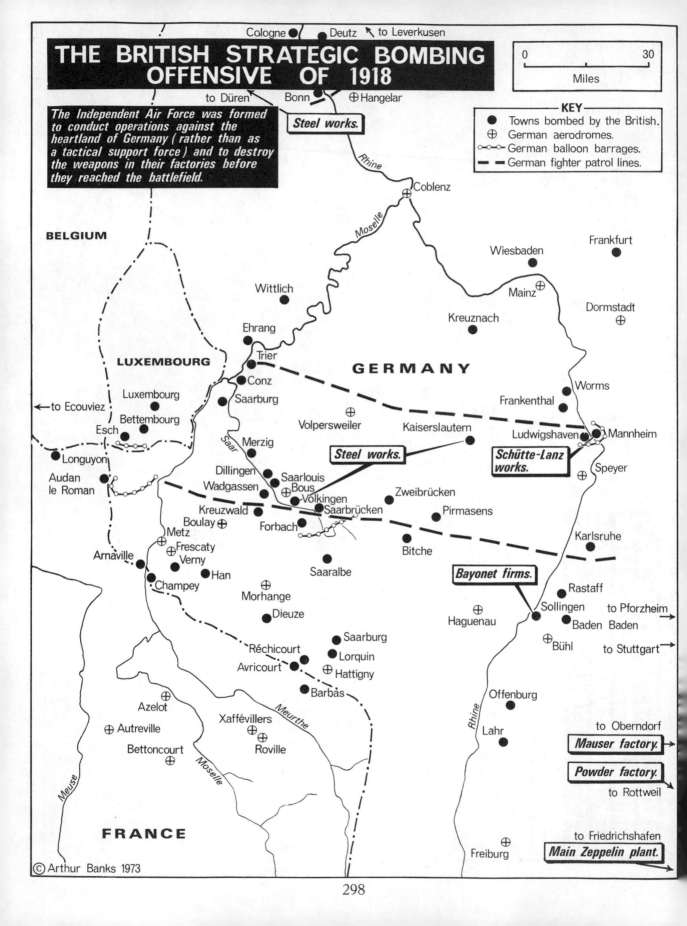

THE BRITISH STRATEGIC BOMBING OFFENSIVE OF 1918

The Independent Air Force was formed to conduct operations against the heartland of Germany (rather than as a tactical support force) and to destroy the weapons in their factories before they reached the battlefield.

KEY
- ● Towns bombed by the British.
- ⊕ German aerodromes.
- ⊶ German balloon barrages.
- – – – German fighter patrol lines.

0 — 30
Miles

Cologne · Deutz ↖ to Leverkusen

to Düren · Bonn · ⊕ Hangelar

Steel works.

Rhine

⊕ Coblenz

Moselle

BELGIUM

Frankfurt

Wiesbaden

Wittlich

Mainz ⊕

Dormstadt

Kreuznach

Ehrang

LUXEMBOURG

Trier

GERMANY

Conz

Worms

Luxembourg

Saarburg

Frankenthal

to Ecouviez →

Bettembourg

Volpersweiler ⊕

Kaiserslautern

Ludwigshaven

Mannheim

Esch

Merzig

Longuyon

Saar

Steel works.

Schütte-Lanz works.

Audan le Roman

Dillingen

Saarlouis

Speyer ⊕

Wadgassen

Bous

Zweibrücken

Völkingen

Kreuzwald

Saarbrücken

Pirmasens

Boulay ⊕

Forbach

Karlsruhe

Metz ⊕

Frescaty

Verny

Bayonet firms.

Arnaville

Han

Saaralbe

Bitche

Rastaff

Sollingen

to Pforzheim →

Champey

Morhange ⊕

Baden Baden

Haguenau ⊕

Bühl ⊕

to Stuttgart →

Dieuze

Saarburg

Réchicourt

Lorquin

Avricourt

Hattigny ⊕

Offenburg

Barbás

Rhine

Azelot ⊕

Xaffévillers

Lahr

to Oberndorf

⊕ Autreville

Roville ⊕

Mauser factory.

Bettoncourt ⊕

Moselle

Powder factory.

Meuse

to Rottweil

FRANCE

to Friedrichshafen

⊕ Freiburg

Main Zeppelin plant.

© Arthur Banks 1973

298

DEVELOPMENTS IN AERIAL SURVEYING 1914-1918

❶ Balloon Photography

BALLOON
CAMERA
OBLIQUE ANGLE
ENEMY POSITIONS

From the cartographic viewpoint, this method was unsatisfactory due to distortion of scale. What was required was overhead 'plan view' photography.

❷ Overhead Photography

ENEMY POSITIONS

By utilising aeroplanes and airships, overhead views could be obtained. Battle maps improved both in scale accuracy and in detail shown.

❸ The Mosaic Map

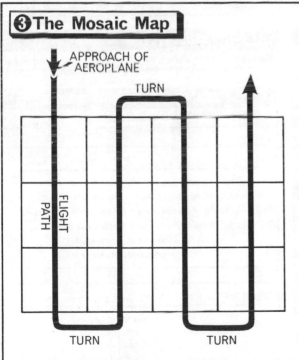

APPROACH OF AEROPLANE
TURN
FLIGHT PATH
TURN   TURN

To cover large areas, photographs were butt-jointed together to form one vast panoramic spread.

❹ The Overlap Refinement

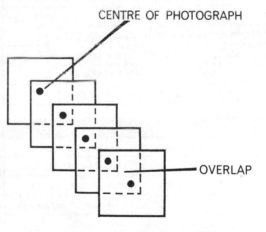

CENTRE OF PHOTOGRAPH
OVERLAP

The mosaic map left much to be desired as only the centres of photographs were true to scale, and these varied individually. By regulating camera shutters at fixed intervals while aircraft maintained a consistent height, resulting prints could be overlapped to register uniformly.

THE FIGHTER 'ACES'

Note: main decorations only shown.

THE INTERNATIONAL TOP TEN SCORERS

POSITION	NAME	COUNTRY	'KILLS'
1	RICHTHOFEN	GERMANY	80
2	FONCK	FRANCE	75 ?
3	MANNOCK	BRITAIN	73 ?
4	BISHOP	CANADA	72
5	UDET	GERMANY	62
6	COLLISHAW	CANADA	60
7	McCUDDEN	BRITAIN	57
8	BEAUCHAMP-PROCTOR	SOUTH AFRICA	54
8	MacLAREN	CANADA	54
8	GUYNEMER	FRANCE	54

GERMAN TOP SCORERS

1	Rittmeister Manfred von Richthofen	80 kills
2	Oberleutnant Ernst Udet	62 kills
3	Oberleutnant Erich Loewenhardt	53 kills
4	Leutnant Werner Voss	48 kills
5	Hauptmann Rudolph Berthold	44 kills
6	Leutnant Paul Bäumer	43 kills

All six aces won *Pour le Mérite* (in Germany an 'ace' implied 10 or more victories).

FRENCH TOP SCORERS

1	Capitaine Rene Paul Fonck, L d'H, C de G with 28 Palms, MC, CK	75 kills
2	Capitaine Georges M.L.J. Guynemer, L d'H, MM, C de G (26 Palms)	54 kills
3	Lieutenant Charles E J M Nungesser, L d'H, MM, C de G	45 kills
4	Capitaine Georges Felix Madon, L d'H, MM, C de G	41 kills
5	Lieutenant Maurice Bayau, L d'H, MM, C de G	35 kills
6	Lieutenant Michel Coifford, L d'H, MM, C de G	34 kills

BRITISH EMPIRE TOP SCORERS

1	Major Edward Mannock, VC, DSO and 2 bars, MC and bar	73 kills
2	Lt. Colonel William A. Bishop, VC, DSO and bar, MC, DFC, L d'H	72 kills
3	Lt. Colonel Raymond Collishaw, DSO and bar, DSC, DFC, C de G	60 kills
4	Major James T.B. McCudden, VC, DSO and bar, MC and bar, MM	57 kills
5	Captain Anthony W. Beauchamp-Proctor, VC, DSO, MC and bar	54 kills
6	Major Donald R. MacLaren, DSO, MC and bar, DFC, L d'H, C de G	54 kills

RUSSIAN TOP SCORERS

1	Staff Captain Alexander A. Kazakov, (13 Russian), DSO, MC, DFC	17 kills
2	Captain d'Argüeeff (Argeyev ?), Order of St. George	15 kills
3	Lt. Commander Alexander Prokofieff de Seversky, (all high Russian)	13 kills

THE RED BARON

Manfred von Richthofen was the highest scoring German fighter pilot 'ace' of the 1914-1918 war. He was credited with 80 enemy aircraft destroyed, and although the majority of these were reconnaissance machines, this total made him the top individual scorer of any country involved in the war.

He began flying as an active fighter pilot in March 1916, and was associated with the red Fokker triplane, the machine gun of which was synchronised to fire through the propeller.

He formed the group of squadrons known by the British as Richthofen's "circus", and was awarded the Pour le Mérite (the Blue Max) in February 1917. He was finally shot down on 21 April 1918, and was buried by the British with full military honours at Bertangles in France.

After the war he was reburied with much pomp and ceremony in Berlin.

AUSTRO-HUNGARIAN TOP SCORER

Hauptmann Godwin Brumowski	40 kills

BELGIAN TOP SCORER

Second Lieutenant Willy Coppens de Houthulst, DSO	37 kills

ITALIAN TOP SCORER

Maggiore Francesco Baracca	34 kills

UNITED STATES' TOP SCORER

Captain Edward V. Rickenbacker, CMH	26 kills

DECORATIONS: abbreviations employed here

VC = Victoria Cross.
MC = Military Cross.
DSO = Distinguished Service Order.
MM = Military Medal.
DSC = Distinguished Service Cross.
L d'H = Légion d'Honneur.
DFC = Distinguished Flying Cross.
C de G = Croix de Guerre.
CK = Cross of Karageorgevitch.
CMH = Congressional Medal of Honor.

EUROPEAN RANKINGS: Approx. equivalents

note: army ranks

Rittmeister = Cavalry captain.
Hauptmann = Captain.
Oberleutnant = Lieutenant.
Leutnant = Second Lieutenant.
Maggiore = Major.
Capitaine = Captain.

© Arthur Banks 1973

THE LOOP

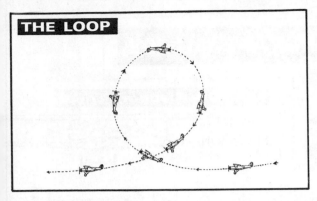

HALF ROLL ON TOP OF LOOP

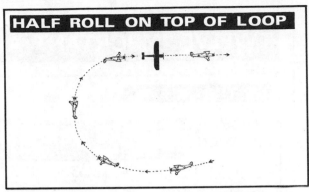

SLOW ROLL

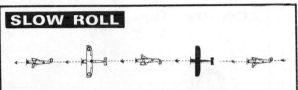

THE TOP SCORER : AN ANALYSIS

MANFRED VON RICHTHOFEN: THE RED BARON

HIS TALLY

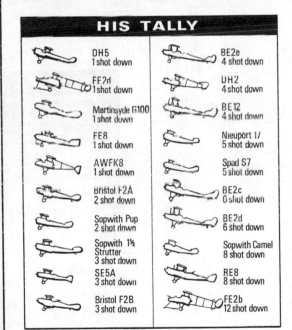

DH5 — 1 shot down	BE2e — 4 shot down
FE2d — 1 shot down	DH2 — 4 shot down
Martinsyde G100 — 1 shot down	BE12 — 4 shot down
FE8 — 1 shot down	Nieuport 17 — 5 shot down
AWFK8 — 1 shot down	Spad S7 — 5 shot down
Bristol F2A — 2 shot down	BE2c — 6 shot down
Sopwith Pup — 2 shot down	BE2d — 6 shot down
Sopwith 1½ Strutter — 3 shot down	Sopwith Camel — 8 shot down
SE5A — 3 shot down	RE8 — 8 shot down
Bristol F2B — 3 shot down	FE2b — 12 shot down

ATTACK FROM ASTERN ❶

FIXED MACHINE GUN FIRING FORWARD.

LINE OF ATTACK

HEIGHT ADVANTAGE (CLEAR VIEW).

This position was advantageous to the rear aircraft when the front machine carried only one occupant.

ATTACK FROM ASTERN ❷

OWN FUSELAGE IMPEDES REAR MACHINE GUNNER'S LINE OF FIRE.

LINE OF ATTACK

This position was advantageous to the rear aircraft when the front machine carried two occupants.

THE DECEPTIVE SIDE TURN   PLAN VIEW

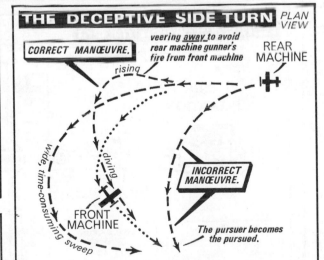

CORRECT MANŒUVRE.

veering *away* to avoid rear machine gunner's fire from front machine

rising

REAR MACHINE

wide, time-consuming sweep

diving

INCORRECT MANŒUVRE.

FRONT MACHINE

The pursuer becomes the pursued.

This diagram illustrates problems confronting a pilot when his quarry turned or banked to escape attack.

SOME OTHER FAMOUS 'ACES'	KILLS
AUSTRALIAN Captain Robert A. Little, DSO and bar, DSC, C de G	47
BRITISH Captain Albert Ball, VC, DSO and 2 bars, MC	44
GERMAN Hauptmann Oswald Boelcke, Pour le Mérite	40
GERMAN Oberleutnant Max Immelmann, Pour le Mérite	15

TWELVE IMPORTANT AIRCRAFT 1914-1918

BRITISH B.E. 2C

FRONT ELEVATION

SIDE ELEVATION

PLAN VIEW

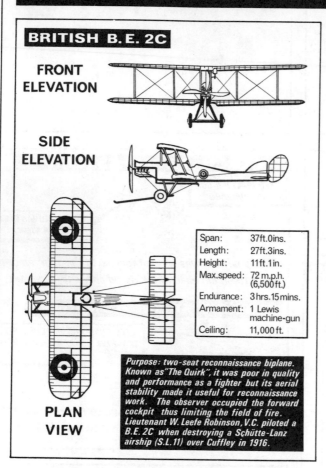

Span:	37ft.0ins.
Length:	27ft.3ins.
Height:	11ft.1in.
Max.speed:	72 m.p.h. (6,500 ft.)
Endurance:	3 hrs. 15 mins.
Armament:	1 Lewis machine-gun
Ceiling:	11,000 ft.

Purpose: two-seat reconnaissance biplane. Known as "The Quirk", it was poor in quality and performance as a fighter but its aerial stability made it useful for reconnaissance work. The observer occupied the forward cockpit thus limiting the field of fire. Lieutenant W. Leefe Robinson, V.C. piloted a B.E. 2C when destroying a Schütte-Lanz airship (S.L.11) over Cuffley in 1916.

FRENCH Nieuport 17 C.1

FRONT ELEVATION

SIDE ELEVATION

PLAN VIEW

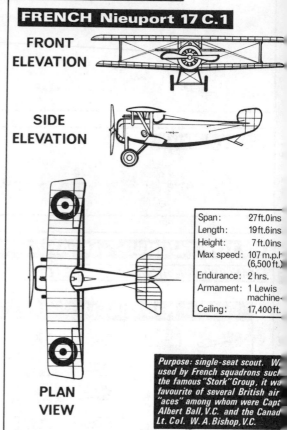

Span:	27ft.0ins
Length:	19ft.6ins
Height:	7ft.0ins
Max speed:	107 m.p.h. (6,500 ft.)
Endurance:	2 hrs.
Armament:	1 Lewis machine-
Ceiling:	17,400 ft.

Purpose: single-seat scout. W used by French squadrons such the famous "Stork" Group, it wa favourite of several British air "aces" among whom were Capt Albert Ball, V.C. and the Canad Lt. Col. W. A. Bishop, V.C.

GERMAN Albatros D-1

SIDE ELEVATION

PLAN VIEW

FRONT ELEVATION

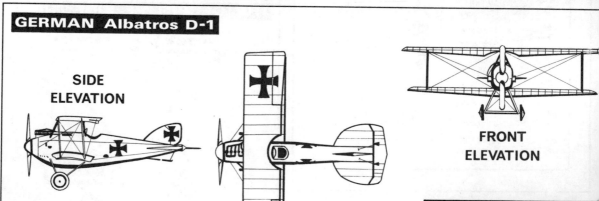

Span (upper):	28ft.3ins.	Max.speed:	110 m.p.h. (sea level)
Span (lower):	25ft.11ins.	Endurance:	4 hrs.
Length:	24ft.0ins.	Ceiling:	12,000 ft.
Height:	9ft.6ins.		
Armament:	Twin Spandau machine-guns		

Purpose: single-seat scout. First deliverie to squadrons commenced on 3 September and the famous German "ace" Oswald Boelc shot down eleven Allied aircraft within a sh period of 16 days. It was supreme during winter of 1916-1917 and its twin synchron guns feature became incorporated into the design of all subsequent German and All fighters.

BRITISH Bristol F.2B

SIDE ELEVATION

FRONT ELEVATION

PLAN VIEW

Span:	39ft.4ins.	Armament:	1 Vickers machine-gun for the pilot
Length:	26ft.2ins.		
Height:	10ft.1in.		1 or 2 Lewis guns for the observer
Max.speed:	125 m.p.h. (sea level)		
Endurance:	3 hrs.		Racks for light bombs
Ceiling:	20,000 ft.		

Purpose: two-seat fighter/reconnaissance aircraft. Possibly the finest all-round fighter of the Allies in the war, it was extremely manœuvrable and carried the advantage of a "sting in the tail". Known as the "Brisfit" or "Biff", it was a favourite of British "ace" Captain McKeever who won most of his thirty victories with this type.

FRENCH Spad S-7 C.1

SIDE ELEVATION

FRONT ELEVATION

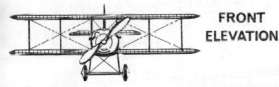

PLAN VIEW

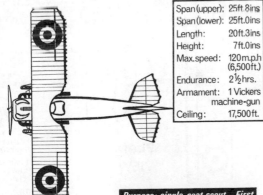

Span (upper):	25ft.8ins
Span (lower):	25ft.0ins
Length:	20ft.3ins
Height:	7ft.0ins
Max.speed:	120m.p.h (6,500ft.)
Endurance:	2½ hrs.
Armament:	1 Vickers machine-gun
Ceiling:	17,500ft.

Purpose: single-seat scout. First flown in July 1916, over 5,000 Spad S-7's were built in France, and 400 in England. The famous French "Stork" Group, of which the "ace" Georges Guynemer was a member, flew this type.

GERMAN Fokker Dr-1 Triplane

FRONT ELEVATION

SIDE ELEVATION

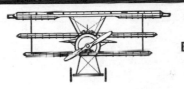

PLAN VIEW

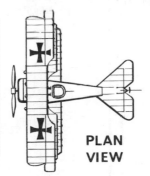

Span (upper):	23ft.7ins.
Span (centre):	20ft.6ins.
Span (lower):	18ft.9ins.
Length:	19ft.0ins.
Height:	9ft.0ins.
Max.speed:	122 m.p.h. at 8,000 ft.
Endurance:	2hrs.30mins.
Armament:	Twin Spandau machine-guns
Ceiling:	20,000 ft.

Purpose: single-seat scout. First employed in August 1917, it was a favourite of German "aces" such as Manfred von Richthofen and Werner Voss and was the supreme German "dogfighter" of the war.

TWELVE IMPORTANT AIRCRAFT-continued

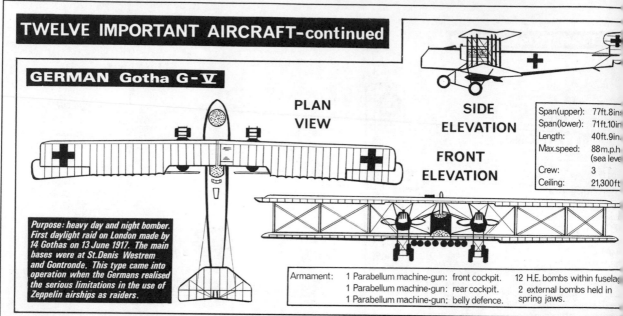

GERMAN Gotha G-Ⅴ

PLAN VIEW

SIDE ELEVATION

FRONT ELEVATION

Span(upper):	77ft.8ins.
Span(lower):	71ft.10ins.
Length:	40ft.9in.
Max.speed:	88m.p.h. (sea level)
Crew:	3
Ceiling:	21,300ft

Purpose: heavy day and night bomber. First daylight raid on London made by 14 Gothas on 13 June 1917. The main bases were at St.Denis Westrem and Gontronde. This type came into operation when the Germans realised the serious limitations in the use of Zeppelin airships as raiders.

Armament:	1 Parabellum machine-gun: front cockpit.	12 H.E. bombs within fuselage.
	1 Parabellum machine-gun: rear cockpit.	2 external bombs held in spring jaws.
	1 Parabellum machine-gun: belly defence.	

BRITISH Sopwith F.1 "Camel"

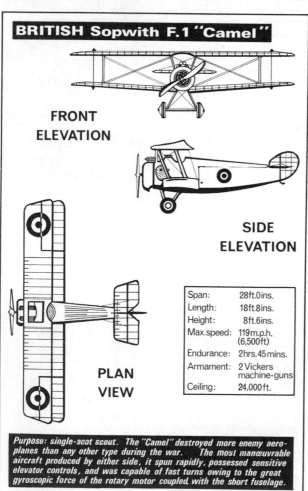

FRONT ELEVATION

SIDE ELEVATION

PLAN VIEW

Span:	28ft.0ins.
Length:	18ft.8ins.
Height:	8ft.6ins.
Max.speed:	119m.p.h. (6,500ft)
Endurance:	2hrs.45mins.
Armament:	2 Vickers machine-guns
Ceiling:	24,000ft.

Purpose: single-seat scout. The "Camel" destroyed more enemy aeroplanes than any other type during the war. The most manœuvrable aircraft produced by either side, it spun rapidly, possessed sensitive elevator controls, and was capable of fast turns owing to the great gyroscopic force of the rotary motor coupled with the short fuselage.

BRITISH S.E.5a

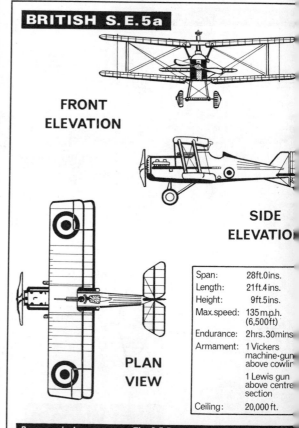

FRONT ELEVATION

SIDE ELEVATION

PLAN VIEW

Span:	28ft.0ins.
Length:	21ft.4ins.
Height:	9ft.5ins.
Max.speed:	135m.p.h. (6,500ft)
Endurance:	2hrs.30mins.
Armament:	1 Vickers machine-gun above cowling
	1 Lewis gun above centre section
Ceiling:	20,000ft.

Purpose: single-seat scout. The S.E.5a was remarkable for its "dogfighting" qualities. Although less manœuvrable than the Sopwith F.1 "Camel", it was notable for its marked stability as a gun-platform. It is to be noted that the famous "aces" Major E.Mannock,V.C. and Major J.T.B.McCudden,V.C. scored most of their victories in this scout.

GERMAN Fokker D–VII

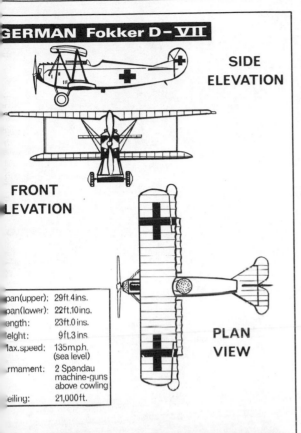

SIDE ELEVATION

FRONT ELEVATION

PLAN VIEW

Span(upper):	29ft.4ins.
Span(lower):	22ft.10ins.
Length:	23ft.0 ins.
Height:	9ft.3 ins.
Max.speed:	135m.p.h. (sea level)
Armament:	2 Spandau machine-guns above cowling
Ceiling:	21,000ft.

Purpose: single-seat scout. Possibly the finest of all German fighters produced during the 1914-1918 war, it was credited with 565 victims in August 1918 alone. Hermann Goering (also of 1939-1945 war fame) flew this type. By the autumn of 1918 every German scout squadron on the Western Front was equipped with this aircraft.

BRITISH Sopwith 7F. I "Snipe"

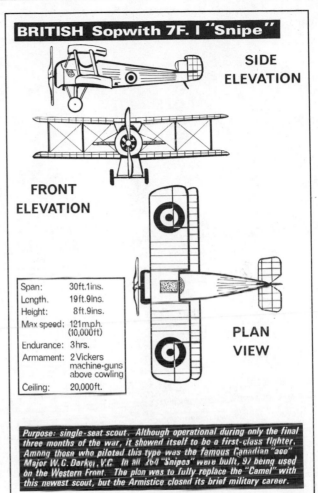

SIDE ELEVATION

FRONT ELEVATION

PLAN VIEW

Span:	30ft.1ins.
Length:	19ft.9ins.
Height:	8ft.9ins.
Max speed:	121m.p.h. (10,000ft)
Endurance:	3hrs.
Armament:	2 Vickers machine-guns above cowling
Ceiling:	20,000ft.

Purpose: single-seat scout. Although operational during only the final three months of the war, it showed itself to be a first-class fighter. Among those who piloted this type was the famous Canadian "ace" Major W.G. Barker, V.C. In all 264 "Snipes" were built, 97 being used on the Western Front. The plan was to fully replace the "Camel" with this newest scout, but the Armistice closed its brief military career.

BRITISH De Havilland 4

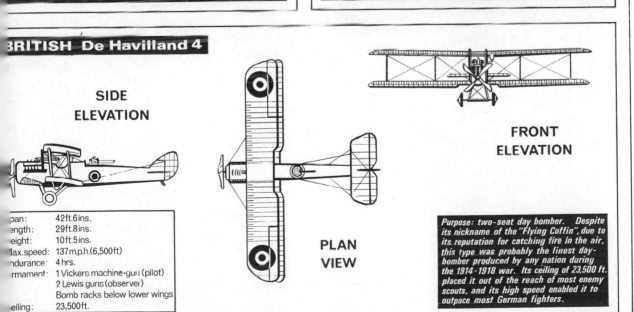

SIDE ELEVATION

PLAN VIEW

FRONT ELEVATION

Span:	42ft.6ins.
Length:	29ft.8ins.
Height:	10ft.5ins.
Max.speed:	137m.p.h.(6,500ft)
Endurance:	4hrs.
Armament:	1 Vickers machine-gun (pilot) 2 Lewis guns (observer) Bomb racks below lower wings
Ceiling:	23,500ft.

Purpose: two-seat day bomber. Despite its nickname of the "Flying Coffin", due to its reputation for catching fire in the air, this type was probably the finest day-bomber produced by any nation during the 1914-1918 war. Its ceiling of 23,500 ft. placed it out of the reach of most enemy scouts, and its high speed enabled it to outpace most German fighters.

General Index *

* Prepared by Mrs Brenda Hall, Society of Indexers.

Ammunition *see under* Munitions
Anafarta Sagir, Gallipoli, 119
Anatolia, 118
Ancre, 17, 182–3
Andlauer, General, 159
Anneux, 174
Anodalu Mejidieh, 110–11
Antenna mines, 278
Anti-aircraft defences
  British fighter airfields, 295; in Germany, 298; round London, 286, 288–9, 290–1, 293, 294; weapons used by, 233–4
Antoine, General, 168
Antwerp
  Belgian withdrawal to, 1914, 13–15, 42; bombardment by siege artillery, 13–15, 41, 61, 115; bombing of, by German airships, 281; fortifications, 26, 29, 30; relation to Western Front lines, 17, 134; siege of, 13–15, 39, 52, 60, 62–3
ANZAC forces
  casualties in Gallipoli, 122, 128; landings, withdrawal, in Gallipoli, 109, 120, 121, 123, 128, 252–3; trench lines, 124–5
Anzac (place), withdrawal from, 109
Apremont, 19, 193, 195
Arab Legion, 179
Arab Revolt, 211, 212–13
Arabia, assault on Turkish territory from, 212
Arbuthnot, Rear-Admiral Sir Robert, 248–51, 257–9
Archangel, inaccessibility through ice, 177
Ardennes, 16, 23
Ardoye, 196
Argentine, dispute with Germany, 215
Argonne, 16, 190, 194, 195
Ari Burnu, 119, 121, 123
Arleux, 169
Armaments
  German 42-cm. H.E. shell, 63; in contestants' divisional-organization, 1914, 34–5, 36–7; in fortifications at Namur, 28; naval, on British Monitors, in battle of the Yser, 69; on early British tanks, 157; *see also* Munitions, *and under individual weapons, and* Armed Forces Index *for individual ships*
Armed liners, British, at Coronel, 240
Armed merchant cruisers, British, at Falkland Islands, 241
Armed trawlers, 266, 268
Armenia, Armenians
  campaigns in, 1914–16, 163; contestants' dispositions, 118; Turkish persecution in, 163

Armentières, 38–9, 64–5, 75–7, 180, 181, 186, 196
Armin, General, von, 186
Armistice, November 1918
  German desire to influence negotiations, 236, 275; signature, 179, 197; terms, 197; Western Front line at, 17
Armour, weight of, on various tanks, 226–7
Armoured cars, 219
Armoured cruisers, 237, 240, 241, 248–51
Armour-piercing shells, 231
Arnaville, 298
Arras, 16, 17, 38–9, 134, 166, 167, 169, 175, 182–3
Arsiero, 202
Arsimant, 43
Artaki Bay, Sea of Marmara, 252–3
Artamanov, General, 92–3
Artillery
  Allied: ammunition supply in contestants' divisional organization, 34–5, 37; bombardment at Loos, 1915, 145; bombardment at St Mihiel, 1918, 193; bombardment of German lines on Somme, 1916, 152–3; evacuation from Gallipoli, 128–9; inadequacy in Gallipoli, 122; *Austro-Hungarian:* strength on Italian front, 200; *British:* in battle of Neuve Chapelle, 136; stations at 2 Ypres, 142; Canadian captures of, at Vimy, 170; contestants' strength in Palestine, 213; effectiveness against concrete defences, 219; *French:* superiority in 1914, 4; *German:* at Caporetto, 202; bombardment by, during battle of the Yser, 67, 68, 69, 71; bombardments in battle of Verdun, 150, 151; domination of action in 2 Ypres, 140–2; contestants' divisional organization, 36–7; in battle of Neuve Chapelle, 137; in bombardment of Paris, 1918, 184–5, 187; in defence of Namur, 1914, 28; infantry, in contestants' divisional organization, 34–5; losses by capture, 170, 193, 197; use at battle of Tannenberg, 91, 92–3; use of siege, in reduction of Belgian, French fortifications, 13–15, 33, 41, 42, 52, 115, 219; *Italian:* pre-war assumptions about role of, 219; shortage of, 199; *Rumanian:* weakness in, 162; *Russian:* shortage of shells, 85–6; strength in United States' divisional organization, 190; strength of contestants' during German offensives, 1918, 182–3; *Turkish:* capture of, in Meso-

potamia, 210; gun ranges, calibres, 112; in defence of Dardanelles, Gallipoli, 110–11, 121; various important weapons in use 1914–18, 4, 33, 220–3; *see also* Anti-aircraft defences *and under individual weapons*
Artois, 131, 144
Arvillers, 182–3
Ashby, air raid on, 296
Ashford, air raid on, 296
Asiago, 200, 201, 202, 203
Atakpame, Togoland, 216
Ath, 16, 181
Athies, 169
Atlantic Ocean, minefields, 276–7
Atlee, Clement, 122
Atrocities
  German commission of, in Belgium, 39; Turkish, in Armenia, 163
Attichy, 58–9
Aube, River, 52, 53
Aubenton, 38–9
Aubercourt, 191
Aubérive, 168
Aubers, 75, 76–7
Aubigny, 182–3
Auchonvillers, 152–3
Audan le Roman, 298
Audenarde, 181
Auffenberg, General, 100, 101, 102
Aulnoy, 197
Aus, German South West Africa, 216
Australian armed forces
  capture of German colonies in Pacific, 108; in battle of Messines, 165; in capture of Damascus, 213; in Gallipoli, *see* ANZAC forces
Austria-Hungary
  alliances in 1914, 1, 2, 3; ambitions in Balkans, 1, 2, 3, 8, 9; annexation of Bosnia, Herzegovina, 7; appeal for aid in Italy, 201; armistice in Italy, 203; declaration of war on Serbia, 11; family history of Hapsburgs, 10; military strength, 1914, 4; mobilization, 11; physical, regional geography, 18; reasons for collapse, 179; reasons for going to war, 1, 2; Russian declaration of war on, 11; significance of racial structure, 4, 5; spread of disaffection in, 179; strategic importance of railways, 21, 99; war plans for Eastern Front, 24; *see also* Austro-Hungarian armed forces
Austro-Hungarian armed forces
  Army advances on Eastern Front, 1914, 103; at Caporetto, 199, 202, 203; casualties suffered by, 99, 201, 202; decision to sue for peace in Italy, 199; defeat in Serbia,

Gallipoli campaign—*contd.*
120, 128–9; contestants' casualties during, 109, 120, 121, 122, 128–9, 254; course of land campaign, 109, 121–9; effect of abandonment on British strength on Western Front, 152–3; effect on land operations of British naval losses, 254; naval bombardments during, 109, 110–11, 129; plan for initial assault, 120; reasons for Allied failure, 109, 121, 122, 123; rejection of initial ANZAC request for evacuation, 252–3; relation to Salonika front, 204; significance of submarine operations, 252–3; strategic concepts, 108, 109, 116–17; trench lines, 122, 124–7; Turkish strength at Suvla, 123; *see also* Dardanelles, Gallipoli Peninsula

Gallipoli Peninsula
extent of Allied penetration, 121; physical features, 119; projected diversionary landing by Royal Naval Division, 116–17; Turkish military dispositions, 118, 119, 121; *see also* Dardanelles, Gallipoli campaign

Gallipoli Strait, Turkish battleship sunk in, 252–3

Gallipoli (town), 120

Gallwitz, General, 160

Gamble, Vice-Admiral, 248–51

Garnier-Duplessis, General, 159

Garua, Cameroon, 217

Gas warfare
construction of shells, 231; first use by British army, 145; first use by German army, 33, 74; German battery at Caporetto, 202, 203; introduction of mustard gas, 173; introduction of phosgene (Green cross) at Verdun, 148–9; Rumanian weakness in, 162; use at Ypres, 1915, 131, 139, 140, 142, 143

Gaza, 213

Geddes, Sir Eric, 140

German armed forces
Army anti-aircraft guns, 234; artillery, 13–15, 33, 41, 42, 52, 115, 197, 219; at end of mobile war, 83, 133–4; 'black day', 191; casualties suffered by, 13–15, 85–6, 143, 147, 148–9, 152–3, 170, 216, 217; concentration of firepower, 1918, 179; concentrations fundamental to Schlieffen Plan, 21, 22; defeat of 'Asia Corps' in Palestine, 199; deployment to aid Austria-Hungary, 103–5; dispositions, strength during contestants' offensives, 1918, 180, 181, 182–3, 193, 194; divisional organization, 34, 36, 161; effect of Brusilov

offensive on strength at Verdun, 161; effectiveness of wireless organization, 85–6, 90, 91, 103, 104; experiments with aircraft, 281; first use of mustard gas, 173; first use of phosgene gas, 148–9; grenades used by, 230; high command, 30; in Africa, 216–18; in offensive at Caporetto, 199, 202, 203; initial advances, 1914, 17, 23, 48–9; limits, lines of advance on Eastern Front, 19, 203; losses by capture of prisoners, 197; machine guns, 219, 224; 'Mauser' (Model 1898) rifles, 228; mining of lines at Messines, 171; movements during 'race to the sea', 64–5; numbers in battle of Neuve Chapelle, 137; offensive in Galicia, 1915, 131, 135; offensive in Serbia, 131, 160; pistols, revolvers used by, 232; pre-war strategic concepts, 2, 13–15, 20–2; problems of supply, communications, 48–9; reasons for failure of offensives, 1918, 182–3; reinforcement of Eastern Front with troops from West, 13–15, 47–8, 96–7, 103, 177; relative strength of infantry divisions, 87; relative strength on Western Front, 1917–18, 179; retreat from Balkans, 1918, 205; retreat on Western Front, 1917–18, 165, 166, 167, 169, 181; Riga offensive, 176; role in 2 Ypres, 138–43; significance of battle of Verdun for, 147; signs of demoralization, 191; tanks, 226; trench lines, systems, 144, 152–5, 168, 175; trench weapons, munitions, 230–1; troop concentrations on Eastern Front, 1914, 32; troop strengths, dispositions on Western Front, 1914, 13–15, 30–1, 45; use of gas in Ypres offensive, 1915, 131, 139, 140, 142, 143
Navy casualties suffered by, 235–6, 250–1, 258; concept of significance of submarines, 235–6, 246, 250–1; demoralization, mutiny in, 179, 236, 275; hazards confronting U-boats, 236, 268; losses at Jutland, 235–6, 258; minefields laid by, 276–7; mines, 278, 279; Pacific squadron, 108; significance of battle of Jutland for, 235–6, 258; significance of defeat at battle of Falkland Islands for, 241; strategy in North Sea, 235–6, 255, 256, 275; submarine losses, 262–5; submarines in North Sea, 1914, 246; units with Turkish fleet, 272; *see also* Armed Forces Index *and* Sea, War at

Air forces casualties among airship crews, 284, 285, 290–1; England Squadron (Kagohl 3), 292, 293; fighter aces, 300, 301; fleet of airships, 281, 282–4; *see also* Air, War in, Aircraft, Airships

German East Africa
campaign in, 199, 217–18; extent in 1914, 6; wireless station at Dar es Salaam, 216, 217

German South West Africa
campaign in, 216; wireless stations in, 216

Germans
minority group in Austria-Hungary, 4, 5; percentage in Austro-Hungarian army, 102

Germany
airship bases, 282, 283, 284; alliances, 1, 2, 3, 131, 160; ambitions to become world power, 2, 5; appeal for aid on Italian front by Austria-Hungary, 201; attempts to persuade Holland into alliance, 132; balloon barrages, 298; blockade of Baltic by, 177; British blockade of, 108, 147, 179; declarations of war by, on, 11, 200, 214, 215; demoralization in 1918, 179; development of commercial submarine by, 280; extent, loss of empire, 6, 108, 199, 216–18; fear of encirclement, 1, 2, 3; fear of war on two fronts, 133; fighter patrols over, 298; food shortages, 178; French occupation of part of, 133; guarantee of Belgian neutrality, 25; idolization of Hindenburg, 85–6; importance of railways to, 13–15, 18, 103, 134; iron ore imports from Sweden, 269; military appraisal, 4; mobilization, 11; naval rivalry with Britain, 1, 3, 5, 7, 21; physical, regional geography of Eastern Front, 18; policies in Balkans, 7, 8; policies in North Africa, 7; reasons for collapse, 179, 197; reasons for going to war, 1, 2; severance of diplomatic relations by Argentine, Peru, 215; strategic bombing of, 281, 298; strategic importance attached to Channel Ports, 66; terms of Armistice, 1918, 197; war plans for Eastern Front, 24; Western Front fortifications, 16, 26; Western frontier, 43, 44; *see also* German armed forces

Gerogette, German offensive, 1918, 180

Gheluvelt, 13–15, 75, 78–82, 172, 173

Ghent, 17, 22, 134, 172, 181, 292, 293

321

322

Namur—contd.
following defeat at, 60; fortifica-
tions, 16, 26, 28; relation to static
Western Front lines, 17, 134;
siege of, 23, 39, 42, 48–9, 51, 115
Namutoni, South West Africa, 216
Nancy, 16, 17, 30–1, 53, 134
Nanguari, Portuguese East Africa,
218
Nanichevanski, General Khan, 88–9
Nanteuil, 47, 48–9, 55–7
Nanungu, Portuguese East Africa,
218
Napier, Rear-Admiral T. D. W.,
248–51
Naples, Zeppelin raid on, 285
Narrows see Dardanelles, Sea of
Marmara
Nasiriya, 207
Naulin, General, 168
Nauroy, 168
Naval blockades, techniques, strate-
gies, 108, 147, 177, 179, 212, 235–6
Naval guns
German ('Long Max'), shelling of
Dunkirk by, 184; German long-
range shelling of Verdun, 150;
Hotchkiss Automatic, on British
Monitors, 69; inaccuracy in trench
warfare, 122; Maxims, on 'London'
Class of battleships, 69; use of
British 6-pounder on early tanks,
157; types used in bombardments
in Dardanelles, 112, 115; 38-cm.
long-range, German, 150; 4-inch,
112; 4.7-inch, 69; 6-inch, 69, 112,
115; 6.4-inch, 112; 12-inch, 69,
112; 15-inch, 115; 3-pounder, 69,
115; 12-pounder, 69, 115
Naval supremacy see Sea power
Nazareth, 213
Neidenburg, 90–3, 94, 96–7
Néry, 47, 48–9
Nesle, 48–9, 180, 181, 182–3
Nets, submarine losses in, 262–4
Neu-Breisach, 26, 31, 45
Neuenburg, 26
Neufchâteau, 16, 26
Neuve Chapelle, 17, 74, 76–7, 134
Neuve Chapelle, battle of, 131, 136–7
Neuve Église, 75, 186
Neuville, 169
Neuville-St.-Vaast, 144
Neuville Vitasse, 167
New York, U.S. embarkation port,
188
New Zealand, coastal minefields,
276–7
New Zealand armed forces
capture of German colonies in
Pacific, 108; in battle of Messines,
165; in Gallipoli campaign, 109;
see also Anzac forces
Newala, German East Africa, 218

Newark, air raid on, 296
Newcastle on Tyne, air raids on, 281,
287, 296
Newcastle under Lyme, air raid on,
287
Newmarket, air raid on, 296
Newport News, U.S. troops em-
barkation point, 188
Newton Pippin rifle grenades,
British, 230
Ngaundere, Cameroon, 217
Ngomano, Portuguese East Africa,
218
Nibrunesi Beach, Gallipoli, 123
Nibrunesi Point, Gallipoli, 119
Nicaragua, Bryan-Chamorro Treaty
with, 214
Nicholas, Grand Duke, 85–6, 147
Nicholas II, Tsar, 147, 177
Nieppe, 75, 76–7
Nieumunster, air base, 293
Nieuport
battle for, 66, 68, 69; inundation
of, 13–15, 70–1, 83; relation to
static Western Front lines, 17
Nieuport 17 C.1 French aircraft,
302
Nigeria, Allied advance into
Cameroon from, 217
Nikolaiev, naval construction yards
at, 272
Nivelle, Robert Georges, 159, 165,
166
Nivelles, 16
Nixon, General Sir J. E., 207
Nonsard, 192, 193
Noord Vaart Siphon, 71
Nordenburg, 87, 88–9
Nordholz, airship base, 282, 286,
290–1
Noreuil, 182–3
Norfolk
air raids on, 286, 296; naval bom-
bardment on coast of, 296
Norroy, 192, 193
North Africa see Africa, North
North Sea
contestants' naval strategies in,
235–6, 255, 256, 275; Franco-
British agreement on naval
supremacy in, 2, 3; German access
to, 5, 21; minefields, 236, 246,
249, 256, 259, 268, 276; U-boats
in, in 1914, 246; see also Sea, War
at, Submarine warfare, and indi-
vidual battles
North Weald Bassett, fighter airfield,
295
Northampton, air raid on, 296
Northern Rhodesia, advance on
German East Africa from, 218
Norwich, air raids on, 287, 296
Nottingham, air raid on, 296
Novo-Georgievsk, 18, 91, 100, 135

Noyon, 16, 17, 47, 48–9, 58–9, 134,
167, 180, 181, 182–3, 197
Nungesser, Lieutenant Charles
E. J. M., 300
Nun's Copse, Ypres, 80
Nurlu, 182–3
Nyamirue, Portuguese East Africa,
218
Nyasaland, advance into German,
Portuguese East Africa from, 218
'Nymphe' class of protected cruisers,
245

Oberleutnant, rank of, equivalents,
300
Oblong Farm, Ypres, 138
Obrégon, Alvaro, 214
Observation balloons, 152–3
Odessa, bombardment of, 272, 273
Offenburg, bombing of, 298
Oil
contestants' strategies for securing
of supplies, 177, 199, 206, 210;
use of burning, in trench warfare,
219
Oise River, region, 16, 17, 52, 53, 190
Oisy, 47
Old Contemptibles, 13–15
Oliezy, 182–3
Olleris, General, 81–2
Omaruru, South West Africa, 216
Omecourt, 158
Oostakker, air base, 292
Oostaverne, 173
Oostnieuwkerke, 75
Oranovski, General, 88–9
Orkanie, Dardanelles, 110–11, 112–
14, 119
Ornes, 148–50
Ortelsburg, 90–1, 95–7
Oscillating mines, 279
Ossowiec, 87
Ostend
Allied bombardment of, 68; battles
for, 181, 197; British attempt to
block harbour, 236, 274; minefield
laid outside, 68; relation to West-
ern Front lines, 17; strategic im-
portance, 66, 68, 172; submarine
base at, 268
Osterode, 96–7
Ostrolenka, 87, 90, 91
Otranto, 236, 271
Ottoman Empire see Turkey
Ouchy, Treaty of, 7
Oudenarde, 197
Ouderdom, 141
Ourcq, River, 16, 54–7
Ourthe, River, 16, 52
Ovillers la Boisselle, 154–5, 156, 158

Pacific Ocean, area
German squadron in, 108, 238;
loss of German colonies in, 108

Padua, 200
Pagan Island, rendezvous of German Pacific Squadron at, 238, 239
Pagny, 192
Pakenham, Rear-Admiral W. C., 248–51, 256–9
Palestine
contestants' strength in, 213; course of campaign in, 165, 179, 199, 211, 213; desertions from Turkish army in, 179; effect of Arab Revolt on Turkish strength in, 212; proposed cavalry advance from Mesopotamia to link with, 210, 211; role of R.A.F. bombers in, 281; strategic concepts, 199
Pan-Slavism, 2, 3
Panderma, 252–3
Pannes, 192, 193
Pannewitz, General, 105
'Panther', sent to Agadir, 7
Papadopoli, 203
Paraná, Brazilian ship sunk by submarine, 215
Pardo, President, 215
Paris
air raids on, 283, 297; bombardment, 184–5; civilian casualties in, 283; fortifications, defences, 26, 27, 190; French government's departure from, 53; Headquarters, U.S. Army General Purchasing Board, 189; in German strategic concepts, 20, 22, 179, 187; relation to Western Front lines, battles, 16, 17, 47, 48–9, 54–6, 179, 187; taxi-cabs, rushing troops to front, 55, 219
Paris, General, 63, 120
'Paris Gun' (Lange 21-cm. Kanone), 184, 185, 187
Pasly, 47
Passaga, General, 159
Passchendaele, 13–15, 75, 78–82, 165, 172, 173, 186
Patey, General, 205
Pau, General, 45
Peissant, 47
Pentagon, French fortifications, 1914, 31
Perenchies, 75, 76–7
Péronne, 16, 17, 48–9, 134, 152–3, 156, 167, 180, 181, 182–3
Pershing, General John Joseph, 188, 193, 214
Persia
Dunsterforce expedition through, 210, 211; Russian influence in, 118
Perthes, 134
Peru, severance of diplomatic relations with Germany, 215
Peruvelz, 38–9
Pétain, Marshal, 144, 165, 179
Peterborough, airship flight over, 287

Peterhead, wireless station, 248
Petit Morin, River, 16, 17, 52, 54–7
Petrograd
German advance on, 1917, 177; name changed to Leningrad, 177; projected bombing of, 281, 283
Pflanzer-Baltin, General, 161
Phalsburg (Pfalzburg), 45
Philadelphia, U.S. embarkation point, 188
Philippeville, 16, 38–9, 43, 48–9
Phosgene gas, 148–9; *see also* Gas warfare
Photography, aerial, development of, 299
Piave, River, region, 179, 200, 201, 203
Pierkenshoek, 196
Pierre Levée, 47
Pierrefonds, 47
Pilckem, 78–82, 138–43, 173
Pilckem Ridge, Ypres, 138
Pilkallen, 88–9
Pill-boxes, concrete, effectiveness against artillery fire, 219
Pimple, The, Vimy Ridge, 170
Pioneer units, in divisional organization, 34, 35, 36
Pirmasens, bombing of, 298
Pistols, types used by contestants, 219, 232
Platana, Turkish supply base, 272
Plava, 201, 202
Plehve, General, 100, 101, 102
Plessier-Romainvillers, 191
Plettenberg, General, 81
Plezzo, 202
Plock, 104–5
Ploegsteert, 75, 78–82, 186
Ploegsteert Wood, Ypres, 80
Ploken Pass, 200, 201
Plumer, Lieutenant-General Sir H., 139, 171, 186
Plummet system of depth-taking, in mines, 278
Plüskow, General von, 105
Plymouth, U.S. debarkation port, 188
Poelcapelle, 75, 78–82, 173, 186, 196
Pola, naval base at, 271, 273
Poland
Central Powers' advances in, 85–6, 135; in contestants' war plans, 24; Russian surrender at Brest-Litovsk, 178; *see also* Poles
Poles
minority group in Austria-Hungary, 5; percentage in Austro-Hungarian army, 102
Polygon Wood, Ypres, 80, 138
Pont à Mousson, 197; *see also* St Mihiel
Pontic Alps, campaigns in, 163
Pontoise, 47

Poplar, London, air raid on, 293
Popović, Vijetko, 10
Port Arthur, Neuve Chapelle, 136–7
Port Fouad, Suez Canal, 212
Port Said, unsuccessful Zeppelin raid on, 285
Port Tewfik, Suez Canal, 212
Portland, Maine, U.S. embarkation point, 188
Porto Amelia, Portuguese East Africa, 218
Portsmouth, naval base, 255
Portugal, coastal minefields, 270
Portuguese army, in Western Front campaigns, 179, 186, 194
Portuguese East Africa, campaign in, 218
Posen, 18, 91, 100
Poti, 211, 272
Potijze, 78–82, 173
Potiorek, General, 85–6
Potsdam, airship construction plant, 284
Pour le Mérite (Blue Max) award, 300, 301
Pozières, 152–3, 154–5, 158
Predeal Pass, 162
Premesques, 75, 76–7
Prince Eitel Trench, Moronvilliers, 168
Princip, Gavrilo, 10
Prisoners of war
numbers taken during final campaigns in 1918, 191, 193, 197; taken in Mesopotamia, 208, 210
Prittwitz, General von, 85–6, 87, 88–9, 90
Prokofieff de Seversky, Lieutenant Commander Alexander, 300
Propaganda, German use of, 132
Prouilly, 168
Provins, 181
Proyart, 182–3
Prunay, 168
Prussia *see* Germany
Przemysl, 18, 85–6, 100–2, 131, 135
Psychological warfare, 57
Puerto Rico, Jones Act concerning, 214
Puisieux, 182–3
Pulteney, Lieutenant-General Sir W. P., 76–7
Pultusk, 87
Putnik, Field Marshal, 24, 85–6, 99
Putz, General, 139

Qala Shadi, 208
Q-ships, 236, 265, 266, 267
Quadrilateral
at battle of Neuve Chapelle, 136–7; in battle of the Somme 152–3
Quast, General von, 186
Quéant, 17

Armed Forces Index *

* Prepared by Mrs Brenda Hall, Society of Indexers.

331